PIAGETIAN RESEARCH
A Handbook of Recent Studies

H·04

PIAGETIAN RESEARCH

A HANDBOOK OF RECENT STUDIES

SOHAN MODGIL

NFER

Published by the NFER Publishing Company Ltd.,
Book Division, 2 Jennings Buildings, Thames Avenue,
Windsor, Berks., SL4 1QS
Registered Office, The Mere, Upton Park, Slough, Bucks., SL1 2DQ
First Published 1974
© Sohan Modgil, 1974
85633 030 2

Printed in Great Britain from Computer composition by
Eyre & Spottiswoode Ltd at Grosvenor Press

Distributed in the USA by Humanities Press Inc.
450 Park Avenue South, New York, N.Y. 10016, USA.

*Dedicated with gratitude, love and
respects to my mother and my father
who sacrificed everything for their children.*

CONTENTS

PREFACE

This book is intended to serve a wide range of needs for both teacher and learner at all levels: for university and college lecturers; post-graduate research students; those training to be educational psychologists; teachers and others following a wide range of advanced diploma courses; and education and psychology students at undergraduate level, following Educational and Developmental Psychology options. Research projects have been included which have implications for rehabilitation and social workers.

In one sense, there are many authors to this book. The research evidence included is dependent on the countless efforts of Piaget's followers. In fairness, my gratitude is extended to those followers whose researches contribute immeasurably to the contents of this book.

I owe a very special debt of gratitude to Geneva University, and to universities here and abroad. Likewise, the inspiration of Professors Piaget and Inhelder, together with the general support of Professors Marcel Goldschmid, Irene Athey and Jorgen Jensen, are acknowledged. Joan Cooper of the Institute of Education, University of London, has provided constant encouragement and moral support over a number of years.

For the endless effort in the basic work of reading the draft manuscript I am indebted to Celia Scaplehorn of Goldsmiths' College, London University, who studied this with patience and fortitude. The chapter on Moral Development is also her contribution.

It is with great respect that I acknowledge the experienced advice of Professor Ruth Beard of Bradford University. She most graciously undertook the task of reading the manuscript. Likewise, my greatest debt is to Dr G. R. Cross of London University for his tolerance, sympathy and understanding at all times. His help in reading and commenting on the manuscript leads to an appreciation greater than I can ever express.

Jeanette Dixon, Editor, NFER Publishing Company Ltd.,

1

Windsor, provided both general and moral support. Mrs. Dixon went through the manuscript with care and gave the benefit of her editing skills and psychological knowledge. I am indebted to her.

Sohan Modgil

August, 1973

INTRODUCTION

This book has many purposes. It is designed to make available a substantial number of Piaget-oriented researches that may be useful for immediate information as well as for long-term reference. The accelerating expansion of Piagetian research has led to an acute need for a source book more comprehensive than the ordinary text book but more focused than scattered periodical literature. More specifically, it should give the reader access to source materials that elaborate upon most Piagetian topics. Likewise, such a book should offer students examples of a variety of approaches utilized by researchers in their efforts to investigate cognitive development. The numerous researches assembled here present experimental subjects whose chronological ages range from birth to 94 years. The intended readership is therefore broad, from those interested in the very young, in adolescents, in the elderly. The present volume, as well as recording the replications and extensions of Piaget's work, includes reflections on, speculations about and analyses of the various problems of the theory. Hopefully, this should in turn provide inspiration for further elaboration, extension and revision. The research worker is provided with a broad spectrum of original sources from which an appreciation in depth of the theoretical, methodological and practical questions relevant to a Piagetian framework can be obtained. While it is conceded that a secondary source is not the ideal way to comprehend the theory, nevertheless it can provide the reader with a basic direction to the problem at hand.

The material gathered here has been heavily drawn from two main sources: University degree theses and published research papers up to and as recent as December 1972*. It became apparent that the subject matter was voluminous and that there were many ways to subdivide the Piagetian cognitive researches. In choosing the articles, the criteria were made as objective as possible, while recognizing that a personal slant is bound to influence the selection. Despite an extensive search it is not unlikely that valuable articles have been overlooked. To these researchers apologies are extended. In assembling these researches the principal objective was to include only those which satisfy one of the following criteria: Piaget-oriented (replications or extensions); developmental in nature; or those which have discussed their findings within the Piagetian framework.

The table of contents reflects a broad range of studies, and represents most of the major subdivisions of Piagetian literature. It must be pointed out that while some articles fall naturally under certain specific headings, others would have fitted simultaneously into more than one section, this being in part due to the inability to distinguish between the analytic and synthetic. Consequently, it was difficult to select one single scheme that would satisfy all readers and many arbitrary decisions had to be made. There is obviously considerable reliance on the use of cross-references.

This is not a book of readings. The compilation covers twelve areas — each chapter focuses on a major aspect of Piaget's work. The main areas covered are: Piaget's Cognitive Theory, Sensori-motor Intelligence, Conservation, Training Techniques, Logic, Space, Handicapped Children, Cross-Cultural Research, The School Curriculum, Morality, Socialization and Test Development.

Each chapter consists of an integrated review of the range of recent studies followed by abstracts of these researches arranged, in the main, chronologically. Where details of early research are essential to illustrate the evolution of a particular area of study, these are not represented by a full abstract, but are included in the introductory review in the relevant chapter. Only previously unpublished researches prior to 1965 (i.e. higher degree theses) are presented in abstract form; elsewhere the early years are covered by references to secondary sources. Chapter Nine, on moral development, includes some abstracts of earlier works, mainly because there has been little documentation in this field of research activity. Although many cross-references to related abstracts are included, the reviews preceding the abstracts are not intended to be fully critical of the validity and reliability of experimental design. This is partly due to the fact that, unless full details are available, (sometimes these have neither been published fully, nor the definition of concepts made meaningful) this would be inimical, and partly because the amount of work involved in a critical evaluation of every study in a work of this breadth would be prohibitive.

In comparison to most publications an unusual amount of detail of researches is made available, and to accompany this with an equal amount of discussion, although essential, could introduce complexity in the aims of the book. Some of the abstracts (indicated by an asterisk) have been written by the authors themselves and reproduced in their entirety. It is realized that

4

some abstracts are of only marginal importance, yet their inclusion is essential to show general developmental patterns.

It is the author's intention that the reader, having investigated the range of available material, would then consult the original research according to his specific interests. Advanced research depends a great deal on what sources and data are available for study, and there is a consequent tendency for some parts of the field to be ploughed over and over again, while others remain virtually untouched.

A comprehensive bibliography encompassing over 1,500 references concludes the book. While it may be argued that sectionalized bibliographies at the end of each chapter would have been more convenient for the reader, such an arrangement would have resulted in repetitive references throughout the book.

Every care has been taken to report the results of the researches as accurately as possible — any misinterpretation of the results is accidental. It must be conceded that all the studies included do not receive equal coverage. While the overall response to the circulated requests was excellent, some shortcomings in the book are due partly to some failure of response. While deficiencies of the final product are my own responsibility, they exist in spite of a number of advisers who gave their time generously.

*The author has been alert to studies appearing up to August, 1973 (after the completion of the main manuscript) and brief details of further selected researches have been added in order to enrich particular areas of inquiry and discussion. Hopefully, researches within this category will receive full treatment in an anticipated follow-up volume.

CHAPTER ONE
THE DEVELOPMENTAL THEORY OF
JEAN PIAGET

Great intellectual stature can be attributed to Jean Piaget. It can be speculated that his influence will pervade future research for many decades to come and occupy a most significant role in the history of the evolution of human understanding. His deep insight with respect to children has caused him to be regarded as the outstanding child psychologist in the world today.

Piaget's thinking is multi-disciplinary and he is able to integrate his ideas from varied sources including philosophy, biology, mathematics and logic. As a result his thought and work have become relevant to many professions – psychology, sociology, psychiatry, paediatrics and, obviously, education.

As a developmentalist interested in the organism's adaptation to the environment through intelligence, Piaget, in the course of more than 50 years of concentrated research on mental development, has evolved a theory of intelligence. He established a sequence of age-related stages, from the early sensori-motor coordinations of infants to the abstract intelligence of adults. The stages are assumed to reflect maturational changes in forms of thinking, and the gradual acquisition of concepts reflects the influence of the physical and social environment.

Piaget states, 'I would . . . define intelligence not by a static criterion, as in previous definitions [here he was referring to Claparède and Karl Bühler] but by the direction that intelligence follows in its evolution, and then I would define intelligence as a form of equilibration . . . toward which all cognitive functions lead . . . equilibration is not an exact and automatic balance, as it would be in Gestalt theory; I define equilibration principally as a compensation for an external disturbance' (1961). He goes on to argue that the compensation implies the fundamental idea of reversibility, and this reversibility is precisely what characterizes the operations of intelligence. An operation is always subordinated to other operations, is an internalized action, but is also a reversible action. Thus, Piaget defines intelligence in terms of operations and the co-ordination of operations.

He describes cognitive development in terms of stages, the criteria of which can best be defined in Inhelder's terms:

1. 'Each stage involves a period of formation (genesis) and a period of attainment. Attainment is characterized by the progressive organization of a composite structure of mental operations.

2. Each structure constitutes at the same time the attainment of one stage and the starting point of the next stage, of a new evolutionary process.

3. The order of succession of the stages is constant. Ages of attainment can vary within certain limits as a function of factor of motivation, exercise, cultural milieu and so-forth.

4. The transition from an earlier to a later stage follows a law of implication analogous to the process of integration, preceding structures becoming a part of later structures.' (1962)

Piaget distinguishes four stages in the development of intelligence: first, the sensori-motor period before the appearance of language; second, from about two to seven years of age, the pre-operational period which precedes real operations; third, the period from seven to 12 years of age, a period of concrete operations; and finally, after 12 years of age, the period of formal or 'propositional' operations.

Sensori-Motor Stage

Children in the sensori-motor period demonstrate a certain number of stages, which range from simple reflexes to the co-ordination of means and goals. Sensori-motor intelligence lays its premise mainly on actions, movements and perceptions without language. However, these actions are co-ordinated, in a relatively stable way, under what Piaget calls 'schemata of action'. This sensori-motor system is made up of displacements which, although they are not reversible in the mathematical sense, are nonetheless amenable to inversion ('renversables'). The child can return to his starting point and attain the same goal by different routes. In the co-ordination of these movements into a system, the child comes to realize that objects have permanence whatever their displacements.

Briefly then, the sensori-motor stage (approximately birth to two years) is characterized by development from a state of reflex activity to an organized sensori-motor action system which permits increasing mastery of objects in the environment.

Related studies include Decarie (1965) who constructed an object permanence scale, and whose findings lend further credence to Piaget's conclusions. Uzgiris and Hunt (1966) devised ordinal scales of the infant's psychological development (IPDS), which are receiving increasing attention. (See also Uzgiris, 1973). Roberts and Black (1972) employed the scales while investigating the effect of naming and object permanence on toy preferences. Wachs (1970) concluded '... its potential [i.e. that of the IPDS] for applicability . . . must be considered favourable.'

It is encouraging to note that the development of sensori-motor intelligence is receiving increased cross-cultural attention. The IPDS is currently being administered in Teheran and Israel (Dasen in personal communication with McV. Hunt, 1972). A study of object construction and imitation under differing conditions of rearing in Athens (Paraskevopoulos and Hunt, 1971) demonstrates high intercorrelations between levels of development in object permanence, vocal imitation and gestural imitation.

More recently, Woodward (1972) analysed the problem-solving strategies utilized by normal and severely sub-normal children in tasks demanding rapid reasoning. Chronologically, the subjects were in the period between the end of Piaget's sensori-motor stage and the beginning of the intuitive. (The study is described in Chapter Seven).

Pre-Operational Stage

The pre-operational stage (approximately two to seven years) has received less attention than the sensori-motor stage. It is a transition period from the predominantly autistic and egocentric stage of early childhood to the early forms of social behaviour, sociocentric speech, and conceptual thought, which become more obvious toward the end of the pre-operational stage. Many of the problems which the infant faces at the sensori-motor stage reappear, since the child in the pre-operational stage must learn to adapt to the thoughts of others and to conceptualize his own experiences on a higher level of development.

This period is characterized by symbolic activity. The child develops symbolization and acquires more facility in language. During the pre-operational stage the child does not use logical operations in his thinking. Instead, he is perceptually oriented, makes judgements in terms of how things appear, and generally can deal with only one variable at a time. Thinking at this level of functioning is rigid.

This stage can be divided into two further stages, namely the pre-conceptual stage (two to four years) and the stage of intuitive thinking (four to seven years). At the pre-conceptual stage the child operates on the principle of transduction: he is closely tied to the perceptual aspects of individual situations, and he is unable to form concepts. He has some general ideas, which Piaget calls 'preconcepts', i.e. a way of thinking midway between reference to specific objects and a genuine understanding of classes. Piaget believes that the development of mental imagery plays an important role in enabling children to anticipate recurring events and to plan actions in advance.

The second, more advanced phase (four to seven years) of the pre-operational stage is that of intuitive thought or intuitive use of concepts. The differentiation from the previous phase is a refined one. The judgement of the child at this stage is intuitive and subjective but deals with somewhat more complex configurations than in the previous stage. Piaget (1950) maintains, 'Intuition, at first dominated by the immediate relations between the phenomenon and the subject's viewpoint, evolves towards decentralization. Each distortion, when carried to an extreme, involves the re-emergence of the relations previously ignored. Each relation established favours the possibility of a reversal . . . Every decentralization of an intuition thus takes the form of a regulation, which is a move towards reversibility, transitive combinativity and associativity, and thus, in short, to conservation through the co-ordination of different viewpoints . . . which progress towards reversible mobility and pave the way for the operation' (pp 138-9).

Stage of Concrete Operations

Around seven years of age, the construction of operational structures gives the child the means to know the world within systems of logical classification, seriation, numbers, spatial and temporal co-ordinates and causality. These systems and operations include such acts as those of compensation, identity and reversibility, all characteristic of children demonstrating full operativity. However, these operations do not deal with propositions or hypotheses, which appear only in the last stage of formal operations.

An illustration of these concrete operations is that concerned with classifying objects according to their similarity and their difference. This is accomplished by including the subclasses within larger and more general classes, a process that implies inclusion and is only fully operational around CA seven to eight years.

Therefore, during this period of development one can follow the genesis of thought processes. Nevertheless, it is still a long time before these structures can be applied with full operativity to all possible concrete contents. For example, the principle of invariance (constancy, conservation) is applied to the quantity of matter earlier than to weight, and to volume still later.

Briefly, during the stage of concrete operations (approximately seven to eleven years) mobile and systematic thought organizes and classifies information. Thought is no longer centred on a particular state of an object. It can follow successive changes

10

through various types of detours and reversals, but because the operations are tied to action they are concrete rather than abstract. The attainment of the act of reversibility is the main feature in the development of the child's transition from pre-operational to concrete-operational thought.

Bruner (1959) comments 'in a general sense, by concrete operations we mean actions which are not only internalized, but are also integrated with other actions to form general reversible systems'.

The importance of conservation is well illustrated by Lunzer (1968) when he outlines the work of Piaget and others on conservation and observes: 'The importance of these experiments derives largely from the fact that they appear to bear out the appearance of invariants, which can serve as elements in the logical conceptualization of the world in terms of its quantifiable, spatial and physical properties'.

It should be mentioned here that alongside conservation there appears what Lunzer (1968) terms: '. . . a facility in applying certain logical relations both to objects and to these invariant properties. These logical relations are said to constitute well defined "structures" involving the operations of classification and seriation.'

Piaget (1953) argues that the period of concrete operations sees eight 'groupements' of classes and relations, each of equal value in the study of behaviour at this period. Peel (1960), following Piaget's 'Traité de Logique' illuminates further the nature of operational thought when he gives an outline of the logic of classes and differences together with the logic of the substitution of equivalent or symmetrically related elements. It is, of course, Piaget's thesis that there is a parallel between logical structure and mental structure which is operational. The case is strongly presented by Piaget (1950, 1952, 1953, 1964). A large number of cross-cultural studies within the framework of the concrete operational stage have been carried out. These are described in Chapter Eight. Some of these studies have produced evidence that some subjects, even in the higher age group (12 to 18) do not reach the concrete operational stage. Dasen (1972) maintains '. . . it may be considered surprising, and a limitation of the universality of Piaget's stages, to find more and more evidence accumulating to show that concrete operational thought is not necessarily attained'.

Stage of Formal Operations

The last stage of intellectual development begins, on average, at 11 or 12 years of age and is characterized by the development of formal, abstract thought operations. The child becomes capable

11

of reasoning, not only on the basis of objects, but also on the basis of hypotheses and is able to perform 'operations on operations', in a systematic manner. The formation of hypotheses and of deducing possible consequences from them, leads to a 'hypothetico-deductive' level of thought which expresses itself in linguistic formulations of propositions and logical constructions.

Combinatorial logic and proportionality are examples of formal thinking. In the experiment on combinatorial logic, the child is presented with five bottles of colourless liquid. The first, third and fifth bottles, combined together, will produce a brownish colour; the fourth contains a colour-reducing solution, and the second bottle is neutral. The child's problem is to find out how to produce a coloured solution.

In experiments on proportionality, the adolescent is given a candle, a projection screen and a series of rings of different diameters; each ring is on a stick which can be stuck into a board with evenly spaced holes. The instructions are to place all the rings between the candle and the screen in such a way that they will produce a single 'unbroken shadow' on the screen — the shadow of a 'ring'.

Briefly, it is around CA 12 that the child begins to comprehend in mathematics the knowledge of propositions, and becomes capable of reasoning by using different systems of reference simultaneously. The system remains flexible and can be elaborated indefinitely.

'The four principal stages of the development of intelligence of the child progress from one stage to the other by the construction of new operational structures, and these structures constitute the fundamental instrument of the intelligence of the adult' (Piaget, 1961).

Lovell (1968) maintains that a proportion of adolescents either do not reach formal operational thought at all or attain it in limited areas or for short periods. He cites the work of Hughes (1965) which involved a four-year longitudinal study of pupils, and stresses the slow cognitive advance among ordinary and even abler secondary modern school pupils; similar findings have been reported by Tomlinson-Keasey (1972), Stephens et al (1972). (See Chapters Five and Seven, respectively.) A recent monograph by Peel (1971; described in Chapter Nine) draws attention to the few systematic investigations into the growth of thinking during adolescence, and describes a number of verbal situations which he, together with his students, has constructed for assessing the conditions under which adolescents make judgements.

A few cross-cultural studies have been conducted on formal thought — Goodnow (1962), Peluffo (1967), Were (1968) and Kelly (1970). These are discussed in Chapter Eight. Such research evidence lends credibility to Piaget's 'prediction' (1966, p. 13; 1968, pp. 97-99) that the reasoning of 'primitive' peoples would not develop beyond the stage of concrete operations.

By way of summary, it appears that the weight of evidence produced by the Geneva Centre, for the unity and interconnectedness of mental structures, needs to be set beside the wealth of evidence available on individual differences. It is suggested that there is an absolute need to extend Piaget's theory so as to take account of personality, environmental, socialization and motivational effects on mental structures.

Tuddenham (1969), cited in Dockrell (1970), observes: 'I must confess that I am pleased rather than dismayed that the intractable individuality of human beings, which has plagued normative psychologists . . . continues to assert itself, even in the face of Piaget's elegant normative theory'.

The reader who is unfamiliar with Piaget's theory will find a more detailed account in Flavell's 'The Developmental Psychology of Jean Piaget' (1963), Beard's 'An Outline of Piaget's Developmental Psychology (1969), Ginsburg and Opper's 'Piaget's Theory of Intellectual Development' (1969) and Piaget and Inhelder's 'The Psychology of the Child' (1969).

As early as 1930, Hazlitt and McCarthy criticized Piaget's 1920s work for its heavy reliance on the interpretation of verbal statements, and the tendency to 'project' the experimenter's ideas into these interpretations. Commenting on these views, Dodwell (1960 p. 191) maintains that the 1952 English translation of Piaget's 'La Genèse du Nombre chez l'Enfant' (1941) '. . . .is an improvement on Piaget's earlier studies in at least two respects. First, the theoretical background is much more precise, but at the same time more elaborate than his earlier themes of cognitive development, and secondly the empirical investigations are more objective, described in sufficient detail to be essentially repeatable . . . .' In the 1940s, Piaget began to revise his earlier linguistically-oriented approach by posing questions concerning concrete materials instead of imagining these objects merely on the basis of a verbal description. Pufall, Shaw and Syrdal-Lasky (1973) draw attention to Piaget's concern for the refinement of his earlier themes and, focusing on the development of number conservation, they state, 'In his original volume on number, Piaget (1952) identifies three stages in the development of lasting equivalence, while in a subsequent article (Piaget, 1968) he identifies a fourth stage which precedes the other three' (see Chapter Three). Likewise, Berzonsky (1971) underlines Piaget's constant redefinement and elaboration of his theoretical formulations with his description of Piaget and Inhelder's 'The Growth of Logical Thinking in Childhood and Adolescence' (1958) as a 'pinnacle of sorts' reached from Piaget's 1926, 1928, 1929, 1930, 1932, 1950 and 1953 works. (Details of 'The Growth of Logical Thinking' and Berzonsky's investigations appear in Chapter Five.)

Flavell (1963), in a critique relating to Piaget outlines the various shortcomings of the latter's approach surrounding 'matters of theory and interpretation; matters of experimental design and data analysis and matters of the upward and downward relating of data to theory and interpretation'.

Whether or not the revised clinical method gives a reliable assessment of the child's abilities continues to be debatable. Some psychologists feel that the method is still too verbal (Braine, 1962) while others have demonstrated the reverse (Fleischmann, Gilmore and Ginsburg, 1966, pp. 353-68).

Wallace (1972) states '. . . he (Piaget) appears to have failed to resist the supreme temptation of capitalizing on the ambiguity of verbal response to derive support for his preconception . . . although verbatim protocols for a number of subjects are usually presented in his work on intellectual development, there is little indication that Piaget followed a systematic inductive strategy in moving from this data to the formulation of his theory of stages. On the contrary there is a case for viewing the children's verbalizations cited as simply illustrations of the appropriateness of a preconceived theory.'

Further, Wallace draws attention to the question of the existence of stages which, he considers, 'remains as baffling as ever'. He reflects that the cross-sectional studies carried out by Piaget and his followers can never illuminate the child's development in conceptualization and that a longitudinal approach would give more definite results. (Later chapters in the present book reveal initial and increasing attempts to carry out longitudinal studies.) Wallace calls for greater flexibility in aims for research studies lying in 'the acceptance of the inevitability of inconsistencies and individual variations in subjects' responses and in a consequent adjustment in the criteria employed in identifying developmental stages . . . this approach entails rejection of the aim of assigning particular individuals to single stages characterizing their performance across all situations and based on hypothesized underlying structures with the constraints on the order of acquisition of inference patterns which this involves'. However, to balance Wallace's and other criticisms, attention needs to be drawn to Piaget's writings (1969) on the value of the developmental stages in education and science. So far as questions about natural phenomena are concerned Piaget comments, '. . . such a development of response would seem to bear witness to a structural transformation of thought with age'. He acknowledges that the same results have not been observed everywhere (this is evidenced in many chapters in this book) and that inconsistencies must be recorded — however, if the reactions of younger children are compared with those of older, the existence of a maturing process has to be accepted. Nevertheless, Piaget comments that to posit, from this, the existence of inflexible stages characterized by invariable chronological age limits and a permanent thought content, is to proceed to extremes. He states that characteristic ages are never more than average, that there are overlaps when passing from one test to another — '... these overlaps ... probably exclude the possibility of establishing generally applicable stage limits ...' — further, that 'each stage of development is characterized much less by a fixed thought content than by a certain power, a certain potential activity, capable of achieving such and such a result according to the environment in which the child lives'. Piaget continues that we can never obtain anything more from experiments than sorts of 'mental phenotypes' and that reactions are not absolute characteristics of a given stage. Nevertheless, it is apparent that common features can be determined and 'are in fact an index of the potential activity differentiating each stage from the other.'

Flavell (1972) offers 'some proposals' concerning the classification and explanation of developmental sequences of cognitive acquisitions. He discusses the constituents of a cognitive-developmental sequence and some of the methodological problems in the empirical validation and examines the difficulties of explaining an invariant or near-invariant cognitive-developmental sequence. He also argues that human cognitive development 'may exhibit significant asequential features in addition to the obvious sequential ones, and that a realistic, balanced view of such growth should take account of both sorts of features'.[1]

A variety of findings has emerged with respect to the existence of the stages described by Piaget and these are reported throughout most of the following chapters.

Flavell (1963) considers that Piaget's system, theory and experimentation has repelled many and that 'Piaget has not been the best of salesmen for his own wares'. However, replication of Piaget's studies would not be 'such a popular (and such a necessary) pastime had these shortcomings not been present'. The many studies reported throughout this book bear witness to this assertion.

The momentum of Piaget's work has been increased by the interest shown by educators — first and foremost by educators involved with young children (Susan Isaacs was much involved in correspondence with Piaget) but increasingly (as is shown in later chapters) by those concerned with older children. Although the majority of replication and extension studies are carried out within the universities, the progressive involvement of teachers and college of education lecturers in advanced courses and research degrees implies a stimulation within the schools. When Piaget began his studies of genetic epistemology he was not concerned with educational problems and during the years has only occasionally commented on educational practices. Therefore, as with many other theories, educators have had to draw their own implications with respect to educational philosophy and practice.

Piaget has provided a conceptual framework and schema from which to view educational problems. It will be observed throughout the book that many experimenters carrying out Piagetian studies have drawn educational implications from both the work of Piaget and their own investigations.

Arising from Piaget's theory, educators have placed increasing emphasis on the child being active in his learning with the teacher's role involving stimulating to help the child to establish new levels of understanding. The teacher familiar with the stages is likely to be more appreciative of the disparity between language and thought, relative to the child's particular level of cognition. The importance of the early years for later cognitive growth is also realized as a result of Piaget's work, together with the important factor of the continuity of intellectual growth. Piaget's emphasis on social interaction as a necessary condition for cognitive growth has supported other influences in establishing learning situations in schools where pupils are encouraged to interact. (Such research evidence has been assembled in Chapter Eleven) (Beard, 1969, Athey, 1970; Elkind, 1970; and Furth, 1970 together with others have further discussed the educational implications of Piaget's theory.)

However, Vinh-Bang (1971) draws a distinction between the interests of Piaget as he studies the child and those who would like to contribute directly towards change in the teaching–learning situation. He questions the practice of direct application of Piaget's research techniques into exercises for students and considers that this reveals a lack of understanding of developmental psychology. He concludes: 'The research of Piaget in developmental psychology has provided a theoretical foundation. It is left to us to project his theoretical models into the reality of the schools; in other words to make the solutions operational for the schools. In this way, the thought of Piaget will remain intact, yet his work will have a determining influence on the educational system.'

More recently, with the publication of 'The Science of Education and the Psychology of the Child' (1970) together with an article written for a series of studies prepared for the International Commission on the Development of Education, for

16

Unesco (1972), Piaget has revealed an interest in the school curriculum. Within this sphere he reaffirms his approach to the development of intelligence as being of a 'constructivist nature (attributing the beginnings of language to structures formed by the pre-existing sensori-motor intelligence). It recognizes neither external preformations (empiricism) nor imminent preformations (innateness), but rather affirms a continuous surpassing of successive stages. This obviously leads to placing all educational stress on the spontaneous aspects of the child's activity.' Piaget draws attention to the proportionally small number of students following courses in science as opposed to liberal arts. He advocates a complete revision of methods and aims in education involving pre-school education — more active methods, the application of child and adolescent psychology and interdisciplinary curricula as opposed to 'compartmentalization'. He commends practice in observation at the pre-school level; more active methods which involve the child and adolescent learning every new truth by discovery and reconstruction with the teacher creating the situations and being 'a mentor stimulating initiative and research'. An approach to subjects from an interdisciplinary point of view, with more flexibility between the human and natural sciences and an upgrading of the teaching profession at all levels (to include a full university training and the acquisition of adequate psychological knowledge) are also recommended. Piaget is particularly appreciative of the primary teacher's role 'for the younger the students are, the more difficult the teacher's task, if it is taken seriously'. (An extended account appears in Chapter Nine.)

The following chapters provide evidence that Piaget's theory is in full vigour; the research journals abound with further validation or extensions of Piaget's work, in a continuing search for further understanding of the issues raised by Piaget. The name of Piaget is likely to be heard for many decades to come. His theory allows optimism and the possibility of continued growth in many spheres. A challenging objective has been formulated by Goldschmid (1970, 1971, in private communication): 'The Freudians and Neo-Freudians, the "social role" and "socialization" people have never produced a meaningful theory of thought development. Studies of the relationship between Piagetian concepts and other variables in child development are still very rare, yet most desirable if one is to develop a "psychological theory" of child development as opposed to a "cognitive" or "social" or "emotional" theory of child development on an empirical basis.' (See Chapter Eleven.)

[1] A full discussion of the concept of stages can also be found in Mischel, T. (Ed.) (1971). 'Cognitive Development and Epistemology', pp. 25-60; and in 'Cognitive Development in Children', (1970) Society for Research in Child Development, pp. 55-73.

CHAPTER TWO
'SENSORIMOTOR' OR 'PRACTICAL' INTELLIGENCE

Piaget (1967) considers that the period that extends from birth to the acquisition of language is 'marked by an extraordinary development of the mind.' The importance of this period is sometimes underestimated because 'it is not accompanied by words that permit a step-by-step pursuit of the progress of intelligence and the emotions, as is the case later on'. Piaget emphasizes that this early mental development determines the entire course of psychological evolution. In fact, it is no less than 'a conquest by perception and movement of the entire practical universe that surrounds the small child'.

Piaget cites three stages between birth and the end of the first period: the reflex stage, the stage of the organization of percepts and habits and the stage of sensorimotor intelligence itself. At birth, mental life is limited to 'hereditarily determined sensory and motor coordinations that correspond to instinctual needs, such as intuition'. Piaget stresses that these reflexes are not by any means passive, for from the outset they show genuine activity. Further, they reveal the existence of 'precocious sensori-motor assimilation': for example, the sucking reflexes become refined and improved over time. The sucking reflex also becomes generalized to other sucking activities. 'The infant assimilates a part of his universe to his sucking to the degree that his initial behaviour can be described by saying that for him the world is essentially a thing to be sucked . . . this same universe will also become a thing to be looked at, to listen to, and, as soon as his own movements will allow, to shake.'

This reflex stage soon becomes integrated into habits and organized percepts: the child turns his head in response to a sound, follows a moving object and gradually begins to recognize certain persons as distinct from others. He does not, however, conceptualize a person or even an object. Piaget stresses the essential role of 'circular reactions' at this stage: 'the infant's random movements fortuitously producing something interesting (interesting because it can be assimilated into a prior schema) for him to repeat these new movements

19

immediately' and representing a more advanced form of assimilation.

The third stage, 'which is even more important to the course of development': the stage of practical and sensorimotor intelligence itself. Intelligence actually appears well before language, that is to say, well before internal thought, which presupposes the use of verbal signs (internalized language). It is an entirely practical intelligence based on the manipulation of objects; in place of words and concepts it uses percepts and movements organized into 'action schemata'. Piaget considers that the stage of sensorimotor intelligence leads to the 'construction of an objective universe in which the subject's own body is an element among others and with which the internal life, localized in the subject's own body is contrasted'. (Piaget subdivides these stages even further and gives detailed accounts of each in 'The Origin of Intelligence in the Child', 1953.)

Piaget describes four fundamental processes which characterize the sensorimotor period: the construction of the categories of the object, of space, of causality and of time. He adds the proviso that these refer to purely practical or action categories and not, of course, to ideas or thinking. The elaboration of space is derived from the coordination of movements; causality, the link between an empirical result and some action that has brought it about, and the objectification of time enabling 'the nascent mind' to be extricated 'from its radical unconscious egocentricity' and to be placed in a 'universe'. (Further details of these fundamental processes appear in 'The Construction of Reality in the Child, 1955.)

(The few studies relating to the sensorimotor stage as a whole are reported within the Introductory section, namely: Woodward, 1959, 1972; Uzgiris and Hunt, 1966; Wachs, 1970; Golden and Birns, 1971; Paraskevopoulas and Hunt, 1971.) Kephart (1960), working independently from Piaget, concluded (as had Piaget before him) 'that normal sensori-motor development is a pre-requisite to orderly symbolic functioning'.

The Development of Object Concept

The formation of the scheme of the permanent object is closely related to the whole spatio-temporal and causal organization of the practical universe. The six stages as postulated by Piaget (1955) of the development of the object concept correspond to those of intellectual development in general. Piaget summarizes the stages as follows: 'During the first two stages . . . The infantile universe is formed of pictures that can be recognized but that have no substantial permanence or spatial organization'. 'During the third stage . . . , a beginning of permanence is conferred on things by prolongation of the movements of accommodation . . . but no systematic search for absent objects . . . During the fourth stage . . . there is searching for objects that have disappeared but no regard for their displacements . . . During a fifth stage . . . the object is constituted to the extent that it is permanent individual substance and inserted in the groups of displacements, but the child still cannot take account of changes of position brought about outside the field of direct perception. In a sixth stage (beginning at the age of 16 to 18 months) there is an image of absent objects and their displacements.'

Stage IV marks an important transition. Before Stage IV, the infant lacks object permanence and knows an object and its location only in the context of his ongoing actions: he cannot find hidden things or can only find them if he has begun to reach for them before they disappear. In Stage IV, the infant is aware of object permanence: when he observes an object disappear, he searches for it even when he has not begun to reach for it before its disappearance. In Piaget's experiments an object is hidden in one place (A) and then in a second place (B). After the infant finds the object at A, he watches the object being hidden at B. However, when the object disappears from view, the infant searches at A. This establishes the pattern of success at A and failure at B and is referred to as 'AB'.

Of the follow-up studies, the majority have demonstrated that the task of finding an object hidden only at 'A' (object in one place) is relatively easier than the task of finding an object hidden both at 'A' and 'B' ('B' refers to the object transferred to a second place). Such studies include those of Decarie (1965), Bell (1968), Escalona and Corman (1967), Miller, Cohen and Hill (1969) and Smith (1970). These studies, however, did not provide convincing evidence as to whether unsuccessful behaviour at 'B' is followed by exploration at 'A', or termination of the search. Furthermore, the universality and age-relatedness of such a phenomenon is uncertain. For example, only two of 25 eight-and-a-half-month-old infants in Bell's study (1968), who searched successfully at 'A', failed at 'B'. However, it was not made clear whether either of the two infants failed 'B' by searching at 'A' or simply terminated the search. Other studies, e.g. Appel and Gratch (1969), Bower (1967), and Charlesworth (1966), who also examined the development of object-permanence, recorded their observations in a one-position situation only. Of particular interest is Charlesworth's study, in which a 'trick condition' was introduced involving a small foot-operated 'trap door' in the tray of the child's high chair. This enabled a 'more sensitive measure of a child's cognitive progress' (see Flavell, 1971).

Gratch and Landers' investigation (1967) concluded that 'the visual orientation of infants during the delay between hiding and searching was related to their successful searching behaviour in the AB experimental paradigm' (i.e. a pattern of success at A and failure at B). In continuation, Landers' study (1971) involved infants' 'playing a two-position hidden-object game. Infants who had much experience of reaching and finding an object at the "A" position made longer error runs at this position than infants who had little searching experience at "A" or infants who had much experience just observing objects hidden at "A" but no experience searching for them'. (The study is discussed fully later in this chapter.) In an attempt partly to replicate and partly to extend Landers' study, Gratch and Landers (1971) generally confirmed Piaget's (1954) Stage IV in the development of object concepts. (Full details appear later in the chapter.)

Luria (1959) reported a phenomenon similar to Piaget's Stage IV behaviour in 16- to 18-month-old children. A study of Webb, Massar and Nadolny (1972) revealed that, if the child is permitted to continue his search, he is observed to make 'predominately correct second choices after making an initial error'. (See also Evans and Gratch, 1972, and Roberts and Black, 1972.)

Le Compte and Gratch (1972) were intent to investigate directly the development of object identity, by varying the object rather than its spatial position. They note studies (namely Appel and Gratch, Charlesworth, Evans and Gratch) which question the assumption that infants in and beyond Stage IV know that the reappearing toy is the same toy as that which was hidden. Tricking the child, by hiding one toy and having him find another, violates a rule of permanence. Older infants reacted with 'high puzzlement and searched for the missing toy and the causes of its disappearance. Younger infants were mildly puzzled but only focused on the new toy.' Piaget's contentions concerning the development of the object concept were upheld. (The study is described later in this chapter.)

Bower (1967) has, in part, criticized Piaget's concept of object permanence. Through a series of ingenious experiments, Bower has published convincing evidence which suggests that two- to three-month-old infants have a perceptual version of the concept of object permanence. Bower is in agreement with Piaget in finding that if an object disappears in an abrupt, discontinuous manner, the infant acts as if it no longer existed for him. However, if it disappears gradually and continuously, the infant behaves for a short period as though it were still present or would reappear. Bower concludes that 'these primitive, perception-based discriminations regarding permanence and impermanence are later subordinated to conceptual rules to the concept of object permanence. Unlike the three-month-old, the 12-month-old has come to believe in the continued existence of certain objects (e.g. his mother), regardless of the psychophysical properties of their disappearance — even when his lower-order, perceptual operations have given him a verdict of out-of-existence rather than out-of-sight'. More recently, Bower and Paterson (1972), after supporting the hypothesis 'that there is an object concept developing from birth onwards and that facilitatory intervention at one point will speed development at later points', draw attention to the need to devise a theory to link the various stages of the development of the object concept. (Interesting extensions are reported in Bower and Paterson, 1973.)

Bell (1970) showed that infants tended to be more advanced in the concept of persons than in the concept of inanimate objects as permanent. Furthermore, individual differences in the rate of development of person permanence were related to the quality of attachment that an infant showed toward his mother. In turn, this affected the development of object permanence. She concluded 'the quality of a baby's interaction with his mother is one of the crucial dimensions of "environmental influence" to affect this type of sensori-motor development'. (Details are given later in this chapter.)

Golden and Birns (1971) examined infants between 18 and 24 months of age from different SES groups on the Cattell and Piaget object scales. The authors concluded that social class differences in cognitive development were not evident during the sensori-motor period; further, that SES differences emerge from CA 18 to CA 36 months when language develops. (Details are given later in this chapter.) Baliska (1965) has extended the research beyond the sensori-motor stage six. She considers that object concept is not fully operative until about three years of age — a research area termed by Flavell (1971) as 'Beyond the Object Concept'.

The development of the concept of object as related to infant-mother attachment
S. M. Bell, 1970

Piaget's contentions (1937; 1954) are that the development of the object concept does not proceed at the same rate with respect to all objects (Bower, 1967, Smith, 1970). Bell (1970) investigated the patterning between the development of person and· object permanence and the attachment of an infant to his mother. Other researchers who have reported similar findings are Saint-Pierre (1962), Ainsworth and Bell (1970) and Ainsworth and Wittig (1969).

The inquiry was addressed to the following hypotheses:

23

(a) that infants tend to be more 'operational' in the concept of person than in the concept of inanimate objects;

(b) that differences in the rate of development of person permanence are affiliated to the quality of attachment behaviour that an infant demonstrates towards the mother; and

(c) that differences in the rate of acquisition of person permanence can affect, subsequently, the development of the concept of object permanence.

SUBJECTS/Twenty-one boys and 12 girls (CA eight-and-a-half months to 11 months) of middle-class parents took part in the study. In order to assess object and person permanence the author devised two scales. These scales were drawn partly from Decarie (1965) and were subsequently found to be closely comparable to Escalona et al. (1967) and Uzgiris and Hunt (1966b). The Griffiths Test of Infant Intelligence (1954) was administered and retarded infants (below IQ 75) were not included.

METHOD/The infants were assessed at home three times between the ages of 8.6 months through to 11 months. Information from mothers was also obtained. Seven days after the third interview, infants were introduced to a strange situation. This was used to evaluate and observe attachment behaviour. At 13½ months some of the infants were further assessed for the development of the object concept. Full details of the two scales are given by the author in her published work (1970; page 296, Table 1).

Criterion of Attachment: Behaviour in a 'Strange' Situation. For the purposes of the present study, the author adopted, with success, the 'strange' situation devised by Ainsworth and Wittig (1969) to elicit exploratory behaviour at first, 'but then to tip the balance toward attachment behaviour through a series of increasingly stressful episodes'. (The reliability of this procedure has been demonstrated further by Ainsworth and Bell, 1970, and Ainsworth, Bell and Stayton, 1971.)

RESULTS/The results of Bell's study lends further credence to the contentions of Piaget (1937) — that the development of person permanence is homologous with that of object permanence with a variability in time and progression rates. Perhaps the most significant finding of Bell's study was that the development of the object concept was intimately associated with the attachment of a baby to his mother. Over and above this finding, all the three hypotheses, stated in the beginning of the study, were substantiated.

24

Social class, intelligence and cognitive style in infancy
M. Golden and B. Birns, 1971

The study involved infants who were examined under both standard and optimal conditions. Three issues were investigated:
(a) that welfare children should obtain significantly lower Cattell and (Piaget) Object Scale scores than middle-class subjects under standard conditions;
(b) that welfare children should show significantly greater improvement in intellectual performance from standard to optimal conditions; and
(c) that there should be no socio-economic status differences under optimal conditions.

SUBJECTS/The 54 infants ranged in age from 18 months to two years. Eighteen subjects each were grouped in each of the three socio-economic status groups as follows:
(1) black welfare families; (2) black higher-educational-achievement families; (3) white higher-educational-achievement families (upper middle class).

METHOD/Test Scales. Each child was seen individually under standard conditions by one examiner and was retested seven days later by another examiner under optimal conditions. The tests employed were Cattell and Piaget Object Scales. (Fuller details of the experimental procedure are given elsewhere: Golden and Birns 1968; Golden, Birns, Bridger and Moss 1971).

RESULTS/Golden and Birns state 'while there was significant improvement in Cattell and Object Scale performance from standard to optimal conditions for all Ss, there were no significant SES differences under either testing conditions, nor were there significant SES differences in the amount of improvement from standard to optimal conditions; . . . when tested under identical conditions, 18- to 24-month infants from black welfare families did not differ in their intellectual performance from upper-middle class white infants; . . . there were no significant differences in intellectual performance between the black and the white infants even though the examiners were both white'. They conclude that 'social class differences in intellectual development . . . are probably not present during the sensori-motor period, and that SES differences emerge somewhat between 18 and 36 months of age, when language enters the picture'.

Stage IV of Piaget's theory of infant's object concepts: a longitudinal study
G. Gratch and W. F. Landers, 1971.

Gratch and Landers (1971) addressed their inquiry to the following two objectives, which are best described in the authors' own words:

(a) 'Is AB a step in an age-graded sequence of responses to disappearing objects?'

(b) 'How do infants shift from AB to successful search at A and B? Do they follow the course that Piaget described, that is, orient to A, orient sometimes to A and sometimes to B, and orient to B?' (The symbols A, B, AB, in this context refer as follows: when the object is hidden first in one place (A) and then in a second place (B), Piaget postulates that, after a child has found the object at A, he attentively watches the object being hidden at B. However, when the object disappears from view, he searches at A. This establishes the pattern of success at A and failure at B which is here referred to as AB.)

SUBJECTS/Thirteen Caucasian infants were selected, aged five months, 29 days to seven months, 16 days. All parents were college-educated and by the time the observation sessions were concluded, the infants ages varied from 10 months to 14 months and 12 days. The median number of sessions per child was 11.

METHOD/Gratch and Landers undertook their study utilizing a longitudinal strategy and observed some important controls, e.g. the length of time the object was out of view (a 'delayed-reaction situation with a three-second intra-trial interval'). The authors stress the systematic control side of hiding, assessed side-going preferences, and oriented the infant to the situation in a systematic manner.

PROCEDURE AND APPARATUS/Each child was seen individually, and seated in a high chair. A table in front of the child had a tray with two wells 12 inches apart. The wells were covered with white washcloths.

Any one session consisted of the following sequences and lasted 30 minutes: (a) warm-up, (b) A trials, (c) B trials, (d) AB trials. (Fuller details of procedure are described by Gratch and Landers, 1971, pp. 363-64.)

RESULTS AND DISCUSSION/The results substantiated Piaget's contention that initial operativity in finding an object at one place is associated with a tendency to search at that place even when the infant sees the object hidden in a second place. Gratch and Landers argue that their various results support Piaget's findings of the development of the infant's search for an object hidden in one of two places. It is interesting to note that Gratch and Landers' experimental procedures were not similar to Piaget's, despite their identical results. Gratch and Landers maintain that the stage IV phenomenon is part of an age-related sequence of responses to hidden objects. Further, Piaget's explanations of AB are also generally upheld by the results of the present study, apart from certain reservations. For example, 'If the likelihood of AB does not vary with the length of the delay interval, then Piaget's position would be supported. However, if the length of delay does influence AB, then Piaget's explanation would have to be considered either incorrect or incomplete' (c.f. Schofield and Uzgiris, 1969).

Effects of differential experience on infants' performance in a Piagetian stage IV object-concept task
W. F. Landers, 1971

Landers addressed his inquiry to the following objectives:
   (a) 'What are the effects on the AB behaviour pattern of variations in A experience. Related to this, what are the effects of "active experience" (i.e. searching for the hidden toy) versus "passive experience" (i.e. observing but not searching) on the AB behaviour?'
   (b) 'What is the relationship of the infant's visual orientation to AB behaviour and differential A experience?'

   SUBJECTS/Twenty-two females and 20 males of white middle-class parents were involved in the study, between the ages of 7½ and 10½ months.

   METHOD/Each subject was assigned to one of three groups, comprising 14 subjects each, which portrayed the varied degrees of A experience, as indicated by Landers (1971). The three groups were matched for sex, age and 'side preference'. Children were seen at home. After an initial period of familiarization with the subjects, the session consisted of three phases; (a) warm-up trials, (b) A-hiding trials, (c) B-hiding trials. Only the A-trials were different for each of the three groups. (General procedure was identical to Gratch and Landers, 1971.)
   Group I, designated the 'low A experience group' was administered the A-hiding trials, consisting of two consecutive successful searching trials to the A side. The main experimental procedure is best described in the author's own words. 'On each

trial the experimenter showed the object to the infant and moved it into position over the A-hiding well of the tray. With the tray beyond the subject's reach, the experimenter raised and lowered the object into the A well to ensure attention to the place of hiding. On the third lowering, the well was covered with the white wash cloth (the other well — B — had been covered prior to the baiting). After covering the well, the experimenter stood motionless at the midline for a three-second delay, then moved the tray forward enabling the subject to reach for the toy. If the subject found the toy, he was allowed to play with it briefly before the next trial started. If the subject did not find the toy, the tray was moved out of reach and the experimenter drew the subject's attention to another toy and allowed him to play with it until the next trial. When a subject searched unsuccessfully . . . on an A-hiding trial, he was given an extra A trial in order to reach the appropriate number of consecutive successful searching trials to the A side. This procedural criterion was used for subjects in all three groups. At the end of the inter-trial interval . . . the examiner recovered the toy from the infant in order to begin the next trial. The amount of A experience for Group I subjects reflected the amount Piaget's infants typically received.'

Group II was designated as 'high-active A experience Group'. The general procedure was identical to that of Group I, apart from the fact that A-hiding trials comprised of either eight or 10 consecutive successful searching trials.

Group III was designated as the 'high-passive A experience group'. Subjects received six or eight observing trials and two searching trials. Overall, the general procedure was similar to that for Group I, described above, apart from certain modifications.

Following A-hiding trials, all subjects received the same B-hiding trials, where the object was hidden on the B side in the identical manner described for Group I A-hiding trials. Only slight modifications were observed. (Fuller details of exact experimental procedure, including the classification of the subject's behavioural visual orientation are given elsewhere, in Landers, 1971 pp. 50-1.)

RESULTS/Landers' study generally indicated a positive relationship between differential A experiences and differences in the AB behaviour pattern of Piaget's (1954) stage IV of object-concept acquisition. The results lend further credence to Piaget's contentions. However, Landers concludes that further investigations related to Piaget's Stage IV of object-concept development are needed 'to establish empirical parameters, (which) would provide greater understanding and explanation of the genesis of cognitive processes in infancy'.

The stage IV error in Piaget's theory of object concept development: difficulties in object conceptualization or spatial localization?
W. F. Evans and G. Gratch, 1972

AIMS/With respect to the phenomenon of the AB error the authors were intent to evaluate the relative merits of Piaget's explanations for this error, namely: (a) the infant's confusion about the relation between thing and place because he understands the nature of things and their locations only in terms of where he has successfully acted upon them in the past, and (b) that the infant localizes objects in terms of his prior actions.

SUBJECTS/twenty-four infants aged between 8½ and 10½ months.

METHOD/For half of the infants an object was introduced at B discriminably different from the object hidden at A. For the remaining half, the same object was hidden at both A and B. The authors reasoned that 'if the AB error occurs because the child associates a particular object with his action at A, then introducing a new object at B should lead to fewer errors because the new object will not have become associated with a place. On the other hand, if the child errs because A has somehow become a special place, then introducing a new toy should have little effect on the error.' (Full details of the procedure and apparatus can be found in Evans and Gratch pp. 684-5.)

RESULTS/The results supported 'the notion that the AB phenomenon occurs because A has somehow become a place where hidden toys are found, rather than because, as Piaget has argued, the particular object belongs at A. If Piaget's "thing of place" argument were correct, then the fact that the child sees a new object hidden at B should increase the probability that he will search correctly since no previous action by the child has endowed the new object with a place. The fact that introducing a new toy has no effect on AB suggests that A has become something more than a place where a particular toy is to be found. It has, instead, become a place where the child goes when things are hidden; it has become a special place.'

The authors draw attention to further research they are undertaking to resolve the issue that active search at A is essential to the AB phenomenon. They are comparing a group of subjects allowed to search actively at A with another group permitted only to see the toy hidden and uncovered at A. 'If only the active searchers err, then additional support will be given to the part of

Piaget's theory which says that Stage IV infants tend to localize hiding places in terms of their recent action sequences.'

Violation of a rule as a method diagnosing infants' levels of object concept
G. K. LeCompte and G. Gratch, 1972

AIM/The purpose of the study was to investigate the development of object identity by varying the object rather than its spatial position. The child was 'tricked' by one toy being hidden and another found. The authors were intent to establish the age at which infants reacted to the transformation of the object and the manner in which they reacted to the transformation. They hypothesized that initial and subsequent reactions to the 'trick' would be correlated and that age-related levels of development of the permanence of the object be established conforming to Piaget's account.

SUBJECTS/Thirty-six babies aged 9, 12 and 18 months to correspond with stages IV, V and VI respectively in Piaget's sensori-motor development scheme.

METHOD/Large, colourful noisy toys were contrasted with small, drab-coloured plastic objects. The 'trick' box enclosed two sliding trays: only one of the trays showed in the hole at one time. The subjects' reactions were recorded on videotape. (Full details of the procedure can be found on pp. 388-9.) Familiarity with the toys was established and warm-up trials carried out.

RESULTS/Infants at all ages reacted differently on the 'trick' trials and reacted more noticeably when a large, colourful toy was 'transformed' into a small drab one. The reactions to the tricks were related to age and they supported Piaget's account of the development of object permanence. The authors, however, draw attention to aspects needing further clarification, including the use of alternative measures to assess the infants' cognitive understanding of the hiding game situation.

CHAPTER THREE
EXPERIMENTAL VALIDATION OF PIAGETIAN CONSERVATION

Introduction

The plethora of studies relating to conservation acquisition in young children indicates its popularity in cognitive developmental research. This is due to the central role it has played in the research and theorizing of Piaget and the consequent interest of teachers. Piaget uses evidence of conservation acquisition as an indicator of sequential cognitive progress through several stages which terminate in succeeding levels of equilibration. For example, he proposes (1960, 1967) that the child passes through three stages of equilibration in achieving a conservation. Initially, the child adopts a 'strategy' of responding to a single dimension even in the face of continued transformations. Secondly, judgements fluctuate between both dimensions, either on the same problem or on varied problems. Finally, both dimensions are related simultaneously and their transformational relations are realized.

I. Number

Piaget (1952b) analyses three stages in the development of the conservation of number. Piaget (1968) identified a fourth stage concerned with judging numeric relations in terms of topological relations of 'extension' (length) or 'crowding' (density) which he described as preceding the stages to be expounded. Stage II is characterized as the period of global quantification wherein properties are not interrelated systematically. Stage III is manifested by a period of intuitive quantification when thinking is quasi-operational. Finally, the child establishes permanent equivalence when he holds several dimensions simultaneously in the acquisition of concept development.

'There is no connection between the acquired ability to count and the actual operations of which the child is capable . . . If the child has not yet reached a certain level of understanding

31

which characterizes the beginning of the third stage (Lasting Equivalence), counting . . . has no effect on the mechanism of numerical thought' (Piaget, 1952b).

Wohlwill (1960b), considering Piagetian situations to be rather flexible, undertook a scalogram analysis of the development of the concept of number. He maintains: '. . . the results of our study confirm . . . the theoretical views of Piaget in demonstrating the existence of a relatively uniform developmental sequence in the area of number concept'. Wohlwill's findings contradict the findings of Estes (1956), who presented an entirely negative account. No stages were reported in the growth of the number concept: all the six-year-olds had full understanding (details of the study appear later in this chapter). However, Estes designed her experimental situations upon the structure of the three tasks mentioned by Piaget in a short article, published in the 'Scientific American' (1953), rather than on his original set of tasks in the classic work 'The Child's Conception of Number', (1952b). Moreover, she lists only two other references for her study, neither of them directly concerned with number, and only one of them experimental in nature. L'Abate (1962) and Flavell (1963), likewise, point out some of the shortcomings of Estes' replicatory study: restricted age samples, failure to follow strictly the Piagetian tasks, and 'a generally inimical attitude'. Further, Estes' report of her procedure was rather inadequate: 'apparently the manipulations required of her subjects were very limited' (Dodwell, 1960).

Dodwell (1960, 1961) was able to implement the Piagetian contention that the operation of counting is no guarantee of the concept of number or even the concept of conservation of quantity. He also confirmed the emergence of the Piagetian operational stages, but pointed out that age levels of attainment are not so clear-cut as Piaget maintains. A significant correlation was obtained between the Piagetian number concept test and a teacher-made arithmetic test and Dodwell considers the Piaget tests to be a satisfactory measure of 'arithmetic readiness' (further details are given later in this chapter). However, doubt is cast on the validity and reliability of the teacher-made test.

Among studies dealing specifically with conservation, cardination and counting as factors in mathematics achievement, mention is also made of Hood's (1962) study. He was interested in the relationship between the presence of number concepts and ability in arithmetic. Hood compared the stage placement of 120 children, aged four to nine years, with teacher ratings of the children's arithmetical understanding. He concluded that conservation of number is the key factor in number readiness. However, some weaknesses of the study must be mentioned.

Teacher judgements were used to assess ability in arithmetic. The teachers were asked to make global judgements which they may have been basing on different standards. However, Hood's method in this respect is slightly better than using teacher's term marks of students which Dodwell (1961) found to be useless. With a better method of assessment, the relationship between number concepts and ability in arithmetic might have been more pronounced (fuller details of Hood's study appear in Chapter Seven). Hood also noted a tendency for young children to choose the last alternative in a series, especially if the situation with which they were confronted involved difficult questions. Siegel and Goldstein (1969), discussed later, examined this 'recency' hypothesis.

The importance of Piaget's concept of conservation of number as a predictive index of arithmetic achievement was demonstrated by Wheatley's study (1968). The author concludes that counting is a poor basis for judging potential in arithmetic and that often counting is a meaningless set of responses (details of the study appear later in this chapter).

Williams (1968) maintains that, 'number . . . is concerned with the child's way of thinking about the relationships within and between quantities. Piaget is concerned about the extent to which the child appreciates the fundamental nature of the relationships between these quantities. Arithmetic, which is the conventional language of number, is not Piaget's concern but using his criteria we are able to assess the extent to which the child's developing quantitative notions can form the basis for arithmetical activities at the concrete operational level' (Williams' 1958 study is described in Chapter Seven).

In an unpublished report, 'The performance of first-grade children in four levels of conservation of numerousness and three IQ groups when solving arithmetic addition problems', Steffe (1966) classified 132 first-grade children into four levels of number conservation. Children who performed at a lower level of operativity (level four) scored significantly lower on a problem solving test, than children with hierarchical levels of operativity (levels three, two and one), respectively.

Almy's study (1966) investigated the relation between conservation of quantity and school achievement (the study is described more fully in Chapter Nine). The correlations of conservation scores with the two parts of a second grade mathematics achievement test were calculated. For the middle-class school, the correlations were 0.26 and 0.53 and for the lower-class school, they were 0.41 and 0.38. It is likely that the correlations would have been more valid if the verbal factor had been controlled. For further criticisms of the Almy study, refer to Gaudia (1972), and Almy abstract in Chapter Nine.

Overall, with the exception of Estes (1956), the above studies, together with Churchill (1958, cited in Lunzer 1960), Lovell and Ogilvie (1961, discussed later) and others, are in agreement with Piaget's earlier interpretations of the stages of mental structuring, systems of operations and the concept of conservation. Further, the specific stages and levels of operations are neither rigid nor mutually exclusive, and are generally applicable to children at much earlier ages than Piaget maintains.

Piaget, more recently, shows a similar realization: 'But progressive construction does not seem to depend on maturation, because the achievements hardly correspond to a particular age. Only the order of succession is constant' (Piaget, 1961).

Although extensive research has been undertaken into the number and quantity concepts of conservation, these investigations have generally been restricted to children four years of age and older, with most studies dealing with children not younger than five years (see Flavell, 1963; Mehler and Bever, 1967).

The primary reason for this exclusion of the younger ages appears to be that Piaget (1952b) had concluded that conservation of number and quantity are not usually present until age six or seven, and therefore, that nearly all four-year-old children are in the earliest stages of conservation. These contentions, as well as the findings of most investigations (Elkind, 1961; Gruen 1965; Hood, 1962; Rothenberg, 1969; Wohlwill and Lowe, 1962) have demonstrated that conservation operativity is not commonly present at least until age six.

However, authors like Braine (1964) Braine and Shanks (1965), Bruner (1966) and Mehler and Bever (1967) have provided contrary evidence. In Braine's (1964) and Bruner's (1966) studies, the authors have suggested that children of age four are able to conserve, while Mehler and Bever's (1967) study dealt with changes in age in the development of the conservation of number concepts. They suggested that children between the ages of two years six months and three years two months were able to conserve, but that this ability was then lost until the age of four years, six months and reacquired after that (the details of the study appear later in this chapter).

There are many aspects of the assumptions, design and method reported by these authors that seem questionable. For example, in Mehler and Bever's tasks it is always the more numerous row that is manipulated. This tends to violate, at least in part, the Piagetian experimental procedures and the inconsistency in the overall analyses of the behavioural responses. Moreover, Mehler and Bever used a single biased question to assess operativity.

However, in regard to Braine's study (1964) and Bruner's

study (1966), Gruen (1966) had demonstrated that the difference in criteria of conservation between these studies and others (for example, Smedslund, 1961, 1963, 1965) is the reason for the varied results. Smedslund's criteria for conservation operativity consist of both conserving judgement and an adequate explanation for the judgement, while Braine's (1964) and Bruner's (1966) studies necessitated only a conserving judgement (c.f. Fogelman, 1968 and Rothenberg, 1969).

Rothenberg (1969) demonstrated that conservation was rarely present among four- and five-year-old children, when justification is required. She argued that data showing conservation in very young children (e.g. Mehler and Bever, 1967) are confounded by the fact that subjects tend to agree with the investigator more frequently than they disagree. Moreover, Rothenberg suggested that the ideal sequence of conservation assessment questions should be structured so that subjects must both agree and disagree with the investigator, to be judged conservers (details of the study appear later in this chapter).

The results of Mehler and Bever's (1967) study (op. cit.) were uncorroborated by Rothenberg and Courtney (1968) commented upon by Piaget (1968), questioned by Lovell (1971), not upheld by Goldschmid and Buxton-Payne (1968), challenged by Beilin (1968), and partially substantiated by Calhoun (1971). For example Beilin (1968) and Piaget (1968) rejected the application of the term 'conservation' to the Mehler and Bever results. This was based on the fact that the Mehler /Bever procedure did not elicit conservation behaviour, but responses to addition and 'relocation' (Beilin, 1968) or to 'crowding' (Piaget, 1968).

Piaget maintains that Mehler and Bever's experiment has nothing to do with conservation, and finds it difficult to understand why Mehler and Bever conclude that the answers that coincide with the correct numerical quantities exhibit conservation. 'They probably think that, since the usual obstacle to number conservation is evaluation by length, it suffices to show that children from two years six months to three years do not evaluate quantity by length to conclude that they possess the notion of conservation.'

He cites in support of his criticisms an experiment in which he interviewed 29 children between the ages of two years three months and three years ten months, utilizing both Mehler and Bever's techniques and the typical Genevan procedures. Unlike Mehler and Bever, not only unequal collections were presented to the children, but also equal collections. One row had its elements spaced out (length) and the elements of the other row were grouped together. Mehler and Bever's evidence was not substantiated.

35

'To conclude, Mehler and Bever invoke an innate structure which supposedly accounts for early correct answers (we have interpreted these answers in a different way) and for the final successes but which does not explain why the structure is overpowered so easily during the intermediate stages, or why the final structure is richer than the initial one. I maintain that when these facts are explained, the concept of an "innate structure" becomes superfluous, that an innate functioning is sufficient' (Piaget, 1968). Rather an unfavourable and not too penetrating a reply is forwarded by Mehler and Bever (1968) and Mehler and Epstein (1968) to these criticisms of their study, although they acknowledge that their use of the term 'conservation' was unorthodox.

Goldschmid and Buxton-Payne (1968) replicated Mehler and Bever's study. However, the authors made certain modifications, which Mehler and Bever's study did not observe. These included a comprehension of relational terms; questions were rephrased without violating the underlying principles of Mehler and Bever's inquiry, together with a more sophisticated analysis of the behavioural responses. The results indicated that older subjects performed at a much higher level of operativity than the younger ones. Furthermore, not enough evidence emerged to demonstrate a reversal of the developmental sequence of Piaget's cognitive stages.

Calhoun (1971) cites the work of Pratoomraj and Johnson (1966) and Uzgiris (1964). An attempt was made to elucidate the effects of the mode of responding and of age on the number conservation responses in the very young children. A clarification was also sought of the decrement in conservation behaviour, as indicated by Mehler and Bever's study, together with certain aspects of the Rothenberg and Courtney study (1968). Overall, the results substantiated the findings of Mehler and Bever.

Calhoun maintains 'In their replication of the Mehler and Bever study, Rothenberg and Courtney may have confounded the effects of stimulus materials and mode of responding. Although studies with very young subjects are lacking, findings with older subjects suggest that the materials used and the mode of response used can have significant effects on the number conservation responses obtained.'

More recently, however, Willoughby and Trachey (1972) failed to substantiate Mehler and Bever's study. They found (a) that children below three years eight months demonstrated no tendency to select the row containing more objects in any of the three test conditions; (b) that children between three years eight months and four years seven months indicated a significant tendency to select the row containing 'more' when 'M & Ms' were used as objects but not when clay pellets were used; (c) that only the older children (three years eight months and above) chose to eat the row with six sweets in it with any reliability, and (d) that older children were affected by the sequence in which the 'M & M' and clay pellets tests were presented.

Bryant (1972, described in Chapter four) demonstrated that very young children 'do have an effective grasp on the invariance principle and can use it. This is an important conclusion, since this is the first strong evidence for the understanding of invariance at such an early age. Other attempts to demonstrate the invariance principle in very young children (Bever, Mehler and Epstein, 1968; Mehler and Bever 1967) have been shown to be fraught with methodological errors (Rothenberg and Courtney, 1968; Siegel and Goldstein, 1969). The result supports the hypothesis conflict analysis of performance in conservation tasks.' (Lunzer's criticisms, 1972, of Bryant's study are also reported in Chapter Four. Siegel and Goldstein's study is described later in this chapter.) Siegel and Goldstein maintain that the techniques used by Mehler and Bever 'involved both the addition to, and transformation of, a group of objects. This procedure tests the understanding of the relational concept of "more" but not the ability to make conservation responses which involve recognizing identity.'

Overall, the above studies point to certain features of Piaget's concept of conservation. Piaget (1952b) has demonstrated the essential properties of the growth of the number system that indicate a comprehension of number rather than just the ability to use number. Dodwell (1961) and Wheatley (1968) suggest that number conservation tasks may be a relevant measure of arithmetic readiness.

Others (Dodwell, 1960; Elkind, 1961; Hood, 1962; and Goldschmid, 1967) demonstrate that number conservation ability is positively related to intelligence. Further, that both CA and MA should be involved in the evaluation of children's understanding of conservation concepts (Keasey and Charles 1967). Several studies have demonstrated that conservation is not present until CA six (Elkind, 1961; Gruen, 1965; Hood, 1962; Rothenberg, 1969 and Wohlwill and Lowe, 1962), while contrary evidence has been presented by Braine (1964) and more recently by Bryant (1972). However, Gruen (1966) has stressed that the reason for the different results may be due to the difference in criteria employed for an assessment of conservation. Finally, Rothenberg (1969) has pleaded for further research into the nature of the transformations utilized to assess conservation.

Some mathematical and logical concepts in children
B. W. Estes, 1956

SUBJECTS/Estes' study involved a total sample of 52 children consisting of 14 four-year-old children, 20 five-year-olds, and 18 six-year-olds. Warner—Meeker—Eells Index of Status Characteristics (1949) classified 31 children in the middle socio-economic group and 21 in the lower socio-economic group.

METHOD/Four Piagetian problems were administered to the subjects individually. These were as follows:
(a) each child was asked to count ten small green blocks placed in three separate spatially oriented arrangements – in a straight line; in a pile; and in a diamond shape;
(b) the examiner placed eight white chips on the table and the subject was asked to take an equal number from a box containing red chips. The white chips were arranged (a) close together, (b) two inches apart, and (c) in a pattern resembling a parallelogram;
(c) the third task was identical to Piaget's concept of space (construction of the Projective Straight Line) (Piaget 1956, p. 156).

RESULTS/Estes states that in her study, if the children were able to count the spatial orientation of objects, this did not hinder their operativity (seven of the 14 four-year-olds, 17 of the 20 five-year-olds, and all of the six-year-olds demonstrated the ability to count with all three arrangements). Secondly, no stages were found in the growth of the number concept (12 of the 14 four-year-olds had full understanding of number concept; four children at four and five years who showed no ability to count were non-operational). Thirdly, her children did not mistake an apparent increase for a true increase in number (10 of the 14 four-year-olds, 15 of the 20 five-year-olds and all of the six-year-olds followed this pattern). Lastly, if the children could project a straight line in one direction, they could project it in another direction as well. This was found to be true for four of the 14 four-year-olds, 15 of the 20 five-year-olds and all of the six-year-olds.
Estes finally concludes 'the performance of eight of the 10 five-year-olds and all of the six-year-olds in the lower economic group was the same as that of the middle group. Thus economic level does not appear to be a variable.'

Children's understanding of number concepts: characteristics of an individual and group test
P. C. Dodwell, 1960, 1961

AIM/Dodwell's studies related to the experimental validation of Piaget's theory as it applies to the area of mathematics.

SUBJECTS/Two hundred and fifty children from five Canadian schools were involved in the study, representing all socio-economic levels and ranging in age from 5.1 to 10.1 years. The class teachers concerned provided each child with ratings of either 'above average', 'average' or 'below average'.

METHOD/The experimental procedure was similar to the Geneva school. Some degree of flexibility was observed in the administration of the five standardized tests, consisting of 54 questions in all. The five main tasks were as follows:
    (a) Relation of perceived size to number. Materials included beakers and beads.
    (b) Provoked correspondence. Materials included eggs and eggcups.
    (c) Unprovoked correspondence. Materials included red and blue poker chips.
    (d) Seriation. Dolls and canes of graded size were used as materials.
    (e) Cardination and ordination. Wooden cubes and dolls were used as materials.
(Fuller details are given in Dodwell, 1960, pp. 195-97 inc.)

RESULTS/An analysis of the responses indicated emergence of the three stages of thought. However, there were marked variations from task to task. Eighty per cent of the children at five years, ten months demonstrated operativity with the eggs and egg cups (task (b) above) while 80 per cent gave operational responses in the experiment with the beads (task (a) above). Seriation and cardination and ordination (tasks (d) and (e) above, respectively) indicated even less clear age patterns than the conservation tasks. Dodwell was able to implement the Piagetian contention that the operation of counting is no guarantee of the concept of number or even the concept of conservation of quantity. He also confirmed the emergence of the Piagetian operational stages, but pointed out that age levels of attainment are not so clear-cut as Piaget states. Children may also be in one Piagetian stage for one test situation and in a different one for another at one and the same time (Dodwell, 1961).
    When reassessing the 1960 data (op. cit.), Dodwell argues that the difficulty per se of the tasks may not be entirely

responsible for the differences observed. He concluded that 'the pattern of development of number concepts does not follow the sequence described by Piaget with great regularity . . . It is shown that the test is satisfactorily reliable, and valid for predicting arithmetic progress in Grade One'. Thirty-four children were subjected to a teacher-made arithmetic test administered seven months after his 1960 study. This test included such items as number recognition, counting, drawing different numbers of objects, etc. Scores on this test were computed with the Piagetian number concept test, and a correlation of .59 was obtained. Dodwell maintains this to be a satisfactory measure of assessing 'arithmetic readiness'. However, the reliability and validity of the teacher-made test casts doubts and in this respect the findings should be taken with caution.

Cognitive capacity of very young children
J. Mehler & T. Bever, 1967

The authors administered a series of number concept tasks to 200 children.

SUBJECTS/Seven age groups of children with CA two years, four months to four years, seven months were examined.

METHOD/The child was shown two parallel and corresponding rows of four clay and chocolate pellets (M & M's) and equivalence was required (one of the experimental sequences for each child had clay pellets while the other had chocolate pellets). The arrays were modified so that there was a short row of six, parallel to a longer row of four. In the clay pellets item, the examiner asked the child 'to take the row you want to eat and eat all the M & M's in that row'. The orientation of the arrays on the table in front of the child and the presentation of the clay and the M & M items was consistent for each age group (for fuller details of the experiment, refer to Mehler and Bever, 1967, pp. 141-2).

RESULTS/The responses were summarized by age and the results demonstrated a decrease in conserving responses by age, which are at a minimum in the group between three years, eight months and three years, 11 months. 'Thus, as the children get older than two years, six months they get worse, rather than better, at quantity conservation.' The authors further suggested that the 23 youngest children (under two years, eight months) demonstrated higher frequencies of conserving responses — 100 per cent of verbal responses on the quantity of clay pellets and 81 per cent for the sweet rows. The decrease in the CA is significant for the verbal judgements (P<.001 by χ^2 comparing the ages $2 - 4$ to $2 - 7$ and $4 - 0$ to $4 - 3$ for verbal judgements) and non-significant for responses to sweets. At CA four years, six months, children again demonstrated operativity for both kinds of quantity judgement (significance of increase in conservation of clay pellets between $4 - 0$ to $4 - 3$ and $4 - 4$ to $4 - 7 = $ P<.01; for sweets, P<.01 by χ^2).

The authors argue that their results suggest the act of non-conservation to be not a permanent phase in the general cognitive development of the child. 'The study shows that under three years two months, children exhibit a form of quantity conservation; they lose it as they get older and do not exhibit it again until they are about four years six months . . . The fact that the very young child successfully solves the conservation problem shows that he does have the capacities which depend on the logical structure of the cognitive operations.'

They further maintain that the temporary inability to solve the conservation problem reflects a period of over-dependence on perceptual strategies. However, the child can overcome his handicap when he is required to respond in what would seem to be a motivating and attention-arousing manner, that is, eating!

Conservation of number in very young children: a replication of and comparison with Mehler and Bever's study
B. B. Rothenberg and R. G. Courtney, 1968

Rothenberg and Courtney aimed to replicate the methods used by Mehler and Bever (1967).

SUBJECTS/The subjects were 117 pre-school children. The ages ranged from two years four months to four years seven months and the subjects were divided into seven groups at four-month intervals, as in the Mehler and Bever study (1967). The total sample had 60 lower-class and 57 middle-class children.

METHOD/The Mehler Bever techniques were administered first, followed by the Rothenberg task. The details of the Mehler/Bever experimental tasks have already been discussed in this section. The Rothenberg task details were identical to Piaget's (1952b) number procedure. However, for the present study only the dichotomy of conserving (CONS) versus nonconserving (CNC) was utilized.

RESULTS/An analysis of the total sample suggested a trend

similar to Mehler-Bever's. Sixty per cent of the children in Rothenberg's sample were operational on the clay item as against 59 per cent for the Mehler-Bever study. General trends in respect to SES were also observed. The lower SES children computed 62 per cent operational responses, while the middle SES group obtained 58 per cent of the clay item. Seventy-five per cent and 65 per cent respectively of the lower- and middle-class subjects were correct on the sweets items.

The two orientations of array varied in their effect of operational responses. An analysis of the total sample of children demonstrated that differences between the easiest and the more difficult conditions were significant for both clay pellets ($Z = 3.57$, $p<.001$) and sweet items ($Z = 3.31$, $p<.01$). The results of the replication demonstrated that, although a similar percentage of the total sample 'conserved' in both the original and the replicated studies, the age trends noted in the original study were not substantiated. A comparison with the results of all conservation tasks indicated that only a small percentage of subjects aged two years, four months to four years, seven months could actually be classified as conservers. Finally, the authors conclude that there were no sex differences in any of the aspects of conservation of number measured. This lends further support to other findings (Braine, 1959; Pratoomraj and Johnson, 1966; Shantz and Siegel, 1967, and Rothenberg and Orost, 1969).

Conservation, cardination and counting as factors in mathematics achievement
G. H. Wheatley, 1968

AIM/The importance of Piaget's concept of conservation of number as a predictive index of arithmetic achievement is demonstrated by this study.

SUBJECTS/Twenty-one boys and 20 girls were selected at random from two Delaware schools of a total population of 286 children. The subjects were representative of the various ethnic and socio-economic groups.

METHOD/Tests/The three tasks administered were the Greater Cleveland Mathematics Programme, the Number Concept and the Stanford Achievement Test.

RESULTS/The author was interested in the Number Concept Test (NCT) as a predictor of achievement in young children ('first-grade level').

Evidence suggested that the NCT was measuring factors different from those evaluated by the intelligence test used. The correlations between the NCT and SAT (Arithmetic Part) was .75. This was significant at the .001 level and the 95 per cent confidence interval was .57 to .86. Holding constant the effects of intelligence still retained the significance (the correlation was .65 significantly different from zero at the .001 level). The results further indicated the important role that conservation plays in measurement. All correlations between NCT and SAT (four subsections) computed a coefficient of .59, except for NCT with Measurement, which was .76. 'Conservation appears to be the best single predictor of achievement. Although the differences between the correlations are not significant, they approach significance at the .05 level in some instances.' The necessity of the concept of conservation as an essential pre-requisite in the acquisition of the concept of number was, therefore established. The author concludes that counting is not only a poor basis for judging potential in arithmetic but often consists merely of a meaningless set of responses (c.f. Piaget, 1952b; Dodwell, 1961).

Conservation of number among four-and five-year-old children: some methodological considerations
B. B. Rothenberg, 1969

AIMS/To elucidate some of the methodological problems associated with conservation and to examine the growth of number concept development among four- and five-year-old children.

SUBJECTS/Rothenberg's investigation drew on 210 children of lower- and middle-class backgrounds. The children were selected from private nursery schools, preschool groups and kindergartens. The sample included 80 preschool children, with CA four years three months to five years, mean age four years eight months; 130 kindergarten children, with CA five years, three months to six years, mean age five years seven months.

METHOD/The conservation of number technique was patterned after Piaget (1952) and incorporated the modifications of procedures and materials argued and commented upon by Flavell (1963).
The Peabody Picture Vocabulary Test was also adminstered to the total sample of children, who were divided into two equal groups and matched for SES, CA and sex. Group A children were administered the instructional section and the five test trans-

formations (blocks) followed by transformations 3 – 5 repeated with toys. Group B children undertook the instructional section, the five test transformations with toys and followed by transformations 3 – 5 with blocks. 'The purpose of this variation was to evaluate the effects of materials and previous experience with the same transformation on children's ability to conserve number.' However, Rothenberg does not report these results in this study.

RESULTS/The categories of reasons utilized to explain answers to the conservation questions were: symbolic; number; matching; perceptual; limited verbal; don't know; and magical. This was patterned after Shantz and Sigel (1967). The categories of manipulations employed to make both rows have the same number were: matching; incomplete match; adding or subtracting; meaningless and no change.

Overall, Rothenberg's study indicated:

(a) that an identification of full operativity is a function of the conservation question/questions presented and on the number of transformations requested;

(b) inaccurate assessment in terms of 'conservation status' is more likely to be applied to lower-class children than the middle-class subjects;

(c) in the total sample of 210 children, only 13 subjects demonstrated full operativity.

The author concludes the study with a critical review of the methodological considerations in conservation assessments.

Number conservation in very young children: the effect of age and mode of responding
L. G. Calhoun, 1971

AIMS/Calhoun addressed his inquiry to the following two objectives:

(a) a verification of the decrement in conservation operativity as demonstrated by Mehler and Bever (1967) between CA three years three months and four years four months;

(b) 'a study of the effect of two different modes of responding on number conservation in order to clarify possible confounding of stimulus and response variables by Mehler and Bever (1967) and by Rothenberg and Courtney (1968)'.

SUBJECTS/A total sample of 56 Children (26 boys and 30 girls) was involved, eight in each of the seven age groups as follows: two years four months to two years seven months; two years eight months to two years eleven months; three years to three years three months; three years four months to three years seven months; three years eight months to three years eleven months; four years to four years three months; four years four months to four years seven months. To some degree, SES and IQ were controlled.

METHOD/The materials used and the general experimental procedures followed were patterned after Mehler and Bever's 1967 study. Five conservation tasks were utilized under each of the following two modes of response: (a) the child was requested to put his finger on the row that had more; and (b) the child was requested to eat all the candies in any row he preferred.

RESULTS AND DISCUSSION/Overall, Calhoun's results substantiate the findings reported by Mehler and Bever (1967) and Bever et al. (1968). Calhoun, however, draws attention to the difficulty of categorizing accurately the responses of the youngest age group. 'It would seem that the assessment of conservation ability of the youngest children becomes exceedingly difficult because the children may be unable to decode verbal directions of a sufficiently complex level to allow adequate evaluation of conservation. The use of completely nonverbal methods of assessment may prove to be a way of approaching the problem of decoding and encoding of verbal instructions and responses.'

In Calhoun's study there was a decrement in performance between CA three years and three years seven months. However, Mehler and Bever (1967) found a similar decrement between CA three years eight months and four years three months. The author argues that this may be due to the stimulus materials employed (c.f. Goldschmid, 1967; Lovell et al., 1962; Uzgiris, 1964) and population sampling, and that attention and past experience may account for the performance decrement.

Results also indicated that children do conserve when very young; there is then a period of time when some impairment is observed before the ability is regained. However, an 'attention-arousing mode of responding' does produce some enhancement in conserving ability during the period of impairment.

Finally, Calhoun suggests that the disagreement with other related studies may be due to the varied criteria employed by researchers. The author recommends a distinction of two types of number conservation as a solution to conflicting criteria for number operativity and draws attention to the work of Braine and Shanks (1965).

The sequence of development of certain number concepts in preschool children
L. S. Siegel, 1971

AIMS/The inquiry is addressed to the assessment of sequential development of some quantitative concepts in young children; and to the examination of the inter-relationships among tasks which purport to measure number understanding.

SUBJECTS/Seventy-seven children from nursery schools were involved in the study. Their ages ranged from three years to four years eleven months and they had middle-class backgrounds. These children were further divided into four age groups: three years to three years five months; (six girls and seven boys); three years six months to three years eleven months (seven girls and nine boys); four years to four years five months (7 girls and 14 boys); four years six months to four years eleven months, (sixteen boys and eleven girls).

METHOD/The tasks included magnitude discrimination continuous, magnitude discrimination discrete, equivalence, conservation, ordination, seriation and addition. One half of the children in each age group received the continuous magnitude discrimination task first while the other half received the task of discrete magnitude discrimination first (fuller details of experimental procedure are given in Siegel, 1971, pp. 358-9).

RESULTS/No significant differences were computed between the magnitude continuous or discrete tests, at any age. Likewise, no such significant differences were observed between performance on magnitude and equivalence tasks. However, the ordination task was also significantly more difficult than the magnitude discriminations and equivalence tasks for all age-groups, apart from the four years to four years five months group. The ordination task was also significantly easier than seriation and addition tasks in all age groups, apart from the three years to three years five months group. No sex differences were noted in any of the tasks in any age groups.

Siegel further qualifies the results by suggesting the effect of other variables, e.g. the degree of similarity between tasks and 'the elimination of the possibility that differences in performance among the tasks were due to linguistic factors rather than differential development of the conceptual ideas tested by the tasks ... By testing the child's ability to learn a concept through operant conditioning techniques, rather than by determining the presence or absence of the concept at a particular development level, the possible discrepancy between a child's linguistic and quantitative concepts can be minimized'.

The development of the understanding of certain number concepts
L. S. Siegel, 1971a.

Siegel's earlier study (see above) demonstrated that in preschool children, aged three years to four years eleven months, the concepts of magnitude and equivalence developed simultaneously, followed by the conservation operativity. Ordination developed later than equivalence, magnitude and conservation, and preceded the development of seriation and addition.

AIM/The author's present study was an extension of her previous findings to older children. A clarification of the relationship between the acquisition of the concepts of ordination, seriation and addition was also attempted.

SUBJECTS/Eighty-six children from Ontario were involved and were assigned to the following age groups: five years to five years five months (22); five years, six months to five years, eleven months (22); six years to six years, eleven months (22); seven years to seven years, eleven months (20).

METHOD/The general experimental procedure was identical to Siegel (1971, op. cit).

RESULTS/The data were subjected to a mixed-design analysis of variance. Significant effects of age ($F = 30.7$, df = 3/82, $P<.001$) and task ($F = 109.4$, df = 2/164, $p<.001$) were computed. A significant interaction between these two variables was also observed ($F = 4.57$, df = 6/164, $p<.001$). Significant differences among the means for each task at each age group were shown.
A scalogram analysis was also performed to establish a 'meaningful developmental sequence'. The coefficients of reproducibility for the seven tasks administered to the five years to five years five months and the five years six months to five years 11 months groups, were .96 and .98 respectively, and 1.00 for the three tasks administered to both the six years to six years 11 months and the seven years to seven years 11 months groups,
Siegel remarks that the full operativity of ordination or ordinal position precedes a full comprehension of seriation. 'The understanding of the concept of addition develops later than the concepts of seriation and ordination ... and the present study confirmed the results of the earlier one with respect to the sequential development of magnitude, equivalence, and conservation concepts.'

II. Variations in Experimental Design

Lovell (1971) agrees with the results of Goldschmid and Buxton-Payne (op. cit.). He maintains that there is a lack of empirical research evidence to suggest that a reversal of the developmental sequence as postulated by Piaget of the cognitive stages, is feasible. He cites evidence from the work of Donaldson at Edinburgh, who demonstrated that children at CA three years do not comprehend the word 'more', and that 'without understanding a term such as "more" it is difficult to see the validity of the Mehler and Bever data'. For example, Donaldson and Balfour (1968) found that young children respond' to questions using 'less' as if the word 'more' had been used, that is, the meaning of 'less' appears to be synonymous with 'more'. This is in contradiction to Harasym, Boersma and Maguire's (1971) study. Further, Rothenberg (1969, op. cit.) demonstrated that the majority of the four-year-old children demonstrated a lack of comprehension of the necessary concepts 'same' and 'more'. She argued that this deficiency in their basic understanding of the language terms corresponded to a great percentage of inconsistent non-conserving responses in the five conservation tasks. This pattern was demonstrated in her 'warm-up items', where the items were administered '. . . partly to provide base-line data on the S's understanding of the necessary concepts "same" and "more".' Griffiths, Shantz and Sigel (1967) showed that 'more' is used correctly with greater frequency than 'less' but in Harasym, Boersma and Maguire's (1971) study, (discussed later) children appeared to be more competent in using 'less'. Such differences in these various studies may lie partly in the use of testing techniques. The semantic differential technique patterned after Osgood, et al. (1957) was used in the Harasym et al. study, as contrasted with the subjective methods involving personal questioning and performance in the other investigations cited. Moreover, the chronological ages of the various subjects may, in part, be responsible for the differences: some of the studies involved school age children, while others examined pre-school subjects. Likewise, attention has been drawn to the language structure of the questions which contain a number of separate parts, viz. 'Does this row have more, or does this row have more, or do they both have the same number?' (Wallach and Sprott, 1964; Zimiles, 1966), and two-part questions, 'Do these two rows have the same number or does one have more?' (Fleischmann, Gilmore and Ginsburg, 1966).

Pratoomraj and Johnson's study (1966) investigated the kinds of questions and types of conservation tasks as related to children's conservation responses. The questioning of the four sub-groups was varied, being framed around the phrases 'Is it the same?', 'Is there more?', 'Is there less?" 'Are they different?'. The study indicated that the proportion of children's operational responses was not affected by the kind of question asked. Piaget's contention that children's predictions, judgements, and explanations may be used interchangeably as predictors of conservation operativity/non-operativity, was not substantiated (the study is described later in this chapter). Siegel and Goldstein (1969) demonstrated that young children did not show conservation of number. These children showed recency response strategies by choosing the latter of two alternatives offered them. Until CA four years seven months the majority of the children did not respond correctly to quantitative relational terms such as 'more', 'less' and 'same' (the Siegel and Goldstein study is described later in this chapter).

Kinds of questions and types of conservation tasks as related to children's conservation responses
S. Pratoomraj and R. C. Johnson, 1966

AIMS/The authors were interested 'to establish the influence of the kind of question concerning conservation (e.g. "is it the same?" "is it different"?) and of the type of conservation task (prediction, judgement or explanations) on the maturity of Ss' responses to a number of problems at each of a number of age levels'.

SUBJECTS/16 boys and 16 girls at each age level from four to seven years were involved. Children in each age group were divided into four subgroups of eight children each.

METHOD/Tests/Five tasks were administered, patterned after Inhelder and Matalon (1960) and Piaget (1952, 1953). Briefly, these were as follows:
1. Conservation of Substance (plasticine). Two plasticine balls, equal in size and shape were placed before the child, who establishes equivalence. After prediction question (1), one of the balls is rolled into a sausage. This is followed by Questions 2 (judgement) and 3 (explanation). Children in each sub-group were administered subgroup questions as follows: 'Subgroup I (All questions framed around the phrase, "Is it the same?") Question 1: "Suppose one of the balls is made into a hot dog (E makes the gesture), will the amount of plasticine in the ball be the same as the amount of plasticine in the hot dog?" If S did not respond, S was asked: "Will there be as much plasticine in the ball as in the

hot dog?" The first of the two questions under each heading here and below, was asked first in each case. It was only if S did not respond that S was asked the second question.'

'Question 2: "Is the amount of plasticine in the ball the same as that in the hot dog? Is there as much plasticine in the ball as in the hot dog?" '

'Question 3: "Why is that?" "Why do you think that?" Each subgroup was asked the same questions in this and the four problems described below, except that for Subgroup II the questions were framed around the phrase, "is there more?" Subgroup III "Is there less"? and Subgroup IV "Are they different?" '

2. This conservation test involved two towers of cube blocks of the same height (seven blocks each). The basic aim was to establish whether the child continued to establish equivalence of height, under different orientations and manipulations.

3. This task was the conservation of liquid. The aim was to establish whether the child continued to establish equivalence of water when poured into a differently shaped container.

4. This problem was basically the conservation of length and the aim was to establish whether the child believed the blocks to be equal in length, when each overlapped one of the ends of the other block.

5. This task involved the basic principles of the concept of conservation of distance, where the distance from A to B is equal to distance from B to C. The aim was to establish if the child believed the distance AB to be equal to BC, when an object is placed between A and B.

(Fuller details of the experiments including general experimental procedure and scoring techniques patterned after Kooistra 1964, are described in Pratoomraj and Johnson, 1966 pp. 344-7.)

RESULTS/The overall results lent added credibility to Piaget's contentions that children demonstrate the concept of conservation more often as age increases. No sex differences were noted, and likewise the proportion of children's operational responses was not affected by the kind of question asked. Children demonstrated more conservation responses to questions involving prediction than to questions involving judgement and explanation, except for the four- and five-year-old group. In this respect, 'the findings of the present study are in opposition to Piaget's contention that children's predictions, judgements and explanations can be used interchangeably as signs of conservation or non-conversation' (Pratoomraj and Johnson, 1966, p. 352).

Tests of development in children's understanding of the laws of natural numbers
P. G. Brown, 1969

AIM/The aim of the investigation was to study the course of development of understanding of the laws of natural numbers in primary school children.

SUBJECTS/The study involved 180 children aged from six to 11 years, 36 from each of the top infant and four junior year groups of an infant and junior school. Two groups of 40, each with eight children randomly selected from each of the five year groups, formed an experimental and a control group respectively.

METHOD/Two main groups of tests were administered to 180 children.

(a) A written group test with parallel forms 'consisting of 65 items in seven sections, respectively concerned with identity, commutative and associative laws for addition and multiplication and with the distributive law'.

(b) Nineteen Piagetian tests of conservation, spontaneous correspondence, additive composition and tests for the law of closure. These situations paralleled the written test in (a) above.

The experimental group was individually tested on the Piagetian tests and the written test was administered to the whole group of 180 children. The author made comparisons between the performances in the written and Piaget-type tests and between the performances of the experimental and control groups in a written re-test.

The results of the study were as follows:

(a) the achievement performance was positively correlated with an increase in age, with some reservations. For example, in each year group there were exceptional children whose performances were advanced or retarded by up to four years compared with their peers;

(b) children who appeared to understand certain laws of number failed to appreciate closely related non-examples of the laws. The author indicates the latter as a valuable criterion from which to confirm fuller understanding;

(c) the understanding of closure preceded the understanding of identity at seven years of age. This was followed by commutativity and associativity between eight and 10 years of age. Addition usually preceded multiplication. However, this order was not irreversible and depended on the nature of the test. Few children before the age of 10 years understood distributivity;

(d) there was a lack of consistent patterning of evidence that

51

the children who took the Piagetian-type tasks made a greater improvement than those who had not;

(e) the laws of natural numbers appeared to be more difficult than Piaget's concept of conservation operativity.

Conservation of number in young children: recency versus relational response strategies
L. S. Siegel and A. G. Goldstein, 1969

AIMS/Siegel and Goldstein attempted to reconcile Piaget's (1952) and Mehler and Bever's (1967) positions. Piaget maintains that a child does not reach conservation operativity until the age of six or seven, whereas Mehler and Bever's study demonstrated that children as young as two years and four months showed conservation behaviour. Further, Siegel and Goldstein examined the 'recency' hypothesis: that is, young children will select the last alternative presented to them rather than the correct relational one (cf. Hood, 1962).

SUBJECTS/Sixty-six middle-class children of above average intelligence were involved. The distribution of subjects, at each age level was as follows: seven subjects at two years seven months to three years; six subjects at three years one month to three years six months; eight subjects at three years seven months to four years; nine subjects at four years one month to four years six months; 12 subjects at four years seven months to five years; 16 subjects at five years one month to five years six months; and eight subjects at five years seven months to six years one month.

METHOD/Tests/Two tests were adminstered. The first test was intended to assess the understanding of children's knowledge of 'more' and 'less'. Four questions were involved: the first two asked the subject to specify which row had more pennies; and the next two questions required judgements of which row had fewer pennies; e.g. 'which row of pennies has more (less), this one or this one?' The second was a conservation of number test, and three main questions were asked e.g. the child was shown two parallel rows of equal length, each with six pennies, and asked 'Are there the same number of pennies in each row, or does one row have less or more pennies than the other row?' (fuller details of the experimental procedure may be found in Siegel and Goldstein, 1971, page 129).

In order to examine the 'recency' hypothesis, the position of terms 'more' and 'same' was varied in an organized manner for each subject, e.g. if 'more' appeared last in Question One, it occurred first in Question Three. The authors also made certain that the children understood the term 'same'. 'For Question Two, half of the subjects had 'same' first and 'more' last, and the other half had the reverse order. This procedure did not depend on the temporal position of the correct alternative.' (Question Two was identical to Question One, apart from the fact that the row of pennies closest to the child was gathered together, in full view of the child.)

RESULTS AND DISCUSSION/The data were subjected to analysis of variance and showed a significant interaction between the relational and recency strategies as a function of CA ($F = 5.97$, df = 6/59, p<.001). Younger children tended to choose the most recent stimulus but this pattern decreased with increasing CA. 'More' and 'less' were fully comprehended by older children. Results indicated that, until the CA four years seven months, the majority of children did not comprehend the meaning of 'same'. Likewise, the percentage of conservation responses advanced at each age group revealed that it was not until the age of five years seven months that the majority of the subjects showed number operativity.

Siegel and Goldstein finally conclude '. . . it appears that young children do not show conservation of number as previously reported by Mehler and Bever if the understanding of the words "more", "less" and "same" is controlled. Instead, young children tend to respond on the basis of positional preferences for the last alternative.'

Verbal factors in compensation performance and the relation between conservation and compensation
G. Y. Larsen and J. H. Flavell, 1970

AIMS/The authors argue that 'The Bruner-Braine hypothesis that conservation performance can be improved if abstract verbal terms are avoided must be regarded as unproven until the compensation – conservation issue is cleared up, or until a more direct test of the relation between abstract verbal terms and conservation can be made. The more general contention, however, that the verbal terms used to present a task to a child influence the child's performance on the task can be tested in relation to the anticipation-of-levels task itself. The major part of the present study was concerned with examining this contention. It was expected that the more abstract the terms used, the more difficult the task would become.'

SUBJECTS/One hundred and twelve children from a middle-class background were involved in the study. Of these, 80 children were from a kindergarten with CA range five years one month to six years and 32 were second-grade children with a CA range seven years one month to eight years one month.

METHOD/Compensation of Displacement and Conservation of Length/Prior to the anticipation of levels task, each child was administered the conservation of length task, then the compensation of displacement test and finally was re-tested for length conservation. The materials consisted of two sticks, a block of wood and a board.

'The sets of sticks represented different ways the child might imagine the appearance of the halves of the two three-inch sticks covered by the block of wood after one stick had been displaced ¾ inch. The two sticks were placed in front of the child parallel to each other and perpendicular to the child's line of sight, and with the ends matching. After obtaining the child's agreement that the two sticks were the same length, E displaced one stick to the right, and asked again if they were equal and why. Then E realigned the sticks, placed the block of wood over the left half of the sticks, and moved the bottom stick ¾ inch to the right. The child was shown the board with four sets of sticks at various displacements in relation to each other, and asked to indicate which of the four sets of sticks "looks like the part of the sticks underneath the tunnel". After obtaining the child's response the block of wood was removed, and the child was again tested for conservation of length.'

Anticipation of Levels/The materials for this task were as follows:

(a) six transparent rectangular plastic containers were used: two standard containers, and two comparison containers for each standard, one narrower and one wider. Each child was asked to form a prediction and to justify the prediction advanced, of the level of water for both the wider and narrower comparison containers for each standard.

The three modes of presentation were as follows:

1. 'This water' — for each estimation the child was asked, 'If I poured this water (E points to the water in the standard) into here (E points to the comparison container) how high would it come up to? Why do you think it would come up to there?'

2. 'Same Amount' — E asked the child, 'If I put the same amount of water in here (E points to the comparison container) as there is in here (E points to the standard), how high will the water come up to? Why?'

3. 'Fair Share' — E said 'Let's pretend that this (E points to

the comparison container) is Mary's jar, and that this (E points to the standard) is John's jar. Now I want to give Mary a fair share of water. How high should I fill Mary's jar so that Mary will have a fair share? Why do you think so?'

The fourth and fifth groups were administered the 'same amount' and 'fair share' presentation, but in these groups the E actually filled the comparison containers until the child told him to stop (the participation version).

(Fuller details of the experimental procedure, including the scoring techniques are described in Larson and Flavell, 1970, pp. 967-970, and in Cohen, 1967, pp. 150-154.)

RESULTS/Anticipation-of-Levels Task/Presentation condition ('this water' vs. 'same amount'), grade level (kindergarten vs. second grade) and direction of comparison (narrower vs. wider) were analysed. Performance improved considerably with age or grade level. A significant main effect was found for the presentation conditions, but there was also a highly significant interaction between presentation condition and the narrow-wide factor: the significant difference between presentation conditions was present only when the estimation was of the level of water in the wider container. In this case the 'same amount' condition was significantly more difficult than the 'this water' condition, the 'fair share' condition being intermediate in difficulty.

The effect of using a 'participation' version of the task erased the difference found between the narrow and wide comparison.

Compensation of Displacement and Conservation of Length/ There was little evidence that compensation necessarily precedes or accompanies conservation or vice-versa.

Semantic differential analysis of relational terms used in conservation
C. R. Harasym, F. J. Boersma and T. O. Maguire, 1971

AIM/The authors' main aim was to investigate the relationship between qualitative and quantitative relational terms and conservation operativity utilizing the semantic differential.

SUBJECTS/Forty-two boys and forty-three girls were selected from grades 1, 2 and 3 for the purposes of this study. The Conservation Concept Assessment Kit, Form A was administered to the total sample of 85 children whose mean CA was seven years nine months.

METHOD/The Kit has been devised by Goldschmid and

Bentler (1968) and comprises eight conservation tasks: Two-dimensional space; Number; Substance; Continuous quantity; Weight; Area: Length and Discontinuous quantity. On the basis of their score, children were classified as either Logical Conservers (LCs); Intuitive Conservers (ICs); or Nonconservers (NCs).

Semantic Differential Testing/The concepts 'more', 'less', 'same', 'different', 'mother' and 'school' were selected from the semantic differential which consists of six concepts and 12 scales. 'More' and 'less' represented 'qualitative concepts'.

Six scales 'low-high', 'long-short', 'wide-narrow', 'big-small', 'thin-fat' and 'up-down' (concrete scales) were selected. The abstract scales consisting of 'bad-good', and 'noisy-quiet' were also used. The general procedure of administering the semantic differential was patterned after Osgood et al. (1957). Other relevant details of modified procedures have been described by Harasym, Boersma, and Maguire (1971, pp. 770-771).

RESULTS/It was argued by the authors that LCs would advance finer discrimations of 'more' and 'less' than ICs and NCs. The results indicated that 'less' was utilized consistently by all the three groups of LCs, ICs and NCs 'while the profile for "more" is increasingly dissociated from "less" with attainment of conservation. Therefore, for NCs "more" is associated with "less"; for ICs, "more" hovers around the neutral point of the scale; while, for LCs "more" is opposite to "less".'

Finally, Harasym, Boersma and Maguire (1971) concluded that 'logical conservers (LCs) were able to distinguish between qualitative and quantitative differences better than either Intuitive Conservers (ICs) or Nonconservers (NCs), and that there was an apparent developmental progression in the use of these terms reflecting Piaget's stages of Conservation attainment. Thus it appears that conservation status and the ability to use relational terms are related.'

III. Identity and Equivalence Conservations

Elkind (1967) maintains the existence of two kinds of conservation: identity and equivalence conservation, details of which are given later in Moynahan and Glick (1972; see below). Recent studies which have attempted a developmental comparison of identity and equivalence conservation include those of Hooper (1969a and 1969b). In his (1969b) study, Hooper administered tasks of one identity and two equivalence problems to young children. It was concluded that equivalence conservation appeared later than identity conservation. Among the low socio-economic status subjects (CA five years six months to six years six months), the same general trend was observed (1969a). Seventy-five per cent of the children failed both identity and equivalence tasks for conservation of discontinuous quantity and 13.75 per cent were operative on both the tasks. 11.25 per cent passed identity and were non-operative on equivalence, whereas no child passed equivalence but failed identity. Moynahan and Glick (1972) report '... Hooper's (1969b) task analysis may not describe the cognitive processes actually used in solution of equivalence conservation tasks, while logically valid, Hooper's model may not be valid as a model of psychological processes' (see below).

Schwartz and Scholnick (1970) investigated the effect of the stimulus situation on quantitative identity and equivalence conservation. Children were required to make direct comparisons, identity, and equivalence judgements under two conditions in which: (a) the glasses to be judged were the same in diameter and (b) the glasses to be judged were of different diameter. The results demonstrated that when the containers were of identical diameter, identity and equivalence judgements were of equal difficulty. However, when the comparison containers differed in diameter, judgements of equivalence were more difficult than identity judgements (see below).

However, Teets (1968) did not find the priority of identity conservation among 120 young children from two socio-economic levels on weight identity and equivalence conservation tasks. Likewise, Northman and Gruen (1970) did not support the hypothesis that identity conservation, being a simple task, was attained developmentally prior to equivalence conservation. Sixty children (mean age eight years) were administered three identity and three equivalence conservation tasks. However, that identity and equivalence conservation emerge simultaneously, as postulated by Inhelder and Piaget (1956), was given added credibility (details of the study appear below). Additionally, an investigation by Murray (1970) failed to find any significant differences between identity and equivalence number performances in four presentation modes. (See also Nair, 1966, who examined the priority of the qualitative identity concept described by Bruner, 1966, and by Piaget, 1968.)

In continuation, Papalia and Hooper (1971) studied the developmental priority of identity conservation with equivalence conservation, employing quantity and number conservation tasks. Sixty subjects, with an age range four to six years, were drawn from a middle socio-economic class background. The authors concluded that identity concepts developed prior to equivalence concepts in the quantity conservation area. However, no conclusive evidence emerged in respect to number conservation (the study is described below).

Moynahan and Glick (1972) maintain that the tasks in Hooper's (1969b) study (op. cit.) involved discontinuous quantity, a relatively early conservation. Their own study examined a variety of types of conservation tasks, since they anticipated that the relation between identity and equivalence conservation might vary with the content domain of the task. Tests within the four conceptual domains comprised: number, length, continuous quantity and weight. The overall results indicated that identity conservation did not precede equivalence conservation, rather the two conservations tended to co-occur (the study is described below).

Likewise, Bright (1972) was intent to clarify Elkind's (1967) classification of conservation skills. Elkind's (1961) tests were administered, with slight modifications, to prospective elementary school teachers. The results indicated that the conservation of identity was attained by more subjects than conservation of equivalence and that the former preceded the latter.

More recently, however, Elkind and Schoenfeld (1972) have attributed the conflicting results of the above studies to a 'misunderstanding'. They maintain that 'investigators who have failed to find the identity equivalence discrepancy did not appreciate that the discrepancy was predicted only for pre-operational and not for concrete operational youngsters. The first author of the present study must bear some of this responsibility for this misunderstanding by not making this point sufficiently clear in the original publication (Elkind, 1967).' Their 1972 study, therefore, involved 22 four-year-old and 22 six-year-old children. The subjects were tested for judgements regarding the conservation of identity and equivalence for four types of quantity: number, length, liquids and mass. Elkind and Schoenfeld conclude, 'identity and equivalence conservation require different mental processes and that the difference between these types of conservation should be more apparent among younger than among older children'.

Relationship between identity and equivalence conservation
J. Northman and G. Gruen, 1970

The authors state that Elkind (1967) has advanced two kinds of conservation. 'In the equivalence conservation task, two identical beakers (S_1 and S_2) are filled equally with liquid. The contents of one (S_1) are then poured into a third, differently shaped container (V). The child is then asked whether or not the amounts of liquid in S_2 and V are still equivalent. On the other hand, if the child were asked to compare the content of V to itself in the original beaker (S_1) the task would be one of identity conservation.' Further, 'that identity conservation is a necessary but not sufficient condition for equivalence conservation. Transitivity is the critical mental operation which the child must perform in an equivalence task but not in an identity task.'

AIM/Northman and Gruen attempted an assessment of the possibility that identity conservation may be attained developmentally prior to equivalence conservation.

SUBJECTS/Sixty children with a CA range of six years eleven months to nine years eight months (mean age eight years), were drawn from an urban school, with working class background. All children showed comprehension of relational terms 'more', 'less', and 'same' in a pre-test.

METHOD/Tests/All subjects were examined individually on three identity conservation and three equivalence conservation tasks.

RESULTS/The main hypothesis that conservation of identity precedes conservation of equivalence was not substantiated. The results supported Piaget and Inhelder's contentions (1956) that these two types of conservation emerge simultaneously. Likewise, 'transitivity, as a mental operation . . . emerges about the same time as the operation(s) necessary and sufficient for conservation of identity'.

Scalogram analysis of logical and perceptual components of conservation of discontinuous quantity
M. M. Schwartz and E. Kofsky Scholnick, 1970

AIM/An attempt was made to establish the interrelations of numerous logical operations and perceptual features of the conservation of discontinuous quantity. A scalogram analysis was employed.

SUBJECTS/Forty children from private nursery and kindergarten schools were involved in the study. The sample comprised eight boys and 32 girls, with a CA range of 53 to 76 months (mean age = 65.8 months).

METHOD/Each child was seen individually. Three tasks were administered in the same session: non-verbal pre-training non-verbal experimental tasks, and a verbal conservation task. These were presented prior to pre-training and repeated at the end of the session.

Verbal Conservation/This task involved the concept of the conservation of discontinuous quantity and the general experimental procedure was patterned after Piaget (1952).

Pre-training/'Both pre-training and experimental tasks used a two-choice discrimination format. The child was seated in front of a 73 x 63 cm piece of black hardboard which was mounted on a base. The Board contained two rectangular 8 x 15 cm windows. Two white hardboard covers were attached by a hinge over each window. On one window, the top cover showed a drawing of a happy face, and the bottom cover, a drawing of a sad face. The position of each was reversed on the second window... Pre-training was designed to teach S to associate judgements of quantity with each of the faces. The child was told he was going to play a game about a boy named Billy who makes a happy face when he gets as much as E does to eat and is sad when he gets less than E. The child was to look at E's candy and Billy's and decide whether Billy would be happy or sad. Then S was to point to the appropriate face and lift the cover. If his judgement was correct he would find a candy. Four pairs of ... cards were employed as stimuli ...'

Experimental Tasks/Seven tasks were presented four times each. They differed in whether they demanded direct comparison of amounts (C), identity judgements (I), or equivalence judgements (E), and in whether the glasses to be judged were the same (S) or different (D) in diameter (fuller details of the Verbal Conservation, Pre-training Phase and Experimental Tasks, including experimental procedure and scoring techniques are described in Schwartz and Kofsky, 1970, pp. 696-699).

RESULTS/The authors discuss their findings in conjunction with related studies and cite the work of Elkind (1967), Wallach (1969), Gelman (1969), Osler and Kofsky (1965) and Flavell and Wohlwill (1969). They conclude as follows: 'The tasks formed a Guttman scale. The easiest items involved identical containers. There was a significant interaction between stimulus setting and judgements. When identical containers were used, identity judgements were least accurate, but when the two containers differed, identity was easiest, followed by equivalence and comparison judgements.'

A developmental comparison of identity and equivalence conservations
D. E. Papalia and F. Hooper, 1971

AIM/The authors addressed their inquiry to the exploration of relationship between identity and equivalence conservations, as defined by Elkind (1967). Particular attention was paid to the order of task acquisition and it was hypothesized that such an order might be qualitative identity, quantitative identity, and equivalence conservation for the content areas of substance and number conservation.

SUBJECTS/The total sample of 60 children comprised ten boys and ten girls of middle-class background, with CA range of four to six years. The mean IQs for the four-, five- and six-year-old groups were 114.6, 112.0 and 114.7, respectively (Peabody Picture Vocabulary Test).

METHOD/Tests/All subjects were seen individually on a battery of six conservation tasks. Children were also assessed on their comprehension of relational terms (patterned after Hooper, 1969). Scores of the Peabody Picture Vocabulary Test (PPVT) were also obtained. The tests involved Qualitative Identity, Quantitative Identity and Equivalence Conservation in both Substance and Number. Children were asked to advance justifications for their responses. Children who were to be scored at the higher level of conservation operativity had to show evidence of their ability to perform one of the following acts: reversibility, compensation, identity, addition/subtraction and counting (fuller details of the experimental procedure, including scoring techniques are described in Papalia and Hooper, 1971, pp. 351-353).

RESULTS/The authors discuss the results of their study in relation to other parallel investigations and cite the work of Northman and Gruen (1970), Teets (1968), Gruen (1966) and Hooper (1967, 1969). They conclude the results as follows: 'For the quantity battery, under the "without justification" condition, conditional probabilities and significant performance differences in the mean number of trials passed indicated that the order of acquisition of quantity tasks did conform to the hypothesized sequence: qualitative identity, quantitative identity, and equivalence conservation. No significant performance differences for number concepts were noted for both "justification" and "without justification" conditions. Scalogram analyses performed upon the combined quantity number task array indicated a scale or quasi-scale in the predicted order of difficulty (and) ... that identity concepts develop prior to equivalence concepts when the content area is quantity conservation. In contrast, clear-cut conclusions cannot be made about number conservation.'

Relation between identity conservation and equivalence conservation within four conceptual domains
E. Moynahan and J. Glick, 1972

AIM/An attempt was made to establish the relation between identity and equivalence conservation by utilizing four conservation tasks.

SUBJECTS/The sample of 57 kindergarten children of middle-class background comprised 33 boys and 24 girls. Another sample of 39 first grade children comprised 21 boys and 18 girls. The mean age of the kindergarten group was five years 11 months; of the first grade children six years nine months; and of total sample six years three months.

METHOD/Tests/In the concepts of length, number, weight and continuous quantity, both an identity and an equivalence conservation task were administered.

Identity Conservation/Moynahan and Glick cite the work of Elkind (1967) and state 'Identity Conservation is the realization that transformations of certain attributes of a single object (e.g. its shape) leave other attributes (e.g. weight) of the same object unchanged'.

The child was requested to observe the attribute when an object was presented, e.g. 'See this straw and see how long it is'. After transformation E questioned the child 'Is this straw the same length as it was before when it was over here, or is it a different length?' Justifications were always requested for their responses.

Equivalence Conservation/In citing the work of Elkind (1967), Moynahan and Glick report 'Equivalence conservation is the realization that two objects (A and B), initially equivalent with respect to an attribute, are still equivalent in this respect after certain other attributes of one of the objects have been changed (i.e. after B is transformed into C). Both tasks require that the subjects understand the irrelevance of the transformation performed. However, both Elkind (1967) and Hooper (1969) have argued that equivalence conservation requires the additional ability to make transitive inferences (i.e. if A = B and B = C, then A = C) since the subject is not directly asked if the transformed object is changed (if B = C) but is instead questioned about the equivalence of the two objects and A and C.'

The child was asked to establish equivalence after two identical objects were presented. After transformation the child was questioned 'Are these two straws the same length as each other, or are they different lengths?'

Two trials were involved in each of the four tasks of length, number, weight and quantity. Different transformations were involved, but the materials for the corresponding tasks both in Identity and Equivalence experiments were identical (fuller details of the experimental procedure and scoring techniques are described elsewhere, Moynahan and Glick, 1972, pp. 248-249).

RESULTS/The results showed that, of the eight comparisons, only length transformation revealed a significant trend for identity conservation to be present without equivalence conservation. Furthermore, evidence also indicated that identity and equivalence conservation were present simultaneously in the majority of the tasks '. . . also that within both the identity and equivalence conditions, the length, quantity, and weight tasks were of similar difficulty level, but the number tasks were considerably easier than these others'.

This finding supports those of Northman and Gruen (1970), but is at variance with those of Hooper (1969) and McManis (1969).

Moreover, the contention that the relation between identity and equivalence conservation varies with the 'conceptual domain' was only partly substantiated. Moynahan and Glick conclude 'it is surprising that the inference requirement generally did not affect task difficulty. Perhaps the ability to make transitive inferences is so readily available to conservers that the equivalence task, despite its inference requirement, is no more difficult for them than the identity task is. This possibility is consistent with Piaget's (1970) view that conservation and transitivity should occur concurrently since the two concepts are based on groupings which are structurally interdependent.'

IV. Substance, Weight and Volume

Piaget and Inhelder (1941) state that children attain conservation of substance at about age seven, conservation of weight at about age nine, and conservation of volume at about age 12. An early British attempt to investigate the development of the Piagetian concepts of substance, weight and volume was made by Lovell and Ogilvie (1960, 1961) with children of junior school age. The overall results indicated the presence of the three stages in the development of the concept of substance. An examination of the protocols showed the pattern of reasoning of British children to be identical to that of the Swiss subjects. The authors maintain, 'on the other hand, our evidence does not always agree with that of Piaget, nor does it enable us to prove or disprove the assumption that the child arrives at the concept of conservation because he is able to argue logically in concrete situations'. The concept of volume was also investigated, the general procedure being patterned after Piaget, Inhelder and Szeminska (1960). The results substantiated Piaget's contentions that it is not until CA 11 − 12 years of age that the concept of physical volume (which embraces interior occupied and displacement volume) is attained (the studies are described below). Modgil's (1965a, b, c) study among 26 ten-year-old British children in Northumberland, of the development of the concepts of substance, weight and volume, substantiated the results reported by Piaget and Inhelder.

Elkind (1961) replicated Piaget's tasks of mass, weight and volume among 469 junior and senior high school students from a lower middle-class background. He found that, while his results agreed with those of Piaget with regard to the conservation of mass and weight, only 27 per cent of the 11-to 12-year-old junior school children, 47 per cent of high school subjects, and 58 per cent of the college students had abstract conceptions of volume. Furthermore, he reported a significant sex difference in the attainment of the concept among the college students, with men performing at higher levels than women (details of the study appear below).

Hall and Kingsley (1968) reported that 29 per cent of psychology graduate students and 26 per cent of psychology 'upper class men' failed a conservation of volume question similar to that of Elkind.

Elkind's (1961) study was replicated by Towler and Wheatley (1971). The behavioural responses of the 71 college students were identical to those reported by Elkind, with only 61 per cent of the students demonstrating volume operativity. The authors concluded a 'poorly formed concept of atomism is hypothesized to be the reason for the failure of the subjects to score highly on these conservation tests' (details of the study are given below).

More recently, Nadel and Schoeppe (1973) substantiated the results obtained by Elkind. In both studies, for the same mean age group (13 years and six months), only 29 per cent of the subjects were operational in the conservation of volume tasks.

Uzgiris (1964) has also supported Piaget and Inhelder (1941), with regard to the sequence and also the time of the attainment of substance, weight and volume. She points out that studies like those of Beard (1957), Hyde (1959, described in Chapter eight) and Lovell and Ogilvie (1960, op. cit. and described later in this section) have 'mentioned, mostly parenthetically, that some children who demonstrated conservation of a particular concept with the plasticine balls did not show conservation of the same concept when confronted with a different material or vice-versa'. She, therefore, examined systematically the effect of varying the materials used to test for the conservation of substance, weight and volume. Overall, the results indicated that when different materials were used there was a significant difference in the conservation responses of children.

Uzgiris comments, 'Individual past experience may well underlie situational differences and account for the observed inconsistency across the various materials. It may well be that when a schema is developing, specific contacts with the environment will lead it to accommodate more in certain areas than in others, producing situational specificity in terms of specific past experiences of the individual' (p. 840). This emphasis on specific contacts of the environment leads to the study by Price-Williams, Gordon and Ramirez (1969) which included in its objectives an investigation into the different kinds of environment which may enhance or inhibit conservation operativity. The authors hypothesized that the 'potters' children would show an early acquisition of the concept of substance, 'while it was an open question as to the transfer to other types'. Generally, the results indicated an early age for the acquisition of the conservation of weight and volume among the 'potters' children (the study is described below).

Pertinent here is an interesting extension by Graves (1972), who attempted to establish whether race, sex and education had an effect on the degree of conservation of mass, weight and volume in minimally educated adults. One hundred and twenty adults (30 white women, 30 black women, 30 white men and 30 black men) with a mean age of 33.25 years were involved in the study. The subjects were categorized into three levels, based upon their performance on the 'Adult Basic Learning Examinations'. The results showed that 75 per cent conserved mass, 67 per cent conserved weight, and only 24 per cent conserved volume. Generally, no significant racial effects were observed and only for conservation of mass was the level of education a significant factor. Sex differences in favour of males were found in the acquisition of the volume concept. Graves reported that the development of conservation of quantity could not be explained by maturation.

A study of the conservation of substance in the junior school child
K. Lovell and E. Ogilvie, 1960

AIM/The authors attempted to outline the development of the concept of substance and to examine the justifications advanced by the children.

SUBJECTS/A total of 322 British children were involved. The sample consisted of 83 children (mean age seven years eight months); 65 children (mean age eight years ten months); 99 children (mean age nine years nine months); and 75 children (mean age 10 years eight months).

METHOD/Tests/Three experiments were administered. These were as follows:
(a) the concept of conservation of substance;
(b) an experiment to establish if an understanding of addition and subtraction of pieces of plasticine produces the concept of conservation;
(c) an experiment to examine whether a non-conserver of plasticine will have the same status in another situation involving the amount of rubber in a rubber band.

The main experiment (a) was typically Piagetian and the general experimental procedure was identical to the Geneva Centre (fuller details of all experiments, including (b) and (c) are given elsewhere: Lovell and Ogilvie, 1960, pp. 110-117).

RESULTS/The results substantiated the three main stages postulated by Piaget. The authors further analyse the justifications advanced by the subjects. An examination of the protocols revealed that children performing at a higher level of conservation operativity tended to employ such acts as reversibility, identity, plus/minus weight and shape. The explanations forwarded by non-conservers and transitional children are also analysed. 'Centering' on one dimension was the predominant feature of such subjects.

An interesting aspect of Lovell and Ogilvie's study demonstrated that 'reversibility does not necessarily produce conservation in spite of the fact that it is given as a reason for conservation among conservers. Thus, 70 children can show reversibility as we have defined it, but draw no conclusion from it and remain at the non-conservation or transition stages.'

Moreover, many children in the sample in the first two years of junior school did not show conservation of substance. Children of seven and eight show considerable mental confusion of such terms as 'longer', 'fatter', 'shorter', 'bigger', 'thicker' and 'smaller'.

Lovell and Ogilvie conclude 'our evidence does not always agree with that of Piaget, nor does it enable us to prove disprove the assumption that the child arrives at the concept of conservation because he is able to argue logically in concrete situations'.

Quantity conceptions in junior and senior high school students
D. Elkind, 1961

AIM/Elkind attempted to replicate Piaget's concepts of substance, weight and volume among 12- to 18-year-old adolescents; further, to examine the influence of CA, sex and IQ on the attainment of abstract conceptions of quantity.

SUBJECTS/Four hundred and sixty-nine junior and senior high school students (265 girls and 204 boys) from Massachusetts with lower-middle class background were involved in the study.

METHOD/Tests/Each child was administered the following three experiments.
1. Test for the conservation of substance (Mass). This was a typical Piaget type of task concerned with two identical balls of plasticine, one of which was rolled into a sausage, whereupon the child was questioned. Four types of questions were involved: identity, prediction, judgment and explanation.
2. Test for the conservation of weight. E rolls the sausage back into a ball and the general procedure as for substance is repeated. 'Weight' is substituted for 'amount'.
3. Test for the conservation of volume. E rolls the sausage back into a ball and the general procedures for substance and weight are repeated. 'volume' and 'same room or space' are substituted for 'substance' and 'weight' (fuller details of the experimental procedure are given elsewhere, Elkind, 1961, pp. 552-553; and Piaget and Inhelder, 1941).
Scoring/Subjects were identified as performing at the highest level of conservation if they demonstrated operativity in respect to identity, prediction, judgement and explanation questions.

RESULTS/An examination of the protocols revealed that some students who understood questions related to the substance and weight experiments, failed to comprehend and generalize their judgements, predictions and explanations to volume conservation. However, such students who showed conservation operativity for substance and weight did so through the acts of addition/subtraction, identity and compensation.
Further analysis demonstrated that students who performed at the lowest level of conservation performance did so, not due to a lack of verbal misunderstanding but 'rather because they failed, in Piaget's terms, to dissociate their subjective sensori-motor conceptions (impact, compression) of weight and volume from their objective (molecules) logical mathematical conceptions'.

Elkind further reports the percentage of subjects assessing conservation. Of the 469 students, 87 per cent showed conservation of substance and weight, but only 47 per cent performed at the highest level of volume conservation. A test of the difference between the three percentages yielded chi-square of 254.2, significant at the .001 level. The volume task proved difficult for all but the oldest age group.

Variables Influencing Volume Conservation/1. Age. There was a progressive increase with CA in the percentage of students who attained volume conservation. 2. Sex. For each age level the percentage of boys demonstrating volume operativity was higher than the percentage of girls. 3. IQ. 'The point biserial coefficient for the correlation of IQ (Kuhlmann-Anderson) with passing the volume test was .31, significant beyond the .01 level.'

Elkind finally raises two issues which he discusses and elaborates within the Piagetian genetic psychology framework — 'why do significantly more students attain abstract conceptions of mass and weight than attain the abstract conception of volume?' (b) 'In what respect are age, sex and IQ related to volume conservation?'

The growth of the concept of volume in junior school children
K. Lovell and E. Ogilvie, 1961

SUBJECTS/This study involved 191 junior school children drawn from a North of England town. Of these 191 children, 51 were first- 40 second- 45 third- and 55 fourth-year children. The authors admit, however, that the sample was not entirely representative of English children in general.

METHOD/Tests/The authors investigated the concept of volume under five sub-headings. These were Internal Volume, Occupied Volume, Complementary or Displacement Volume. Each child was also questioned as to whether any water would spill over if just one cube was lowered into the full pint can and into the full gallon can. Finally, if the subject retained equality in relation to the amounts of water spilt in Displacement Volume, above, further questioning followed in regard to the amounts of water spilt if (a) the cube was used in the experiment, and (b) a cube of exactly the same size and shape but made of lead, and thus much heavier, were immersed into the full pint can. The questions were put in respect of the full pint can rather than the full gallon can.

All tests and sub-tasks were administered individually and responses recorded verbatim. The general procedure was similar to

68

the Geneva school.

The authors attempted to analyse various questions in relation to the number of children passing each set of questions and sub-questions, the criterion being operativity and non-operativity, in several situations.

RESULTS/The evidence produced by the study demonstrated that the concept of physical volume (which embraces interior, occupied and displacement volume) develops slowly during the junior school period. The authors point to the child's ability to eliminate irrelevant cues in the full acquisition of the concept of volume. Lovell and Ogilvie's study supports Piaget's contention that it is not until 11-12 years of age that a well-developed concept of physical volume is attained.

Situational generality of conservation
I. C. Uzgiris, 1964

AIM/A systematic examination was undertaken of the effect of varying the materials employed to assess the sequential acquisition of conservation of substance, weight and volume.

SUBJECTS/The total sample of 120 subjects consisted of 20 children (10 boys and 10 girls) each from first through sixth grade in a parochial school in Illinois. A wide range of socio-economic background was represented.

METHOD/Guttman's technique of scalogram analysis, and Jackson's Plus Percent Ratio (PPR) was used in the study.

Materials/(a) Plasticine balls, 2in. in diameter, of green colour; (b) metal nuts, ½in. across and ½in. high and served as metal cubes; (c) wire coils, 1¼in. in diameter, 3 coils high, made of multi-stranded, twisted wire; (d) straight pieces of red, plastic-insulated wire, 6in. long and $\frac{1}{16}$in. in diameter. Two glass jars were also used.

Tests and Procedure/Three tasks were administered to each child. These were the concepts of conservation of substance, weight and volume. The materials were presented one at a time, in a counterbalanced order. For any one material, questions regarding the conservation of substance were always asked first, then those about weight conservation, followed by volume. The questions were modified for each type of quantity and each material. Three deformations were performed on each material for each of the three concepts. Each child was seen individually and all responses were recorded verbatim. The details of the experiments including the general experimental procedure were patterned after Piaget and Inhelder (1941). Fuller details are given in Uzgiris (1964) pp.832-4.

Scoring Technique/Children to be classified as performing at the highest level of conservation operativity had to answer correctly all the questions — initial equivalence, prediction, explanation and justification.

RESULTS/Piaget's contentions of the sequential cognitive development of the conservation of substance, weight and volume were confirmed. The results also substantiated Piaget's suggested ages at which such concepts are acquired. However, in respect to volume concept, results were only partly in agreement with Piaget's findings, with Lovell and Ogilvie (1961) and with Lunzer (1960), but they fully supported Elkind's (1961) results. Furthermore, the conservation of substance, weight and volume were acquired in the same sequential order, regardless of material. Uzgiris's results also lent support to Smedslund's (1961) study — that the conservation of substance is first acquired with discontinuous materials followed by the continuous. Finally, Uzgiris argues, 'the finding that variation across materials is greater at some age levels than others suggested that a relation between situational variables and conservation behaviour may be most evident during the formation of a conservation scheme'.

Skill and conservation: a study of pottery-making children
D. R. Price-Williams, W. Gordon and M. Ramirez, 1969

SUBJECTS/Twenty-eight Mexican children from two areas were involved. There were 12 children in the experimental and control groups from the town of Tlaquepaque. All were boys and comprised three children in each of the four age groups, from six to nine, inclusive. In the San Marcos sample there were 16 children in each of the two groups, 4 from each year group of six to nine.

Children in the experimental group 'had grown up in the pottery making families'. The children in the control group, who were matched for CA, SES, years of schooling, belonged to 'families engaged in skills other than pottery making'.

METHOD/Tests/The tasks administered involved the conservation of Number, Substance, Weight, Volume and Liquid.

The general experimental procedure was identical to the Geneva Centre. The tests were presented in the Spanish language.

The authors maintain 'the guiding principle behind the choice of selecting children versed in pottery making was that of the role of experience and specifically manipulation in the attainment of conservation. It was predicted that experience in pottery making should promote for these children earlier conservation in at least the concept of substance (in which clay is the experimental medium), while the question of transfer to other concepts of number, liquid, weight and volume was left open.'

RESULTS/The data from the Tlaquepaque sample were subjected to Fisher's exact probability test. Nonsignificant results were observed on the tests of number, liquid, weight and volume. However, significant differences were computed for substance ($p<.05$), in favour of the Pottery group. Although, on all five tasks, children belonging to the pottery families showed more frequent conservation responses, these were not significant. Similarly, the quality of justifications advanced by the pottery group sample was superior to the non-pottery group. In the San Marcos sample, out of a possible 80 total, composed of five tasks for the 16 subjects, 77 of the sample demonstrated conservation operativity in the pottery group. No such trends of this magnitude appeared in the non-pottery group. Likewise, the quality of responses of the conservers in the pottery-group was superior to those advanced by the subjects in the non-pottery group.

The authors conclude that 'the role of skills in cognitive growth may be a very important factor. Manipulation may be a prior and necessary prerequisite in the attainment of conservation, but a skill embodies a set of operations with a recognizable end. . .'

Conservation concepts in college students: a replication and critique
J. Towler and G. Wheatley, 1971

AIM/Towler and Wheatley (1971) attempted to replicate Elkind's three investigations (1961, 1961a, 1962) in order to check the reliability of Elkind's results with college students. Elkind repeated the Piagetian task of mass, weight and volume with school children, high school pupils and college students. Elkind's findings substantiated Piaget's contentions with regard to the concepts of mass and weight. However, so far as the concept of volume was concerned, only 27 per cent of the 11- to 12-year-old school children, 47 per cent of the high school pupils and 58 per cent of the college students demonstrated full operativity. Sex differences were also indicated in favour of the male population.

SUBJECTS/Seventy-one female University students, with an age-range of 17 to 27 and median age of 18.

71

METHOD/Tests/The three tasks administered, of the concepts of mass, weight and volume, were identical to those used by Elkind (1962).

RESULTS/All 71 subjects performed at the highest level of operativity in the conservation of mass tasks, as compared with 68 in the conservation of weight. However, with conservation of volume tasks, only 44 out of the 71 students showed full operativity. This finding of 61 per cent who performed at the stage of conservation lends further credence to Elkind's (1962) findings where 58 per cent indicated volume operativity. Another feature common to both the Elkind and the Towler/Wheatley study was the nature of the responses advanced by the non-conservers. These students who performed at a lower level of operativity showed a rigidity of mental strategies. They were unable to transfer the acquired concepts of mass and weight in order to achieve volume operativity.

The authors point out the weaknesses in the methodological procedures utilized by Elkind, specifically the inclusion of a 'special check' question in the test of volume. The students were asked to assess 'whether the water levels in two identical jars filled equally high would rise equally or unequally if the "sausage" were placed in one and the ball in the other'. Towler and Wheatley have argued that Elkind did not consider the differentiation between 'interior volume' and 'occupied volume', as demonstrated by Piaget (1960, pp.375-85). Further, that Elkind explains the non-conservers' performance in terms of sex differences and that 'Elkind does not offer to deal with the reason behind this inability'. Towler and Wheatley maintain that the reasons may be, at least in part, in the inadequately formed concepts of atomism, 'since nearly all of the erroneous explanations centre on molecules, density, or the surface area of the clay'.

V. Miscellaneous Related Studies

Piagetian tests and sex differences
K. R. Fogelman, 1969

AIM/This study investigated the concept of conservation of quantity. The author discusses differences among subjects and experimental techniques.

SUBJECTS/Six- and seven-year-old children, randomly assigned to one of two groups. Fuller details appear in Fogelman's (1969) study.

METHOD/Piaget's (1941) test of conservation of quantity was administered. A variation in the manner in which the test was administered was utilized. The first group followed the 'active' procedure, in which children actually manipulated the materials. The 'passive' group however, watched the experimenter carry out the manipulation.

RESULTS/No differences in children's performance were observed. However, the author qualifies the statement by suggesting that possible effects are complex and the interaction of other variables might be responsible. Special attention was paid to sex differences.

Age characteristics of the four sets of children showed no difference. The overall performance of the 'active' group and 'passive' group was similar, if not identical. However, it was noted that the boys did better under the 'active' condition and the girls were superior under the 'passive' condition. This superiority was significant at the five per cent level. Moreover, girls who reached full operativity justified their judgements with greater mobility of thought.

The study demonstrated that girls perform better on a test of conservation of quantity when they observe or are attentive to the manipulations of the materials by the tester and boys are more operational when the manipulations of the materials are performed by themselves.

The author draws attention to the necessity of taking sex differences into account, when considering possible standardizations of Piagetian tests as scales for measuring efective intelligence.

Eye movements, perceptual activity and conservation development
K. G. O'Bryan, 1971

AIM/An investigation was undertaken to extract information about the relationship of perceptual activity to conservation and, further, to attempt to establish the development of a non-verbal, noncued means of determining conservation. 'The medium chosen was eye movements (EM) recording by means of a MacWorth (1967) stand-mounted camera. The general questions asked were: Do conservers and non-conservers identified by Piagetian techniques display different movement patterns (EMPs) while engaged in conservation tasks? Should they do so, what is the nature of the differences? And what light might these findings shed on the conservation problem?'

SUBJECTS/A total of 92 girls with CA range 75-122 months were involved in the study. NCI referred to children assessed as 'strong non-conservers', NC2 were transitional subjects, and C were children pérforming at the highest level of conservation operativity.

METHOD/The pre-training phase consisted of a game in which two strips of cardboard were held before the child. The child was questioned whether one waš longer, shorter or the same as the other. The subjects were asked to close their eyes as soon as they responded. This was repeated with plasticine, glasses of water and cardboard pieces. 'Thus Ss were trained to close their eyes upon reaching an answer so the EM closure would indicate when S had reached solution to a conservation question during the EM recording session. . .Ss were taken to the laboratory, seated at the EM recorder, and asked to make an impression on dental compound covering a "child-size" bite bar. The S received instructions through a headset that the game she had learned was now on a movie film and that she was going to play it "just like before". The movie film and recorded directions were synchroniz-ed by an assistant. A series of five two-element figures were displayed on the EM recorder screen. The number of stimuli varied. . .The S was asked to judge the equality of the elements and to close her eyes as soon as she had an answer. . .After this training. . .the S was shown filmed Piagetian conservation tasks of length, area, and continuous quantity (solid and liquid). . .with the actual transformation presented in movie form and stop-action exposure used during the question and discussion period. . . Instructions. . .were those used by Piaget. . .the exception being that S was required to close her eyes, to indicate that she recognized the initial equivalence of the transformed elements. Immediately upon completion of the transformation, S was asked the standard conservation question and then EM recording began. . .' (fuller details of the experimental procedure, definitions of the terminology used and analyses of verbatim and recorded responses are described elsewhere, O'Bryan, 1971, pp.159-161).

RESULTS AND DISCUSSION/The results indicated that for all tasks, NCI subjects fixated on the greater significantly more often than on the lesser ($p < .01$), while for NC2 children identical results were observed for only two of the four tasks. No significant differences were computed between transformed and non-transformed for those showing conservation operativity over total solution time.

'The. . .results on fixations and mean length of run suggest that perceptual activity (in the form of EMs) is least in NC1, somewhat variable in NC2 and greatest in C Ss ... a steadily decreasing centration effect appears to be occurring as one proceeds from a condition of nonconservation to logically justified conservation ...'

Furthermore, children performing at the highest level of conservation operativity, demonstrated significantly more 'couplings' than either NC1 or NC2 children on every task (p<.01). Conservers were more active in perceptual activity; NC2 children displayed more 'couplings' than NC1 subjects on two tasks (p<.05) and tended to be in a transitional period of increasing decentration. Conservers showed a restricted number of fixations and indicated that centration altered to decentration at the operational level. (O'Bryan illustrates further patterns by quoting more case protocols. Details of these appear on pp. 164-167, including plots of EMPs of horizontal décalage on conservation tasks.)

O'Bryan's results are consistent with 'Piaget's (1950) argument on the nature of developing decentration, as well as with Wohlwill's (1962) suggestions of perceptual distortion giving way to conceptual certainty ... in the presence of the transformed stimulus, non-conservers are distracted by the dominant perceptual cues that are usually irrelevant to a conservation judgement; however, true conservers apparently adopt a scanning strategy so that their judgement is not based on only one dimension nor distorted by the irrelevant perceptual cues'.

Performance of culturally deprived children on the concept-assessment kit-conservation
B. Wasik and J. Wasik, 1971

AIM/The authors investigated the performance of culturally deprived children, on Goldschmid's Concept-Assessment Kit-Conservation (1968b). Furthermore, to compare their performance to the already established norms of the Concept-Assessment Kit.

SUBJECTS/One hundred and seventeen subjects (half white and half negro children) from a primary school for culturally deprived children were tested. All children were tested individually by experienced personnel.

METHOD/Concept-Assessment Kit-Conservation/Form A of the kit was administered. The kit measures eight areas of conservation: two-dimensional space; number; substance; continuous quantity; weight; area; discontinuous quantity; and length (fuller details of the tests, including experimental procedure and scoring schedules are described in Goldschmid and Bentler, 1968b).

RESULTS AND DISCUSSION/An analysis of the assembled scores demonstrated that in seven out of the eight tasks the culturally disadvantaged group performed at a significantly lower level than did the norm group. Only the youngest male children showed no such pattern. The two groups of subjects, when compared, revealed that children at every CA level lagged one to two years behind the norm data.

The authors argue that their findings lend support to a 'Piagetian interpretation which would assume that some environments expose children to intellectual tasks which compel the child to organize his thinking more often than others (Smedslund, 1961) . . . some children in this study were in their third year in special classes for the culturally deprived . . . their scores still indicate considerably less facility with the tested concepts than the normal population . . . even with an enriched learning experience, this lag in acquistion of conservation concepts had not been advanced by any appreciable degree . . . we caution those who work with children from culturally deprived populations to recognize the discrepancies in cognitive development between these children and other children with different cultural backgrounds . . . those who work with these children should be better able to plan realistic learning experiences.'

CHAPTER FOUR
TRAINING TECHNIQUES

Introduction

Although training may serve to accelerate concept acquisition, most supporters of Piaget would argue that it is impossible to alter the sequence or bring about too rapid a change. For example, Freeberg and Payne (1965 p.80) focus on Bruner's (1960) position in that 'almost any subject matter, if properly organized can be taught at the pre-school level . . . At somewhat the other extreme is the essentially maturational position of Inhelder and Piaget (1958) who argue for specific levels of cognitive development that must be achieved before certain conceptual strategies can be learned (e.g. those basic to inductive reasoning)'. Freeberg and Payne further draw attention to Ausubel who would also doubt the likelihood of inducing certain concepts at the 'pre-operational' stage in Piaget's system. However, he looks upon these conceptual stages as 'nothing more than approximations' that are 'susceptible to environmental influences' (Ausubel, 1965 pp.11-12).

Piaget (1964) has discussed three criteria as vital in ascertaining whether a researcher has '. . . succeeded in teaching operational structures' (p.17). The first is the durability of learning. Some studies have demonstrated that provoked conservation could be sustained three weeks to six months after training (Fournier, 1967; Gellman, 1967; Goldschmid, 1968a). Goldschmid (1969) concludes that '. . . it is indeed possible to accelerate the long-lasting acquisition of certain Piagetian concepts'. However, other researchers do not agree with Goldschmid. Lovell (1969) maintains 'the evidence . . . as to whether training on conservation leads to improvement on performance in respect to seriation, classification etc., is only meaningful if the relevant schemata are related in a general structure. If they are not, then these involve independently learned skills . . . Piagetian test items have no more and no less rationale than those employed in the Binet scales — namely, they are tasks which children at certain ages can perform. While, then, there is evidence that training can induce a cognitive schema, which has durability and at best limited transfer, the evidence is still — and Goldschmid himself admits to this — not at all clear as to whether there is a change in the operational structure in a strictly Piagetian sense ... Training which generates these rather narrow schemas at first may well be advantageous to the child. Operative thought may be extended to other areas earlier, but this I don't know.' He agrees with Goldschmid concerning the need for longitudinal studies of children who have experienced training and would like training to be extended to such concepts as time, temperature and space.

The second criterion postulated by Piaget (1964) concerns the vital issue of generalization or transfer to related cognitive strategies. The studies of Fournier (1967), Gellman (1967) and Goldschmid (1968a) have shown training to enhance the acquisition of conservation concepts with varied degrees of transfer to related and hierarchical concepts and sub-concepts. In Goldschmid's study (1969, op.cit.) two types of transfer tests — Scales A and B (Goldschmid and Bentler, 1968a; 1968b) included six tasks which were intercorrelated and homogeneous (refer to Conservation Assessment Kit, described in Chapter Twelve). The training involved three of these tasks. Post-tests demonstrated that performance improved significantly not only on the trained tasks but on all six tasks of the scales. A more remote transfer also occurred to another dimension of conservation as measured by scale C. However, the study has encountered many criticisms (Lovell, 1969; Inhelder, 1969; Beilin, 1969; and Elkind, 1969).

Piaget's third criterion is best described in his own words: 'In the case of each learning experience what was the operational level of the subject before the experience and what more complex structures has this subject succeeded in learning? ... We must look at each specific learning experience from the point of view of the spontaneous operations which were present at the outset and the operational level which has been achieved after the learning experience' (Piaget 1964).

Another criterion is formulated by Smedslund (1961) as 'the resistance to extinction'. In an experiment designed to induce conservation of weight he found that children who were operational on conservation after training tended to extinguish their conservation behaviour when the examiner surreptitiously removed some clay from one of the two objects. Whereas another group of children, who were operational on conservation spontaneously, tended to resist extinction. Goldschmid (1969) employed the same extinction test as Smedslund for weight (1961b) and casts doubt on Smedslund's findings, whereas Kohnstamm (1966) has suggested that if he were to apply this criterion of extinction, he would only do so '... after having accustomed the young child to the idea that the stranger (E) sometimes systematically tries to mislead him, otherwise the timid child may fall back on the old answer which E definitely suggests to be correct, while the self-confident child may resist. Variables of personality or child-adult interaction should not interfere with the testing for quality of cognitive growth' (p.63). Two other critics of Smedslund's (1961b) study concerning conservation and resistance to extinction are Hall and Simpson (1968). They argued that this study has had to '. . . bear a very heavy empirical and theoretical burden'. Hall and Simpson agreed that conservation can be extinguished, drawing on the results of several extinction studies of their own. They proposed a learning explanation for the development and extinction of conservation. However, Smedslund (1968) comments briefly on the theoretical issues involved and on Hall's and Simpson's failure to replicate his findings. 'I still believe that the findings of my original pilot study can be replicated . . . However, a replication would seem to require a very careful balancing of emphasis on standardization of procedures and consideration of the subtleties of the experimenter-child interaction.' Moreover, he maintains that conservation can never be extinguished, since a defining property of true conservation is that it is logically necessary and therefore unextinguishable. Miller (1971) attempts to elucidate some of the issues involved in the Hall and Simpson/Smedslund controversies. He maintains that, 'the major criticism that can be directed against previous studies is that their criteria for assessing extinction have been too limited; the possibility of a socially compliant "pseudo-extinction" has correspondingly been too great' (p.48). Miller's (1973) study 'attempted to minimize demand pressures in a situation utilizing a number of different measures' (p.48). (Cf.Brison and Bereiter (1967) and Sullivan (1967) who used the resistance to extinction procedure and demonstrated that the conservation concept can be achieved through training. Sullivan induced conservation by having film-mediated models explain the principles of conservation. When Brison and Bereiter trained retarded, normal and gifted on conservation tasks there were no significant differences in trainability as a function of IQ. Moreover, the retardates were only slightly more susceptible to extinction than the others.)

More recently, an attempt to extinguish conservation of weight in College students has been demonstrated by Miller, Schwartz and Stewart (1973, p.216), who discuss discrepancies in their results with those of Hall and Kingsley (1968).

I. Number

Whiteman and Peisach (1970) draw attention to the fact that researchers like Kingsley and Hall (1967) and Sigel (1966)

79

demonstrate that a combination of training procedures facilitates conservation behaviour. That reversibility training may be more successful when presented as a sensori-motor rather than as a perceptual experience has been demonstrated by Greenfield (1966) and Sonstroem (1966). Whiteman and Peisach administered number and substance tasks incorporating perceptual cues and sensori-motor experience to compensate for the absence of such underlying cognitive schemata as compensation, atomism and reversibility among children of low socio-economic status. The authors maintain that sensori-motor cues are of relatively greater help to younger children closer to the sensori-motor stages, while perceptual cues are of more aid to older children. The results also demonstrated that 'the situational supports were compensatory for cognitive inadequacies only on the number conservation items, the older children improving on both judgement and explained judgement scores, the younger children only on the judgement score.' Wallach, Wall and Anderson (1967) were intent to determine the nature of training necessary for the inducement of the conservation of number. Wallach and Sprott (1964) indicated that 'conservation under operations that remove defining attributes could be induced through experience with reversibility of these operations'. However, Wohlwill and Lowe (1962) and Smedslund (1962), proposed that experience with addition and subtraction may be critical for conservation. The results of Wallach et al. indicated that reversibility training was effective in the inducement of number and that such a training did not need to be accompanied by experience with the act of addition/subtraction. Further, in the absence of reversibility training, training in addition/subtraction by itself did not prove successful in facilitating the acquisition of number conservation. However, certain reservations were suggested by the authors (full details of which are given later in this chapter). Roll (1970) further investigated the effect of training in reversibility on the conservation of number. He concludes that the training resulted in a significant increase in conservation response but not in increased verbalization of conservation principles (details are given later in this chapter).

Rothenberg and Orost (1969) attempted an approach to the teaching of the conservation of number through the presentation of a logical sequence of component concepts or steps evaluated in a series of three experiments. Training sessions involved reinforced counting (Wohlwill and Lowe 1962); addition and subtraction of one object at a time (Gruen 1965); and verbal training on the concept of 'more' (in number) versus 'longer' (in length). The results of the study implied that conservation of number can be taught to young children; moreover, the effect of training lasted as long as three months and increased the understanding of related problems (details are given later in this chapter).

Lally (1968) investigated Braine and Shanks' (1965) hypothesis that verbal stimulation and feedback information accelerate conservation of number and enable children to distinguish between real and phenomenal appearances (details of this study appear below).

In Beilin's (1965) study, subjects were trained on length and number conservation using non-verbal reinforcement, verbal orientation reinforcement, verbal rule instruction and 'equilibration' methods. The results indicated that 'correct verbalization of the conservation principle, both before and after training, was less predictive of correct performance in conservation tasks than the reverse. On the pre-test, there was little convergence of conservation performance for children who did not fully conserve. Training materially increased convergence, but not to the extent represented among conservers who acquired the capacities less formally' (see below . . .). (Cf.Mason (1969) later in this chapter, and Figurelli and Keller (1972), who report 'the lack of a significant training effect on transfer test performance indicates that training of the type employed did not transfer from one set of conservation tasks to a dissimilar set of conservation tasks. Similar results were reported by Beilin (1965). It is quite likely that training with this simple procedure results in acquisition that is separate and independent for each conservation concept – and perhaps for each task within a given concept'.)

Winer's (1968) study addressed itself to the effect of 'set' on the acquisition of conservation of number. The general experimental procedure involved addition/subtraction training, perceptual-set training or no-set training together with conflict trials and post-tests. The main investigation comprised two studies: with respect to the first, a significant relationship between performance and training conditions was evidenced, the performance of the addition/subtraction group differed significantly from the performance of the perceptual and control groups. The second study revealed a non-significant difference in favour of the groups receiving the conflict trials (details are given later in this chapter).

A discrimination test was employed by Halford and Fullerton (1970) in order to induce conservation of number. Minor modifications were made to the 'beds and dolls' task and results indicated that the training method induced two-thirds of the subjects to acquire conservation of a 'stable' kind.

Curcio, Robbins and Ela (1971) showed that a combination of readiness and body-part training (i.e. use of fingers) was the most effective for pre-school children in facilitating number conservation with external objects (details of the study are given later in this chapter).

Bryant's (1972) study has the implication 'that the emphasis should be shifted to training children how to form judgements properly instead of teaching them invariance'; further, that previous attempts to train invariance have, on the whole, been unsuccessful ' . . . because the experimenters were trying to teach children the wrong thing, to teach them, in fact, something which they knew already'.

That children as young as three years of age can manipulate the invariance principle has been demonstrated by Bryant (this and other partly-related studies are referred to in Chapter Three). Bryant also indicated 'that training that some cues provide a more reliable basis for quantity judgments than others, enables young children to transfer quantity judgements over perceptual transformations much more effectively than they had previously' (details of the study appear below).

With respect to number conservation, an interesting extension among the varied training approaches is the study by Feigenbaum (1971) who explored the hypothesis that 'successfully training a child to show conservation will improve his ability to take different social roles and conversely that successfully training a child to take different social perspectives will improve his ability to conserve'. The results indicated a relation between the two aspects of development (details are given later in this chapter).

Pertinent here is a reflection by Curcio, Kattef, Levine and Robbins (1972), in relation to some of the above-mentioned studies, viz. Beilin (1965), Curcio, Robbins and Ela (1971) and Whiteman and Peisach (1970). Curcio et al. argue that ' . . . these investigators have relied directly upon the age of the child as an index of susceptibility or differentiation of total non-conservers from partial conservers. Thus, the specific factors responsible for differential susceptibility to conservation training remain open to question because so many conservation-relevant abilities, such as memory, language etc. can covary with these general variables'.

Learning and operational convergence in logical thought development
H. Beilin, 1965

SUBJECTS/Beilin's study comprised a total number of 170 kindergarten subjects. The children were selected from six classes from a school in the city of New York. All except 10 were white, and were drawn from a 'middle-income housing project' area. The median age of the sample was five years and four months.

METHOD/The children were randomly assigned to the four

training groups of Non-Verbal Reinforcement, Verbal Orientation/ Reinforcement, Verbal Rule Instruction and Equilibration. The numbers of children in each of the training groups were 31, 33, 33 and 34 respectively. A control group of 33 children was also included. Each child was tested and underwent training individually. Each training session averaged about 40 minutes and each child faced 10 sessions in all.

So far as the basic principles were concerned, the number conservation task was identical to that utilized by Wohlwill and Lowe (1962), apart from slight modifications. The length conservation task was consistent with the Piagetian type situations, apart from the inclusion of a larger array of spatially distorted arrangements than is used by the Geneva school. The task for the conservation of the concept of area did not depart from the Piagetian principles. The apparatus and the experimental procedures are more fully described by Beilin in his 1964 published work.

RESULTS/The analysis of the results indicated that the verbal-rule instructions technique demonstrably enhanced conservation acquisition. However, no such evidence was present in the area conservation tasks. Beilin further concludes that 'correct verbalization of the conservation principle, both before and after training, was less predictive of correct performance in conservation tasks than the reverse. On the pre-test, there was little convergence of conservation performance for children who did not fully conserve. Training materially increased convergence, but not to the extent represented among conservers who acquired the capacities less formally'.

Number conservation: the roles of reversibility, addition-subtraction, and misleading perceptual cues
L. Wallach, J. Wall and L. Anderson, 1967

Relating to the inducement of the concept of number conservation, Wallach, Wall and Anderson argued that a comprehension of the act of reversibility is necessary for the acquisition of the concept of number conservation. The authors, in attempting their experiment, wanted to unravel debatable issues from a previous study (Wallach and Sprott, 1964) in which number conservation was successfully induced. They state that Wallach and Sprott interpreted the results 'as indicating that conservation under operations that remove defining attributes could be induced through experience with reversibility of these operations. However, it has been proposed (Wohlwill and Lowe, 1962; Smedslund, 1962) that experience with addition and subtraction may be critical for conservation and such experience, as well as experience with reversibility, was involved in the training procedure' (page 426). In the light of this, four main hypotheses were formulated as follows:

(a) whether conservation could be induced, by training in reversibility alone;

(b) whether conservation operativity could be enhanced, by training in the acts of addition and substraction alone. No training in the act of reversibility was envisaged;

(c) whether such an inducement would stand the test of transfer to related and hierarchical sub-concepts;

(d) whether conservation of the quantity of a liquid could be fostered, by training in the act of reversibility.

SUBJECTS/Fifty-six children of middle-class background were involved in the study with a CA range of six years one month to seven years eight months, with a mean of six years 11 months.

METHOD/Pre-tests/Two tasks, the Doll Pre-test and the Liquid Pre-test, were administered. The experimental procedure was identical to that of Piaget and Inhelder (1964).

The full details of the various training phases are lengthy and it is proposed to give a general outline only as stated by the authors themselves (detailed procedures are given elsewhere — in Wallach, Wall and Anderson, 1967, pp. 427-35).

'Participation in the experiment ended with the pre-test for Ss in the "not meeting criteria" and "conservation" categories. The Ss in the other categories received additional training and testing as follows: The "non-conservation" Ss and the "partial conservation — liquid" Ss were divided within each category by alternating assignment (the order of Ss was at the convenience of the teacher) the groups receiving doll reversibility training and doll addition-subtraction training. Immediately following the training, both groups were given an immediate post-test, which, except for the delayed post-test, was the end of the experiment for the "partial conservation — liquid" Ss. "Non-conservation" Ss who did not show conservation in the doll post-test were then given liquid reversibility training and subsequently a liquid post-test. "Non-conservation" Ss who did show conservation in the doll post-test were immediately given the liquid post-test to test for direct transfer. If direct transfer did not occur they were then given training on the transfer series, and, if this also did not lead to liquid conservation, they were given liquid reversibility training and the liquid post-test was repeated. The subjects in the "partial conservation-dolls" category were given liquid reversibility training and then the liquid post-test immediately following the pre-test.

"Non-conservation" and both "partial conservation" groups of Ss were given both doll and liquid delayed post-tests two to six weeks after the training.'

RESULTS/The results indicated that reversibility training was effective in the inducement of number conservation (more so with Ss receiving training with dolls than with liquid) and that such a training did not need to be accompanied by experience with the act of addition/subtraction. Further, in the absence of reversibility training, training in addition/subtraction by itself did not prove successful in the enhancement of number conservation. Moreover, number conservation inducement was not transferable to operativity in the liquid task. However, the authors take care to point out certain reservations; for example (a) the reasons advanced for operational answers, and (b) the failure of liquid reversibility training to be effective. In respect to (a) such justifications that the two dolls were 'sharing' a bed led the authors to argue that 'the doll reversibility-training pro-cedure . . . may well have been successful, not because it led the Ss to recognize reversibility, but because it led them to stop relying on a misleading cue . . . It is not clear to what extent the recognition of reversibility resulted from the experience with reversibility provided by this training procedure, and to what extent it was due to prior experience . . . recognizing reversibility as well as not using misleading perceptual cues would seem to be necessary for conservation'.

The effects of supplementary verbal stimulation on the de-velopment of concepts of number
V.M. Lally, 1968

AIMS/In two articles on the conservation of size and shape in 'The Journal of Verbal Learning and Verbal Behaviour' (1965) and 'The Canadian Journal of Psychology' (1965) respectively, Braine and Shanks made the following proposals:
(1) with the aid of verbal stimulation, children are capable of conserving earlier than is suggested by Piaget;
(2) verbal stimulation and feedback information enable the majority of children to distinguish between real and phenomenal appearances two or three years earlier than Piaget's age norms for conservation;
(3) additive and transitive properties need to be sharply distinguished from conservation.
These hypotheses were suggested as a result of a number of experiments on 'size' and 'shape'.

The verbal stimulation of the words 'looks' and 'really' was employed with emphasis in order to aid the child to differentiate between real and phenomenal appearances.

METHOD/The present study investigated the above hypotheses in the field of number. Experimental work was undertaken, using some of Piaget's number tasks from The Child's Conception of Number (1952b). The experimental work was done in three phases: (a) pre-test involving 12 children; (b) training phase involving 50 children (25 in each group experimental and control); (c) post-test and transfer task involving 40 children (20 in each group).

RESULTS/The major findings of the experiment were as follows:
(1) the verbal stimulation of the words 'looks' and 'really' does not appear to aid conservation development;
(2) conservation does not appear to be dependent on a real-phenomenal distinction, in the manner suggested by Braine and Shanks;
(3) it seems that a sharp distinction cannot be drawn between additive and transitive properties and conservation;
(4) feedback information appears to aid conservation development, but not in the manner suggested by Braine and Shanks;
(5) (i) in this experiment the children conserved one year earlier than Piaget suggests, (ii) it would appear that conservation can be accelerated to two years earlier than Piaget's age norms, with the aid of feedback information.

Induced set and the aquisition of number conservation
G.A. Winer, 1968

AIM/Winer's study addressed itself to the effect of 'set' on the acquisition of conservation of number. The main investigation comprised two studies.

SUBJECTS/The first study had a sample of 87 children from Worcester (USA) who were drawn from lower-middle class. Forty-two non-conservers (on the main conservation test), who were operational on the Addition/Substraction (A/S) pre-test (Smedslund 1961a, b, c, d), were randomly assigned to one of the three training groups: addition/subtraction group with a mean age of five years 10 months; perceptual group with a mean age of five years 11 months; and the control group (five years 11 months). The second study drew the subjects from the same catchment area. Twenty-eight children, from a total sample of 74 subjects, who passed the addition/subtraction pre-test but were non-conservers on the main conservation test, were randomly assigned to one of the two training groups. The mean age of the subjects in each group was five years, 10 months.

METHOD/The general experimental procedure consisted of pre-tests, 'set' training, conflict trials and post-tests. Briefly, the pre-tests had a two-fold purpose. The first was to establish the subject's ability to respond to addition/subtraction manipulations and the second to determine the initial presence or absence of number concepts. The basic principles were consistent with those of Smedslund's studies (1961a, b, c, and d). In the 'set' training phase, only those children who passed the addition/subtraction test but were non-conservers of the number concept were administered the remaining sequence of trials. These children were randomly assigned to one of the three training groups: A/S set training; perceptual-set training; and the control (no-'set' training). The training trials were followed by conflict trials. 'Each conflict trial started with two equivalent rows of chips. The experimenter then made an A/S manipulation and a contrasting length manipulation so that the shorter row had more chips than the longer row.' In all cases, the larger A/S change was paired with the longer length manipulation. The post-tests were essentially identical to the pre-tests.

RESULTS/In respect to the first study, an overall χ^2 analysis demonstrated a significant relation between performance and training conditions ($\chi^2 = 13.2$, p<.01). The performance of the A/S group differed significantly from the performance of the perceptual ($\chi^2 = 9.2$, p<.01) and control ($\chi^2 = 5.2$, p<.05) groups. However, there was no difference between the performance of the perceptual and control groups (p>.3 by Fisher's exact test). In the second study a non-significant difference in favour of the groups receiving the conflict trials was observed. Winer's 1968 study casts doubt on the 'conflict-resolution interpretations' of the acquisition of conservation as formulated and established by Smedslund's 1961a, b, c, and d studies.

A study of acceleration of concepts of number in young children through group treatment
J. Mason, 1969

INTRODUCTION/The study reported here is based on work carried out by Wallace and reported in his doctoral, 'An inquiry into the development of concepts of number in young children involving a comparison of verbal and non-verbal methods of assessment and acceleration' (1967).

Wallace showed in a 'short-term' longitudinal study that it was possible to accelerate the course of conceptual development and that non-verbal methods, in this instance, were superior to verbal methods. 'It seems reasonable in the current state of our knowledge to advance as a working rule that non-verbal methods should be largely employed with children under five years of age' (Wallace, 1967).

With such results as obtained by Wallace, it seems imperative that this acceleration technique should be made available to teachers in charge of young children. With the present teacher-pupil ratio the method adopted would not be practicable. No teacher could afford to spend 30 minutes on eight successive school days with one child! On the other hand, if the same results were obtained by using group treatment, this acceleration process would become a practicable proposition for teachers of young children. This investigation was designed to focus its attention on this problem. The non-verbal acceleration process was modified and presented to children on a group basis.

EXPERIMENTAL DESIGN/In the case of experimental design, the shortcomings of cross-sectional studies have been highlighted in the literature. As long-term longitudinal studies are fraught with difficulties, the adoption of the 'short-term' longitudinal study as a compromise appears eminently suitable. The development of number conservation is a theme which is well-suited to this approach since the available data indicate that it takes place in a relatively short period of time in the region of five to seven years of age.

The general features of the short-term longitudinal approach are also in accordance with some of the requirements of the acceleration issue. The desirability of determining the stability and permanence of any changes produced by the experimental treatments adopted, decrees that at least two post-tests, separated by a reasonable interval of time, should be a feature of the design. In addition, the problem of acceleration makes demands of its own experimental design. A study involving a single experimental group and a control group poses the problem of devising a treatment for the control group which will compensate for the action of the Hawthorne effect on the performance of the experimental group. It seems desirable, therefore, to have two experimental groups and thus the results of each treatment can be compared with those of another as well as with the results of a control group. The above considerations led to the adoption of the following design:

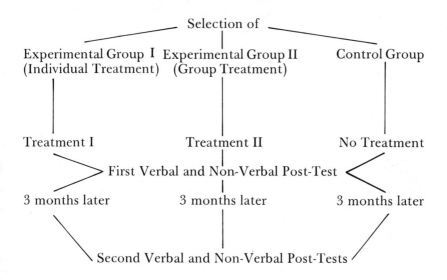

Since it was necessary to establish the effectiveness of the non-verbal acceleration treatment when used with a group of children, a uniform mode of presentation was adopted. A single teaching machine, designed and first used by Brimer (1967), acted as the reinforcing agent for the children's responses. Cards were positioned on the machine by two locating holes on each side. Six coloured lines (blue, black, green, red, white and yellow) appeared on each card and one of these colours was also displayed on the slide being shown to the children. Under each colour band there were three holes which registered with a hole in the machine when the card was positioned. Six sets of such cards were used for each child in the group. The total effect of the machine was that the bulb lit when a plunger was inserted in the correct hole in each row. ('A further feature of the machine was that it allowed nine different sequences of correct hole position which could be selected by differential registration of display cards upon fixed studs in the machine' Brimer 1967).

As the non-verbal acceleration technique devised by Wallace was selected for use with both experimental groups, the theoretical work that was behind the technique was the same for both groups hereafter referred to as Experimental Group I (Individual Treatment) and Experimental Group II (Group Treatment).

What then was the difference between treatments? The

transfer of an individual technique to a group situation involves not merely technical difficulties but changes in the conditions for learning. While the technique devised by Wallace emphasized the non-social circumstances, as determinants of learning, his procedures inevitably involved an inter-personal relationship between teacher and child. The teacher established rapport, manipulated the model environment and was instrumental in reinforcement. The proposal to transfer to a group technique alters the situation radically.

The first major difference is one of relationships. Experimental Group I was seen on an individual basis, there was always a one-to-one correspondence between adult and child. Leith and Bassett's (1967) work suggests this may not be the situation best suited for learning. Experimental Group II was treated as a group. There was one adult in the room and eight children. They were permitted to talk and they each had to demonstrate, on the machine described above, their comprehension of the tasks used in the presentation of the experimental problems. The atmosphere was relaxed and the adult was merely an operator of the projector. Boyce (1968) obtained encouraging results using a similar technique.

The first hypothesis was that group treatment aimed at accelerating the development of number concepts in young children would be as effective in terms of results as a similar individual treatment, and that group and individual treatments would be more effective than no treatment. Also, group treatment would be more efficient than individual treatment.

SUBJECTS/The subjects were 24 children drawn from an Infants' School in the west of England. It was assumed that these children would be selected from the intake of 60 children entering school in September 1969. It was found that the inability of these children to count to six, seven or eight, made it necessary to widen the field to children who had been in school for 18 months. Also a pre-'pre-test' had to be instituted. To qualify for the pre-test, the ability to name correctly a collection of eight shells was a prerequisite. To find the necessary 24 children to proceed to the pre-test, 150 children, with an age range from four years 11 months to six years two months, had to be pre-tested.

CONCLUSIONS/1. Group treatment aimed at accelerating the development of number concepts in young children is as effective in terms of results as a similar individual treatment; group and individual treatments are more effective than no treatment. Also, group treatment is more efficient (two and a half hours) than individual treatment (20 hours).

2. Subjects treated on an individual basis showed the greatest improvement on the first post-tests. Subjects treated on a group basis showed the greatest improvement on the second post-tests.

3 The results of this investigation and Wallace's doctoral thesis (1967) have far-reaching implications for all teachers of young children.

4. As counting plays an important part in the development of conservation of number in young children, further research into the strategies of counting adopted by young children should be investigated.

The training of conservation of number in young children
B. Rothenberg and J. Orost, 1969

AIM/Rothenberg and Orost attempted an approach to the training of conservation of number through the presentation of a logical sequence of component concepts, or steps, evaluated in a series of three experiments.

SUBJECTS/The 130 kindergarten children with middle- and lower-class backgrounds and with an age range of four years 11 months to six years six months were given individual instruction by the authors.

METHOD/In the training sessions, Wohlwill and Lowe's (1962) technique of reinforced counting was used — the subjects were first given practice in counting aloud and then in counting small groups of objects to promote a tentative concept of 'same number'. Addition and subtraction of one object at a time was presented, using a technique similar to that of Gruen (1965). Verbal pre-training on the concept of more (in number) versus longer (in length) was given, a variety of situations being presented to teach this concept. The contentions of Zimiles (1966) were also observed, that is, 'the initial presentation of small aggregates enhances a comprehension of numerosity independent of spatial distortions'.

RESULTS/The results of the study implied that conservation of number can be taught to kindergarten-age children. Moreover, the training was effective — its effects lasted as long as three months and significantly increased the understanding of the related problems of conservation of quantity. The sequence of concepts and the style of teaching used seemed to present a reasonable and workable series for the teaching of number conservation. These results do not prove, however, that the developmental sequence of learning presented in this study contains the only acceptable steps to attaining conservation of number. No sex differences were found and only slight differences were demonstrated in conservation learning between socio-economic status groups. It must be pointed out, however, that in Rothenberg and Orost's study the lower-class subjects were all negro and the middle-class subjects were white. How far the cultural variations may have contributed one way or the other is open to question.

A discrimination task which induces conservation of number
G.S. Halford and T.J. Fullerton, 1970

AIM/The study employed a discrimination task in order to induce conservation of number.

SUBJECTS/The study drew 24 children from a school in a working-class socio-economic area. Twelve subjects were randomly allocated to the experimental group, and 12 to the control. For experimental subjects, the mean age was 75 months with SD = 9.7 and the mean IQ 90.6 with SD = 9.3. For control subjects the mean age was 77 months with SD = 9.2 and the mean IQ 91.1 with SD = 7.9.

METHOD/The conservation of number pre-test consisted of the typical Piagetian 'beds and dolls' task. Five dolls were each assigned to five beds. After the child had established the equivalence of dolls and beds, one of the arrays of beds/dolls was spatially distorted, and the child was asked for the equivalence. The responses were recorded verbatim and the general procedure followed that of the Geneva school. With respect to the training apparatus, minor modifications were made to the 'beds and dolls' task, without violating the basic principles inherent in the Piagetian conservation concept. Details of these modifications are given by the authors in their published work (Halford and Fullerton, 1970, pp.205-13). The actual procedure involved one individual session per day over a period of five consecutive days. Extensive training sessions were employed to establish complete operativity. The post-tests were essentially the same as the pre-tests, with the addition of two identical items. In the additional items, one difference was the increase in the number of dolls and beds from five to 11.

RESULTS/The results indicated that the training method induced two-thirds of the subjects to acquire conservation of a 'stable' kind (eight out of 12 controls). See also Wallach and Sprott (1964); Wohlwill and Lowe (1962); Smedslund (1962); Wallach, Wall and Anderson (1967) and Roll (1970). Halford and Fullerton's study could be seen as related to Piaget's equilibration theory and may also be seen partly as an attempt to transform Smedslund's (1961a) techniques into a 'simultaneous discrimination' (see also Halford, 1971).

Reversibility training and stimulus desirability as factors in conservation of number
S. Roll, 1970

AIM/Roll investigated the effect of training in reversibility on conservation of number.

SUBJECTS/The study involved 87 subjects in a private middle-class school in Colombia in South America. Equal numbers of children of either sex were represented, and ranged in age from five years, seven months to seven years, 11 months, with a mean of six years, seven months.

METHOD/Tests/Various tasks were administered to the subjects, such as 'production', 'equivalence' and 'recognition'. Each child was then given six trials to test for conservation of number. General procedure in the overall administration of the tasks followed very closely that of the Geneva school. All instructions were given in Spanish by the experimenter. The subjects were finally categorized as either 'conservers', 'non-conservers' or 'partial conservers'.

It was with the 44 'non-conserving' children that Roll examined the effect of training in reversibility on conservation of number, by dividing the children into one training and two control groups. The typical Piagetian task of 'dolls and beds' was administered, with extensive training in favour of operational responses. During any one month, each child received four trials per day for 11 non-consecutive days. Children in control group I were individually tested, were permitted to familiarize themselves with the materials and followed the same number of sessions utilized in training. However, control group II received only the pre-and post-tests. The post-tests were essentially the same as the six conservation tasks used in the conservation pre-test, apart from a change in the materials.

RESULTS/Roll concludes that the training resulted in a significant increase in conservation responding ($<.01$) but not in an increased verbalization of conservation principles.

Perceptual and sensori-motor supports for conservation tasks
M. Whiteman and E. Peisach, 1970

AIM/Whiteman and Peisach examined the following hypotheses:

(a) that conservation tasks may be operated upon with greater facility when involving numerous supporting cues and experiences;

(b) that the level of conservation operativity is affected by the inter-action between supports and schemata;

(c) 'that sensori-motor cues are of relatively greater aid to younger children who are closer to sensori-motor stages, while perceptual cues are of more aid to older children who are closer to the later developing perceptual stages';

(d) that children performing at a lower level of conservation are more dominated by 'salient perceptual characteristics' in their conceptions of greater quantity.

SUBJECTS/Thirty-two kindergarten children, (13 boys, 19 girls) and 31 third-graders of lower SES (16 boys, 15 girls) were involved in the study. These negro children were of average intelligence on the Stanford-Binet scale (mean IQs for the kindergarten and third-grade children were 94.05 and 98.08, respectively). The mean age of the kindergarten group was five years, 10 months (range from five years to six years, five months); of the third-grades, nine years, two months (range from eight years, six months to nine years, eight months).

METHOD/Two tasks of conservation were administered — mass and number. In both of these tests sweets were used 'to add a note of realism'.

Slight modifications were used in the number conservation items: '. . . it was felt that one-to-one correspondence might be enhanced through between-pair perceptual cues based on colour and guide lines. In the case of the colour cue, each candy in the row in front of the child was aligned with the candy of the same colour in the row in front of the experimenter . . . the red candy from the experimenter's row was placed opposite the red candy in the child's row. . . . In the case of the guide lines, corresponding candies from the elongated and compact rows were connected by lines drawn on the oak-tag rectangle on which the candies were placed . . .'.

Experiences in respect to the act of reversibility comprised

94

two types — unilateral and bilateral. In the former, 'the experimenter had the child use one hand to move each candy from the elongated to the compact position and back, once without guide lines, and once with guide lines'.

In the latter, '. . . the experimenter had the child use both hands simultaneously to move pairs of adjoining candies, one member of a pair from the experimenter's and the other from the child's row. The candies were moved to the elongated position and then back to the compact positions along the guide lines . . .'.

In order to increase the number of supports, the following order was observed by Whiteman and Peisach:

(a) standard conditions, candies of identical colour, no reversibility experience; (b) colour cue; (c) colour and unilateral reversibility experience; (d) colour and guide lines; (e) colour, guide lines, and unilateral reversibility experience; (f) colour, guide lines, and bilateral reversibility experience.

In the typical tasks of mass conservation the following sequence was followed: (a) standard condition, without colour cue or reversibility experience; (b) colour cue; (c) colour cue and reversibility experience. (Fuller details of the experimental procedure are given in Whiteman and Peisach, 1970, pp.249-50.)

RESULTS AND DISCUSSION/The results lent support to the first hypothesis, i.e. that cumulations of cues and experiences would foster conservation operativity. This, however, was true with number conservation tasks only. It was also true in the case of the younger children, but only if the judgement rather than the explained judgement score was used. This may, in part, be due to the fact that the supports given to the children were perceptual and sensori-motor, rather than linguistic. The authors have argued that the perceptual and experimental supports may be more effective with an easier task (the number task proved easier than the mass conservation task). Moreover, the authors maintain that all such supports as colours, guide lines, reversibility experiences 'can be conceived as maintaining the child's focus on the one-to-one correspondence between the adjoining elements of the two rows'.

The study also produced evidence demonstrating that the sensori-motor experiences tended to facilitate the younger subjects' performance at a lower level of conservation operativity, whereas perceptual cues were more beneficial to older subjects of non-conservation status. Whiteman and Peisach defend this finding when they argue that '. . . this makes sense in the light of the stress of developmental theories on cognitive stages proceeding from sensori-motor to perceptual levels. If the older child is closer to a perceptual level, then perceptual cues may be more effective than sensori-motor feedback from activity, which is more in keeping with the younger child's proximity to sensori-motor levels'. Moreover, older children tend to possess greater readiness to resist spatial orientations than younger subjects.

Finally, the authors maintain that a combination of training techniques may prove more appropriate in the overall enhancement of conservation operativity.

The role of body parts and readiness in acquisition of number conservation
F. Curcio, W. Robbins and S. Ela, 1971

AIM/To determine whether number conservation with body parts (fingers) preceded number conservation with external objects.

SUBJECTS/One hundred and sixty-seven nursery school-children with an age-range of 42 to 64 months were involved in the study.

METHOD/Materials/In all tasks red and yellow pipe cleaners (PCs) were used. The subject was allowed to choose his favourite colour. These were placed in front of the S and the remainder in front of E. Depending on the nature of the task, various numbers of PCs from each pile were placed to the centre of the table.

Pre-Training/In this phase five tasks were presented to all children. These were: 1. counting; 2. one – one correspondence; 3. number conservation with objects; 4. addition/subtraction; 5. number conservation with fingers.

Test 1 was simple counting, while tests 2, 3 and 4 were typical Piaget-type situations. In Test 5, the child was asked to hold up his hands with the fingers slightly apart. 'Do you have more fingers on this hand (left hand) or on this hand (right hand), or do you have the same number of fingers on both hands?' S was then asked to spread apart his left hand, while the right hand fingers were left together. The child was again requested for the equivalence.

Results demonstrated that number conservation of fingers preceded number conservation of external objects.

Training/From the pre-training sample, three groups of 16 children each, participated in the training and post-testing phases. Thirty-two Ss who were operational on counting, addition/subtraction and correspondence tasks but were non-operational on both conservation tasks were assigned either to rote-counting (RC) or addition/subtraction (A/S) training groups. (Fuller details of the rote-counting (RC) and addition/subtraction (A/S) training procedures are described elsewhere, Curcio, Robbins and Ela, 1971, pp.1642-3).

Post-Tests/All training groups were presented with two identical post-tests of number conservation with objects. These were typical Piaget-type situations and once again pipe-cleaners (PCs) were used as materials. These were administered soon after the training and again seven days later.

RESULTS/The authors conclude, '. . . the strongest training effect emerges when the following groups are compared: Ss who possess number conservation with fingers trained to generalize this ability, and Ss who do not possess finger conservation trained on A/S or RC procedures. When closeness or readiness is equated and training is different, the BP (body parts − fingers) training group tends to maintain acquisition of number conservation one week later, while the other groups do not, which suggests the special contribution made by this type of training . . . when readiness of a child is coupled with a form of training appropriate to the child's current level of development, acquisition of number conservation is strongest. . . . Concerning the horizontal décalage between number conservation with fingers and that with external objects, perhaps the 'provoked correspondence' (Piaget 1952) in pairing thumbs, index fingers, . . . contributes to the recognition of number conservation with fingers before that with external objects.'

Pilot investigation of the effects of training techniques designed to accelerate children's acquisition of conservation of discontinuous quantity
K. Feigenbaum, 1971

AIMS/Feigenbaum's study addressed its inquiry to the following three objectives:
(a) to investigate 'trainings' aimed at an enchancement of conservation of discontinuous quantity in children;
(b) to examine 'trainings' aimed at fostering the ability in children to take varied social roles; and
(c) to establish whether an effective training in conservation will facilitate children to take varied social roles, and vice-versa.

SUBJECTS/One hundred and three children were involved, with an age range of 45 to 64 months, averaging 53.9 months. The total sample was divided into seven training groups and one control. All groups were roughly matched for CA, SES and IQ (Peabody).

METHOD/The battery consisted of the following tests:

(a) The Peabody Picture Vocabulary Test.

(b) Piagetian tests of Conservation.

(c) Field Dependence (WISC). (The Picture Completion Sub-test).

(d) Use of figures in retelling a story. Briefly, a story is told using cut out figures of 'mummy, daddy, brother/sister, baby'. The subject is requested to retell the story. The child is encouraged to use the cut-out figures. A score of one was awarded when the 'S could not relate a coherent plot'. The maximum score of six was awarded when the 'S told the story correctly . . . the feeling of the characters, and included interpretations of the motivation behind the characters' actions'.

(e) Role-Play Test. The child is asked to play the role of the parent and the sibling of the same sex as the subject.

Training/Seven training groups, with between 11 and 15 children in each, were trained in different 'combinations of conditions' (reversibility-reciprocity; physical perspective-taking; and social role-playing) over a period of six weeks, in one half-hour session per week. The control group consisted of eight subjects. Training was specifically given to enhance a child's performance on tests of conservation, correspondence conservation, role-play and retelling, conservation with beads and glasses, and physical perspective-taking.

Post-testing was carried out within three weeks of the initial training. Feigenbaum gives an example of the teaching of perspective-taking as follows: '. . . a large box was placed in the centre of the floor: on two opposite sides were one big black dot, and two dots (on white field) respectively; on the other two opposite sides, the plain colours black and green. The children were shown all sides. Then a child sat facing each side, close to the box. 'Extras' stood behind each sitting child. Extras then asked each sitting child what the opposite child saw. The 'extra' went around to check, and said if the child was right. The children then switched both standing and sitting positions and the exercise was repeated'.

RESULTS/The data gathered were subjected to Wilcoxon tests of significance of differences between the pre- and post-training performance. Significant improvement was observed on some of the conservation tasks. More specifically, the reversibility-reciprocity training enhanced the acquisition of conservation of discontinuous quantities.

Further, no training techniques devised by Feigenbaum fostered children's ability to take different social roles. The overall results were inconclusive. Children given role-play and physical-perspective training significantly regressed in role-taking ability. The control group demonstrated moderate improvement. The role-play training group showed no improvement in role-taking ability. However, tests of significance of difference on combinations of groups in which reversibility-reciprocity training was administered, demonstrated consistent improvement in social role-taking and physical perspective-taking ability.

No consistent patterns emerged between children's ability to conserve and their ability to take different social roles. Likewise, with regard to the relation between physical perspective-taking and social perspective-taking, the pre-treatment correlation computed a small significance (.05), while the post-treatment correlation was not quite significant at the .05 level.

The understanding of invariance by very young children
P. E. Bryant, 1972

Bryant argues that '... the number conservation problem ... involves a transformation from a display which normally produces a judgement that the rows are equal, into a display which normally produces a contrary judgement that they are unequal. If we assume ... that the child does understand invariance we can suggest that the transformation faces him with a conflict between two judgements, the first that the rows are equal, the second that they are not. He can only adopt one of these two incompatible judgements and realizes that one of them must be wrong. ... Faced with this dilemma he falls back on the more recent of the two ... The solution is to find displays about which young children appear to have no consistent hypotheses at all, displays with which their behaviour is quite random. It is then possible to transform a display which does produce a consistent judgement into one of these displays which does not. This transformation avoids hypothesis conflict, and yet tests invariance. ... The aim ... was to institute such a transformation and to compare performance on it to performance on more traditional kinds of transformations.'

Experiment One

SUBJECTS/Fifteen children, each at age level three to six years, were involved in the study. They were drawn from two nursery and two infant schools in Oxford, with an age range from three years, six months to six years, eight months.

METHOD/Three types of displays were presented involving coloured counters placed on a board. Each display consisted of two parallel rows of counters. The displays were 'the above chance display (A)', 'the below chance display (B)'; and 'the chance display (C)'. Three sessions and three displays were used in the experiment. 'The pre- and post-tests established baseline levels for the three displays. In the experimental session the above chance display (A) was transformed into either the below chance (B) or the chance (C) displays. Thus the transformation in A-B trial was from a display which produces one hypothesis into a display which produces a contrary hypothesis. In A-C trials the transformation was from a display which produces a consistent hypothesis into a display which produces no consistent hypothesis at all. If, in either the A-B trials or the A-C trials, Ss make more correct responses with the B or C displays than they do in the baseline pre- and post-tests, they will demonstrably have transferred information about quantity across a perceptual transformation.'

Experiment Two
SUBJECTS/Sixteen children, at each age level three to six were involved in this experiment. They were also drawn from two nursery and one infant schools in Oxford. The CA ranged from three years, nine months to six years, eight months.

METHOD/The tasks and displays were identical to Experiment One, apart from minor modifications.

Experiment Three
SUBJECTS/The four- and the five-year-old groups consisted of 20 children, with an age range of four years, nine months to five years, 11 months. These were further divided into two sub-groups of 10 subjects each. The children were drawn from one nursery and one infant's school in Oxford.

METHOD/The general problem was to establish if experience with the two kinds of transformations (A-type and B-type displays) would affect the child's level of operativity from pre- to post-tests. There were four phases involved in the general procedure as follows: (a) pre-test; (b) training (A-type display); (c) training (B-type display); (d) post-test. (Fuller details of the experiments, the displays, the general experimental procedure and the statistical treatment of the data gathered, is described in Bryant 1972, pp. 80-91.)

OVERALL RESULTS AND DISCUSSION/Bryant discusses the main results in terms of the hypothesis conflict theory, and reports the results as follows:

(a) 'that children as young as three can maintain a quantity judgement over a transformation';

(b) '. . . that they do not do so when the response characteristically produced by the second display is opposite to that produced by the first';

(c) '. . . that training that one cue is more reliable than the other enables young children to maintain a judgement based on the more reliable cue at the expense of using the less reliable one'.

Bryant argues that children should be trained in the formation of judgements rather than teaching invariance and cites in criticism the work of Smedslund (1961) and Wallach (1969). The author further stresses the 'gap between competence and performance. It seems that young children's performance with some invariance problems lies far behind their competence. It is their developmental task between the ages of three and eight years not to acquire the competence but to bring their performance more in line with their competence.'

Lunzer (1972) has argued that Bryant's study contained many omissions and distortions and that 'Bryant's novel interpretation coincides with what has been said by Piaget himself'. Moreover, he maintains that Bryant has made the case that 'right from the start the child has conflicting hypotheses in the conservation situation, and simply prefers that hypothesis which is supported by more recent cues. He would need to show that the two hypotheses do indeed co-exist and conflict. The evidence is that the pre-operational child is not in conflict at all. The conservation of amount hypothesis is simply discarded . . . Bryant would have us believe that the two cues of one-to-one correspondence and of relative length are both perceptual in origin. To begin with they are equipotent, but the former gradually becomes prepotent because it happens to be consistent . . . But the facts are quite otherwise . . .'.

Finally, Lunzer points out four main flaws in respect to Bryant's third experiment. These are respectively: a weak conservation criterion; no late post-test was administered; training and test tasks were presented too close to each other and with identical material and spatial orientations; and the study was not strictly 'blind'.

A reply to Lunzer's criticism has been advanced by Bryant (1972).

II Substance

Smedslund's (1961a) study succeeded in inducing the concept of the conservation of substance by employing the 'cognitive conflict' theory. This provides the greatest promise for success because of its similarity to Piaget's theory of adaptation. Moreover, both adaptation and cognitive conflict processes employ the disequilibrium – equilibrium model. . . . This is the system, according to Smedslund, of 'competing cognitive strategies' and he has argued that the creation of such conflict would enhance cognitive reorganization to the extent of inducing the concept of conservation. Smedslund conceives of cognitive conflict as being similar to Festinger's (1957) 'cognitive dissonance'. Smedslund's argument is that, if a child believes that the lengthening of a piece of plasticine makes it heavier (because it is now longer) and yet knows that subtracting a piece from the object makes it lighter, then in those cases where both of these schemata are activated with precisely the same strength, cognitive conflict will occur. However, Smedslund's cognitive theory has not been entirely supported. See, for example, Winer's (1968) study and Hall and Simpson (1968, op. cit.).

Beilin's (1965) training procedure appears to violate Piagetian theory directly. The 'verbal rule instruction provides the child with a statement of the rule to be applied to the problem in each instance of an unsuccessful trial response on a conservation task'. (p. 326) The study is discussed earlier in the chapter.

Bruner's (1964) 'language activation' training involves experimental procedures, which also appear to be inconsistent with Piagetian theory. (Details of Bruner's training procedures may be found in 'The Course of Cognitive Growth', American Psychologist, 19, 1964 pp. 2-15). Bruner's position on training is that adequate linguistic experiences would facilitate the concept of conservation. Activation of language habits would enable the child to be in full mental control of the irrelevant perceptual cues and would encourage the child to employ symbolic processes. '. . . Improvement in language should aid this type of problem solving.' This differs from Piagetian theory (1967) in that Piaget believes that the mental structure precedes language development.

Sigel, Roeper and Hooper (1966) also succeeded in inducing the concept of conservation of substance by employing a technique which incorporated aspects of the techniques of Smedslund (1961a), Gruen (1965), Bruner (1964) and Wallach and Sprott (1964). The sample was unexpectedly small – 10 children were randomly assigned to two groups of five each. Piagetian task of conservation were administered.

The authors claimed that the acquisition of conservation of substance followed the acquisition of simpler structures such as multiple labelling, multiple classification, multiple relations and reversibility. More specifically, they maintained that training in these structures, in the order stated, should facilitate the acquisition of conservation. However, an important feature has been pointed out by Lovell (1971) in regard to the Sigel-Hooper study (1966): '. . . pupils involved had IQs of 130 plus, and they may very well have been at or near the transitional stage anyhow. I think this is a point that one has often overlooked in connection with the Sigel study.' Sigel has modified his position on acquisition of conservation. Rather than suggesting that multiple labelling, classification, seriation and reversibility training, in that order, facilitate conservation, he now suggests that classification and discrimination learning may be among the several variables for conservation. It is interesting to note that Piaget's (1952b) contentions are that for operativity to occur, the child must be able to perform multiple classification, multiple relationality, atomism, reversibility and seriation. It must be pointed out, however, that Sigel's (1966) training originated, at least in part, in the Piagetian theory.

Mermelstein, Carr, Mills and Schwartz (1967) hypothesized that the training procedures, described above, would not be effective in the inducement of the concept of the conservation of substance. However owing to the greater congruence of Smedslund's (1961a) position with Piagetian theory, they hypothesized that such training would be more successful than the other three training procedures – that of Sigel (1966), Beilin (1965) and Bruner (1964).

The authors concluded that none of the four training techniques facilitated the concept of conservation of substance. It was further suggested that language interferes with, rather than facilitates, acquisition of the concept (details are given later in this chapter).

Brison (1966) attempted to induce the concept of substance in 24 non-conserving subjects. The control group consisted of 26 children who received no training. Twelve of the experimental subjects demonstrated evidence of conservation operativity. The author concludes 'five of these subjects gave at least four of five correct conservation predictions. The concept transferred to substances (clay, sand) not used in experimental group. The five experimental subjects with four correct predictions performed similarly to subjects possessing conservation before the experiment on an extinction item.'

Training techniques for the concept of conservation
E. Mermelstein, E. Carr, D. Mills, and J. Schwartz, 1967

AIM/The authors employed the following training techniques in their investigation: Smedslund's (1961a) 'cognitive conflict' technique; Bruner's (1964) 'language activation' procedure;

Beilin's (1965) 'verbal rule instruction'; and Sigel's (1966) 'multiple classification' technique.

SUBJECTS/One hundred and twenty children were selected and were operationally defined as between five years and six years two months of age.

METHOD/Equal numbers of children of either sex were assigned to each of the four training conditions: 'cognitive conflict'; 'language activation'; 'multiple classification'; and 'verbal rule instruction'. Twenty children were assigned randomly to each of two control groups and each of the four training techniques. Non-white children were not included in the study in order to mitigate any milieu differences. The training apparatus was similar, if not identical, to that of Smedslund, Bruner, Beilin and Sigel. Although some modifications were made, the underlying principles of these techniques were not violated. Post-test tasks were typical Piagetian tasks of conservation of discontinuous substance (Piaget and Inhelder, 1941). Children were tested in all the six groups one week, eight weeks and six months after the last training session. This study satisfied Piaget's (1964) criteria for ascertaining whether the concept of conservation was induced, especially the first two criteria regarding transfer and durability (discussed earlier in the Chapter).

RESULTS/The authors concluded that the Piagetian concept of conservation of substance, as measured by the specific criteria described, was not induced by a variety of training techniques. It was further suggested that language interferes with, rather than facilitates, acquisition of the concept of conservation of substance.

III Weight

Among training studies, the majority have dealt with conservation of number and substance, and relatively few have been concerned with the concept of weight. Smedslund (1961b) carried out several experiments which attempted to teach conservation of weight. The first group comprised 11 children successfully trained in the conservation of weight. They were compared with 13 children who had demonstrated conservation operativity on the pre-test. The extinction manipulation consisted of the surreptitious removal, during the conservation transformation, of a piece of clay from one of two balls, initially equal in weight, followed by a weighing which demonstrated that the weights were now unequal. The subject was required to advance an explanation for the inequality, and he was judged to have extinguished if he did not succeed in giving an acceptable explanation. All 11 trained children extinguished by this criterion; in contrast, six of the 13 natural conservers successfully resisted extinction.

Wallace (1972) draws attention to Piaget's (1959) discussion of Smedslund's attempts to accelerate the development of the conservation of weight and makes the deduction that Piaget would agree with training, provided that the treatment was not regarded as a sufficient feature and that encouragement was given to the establishment of conceptual conflict which would lead to structural reorganization and be conducive to the process of equilibration.

Kingsley and Hall (1967), using training based on Gagné's (1962, 1963) learning set procedure, which depended heavily on experience rather than on Piaget's maturational structures[1], yielded highly significant training effects on weight and length conservation and its subsequent transfer to substance conservation. (Details are given later in this Chapter. See also Caruso and Resnick, 1972, p. 1307.)

Smith (1968) reported that Beilin's (1965) methods (op. cit.) improved significantly the performance of both non-conservers and transitional conservers, whereas Smedslund's (1961a, op. cit.) procedure produced no effect on the conservation performance of either group. (Details are given later in this chapter. See also Miller, 1973, who discusses and compares his results to those of Kingsley and Hall, op. cit. and Smith, op. cit.)

An attempt to induce the concept of conservation of weight in ESN children was made by Lister (1969). Results demonstrated that '. . . it is possible to develop a concept of weight conservation in ESN children using a teaching method, which included active manipulations by the learner and verbal representation with emphasis on identity, subtraction/addition and reversibility' (details are given later in this chapter).

Appropriate here is the study by Lister (1972) in which she extends her 1969 and 1970 findings to an investigation concerned with the development of ESN children's understanding of conservation. She concludes 'post-tested after one week and then two months, 30 of the 34 instructed children consistently recognized, generalized and gave reasons for conservation on both post-tests. No control child improved in understanding of conservation by the time of the second post-test' (details are given later in this chapter).

Training conservation through the use of learning sets
R. C. Kingsley and V. C. Hall, 1967

AIMS/The authors contend that most of the training attempts have ignored the large amount of 'background knowledge' necessary and thus time is needed to train children for conservation mastery. Their attempt was designed to test this position through the use of training based on Gagné's (1962, 1963) learning set procedure. Gagné's analysis of learning sets depends much more heavily on experience than on Piaget's maturational structures.

SUBJECTS/The study involved 86 boys and girls aged five to six years.

METHOD/Thirty-six children were assigned to each of the two control groups and a training group. Similarly, 24 children aged six years were randomly assigned to the various groups and given a pre-test and two post-tests. Half of these children were extensively trained while the others served as controls. The authors also established an additional group of 15 children who were completely operational on all conservation tasks and were examined according to Smedslund's extinction technique (1961a). However, the age of this additional group ranged from six to 12 years.

The pre-tests were administered in the order of weight, length and substance. The authors have argued that, because the concepts of substance and weight generally co-vary, the concept of conservation of length would interpose between them. These three tasks of weight, substance and the concept of length were typically Piagetian and were consistent with the basic principles of conservation operativity.

The training phases lasted for a maximum of nine individual training sessions of 20 minutes' duration. The authors give full details in their published work (Kingsley and Hall, 1967, pp. 1117-1120). Post-tests of the Piagetian type were administered after a minimum of three days had elapsed between the last training session and the first post-test. The general procedure followed involved the children in the experimental group being pre-tested on knowledge hypothesized to be necessary for mastery of weight and length conservation along with actual conservation tasks in length, weight and substance. They were then trained on weight and length conservation only and post-tested twice to determine (a) training effects on weight and length conservation acquisition and (b) effects of training weight and length conservation on substance conservation.

RESULTS/Analysis of results using both parametric and non-parametric techniques (Kruskel-Wallis one way analysis of variance by ranks; Mann-Whitney U test and an analysis of covariance in Siegel, 1956, and Winer, 1962, respectively), yielded highly significant training effects. Experimental groups improved significantly more than control groups in substance conservation and the authors presented evidence to demonstrate that this was due to the similarity of substance and weight tasks.

The effects of training procedures upon the acquisition of conservation of weight
I. D. Smith, 1968

AIM/Smith also reported successfully teaching a concept of weight conservation by using Beilin's (1965) 'verbal rule instruction' method. The study was also addressed to determine the relative efficiency of Smedslund's (1961a) addition/subtraction method.

SUBJECTS/The study involved 139 subjects drawn from three first-grade classes and one second-grade class.

METHOD/The children were randomly assigned to various groups. There were three training procedures: (a) addition/subtraction (Smedslund, 1961a); (b) reinforced practice, and (c) Beilin's (1965) 'verbal rule' instruction. All training was administered in one session, lasting about 20 minutes. The control group was not subjected to any training phases.
Each child was tested individually and an understanding of the concepts like 'heavier', 'lighter' and 'sameness' was established. The responses were recorded verbatim and the general procedure followed that of the Geneva school. The recorded responses were later examined to establish patterns and branching relationships. The training was undertaken in two stages. Stage One consisted of Smedlund's (1961a) addition/subtraction technique, Reinforced Practice and Beilin's (1965) 'verbal rule' instruction. The second stage comprised the 'counter-suggestion' phase.

RESULTS/Beilin's (1965) method improved significantly the performance of both non-conservers and transitional conservers, whereas Smedslund's (1961a) procedure produced no effect on the conservation performance of either group. The authors also found that neither formally trained conservers nor informal conservers proved to be resistant to the counter-suggestion involved in a demonstration of apparent non-conservation.

The development of a concept of weight conservation in ESN children
C. M. Lister, 1969

AIMS/Lister attempted to clarify elements important in the development of the concept and to discover how to enhance the acquisition of such concepts by slow-learning children.

SUBJECTS/The study involved 44 children drawn from a school for ESN children and aged between 13 and 16 years with IQs between 42 and 79.

METHOD/These subjects were pre-tested for conservation judgements in the Piagetian situations. Twelve children who gave non-conservation judgements on all the questions of the pre-test were selected for special study. Six experimental subjects were matched as closely as possible by six control subjects with respect to CA and IQ. The six experimental group subjects were taught and then post-tested twice. When the experimental groups were given the post-test for a second time, the six control group subjects were re-pre-tested; then they too were taught and post-tested twice. Eight months later, 11 of the 12 original subjects were followed up and tested further. The conservation of weight acquisition was tested in the usual Piaget-type situations. The materials utilized were familiar and simple: plasticine, pencil, car, balloons, plastic cups, wooden cubes and others. The pre-testing tasks were identical to those of Piaget and Inhelder (1941, Chapter 2). The responses were later examined for any patterning of relationships. The teaching phase involved sequence of steps. These were the handling of unequal weights, equalizing weights of materials, experiencing the distinction between size and weight, the manipulation of transformations of continuous and discontinuous quantities, predicting and observing demonstrations of conservation. The materials were varied in contents and texture. All experiences were discussed and refined whenever the need was felt. The post-tests were identical to the pre-tests.

RESULTS/Results demonstrated that '. . . it is possible to develop a concept of weight conservation in ESN children using a teaching method, which included active manipulations by the learner and verbal representation with emphasis on identity, subtraction/addition and reversibility'.

The development of ESN children's understanding of conservation in a range of attribute situations
C. M. Lister, 1972

AIMS/The author addressed the inquiry to four main objectives.
Lister's (1970) work revealed that ESN children 'appreciate' substance conservation before weight and before volume. She wanted to examine
(a) if this sequential development extended to number, length, distance and area concepts;
(b) the influence of specific task variables;
(c) how effective two independent schemata of instructions can be, following pre-testing; and
(d) whether any degree of generalization acquired through instruction, is transferable to related problems.

SUBJECTS/One hundred and fifteen ESN children (IQs 47 to 81) with CA eight to 16 were involved in Lister's study.

METHOD/Each child was pre-tested on number, substance, length, distance, area, weight and volume tasks. Fifty-one children out of 115 total population, showed non-operativity with two or more of these attributes. These 51 children were allotted to three matched groups. 'Each child was matched by a child in each of the other two groups according to CA, IQ and level of understanding of conservation. Age differences were less than 15 months and IQ differences less than 16 points. Each group contained 17 children, nine who had failed on area and volume tasks, three who had failed on area, volume, and weight, one who had failed on area, volume, weight and length, two who had failed on area, volume, weight, length and substance, and two who had failed on area, volume, weight, length, substance and number. One group was then given one scheme of instruction while a second group was given another instruction scheme and the third group, the control, was seen by the experimenter for practice in reading.'
The two groups who received instructions were post-tested after intervals of one week and eight weeks. At the time when the post-testing took place (at eight weeks), the control group was administered the pre-test again.
(i) Pre-testing/The Piaget tasks included number, substance, length, distance, area, weight and volume. Children were classified as conservers or non-conservers. For full conservation operativity, a child had to answer correctly and advance logical justifications. A conserver had to show his ability to perform either the acts of reversibility, identity or compensation. An analysis of the

responses of the various tasks, revealed a developmental sequence, i.e. that children appreciated conservation of number before substance, length, weight, volume and area. However, the influence of the specific task variable did not produce any consistent patterns. Generally, differences in the material situations presented influenced some children's recognition of conservation operativity. Likewise, 'differences in the transformations made influenced recognition of continuing equality'. (Lister gives full details of such effects on the various tasks employed in her published article, 1972, page 17.)

(ii) Teaching/In this phase 51 children who demonstrated non-operativity in two or more attributes were divided into three groups of 17 children as follows: E1, E2 and C. Children in group E1 were given instruction according to scheme 1: 'this scheme was designed to develop a broadly general understanding of conservation of quantity and it deployed various attribute situations while avoiding detailed discussion of the particular attributes'. Children in group E2 were given instructions according to scheme 2: 'this aimed explicitly at only conservation of area and it deployed only Piaget-type area situations'. Children in group C received no such instruction but answered questions on reading, which they were encouraged to do for the same length of time as groups E1 and E2.

Both schemes involved explanations and experiences. The type of explanation included: acts of identity, reversibility, compensation, fact, addition/subtraction. The types of experience were: verbalization of reasons; observation of spatial orientations; use of external criteria and manipulation of reversible transformations. The objective was 'to help all children to appreciate the grounds for conservation judgements, to look for evidence of conservation or non-conservation, to develop verbal arguments . . .'.

Scheme 1 comprised six situations and included number, substance, length, area, weight and volume. These were identical to the pre-test tasks. Scheme 2 comprised the two area situations from the pre-tests.

(iii) Post-testing/Children in groups E1 and E2 were given post-tests one week and eight weeks after instruction. Thirteen of the pre-test situations, seven new material situations and six conservation of inequality tasks were administered. (Fuller details appear in Lister, 1972, page 19.)

RESULTS/The results indicated that 15 out of 17 children in each of groups E1 and E2 demonstrated conservation operativity in all situations of the post-test, both one week and eight weeks after instruction. 'So, for 30 of the 34 children, either scheme was equally effective in developing a generalized and durable understanding of conservation.' Lister further argues that these children who showed operativity advanced reasons which included the acts of reversibility, addition/subtraction, identity, fact and compensation. The 17 children in the control group remained rigid and continued to perform at the non-conservation stage. 'This lack of "spontaneous" development is a matter of practical educational concern because it indicates the extent to which ESN children depend on explicit teaching for their mental advancement.'

IV Liquid

Frank (1966) tested children from the ages of four to seven on the classic test of conservation of liquid quantity. In one condition the materials were in full view, and for several conditions the beakers were screened. In the screening conditions, the S was asked to verbalize what he observed with only the tops of the beakers visible. Under the screening conditions there was an increase in the operational response for each age group. Furthermore, 80 per cent of the five-year-old children and virtually all of the six- to seven-year-olds maintained conservation when the screen was removed. A post-test on an unscreened, transfer task demonstrated a pronounced enhancement in conservation response for the five- to seven-year-old Ss, when compared to pre-test norms. The author maintained that the study demonstrated the potential contribution of verbalization to the acquisition of liquid conservation.

The effects of the three training conditions, initially attempted by Frank, on the acquisition of the concept of conservation were further investigated by Strauss and Langer (1970). The results demonstrated that the screening of misleading cues did not facilitate conservation operativity and no credibility was added to Bruner's 'modes of representation conflict hypothesis'. Furthermore, children at the transitional stage were more likely to conserve and 'change progressively'. (Strauss and Langer's study is described later in this chapter. Also see Minichiello and Goodnow, 1969, discussed later in this chapter, and Inhelder and Sinclair, 1969.)

A more recent study by Siegler and Liebert (1972), investigated the effects of presenting relevant rules and complete feedback on the conservation of liquid quantity task. The authors maintained that 'both rules and feedback facilitated production of correct answers and explanations, with the two treatments operating additively'. Furthermore, results of a one-week follow-up demonstrated that the effects were 'temporarily stable'. However, Overton and Brodzinsky (1972, described in Chapter Five) argue 'it should be noted that while other studies have also demonstrated positive effects for various training conditions — e.g. Frank (1966) showed that a technique for screening misleading cues resulted in better performance on (liquid) conservation tasks — there has been in such studies a general lack of empirical inquiry into whether these effects are general across several years or are limited to the transitional children. This distinction is important because findings of general effect across development suggest that the behaviour involved is in fact learned through the techniques employed, whereas, on the other hand, the limitation of the effect to a specific period suggests that these techniques are activating already present cognitive structures'. (See also a more recent study by Miller (1973) who investigated the role of attention to stimulus dimensions in the conservation of liquid quantity and discussed results in terms of Gelman's, 1969, study in which attentional training successfully induced conservation operativity.)

Effect of an 'action' cue on conservation of amount
M. D. Minichiello and J. J. Goodnow, 1969

AIM/The authors investigated the effect of an 'action' cue on conservation of amount. They sought to clarify the source of any such improvement and to establish whether the same differences would be evidenced in a comparison of 'regular' and 'actions' procedures.

Minichiello and Goodnow cite the work of Inhelder and Piaget (1963, pp. 68, 97). The study reports two procedures ('regular' and 'actions') that give different results on some conservation tasks. In the liquid conservation task, four per cent of five-year-old children and 18 per cent of six-year old children conserved with a 'regular' procedure; 23 per cent and 46 per cent conserved with an 'actions' procedure. Likewise, similar gains from 22 per cent and 54 per cent to 60 per cent and 93 per cent are reported for conservation of discontinuous quantities.

SUBJECTS/Seventy-four children, five- and six-year-olds (mean age of total group five years nine months) were examined from two schools.

METHOD/Tests/Two tasks were administered to each child. These were: (a) Task 1 — Discontinuous quantities: children were given either regular or action procedure. (b) Task 2 — Continuous quantities: children were given only regular procedure.
'Performance on Task 1 allows a measure of any direct improvement from an action procedure. Performance on Task 2 allows a measure of any transfer effect to another task. Task 2 is

like Task 1 in asking for conservation of quantity, but differs in its stimulus material and in its level of difficulty.'

The authors describe the 'regular' and 'actions' procedures as follows:

' "Regular"/The child is shown two identical containers, A and A', already equally filled. He watches as E pours the water from A' to B, a container with a different shape from A. The child is asked if A and B have the same amount.

"Action"/The child is shown two differently shaped containers, A and B, both empty. He watches as E takes paired cups of water and pours them, in a simultaneous one-one fashion into the containers. The child is asked if A and B have the same amount.' (The fuller details of the experimental procedure in this study are given elsewhere, Minichiello and Goodnow, 1969 pp. 200.)

RESULTS/In the first conservation task, the use of actions had a two-fold effect:

(a) An improvement was observed in the number of operational responses on the specific task. However, this was only true of kindergarten children, and was statistically significant at the .05 level (one-tailed 't' test).

(b) It also increased the number of correct judgements on a second task. This was true with the first-grade children and the transfer effect was statistically significant at the .02 level (one-tailed 't' test). No transfer was noted among the kindergarten children.

DISCUSSION/The authors argue that the type of explanation advanced by Berlyne (1965) 'is a fruitful way of accounting for the effect of the "actions" procedure in the present study . . . the judgement situation at the end of the task can be regarded as a balance between relevant and irrelevant cues. In the usual Genevan procedure, the child's attention is drawn to the irrelevant cue of level, a cue difficult for children since it is sometimes useful and sometimes not. In the "actions" procedure, the child's actions draw attention away from the irrelevant cue, a function described as the "decentering" role of action in Piagetian terms (c.f. Piaget and Inhelder, 1956, p. 35) . . . they serve a function not stressed in Piagetian theory, namely, a positive drawing of attention to a relevant part of the stimulus, the equivalent composition of the two original amounts.'

The authors addressed their inquiry to the following hypotheses.
'(a) Conflict, with or without screening misleading cues, will lead to significant progressive change in conservation concepts.

(b) Screening misleading cues will lead to significant progressive change.

(c) Transitional children will be more likely to progress and conserve than preoperational children, regardless of the interviewing training condition to which they have been subjected.

(d) Only partial progress will be induced by the conditions used.'

SUBJECTS/One hundred and five children from lower- and middle-classes, both black and white, were involved in the study. The CA range was from five years six months to eight years 10 months (mean age seven years four months). Pre-test results placed 56 at the preoperational and 49 at the transitional stages. The subjects were assigned to one of six groups: preoperational and transitional children were randomly assigned to each of the four training conditions. Two groups were used as controls.

METHOD/Pre-test/In this phase, the concept of conservation of liquid task was administered to each child. Briefly, the child was shown two identical containers with the same amount of liquid in each. After the child had established the equivalence, the liquid from one of the identical containers was poured into a narrower and taller jar. The child was then questioned regarding the amount of liquid (conservation question). Justifications were asked and those who demonstrated conservation operativity were subjected to counter-suggestion. In the second part, seven cylindrical containers were shown to the child, two of which were identical. The liquid from one of these identical containers was transferred into the remaining five containers. The child was questioned again regarding the amount of liquid, followed by a counter suggestion. Fuller details are described elsewhere (Strauss and Langer, 1970, pp. 166-8). Children performing at the highest level of conservation operativity were excluded. Those who conserved on one part of the concept of liquid conservation were assigned as transitional. The preoperational group consisted of children who failed on both parts of the test.

Training Conditions/(a) Conflict and screening (patterned after Frank's (1966) third procedure). (b) Conflict and no screening. (c) No conflict and screening (patterned after Frank's (1966) first procedure). (d) No conflict and no screening (patterned after Frank's (1966) second procedure).

'The pre-test and the first and second post-tests, but no training, were administered to one control group (control one). The second control group (control two) took the pre-test and the second post-test to guard against the possibility that the first post-test might have influenced the judgements on the second post-test.'

Post-tests/These were identical to the pre-test. First post-test was presented one day after training. The second post-test was administered 10 to 14 days after the first post-test.

RESULTS/The authors summarize their findings: '(a) screening misleading cues did not induce conservation; (b) Bruner's modes of representation conflict hypothesis was not substantiated; (c) transitional phase Ss were more likely to conserve and change progressively; and (d) using the present procedures, it was not possible to assess definitively whether only partial progress could be induced.'

This indicates a departure from the results reported by Inhelder and Sinclair (1969), who demonstrated that 12.5 per cent of the preoperational children changed developmental level but without elements of logical strategies being evidenced in their justifications; and that 75 per cent of the transitional children benefited from the learning tasks, together with at least half the number who were able to advance logical judgements.

V Length

Piaget and others, such as Murray (1965), have shown that the age for the acquisition of conservation of length is between seven and eight. However, Braine (1959) has demonstrated that by using non-verbal techniques it is possible to lower some of Piaget's age norms by more than two years. If Braine's conclusions are valid (see Smedslund 1963 for a detailed critique), it might be reasonable to hypothesize that the use of essentially non-verbal techniques would allow the child to reveal his acquisition of the conservation of length at an age somewhat younger than seven or eight. More recently, Smedslund (1965) has commented on Braine's reply regarding the development of transitivity of length. Braine's position is that 'children normally become capable of making transitive inferences of the types $A{>}B. B{>}C{:}{\supset}{:}A{>}C$ and $A{<}B. B{<}C{:}{\supset}{:} A{<}C$ (where '$>$' means 'longer than' and '$<$' means 'shorter than') around the age of five years'.

Further complications were added to the already conflicting data of Braine and Smedslund by Sawada and Nelson's (1967) study. The authors developed a non-verbal method for training and assessing conservation of length. Their data showed that nearly 100 per cent of the children between the ages of seven years two months and eight years, were conservers of length. Nearly 70 per cent of the children between six years three months and seven years one month were conservers, and about 60 per cent of the children between five years four months and six years two months could conserve. 'It appears safe, therefore, to conclude that the threshold age for the acquisition of conservation of length is between five and six. The hypothesis about the efficacy of non-verbal techniques is therefore accepted.'

Jensen (1969) focuses upon Danset and Dufoyer's (1968) study and makes comparisons of their respective methodologies. Also intent to devise non-verbal methods of assessing transitivity, Danset and Dufoyer centred on bi-directional transitivity. However, Jensen limited his investigation to uni-directional transitivity. His design utilized a training and a test phase. The former was used to establish the relevant dimension upon which the child must attend in order to obtain a lead, the latter consisted of eight trials, in which the elements A, B and C were displayed in a systematic variation. A subject was said to display transitivity when he chose the longest of the three sticks A, on the basis of the information A>B and B>C. When this happened more than five times in the eight test trials, the subject demonstrated transitivity. 'In a group of 20 children, varying in age between 52 and 80 months, half of the group, which was socio-economically upper-middle class, displayed transitivity of length. However, the youngest child displaying transitivity with six correct test trials was 5½ years old. The youngest child displaying transitivity with eight correct trials was 6¼ years old.'

VI Logic

Kohnstamm's studies in 1962 and 1966 (Kohnstamm, 1967) demonstrated the facilitative value of the training programmes involving verbal explanation, in class-inclusion tasks. Although several other researchers have attempted to bring forth the inclusion response (Ahr and Youniss, 1970; Wohlwill, 1968, all described in Chapter Five), these have not succeeded in establishing conclusively that young children five to six years of age can acquire the ability to comprehend inclusive relation of classes. Hatano and Kuhara (1972) have criticized Kohnstamm's studies (op. cit.) 'The first is that he explained to children, and then asked them to explain the inclusion response in terms of number of two given classes . . . numbers obtained by counting do not imply any logical relation between two classes. . . . Though he used varieties of transfer items, most of them could be solved by mere generalization of the response and this left a possibility of interpreting the findings as mere response learning.' Hatano and Kuhara utilized an extensive training programme on class-inclusion problems, among 13 five- to six-year-old subjects. The authors' 'most important conclusion is that children of five to six years of age can acquire the ability to grasp inclusive relation, as typical of logical relations of two classes. Using more adequate methodology than Kohnstamm's, we confirmed this assertion that an intensive training programme is effective' (see also Okonji's study on the effect of special training on the classificatory behaviour of some Nigerian Ibo children, 1970, described in Chapter Eight).

Sigel, Roeper and Hooper (1966, discussed earlier) agree on the feasibility of training children to conserve, and they indicate the need for two other experiences; multiple classification and multiple relationship. These operations are prerequisites for logical reasoning.

Several researchers have attempted to teach multiple-classification skills. A series of studies, directly or indirectly related to the teaching of the completion of a matrix utilizing two attributes, were undertaken by Jacobs and Vandeventer (1968, 1969, 1971, 1971a). Their 1968 study indicated that an overall enhancement in the manipulation of double-classification problems could be achieved by altering certain features in the training phases. In continuation, Jacobs and Vandeventer (1971) established a number of training sequences, each of which permitted more individualization of instructions and involved more verbalization. A new test of double-classification skill was substituted for Coloured Progressive Matrices. Children in the experimental group (with highly structured and individualized training) performed at a higher level of classificatory operativity involving colour and shape relations than children in the control group. This acquired ability in the experimental subjects was also transferable to related post-tests involving new stimuli, both immediately and four months later. (The study is described later in this chapter. See also Caruso and Resnick, 1972, p. 1307.) Jacobs and Vandeventer (1969) carried out a survey of the actual rules employed in current double-classification test items. They were able to establish a 'universe', within which transfer could more meaningfully be assessed. The authors in their 1971a study, defined a 'universe', 'as consisting of all possible pairings of twelve logical relations . . .'. They wanted to assess transfer from the training procedure of their 1971 study within this 'universe'. An evaluation of the effects of more extensive training together with the effectiveness of different trainers was made. The results indicated that ' "regular-training" subjects significantly out-performed control subjects throughout the universe of relations. "Extended training"

117

produced significantly more transfer than "regular training". The two trainers did not differ in effectiveness. Transfer effects for regular and extended training were found to hold up three months later.'

Parker, Rieff and Sperr (1971) examined the effectiveness of a hierarchical instructional programme in multiple-classification. Overall, the evidence indicated an enhancement in the ability of the six- and seven-year-olds from the training programme. However, the four-and-a-half-year-old children demonstrated little increase in multiple-classification ability. The authors, in explaining the latter finding, advance two possible explanations: first, that the four-and-a-half-year-old children were too young to profit from multiple-classification instruction, and second, that the training programme needed revision (details appear later in the chapter).

In continuation, Parker, Sperr and Rieff (1972) employed two multiple-classification training programmes: an individual sequenced instruction (patterned after Gagné, 1965, 1966; Resnick, 1967) and terminal objective instruction (patterned after Jacobs and Vandeventer, 1968, 1969). Seventy-two children who were non-operational on multiple-classification problems, each at ages five years six months, six years six months and seven years six months were involved in the study. Overall, the results demonstrated that 'both individual sequenced instruction and terminal objective instruction groups performed significantly better after training than the contact control group, but that the individual sequenced instruction and the terminal objective instruction groups did not differ from each other on total score, criterion performance, or transfer tasks'. Moreover, the children aged six years six months and seven years six months benefited more from the training programme than the five-and-a-half-year-old subjects.

Brainerd (1970) and Brainerd and Allen (1971) suggested that the conservation problems may be categorized into those which are solved during the 'concrete' operations and those of 'formal' operations. An attempt to train the formal operational concept of density conservation was made by Brainerd and Allen (1971a) while investigating the effects of feedback and consecutive similar stimuli. A highly significant training effect was evidenced for the feedback treatment. 'The nontrivial nature of the training concept was demonstrated via significant ($p<.005$) pre- to post-test improvements in the feedback subjects' rationales for their answers (intraconcept generality) and via significant ($p<.005$) transfer of density training to solid volume conservation (interconcept generality)'. Details of this study are given later in this chapter. (See also Tomlinson-Keasey, 1971, described in Chapter Five, who demonstrated that the training procedure

118

utilized, produced an overall enhancement in tasks of formal operations, in adult females aged 11 to 54 years. However, such an acquired ability was not transferable to related, but delayed post-tests.)

Training and generalization of density conservation: effects of feedback and consecutive similar stimuli
C. J. Brainerd and T. W. Allen, 1971a

Brainerd and Allen selected density conservation (formal conservation) to be trained in subjects with CA 10 to 11 years seven months. The general design consisted of dividing the density conservation experiment into three phases: pre-tests, training and post-test. Only subjects who were non-operational in density, solid and liquid volume conservation were included.

SUBJECTS/Subjects from an elementary school were involved, with CA ranging from 10 years two months to 11 years seven months.

METHOD/Pre-tests/Briefly, the child had to predict if a blue clay ball would float when placed in the water-filled beaker. The child could see the ball sank when placed in water. E then flattened the same ball into a 'raft' and questioned the child 'Do you think that this raft will float?' 'Why?' 'Do you think this raft will sink?' 'Why?' This was followed by a small piece being subtracted from the 'raft', and questioned in the same manner. Later, the 'raft' was reduced to the size of a 'dime', followed by identical questioning. Those who answered correctly in all modifications of the experiment were also asked, 'Do you think that we could ever get a piece of this clay small enough so that it would float?' Subjects who responded 'No' were judged as operational and were excluded from the training phase. In all, 40 children showed non-operativity on the pre-tests, and were subjected to the training phase.

Next, E immersed a red clay ball in water, causing the water level to rise to a new height which was marked with the help of a rubber band. The same ball was then rolled into a sausage and the child was questioned as follows: (a) 'If I place the sausage in the glass, will the water rise above the rubber band?' 'Why?' (b) 'If I place the sausage in the glass, will the water go below the rubber band?' 'Why' (c) 'If I place the sausage in the glass, will the water go right back to the rubber band?' 'Why?'

The typical liquid volume pre-test, consisted of the child establishing equality of water in two identical beakers. After

119

which water from one of the beakers was poured into a differently shaped container and the child questioned again. 'Does the water in these (pointing) two beakers take up the same amount of space or room?' 'Why?' (b) 'Does the water in one of these beakers take up more space or room?' 'Why?' (Fuller details of these experiments are described in Brainerd and Allen, 1971a, pp. 696-8.)

Training/The 40 children who were assigned as non-conservers in all the pre-tests, described above, were included in the training phase. The difference between the pre-test and training phases was the introduction of two training variables, over and above the four repetitions of the density evaluation during the pre-tests.

Feedback was the first variable. Each of the 20 subjects who made a 'float-sink' prediction, was able to observe the piece of clay being placed in water and note whether his prediction was correct or incorrect. The remaining 20 children were not permitted any such observations. Consecutive similar stimuli constituted the second training variable. 'The 20 Ss, given consecutive similar stimuli, saw balls of the same colour on adjacent trials (brown, brown, green, green; or green, green, brown, brown)· while the remaining 20 Ss saw balls of different colours on adjacent trials (brown, green, brown, green; or green, brown, green, brown).'

Post-tests/The procedure here was identical to the pre-tests.

RESULTS/The post-test data indicated that feedback induced operativity in density conservation performance (F = 143.07, df = 1/36, p<.0001). However, similar stimuli did not indicate any such patterning (F<1).

Transfer of Training/Density training also enhanced solid volume operativity. Levels of solid volume operativity of the feed-back subjects were compared with the performances of their controls. The feedback advanced higher operativity (T = 3.21, df = 38, p<.005). However, density training did not facilitate liquid volume conservation. Generally, there was reliable evidence that density training transferred to conservation of a dissimilar concept.

Improvements in Control Subjects/Significant improvement in control group behavioural responses across various trials was also noted. The difference between pre-test and post-test performance was significant (matched t = 1. 86, df = 19, p<.05).

The learning and transfer of double-classification skills by first graders
P. Jacobs and M. Vandeventer, 1971

Studies by Jacobs (1966) and Jacobs and Vandeventer (1968) included the use of Raven's Coloured Progressive Matrices — a test which includes many double-classification items. Generally, these studies demonstrated an overall improvement with generalizability in skills of double-classification tasks, but, however, that these improvements were subject to altering certain features like training and the criterion employed. Modifications were made to the Coloured Progressive type of problems, with stress on more individualization of instruction and more verbalization in its training phases.

SUBJECTS/Forty-two children were selected on the basis of high scores on a test of double-classification.

METHOD/Training/On each card all cells contained a coloured shape, except for one cell which was empty. In all, six different colours and 20 different shapes were represented in the whole series of cards. The child was requested to select the shape suited to the empty cell. This was generally patterned after Raven's Progressive Matrices tests (1938). (Fuller details appear in Jacobs and Vandeventer, 1971, pp. 150-3). In the testing phase, an eight-item task was administered in order to evaluate directly the effects of training. The general layout of the matrices was similar to that of training cards. The matrices involved rules based on shape and colour, apart from combinations which were not identical to the training cards. Further, similar colours or shapes were not employed in the same item.

The eight-item test also assessed transfer of training (Transfer Tests). An assessment to record remote transfer was also undertaken employing items B6-B11 from Raven's Coloured Progressive Matrices (CPM) test. Fuller details appear in Jacobs and Vandeventer (1971, pp. 150-3).

All 56 first-grade children were pre-tested individually. Two of the three tasks from the Testing cards series were administered. Fourteen of the lowest scoring children were given various training techniques which were arrived at by 'individual informal try-out'. Further, 'it was felt that if the technique were successful with these particular subjects, it was likely to work with all Ss in the study'.

Forty-two of the subjects were paired by the total sum-score on the two tests. A child in each of the pairs was randomly assigned to each of the experimental and the control group, respectively.

All experimental subjects were trained individually after five to eight weeks of pre-testing. Each child passed through the identical sequence of stages, in its training phase. During these

121

training periods the E 'played a non-relevant game with the control Ss'. Another examiner who had no knowledge of the status of the child (experimental or control) administered the post-test. This involved the 'Testing Cards Series' and both 'Transfer Tests'. The instructions were as follows: 'Up here (E points) is a pattern, and here a piece is missing. One of the pieces down here is the one that is missing. I want you to think about which piece is missing, and then point to it.'

Retention testing was administered four months after the post-test. Two forms from each of the 'Testing Cards Series' and 'Transfer Tests' respectively were employed. The general procedure here was patterned in a right — wrong format (Jacobs and Vandeventer, 1968).

RESULTS/Jacobs and Vandeventer conclude that short training phases enhance the overall performance in young children on double-classification tasks. Children were able to transfer the learned strategies to solve related subconcepts. Piaget and Inhelder's (1964) findings were also partly substantiated. Jacobs and Vandeventer's results also lent further support to the three criteria which Inhelder and Piaget (1964) state for the presence of operational solutions in respect to double-classification problems. Further, the authors (Jacobs and Vandeventer) discuss the implications of their results for intelligence testing and point out the salient features, as follows:

(a) an awareness of the double-classification principle;
(b) a familiarity with rules common to double-classification items;
(c) teaching children how to sort out combinations of these rules;
(d) teaching children how to infer new rules; and
(e) teaching the strategies to overcome perceptual confusion.

Lastly they draw attention to the practical feasibility of the features (a) to (e), above, in one of their other researches (Jacobs and Vandeventer, 1969).

The learning and transfer of double-classification skills: a replication and extension
P. Jacobs and M. Vandeventer, 1971a.

AIM/'The primary purpose of the present research was to assess transfer from the training procedure of an earlier study (Jacobs and Vandeventer, 1971) throughout a universe consisting of combinations of 12 basic relations. Subsidiary purposes were to evaluate the effects of more extensive training and to investigate

122

the effectiveness of different trainers.'

SUBJECTS/The sample of 61 children comprised 31 boys and 30 girls in first grade in an elementary school.

METHOD/Materials/Experiment One was basically concerned with certain methodological and procedural issues. It attempted to estimate the degree of practice effects in order to determine the length for the pre-test of experiment two. Furthermore, it provided some indication of any sex differences and an estimate of the relative difficulty of the set of transfer tasks.

A 57-item double-classification test was used. The child was asked to show what belonged in the empty cell. Four alternatives were offered: the right answer, the figure directly above the missing cell, the figure directly to the left of the missing cell, and a 'relevant other'. The 57 matrices were assembled into 12 sets based on the relationships involved. Within each set, colour and shape were each paired with one of nine basic relations: size, shading, elements of a set, number series, addition, added element, reversal, flip-over or movement in a plane.

The general procedure was as follows: 'Up here (E points) is a pattern, and here (points) a piece is missing. One of the pieces down here (runs finger across four pieces from left to right) is the one that is missing. Look carefully and think about which piece is the missing piece and then point to it'. (Fuller details of the matrices and general procedure are described in Jacobs and Vandeventer, 1971a, pp.242-5.)

Experiment 2

The main objectives of this experiment were 'to assess whether relatively brief double-classification training with the colour and shape relations produces transfer throughout a universe containing all possible pairings of nine other relations . . .'.

SUBJECTS/A total of 57 subjects were involved, comprising 32 boys and 25 girls in first grade.

METHOD/Materials/Regular training involved a 2 x 2 or 3 x 3 matrix. Each cell contained a shape painted in colour except for one empty cell. The shapes and colours varied from cell to cell, 'such that in one direction (across rows or down columns) shape was the relevant relationship while in the other direction colour was the relevant relationship'. (Fuller details appear in Jacobs and Vandeventer, 1971a.) The extended training was similar to regular training cards, with additional materials of sorting cards; supplementary training was similar to regular training cards,

123

with additional materials of sorting cards, supplementary training cards, and build-a-matrix tasks. Ten matrices were constructed, identical to those described in experiment one.

The eight-item pre-test was constructed on shape and colour relations, together with four items based on size, movement in a plane, and addition relations. The post-test and the retention test were identical, comprising one set of eight items and 13 sets of four items each (Fuller details appear in Jacobs and Vandeventer, 1971a).

Procedure/'All Ss were individually administered the pre-test by E. The instructions to Ss were the same as those used in Experiment 1. Ss were then rank-ordered by the pre-test score. Among the highest three, one was assigned at random to the regular training, one to the extended training and one to the control groups.'

RESULTS/Jacobs and Vandeventer conclude their main results as follows: 'Regular training Ss significantly out-performed control Ss throughout the universe of relations. Extended training produced significantly more transfer than regular training. Transfer effects for regular and extended training were found to hold up three months later. Transfer was also found to Raven's Coloured Progressive Matrices, which was administered for the first time at this stage of the experiment.'

Teaching multiple classification to young children
R.K. Parker, M.L. Rieff and S.J. Sperr, 1971

The main aim of the inquiry was 'to evaluate the effectiveness of a hierarchically arranged instructional program in multiple classification'. More specifically, the following hypotheses were tested:

(a) that trained children at each level, four years six months to seven years six months, would perform at a higher level of operativity than the control children;

(b) that trained subjects would perform better on criterion performance tasks than on transfer tasks; and

(c) that the training schedules would vary in their effectiveness, the older children demonstrating higher operativity levels than the younger ones.

SUBJECTS/Sixty children with a white middle-class background, 20 children (mean ages four years six months, six years, and seven years six months), were randomly assigned to training and control groups. Each group comprised 10 children of each mean age.

METHOD/Children in the experimental group underwent a pre-test, training and a post-test. The control group subjects received a pre-test, 'contact control' (no training, but equal contact with E playing a game), and a post-test.

Pre-test/The pre-test, which was patterned after Inhelder and Piaget (1964) in its presentation and general experimental procedure, aimed at selecting children who showed similar ability in the development of the multiple-classification skill. The pre-test was administered to all subjects.

Training/Parker, Rieff and Sperr describe the main features of the training phase as follows: 'The S was taught the conjunctive classification skill using a matrix format in which his task was to combine the commonality of the row and column in order to pick the correct stimulus choice . . . the training programme was divided into 13 steps and arranged according to presumed difficulty . . . two other procedures were used to arrange the training steps according to difficulty . . . a 3 x 3 matrix was used early in training prior to fading to a 2 x 2 matrix . . . the training programme was developed with special emphasis on "remedial" loops. When S failed to reach criterion performance on any step, he was branched to a remedial loop consisting of a set of substeps designed to review those skills considered prerequisities to the mastery of the step.' (Fuller details of all the 13 steps employed in the training phase are described by the authors on pp.1783-5.)

Post-test/The post-tests were administered one to four days after the training sessions to all the children.

RESULTS/The overall results of the study demonstrated that the training programme enabled the seven-and-a-half-year-old children to perform at a higher level of classification operativity than the six-year-old subjects. However, the four-and-a-half-year-old children indicated no overall improvement in their performance on tasks of multiple classification. The latter finding is discussed fully by the authors and they cite the results of other investigations, including Inhelder and Piaget (1964); Kofsky (1966); and Shantz (1967).

Conclusion

A diversity of opinion exists on how adequate the training procedures in the above studies have been. Inhelder (1969) argues that cognitive learning depends very much on the level at which the child is when interviewed. Inhelder cites a conservation experiment in which she offered training to completely pre-operational children and found that the great majority (87.5 per cent) did not make any real progress, while a minority (12.5 per cent) attained an intermediate level. The situation was rather different for those children who performed at the intermediate stage. 'Of the latter group, only 25 per cent made no progress at all but as for all the others, 75 per cent benefited from the learning procedures in varying degrees. For half of the latter group — 38 per cent — the acquisition of the conservation concept was no more than an extension of the structuration that had already begun at the time of the pre-test. But for the other half, true, progressive elaboration took place of which it is easy to follow the successive moments of integration during the learning sessions. So it is not that children learn nothing, but really it depends very much on their developmental level — the integration that is going on' (Inhelder and Sinclair, 1969).

Strauss and Langer (1970, described above) argue that 'the Inhelder and Sinclair (1969) study was missing a crucial control condition to partial out repeated trials which might have revealed that the observed change in their transitional Ss was not due to training. Rather, it may at least in part, be due to increased familiarity with the examiners and the testing procedures (cf. Zigler and Butterfield, 1968)'.

An analysis of the foregoing studies reveal certain patterns, the success of which might depend on: (a) the child's level of development at the beginning of training, (b) the training method employed, (c) the particular tasks used, (d) the amount of training, and (e) the criteria used to evaluate success.

The field of training efforts in concept inducement is a complex one and with greater sophistication in research techniques the researchers have tended to modify their original thinking. In this respect, Smedslund (1966) has modified the position he held (at the time of his 1961a study), that is a conversion from 'organism-object conflict' to 'organism-organism conflict', (1966). This shift in Smedslund's thinking in fact now renders it identical rather than similar to Piaget's.

Inhelder (cited in Green, Ford and Flamer, 1971, Eds.) objects to the artificial dissociation of reversibility, compensation and identity for experimental purposes. She further maintains (and justifiably), that a comprehension of conservation as a whole necessitates the development of numerous interrelated processes, '. . . so if you accentuate (deliberately or accidentally) one aspect at the expense of others, you sometimes have distortions and later on there may even be a kind of breakdown'. However, while such an argument is sound and logical, the need for objectivity in research necessitates selection among the many areas that might be explored.

More recently, Piaget (1972), commenting on stage acceleration, states that all education is just an acceleration, 'but it remains to be decided to what extent it is beneficial. It is not without significance that it takes man much longer to reach maturity than the other animals. Consequently, it is highly probable that there is an optimum rate of development, to exceed or fall behind which would be equally harmful. But we do not know its laws, and on this point as well it will be up to future research to enlighten us.'

[1] For a comparison of the learning theories of Gagné and Piaget, See Strauss (1972).

CHAPTER FIVE
THE GROWTH OF LOGIC

Introduction

Three major works of the Geneva Centre in the field of Logic are: 'Logic and Psychology' (Piaget, 1953); 'The Growth of Logical Thinking' (Inhelder and Piaget, 1958) and 'The Early Growth of Logic in the Child' (Inhelder and Piaget, 1964). The first is a theoretical discourse given originally as three lectures at Manchester University and later published with an introduction by Mays outlining the fundamentals of propositional logic. The second is an account of the construction of formal operational structures (details of which are given later in this chapter). The most recent publication examines the evolution of systems of classification and seriation in children. In their own introduction, Inhelder and Piaget postulate four hypotheses regarding the contribution of language, maturation, perceptual factors, and the earlier sensori-motor schemata in the evolution of systems of classification and seriation.

They argue that language merely accelerates the formation of classes. Although language is an important factor in building logical structures, it is not the essential factor (they note experiments with deaf children, namely Vincent-Borelli and Oléron discussed in Chapter Seven).

Whilst maturation plays a part in the remarkable changes which take place about seven or eight years of age, it can do no more than create conditions for a continued expansion of the field of possibilities. 'The realization of these possibilities demands not only the action of the physical environment (practice and acquired experience) but also the educational influences of a favourable social environment.'

In considering the role of perception, they dismiss the hypothesis that perceptual knowledge exists before any other form of knowledge and state the case for perception bound up with, and influenced by, action schemata. They further emphasize that visual perception is intimately bound up with haptic (or tactile kinaesthetic) perception.

They conclude that the origins of classification and seriation are to be found in the sensori-motor schemata as a whole and suggest that these origins can be traced before the evolution of language and symbolic representation.

The actual experimental work begins with a study of graphic collections. Intensive properties are defined as properties which are common to the members of the given class and those of other classes to which it belongs: properties which are specific to the members of the given class, and which differentiate them from members of other classes. Extensive properties are those which deal with part-whole relations of class membership and inclusion (e.g. 'all' and 'some'). These properties are involved in the constitution of a class. A graphic collection is essentially a spatial arrangement of the elements to be classified. Coloured geometric shapes and small toys were used, the child being presented with the problem: 'Put together the things which are alike' or 'things that go together'.

Several stages are noted within the 'graphic collections' phase by Inhelder and Piaget, which, they say, tend to overlap and are not necessarily sequential. During the first stage, the child tends to arrange the stimuli in a continuous or discontinuous line. 'Collective objects' are characteristic of the second stage, involving a two- or three-dimensional arrangement rather than a single line. In the third stage, the child forms 'complex objects' groupings, in which he becomes distracted by the shape of the whole and begins to construct without attention to similarity. Inhelder and Piaget found that 'graphic collections' generally occur between the ages of two years six months and five years. The authors concluded that young children are guided by what they perceive, and are unable to co-ordinate intension and extension, but tend to oscillate between them.

Non-graphic collections form the next stage, which is described as quasi-classificatory. Four types of non-graphic collections have been observed by Inhelder and Piaget. First, only a portion of the stimuli are arranged into a number of different groups based on varied criteria. Next, all of the stimuli are assembled into a number of different groups based on different criteria. Third, all stimuli are formed according to the same criterion. Finally, all groups are based on the same criterion and, then, are further sub-divided according to the same second criterion. Inhelder and Piaget found that non-graphic collections generally occur between the ages of five and seven or eight. The authors then turn to an investigation of the conditions of class inclusion and remark: '. . . if children have difficulty with class inclusion, it is because they find it difficult to adjust their use of "all" and "some" to the intensive properties of the

129

elements to which these qualifiers are being applied'.

The stage of class inclusion and hierarchical classification makes clear the difficulties the child encounters in co-ordinating intension and extension, and discovers how far he is able to quantify the extension of class. In the 'nesting' experiments Piaget found different performances in the classification of animals and the classification of flowers.

Complementary classes logically follow order relations and class-inclusion. Perhaps the most important development is the realization of negation, that is, what lies outside a class: the ability to discriminate that which is not included. Piaget and Inhelder show how complementarity is related to inclusion.

A further aspect of classification is that of multiplicative classifications. These are more complex than the preceding additive classifications, but they appear to be mastered at approximately the same time. Inhelder and Piaget claim that these two structures constitute 'a single operational organization in spite of differences in graphic power and complexity' — a claim which the authors reiterate when later dealing with additive and multiplicative operations of order relations.

The 'investigation' into flexibility in hindsight and foresight involves rearrangement of classes caused by the addition of new elements; rearrangement due to changes of criterion; anticipation, execution and changes of criterion in partly spontaneous classifications. The authors claim that the development of operational schemata is related to the retroactive and anticipatory processes revealed in these experiments.

The main interest from the classification of elements by touch arises through the nature of such an activity. Tactile perceptions can only occur successively and not simultaneously. The experiments demonstrate that classification iş an active process and not merely a perceptual one. Children from the age of eight or nine were able to anticipate and abstract as many as three criteria. This is due to the interplay of hindsight and foresight, and there is a remarkable parallel between visual and tactile classification which, the authors claim, support the operational nature of the process.

The authors finally investigate the operations of seriation and multiple seriation. It suffices to mention that seriation appears a little before classification (seven or eight years). With regard to seriation and multiple seriation, Piaget and Inhelder conclude: (i) 'children reach an operational level in the multiplication of series about the same period as cross classification (seven to eight years)'. (ii) 'nevertheless the first of these schemata does entail a problem of its own, a problem of spatial symbolism and not one of logical structure . . . Finally there are four principle 'groupings' in the logic of classes and relations, corresponding with simple and multiple classification and simple and multiple seriation'.

I. *Studies in 'The Early Growth of Logic in the Child'*
(a) *Class-Inclusion*

Inhelder and Piaget (1964) examined the development of subclass to total-class comparison using a variety of stimuli. Children who demonstrate lower levels of such behaviour, '... reflect the absence of the requisite structures of logical thought that enable a child to compare a subset with the total set of which it is a part, which in effect entails the logical operation of the addition and subtraction of classes'. Wohlwill (1968) found that, for class-inclusion tasks, presenting the problems verbally rather than pictorially, enhanced the performance of the transitional children. This was true of the results in three of four experiments among children aged five to six years. Wohlwill also argues that for Piaget, all concrete operations are intrinsically bound, so that consistent inter-relations may be expected between class-inclusion perform-ance and, for example, conservation tasks. However, Dodwell (1962) reported negative findings in this respect. (Both the Wohlwill and the Dodwell studies are described later in this chapter.)

In continuation, Ahr and Youniss (1970) obtained results similar to Wohlwill's for class-inclusion problems, although using a correction procedure. (Ahr and Youniss' study is described later in this chapter.)

Relations between the understanding of the logic of classes and of cardinal number in children
P.C. Dodwell, 1962

AIM/The author's investigation concerned: '... the extent to which young children, in developing concepts of number, and of "conservation" of physical quantities, also develop the concept of "class of objects", and the operations and linguistic skills which allow them to deal with the elementary logic of classification and the composition of classes'.

SUBJECTS/Sixty children of CA five years two months to eight years eight months took part in the study, their IQ range being 81-118 (mean IQ 99.4). However, 20 of these children from a kindergarten school were not assessed for intelligence.

METHOD/The materials used were: (a) Toy plastic dolls, four inches tall, both boys and girls. (b) Toy garden tools, rakes and shovels, eight inches long. (c) Toy cars, both yellow and red.

The children in the present study had been assessed previously by Dodwell in his investigations (1960, 1961). Following the administration of the number concept tests, each child was seen individually 'to ascertain the extent of his understanding of the additive composition of classes'. The general procedure was identical to that of Piaget, with attempts being made to minimize the ambiguity of the questioning. With the materials described in (b) above, some of the standardized questions were as follows: 'Here are some garden tools. Do you know what they are called?' 'Show me all the rakes. Show me all the shovels.' 'Are they all garden tools? Show me all the garden tools.' 'Are there more rakes, or more tools, on the table?'

An identical procedure was followed with the groups of dolls and cars.

RESULTS/The responses were scored either 0, 1, or 2 according to the understanding of the operation, e.g. complete operativity gained a score of 2 and non-operativity behaviour scored 0. Three types of responses were observed, identical to the stages in number concept development of global comparison, operational judgement and intuitive judgement respectively.

Using a χ^2 test, no significant correlation was observed of differences between frequencies of correct answers for the different materials and different numbers in the sub-groups. Likewise, no sex differences were noted.

Moderate correlations were observed in respect to age and IQ. Older children, and the more intelligent performed at a higher level of operativity. (Age comp. r = .238, N = 60, p<.05. IQ: comp. r = .338, N = 40, p<.01.)

'The biserial correlation between "logic" scores and provoked correspondence is .19; between "logic" scores and unprovoked correspondence, .20. Neither is significant. It could be argued that the correlations do not tell us precisely how the two types of concept are related . . . It might be the case that understanding of the logical compositions is a necessary condition for understanding numbers (as seems to be implied by Piaget) but not conversely.'

Responses to class-inclusion questions for verbally and pictorially presented items
J. F. Wohlwill, 1968

EXPERIMENT ONE/The first experiment was designed to

verify the facilitative effect of the verbal condition, demonstrated in the pilot study.

SUBJECTS/Twenty children (11 boys and nine girls) with a mean CA five years 11 months were selected.

METHOD/Two sets of cards were employed. The items in Set A involved such tasks as: (a) Four owls and two pigeons. Q: 'Are there more birds or more owls?' Set B contained such items as: (a) Four forks and two spoons. Q: Are there more pieces of silverware or more spoons?'
Set A and Set B were administered to each half of the children, respectively. Within each group, half were given the items first in verbal form, the other half in pictorial form. Two weeks after initial testing, 18 of 20 children were administered a retest on the alternate set, under both verbal and pictorial conditions. A period of extensive practice was extended to half the children in abstracting class and ordinal relations.

EXPERIMENT TWO/Wohlwill argues that the results of Experiment One, 'might be interpreted as showing a faulty perceptual set on the part of the child: given two subsets unbalanced as to number, he automatically tends to translate the class-inclusion question into one, referring to the two subsets. According to such an interpretation, one should expect beneficial effects from practice in this task, preceded by instructions to the child to count the number of objects in the superordinate class and in the majority subclass. This following experiment was designed to verify such an interpretation.'

SUBJECTS/Sixty-one children (34 boys and 27 girls) were selected from a lower middle class school in Worcester, Massachusetts. Their mean CA was six years one month.

METHOD/Set A items (as in Experiment One, above) were administered for a total of four trials. The pre-test (the first trial) was administered in the usual manner. Trials 2 and 3 involved counting the elements of superordinate and subordinate class. In Set A, item C was modified thus: 'How many flowers are there on this card?' 'How many roses are there on this card?' 'Are there more flowers or more roses?' Trial 4 (the post-test) followed the standardized form, followed by identical items presented verbally.

EXPERIMENT THREE/The aim here was to provide a comparison of the same pictorial items administered under three conditions. 'Under Condition A, all instances of each subset were

133

identical and were spatially segregated from those of the other subset. Under Condition B, the instances of a subset varied in colour, type, size etc., and were intermingled with those of the other subset.' Condition C items were identical to those utilized in Condition B.

SUBJECTS/Fifty-four children were divided into three groups of 18 subjects each, with mean ages five years five months, five years nine months and six years 10 months respectively. The children were selected from a school in Massachusetts, with a lower middle class background.

METHOD/A new set of 12 items, with three versions of each item, was used. Each set corresponded to different perceptual contrast conditions: 'A (identity within and segregation between subsets), B (similarity within and intermingling between subsets), and C (as in B, plus two extraneous objects)'.

RESULTS/Wohlwill finally concludes that children between CA five and seven in his study demonstrated 'A consistent, highly significant superiority of the verbal condition over the pictorial one, which was attributed to the weakening of a subclass-comparison set engendered by the perception of majority and minority subclasses in the standard pictorial condition'. Practice in counting subclass and total class together with an introduction of extraneous elements, combine together to produce enhancement in operativity, and were interpreted by the author, 'as supporting this perceptual-set interpretation'.

Reasons for failure on the class - inclusion problem
P.R. Ahr and J. Youniss, 1970

AIM/The authors examined the general premise that Piaget's analysis of class-inclusion behaviour was correct theoretically but was in need of methodological explication.

SUBJECTS/The study employed two experiments. In the first experiment 10 girls and 10 boys were sampled from each of three age levels; CA six years five months, eight years five months and 10 years five months. The children were from a parochial school in a middle-class area in suburban Washington DC.

METHOD/When presented with cut-outs of cats and dogs the children were asked the question 'Are there more/fewer pets or dogs?' Children of CA six and eight consistently responded as if the E had asked them to compare dogs with cats. On the other hand children of CA 10 responded accurately to the intended class-inclusion relation. For the two younger groups of children, incorrect responses increased as the numerical difference between cats and dogs increased. This, however, was not evident with children aged 10. The 40 children aged six and eight who took part in the first experiment were involved in the second experiment, which was designed to establish whether the non-operational six- to eight-year-old children who exhibited no inclusion behaviour in Experiment One could demonstrate inclusion operativity after training. Nineteen of these children were subjected to extensive training and 21 were given correction training. It was evident that after correction training, but not after new question training, children who were initially non-operational exhibited the act of operativity.

CONCLUSIONS/The results of both experiments confirmed the view that the non-operational children persistently compared subclasses to the exclusion of considering one subclass in relation to the supraordinate class. The authors finally conclude '. . . the complex situation requiring proper referencing of words with pictorial symbols on the class inclusion test was shown to be a performance deterrent, and comprehension of the inclusion relation was shown to be independent of initial performance'.

Cognitive style and classification
J. Garrettson, 1971

AIM/A possible relationship between Piagetian cognition and 'cognitive style' is examined. Piagetian tasks of the logic of classification Inhelder and Piaget (1964), Kagan's (1963) conceptual style test, and Olver and Hornsby's object sorting tasks (1966) were administered. Further, the children's scores on the Piagetian and cognitive style tasks were compared with the reading achievement scores.

SUBJECTS/Sixty boys (CA seven years three months to eight years two months) from middle-class families were randomly selected from a suburban public school.

METHOD/Three Piagetian tasks were employed. The first consisted of assessing the child's ability to classify things according to their properties. The second and the third were class-inclusion type tasks administered to test the child's comprehension of the hierarchic or class-inclusion aspect of classification. Full details of

135

these tasks are described in 'The Early Growth of Logic in the Child', by Inhelder and Piaget (1964).

Kagan's (1963) Conceptual Style Test consists of 19 items. Each item consists of three line drawings on a card. The child is required to say which two 'go together'. Justifications for the responses are also requested. Kagan suggests three possible types of response: analytic, relational, and inferential. Full details of the test and scoring techniques are described in Lee, Kagan and Rabson (1963) and Kagan, Moss and Sigel (1963).

The Objects Sorting Task (Olver and Hornsby, 1966) involves presenting the child with a 6 x 7 array of 42 water colour drawings of familiar things, each on a 3 x 5 card. The child was asked to make a group in some way from the array of things presented. Justifications were asked for the groupings made. Once a group was established, the pictures were returned to the original array. Next, the child was requested to make new groupings, to a maximum of 10. Each such grouping formed was scored according to (a) whether it was supraordinate or complex and (b) whether it was 'perceptible', 'functional', or 'nominal'. Fuller details are described in Olver and Hornsby (1966).

RESULTS/The results of the study have been discussed by Garrettson under (a) Cognitive Style and Piagetian Performances; (b) Reading Achievements; and (c) Comparisons between Styles described by Kagan and Bruner.

The correlations ranged from − .02 to + .13. However, moderately significant correlations were noted between the Piagetian and Olver and Hornsby tasks. The correlations ranged from + .11 to + .37, four of the six being significant at the .05 level. Further, children who performed at a higher level of Olver/Hornsby classification tasks, also demonstrated sound elements of logical thinking and rapid reasoning in two of the three Piagetian tasks. Likewise, boys who constructed more nominal groups also performed better on Piagetian matrices and direct inclusion problems but not on the 'all' inclusion items. Olver/Hornsby's contention about the relative superiority of the nominal style of making classes, was therefore partly substantiated.

Reading scores on the Metropolitan Reading Achievement Test, Primary I Battery were available from school records. Two of the Piagetian tasks and the Reading Scores appeared to 'tap some of the same cognitive operations', e.g. boys' matrices scores and 'all' inclusion performances were significantly related to their achievement in reading (.30 and .41 respectively). However, this was not the case with the Piagetian direct inclusion tasks (r = .08).

Garrettson finally draws attention to the large variability of

136

responses on the various tasks utilized in the study. 'This type of inconsistency from one task to another has been observed in other studies and it emphasizes the necessity for caution in classifying children on the basis of performance on one Piagetian task as "preoperational" or "concrete operational" . . . especially when the child is near a "transitional"period, it would seem wiser to limit any such classification to the child's ability level on the specific tasks on which he was tested.'

It must be pointed out, however, that all subjects in Garrettson's study were boys and that they were at or near the Piagetian 'transitional stage'.

(b) *Classification*
The study by Annett (1957) involved the administration of classification tasks among children aged five to 11 years and adults aged 18 to 73 years. The results demonstrated that refinement in groupings progressed as a function of age. Furthermore, that the order of classification development is through a series of stages (further details appear later in the Chapter).

Kofsky's (1966) study aimed both to discover whether children capable of mastering tasks involving difficult logical operations were able to perform all the less complex problems and to establish the order of difficulty of Piagetian classificatory tasks. Kofsky remarks that variations in instructions and materials could easily affect results. Her findings demonstrated that a significant correlation exists between the number of tasks mastered and the subjects' age, but there was not a set order to mastery on the various tasks. These findings, at least partially, provide some substantiation for the system advanced by Gagné (1968, p.184). (Details of Kofsky's study appear later in this section.)

Kofsky and Osler (1967) investigated: (a) ability to classify stimulus sets, (b) ability to shift criteria after an initial classification and (c) the size of class formed. They studied free classification in five-, eight- and 11-year-old children, using material with a variety of attributes. The authors concluded that children between five and 11 years were able to sort sets into logical groups. Secondly, the five-year-olds sorted more poorly than the two older groups and experienced great difficulty in shifting criteria for sorting. Thirdly, within the age ranges and stimulus values tested, uncertainty and structure have little effect on the frequency of adequate sorts and shifts. These findings lay stress on the effect of test content on performance. The authors conclude their study with a discussion of the consequences of their findings for concept attainment.

More recently, Denney (1972) studied free classification in

108 two- to four-year-old children. The subjects were presented with a classification task similar to Inhelder and Piaget (1964). The author argues that many of the responses evidence by them were not observed in her study. The main findings were: '(a) graphic responses do not always appear to precede grouping according to similarity and (b) grouping according to one dimension does not appear to precede grouping according to two dimensions'.

In continuation, Denney and Lennon (1972) compared free classification in middle-aged (25-55 years) and elderly (67-95 years) subjects. The geometric figures varied in colour, size and shape. The authors concluded: 'whereas middle-aged individuals tended to group the entire stimulus array into piles of similar items, the elderly individuals grouped very much as young children do — arranging only a portion of the stimulus array into elaborate designs'. It was suggested that young children and elderly adults may categorize according to different criteria from older children and middle-aged adults.

The classification of instances of four common class concepts by children and adults
M. Annett, 1957

AIMS/Annett addressed the inquiry to the behavioural sortings and explanations of 303 children, of CA five to 11 years and 42 adults, aged 18-73 years. The study had three main issues: (a) given as little direction as possible about general sorting strategies, to find how normal subjects classify a group of common objects; (b) age and intelligence as a function of modes of classification change; and (c) the influence of instruction on specific resultant patterns.

SUBJECTS/The 303 children in the city of Bath were as follows: 92.4 per cent from local education authority schools; 1.3 per cent from schools for the ESN and 6.2 per cent from independent schools. Age, sex and vocabulary means and standard deviation were obtained, using norms found by Dunsdon and Roberts (1957).

The adults were selected from an orthopaedic hospital. These were subdivided into two groups — those under and above CA 40 years, respectively. The Mill Hill A and A scores assigned the adults to three vocabulary grades, (Raven, 1943).

METHOD/The material consisted of 16 cards as follows: (a) animals (cow, bird, fish, butterfly); (b) plants (tree, flower, apple, toadstool); (c) vehicles (car, train, ship and aeroplane); (d) furniture (chair, desk, clock and television).

The classification tasks were administered individually and all responses recorded verbatim. Questions were as follows: 'Some of these cards belong together. Sort them into groups so that the ones that go together are in the same group.' The subject's groups thus formed, were again laid before him in turn and he was asked 'How do these belong together?'

RESULTS/Annett concludes the investigation with the following main features:

(a) that the diversity of groupings employed by younger children decreases with an increase in the chronological age;

(b) 'that although concepts may develop through the acquisition of facts about objects, facts about where objects are to be found and what they do are always of greatest interest;'

(c) that the order of development is through a series of 'stages' and mainly through no explanation, enumeration, contiguity, similarity and class name;

(d) that many adults employ more than one method of explanation and shift from one to the other without any awareness of doing so, or that one strategy may be better than another.

'Until more descriptions of response to everyday materials have been made, it is unlikely that pertinent hypotheses about the growth of real concepts can be formulated.'

A scalogram study of classificatory development
E. Kofsky, 1966

Kofsky (1966) had already used the method of scalogram analysis to investigate Piaget's theory that there is a fixed order in which classificatory concepts are acquired.

AIMS/The aim of her study was to discover whether children capable of mastering tasks involving difficult logical operations were able to perform all the less complex problems and whether in fact the order of difficulty of eleven classificatory tasks corresponded to the developmental sequence described by Piaget.

SUBJECTS/One hundred and twenty-two children between four and nine years of age were tested. The sample comprised 10 girls and 10 boys at each age level between four and nine years, except in four-and seven-year-old groups which contained an additional child.

METHOD/The various tasks were as follows: (a) resemblance sorting; (b) consistent sorting; (c) exhaustive sorting; (d) conservation; (e) multiple class membership; (f) horizontal reclassification; (g) hierarchical classification; (h) 'some' and 'all'; (i) whole is the sum of its parts $(A \doteq A^1)$; (j) conservation of hierarchy $(B - A^1)$; (k) inclusion $(B > A)$.

RESULTS/Generally, the percentage of subjects in each age group passing each task tends to support Piaget's contentions. An analysis of variance of age effects $(F = 17.27, df = 5/116, p<.01)$ and correlation of age with score $(r = .86, p<.01)$ were both significant. Tukey's test indicated that the age continuum was divisible into three phases. Higher operational performance was exhibited by the nine-year-old group, followed closely by seven- and eight-year-olds and those under seven years, in that order. However, it is important to realize that there were only ten boys and ten girls at each level. Kofsky remarks that variations in instructions and materials from task to task could easily affect results (cf. Lovell, Mitchell and Everett, 1962, who made a similar observation).

(c) *Multiplicative classification*

The role of perceptual factors (stimulus preference) in the acquisition of multiplicative-classificatory problems was investigated by Overton and Jordan (1971). (Multiplicative classification or cross-classification refers to the simultaneous classification of an object into two or more categories.) 'The findings offered no support for the hypothesis that degree of preference for a given stimulus category enhances performance along that dimension at the four-year level and results in poorer performance at the six-year level'. (Details of the study appear later in this Chapter.)
    Overton and Brodzinsky (1972) used two forms of the matrix-completion task to study the development of multiplicate classificatory skills in children. Inhelder and Piaget's hypothesis that there are figural or perceptual conditions in testing situations which facilitate classification behaviour prior to the development of logical class multiplication abilities, was not confirmed. (Cf. Parker and Day, 1971, who examined the use of perceptual, functional and abstract attributes for multiple classification within the format of a matrix task—performance on the matrices improved with age. Combination of perceptual attributes was found at an earlier age than combination of functional attributes. The combination of abstract attributes emerged last. Details of this study are described later in the Chapter.) However, Overton and Brodzinsky suggested the existence of a transitional phase

prior to logical solutions, and that these transitional children were recognized by their significantly better performance on matrices with a minimum perceptual symmetry in contrast to the traditional matrix task. They cite the evidence of Flavell and Wohlwill (1969) who '. . . suggested that the transition period between pre-operations and concrete operations extends from the point at which logical structures are "first-in-competence" up to the point that they are "always-in-performance", and that during this time the child's behaviour is most susceptible to task-related variables. This phase as suggested by Overton, Wagner and Dolinsky (1971)' (and described later), 'may be thought of as a time during which the introduction of various task variables will lead to the activation of already present structures, and consequently, to the enhancement of performance which would be impossible prior to the emergence of cognitive structures and meaningless once such structures are "always-in-performance".[1] 'This standpoint is suggested by the present study, that the linear-rule instruction condition was effective in improving performance only at six- to seven-year level.' This variable was not effective at either the four- to five-year or eight- to nine-year levels (Overton and Brodzinsky, 1972: the study is described later below).

A study of the function of two forms of a matrix-completion task, CA and SES in the development of multiplicative classificatory skills was carried out by Overton, Wagner and Dolinsky (1971). An important feature of this study which confirmed Overton and Brodzinsky's (1972) findings has already been mentioned above. Other results showed that Negro children of the lower class performed at the lower levels of classificatory operativity at age eight to nine in contrast to the middle-class white subjects. However, no such superiority in the performance of multiplicative classification tasks was observed at ages four to seven, inclusive. (Details of the study appear later in this Chapter.)

Siegel and Kresh in their 1971 study investigated children's ability to deal with a variety of classification skills within a matrix format. Stimuli comprised nine combinations of three shapes and three colours and the six attribute stimuli. Four-year-old children performed at the lowest levels of classificatory operativity, whereas the eight-year-old children performed at the higher levels. In the sample of children from 'lower-middle-upper lower' socio-economic backgrounds, all attending an experimental school in a 'disadvantaged' area, it was found that the performance of white children was slightly, but not significantly, superior to that of Negro children at all age levels on all tasks. (Details are given later in this Chapter.)

Piaget's (1964) contention that complete multiplication will

141

be a prior development in the child to partial multiplicative classification was not wholly substantiated by Findlay's (1971) study. She argues that '. . . the sequential appearance of complete and partial multiplicative classification may be due to the experimental situations used, and therefore complete multiplication as a necessary prior development to partial multiplication remains an open question'.

An investigation of the emergence of ability for partial and complete multiplication of classes in young school children
A.D. Findlay, 1971

AIM/The author of the study was interested in Piaget's (1964) theoretical contention which assumes that in the child complete multiplication will be an earlier development than partial multiplicative classification. Findlay discusses Piaget's reasoning in the course of such a development, and in order to test the hypothesis that 'the finite choice situation would show a higher level of operativity than the creative response situation', she replicated Piaget's experiment, with extensions. One set of children followed the general procedures identical to Piaget's, and the other half were given an array of pictures from which to choose the correct alternative.

SUBJECTS/Ninety-six children ranging in age from five years to 10 years 11 months were selected from a primary school in Scotland. A random selection from three age-group classes formed three groups of 32 with a mean age of six, eight and 10 years respectively. Each of these three groups was again divided randomly to form the two main groups. These were termed as 'finite choice' and 'creative response' groups, respectively.

METHOD/The general experimental procedure and the materials used were identical to those employed by Inhelder and Piaget (1964). Two sets of cards were used. Set one consisted of eight cards, four of which portrayed green objects (a book, pear, tulip and cap) and the remaining four, pears of different colours (pink, yellow, violet and blue). Set two comprised 10 cards, five green and five pink objects (a pear, tulip, book, cap and leaf). The general mode of questioning was identical to that of the Geneva School for all the 96 children, irrespective of whether they were assigned to the 'finite choice' or 'creative response' group. Every child was requested to fill in the empty cell left at the point where the two rows met with an object that 'fits in with everything' in each of the two rows (i.e. a green leaf). 'Here the procedure differed for the 'creative response' and 'finite choice' groups; the latter having 10 alternatives from which to choose.'

RESULTS/Findlay's results substantiated the hypothesis that children find simple multiplication easier in the finite choice situation than the creative situation. However, she argues that this may not be the only explanation for later development of simple multiplication. 'Piaget may be right . . . that simple multiplication means abstracting a portion of the total system of complete multiplication . . . (also) . . . that since the situations which call for simple multiplication are less favourable to perceptual properties, the development of simple multiplication will . . . be later than that of complete multiplication'. She further maintains that Piaget has failed to verify the hypotheses experimentally. The results of Findlay's study have demonstrated 'that the sequential appearance of complete and partial multiplicative classification may be due to the experimental situations used, and therefore, complete multiplication as a necessary prior development to partial multiplication remains an open question'.

Stimulus preference and multiplicative classification in children
W.F. Overton and R. Jordan, 1971

AIMS/The authors considered three points: (a) the role of stimulus preference in the operativity of multiplicative classification problems at two age levels; (b) that matrices containing drawings of realistic objects will be solved more readily by the four-year group than matrices containing drawings of geometric objects; and (c) the roles of sex, the number of relevant stimulus categories and types of categories in the matrices at each age level.

SUBJECTS/A total of 120 subjects were involved. Sixty at CA range four years to four years 11 months and 60 at CA range six years to six years 11 months. The samples contained equal numbers of children of either sex from a middle-class background.

METHOD/Each child was presented with three booklets. The first booklet contained stimulus-preference demonstration material and a stimulus preference test. Briefly, the preference test contained 30 ambiguous matching problems. 'In each problem there were three equidistantly arranged items which could be paired in two different ways, each pair being alike according to one stimulus category, for example, a blue triangle, a blue square, and a red square could be paired according to colour or form. The categories tested were colour, form, number and size. These four categories yielded six problem combinations and each combination was replicated five times . . . The purpose of (the demonstration materials) was to demonstrate to the child the manner of responding to the matching problems.'

The second and third booklets contained 40 standard 2 x 2 test matrices: '. . . each accompanied by a choice set of four items, one of which correctly completed the matrix. The matrices varied in three ways: (a) according to the particular stimulus categories incorporated in a matrix (colour, form, number and/or size), (b) according to number of stimulus categories (i.e. two categories or three categories), and (c) according to type of drawing (realistic or geometric figures). The two-category matrices included the six possible category combinations of colour-form, colour-number, colour-size, form-number, form-size, and number-size; the three category matrices included the four possible category combinations of colour-form-number, colour-form-size, colour-number-size, and form-number-size.'

Tests were presented in groups at each age level. The same children were seen in three consecutive sessions one week apart. The preference demonstration and stimulus preference test were administered during the first session. One of the two matrix tests was administered in each of two subsequent sessions. (Fuller's details of the experimental procedure including the scoring techniques are given elsewhere. Overton and Jordan, 1971, pp.506-7.)

RESULTS/Overall, the results indicated that a strong preference for colour demonstrated a lower level of cognitive organization than preference for other stimulus categories. Further, rich experiences of form would enhance the child's early functioning of qualitative dimensions in his environment. Finally, the authors conclude that 'matrices composed of realistic figures are more readily solved than those composed of geometric figures. This finding is of particular interest in view of the tendency in the field of education to begin teaching cross-classification via the employment of simple materials, that is, geometric forms, and only later to progress to more complex realistic figures . . . The finding that two-category matrices are more readily solved than three category matrices was not unexpected. This supports earlier results by Inhelder and Piaget (1964).'

Social class differences and task variables in the development of
multiplicative classification
W.F. Overton, J. Wagner and H. Dolinsky, 1971

AIMS/The study investigated the performance of lower-class
Negro children and middle-class white children on multiplicative
classification. Further, a generalization was sought with regard to
the findings reported by Sigel, Anderson and Shapiro (1966) and
Sigel and McBane (1967).

SUBJECTS/The total sample of 96 subjects was comprised as
follows: 32 children from each of the following age levels: four to
five years (mean age five years one month); six to seven years
(mean age six years nine months) and eight to nine years (mean
age eight years four months). Equal numbers of either sex were
represented at each level. Furthermore, half of the children at each
age level were lower-class Negro and half were middle-class white.

METHOD/The matrix-completion task administered was
patterned after Inhelder and Piaget (1964). 'In this task, the S is
presented with stimulus objects in the form of a 2 x 2 matrix with
the bottom right cell being empty. The problem for the S is to
choose the stimulus object from a choice set that completes the
matrix — that is, that simultaneously classifies the object as a
member of both the class formed by the horizontal dimension and
the class formed by the vertical dimension.' (Fuller details of the
experimental procedure are described by Inhelder and Piaget,
1964, and Overton, Wagner and Dolinsky, 1971.)
Both forms of the matrices were administered individually to
each child. Half of the children at each age and social class
received the five object matrices, followed by the five pictorial
matrices. The order was reversed for the other half of the children.

RESULTS/The results of the study did not substantiate
Sigel's (1966, 1967) findings. Free classification did not generalize
to multiplicative classification. Sigel had reported results demonstrating that lower-class children performed at a lower level of
operativity than middle-class children when the stimulus material
consisted of two-dimensional pictorial representations of objects
rather than the actual three-dimensional objects. Overton, Wagner
and Dolinsky argue the reasons for this departure from the results
of Sigel's study '. . . the matrix-completion task is more highly
structured, in that the categories are already provided, giving the
child a framework within which to make inferences about class
relationships . . . in the free classification task . . . the child is
required to construct his own categories on the basis of a

disordered array of objects'.

No significant differences in the performance of the middle-and lower-class children were observed, at the CA four to five and six to seven in tasks involving multiplicative classification. However, the CA eight to nine group showed children of the lower-class performing at a much lower level of classification operativity. Overton, Wagner and Dolinsky argue that 'The first explanation concerns the activation of already present cognitive structures while the second involves the actual development of cognitive structures'.

In conclusion, the authors discuss in detail the explanation alternatives for such differences.

The use of perceptual, functional, and abstract attributes in multiple classification
R.K. Parker and M.C. Day, 1971

AIMS/The authors were interested in the investigation of the utilization by children of perceptual, functional, and abstract attributes for classification within the format of a matrix task. Specific hypotheses were: (a) that classificatory operativity would improve as a function of age; and (b) that children would be able to combine perceptual attributes at an earlier age than functional attributes, and functional attributes at an earlier age than abstract attributes; (c) an assessment of the types of error was also investigated.

SUBJECTS/Eighty children of above-average intelligence were involved in the study. All subjects were Caucasian, except for one Mongoloid, and were of middle-class background. The CA ranged from six years one month to nine years and almost equal numbers of boys and girls were represented at each of the age levels six, seven, eight and nine.

METHOD/The stimuli were a series of 42 incomplete matrices composed of three cards in a column and three cards in a row. Three cards representing choices to fill the intersection were presented. The three objects pictured in the row had one common attribute while the other three objects in the column had a different common attribute. The three attributes of the matrices were: (a) perceptual (shape, colour, identity); (b) functional; (c) abstract.

'Combinations of these three types of attributes yielded six types of matrices: Perceptual x Perceptual, Functional x Functional, Abstract x Abstract, Perceptual x Functional, Perceptual x

Abstract, and Functional x Abstract.' (Fuller details are described in Parker and Day, 1971, pp. 313-4.)

Initially, some practice items were presented to the child. 'Then the three pictures with the same perceptual attributes were arranged in a row and the three pictures of objects with a common function in a column. The row and the column met at a blank intersection. The E said: "I am going to put these pictures which are alike in a line here and these three pictures which are alike in a line here. I'm going to put three choices down here." Three pictures were placed below and to the right to the matrix. Two of the choices were those two pictures previously placed with the two groups of like pictures; thus one picture had the attribute of the row alone, the other the attribute of the column alone. The third choice combined both attributes and correctly filled the intersection. "I want you to pick the picture that goes with both groups and put it in this blank space. There is one picture that goes with both groups. Which one is it?" If the subject was incorrect or did not make a choice, the E asked him the common attributes of both the row and the column and again asked which picture had both attributes. The experimenter then pointed out the answer and carefully explained the reason if the S still could not choose the correct intersect. The stimuli were then arranged in the two remaining types of matrices (Functional x Abstract and Perceptual x Abstract). And the same procedure was followed.' (Fuller details are given in Parker and Day, 1971, pp. 314-315).

RESULTS/The results substantiated the hypothesis that an improvement occurs with CA in the number of correct solutions and the relevance of types of attributes on ability to combine attributes. Likewise, it was verified that errors would be made by selection of developmentally 'preferred' attributes.

The authors maintain that the developmental changes in classificatory operativity as a function of age confirms the contentions of Inhelder and Piaget (1964), Kofsky (1966) and Lovell, Mitchell and Everett (1962). Further, the finding that children can combine specific attributes and not others at specific ages corroborates Piaget's 'horizontal décalage'.

Finally, Parker and Day conclude: 'Combination of perceptual attributes was found at an earlier age than combination of functional attributes, and the combination of abstract attributes appeared last. When children made errors, they tended to choose the picture representing the type of attribute most frequently used to categorize in object-sorting tasks by other children at the same developmental levels.'

Children's ability to operate within a matrix: a developmental study
A. W. Siegel and E. Kresh, 1971

AIMS/The authors addressed their inquiry to investigate the developmental patterning about children's ability to deal with varied classification skills within a matrix format involving nominal dimensions. In respect to Piaget's experimental data regarding matrices, Siegel and Kresh framed two questions as follows: (a) 'Does Piaget's general finding hold for matrix situations other than the one he has studied?' Or, (b) 'is there a differential pattern of development as a function of the particular type of matrix manipulation used?'

SUBJECTS/Eighty pre-school and elementary school children, 16 at each of the five age levels from four to eight years were involved. They were all 'mainly average' children with lower-middle/upper-lower socio-economic backgrounds. Equal numbers of either sex were represented in the sample of 80 which comprised 43 negro and 37 white subjects.

METHOD/The apparatus comprised 15 opaque white 'Lucite' boxes, set in a plastic tray and measuring three inches square and an inch high. Stimuli were pieces of cardboard varying in colour and shape. 'Since a matrix format was used, the stimuli employed in the matrix cells were different from those in the attribute cells . . . stimuli for the shape attribute cells were a circle, a square, and a triangle . . . Stimuli for the colour attribute cells were three different irregularly shaped pieces (one red, one blue, one yellow) . . . Stimuli for the matrix cells were three circles (one each of red, blue, and yellow) three squares and three triangles . . .'

The main experimental tasks were presented after the preliminary exercises 'with the aim of assessing logically simpler, but selected classification abilities'. The nine-cell matrix with its six attribute cells was constructed. In the first task, the child was asked to define the attribute values of the object belonging in a particular cell. In the second task, he had to discover the cell in which a particular object belonged. Three other phases of the main experiment were:

Covered Matrix/The matrix cells were completed with the nine stimuli and covered; the attribute cells were filled, but open and visible to the child. Duplicates of the nine-matrix stimuli were set near the matrix.

Uncovered Matrix/The matrix cells were empty and not covered; the attribute cells were filled and uncovered. An array of nine objects was displayed at the side of the matrix.

Attribute Recognition/This was included in order to assess the 'intensional' aspect of classification — the child's ability to specify the common property that accompanied the members of a row or column. (Fuller details of the experimental procedure are described in Siegel and Kresh, 1971, pp. 234-5.)

RESULTS/The overall results demonstrated that the ability to operate within a matrix of two nominal dimensions improves from minimum ability at CA four to maximum at CA eight. This finding lends further verification to Piaget's contentions. The younger child revealed that when presented with what is a difficult task for him, his thinking is focused on a single dimension only. Also, for the younger children (CA four to five and six to seven), a positive correlation was observed among tasks requiring the same kind of mental operational strategies. This pattern appeared for the covered and uncovered matrix tasks and the uncovered matrix and attribute recognition tasks. However, for the eldest group tasks demanding the same kind of mental strategies were not related (covered — uncovered matrix). This was also true of tasks that were similar in feedback characteristics (uncovered matrix — attribute recognition).

Siegel and Kresh further discuss the possible reasons as to the relation/non-relation of the tasks among the eight-year old subjects. In their arguments they cite the work of Smedslund (1967) and finally conclude: '. . . the performance of younger children (as shown in the task intercorrelations) was more determined by task variables such as feedback and type of ability (purportedly) tapped, whereas the performance of older children was more determined by the kinds of mediators the tasks required'.

Perceptual and logical factors in the development of multiplicative classification
W. Overton and D. Brodzinsky, 1972

AIMS/Generally, the study attempted to elucidate the problem of developmental changes in multiplicative classification. Overton and Brodzinsky sought to test Inhelder and Piaget's (1964) hypotheses concerning multiplicative classification:

(a) 'that there are some figural or perceptual conditions in testing situations which enhance classification performance prior to the acquisition of logical strategies; and

(b) that there is a transitional phase which occurs between

the time that perceptual solutions are utilized and the introduction of logical operativity.'

SUBJECTS/The total sample of 90 children from nursery and elementary schools was drawn from a middle-class background. Three age levels, each consisting of 30 subjects were examined: four to five years; six to seven years; eight to nine years (mean age 4.8; SD = .28; mean age = 6.4; SD = .35; and mean age = 8.6; SD = .35 respectively). Three groups were used at each CA level. Group I received the traditional 2 x 2 matrix and perceptual supportive instructions; Group II received the traditional 2 x 2 matrix and rule instructions; and Group III received the linear matrix and rule instructions. Equal numbers of boys and girls were represented in each experimental group.

METHOD/Two demonstration matrices and four test matrices were administered, patterned after Inhelder and Piaget (1964).
The discrimination test was presented first, followed by the demonstration matrix composed of two and then three dimensions.
Group I subjects were requested to choose, from the choice set, the picture that best fit (in the empty cell) going 'this way' (pointing horizontally) and 'this way' (pointing vertically).
Group II subjects 'were told to observe how the picture on the top left (pointing to the cell) changed to make the picture adjacent to it (pointing to the top right cell). This change they were told, was a rule and by following the rule, they could change the next picture (bottom left) into one of the choice set pictures (pointing to the bottom cell and then to the choice set). The subject was then encouraged to choose, from the choice set,.the best one which the picture would be changed to by following the rule.'
Group III subjects were instructed in the same manner as for Group II subjects, apart from the fact that the E started with the far left cell and advanced to the adjacent horizontal cells. (Fuller details of the experimental procedure are described in Overton and Brodzinsky, 1972, pp. 105-7).

RESULTS/The first hypothesis, whether there are perceptual solutions to the matrix task prior to logical class multiplication showed no added credibility (no significa t task differences at the CA four to five were noted, χ^2 = 1.28, df = 2, p>.05).
'Furthermore, analysis of each task condition at each age level by means of binomial tests indicate that only under the most perceptually involved conditions, that is, the 2 x 2-perceptual supportive instructions, do correct solutions not significantly rise

150

above the chance level. This occurs at both the four to five year (Z = 1.06, p = .145) and six to seven year levels (Z = 1.06, p = .145). It seems . . . that at both four to five and six to seven year levels perceptual factors do not facilitate and possibly hinder successful performance.'

Finally, Overton and Brodzinsky cite the research evidence produced by Wohlwill (1968), Ahr and Youniss (1970), Flavell and Wohlwill (1969), when elaborating the findings of their 1972 study. The second hypothesis — that there might be a transitional phase which occurs between the time that perceptual solutions are utilized and the introduction of logical operativity (supported by the evidence of the present study) — is further discussed in terms of Overton, Wagner and Dolinsky (1971) results. '. . . this phase may be thought of as a time during which the introduction of various task variables will lead to the activation of already present structures, and consequently, to the enhancement of performance which would be impossible prior to the emergence of cognitive structures and meaningless once such structures are "always-in-performance". Such a viewpoint is supported by the findings of the present study that the linear-rule instruction condition was effective in improving performance only at the six to seven year level.'

d) *Simple and multiple seriation*

An attempt was made by Siegel (1972) to establish that children as young as three years can manipulate the concept of seriation when the verbal requirements of the task are minimized. The Geneva evidence demonstrated that children below the age of four or five do not have the concept of seriation, even when presented with a small array of objects. However, Siegel's study (described later in this Chapter) concluded. 'The end positions of the series were significantly easier to identify than the inner positions. The four-stimulus series was significantly more difficult to learn than a three-stimulus series only in the cases in which the subject was required to identify an inner position, but not when he was required to recognise an end position' (Cf. Siegel, 1971, described more appropriately in Chapter Three).

That seriation and the use of a relative frame of reference are 'cognitively confounded', was demonstrated by O'Reilly and Steger (1970). Subjects over the age of five could seriate in the presence of an 'anchor or frame of reference'. However, children aged five or below could not seriate or use the 'anchor as a point of reference'. Smedslund's (1963) suggestion that seriation facilitates transitivity was supported by O'Reilly and Steger, since their anchor-type method demanded seriation. (The study is described later in this chapter.)

Piaget (1950 and 1964) maintains that the stage of concrete operations is characterized by a cognitive organization within which simple and multiple classification and simple and multiple seriation become operational at roughly the same time. Mackay, Fraser and Ross (1970) investigated the development of the ability for double seriation in young children. The results indicated a developmental lag between the emergence of the ability for cross-classification and that for double seriation. The results also helped the authors '. . . to relate (these) to the differences existing between the Geneva (Piaget, 1950; 1964) and Harvard (Bruner, et al. 1966) approaches to interpreting cognitive growth.' (Details of the study appear below.)

Matrices, three by three:classification and seriation
C. K. Mackay, J. Fraser and I. Ross, 1970

AIMS/Mackay, Fraser, and Ross wanted (a) to assess the CA at which normal school children are fully operative in multiple seriation tasks; (b) to compare this operativity with the age at which they develop simple cross-classification; and (c) to discuss their findings in relation to the Geneva and Harvard interpretations of cognitive development.

EXPERIMENT I/Subjects/Thirty children were randomly selected at each of three age groups: 5.5 — 6.0 years (six-year group); 6.5 — 7.0 (seven-year group); 7.5 — 8.0 years (eight-year group), respectively. The total of 90 children from lower middle-class background, were drawn from a primary school in Scotland. Each of the three age groups was again randomly divided to form groups A and B respectively.

METHOD/Children in Group A were presented with an array of 3 x 3 arrangement on a wooden board, namely 3 squares, 3 triangles and 3 circles. Each shape was painted red, white or black. Group B was presented with an array comprising nine open-ended grey plastic cylinders, differing in height (six, four and two inches, respectively) and diameter (four, three and two inches, respectively). Fuller details appear in Mackay, Fraser and Ross (1970, pp. 789-90).

Children were required to solve the three tasks of replacement, reproduction and transposition, patterned after Bruner and Kenney (1966). Group A used coloured shapes as described above. Bruner and Kenney apparatus was utilized for Group B. Children who demonstrated partial or full operativity were questioned

152

regarding the strategies they employed in the various tasks.

SCORING CRITERIA/Reproduction/Shape and colour by row and column under condition A and the sequence of height and diameter under condition B, were considered operational when consistency was maintained.

TRANSPOSITION/Condition A: the transposed object remained in position, and the final arrangement maintained the consistency by row and column of shape and colour; Condition B — the transposed cylinder remained in position and the pattern of 'tall-to-short' and 'wide-to-narrow' was retained.

EXPERIMENT TWO/Subjects/The main sampling of subjects was identical as for Experiment One, above. However, 48 children took part in Experiment Two and were sub-divided into groups of 19 five-year-olds, 16 six-year-olds and 13 seven-year-olds.

METHOD/Matrix C comprised nine solid, wooden, painted cylinders varying in height and colour but of constant diameter. Each of the three sets of three cylinders were of height six inches, four inches and two inches, respectively. Each set of cylinders was composed of one red, one white and one black.

The procedure was identical to that for Experiment One, above. Children were requested to perform the tasks of replacement, reproduction and transposition.

RESULTS/The authors summarize the results as follows:

(a) A matrix composed of discrete categories is acquired earlier than one composed of relational variables. The nature of the acquisition is developmental.

(b) Matrices composed of discrete categories in single and dual directions respectively demonstrate equivalent difficulty.

(c) The acts of reproduction and transposition in a matrix composed of discrete categories are of equal difficulty. However, reproduction is easier than transposition in matrices with either one or both continuous variables.

The authors finally conclude '. . . we agree with both Piaget and Bruner that the ability for dual classification is characteristic of the seven to eight-year-old . . . but we strongly disagree with both over the age when serial multiplication develops . . . The décalage implied by our results between the emergence of multiple classification and multiple seriation challenges the important Piagetian principle that transition to the stage of concrete operations necessarily implies the existence of a cognitive structure integrating the four logical groupings corresponding to simple and multiple classification and simple and multiple seriation (Inhelder and Piaget, 1964. p. 279).'

153

Children's use of context in judgement of weight
E. O'Reilly and J. A. Steger, 1970

AIMS/The authors attempted to investigate the child's ability to perform judgements in the presence of an 'anchor', and whether age was a critical factor in such a performance.

SUBJECTS/The total sample of 25 children was comprised as follows: five in each of five ages, five, six, seven, nine and 11 respectively.

METHOD/'A series of five weights from 200 to 400g. in steps of 50g. was used along with an anchor weight of 30g. These were presented in an apparatus which required the subject to pull a lever towards him, and attached to this lever was the specific weight being used. Thus the subject never saw either the weights or the Experimenter change these weights.'

'Since children were subjects the usual category scale, either verbal or numerical, was not appropriate. We therefore designed a five-point category scale by drawing pictures of weights (bell-shaped) that increased linearly in size. Thus, size represented weight. There was no difficulty with this procedure.'

The child was familiarized with the use of the apparatus. The child was to judge the weight of the lever pull (series alone) or the weight of the second pull (anchor-plus-series condition). Furthermore, the subject was asked to point to the picture of the weight that was like the heaviness the child had felt before.

'Each subject was run forst in the series-only condition, six trials each weight in a random order; one week later, each was run in the anchor-plus-series condition, again with six trials per weight.'

RESULTS/The results demonstrated that the ability to seriate stimuli along some stimulus dimension was cognitively linked to the ability to utilize some frame of reference. This substantiates the contentions of Piaget (1952; 1968), Piaget and Inhelder (1959) and Smedslund (1959). However, Smedslund's (1963) results showed that overall, none of his subjects CA five to nine years formed relative judgements of the weights employed. This was not true with the present findings of O'Reilly and Steger. That seriation may foster transitivity was upheld both in Smedslund's and O'Reilly and Steger's studies. Piaget's (1968) contention that children of CA nine cannot seriate weight was questioned by O'Reilly and Steger. Their subjects with CA six and above 'could order the weights, and, if we assume the anchor's shift in judgement reflects transitivity, these children did use this principle'.

Finally, the authors point out three shortcomings of their study. First, only a five-point scale was employed and this restricted the shifting of scaled judgement from the no anchor to anchor condition. Second, no adults over 18 years were involved for comparative judgements with children. Third, 'the need to show the judgemental shift with an anchor heavier than the series, was felt'.

Development of the concept of seriation
L. S. Siegel, 1972

AIM/Siegel's study is a natural extension of her previous investigation (1971), which explored the concepts of seriation, with a minimum amount of verbal instruction being involved. Her 1972 study was operationally defined 'as the child's ability to learn to choose a particular position, for example, smallest in a two, three, or four object series'.

SAMPLE ONE/Subjects/The sample of 90 children comprised 30 children from each of three age levels — three-, four- and five-year-olds. The children were drawn from middle-class backgrounds and were of 'average' or 'above-average' intelligence, according to teachers' assessments.

METHOD/'Each subject was administered three seriation tasks that tested his ability to recognize a particular position in a series. The tasks were administered with a Behavioural Controls 400-SR programmed learning apparatus. There were four response panels covered with clear plastic press panels. The child responded by pressing the panel over the stimulus of his choice. Correct responses were rewarded . . . A non-correction procedure was used and the position of the correct alternative varied randomly from trial to trial. Each child was administered three seriation tasks with two, three, or four stimuli in the series. The stimuli for the tasks were vertical bars of nine discriminably different heights. For all the tasks, the stimuli for each trial were randomly selected from the nine possible so the particular combination of stimuli presented on each trial varied randomly. On a particular trial, the stimuli were not presented to the child in a sequence ordered by size. Depending on his random assignment to an experimental condition, a subject could be reinforced for either the larger or the smaller in the two-stimulus series, either the middle-sized or the largest in the three-stimulus series, and either the largest or the next to the smallest in the four-stimulus series.' (Fuller details of the general experimental procedure are described in Siegel, 1972, pp. 135-7.)

SAMPLE TWO/Subjects/The total sample of 325 children from Ontario comprised 17 boys and 17 girls at age four years; 22 boys and 26 girls at age five years; 24 boys and 30 girls at age six years; 31 boys and 22 girls at age seven years; 36 boys and 31 girls at age eight years; and 32 boys and 37 girls at age nine years. The subjects were 'average' or 'above average' in ability and were drawn from lower- and middle-class backgrounds.

METHOD/The tasks were identical to those administered to Sample One children, apart from the fact that only two tasks were presented. These were the three-stimulus and the four-stimulus series.

RESULTS/Overall, the results revealed that the end positions of the series were significantly easier to identify than the inner positions and that children of CA three years can learn a seriation task, when the verbal requirements during the presentation of the task are minimized. Non-verbal modes of questioning might facilitate the acquisition of the concept of seriation.

II Studies in 'The Construction of Formal Operational Structures'

Inhelder and Piaget state in the preface to their 1958 study that this is a collaborative work based on a convergence between experimental and deductive methods: Inhelder was engaged in a systematic study of the induction of physical laws in children and adolescents, while Piaget was attempting to construct 'a possible symbolic model of the actual processes of thinking'. In comparing the results of their respective work it was realized that Piaget's logical analysis provided a suitable model for the data collected by Inhelder: '. . . while one of us was engaged in an empirical study of the transition in thinking from childhood to adolescence, the other worked out the analytical tools needed to interpret the results'.

Inhelder and Piaget indicate how the data allowed the description of adolescent thought in terms of the structuring of methods of experimental induction not found in the child. These methods of systematic verification were found to be bound up with an entirely new set of operational structures based on propositional logic and a 'formal' mode of thought.

Further, it was found that formal thought was more than verbal reasoning (propositional logic), it also entailed a series of 'operational schemata . . . these include combinatorial operations, propositions, double systems of reference, a schema of mechanical equilibrium (equality between action and reaction), multiplicative probabilities, correlations etc . . . in addition . . . we have to refer to the "integrated structures" on which they are based — i.e. to the dual structure of the lattice and the group of four transformations . . . analysed by the second author in his work on the transformation of propositional operations'. (An analysis of the structures described by Piaget can be found in Boyle, 1969; Flavell, 1963; Ginsburg and Opper, 1969 and Lunzer, 1970.)

By presenting the details of experiments involving such situations as 'The Equality of Angles of Incidence and Reflection', 'The Oscillation of a Pendulum' and 'Combination of Coloured and Colourless Chemical Bodies', Piaget and Inhelder aim to describe the changes in logical operations between childhood and adolescence that mark the completion of the operational development of intelligence. (See also Bruner, 1959 and Parsons, 1960).

Berzonsky (1971) focuses on Inhelder and Piaget's (1958) contentions that logical thinking is (a) dependent on the initial, prevalent stage of precausality and (b) intrinsically unitary. Six- and seven-year-old children were administered measures of physical causality, 'tests of hypothesized component abilities of causal reasoning', Piagetian concrete operational tasks and two of Inhelder and Piaget's formal operational tasks. The results did not support Piaget's claim that children who advance non-naturalistic (pre-causal) explanations do so because they are pre-operational in their thinking. Nor was the unitary nature of logical thinking confirmed. In a later study, Berzonsky (1971a) concluded that a child's familiarity with the objects or events he is being questioned about is a decisive factor in causal reasoning. (Berzonsky's studies are reported in detail later in this chapter.)

Hughes (1965, referred to in Chapter One) identified a general component factor for formal operational skills, in his four-year longitudinal study. Piaget postulates that the stage of formal operations is characterized by the ability to consider all of the possible relationships in a problematic situation. Further, that formal operations, being based on propositions, are internalizable, reversible actions co-ordinated in an integrated system. Likewise, Lovell and Butterworth (1966) using Inhelder and Piaget's tests of proportionality (an aspect of formal thought relating to the understanding of proportions and described by Piaget as facilitating the understanding of complex physical systems) and a variety of tests involving the schema of ratio, arithmetic series or geometric series, confirmed the hypothesis that the schema of proportion 'depends on some central intellective ability which underpins performance on all tasks'. (Details are given later in this chapter.) Brainerd (1971), investigating Inhelder and Piaget's claim that the concepts of volume and density are indexes of the proportionality schema and that the volume index is acquired before the density index, found it to be supported at 'reasonably high levels of confidence'. Likewise, he found that the proportionality schema is acquired between the ages of eight and 15. (The details of Brainerd's study are given later in this chapter. Cf. the study of Pumfrey 1967, which concluded that 'an introduction to the understanding of proportion can be made before the secondary stage of education provided that the structure and content of the materials used are related to the limitations in strategy and hence in the understanding available to the child'. This study is also described below. See also Lowe and Ranyard, 1973.) Using a principal components analysis, Lovell and Shields (1967), in a study involving 50 subjects aged 8.5 — 11.7 years, (verbal IQs 140+ as determined by WISC), found that the Inhelder and Piaget Formal Operational tasks, Equilibrium in the Balance, the Colourless Liquids and the Oscillation of the Pendulum, had fairly high correlations (+.83, +.72, and +.60 respectively). Neimark (1970) attempted to evaluate intercorrelations among a problem-solving task (PS: devised by the author and representing her personal approach to formal operations) and two of Inhelder and Piaget's tasks: combinations of coloured and colourless chemical bodies (CH) and correlations (CO). A 'low but consistent and significant correlation was obtained between PS and CO; CH correlated with neither. Results were interpreted as consistent with the view that formal operations tasks — at least those employed in the present study — are correlated.' The author, however, questioned the appropriateness of the CH task for American children and emphasized the restricted age range.

Based on a consideration of the British studies (namely Hughes; Lovell and Butterworth; and Lovell and Shields) mentioned above, Bart (1971) inferred a unifactor hypothesis with respect to formal operational skills. He administered formal operations tasks, formal operational reasoning instruments (sets of logic items) and a measure of general intellectual ability. The results of the study indicated that 'though the array of formal operations is conceptualized as a "structure d'ensemble", formal operational skills have a bifactor structure. In this bifactor structure the first factor is very substantial and may be viewed as the formal operational factor. The second factor relates to a content factor for in the results of the study, the second factor separated the tasks from the tests.' The component indicating formal thought correlated modestly with the measure of verbal intelligence, in addition to showing non-verbal intelligence components. In a later paper (1972), Bart describes the construction and validation of his paper-and-pencil instrument for formal operational reasoning used in the above 1971 study. The logic items were of the multiple-choice type and related to biology, history and literature. Bart concluded that 'the reasoning tests had substantial content validity, modest concurrent validity and limited construct validity', but that they could 'be employed by educators to select students who are capable of abstract conceptualization and theoretically might profit from a curriculum emphasizing symbolic and verbal instruction and an abstract mode of learning'. (Cf. Tisher, 1971 and Burgess, 1969, described in Chapter 12.)

Research by Hill (1960) produced evidence claiming that 'children at age six, seven and eight are capable of hypothetico-deductive thinking and are by no means limited to "concrete" thought operations'. However, O'Brien and Shapiro (1968) contended that Hill's research was not valid, for they produced evidence to show that, although subjects between six and eight years are able to discriminate between a necessary conclusion and its negation, they are unable to test the logical necessity of a conclusion. In continuation, Shapiro and O'Brien (1970) were intent to investigate 'in what way does the ability to test for logical necessity develop in children up to 13 years of age and how does this developmental pattern compare with that for discriminating between a necessary conclusion and its negation'. The data supported the authors' previous research and they conclude that 'caution should be used in the application of Hill's conclusions'. (The 1970 study is described later in this chapter.)

It is pertinent here to recall the work of Lovell (1968), referred to in Chapter One, who maintained that a proportion of adolescents either do not reach formal operational thought at all or attain it in limited areas or for short periods. He cites the work of Hughes (op. cit.) who draws attention to the slow cognitive advance among some secondary modern school subjects. Tomlinson-Keasey (1972) obtained cross-sectional data on the cognitive levels of females in three age groups (mean ages 11 years nine months, 19 years seven months and 54 years). Sixty-seven per cent of the 19-year-old college students and 54 per cent of the 54-year-old women were at the formal level of operations. An attempt to facilitate the acquisition of formal operations was found to be successful, although there was little generalization to the tasks administered during the delayed post-test, especially among the 54-year-old women. The author concluded that 'it is clear that abilities to use formal operations develop over a period of years. . . . Indeed it is certainly possible that applying the operations characteristic of formal thought to different areas is a life-long endeavour'. (Details are given later in this Section; cf. Brainerd and Allen, 1971a, described in Chapter Four.)

Blanchard and Price (1971) presented 'triadic situations' to subjects judged to be at formal, concrete and pre-operational stages as a result of which 'partial support to a Piagetian interpretation of the development of preference for cognitive balance' was procured. (Details are given later in this chapter.)

More recently, Vickers and Blanchard (1973) confirmed the findings of Blanchard and Price (op. cit.) that formal operational subjects show a preference for balance, while concrete operational subjects demonstrate a 'preference for positivity', p. 189.

Ward (1972) describes the development of a series of reasoning items in the form of a logical game, 'Butch and Slim', devised for the 'Operational Thinking Sub-Scale' for the British Intelligence Scale, described in Chapter 12. The game is based upon the 'combinatorial of 16 binary propositions of p and q' described by Inhelder and Piaget (1958) and 'represents an attempt to integrate developmental material into a factorial framework'. The results 'justify the rationale adopted for the items' and are encouraging so far as reliability and validity are concerned. (The reader's attention is also drawn to Peel, 1971, described in Chapter 9.)

A follow-up study of Inhelder and Piaget's 'The Growth of Logical Thinking'
K. Lovell, 1961b

SUBJECTS/Lovell's study involved 200 subjects with an age range of between eight and 18 years. The sample comprised 34 average and bright primary school children; 14 average and bright preparatory school pupils; 39 grammar school pupils; 50 secondary modern school pupils; 50 comprehensive school pupils; 10 training college students; three able adults whose ages ranged from 25 to 32 years of age.

METHOD/The general experimental procedure followed closely that of the Geneva school. Each subject was seen individually and all responses were recorded verbatim. Modifications were made only when it was felt that more information was needed or where ambiguous responses needed clarification. Lovell repeated 10 of the experiments used by Inhelder and Piaget (1958).

These experiments were designed to investigate: (a) The Flexibility of Rods; (b) Oscillation of Pendulum; (c) Falling Bodies on an Inclined Plane; (d) Effects of invisible Magnetization; (e) Combinations of Colourless chemical Bodies; (f) The Conservation of Motion on a Horizontal Plane; (G) Equilibrium in the Hydraulic Press; (h) Equilibrium in the Balance; (i) Projection of Shadows; (j) Correlations.

RESULTS/Lovell's findings largely confirm those of Inhelder and Piaget, although he is also interested in the educational value of some of his findings. Although Lovell confirmed the main stages as postulated by Piaget and Inhelder, he had reservations about the ultimate attainment of less able secondary modern and comprehensive school pupils. Further, he makes certain recommendations regarding teaching method (e.g. posing of problems) as a result of his findings. He also pleads for a consideration of the effect of strong emotion on logical thinking.

Abilities underlying the understanding of proportionality
K. Lovell and I. B. Butterworth, 1966

The study was initiated with three main hypotheses. These were: (i) that the schema of proportion depends on some central intellective ability; (ii) that specific abilities contribute to the ability to use proportionality in particular tasks; and (iii) that ratio-involving tasks will depend less on the ability as demonstrated under (i) than in the case of the tasks involving proportion.

SUBJECTS/Sixty children from schools in a rural/urban area were drawn as follows: six pupils at each of the ages nine, 10, 11, chosen by their teachers, four being of average ability and two of above average ability in each age group. In the secondary comprehensive school six pupils were selected at the age of 12, and 12 pupils at each of the ages 13, 14 and 15. These children according to their teachers 'were assessed as being within the top one-third of the ability range'.

METHOD/The children undertook 20 tasks in all, many of which involved more than one problem. Some of these tasks dealt with either the schema of ratio, arithmetic, or geometric series. Task 15 — Balance experiment — followed Inhelder and Piaget (1958), Lovell (1961b), Lunzer and Pumfrey (1966); and Task 16 — Rings and Shadow experiment — followed Inhelder and Piaget (1958), Lovell (1961b), and Lunzer and Pumfrey (1966).
All the tasks were administered individually except for Tasks 19 and 20 which were administered to groups of three or four pupils. The procedure was a flexible one, in order to extract detailed reasons for the children's justifications for the various tasks. However, the general approach followed as closely as possible that of the Geneva school.
The authors graded the responses to each of the Tasks 1-18 on a six-point scale, where six represented the most advanced level of response. The tasks were ranked for order of difficulty and

161

an inter-correlation matrix was calculated.

RESULTS/The results indicated that it was not until 14 years of age that 18 out of a possible 72 responses were at or near the level of formal operational thought.

The authors also maintain that the schema of proportion and the schema of ratio were not available in all tasks at the same time. The content and nature of the apparatus together with structures are relevant in tasks where formal thought is required. The study also confirmed the third hypothesis, i.e. that tasks involving ratio will depend less on the intellectual ability than in the case of the tasks involving proportion.

An experimental study of the characteristics of logical thinking of children between the ages of 5 and 15 years.
M. C. Barker, 1969

RÉSUMÉ/Two of the experiments described by Inhelder and Piaget in their book 'The Growth of Logical Thinking from Childhood to Adolescence', namely the Inclined Plane and The Pendulum, were selected for modification and incorporation into a strategy-choice type of experiment, which sought logical operations and their precursors, as described by the aforementioned. Thirty-six children, aged between five and 15 years, took part in the experiment, which used a standardized procedure throughout the range. In the initial design stage of the experiment, it proved impossible to modify the Inclined Plane apparatus as planned, to meet the demands of the new ·procedures, indeed, it proved impossible to get it to work in the manner described by the authors.

Operational strategies of children were recorded when they attempted to match the rate of oscillation of a variable pendulum system with an independent criterion rate provided by electronic apparatus. Matching could be effected by the choice of a particular set of variables built into the pendulum system. Representations of the resulting operational strategies were subjected to a novel technique of qualitative analysis, evolved by Brimer, at the University of Bristol School of Education. The use of an established computer programme in effecting the analysis, allowed consideration of all possible relationships of variables selected within children's strategies, together with categories representing the age levels Piaget assigned to his stages of thinking.

Distinctive modes of operation were revealed in the cluster analysis technique which clearly associated with age, and whose degree of sophistication increased with age also.

The effectiveness of the various techniques used throughout the experiment was demonstrated, and hypotheses were generated by the analysis, which were sufficiently interesting, in relation to the Piagetian model of the growth of logical thinking, to stimulate the planning of a more ambitious experiment incorporating less capricious apparatus, and a larger sample of children.

The growth of the schema of proportionality
P. Pumfrey, 1967

AIM/The author's main aim was to address the inquiry to the developmental sequences involved in proportionality, in the light of Piaget's theory of cognitive development.

SUBJECTS/Eighty children comprised the sample — four boys and four girls at each age level from five to 15 years. The children were drawn from various schools in the Manchester area in England.

METHOD/Each task consisted of a series of situations. In each of these, the child was presented with three of the elements in a proportion and required to predict the fourth. Different equipment was utilized for each of the three Tests.

TEST ONE/Balance/This test was modelled after Inhelder and Piaget (1958). The apparatus consisted of a simple balance and a set of weights. The experimental procedure followed that of Jackson (1963).

TEST TWO/Structural Arithmetic/This test was patterned after a pilot study by Lunzer and Pumfrey (1966). The apparatus was identical to the set of Cuisenaire rods. A 'wall' was constructed, made of a chain of rods of uniform colour and length. The child was 'required to predict the number of rods/bricks of a different colour and length that he would need' in order to build the identical length.

TEST THREE/Pantograph: This test 'required the child to predict the direction and amplitude of the movement of one pointer with respect to the other.'

RESULTS/The author examines the result of the study in terms of two criteria. First, the accuracy of the child's predictions and secondly, the strategy utilized by the child in each prediction. The study points out several strategies which children employed in the three tasks. Some of these have been listed by the author as: Interferes with Balance; Differences; Compensates; Proportion by Symmetry; Simple Addition. The previous findings of another inquiry by Lunzer and Pumfrey (1966) were partly substantiated. The author finally concludes that the findings of the study suggest '. . . that an introduction to the understanding of proportion can be made before the secondary stage of education, provided that the structure and content of the materials used are related to the limitations in strategy, and hence in understanding, available to the child'.

Logical thinking in children ages six through thirteen
Logical thinking in children ages six through thirteen
B. J. Shapiro and T. C. O'Brien, 1970

AIM/Shapiro and O'Brien addressed their inquiry to the following hypothesis: 'In what way does the ability to test for logical necessity develop in children up to 13 years of age and how does this developmental pattern compare with that of discriminating between a necessary conclusion and its negation?'

SUBJECTS/Twenty-four boys and 24 girls were drawn from two Roman Catholic schools from the Cleveland, Ohio, diocese. The children were randomly selected at each of the eight age levels with upper middle-class background.

METHOD/Test A consisted of 100 items in sentential logic, classical syllogism, and logic of quantification. This was patterned after Hill (1960).
The subjects were fully familiarized with the nature of the tasks and each student received a different randomization of the test items to avoid more than three identical responses or two similar principles of logic appearing consecutively. The 12 boys and 12 girls (24 children) were randomly assigned to each of two groups, one of which was administered Test A and the other Test B. Sixty items from sentential logic were administered first, followed by the remaining 40 items from the classical syllogism and logic of quantification.

RESULTS/The authors of the study draw attention to Hill's (1960) findings and maintain that while children at CA six, seven, and eight are able 'to deal effectively with verbal premises that call for hypothetical reasoning', this appears not to be the case so far as the ability to discern logical necessity is concerned. Further, the following points were stressed:
(a) '. . . that hypothetical deductive thinking — at least that

which is consistent with mathematical logic – cannot at all be taken for granted in children of elementary school age';

(b) that children in grades 1-8 'tend to follow some consistent "child logic" of their own which is not the same as "adult" mathematical logic';

(c) that the interpretation of 'if-then' as 'if and only if' needs further research;

(d) that the findings must be read in terms of the child's life experiences – and such experiences were not controlled in this study; and

(e) that 'these findings refer to the current status of thought-operations in children as they result from current and past life experiences. By no means do they indicate what children are capable of since no attempt was made to change the subjects' hypothetical-deductive abilities. Whether these abilities can be altered by some systematic intervention is an open question.'

The role of familiarity in children's explanations of physical causality
M. D. Berzonsky, 1971a

AIM/Berzonsky addressed his inquiry to the investigation of the 'effect of familiarity on causal explanations and to determine whether children would revert to non-naturalistic explanations when they were unable to explain a phenomenon in a "reasonable" manner'.

SUBJECTS/The sample of 84 subjects ranged in age from six years three months to seven years five months. The children were of middle-class background.

METHOD/Three Piagetian-type situations were utilized. In order to assess the child's acquisition of physical causality, a 22-question interview was conducted with each child. All behavioural responses were recorded verbatim. Additional questions were put to elicit further information in respect to vague responses. The experimental procedure involved familiar, remote and malfunctions of objects. The second and third situations consisted of demonstrations and the child had to advance predictions of what would happen, and why. 'These demonstrations were conducted under two conditions: standard and an unexpected reversal condition in which results contrary to normal expectations occurred.' (Fuller details of this are given in Berzonsky, 1969.)

Verbal Tests/Three sub-tests were used. Two were drawn

from the work of Nass (1956). Items dealt with familiar or remote objects. Nass (1956) argues that '... familiar objects are those which a child could have possibly, but not necessarily, experienced directly, whereas remote objects are beyond the direct experience for a child.' The third sub-test was devised by Berzonsky (1970) and dealt with malfunctions of objects. Some of the examples used were: (a) Familiar Objects: 'What makes a clock tick?' (b) Remote Objects: 'What makes the wind blow?' (c) Malfunctions: 'What makes the airplanes crash?'

Teeter-Totter/The test is described by Berzonsky as follows: 'This task consisted of a fulcrum, board, three wooden blocks used as weights, and supports to keep the balance board horizontal during testing. The balance board had hollow compartments in the sides where lead weights could be placed undetected by S. A portable screen was used to shield the apparatus from S when the balance was being arranged. The S was told to close his eyes 'real tight'. The apparatus was then screened from S and E arranged it by supporting the two ends and placed one block on the right end of the balance and two on the left. The screen was removed and S was told to open his eyes. Then E asked: 'If I pull out these blocks (pointing to the two supports) which end (pointing) will fall down? . . . what made that end fall?' Five such trials were used.

Water-level Apparatus/Briefly, the child was asked to advance a prediction and, following a demonstration, to explain which of two objects, when submerged in a transparent jar of water, would raise the water level. Fuller details are given in Berzonsky (1971a, page 709).

RESULTS/The overall results suggested that familiarity with objects or events was a decisive factor in causal reasoning. Fewer non-naturalistic justifications were advanced in respect to objects children could possibly have experienced, than questions about remote, unattainable objects. The results are consistent with the contentions of Nass (1956). Berzonsky further argues that 'a normal function and a malfunction are two different kinds of events with the latter leading to a more physical interpretation'. Piaget's (1967) argument that the divergences in the results of child causality studies may be due, in part, to differences in the modes of analysis, was not substantiated by Berzonsky. Berzonsky states that factors like question wording, testing procedure and familiarity may influence the type of explanations of physical causality advanced by children. 'As Braine (1959) has pointed out, Piaget, in his overriding concern with the process of development, has failed to attend to such factors in his investigations'.

Interdependence of Inhelder and Piaget's model of logical thinking
M. D. Berzonsky, 1971

AIMS/(a) To identify causal reasoning and operational thought factors; (b) to examine the relationship between variations in children's causal justifications and 'structural' differences in their operational strategies of thought; and (c) to study the patterning of children's causal reasoning and logical operativity in a problem-solving situation.

SUBJECTS/Eighty-four subjects with a CA range six years three months to seven years five months were involved. Their measured IQs ranged from 72 to 142 points on the Dominion Group Test of Learning Capacity (Primary).

METHOD/Verbal Tests of Causality/Three Verbal tests of causal reasoning were administered, patterned after Nass (1956). (Fuller details are described in Nass, 1956; and Berzonsky, 1969.)

Hypothesized Causal Components/Ten possible component abilities of causal reasoning were hypothesized and most of these were patterned after Piaget (1928, 1950).

Causal Demonstrations/Two situations were used — teeter-totter, and raising the water level in a container. The child had to advance a prediction, and after a demonstration, justify the phenomenon. (Fuller details are given in Berzonsky, 1969, 1971, p.470.)

Piagetian Concrete Operations Tasks/Two class-inclusion items based on Piaget (1950), were presented to the child. A check adapted from Piaget (1950, p. 133) was also utilized. Two conservation tasks — that of clay and liquid — were also administered. The general experimental procedure, including the scoring techniques, was identical to that of the Geneva centre. Further, a seriation task was also presented, patterned after Elkind 1964).

Piagetian Formal Operational Tasks/In this phase two tasks were administered: the chemical combinations problem and the oscillations of a pendulum. These were taken from Inhelder and Piaget (1958) and the general experimental procedure was also identical to that of the Geneva School.

Intelligence/In order to assess the child's level of general intelligence, the Dominion Group Test of Learning Capacity was also employed.

Descriptive measure/Each child's CA* was represented in months, as a variable in the final analysis. 'The three main sets of tasks, causal demonstrations (A), concrete operational (B), and formal operational (C), were administered in a counterbalanced order according to sex. Thus 14 subjects, seven boys and seven girls, were tested in the order ABC, ACB, then BCA, BAC, CBA and CAB. Items within these main sets were also counterbalanced according to sex.'

RESULTS/The data gathered were subjected to factor analysis and five factors were identified. These were causal reasoning (Factor I); Operational thought (Factor II); Problem solving (Factor III); Causal explaining in concrete situations (Factor IV); and Understanding the Concept of Force (Factor V). Berzonsky suggests that Factor I and Factor IV had very little relation with each other. The high loadings on Factor II which demand the use of concrete operations to solve, substantiate Piaget's (1950) contentions on the unity of operational thought. (Berzonsky's findings are in concordance with Stephens et al. (1972), who attempted a factorial study of Piagetian operational thought, but part from the results reported by Bryan and MacArthur (1967, 1969) in factorial studies of various Piagetian tasks suggestive of concrete operations cf. also Modgil, Dielman and Cattell, 1973, in press).

Further, Factor III lends partial support for the inter-item consistency of Inhelder and Piaget's (1958) problem solving tasks of chemical combinations and the oscillations of a pendulum. Berzonsky suggests that his 'findings bear on the four-phase model of operational thought acquisition proposed by Flavell and Wohlwill (1969)' who have suggested that the consistency between 'operationally equivalent tasks' should vary with the integrity of a stage as revealed at each of the four phases. 'During Phases 1 and 4, intertask correlations should be close to zero since either complete failure or success will occur. During Phase 2, intercorrelations would also be expected to be low since various situational factors would have a profound influence. Only during Phase 3, when structural consolidation has occurred and situational influences have diminished in importance, would intertask consistency appear.'

Berzonsky finally concludes that 'the results fail to support Piaget's (1953) claim that children who give non-naturalistic (precausal) explanations do so because they are pre-operational in their thinking. While both abilities were clearly identified they bear little relationship to each other. The results are also at variance with the unitary nature of logical thinking postulated by Inhelder and Piaget (1958).'

A developmental study of cognitive balançe
E. B. Blanchard and K. C. Price, 1971

AIMS/The authors were interested in examining whether preference for 'cognitive balance' followed a developmental pattern consistent with Piaget's theory of cognitive development. They cite the work of Price (1970). This study involved subjects of three different ages, junior, high school, college undergraduates and middle-age. These subjects who were all in Piaget's formal operational stage were compared on preference for balanced relations. In Price's study no age effect was observed and 'is thus not inconsistent with Piagetian developmental stage interpretation, but does not provide an adequate test of it.'

Blanchard and Price extended the age range of the Price experiment downward.

SUBJECTS/Five different age groups of 24 subjects, with equal numbers of either sex, were involved in the study. The grade levels and mean ages of each group were: first, six years nine months; second, eight years one month; fourth, nine years 10 months; eighth, 13 years 10 months; and undergraduates, 18 years 11 months.

The school children were drawn from middle and lower-class families and were of 'average intelligence'.

METHOD/Subjects in the first and second grades were administered the conservation of quantity (liquid) tests using different coloured liquid and different shaped glasses. The general experimental procedure was identical to the Piagetian situations. Children in the first grade who failed conservation operativity and chidren in the second grade who demonstrated conservation were involved in further experimentation.

Subjects in the eighth grade were administered three tests to assess the presence of formal operational strategies. Questioning and the criteria employed were patterned after Mussen, Conger and Kagan (1969, pp. 453-4) and 'involved use of algebraic versus trial and error methods to solve problems, ability to discuss non-existent objects, and generation of multiple antecendents to an event versus a single cause'. Children in the fourth grade who were non-operational in all three items and children in the eighth grade who were operational in all three items were involved in the study. 'The college undergraduates were assumed to be at a formal operational level of development.'

Triadic Situations/In all, eight triadic situations were administered: 'you (like (+) dislike (−))————; you (like (+), dislike (−)————; you see that ———— and ——— (like (+), dislike (−))

each other.' All possible combinations of positive and negative relations were presented. Modifications were made for the youngest groups. (Fuller details are given in Blanchard and Price, 1971, pp. 344-5.)

RESULTS/The authors finally conclude: 'three different stages in the development of preference for cognitive balance in triadic situations can be identified. In the first, there is a definite preference for balance with the use of extreme ratings. This coincides with the pre-operational stage. In the second stage, there is no preference for balanced over unbalanced situations: instead, subjects tend to respond in terms of positivity. This coincides with the concrete operational stage. Next, there is a transition range which included the eighth graders. Finally, in the third stage there is strong preference for balance but with significantly less use of extreme ratings. This corresponds to older formal operational subjects.'

The development of the proportionality schema in children and adolescents
C. Brainerd, 1971

The main issues were as follows: (a) Inhelder and Piaget (1958) report that a child's volume operativity improves between ages eight and 15. The present study attempted to verify this statement: (b) Do the concepts of volume and density presuppose the same basic cognitive skills? (c) Does the acquisition of volume concept invariably precede the acquisition of density concept? (d) Is the density concept more easily appreciated by older children than by younger subjects?

SUBJECTS/Seventy-two lower-middle class subjects took part in the investigation. Children, who had IQs in the 90-110 range were drawn from three age levels: third grade (mean age = 8.8 years), sixth grade (mean age = 11.6 years) and ninth grade children (mean age = 14.5 years). Boys and girls were represented in equal numbers at each age level.

METHOD/All children demonstrated operativity in number (Piaget, 1952b) and length (Piaget, Inhelder and Szeminska, 1960). The following tasks were administered to the subjects: Density; Solid volume and Liquid volume. (Full details of the experimental procedure including scoring techniques are given on pages 470-2, Brainerd, 1971).

RESULTS/The results indicated no sex differences but a definite improvement in children's conceptions of volume and density between the ages of eight and 15 was noted. 'Although the data suggest some nonlinearity in the acquisition of volume and density, the fact that these non-linear trends were both small ($p < .05$) and restricted to only conservation explanations suggests that they do not merit more extensive consideration.'

Brainerd's study produced further evidence which supported Piaget's general tendency to utilize 'logical' methods of predicting concept growth and development. 'Prima facie, volume seems a more complex concept than density: while density could be conserved merely by thinking 'of it as a simple, invariant characteristic of each substance, volume remains a property that is not so easily conceived. The logic of physics . . . dictates that density is more complex, since density is defined as weight per unit volume. In so far as Piaget typically favours such a "logical" approach, the data of the present study might be construed as supporting a general predictive method, as well as a specific prediction.'

Finally, Brainerd pleads for further research dealing with age differences in the acquisition of density concept.

A Piagetian questionnaire applied to pupils in a secondary school
R. P. Tisher, 1971

AIMS/Tisher examined three issues: (a) the development of pencil-and-paper tests in the assessment of a student's stages of mental development; (b) the utilization of such a test in order to assess the distribution of stages among secondary school pupils; (c) a comparison of resultant patterns obtained through the use of such a questionnaire and the conservation-interview method.

SUBJECTS/The sample of 232 pupils from eight secondary schools comprised 138 boys and 94 girls in Australia.

METHOD/The Piagetian questionnaire was presented to the experimental sample during two consecutive 40-minute periods. Fifty-seven of the subjects were randomly selected and assessed in the typical Piaget Interview sessions. Piagetian tasks of invisible magnetism, equilibrium in the balance, and combination of chemicals were administered (Inhelder and Piaget, 1958), and pupils were classified as 'formal' or 'concrete'.

'Criteria in Inhelder and Piaget were used for the construction of the pencil-and-paper test which contained 24 multiple choice items based on four scientific phenomena or tasks — the bouncing ball, equilibrium in a balance, water levels in connected containers and shadows of rings. Fourteen of the test items were classified as "concrete" (i.e. they would most likely be solved by pupils in the concrete stage of development) and 10 as "formal". To correct for guessing, only those pupils who correctly answered five or more formal items and seven or more concrete ones were classified as belonging to the formal stage of development. The rationale for the procedure appears in Tisher (1962) ... the questionnaire occurred in four phases coinciding with the four sets of questions. Each phase was initiated with a demonstration of the relevant phenomenon. For example, prior to the administration of the items on water levels in connected containers, pupils were shown two connected containers and asked to observe what happened as the researcher moved one or both vessels.'

RESULTS/No sex differences were observed. Significant differences between the number of pupils in the concrete and formal stages for the CA group 12 years to 13 years four months (χ^2 = 56.9, df = 1, p < .005) and the 13 years five months to 14 years nine months age group (χ^2 = 8.1, df = 1, p < .005) were computed. The majority of pupils were in the concrete stage at CA 13 years five months to 14 years nine months. However, there was a significant increase in the proportion in the formal stage.

'That the results are not at variance with those of many other researchers was regarded as an indication of the success of the Piagetian questionnaire. Other indications of its success were that (a) the distribution over stages with ages of the 57 pupils who were interviewed was similar to that in Table One (findings too, were similar); and (b) there was a 77 per cent agreement in classification between the interview and questionnaire techniques ... that pencil-paper tests could be used with advantage.'

Formal operations in females from 11 to 54 years of age
C. Tomlinson-Keasey, 1972

AIMS/The study attempted to obtain cross-sectional data on the level of cognitive development of three age groups. Furthermore, to explore variables which might enhance the growth of formal operations.

SUBJECTS/The sample of 89 comprised sixth-grade girls, college students and women, with mean ages of 11 years nine months; 19 years seven months; and 54 years, respectively.

METHOD/Twenty-four experimental subjects were presented

a pre-test, short-term training experience, immediate post-test, and delayed post-test.

Five tasks were drawn from Inhelder and Piaget (1958). The pendulum balance, and flexibility problems (Inhelder and Piaget, pp. 67-79; 164-81, and 46-66, respectively) were used in the pre-test, training and immediate post-test phases.

In the delayed post-test, another version of the flexibility experiment and chemicals and inclined plane tasks (pp. 107-122 and 182-198 respectively) were administered. These were presented to assess the durability and generalization of the training experience.

Pre-test and delayed post-tests were given identically. The training session involved the following principles: (a) training was suited to the individual; (b) active involvement on the part of the subject; (c) conflict-situations were faced by subjects; and (d) training proceeded from simple to complex concepts.

'The immediate post-test required experimental subjects to teach the next subject, who was a confederate of the experimenter. Thus, subjects were required to produce systematic statements about the problems and to accurately demonstrate their conclusions.'

RESULTS/An examination of the verbatim recorded responses, demonstrated that 32 per cent of the girls were at the formal level with four per cent of their responses at the most advanced stage (III-B, Inhelder and Piaget, 1958). On the other hand, 67 per cent of the college student's responses were at the formal level with 23 per cent at Stage IIIB. And 54 per cent of the women's responses were at the formal level with 17 per cent at stage III-B.

Overall, training produced significant gains for all three age groups from the pre-test to immediate post-test (girls, $t = 8.71$, $p < .01$; college students, $t = 8.41$; $p < .01$; women, $t = 5.52$, $p < .01$). However, on the chemicals and inclined plane experiments in the delayed post-tests, experimental subjects did not differ from the control subjects. Only on the repeated task of the delayed post-test, however, did girls and college students differ significantly from their control counter-parts (girls, $t = 2.36$, $p < .01$, college students, $t = 5.03$, $p < .01$).

Tomlinson-Keasey finally concludes: 'The training procedure was shown to be highly effective for the training tasks. However, little generalization occurred on the different tasks of the delayed post-tests. Attainment of the highest stage of formal operations was rare and seemed to be dependent on available structures, experiences, use and possibly even preference.'

*See also Brodzinsky *et al.*, 1972, who demonstrated the differential effect of shielding stimulus arrays at different age levels. Shielding perceptual cues significantly enhanced performance for the eight- to nine-year-olds and, to a lesser extent, the 10- to 11-year-olds, while it had no effect on the six- to seven-year-olds. This result supports the notion of activation of cognitive structures.

CHAPTER SIX
THE CHILD'S CONCEPTION OF SPACE

According to Piaget and Inhelder (1956) the child's first concepts of space are topological in character, that is, they are based on such characteristics as proximity, separation, order or spatial succession, surrounding and continuity. Children then proceed from topological relationships to a gradual understanding of projective and Euclidean concepts.

Topological space

Initially, Piaget and Inhelder make comparisons between perception and imaginal space, later moving on to define 'haptic perception' as '. . . perception of an object by means of the sense of touch in the absence of visual stimulation'.

In the treatment of elementary relationships the children were asked firstly to draw a man from memory and secondly to copy 21 geometrical shapes. Although the children, of two to seven years of age, were often found to be familiar with Euclidean figures such as circles and triangles, they expressed in their drawings the topological characteristics of proximity, enclosure etc., as in the case of haptic perception, rather than the perceptual features of good gestalt (pattern shape).

The notion of order or sequence is a basic topological relationship and its development is studied through five experiments: (i) reproduction of a simple linear order; (ii) transposition of circular into simple linear order; (iii) establishment of reverse order; (iv) direct or reverse order of stacking; and (v) reproducing a string of beads arranged in a figure of eight, either on a string or on a rigid stick.

The study of the tying of knots was used as a means of discovering the evolution of concepts of surrounding and enclosure and there follows a consideration of the way in which children come to an understanding that the sub-divisions of a line or shape can be infinite and without surface area (a state not

175

achieved until about 12 years of age).

Projective space

For Piaget '... projective space ... begins psychologically ... when an object ... is no longer viewed in isolation, but begins to be considered in relation to a "point of view" ' (1956; p. 153). Piagetian experiments include the construction of the projective straight line, drawing objects whilst imagining what they would look like from different positions; drawing projections of shadows, drawing what a doll is 'seeing' from different positions in relation to a model of mountains; predicting the shapes of sections when cutting various solids and predicting the result of unfolding three-dimensional shapes. The authors demonstrate the lessening egocentricity of the child and his progressive discrimination and co-ordination of different viewpoints (perspectives). The later experiments on geometric sections involve both projective and Euclidean factors. They illustrate that the development of projective and Euclidean concepts take place concurrently.

Euclidean space

Piaget and Inhelder made a systematic study of the development of various Euclidean concepts of parallelism, similarity, vertical and horizontal co-ordinates, and the ability to reconstruct diagrammatical layouts.

Similarity and proportion were first considered with experiments related to similarity of triangles, and the possibility of realizing similarity from parallelism between pairs of sides, from equality of pairs of angles, and from the proportions of pairs of sides. Rectangles were likewise investigated.

Horizontal and vertical co-ordinates also received consideration. These are important frames of reference, closely linked to the topological and projective relationships which are concerned largely with objects themselves and the co-ordination of different viewpoints of these objects. 'Such a co-ordination of objects culminates in the construction of systems of reference or co-ordinates' (Piaget and Inhelder, 1956).

The placing of a doll on a model landscape permitted an investigation into the construction of physical frames of reference. Following this, Piaget and Inhelder contrasted the operations of a spatio-temporal type with thoughts which are logico-arithmetical in structure. According to the authors, operations of the spatio-temporal, also termed 'sub-logical', type are in no sense inferior to logico-arithmetical operations. 'It simply means that their function is to produce the concept of the object as such, in contrast to collections of objects. Such operations deal not with class inclusion, but with part-whole inclusions for single objects.'

Perceptual and conceptual space were differentiated, the former being found in the presence of the object, whilst the latter can exist in its absence. For Piaget, spatial concepts are internalized actions and not merely images of external events or things — or even images of the results of actions. Spatial concepts can only lead to a prediction of these results by becoming active themselves, by operating on physical objects and not simply by evoking memory images of them.

'The image . . . is symbolic in character, plays an increasingly sub-ordinate role as the active component of thought becomes better organized . . . throughout the evolution of spatial operations the image performs an entirely different function from that which it carries out in the case of logico-mathematical operations. A spatial field is a single scheme embracing all the elements of which it is composed and uniting them in one monolithic block whereas a logical class is a collection of discontinuous elements linked by their resemblance, regardless of spatio-temporal location.' (Piaget and Inhelder, 1956.)

Piaget and Inhelder conclude with a consideration of the nature of sub-logical operations and their application to topological, projective and Euclidean space.

One of the most comprehensive attempts to verify some of Piaget's conclusions concerning spatial concepts was carried out by Dodwell (1963). He assessed not only inter-relationships among various spatial problems but also differences among diverse age groups. He concluded that it was not possible to categorize the great majority of children studied as being in any one of the particular stages of spatial concept development described by Piaget. However, the overall ability to deal correctly with spatial concepts improved with age. The author finally concludes that 'such investigations should be supplemented by more intensive longitudinal studies which attempt to unravel some of the threads out of which the fabric of intellectual growth is woven'. (Further details of the study may be found in 'Logical Thinking in Children', Ed. Sigel and Hooper, 1968.)

So far as haptic perception is concerned, Lovell's investigation (1959) merits mention among the early studies. He found that curvilinear shapes were picked out just as easily as shapes involving topological relationships. The verbalizations of his subjects were found to be poor when compared with their Geneva counterparts although their performance on the tests of linear and circular order was superior. In the experiment involving the drawing of shapes, topological properties were better displayed than Euclidean properties, unless attention was confined to curvilinear shapes. Lovell raises questions concerning Piaget's contention that topological relationships necessarily precede projective and euclidean ones and recommends further research. In continuation, Lovell maintains: 'If they (Piaget and Inhelder) are correct, not only have they shown that the "space" of the three to four-year-old is essentially different from that of the adult, but their work implies that we may have to reconsider the activities involving spatial concepts which our nursery and infant school children engage in, and reconsider our teaching of spatial work in the Junior School'. (Details of the study appear in Lovell, 1959, and in Lunzer, 1960.) Peel (1959) also points out that if Piaget and Inhelder's work is true then '. . . the earlier manual and visual skills expected of young children should be those that involve only the main topological ideas of proximity, separation, enclosure, order and continuity.' Mackay (1972), draws attention to the various flaws in Lovell's study (op. cit.).

Page's investigation (1959) into haptic perception among young children discovered that his subjects did not confuse curvilinear with rectilinear shapes as Piaget and Inhelder suggested. The explanation is that children attempt to schematize their touch impressions into a meaningful form by naming them. This is claimed as the reason why topological shapes are easier, since there is a greater variety of possible configurations in topological shapes. Page gives no statistical analysis of his data. (Full details appear in Page, 1959 and Lunzer, 1960.)

Fisher's work (1965) with young children on shape perception suggest that with two-and-a-half-year-old children the most important cues for recognition of objects are textural rather than spatial. Such a contention has now recently been substantiated by Mackay (1972). Fisher casts doubt on Piaget's claim for topological primacy, having shown that when a response is available equally to each of the shape categories under consideration, the topological primacy hypothesis needs to be replaced by one of linear primacy.

Pinard and Laurendeau (1966) used two series of 12 shapes each and mainly analyzed their results in terms of their subjects' total age range (three to 12 years) and of percentage correct responses. Their results substantiated the early acquisition of topological discrimination, but also demonstrated that some simple euclidean discriminations (curvilinear versus rectilinear, indented versus non-indented) were just as easy.

Concannon (1970) reviews the three salient replicative British studies with respect to haptic perception: Lovell (1959), Page (1959), and Fisher (1965). She further focuses on studies in Russia by Boguslavskaya (1963), Zinchenko and Ruzskaya (1961) and Zaporozhets (1965) and those in the United States:

Concannon (1966), Coyle (1968), Fantz (1965), Gibson (1962), Lowenfeld (1945) and Pick (1965). (Concannon's review is summarized later in this chapter.)

Following Piaget and Inhelder's study (1956) of spatial egocentrism (involving a simulated landscape with the requirement that the child describe the perspectives of a doll from various situations), Shantz and Watson were intent to discover the concepts that the young child needs to acquire in order to facilitate the emergence of spatial objectivity. In an initial study (1970), they hypothesized that the ability to predict what another sees from various locations develops from the child's own experience in object relations. The very young child has no expectancy of an object's changing in appearance with a change in his spatial position. Shantz and Watson, in an attempt to assess spatial expectancies, introduced trick situations which resulted in the sample of 48 three- to five-year-old children clearly distinguishing between the 'trick and veridical conditions by their verbal statements'. In continuation, Shantz and Watson (1971) attempted to measure the child's ability to make specific predictions of the position of objects after he himself had changed positions and they hypothesized that this would be positively related to his ability to identify object arrangements from a doll's position. (Details are given below.) The authors conclude that 'the ability to predict object sites when the child moves (a) emerges prior to, (b) is substantially easier than, and (c) is significantly related to the ability to make such predictions from another's viewpoint'. They raise further questions concerning the existence of a necessary or sufficient relation between the two abilities and the factors contributing to the discrepancy in performance on the two tasks.

Partly related is the study by Brodzinsky et al. (1972) who, using a modified version of Piaget's mountain scene task, presented six-, eight- and 10-year-old subjects with both 'single and multiple object arrays under either a shielded or non-shielded condition'. The results demonstrated that shielding perceptual cues significantly enhanced the performance of the eight- to nine-year-old group, and to a lesser extent, that of, the 10- to 11-year-olds while no facilitative effect was observed with the six- to seven-year-olds. Further, no difference was noted between single and multiple object arrays. This result supported the notion of activation of cognitive structures, proposed by Overton et al. (1971, described more appropriately in Chapter Five. See also Houssidas, 1965; Lewis and Fishbein 1969; Laurendeau and Pinard, 1970; Fishbein, Lewis and Keiffer, 1972.)

The development of the water-line concept, (referring to the child's indication that the surface of water — or the water-line — in a container remains horizontal, regardless of the way the container may be tilted) is regarded by Piaget and Inhelder (1956) as evidence that the child has developed a 'Euclidean Coordinate System', enabling him to refer to horizontal and vertical axes when concerned with spatial orientations. Their claim that the acquisition of verticality is synchronous with that of horizontality was challenged by Beard (1964). Her study demonstrated that the concept of vertical precedes that of horizontal. Furthermore, her subjects were not at the stage of immediate prediction of horizontal and vertical in all tasks at the age of 11 years, thereby disagreeing with Piaget's norms. A methodological note relating to the concepts of horizontal and vertical has been forwarded by Mackay, Brazendàle and Wilson (1972, pp. 232-3).

Among the several investigations of the water-line concept are those of Beilin, Kagan and Rabinowitz (1966) who rejected as unlikely the notion that the difficulty in representing oblique lines is a perceptual one, maintaining that the difficulty is mainly conceptual. (The study is described later in this chapter.) However, Mackay, Brazendale and Wilson (1972) suggest '. . . that the difficulty may be both perceptual and conceptual' (p. 236). Shantz and Smock (1966), details of whose study appear below . . . , investigated the relation between water-line prediction and distance conservation which, while supporting Piaget's contentions that the development of the water-line concept depends on the prior development of the conservation of distance, failed to make the distinction between Piaget's prediction procedure (i.e. the child's 'guess' as to how the water will look when the jar is tilted) and the more fundamental perceptual task (the child being requested to depict what he sees, with the tilted jar directly in front of him). Ford (1970), therefore, attempted a systematic comparison between the prediction and perception tasks together with the relation of distance conservation. Contrary to expectations based on Piaget's work, Ford found 'several differences between the prediction and perception tasks and little correspondence between them'. Responses were more advanced on perception than on prediction. 'Results were largely consistent with Piaget's hypothesis that correct water-line performance pre-supposes distance conservation.' (Ford's study is described below.) Larsen and Abravanel (1972), in an examination of the developmental relations between certain spatial tasks (see below), unlike Shantz and Smock and Ford (op. cit.), failed to find any developmental order among the conservation of distance and of length and the awareness of the horizontal and of the vertical, although there were indications that these preceded the measurement of length. Larsen and Abravanel attribute the discrepancy between their findings and those of Shantz and Smock (op. cit.) to differing procedures.

Development of distance conservation and the spatial coordinate system
C. Shantz and C. Smock, 1966

AIMS/(a) To verify Piaget's contention that every child who employs the coordinate system also shows operativity in distance and, further, that every child who is unable to conserve distance is unable to demonstrate the coordinate system concept. (b) To determine the comparability of data relevant to two spatial concepts derived from two-dimensional (drawings) and three-dimensional stimuli (objects).

SUBJECTS/The total sample of 20 subjects comprised 10 boys and 10 girls from a rural elementary school, with CA range from six years four months to seven years 10 months (mean age six years nine months).

METHOD–EXPERIMENTAL MEASURES/Distance Con-servation/Five items each were administered to assess distance operativity as follows: (a) if the distance were filled or empty (FE); (b) if the direction of movement were changed (DM).
In order to assess FE two two-and-a-half-inch trees were placed before the subject, eight inches apart. The child was questioned as to whether the trees were 'far apart' or 'near together'. This was followed by the placement of a board higher than the trees halfway between them, and the child was questioned again, 'And now, are they far apart (or near together)?'. Four more FE tasks were presented, with variations in the type of figures (pigs or trees) and height of interposed object (higher or lower than figures).
The same FE situation was then administered in five drawings. A standard picture showed two trees six inches apart with no interposed object between them. The child revealed whether the trees were 'far apart' or 'near together'. Three more pictures of the identical figures at varying distances were presented. 'Now, here are some trees – some have fences between them and some don't. Now find two trees that are just as far apart (or near together) as these (referring to the standard).' In the assessment of distance conservation with DM the child was questioned whether or not it was 'just as far from here to here (left tree to right tree) as from here to here (right tree to left

tree)'. Four additional tasks were presented with slight modifications.

The five DM tests with drawings were similar to those with objects, apart from minor adaptations.

Coordinate System/Five tests were administered in order to assess the concepts of horizontality (H) and verticality (V). The general experimental procedure was patterned after Piaget and Inhelder (1956). All children were seen individually and the responses recorded verbatim. Briefly, the task consisted of presenting two identical bottles, one half-filled with a coloured liquid. The child was asked to predict the level of the water with respect to the empty bottle, if the filled bottle were tilted at different angles. Prediction was followed by execution. The child marked the level of water at varied degrees of tilt on the outlines of drawings of the bottle at different tilts. Verticality was tested by presenting a clay-covered 'mountain' with a 60 degree slope on which 'trees' were to be planted in a 'nice and straight' line. (Fuller details are described in Piaget and Inhelder, 1956; Shantz and Smock, 1966, pp. 945-6.)

PROCEDURE/Half the children had the tasks presented with objects followed by those with drawings. The remainder had the reverse order of presentation. The tasks of FE, DM, HV were presented in the same order for all subjects.

RESULTS/The authors concluded: 'The impact of the type of stimuli was further evident as an order effect: Ss who had objects first and drawings second performed better than those under the reverse order of stimuli (p< 10). This finding not only indicates the importance of evaluating such order effects in repeated measurement designs but suggests that training of spatial concepts may be most effective with manipulation of objects preceding two-dimensional presentation of tasks. In summary, the data are consistent in general with the hypothesis of the developmental priority of distance conservation to the coordinate system. A longitudinal analysis of the development of these concepts is a necessary next step in the investigation of the ontogeny of spatial representation.'

Effects of verbal and perceptual training on water level representation
H. Beilin, J. Kagan and R. Rabinowitz, 1966

AIM/The aim was to test the effect of perceptual confirmation and verbal methods on the representation of water level, where subjects had previously failed to predict the horizontal 'water-line'.

SUBJECTS/The study comprised nine groups (N = 180) which were matched for IQ, race and SES. CA ranged from seven to eight years.

METHOD/The general method comprised a pre-test, post-test, and transfer test based on an anticipation method, with choice of one water level representation, from a series of drawings of jars in the same orientation. The transfer test employed round-bottomed flasks, but straight-sided jars were utilized in pre-tests, post-tests and training.

The training procedure consisted of two phases — perceptual training and verbal programme training. Perceptual training involved visual confirmation of water level following an antici-pation response, while verbal training involved verbal instruction in the horizontality concept. Four groups were given various combinations of verbal training.

There were also three control groups which received no training.

RESULTS/Perceptual confirmation training was superior to verbal methods but even so, it was more difficult to conceptualize the water level in jars tilted to oblique angles than in jars placed horizontally and vertically. It was argued that for 'the perceptual domain, symbolic imagery, rather than language, served the principal communication function'.

The relationship between spatial ability and performance on some Piagetian tests
R. W. Mycock, 1968

AIMS/The author had several aims in the study. These were: (i) to discover the relationship between performance in certain standardized tests and 'some Piagetian tests of spatial and logical ability; (ii) to ascertain whether factors other than a general factor, and in particular a spatial factor, contributed to performance in the several tests; (iii) to establish whether any significant sex differences occurred in the performance; and (iv) to indicate an order of difficulty for the Piaget tests.

SUBJECTS/The study drew a random sample of 60 children (30 boys and 30 girls) from a Yorkshire junior school.

METHOD/The author administered 10 individual Piagetian

tests incorporating the modifications subsequently published by Lunzer (1970). These included: (a) haptic perception; (b) similarity of triangles; (c) similarity of shapes by classification; (d) horizontal and vertical co-ordinates; (e) linear and circular order; (f) all and some; (g) classification-nesting; (h) multiplicative classification — matrices; (i) intersection — matrices; and (j) multiple seriation.

All the tests were basically drawn from Piaget and Inhelder (1956), and Piaget (1964). These were administered individually and all responses recorded verbatim.

The standardized tests employed were two NFER tests: Primary verbal 1, Non-Verbal 5. SRA Primary Mental Abilities Battery: Perceptual Speed, Reasoning-figure grouping, Reasoning-words, Space, Verbal Meaning — pictures and Verbal Meaning-words.

RESULTS/(i) A substantially high correlation emerged between the two NFER tests and the majority of the remaining tests. However, no such relation appeared between the SRA Space test and the Piagetian spatial tests.

(ii) Four factors were extracted by the method of principal components, in a factor analysis of the 18 tests plus age. Only three factors were identified as: I, a general ability factor; II, variation due to age; III, a spatial factor of a specific kind involving perception of similarity in geometrical figures.

(iii) No sex differences were observed.

(iv) 'The reliability coefficient for the Piagetian tests, correlated for length (each test being considered as one item within the larger test constituted by the Piagetian battery as a whole) was 0.89.'

A review of research on haptic perception
J. Concannon, 1970

In this paper, Concannon has reviewed studies on haptic perception including those which have been inspired by Piaget and Inhelder's (1956) work. She draws attention to the importance of Montessori's studies (1914) in tactual experiences with geometric insets. She points to the methodology of Montessori where there is emphasis on training in tactual perception in early childhood education.

Next, Concannon discusses briefly the stages of development in haptic perception as postulated by Piaget and Inhelder (1956) and considers the weight of evidence for and against the Piagetian frame of reference. She then comments upon haptic studies executed in England, including those of Lovell (1959), Page (1959) and Fisher (1965). (These studies have already received fuller discussion, see above.) In a study by Hermelin and O'Connor (1961) the relationship between mental age and haptic abilities was examined by testing normal and retarded children. An analysis of the data gathered demonstrated that retarded subjects (CA = 12.0; MA = 5.4) performed at a higher level of operativity than normal children in the test which involved manual exploration of haptic forms.

Concannon also cites three Russian studies related to cognition and haptic learning. These studies include those of Boguslavskaya (1963) Zinchenko and Ruzskaya (1961). In these studies children of CA three to seven years were examined, in an effort to analyse their spatial development. The majority of the tasks involved the identification of geometric forms by vision and touch and the results demonstrated that the subjects were more successful on the visual recognition tasks than the tactual. Likewise, Zaporozhets (1965) has summarized several experiments in perceptual development, with specific reference to the role of vision and touch.

Concannon (1966) investigated the development of haptic abilities in pre-school children, but unfortunately her paper is not easily accessible and details are lacking. Subjects participated in a learning programme which involved individual and group instruction in tactual exploration, identification, description and the drawing of geometric forms. These required the full utilization of sight, hearing and touch. Concannon's study demonstrated the following points.

(a) In the pre-test, children in non-Montessori classes performed at a higher level of operativity than subjects from the Montessori classes. However, in the post-test, the results showed a reversal.

(b) the experimental group achieved higher gain scores than the control group.

(c) Individual vs. group treatment did not produce any significant differences for any sub-groups.

(d) 'Increments in CA showed a significant and positive effect on performance in three of the five tests of haptic abilities.'

A follow-up of the children in the Concannon study (1966) was undertaken by Coyle (1968) in order to assess haptic retention. Briefly, retention of haptic learning was observed at six- and 12-month intervals. Likewise, facilitative trends were noted with regard to individual and group instructions. Coyle's results also indicated that 'experimental subjects showed higher mean gain scores on the post-tests than did the control subjects but the latter achieved significantly higher mean change scores. The control subjects continued to experience a natural development in haptic abilities, learning terms as inside, outside, bottom, top, etc.' She draws attention to the need for research into horizontality and verticality in the problem of retention of acquired haptic strategies.

Predictive versus perceptual responses to Piaget's water-line task and their relation to distance conservation
L. Ford, Jr. 1971

AIM/Ford, in the present study, addressed his inquiry to the development of the water-line concept in young children. (The term 'water-line' refers to the child's conviction that the surface of water in a container remains horizontal, regardless of the orientations of the container.) Ford attempted both to compare the prediction and perception tasks more systematically and to establish any branching relationships and patterning of distance conservation to perception and to prediction of water lines.

SUBJECTS/A sample of 20 children (14 boys and six girls) were drawn from a nursery school with a mean age of five years two months and a mean IQ of 120 (Peabody Intelligence Test).

METHOD/All children were seen individually and the water-line prediction and perception tasks were followed by the distance conservation tasks.
The water-line tasks used eight sets of four outline drawings of jars half filled with water. In each set, apart from the set indicating the jars upright, one drawing matched Piaget's Stage IIa (i.e. the line parallel with the base of the jar), one matched Piaget's Stage IIb (i.e. an oblique water-line) and one Piaget's Stage III (i.e. horizontal). The fourth drawing represented one of the incorrect types but with the water-line at a different angle from either of the other two. The right choice appeared once in each of the four feasible locations in each of the first and last four sets. The degrees of rotation from the upright position were: upright, upside down, 90° right, 30° left, 45° right, 60° left and 15° right. (Fuller details appear in Ford, 1971, p. 195.)
For the water-line prediction, the material was similar to that for the water-line tasks. A half-full jar of water was put out of sight of the child and the set of four drawings, as above, was shown to the child. E then said 'Here are four pictures of jars with water in them, but only one looks right. Point to the one where

the water looks just right'. All children were fully operational. E then showed another set of drawings, but this time with the jars upside down. 'Now, here are some drawings of jars that are upside-down. Point to the one where the water looks right.' Similarly, five more sets were administered each with a different angle of tilt.

The water-line perception was similar, apart from the jar being placed on the top of a box with the water-line at the child's eye level. Various rotations were performed by E and the child was asked, 'Point to the drawing where the water looks just like it does in the real jar'. the general procedure followed that of Piaget and Inhelder (1956).

The distance conservation evaluated whether (a) the distance was filled or empty and (b) whether the direction of movement was changed. In respect to (a) the objects (cars, dogs, cups, dolls or soldiers) were placed 12 — 15 inches apart. E said, 'Here are two cars. Are the cars near each other or far apart?' A piece of wood, which acted as the barrier was placed between the objects. 'And now, are the cars near each other or far apart?' In respect to (b) above, the two objects were placed once again 12-15 inches apart 'Is it just as far from here to here as it is from here to here?' E ran his finger from A to B and back again as the question was put. The general procedure, with its full details, appears in Piaget, Inhelder and Szeminska (1960) and Shantz and Smock (1966).

RESULTS/The findings corroborated Piaget's and Inhelder's (1956) results. Children of four years five months have a limited conception of the concept of horizontality of water-lines. Also, operational water-line performance presupposes distance conservation. However, behaviour on the prediction and perception tasks demonstrated a different pattern. Responses on the perception tasks were at a higher level of operational performance developmentally, than on prediction. The two tasks cannot be stated with any degree òf confidence as 'comparable indicators of a geometrical coordinate system'.

Spatial abilities and spatial egocentrism in the young child
C. Shantz and J. Watson, 1971

AIM/The authors hypothesized that the child's ability to predict the location of objects on a model landscape after he had physically moved around the model was positively related to his ability to identify object locations from another's (doll's) point of view.

SUBJECTS/Forty-eight children (29 boys and 19 girls) were involved from two schools. Three groups of 16 children each were formed at each of age levels six to six-and-a-half years (Group I), five to five years 11 months (Group II) and three years eight months to five years (Group III).

METHOD/These children predicted object sites on a covered landscape after moving $180°$ and $90°$ and on two trials were confronted with a 'trick' perspective. A modified version of Piaget's mountain-scene task was also administered as a measure of spatial egocentrism.

The Box Task/In the Box Task, the child had to predict the location of three objects and to check his predictions by looking 'under the three doors', selected while he was at one position. The trials were given in the same order for all children. The Box was introduced to the child with all its contents.

Altogether a child underwent five trials. The first trial consisted of encouraging the child to remember the location of each object after the box-lid had been closed. A paper clip was placed on the 'door' as a marker. Later the child was asked to check his choices by lifting each 'door' in turn. The entire lid was removed for the child to review the whole landscape again. This was practised on trials 1, 3 and 5. (Fuller details appear in Shantz and Watson, page 175.)

The Doll Task/The child was presented with the landscape and the contents were re-observed. A choice board was presented with the explanation that the photographs showed 'how these things look from different places around the table'. Only two trials were utilized in this task. On trial 1 the child was asked to demonstrate which picture 'shows what you see from here'. Errors were corrected by presenting the right picture. In trial 2, the doll was introduced and placed in a different position and the child was asked to select 'the picture that shows what the doll sees from there'. (Fuller details appear in Shantz and Watson page 175.)

RESULTS/The authors conclude: 'There was a significant relation between the number of errors on the two tasks. Of those children who verbally recognized the first trick perspective, significantly more had some success on the egocentrism task compared with the number of children who completely failed it. Generally, predicting object sites when the child himself moves is an easy task in this age range, but identifying object locations from another's view-point is very difficult. There were no significant differences among the three age groups in accuracy on either task.'

An examination of the developmental relations between certain spatial tasks
G. Y. Larsen and E. Abravanel, 1972

AIM/The authors investigated the sequences of competence for individual children on a group of related spatial tasks, using techniques previously employed by Kooistra (1965) and Smedslund (1964). Specific hypotheses were as follows:

(a) successful operation in the construction of a straight line should precede conservation operativity of distance, length, vertical and horizontal coordinates, measurement of length and coordination of perspective relations;

(b) conservation operativity of distance precedes operativity of length conservation and both of these will precede successful measurement of length;

(c) an awareness of the horizontal and vertical axes of space should follow both the distance and length conservations, but precede successful measurement of length;

(d) within the seven spatial tasks administered, the coordination of perspectives would be the last in the order of acquisition.

SUBJECTS/The total sample of 74 children were of average intelligence. This total comprised 15 kindergarten children ($\overline{X}$ = five years eight months; eight boys, seven girls); 17 six-year-olds ($\overline{X}$ = six years four months; eight boys and nine girls); 10 eight-year-olds ($\overline{X}$ = eight years five months; two boys and eight girls); 11 nine-year-olds ($\overline{X}$ = nine years five months, all girls); and 11 ten-year-olds ($\overline{X}$ = 10 years six months, all girls).

METHOD/The hypothesized order of acquisition and the order of presentation was as follows: (a) Conservation of Distance; (b) Conservation of Length; (c) Construction of a Straight Line; (d) Measurement of Length; (e) Awareness of Horizontal; (f) Awareness of Vertical; (g) Coordination of Perspectives.

The experimental procedure was identical to that of the Geneva Centre. Fuller details are described by Piaget and Inhelder (1956) and Piaget, Inhelder and Szeminska (1960).

RESULTS AND DISCUSSION/The tasks were scored and categorized according to the criteria suggested by Piaget et al. (1956, 1960). Statistical techniques as employed by Kooistra (1965) and Smedslund (1964) were used in the analysis of the data. The resultant patterns indicated that distance and length conservation operativity, together with the awareness of the horizontal and of the vertical, significantly preceded the length measurement. However, no developmental order among the four tasks was observed. This finding does not support those reported by Shantz and Smock (1966) who found a priority of distance conservation over the awareness of the horizontal.

Further, there appeared a close correspondence at all ages in the conservation of distance and length. Likewise, appreciation of the horizontal and vertical coordinates of space developed closely in the overall rates of acquisition. Moreover, the construction of a straight line was in advance of operations involved in measurement. Larsen and Abravanel maintain that only sub-patterns of progression in spatial acquisition were evidenced.

However, a big discrepancy in the hypothesized order was observed in the construction of a straight line. Its acquisition was not essential for the concepts of distance, length, nor the horizontal and vertical coordinates, to be fully operative.

CHAPTER SEVEN
THE DEVELOPMENT OF REASONING
AMONG HANDICAPPED CHILDREN

I. Intellectual Handicap

'The Diagnosis of Reasoning in the Retarded' by Inhelder (1968, — French edition 1943) relates Piaget's theory to the area of retardation. She found that severely retarded subjects remained at the sensori-motor stage. Trainable children functioned at a pre-operational level, whereas the retarded educables arrived at the stage of concrete operations. No retardate reached the stage of formal operations because the development of retardates proceeded more slowly than that of normals. Piaget and Inhelder (1947) suggested that retardation may result from a 'partial or total stop in mental functions at a certain level of normal development'.

In an attempt to study severely mentally retarded children and to validate Piaget's sensori-motor stage, Woodward's study (1959) involved 147 subjects whose mental age was less than two years, although their chronological ages ranged from seven to 11. This study investigated a method of classifying the severely sub-normal in terms of the six stages of sensori-motor development which have been distinguished by Piaget (1953, 1955). The stage occurs in normals from birth to approximately two years. The performance was hierarchical, that is, retardates who performed at the most advanced sub-stages had successful performances at all preceding sub-stages. In another attempt, Woodward, in collaboration with Stern (1963), carried out an investigation related to the developmental patterns of severely sub-normal children. They found that severely retarded children who functioned at sub-stage six (highest stage of sensori-motor development) differed significantly from those at sub-stage five and below on a measure of verbal comprehension. Their results support Piaget's contention that the achievements at the sixth sub-stage of the sensori-motor period, a stage which deals with concepts of object permanency, were a necessary prerequisite for the acquisition of meaningful speech. (Fuller details of the study appear later in this chapter.)

Woodward (1972) analysed the problem-solving strategies utilized by normal and severely-sub-normal children in tasks demanding rapid reasoning. The subjects were, chronologically, in the period between the end of Piaget's sensori-motor stage and the beginning of the intuitive. The results were discussed in relation to those reported by Piaget (1955), Luria (1961), and Woodward's results of her earlier studies (1959, 1961, 1962 and, with Stern, 1963). A further discussion of the behavioural responses have been analysed in terms of 'the plan and TOTE unit concept', as postulated by Miller et al. (1960) and discussed in terms of neurophysiology by Pribram (1960). (Full details appear later in this chapter.)

Among studies which replicate Piaget's work on number with educationally sub-normal children, is that of Williams (1958). The study demonstrated how some children performed mechanical 'sums' and arrived at the correct solutions without understanding the basic principles and number relationships in simple operations. This was true for both normal and ESN children. Williams has argued that formal work might prove positively more harmful, under specific circumstances, and goes on to suggest practical programmes in the assessment of 'number readiness'. Another important feature of the study indicated the caution in understanding the term 'activity' within a class-room setting. Williams observed children who demonstrated elements of greater mental strategies and mobility of thought by watching other children attempting to operate a practical task, than by participating themselves. (Further details can be obtained from Williams, 1958 and Lunzer, 1960.)

Consistent with Williams, Mannix (1959) found that the ESN children involved in his study gave pre-operational and operational responses, typical of the Geneva children. The study utilized a scalogram analysis. Results indicated that the full comprehension of number is a single progression, with 'provoked - correspondence' as its starting point and with the conservation of continuous quantities proving more difficult. The item in which the majority of children remained at the non-conservation stage was the additive composition of groups. Mannix concludes that the nature and the discrimination power of the task itself predicts the degree to which a child may fluctuate between operational and pre-operational behaviour. Finally, counting appeared to be the operation preferred by ESN children when faced with a number problem but 'correspondence may be substituted if the test situation makes counting difficult'. (Further details appear in Mannix, 1959, and Lunzer, 1960.)

William's finding (op. cit.), that a number of children can achieve some degree of competence in mechanical arithmetic without a basic understanding of number, was confirmed by Hood's study (1962) which involved 125 normal British children aged five to eight as well as two groups of sub-normals. The Piagetian tasks involved the concepts of conservation of liquid, sets of chips as well as sets of functionally related objects. Hood's study demonstrated the close relation between mental age and cognitive operativity.

Clarke (1962) undertook a series of 10 studies involving subjects who were educationally backward, with a reading retardation of 18 months or more. He attempted to establish levels of operativity in situations involving number and spatial relationships. He examined whether the subjects functioned at a single stage on a series of experimental tasks, or whether they fluctuated from one situation to another. (Details are given later in this chapter. See also studies by Woodward, 1961, and Gruen and Vore, 1972, details of which appear later in this chapter.)

Willington (1967), in an investigation relating to the growth of mathematical understanding in children aged six to 10, identified five main stages. He maintains that 'four of these are common to all the concrete mathematical situations, but the fifth relates only to those tests presented in the algebraical context and to the distributive law'. Willington elaborates that the child's comprehension of mathematics occurs later than the conservation of number and takes place 'over a period of some two to three years for those situations presented in the arithmetical context and which only call for the development of a generally applicable method of calculation'. Most of the 10-year-olds comprehended the basic mathematical principles and the Educationally sub-normal children performed at lower levels of operativity in all situations.

Although proceeding at a much slower rate, retardates' concepts of time were found by Lovell and Slater (1960, and described later in this chapter) to follow approximately the same sequence of development as in normals, when performances on Piagetian assessments were compared with that on standard tests in normals. Another investigation indicating a specific retardation in the sub-normal in the growth of the concept of speed was carried out by Lovell, Kellett and Moorhouse (1962 — details of which appear later in this Chapter). 'It appears that even at school-leaving age, the majority of ESN school pupils have a limited understanding of speed in the sense of distance per unit of time.'

Lovell, Healey and Rowland (1962) administered 12 experiments drawn from 'The Child's Conception of Geometry' (Piaget, 1960) to a population of normal and educationally sub-normal children. The findings broadly confirmed those of Piaget, 'although the numbers of children at the various stages were not always what one might expect from the results obtained from the Geneva children'. It was also found that 14- to 15-year-old ESN children had the operational mobility of about an average seven-and-a-half-year old. (The study is described below.)

Woodward's study (1962) was concerned with the acquisitional patterns of space concepts in the mentally sub-normal, the results of which indicated that the responses resembled those of normal children aged four to seven years. Most subjects performed consistently either at the concrete operational stage or at the intuitive level for all the tasks. (Details are given below.)

A comparison of the performance of ESN with that of normals on classification tasks carried out by Lovell, Mitchell and Everett (1962, and described later in this chapter) demonstrated that the ESN group was more capable in situations involving tactile-kinaesthetic perception than in those involving visual perception. Also, the ESN children experienced difficulty in naming the common quality of the elements after correct classification had been achieved. It was suggested that initial classificatory processes do not rely greatly on language, although later skill in class-extension and class-inclusion does. Operational mobility achieved by the subject was demonstrated by his skill in co-ordinating an increasing number of variables as the criterion for classification changed.

Jackson's (1965) investigation involved retarded educable children aged seven to 15 years, ranging in IQ from 60 to 80. Jackson administered six tasks drawn from Inhelder and Piaget's 'The Growth of Logical Thinking'. He found that 95 per cent of the subjects had not surpassed the initial level of concrete operations, and no retarded subject reached the stage of formal operations. Little improvement occurred in the reasoning of retardates beyond the age of nine; further, some deterioration was observed between the ages of 13 and 15. 'For a good deal of these pupils' school lives, learning consists of a linear series of actions at the level of pre-operational thought, and it is only in later school years that first-order operational schemata develop; and this is only a proportion of these pupils.' (Lovell, 1968, cited in Butcher, 1968, p. 121.)

Piaget (1928) devised two tests to evaluate children's understanding of relations, one dealing with left-right concept and the other with brother-sister concept. He maintains that young children show considerable difficulty in conceptualizing relations, as compared to classes and absolutes. Such thinking has been characterized as egocentric. MacManis (1969, described later) focuses on a number of early studies which attempt to expound the relationship between mental age and relative thinking. He cites the work of Elkind, Kooistra, Lane and Kinder and Prothro respectively, as follows. Elkind's (1961, 1962) results corresponded with Piaget's with no more than a one-year discrepancy on any sub-test. The three stages in the development of left-right conceptions were observed. However, with the brother-sister test, Elkind's seven-year-old subjects demonstrated operativity while Piaget's subjects showed operational behaviour at CA 10. Elkind attributes the discrepancy to family size. Kooistra (1963) attempted to establish the existence of a relationship between MA and relative thinking. The children involved were drawn from four CA levels (four to seven inclusive), with an IQ range of 118-160. While Kooistra's study furnished evidence of the relation between MA and relative thinking by children of superior intelligence, such evidence with retardates is less satisfactory. Lane and Kinder (1939) examined the relationship between MA and relativism in retardates of CA 16, at four MA levels (six, eight, 10, and 12 years). The mean IQs of these groups also differed as follows: 38, 51, 64 and 77 for MA 6-12, respectively. Another group of children with a mean CA of 12 years, one month and a mean IQ of 64, at the eight-year MA level, was also included.

Generally, the results supported those of Piaget, with children of different CA levels. An analysis of the protocols indicated a retardate deficit in certain areas. However, Lane and Kinder's results must be interpreted with some caution. The study contains several design problems: for example, MA and IQ were indistinguishable, since CA was held constant in four of the five groups. Consequently, the separate effects of MA and IQ on the children's relative thinking is difficult to evaluate. Likewise, Prothro's study (1943) does not permit a satisfactory assessment of the MA — relativism relationship. This is partly due to the restricted MA range of the sample. The normal (IQ range 92-136, CA range four to seven) and retarded groups (IQ range 34-46, CA range 17-46) were matched for MA between five years, one month and six years, 11 months. The behavioural responses on Piaget's left-right test were analysed and the two groups demonstrated comparable performance, in that neither IQ group showed relative thinking with respect to right and left.

McManis therefore attempted to overcome the discrepancies with respect to the above studies, while demonstrating the relationship between MA and relative thinking in normal children of average intelligence and in institutionalized retardates. Elkind's (1961, 1962) results were not substantiated in their entirety but some similarities were observed in results obtained by Piaget and Elkind — in that McManis showed an orderly progression from one stage of relational thinking to the next. This was true both for normal and retarded children. He concludes, 'if, as Piaget has stated, the lack of true relational thinking poses an obstacle to the development of operational thinking, efforts to train retardates for community placement could be greatly hampered by such a relational thinking deficit'. (Details are given later in this Section; Cf. Lerner and Lehrer, 1972.)

A survey of the literature reveals limited research into the assessment of the operational processes as they appear or fail to appear in retardates of various age groups. A cross-sectional and longitudinal approach which directed attention to the thought processes of normals and retardates was undertaken in a study by Stephens, Miller and McLaughlin (1969). The results of Phase One revealed that operativity as indicated by normal subjects superseded that of retardates on each reasoning task. The normals performed at a higher operational level than retardates in all the three areas of development measured: reasoning, moral judgement and moral conduct. (The study is described later in this chapter.) Phase Two (1972a) indicates that 'reasoning development proceeded in retardates, ages 16 to 20, although tempo was decelerated; ... differences continued between the operational thought of normals and retardates'. In many instances retardates did not acquire the structures required of concrete logical thought until late adolescence or young adulthood. While the study provided a general indication that young adult retardates continued to make gains in reasoning ability, 'additional longitudinal data to be obtained during waves Three and Four are needed to determine the extent of this growth period' (private communication). This research project has implications for rehabilitation and social workers. The data also indicated that the Piagetian reasoning assessments measure areas distinct from those represented by standard intelligence tests and that 'training programmes should supply activities derived from these factors'. The study by Wachs (1970) involving pre-school retarded children and using the IPDS (see Uzgiris and Hunt, 1966, described in Chapter One), concluded that the Piaget-based IPDS proved a more sensitive measure of the different types of abilities than the traditional IQ tests. This sensitivity was more pronounced within the lower ranges of IQ. Wachs recommends its applicability for the retarded in terms of setting up remediation and training programmes. (The study is described later in this chapter.)

Bovet, 1968, concludes: 'it would seem that well designed exercises, based on what is already known of normal development can have a beneficial effect in certain cases of mental retardation. No doubt, there are limits to the usefulness of such exercises and ... they would have to be used as early as possible ... that even deviations in the course of development are up to a certain point amenable to correction and that optimal conditions of learning can bring about a higher level of development than might have been thought possible.'

The growth of the concept of time: a comparative study
K. Lovell and A. Slater, 1960

AIM/The authors were intent to investigate the concept of time among normals and retardates. The study had a total sample population of 100 children.

SUBJECTS/Ten children were selected at each age level from five to nine inclusive. These 50 normal children were assessed by their respective class teachers to be average to above-average in attainment. Slow-learning children were excluded. The remainder of the children were selected from each of the age groups eight to 11 inclusive, with 10 in the 15-year-old group. These 50 children were drawn from a school for ESN children.

METHOD/The authors administered seven experiments in all.
(a) In order to examine simultaneity, equality of synchronous intervals, and order of events, Lovell and Slater employed three experiments, identical to Piaget (1946).
(b) Two experiments were administered to examine the concept of age. Details of these experiments are given in Piaget (1946).
(c) The development of the awareness of interior time was investigated through a series of two experiments. (i) 'Each child was asked to compare the time spent sitting with eyes closed and arms folded, with a period of equal duration (1 minute) spent looking at a picture book.' (ii) 'Each child was asked to compare the time spent drawing lines, rapidly, with a period of equal duration (1 minute) spent drawing lines carefully and slowly using a ruler.'

RESULTS/Overall, Lovell and Slater's study supported Piaget's (1946) contentions regarding the concept of time in normal and retardates. 'Summing up, we may say that the understanding of simultaneity, equality of synchronous intervals, order of events, age and estimation of interior time follows roughly the same sequence in ESN children as in normal infant and junior school children but the stages in understanding are reached some years later. Our results suggest that, apart from the perception of simultaneity, the 15-year-old ESN pupil is still a little behind the average to bright nine-year-old child in his understanding of the rest of the tasks examined.'

Concepts of number of the mentally sub-normal studied by Piaget's method
M. Woodward, 1961

AIMS/The author was interested in two hypotheses: firstly, that the type of reasoning demonstrated by normal children in the acquisition of the concept of Number would also be projected by sub-normal subjects; and secondly, that an identical type of thinking would be evidenced for all number problems.

SUBJECTS/The subjects included 50 adults and 44 children, who were residents either in hospitals or hostels. The median age of the adults (22 men and 28 women) was 19 years (Q = 2.25). Full-scale IQs on WAIS of 28 of them ranged from 44 to 73 (Median = 49.5, Q = 5). Six without adequate speech had performance scale IQs (WAIS) from under 44-51; the remaining 16, who did not score on WAIS, obtained a mean IQ of 32 (Revised Stanford-Binet Scale; Q = 4.75).

In the group of children — 25 boys and 19 girls — the mean age was 12 years, nine months (Q = 1.4). Forty-three children obtained IQs ranging from 25 to 55 (Median = 34, Q = 6). One child had speech handicaps and on the Performance Scale of WISC, obtained an IQ of under 44. All children were in-patients and attended the hospital training centre.

METHOD/Woodward administered four of the experiments on the growth of the concepts of number, described in 'The Child's Conception of Number' (Piaget 1952b). These tasks were: (a) One-to-one correspondence and equivalence of corresponding sets; (b) Equalizing unequal groups; (c) Seriation; (d) Conservation of continuous quantity.

RESULTS/The results suggested that sub-normal adults and children demonstrated similar types of thinking as normal children of four to seven years when dealing with tasks of number concepts. Behavioural responses also emerged which were identical to Piaget's, specifically in experiments of one-one correspondence, equalizing unequal groups, and seriation. However, this pattern did not emerge in conservation of continuous quantity. Woodward argues that modification in experimental procedure may have been partly responsible for this discrepancy. She finally maintains that '. . . intellectually sub-normal individuals with similar experiences to those of the group investigated reach a relatively advanced level for problems involving a one-one correspondence between two sets of objects, and a belief in the numerical equivalence of the two sets, before they do so for problems involving series and part-whole relations. It is suggested that Piaget's approach has clinical and educational applications to mental subnormality.'

Some aspects of problem solving in older backward children — an introductory note to a series of experiments conducted during the period 1959-1962
D. F. Clarke, 1962

Introduction
    Piaget was the first worker to investigate in a systematic way the development of intellectual awareness in children from a genetic point of view, whilst Bruner tried to gain more precise ideas about concept attainment in mature adults.

    This series of researches was an attempt to follow the two approaches with regard to some 30 older educationally backward children between 11 and 15 years of age, with the initial criteria of backwardness based on reading ages (retarded by 18 months or more) so as to investigate their levels of reasoning in concept formation and the method they tend to use in some aspects of problem solving.

    The writer wanted to find out something about the levels of understanding in these children when they were confronted with situations involving spatial relationships and number; whether they functioned at a single stage throughout the series of experiments or whether they varied from situation to situation. Another objective was to discover if the stages followed the same pattern of development as that described by Piaget and if there was any single factor common to all the tests.

    The spatial tests were adapted from those conducted by Piaget; the two models of farmyards at $180°$ to each other and the model village (Euclidean relationships). The number tests followed Piaget's experiments on the conservation of discrete quantity, number involving cardination and ordination, and additive composition of classes.

    In order to investigate the ways in which these children went about certain kinds of problem solving, two games of 'Battle-ships' were used, with a time lapse of five months between the experimental sessions. These problems involved the use of judgement, foresight and the use of limited resources. It was hoped that some of the characteristic strategies described by Bruner would emerge.

    Problems involving non-verbal and verbal reasoning were also employed, namely the Ravens Progressive Matrices Tests (1947 A, Ab, B) and the Wechsler Intelligence Scale for Children (verbal). Two sessions with the Ravens Progressive Matrices Tests were held with a gap of seven months in between. The second involved verbal reasoning wherein it was hoped to discover if learning took place when verbal explanations were involved, and if any improvement in grades were made since the first test.

All experiments were related to the WISC. The Piaget and Raven Tests were analysed by the Guttman Scalogram technique to see if any single factor dominated and to pinpoint any failures of thinking skills.

The children selected for the series of experiments

A preliminary group of 50 children was selected mainly from the lowest streams of a large city Secondary Modern School (1960-1). The group also included four brighter children and four of the dullest who could be found. The ages of the group ranged from 11+ years to 15 years. The first game of 'Battleships' was administered as a pilot study, followed a month later by the first test of Ravens Progressive Matrices (A, Ab, B). This test was given to form a basis for selecting 30 children for the experimental work. The children who secured the lowest grades were chosen but the four brightest were included to balance the four very dull. The Ravens Test was designed for children up to 10+ to 11 years and so it was considered that any moderate or low grades secured in this procedure would provide reasonable criteria for establishing at least some aspects of backwardness. Low reading ages were also regarded as being indicative where a retardation of greater than 18 months on the Schonell Word Recognition Test was obtained.

The mean score for the first Ravens Test was 25, and for the second test seven months later, when it included verbal reasoning, it was 30.

The first game of 'Battleships' (strategies in problem solving)
Number of children = 50

AIM/(a) To find out the kinds of 'strategies' which backward children tend to use in a problem involving the securing and building up of information from clues, (b) to see how these children use their collected data and whether they bear in mind the limited number of shots they have at their disposal, the kinds of targets they have hit and the kinds of targets left; (c) to discover the overall method in going about the task as a whole, whether a 'safe' method of attack is used or whether risks are taken; and (d) to see if recapitulation forms any part of their scheme.

METHOD/The subject is seated opposite the tester with the table between. The subject has a chart similar to that of the tester — but without the battleships marked in.

A low screen is placed between the tester and the subject so that the subject cannot see the tester's chart, but can speak to him.

A key is drawn on to a paper explaining the number of ships and the values of each in terms of squares. This key is given to the subject for reference. The situation is as follows: the subject is 'defending' an island which is under attack by an enemy fleet. Although he knows the number and types of ships, he does not know their positions. His task is to sink all the ships and he is allowed 70 shots out of the 100 possible targets afforded by the chart. The chart is divided into 100 squares (10 x 10) which are lettered along the top and numbered along the side. The subject gives the letter and number of each square he selects as a target, and the tester tells him if he has secured a hit or sustained a miss. The enemy fleet consists of the following: 1 battleship (5 squares); 2 cruisers (3 squares each); 3 destroyers (2 squares each); 4 corvettes (1 square each).

The squares which make up each ship are next to each other either horizontally, vertically or diagonally. It is necessary to secure five hits to sink the battleship, three to sink each cruiser, two each to sink each destroyer and one for each corvette.

INSTRUCTIONS/The problem was explained to each subject as follows: 'This is a game of "Battleships". The game is that my fleet is attacking your island and you must try to sink all my ships. I have a chart like yours; but mine has the ships marked on it. You can see from the paper (key) how my fleet is made up and the number of squares there are to each ship.

You are defending an island and you have only seventy rounds of ammunition. Your chart has one hundred squares with letters along the top and numbers down the side.

My ships are placed somewhere in these squares. When you choose a square, tell me the letter and the number, and I will let you know if you have scored a hit, or if you have missed. If you get a hit, mark your square with a cross, if you miss, put a 'o'. That way you will slowly build up a picture of my fleet.

Your job is not only to sink my ships, but to find out where they are. If only one ship gets through you have lost . . . Do you understand what you have to do? . . . Any questions? . . . Would you like me to explain once more?'

The second game of 'Battleships' Number of children = 30

AIM/(a) To see if any learning had taken place since the first game (five months earlier); and (b) to introduce a tighter control by introducing a time factor towards the end of the test to discover if strategies were affected in any way.

METHOD/The disposition of the ships was changed. The same remarks were made as in the first game but some additional comments were added to the end as follows. 'I will let you know when you have had 35 shots, when you have 20 left and when you have 10 left. The ships are placed in different positions from the last game.' When 40 shots had been fired an 'urgency' situation was introduced as follows (2nd test). 'Hurry up. Your time is nearly up.' After the testing session (test two) each subject was asked, 'Can you tell me if you were working to any special plan?'

The model farmyards (Euclidean relationships — Piaget) n = 25

This experiment was adapted from Piaget's experiments with Genevan children of normal and superior intelligence. The writer conducted this experiment with a small group of backward children at Leeds University under the guidance of Lovell.

AIM/The aim of this investigation was to find out how older backward children function when confronted with a problem which involves Euclidean relationships in a spatial context. Piaget was concerned to discover if Euclidean and projective concepts evolved together and were mutually interdependent. He pointed to the way in which the simple topological notions, with which the children began to construct the notion of space, developed through projective into Euclidean concepts. The results of the Leeds experiments showed that backward children often got no further than projective concepts in physical frames of reference. It was the purpose of this investigation to discover whether Euclidean concepts develop in older backward children at a later age or whether they get no further than projective (or even topological) ideas of space. These test results were also compared with the strategies used in problem solving in order to see if any relationship existed between certain strategies in focus or conservative scanning and the location of a given object in a situation which involved reversibility of thought. (All the Piaget tests were evaluated by the Guttman Scalogram to reveal any common factors.)

The model village (diagrammatic layouts — Piaget) n = 24

This was adapted from Piaget's experiment with diagrammatic layouts and was used by him as an extension of the model farms test. This test was also used by the writer with the Leeds group.

AIM/To see how the children worked in a situation which involved the reduction to scale (similarity and proportion), of a number of objects placed on a box. The scale plan has to be drawn from an angle of 45° but the problem requires a 90° plan view. This situation involves topological, projective and Euclidean relationships together with concepts of similarity, proportion, parallelism, angles and straight lines.

As with the last problem, it was hoped to compare older children's methods of working in these situations with the earlier spatial problems involving reversibility of thought in physical frames of reference, and the methods of working in 'Battleships' games. The question asked here is: 'do these older children remain at a topological or projective level in their thinking or do they advance to hypothetical deductive reasoning at a later age?'

The peas and jars (conservation of discrete quantity — Piaget) n = 27

This experiment was adapted from Piaget's study into the conservation of discontinuous or discrete quantity with children of normal or above normal intelligence.

AIM/The aim of this inquiry was to discover whether older backward children have the notion of invariance free from perceptual relationship of discrete quantity, or proceed no further than conservation.

As with the experiment regarding physical frames of reference, it was intended to see if older backward children develop much beyond concrete operations, and if their functioning varies within the test situation.

The pink and white beads (additive composition of classes — Piaget) n = 27

AIM/This experiment was again adapted from Piaget. The aim here was to see how the older backward children of the London group functioned in a situation which involved the manipulation of two factors at one and the same moment, namely the relationship of classes and constituent sub-classes. It was hoped to reveal the levels of these children's thinking in this situation, whether operational thought involving reversibility was reached or maintained, and whether 'stages' of thinking fluctuated within the test.

203

The Ravens Progressive Matrices Tests (1st and 2nd sessions)
Number of children for first session = 50. Number of children for second session = 26.

AIM/To find out how the children of the London group scored on this non-verbal reasoning test and how they scored on a repeat, some seven months later when a verbal factor was introduced wherein they had to give the reasons for their selections and were allowed to correct their earlier mistakes. Resulting grades were compared. The first session was also instrumental in establishing the group to be selected for the whole series of experiments. The second session results were given the Guttman Scalogram analysis to see if any governing factors emerged and to aid comparison with the Piaget tests.

The doll and fences (number involving ordination and cardination – Piaget) n = 27
This experiment was adapted from Piaget's investigation of seriation, ordination and cardination, and it included some modifications of his procedure.

AIM/The aim of this inquiry was to find out the stages of reasoning in a group of backward children in problems where they have to relate (a) the cardinal number of a group of fences with the position of a given fence in a series, (b) the ordinal and cardinal numbers of a group of fences determined by the cardinal number of the mats, and (c) seriation of elements when the physical arrangement is disturbed. The relationship of (n + 1) mats to n fences was also involved.
This experiment differed from Piaget's since the fences (or walls) and mats were arranged simultaneously by the tester. This was punctuated by questions about the relationship of mats to fences.
The questioning proceeded in a similar way to Piaget's from then on, except that seriation had to be made after the elements had been disturbed without the fences being handled or being replaced into order again. This introduced a conflict similar to that in the experiment with the peas and jars of perceptual relationships and 'conservation'. The subject had to bear in mind the order of the series when he was faced with the elements out of their correct placing.

General comments and summary of main findings
1. On the whole the group of backward children performed in a characteristic way; they varied in levels of thinking from test to test and from question to question within each test; they

worked in a patchy and 'jerky' sort of way.

2. In problems involving the use of clues (in the 'Battleships' games), they tended to work in two or three typical ways. Most of the children used encircling methods together with recapitulation in utilizing previously secured information. Some persevered, often after the puzzle was under way; a number also seemed to take risks to secure more information or to save time; or perhaps just for a change.

3. Children often went beyond the possible limits of targets and although targets could have been joined together the subjects still probably forgot the nature of that which they were seeking to discover.

4. Children tended, very slightly, to use fewer methods of working in the second game of 'Battleships'. Perhaps some learning had carried over, and possibly a more economical method of attack had been developed. In any case the difference was not great.

5. Most methods seemed common to all quartiles in the IQ range, although perseverance and random approaches were confined to the lower half, and awareness of most or all aspects of the problem was confined to the upper quartile.

6. The profiles showed wide variations of working between and within tests.

7. The more intelligent children showed the highest degree of variation between the sub-tests of the WISC.

8. The WISC scores were about the dull or dull-borderline level but four children secured high scores. The mean IQ was 85.4. The lowest IQ score was 62, the highest four were 101, 114, 121, and 129.

9. In the spatial and Number tests (Piaget) the children worked in ways similar to those described by Piaget.

10. Variation from stage one to stage three occurred between and within tests, with much overlapping.

11. Tests involving reversibility and manipulation of multiple factors proved to be the most difficult for these children.

12. Tests involving projection, conservation and invariance seemed to give less trouble.

13. Relationships between ordination/cardination and seriation were disturbed when visual perception was interfered with, even after demonstration on a model showing exaggerated gradations in a series was carried out.

14. Backward children of 11 to 15, whilst sometimes working at intuitive levels, and mainly at concrete levels of reasoning, can nevertheless pass into the third stage of hypothetico-deductive reasoning under certain circumstances but these are temporary phenomena.

15. On the whole, however, they work mainly at concrete levels of reasoning.

16. The Ravens Progressive Matrices test results showed in the first instance, an average score of 25, and in the second instance an average score of 30.

17. Verbalizing helps in problem solving.

18. The Ravens Tests, when subjected to scalogram analysis, revealed a different order of difficulty from that listed in the manual.

19. Factors other than those of matching and analogies enter in, notably colour, texture, numbers of aspects to be thought of, individual internal configuration of elements, all of which contribute to the problem.

20. The 'gestalt' of each puzzle may well be an important factor.

21. The patchiness of the performance of these children could be due to their lack of sustained and combined application when confronted with new situations. Perhaps we should think not of levels of thinking but of manner of approach when discussing the problem solving of backward children.

22. Perhaps consistency of approach or steadiness of thinking are useful ideas. It will be remembered that these children used a wider variety of approaches in the first game of battleships and a more restricted, but perhaps slightly more controlled approach in the second, where learning effect may have had an influence on performance.

23. Could these varieties of approach have something to do with the shifting of orientation in productive thinking? Is it possible that a more intelligent person 'keeps at it' more consistently only changing his attack when he sees that it is likely to be helpful?

24. Is economy of effort a sign of intellectual strength? Could these varied attacks and shifts of position be a typical wastage of effort due to lack of insight, or aim, or motivation or interest?

25. Does verbalizing help to 'channel' this effort by giving voice to thought leading it in conserving energy?

26. What part does motivation play?

The growth of some geometrical concepts
K. Lovell, D. Healey and A. Rowland, 1962

SUBJECTS/(a) Ten children in the five-year-old age group, and 15 in each of the age groups six, seven, eight and nine, making a sub-total of 70 children, representing all levels of ability. (b) Ten children in each of the age groups nine, 10, 11, 13 and 14 in an ESN school. (c) a sample of 70 children based on the same criteria as (a) above. (d) Ten children in each of the age groups nine, 10, 11, 14 and 15 in an ESN school.

METHOD/The 12 experiments utilized in the study were patterned after Piaget (1960).
(i) Reconstructing relations of distances.
(ii) Conservation of length: the length of lines and the coincidence of their extremities.
(iii) Conservation of length: comparison of length and change of position.
(iv) Measurement of length.
(v) Subdividing a straight line.
(vi) Locating a point in two-dimensional space.
(vii) Angular measurement: measuring angles.
(viii) Angular measurement: measuring triangles.
(ix) A problem of geometrical loci. The straight line.
(x) Subtracting smaller congruent areas from larger congruent areas.
(xi) The measurement of areas. Unit iteration.
(xii) Subdivision of areas and the concept of fractions.

RESULTS/The findings broadly confirmed those of Piaget, although the numbers of children at the various stages were not always what one might expect from the results obtained from the Geneva children. It was found that 14- to 15-year-old ESN children had the operational mobility of about an average seven-and-a-half year old. The authors conclude by drawing attention to the significant educational implications of the various tasks in 'The Child's Conception of Geometry' (Piaget 1960). 'It is not . . . suggested that measurement be postponed until it can be fully understood. Rather, the experiences the child undergoes help to build up "schemas" out of which arises later understanding. The important thing for the teacher is to know to what extent he is performing a given operation with understanding and to what extent he is performing in the rote fashion.'

The growth of the concept of speed: a comparative study
K. Lovell, V. Kellett and E. Moorhouse, 1962

AIMS/The authors addressed their inquiry to the following aspects: (i) the intuition of speed; (ii) the growth of relations of speed in synchronous movements; (iii) the patterning of an understanding of relative speeds; and (iv) the conservation of uniform speeds.

SUBJECTS/A total sample of 100 children was involved: 10 children from each age group five years to 10 years were selected, representing various levels of ability, and making a sub-total of 60. The remaining 40 children were drawn from an ESN school consisting of 10 children each at age levels 10, 12, 14 and 15 years.

METHOD/In order to examine the intuition of speed, Lovell et al. administered five experiments, drawn from the work of Piaget (1946). Briefly, these tasks consisted of: (a) the tunnel experiments; unequal distances, same times; (b) unequal distances; different times; (c) unequal distances; same times; (d) straight and wavy roads, unequal distances, same time; and (e) concentric circles; different distances, same time.

RESULTS/The overall findings indicated developmental patterns as postulated by Piaget (1946), thereby corroborating the Piagetian concepts. The performance of ESN children was, however, slower: '. . . even at 15 years of age, [it] is scarcely equal to that of the seven- to eight-year-olds in the primary school when the whole range of experiments is considered. It appears that even at school-leaving age, the majority of ESN school pupils have a limited understanding of speed in the sense of distance per unit time.'

An experimental study of the growth of some logical structures
K. Lovell, B. Mitchell and I. R. Everett, 1962

AIMS/Lovell, Mitchell and Everett assessed the developmental patterns on various tasks drawn from Piaget's and Inhelder's (1959) book 'La Genèse des Structures Logiques Elémentaires'. Additional experiments were drawn from 'The Child's Conception of Number' (1952b).

FIRST SERIES OF EXPERIMENTS/Subjects/In the first series of experiments the sample population comprised 10 children, in each of the age groups five to 10 years; representing all levels of ability. Another 10 children were selected from an ESN school in each of the age groups nine, 11, 13, 15.

METHOD/This series of experiments consisted of the following tasks: (a) spontaneous classification of geometrical shapes and letters: additive classification; (b) multiplicate classification; (c) anticipation and visual seriation; (d) multiplication of asymmetrical transitive relations; (e) hierarchical classification of animals.

SECOND SERIES OF EXPERIMENTS/Subjects/The second series of experiments, listed below, were administered to 10 children at each age level five years to 11 years inclusive and representing all ability levels. Another group of 25 children in each of the age ranges 10 to 15 years were also involved, drawn from ESN schools.

METHOD/The various tasks administered were: (a) visual classification; (b) tactile-kinaesthetic classification; (c) additive composition of classes involving marked perceptual differences; (d) the use of the words 'all' and 'some' in situations involving colour and weight.

RESULTS/The authors conclude that their findings are in agreement with those of Piaget and Inhelder and lend further support to other studies. 'It has been possible to confirm many of their (Piaget and Inhelder) predictions by giving a number of tests to the same pupils: these pupils being drawn from a known population of school children. In addition the work has been extended to cover ESN special school pupils and it has shown the limited ability of the pupils to develop logical structures.'

Concepts of space in the mentally sub-normal, studied by Piaget's method
M. Woodward, 1962

AIMS/Woodward addressed her inquiry to the acquisitional patterns of space concepts in the mentally subnormal. She postulated that the same kinds of reasoning. in relation to space concepts would be observed in the subnormal children as those found in the Swiss children, over and above an identical sequential development; further, that this type of thinking would be extended to all spatial concepts.

SUBJECTS/The study involved 94 children whose developmental patterns were studied in a previous investigation (Woodward, 1961) together with adults. The median IQ (WAIS) for the adult group, who had a mean chronological age of 19 years, was 49.5. The children, with a mean chronological age of 12 years, had a mean IQ (Revised Stanford-Binet) of 34. Moreover, 20 per cent of the adults and 43 per cent of the children were Mongols. Thirty per cent and 18 per cent of each group respectively demonstrated clinical signs of 'structural or metabolic abnormality of the brain'.

METHOD/Woodward administered three tasks drawn from the work of Piaget and Inhelder (1956):

(a) Linear and Circular Order was investigated in four steps: row in direct order; circular to linear order; row in reverse order; and a figure of eight.

(b) The Drawings task involved 21 figures used by Piaget and Inhelder (1956, p. 54) which were presented to the subjects one at a time, together with the request to copy them.

(c) The Reference Points experiment was identical to Piaget and Inhelder (1956, pp. 125-53). The task was to assess the child's use of external reference points in order to demonstrate the level of water in a jar.

RESULTS/The responses resembled those of normal children aged four to seven years. Most subjects performed consistently either at the concrete operational stage or at the intuitive level for all the tasks. A transitional stage was also evidenced. For example, on the Linear and Circular Order experiment, the pattern of the 94 subjects on the four tasks was as follows: in the figure of eight task, 18 subjects performed at the operational level; 33 subjects were successful in the Reversed Row task; and 55 and 67 passed the Circle task and Direct row displaced, respectively. Woodward argues that the order of difficulty for the upside-down, horizontal and tilted positions (with regard to experiment three) was identical to that described by Piaget and Inhelder (1956). When she made a comparison of the results of the three experiments on concepts of space, Woodward found that in terms of operational with non-operational categories, 73 per cent of the group showed an identical type of thinking for the drawing/spatial order comparison, 96 per cent for drawing/reference points comparison and 62 per cent for the spatial-order/reference points comparison.

Woodward concludes that the Mongol subjects did not differ significantly from non-Mongols in any respect. Likewise, adults were not differentiated from children by their results. Moreover, identical types of responses were found among subnormal subjects and Piaget's Swiss children aged four to seven years, in relation to number and spatial concept development. She also maintains that the spatial concept development indicated the sequence postulated by Piaget and Inhelder (1956).

Developmental patterns of severely subnormal children
M. Woodward and D. J. Stern, 1963

AIMS/Woodward and Stern's study addressed itself to examine the developmental patterns in severely subnormal young children and to evaluate the locomotor, language and social development of children assessed at sensori-motor stages.

SUBJECTS/A sample of 83 children was selected from a Hospital, excluding children with cerebral palsy, gross hydro-cephalus, visual or auditory handicap and those with IQs over 50. The total comprised 51 boys and 32 girls with CA 11 months to eight years, seven months (mean age = 4.85 years). Three children scored 42, 41 and 31 IQs on the Terman-Merrill, 49 subjects failed all six items on the scale and the rest failed one or more of the items on this scale.

METHOD/The general method involved the main classification in terms of Piaget's six sensori-motor stages. Additional data were gathered by administering selected tasks from the Revised Stanford-Binet (Terman and Merrill, 1937) and Merrill-Palmer (Stutsman, 1931).

Gesell's schedule (Gesell, 1940, 1941) was employed in the assessment of locomotor development, although certain items in the locomotor section had either to be modified or omitted (e.g. the imitative items had to be excluded). However, the general principles underlying the schedule were not violated. The language sections of the developmental scales included items of vocalization and comprehension. For speech development the vocalization items were extracted from the Gesell's scale together with the specified age-norms. The development of socialization included the observed behaviour of the child to the E and the hospital staff. Information about the development of feeding skills was collated from the nursing staff.

RESULTS/The severely retarded children who functioned at sub-stage six (highest stage of sensori-motor development), differed significantly from those at sub-stage five and below on a measure of verbal comprehension. Woodward's results support Piaget's contention that the achievements at the sixth sub-stage of the sensori-motor period, a stage which deals with concepts of object permanency, were a necessary prerequisite for the acquisition of meaningful speech. Woodward maintains: 'In the educational field the results indicate that children who have attained the last sensori-motor stage would benefit from attending a training centre, since new developments in language, drawing and performance ability occur during this stage, which appears from this study to be a major event in the development of severely sub-normal children.'

Relative thinking by normals and retardates
D. L. McManis, 1969

AIM/McManis investigated the developmental patterns of relative thinking and reasoning in normals and retardates.

SUBJECTS/Fifteen retarded and 15 normal children at each MA level from five to 10 years were involved. The MA group IQ means were equated within both IQ groups, ranging from 98.40 to 102.33 for the normals and from 56.53 to 59 for the retardates. The normals ranged from 85 to 115 and the retardates from 47 to 73. The CA range of the normals was from five years three months to 10 years 10 months, and of the retardates from seven years eight months to 21 years two months.

TESTS/Two tests were administered — the Right-Left test and the Brother-Sister test. The general experimental procedure was patterned after Elkind (1961, 1962).

RESULTS/On items 1 and 2 of the Right—Left test, normal and retardate children showed operativity at the most concrete level of right-left understanding. However, on items 3 and 4, which demand the application of right-left to two objects from both the subject's and the experimenter's perspectives, the retardate children demonstrated a one-year deficit. A two-year retardate deficit was observed on items 5 and 6, where these items require relational understanding of right-left for three objects from both the subject's and the experimenter's perspectives.

In respect to the Brother-Sister Test, items 1 and 2 measure a comprehension of the symmetry between being and having a brother in the subject's family circle. A one-year deficit occurred in favour of the retarded children. However, a two-year retardate deficit was noted on item 3, measuring the symmetry as in items 1 and 2, but when both relations are given for a fictitious family. When this symmetry is involved in the construction of one relation from the other for a fictitious family (items 5 and 6), a 2-3 year retardate deficit was evidenced. Likewise, a one- to two-year retardate deficit was observed on item 4, which purports to measure the class conception of 'brother'.

McManis concludes: 'Retardates displayed increasing MA deficits in relative thinking as the level of abstractness in the tests increased. Since such thinking is probably mandatory for successful independent functioning in the community, remedial training to alleviate such deficiencies should be included in preparing retardates for community placement.'

Conservation and transitivity of weight and length by normals and retardates
D. L. McManis, 1969a

AIM/The author was interested:
(a) to investigate the order of occurrence of conservation and transitivity of weight, and the order of conservation and transitivity of length;
(b) to examine the order of development of conservation and transitivity across the dimensions of weight and length, by simultaneously classifying children according to whether they demonstrated conservation operativity and transitivity on both dimensions;
(c) to investigate the hypothesis that, with children demonstrating discrepant operativity on any of the tasks, a significantly smaller than chance proportion would show transitivity on either dimensions without also displaying conservation on both dimensions.

SUBJECTS/One hundred and eighty children were involved in the study. Ninety of these were retardates (IQ range 47 to 73 on L-M Form, of the Stanford Binet) and with a CA spread from seven years, eight months to 21 years, two months and an MA range from five years to 11 years, nine months.

The 90 normal children (IQ range 85 to 115 on the Lorge-Thorndike Test) ranged in CA from five years, three months to 10 years, 10 months and in MA from five years, three months to 11 years, 11 months.

The author points out that the sex variable was not controlled. The subjects involved were drawn from a wide socio-economic background, and their fathers' occupations ranged from professional to clerical, skilled, semi-skilled and unskilled. The etiology of the mental retardation included organic, physiological, cultural and psychological factors.

METHOD/Four tests were administered: 1. conservation of weight; 2. conservation of length; 3. transitivity of weight (patterned after Smedslund, 1961); 4. transitivity of length (patterned after Smedslund, 1961).

Generally, Tests one and two were identical to the Piagetian type of tasks, with minor modifications. Children were seen individually and all responses were recorded verbatim. The general experimental procedure was similar to that of the Geneva Centre. (Fuller details are also described elsewhere, McManis, 1969a, pp. 374-7 and Smedslund, 1961.)

RESULTS/McManis argues that the finding that significantly greater numbers of children of average and of inferior intelligence demonstrate weight conservation without transitivity of weight supports Kooistra's (1963) results for children of high intelligence — that there is a sequential order in the acquisition of conservation and transitivity of weight, with conservation emerging first. However, these findings contradict Lovell and Ogilvie's (1961) study which reported that 53 per cent of their subjects at the non-conservation of weight stage were capable of performing the act of transitivity. In relation to Lovell's study, Kooistra has pointed out that 'the criterion employed to assess the presence of transitivity was not stringent to assure that their subjects were not arriving at operational responses through nontransitive hypotheses'.

McManis concludes as follows: 'Among subjects of both IQ levels showing discrepant performance in conservation and transitivity, significantly greater than chance proportions had conservation without transitivity. Retardates attained transitivity considerably later than did normals. . .conservation developed prior to transitivity, with more retardates between MA seven to 10 being in a transitional stage of the sequence.'

The development of reasoning, moral judgement and moral conduct in retardates and normals
W. B. Stephens, C. K. Miller and J. A. McLaughlin, 1969

AIMS/The main aims of this study were (i) to analyse the development of reasoning; (ii) to determine if moral conduct follows an evolutionary process; (iii) to compare the performance of retardates with that of normals on measures of reasoning, moral judgement and moral conduct; and (iv) to establish the relationship among levels of reasoning, moral judgement and moral conduct.

SUBJECTS/A random sample of 150 children was composed of 75 mentally retarded children (IQ 50-75, as determined by the WISC) and 75 normal subjects (IQ 90-110 as determined by the WISC). The mean IQ for the retardates and normals was 66.2 and 100.5 respectively. These two groups were further sub-divided into three age ranges: six-10, 10-14 and 14-18.

METHOD/Reasoning variables/Conservation of substance, weight, volume, length, liquids, length-rod sections, one-one exchange, one-one correspondence and dissolution of sugar. (These were patterned after Piaget and Inhelder, 1941, Piaget

1952, Piaget, Inhelder and Szeminska 1964 and Inhelder 1968.)

Logic Classification/included class inclusion (animals, beads); changing criterion; intersection of classes; relationships — brothers and sisters and right and left. (These were patterned after Piaget, 1964 and Piaget and Inhelder 1959.)

Operativity and Symbolic Imagery/included rotation of squares and beads; transfer from two-to-three dimensions and changing perspectives — mobile and stationary. (These were patterned after Piaget, 1952, Piaget and Inhelder, 1964, Piaget, Inhelder and Szeminska, 1964.)

Formal Operations/Combination of Liquids (Piaget and Inhelder, 1958).

Moral Judgement Variables/included Rules of a Game, lying and justice.

Moral Conduct Variables/included self-control, honesty and persistence and truthfulness.

RESULTS (i) Operativity as indicated by normal subjects superseded that of retardates on each reasoning task. The reasoning of the retardates, however, did not exceed the concrete operational stage. (ii) Moral Judgement and moral conduct were found to be developmental in nature with successful performance increasing with chronological age. (iii) The normals performed at a higher operational level than retardates in all the three areas of development. (iv) Only moderate but significant relationships between and among measures of reasoning, moral judgement and moral conduct, were evidenced.

Report on the utility of a Piaget-based infant scale with older retarded children
T. D. Wachs, 1970

Wachs states that Stott and Ball (1965) have argued that measurement of early intelligence might be more effectively assessed by utilizing tests drawn from the Piagetian framework of early intellectual growth.

AIM/The study investigated the utility of a Piaget-based scale of infant development for older, pre-school retarded children.

SUBJECTS/Sixteen retarded children (mean IQ = 54.73 and mean CA = four years 10 months) were involved. The children were all involved in a pre-school programme.

METHOD/Tests/The Infant Psychological Development Scale (IPDS) was administered as devised by Uzgiris and Hunt

(1966). The IPDS is Piaget-based purporting to measure cognitive growth in seven areas of development. IQ scores of these children were obtained from their school records.

Statistical Treatment/In order to establish any patterning between IPDS performance and IQ, the point-biserial correlation technique was employed. In addition, a product-moment correlation between number of subscales failed and IQ was also computed. Chi-square was also used.

RESULTS/The point-biserial correlation demonstrated a significant relationship between IPDS performance and Binet IQ: $r = +.617$, df = 14, p $<.01$. Likewise, the product-moment correlation between the number of sub-scales failed and IQ was significant ($r = .482$, df = 14, p $<.05$). Similarly, chi-square was significant ($\chi^2 = 5.60$, df 1, p $<.025$). The IPDS was more sensitive for IQs of 50 and below.

Wachs concluded, '... the IPDS, as a Piaget-based scale of intellectual development, seems to be measuring the types of abilities commonly considered to be intellectual in nature ... its potential for applicability to such populations as the retarded must be considered favourable ... the IPDS seems to have a definite potential in terms of setting up remediation programs specifically tailored for each individual child'.

Development of conservation in normal and retarded children
G. Gruen and D. Vore, 1972

AIMS/ (a) To establish whether retarded-normal differences become more evident as comparison tasks increase in difficulty. Piaget's 1950 conservation problems were utilized. (b) To investigate the relationship of IQ, MA, and CA to the ability to conserve. (c) To attempt to resolve 'the conflicting evidence between developmental and defect theorists of mental retardation'.

SUBJECTS/Ninety Caucasian children from upper-lower or lower-middle class socio-economic background from schools in Indiana were involved in the study. The experimental subjects consisted of three groups of familial mental retardates, with MAs of 5, 7 and 9. Ten children were included in each of the three groups, with IQ range of 55 − 80 (Stanford-Binet).

Two types of control groups were also involved. The first group consisted of three groups of 10 subjects each, matched for sex and MA. The second group also consisted of three groups of 10 subjects matched with the experimental subjects by sex and

CA. All subjects in the control groups had IQs ranging from 90-120 (Slosson Intelligence Test, 1963).

METHOD/Testing Battery/The following tests were used: (a) number conservation technique; (b) quantity conservation technique; (c) weight conservation technique. (Details of all the three tests, including scoring schedules, have been fully described by Rothenberg, 1969, and Gruen and Vore 1972, pp. 149-50.)

RESULTS/The authors discuss their findings in relation to results reported by other studies. They cite the work of Zigler (1966), Brison and Bereiter (1967), Keasey and Charles (1967), Feigenbaum (1963) and Goldschmid (1967). Gruen and Vore's results gave added credibility to the general questioning procedure of Rothenberg (1969). The authors conclude their main findings as follows: 'Differences in performance on these tasks were primarily attributable to MA, but not IQ. As expected, conservation of weight was generally more difficult than conservation of water, and the latter was more difficult than conservation of number for both retarded and normal children. However some exceptions to this order were found. Conservation of inequality was typically less difficult than conservation of equality for all concepts.'

Problem solving strategies of young children
M. Woodward, 1972

AIM/Woodward's study attempted to elucidate some aspects of early cognitive acquisition in normal children of one-and-a-half to five years and in severely subnormal children (the period between the end of Piaget's sensori-motor period and the beginning of the intuitive one).

SUBJECTS/Group One/This consisted of 96 children of a larger sample of SSN children (N = 135). The children had CA range of three to 15 years nine months and IQs were under 50. Seven were deaf, two had cerebral palsy and 18 had a severe behaviour disturbance.
Group Two/Forty-two normal children were involved, with an age range of 18-59 months.
Group Three/Forty normal children, 10 in each age group of 36-41 months, 42-47 months, 48-53 months and 54-59 months, with five boys and five girls in each age group, comprised group three.
Group Four/Twenty normal children, 10 in each of the age

groups of 60-65 months and 66-71 months, were involved.

METHOD/Three tasks were administered as follows: (a) A square box, into which 16 cubes fitted closely; (b) A rectangular board, with a row of holes into which six round pegs fitted closely. (Both sets were presented with the objects fitted in the box or board. Either E or S removed these. Children were requested 'to put the objects back'.) (c) The main task consisted of a set of 12 cylindrical cups, ranging in diameter from 1-2¾ inches and in height from 1-2½ inches. 'When the cups were placed in one another, in order of size, they formed a "nest".' (Fuller details of the experimental procedures adopted for the various groups and of scoring have been described by Woodward, 1972, pp. 12-14.)

RESULTS/Behaviour of putting a cup repeatedly in and out of another was common. Twelve SSN (10 under CA five) and two normal children (aged 18 and 25 months, respectively) demonstrated such a pattern. Similar trends were observed in respect to 16 cubes and the box and six pegs and the peg-board. Children employed the following strategies: 'Strategy 1 — Selection of cups from the array in order of size. Strategy 2 — A cup of the wrong size (i.e. not the largest in the array) is held inside the top of the last cup nested, and then returned to the collection, without being dropped in. Strategy 3 — A cup of the wrong size is dropped into the last one nested and then removed and returned to the collection. Strategy 4 — The obstructed cup is taken off the nest and the obstructing cup is removed or several cups are removed: the obstructed cup is then placed in the nest. Strategy 5 — The obstructed cup is taken off the nest and obstructing cup is removed; both are returned to the collection of unnested cups. Strategy 6 — The obstructed cup is taken off and placed underneath the main nest, and then returned to the collection. Strategy 7 — The obstructed cup is taken off and placed successively on cups not nested until it goes into one. Strategy 8 — The obstructed cup is taken off and returned to the collection of unnested cups. Strategy 9 — No action — the obstructed cup is left where it is.'

Operativity by size was achieved by few. Fourteen children in groups 3 and 4 were classifiable as intuitive on either the task of copying a linear spatial order, or of making 1-1 correspondence between the two sets of elements.

Eighteen of 59 operational SSN children employed either strategy 4, 2 or 3 or a combination of these. Furthermore, 23 of the SSN children showed a trend towards complete avoidance of obstruction situations by utilizing strategies 2 or 3. Six children in groups 3 and 4 removed all wrongly sized cups on all trials. Eleven were among the 30 CA four-and-a-half years and above, while none of the 30 under CA four years six months used strategies 2 and 3, a difference which is significant beyond the 0.001 level (χ^2 = 13.46, df = 1).

Furthermore, six of the SSN children were operational by employing strategy 4, which, consistently used, ended in operativity, 'because each time it is used a cup that is larger than that removed is placed in the next and not left on top of the last cup. Eventually, by the continued use of strategy 4 the largest cup of those not nested will be placed in the nest, and so on for the next one ... however strategy 4 fails if cups larger than the obstructed one are removed along with smaller ones, since these will be obstructed later by the cup just placed in the nest.'

The continued use of the inadequate strategies (5-9) contributed to non-operativity. The adequate strategy 4, in the obstruction situation was almost always present in normal children of CA 2.6 years and over, 26 of 31 in Group 2. Likewise, with children in Groups 3 and 4, only five of the 18 children who performed at the lowest level did not employ strategy 4. Of the inadequate strategies, 8 and 9 were most frequently used, contributing to non-operativity: this was evident in all CA groups. No clear-cut patterns were observed. Strategy 7 was not noted in the 'practised' SSN group.

DISCUSSION/Woodward discusses the results of the investigation along with those of Piaget (1955), Woodward (1959), Luria (1961) and Inhelder, *et al.* (1966). A further discussion of the behavioural responses and strategies advanced, have been analysed in terms of 'the plan and TOTE unit concepts', postulated by Miller, Galanter and Pribram (1960) and discussed in terms of neuro-physiology by Pribram (1960).

II Visual Handicap

On the basis of an investigation involving a group of children with visual-perceptual difficulties, Nash (1969) demonstrated that such children functioned at the lower levels of spatial reasoning and 'those with figure-ground difficulties were significantly poorer on number conservation tasks involving figure-ground discrimination at the outset'. Piaget's notion of the logic of developing thought is questioned and the need for further research indicated, with special reference to the factor-analytic studies of Piagetian tasks. [Recent factor-analytic studies include Bart (1971), Kaufman (1971), Stephens *et al.* (1972) and Modgil, Dielman and Cattell (1973, in press). Full details of Nash's study appear below.]

Hughes (1969) investigated the development of spatial concepts and their representation, together with their relation to intelligence tests, in 36 partially-sighted children of Primary School age. The overall results indicated that although the sequential development of the partially-sighted children is identical to that of the normal — the rate of such development is comparatively slower. (Details are given below.)

Gottesman's (1971) study consisted of a comparative developmental investigation of haptic perception patterned after Piaget and Inhelder (1956). Blind and sighted subjects were administered tasks modelled after Page (1959) and Pinard and Laurendeau (1966 p. 244). The overall patterns which emerged demonstrated that the haptic-perception ability of blind and sighted children was similar. However, Gottesman draws attention to the fact that his results should not be generalized, since the subjects were not randomly chosen. (Details are given later in this Section).

Tobin (1972), in an investigation with subjects representing a wide range of degrees of visual handicap from total blindness to partial-sight, found evidence of a developmental lag in the conservation of substance when making comparisons with studies involving sighted subjects. The investigation was not able, without more refined methodology, to exemplify differences attributable to degree of vision.

More recently, Cromer (1973) investigated the concept of conservation in congenitally blind children. He draws attention to the weaknesses in Hatwell's (1966) study in which she found a two-year retardation among the blind in mass conservation. Cromer found no differences among his groups of congenitally blind, blindfolded-sighted children and sighted children. 'However, the manner by which the blind processed the environment differed from the blindfolded-sighted children, as evidenced in some of their non-conservation answers' (p. 241).

Conservation of substance in the blind and partially sighted
M. J. Tobin, 1972

AIMS/To explore the problem of a suggested developmental lag of the visually handicapped child from a Piagetian viewpoint and to evaluate Piagetian-type tasks as simple diagnostic tests for use by teachers of the visually handicapped.

SUBJECTS/One hundred and eighty-nine children registered as blind or partially-sighted aged from five to 17 years.

METHOD/The subjects were assigned to one of three groups according to the degree of visual handicap. The blind group included those who were totally blind and those with 'light perception'. Modifications by Lovell and Ogilvie (1961) and Elkind to the Piaget and Inhelder (1941) conservation of substance procedure were followed.

RESULTS/Conservation responses increased with age. The results suggested 'that while the best of the visually handicapped attain conservation as early as six or seven years and are, therefore, equal to the best of the sighted, there is a greater spread among them, with a substantial number not conserving until beyond the age of nine or ten'. To ascertain how far this developmental lag was due to restrictions in the quality and extent of the child's interaction with the environment was difficult. The author speculates that visual impairment is likely to reduce the number of experiences befalling the child. To engage in training such as the procedures followed by Smedslund (1961) would appear to be a more direct method of investigating this hypothesis. The author further underlines the value of Piagetian conservation tasks for teachers of the visually handicapped as both learning and diagnostic instruments.   •

The study was unable to show any differences attributable to degree of vision — the author comments that these could be found only in segregated groups of totally blind and partially-sighted discriminated through more refined measuring techniques by ophthalmologists.

An analysis using Piagetian concepts, of the responses of partially sighted children of primary school age to the problem of representing their class-room by (a) using wooden blocks, (b) drawing, and their understanding of associated spatial relationships
G. B. Hughes, 1969

This inquiry is concerned with the development of spatial concepts and their representation in a sample of 36 partially sighted children of primary school age. These concepts were investigated by a variety of tests suggested by certain investigations carried out by Piaget and his co-workers.

An examination is made of the relationships between these concepts on one hand, and the children's performance on intelligence tests, mental ages and chronological ages, on the other. The development of spatial concepts in the partially sighted children is also compared with that of normal children on the basis of matched pairs.

It was hypothesized, broadly speaking, that the development of spatial concepts in partially sighted children reveals the same stages and shows the same pattern, as in children without visual handicap, but that this development proceeds at a slower pace; further, that the ability to represent concepts in partially sighted children correlates with scores obtained from intelligence tests.

The writer worked with each child in the sample in order to administer various tests of spatial concepts and of intelligence, and the administration of these tests was spread over a number of sessions with each child. Using a previously agreed rubric, teachers of the various groups helped by administering two group tests of drawing to their own classes. At the school for the partially sighted, information of an ophthalmic nature, details of socio-economic background and psychologist's intelligence ratings were abstracted from the children's records.

The inquiry seems to indicate that the development of spatial concepts in partially sighted children generally follows the same pattern as that outlined by Piaget in his investigations.

Correlation coefficients ranging from +0.808 to +0.442 were found between performance on a variety of spatial tests and the Crichton Vocabulary Scale, Raven's Coloured Progressive Matrices, and Mental Ages derived from a combination of these. Generally, lower correlation coefficients, in this case ranging from +0.465 to +0.157, were found between the spatial tests and chronological age.

When the results of the tests for the whole sample of partially sighted children were compared with the results of other investigators in this field the stages of development reached by the partially sighted children appeared to fall below the standards found elsewhere.

However, strikingly similar standards were found for the performance on most of the tests, when the standards reached by six partially sighted children of average verbal intelligence, were compared with those of six children matched for age, sex and verbal intelligence, but lacking visual handicap. But this similarity was not apparent on tests requiring definitions of positions in space relative to both themselves and an observer.

Some number and spatial concepts of junior school children with visual perceptual difficulties
B. C. Nash, 1969

Piagetian number and spatial concepts tasks were

administered to 130 children in the age range eight to 11 years and WISC IQ range 90 to 126. The tasks were: the conservation of discontinuous quantity, one-to-one correspondence, spontaneous correspondence, seriation, qualitative similarity and ordinal correspondence, the co-ordination of perspectives using the model of three mountains, diagrammatic layouts with two identical landscape models, and the reproduction of the lay-out of a model village; giving a total of 12 sets of responses tasks.

A scalogram analysis of the responses revealed that the tasks must be regarded as independent. No support was found for the existence of Piagetian stages or substages in development. Although the tasks were rigorously Piagetian in design and in the classification of responses, responses to some of the tasks were not similar to those of Piaget's subjects. Often full explanations given by subjects showed different types of reasoning from that suggested to account for Piaget's subjects' responses. Also there were many instances of development of explanations in a completely different order from that suggested by Piaget on the basis of logical structures. Piaget's analysis of the logic of developing reasoning is questioned.

Half of the subjects were classified by their school performance and behaviour, and by the use of the Frostig and the Bender Tests, as having perceptual immaturities. This group was significantly poorer than the control group on the spatial tasks. Those with figure-ground difficulties were significantly poorer on number conservation tasks involving figure-ground discrimination at the outset. This is more supportive of Equilibration Theory than of Piaget's other suggestions of separateness in the development of perceptual and conceptual abilities, although the latter explanation can be accepted more narrowly as relating only to the perceptual constancies.

Using the WISC arithmetic subtest and the Staffordshire Arithmetic Test, Hood's findings that the understanding of number concepts is a necessary, but not sufficient, reason for attainment in arithmetic were only partly confirmed.

There were no differences between the quality of responses given by male and female subjects to the tasks.

There was no significant association between scores on the verbal scale of the WISC and scores on the concept tasks; so that success or failure on the tasks is not a function of verbal ability.

Piaget's notion of the logic of developing thought is questioned. It is suggested that before further studies of order in conceptual development, or the development of standardized tests of concept growth is continued, factor analytic studies of the individual tasks is needed.

223

A comparative study of Piaget's developmental schema of sighted children with that of a group of blind children
M. Gottesman, 1971

AIM/Gottesman was interested in a comparative developmental study of haptic perception based on the research of Piaget and Inhelder (1956). An analysis of the performance of blind and sighted children not allowed to use vision was made with that of the sighted on Piagetian haptic perception tasks.

SUBJECTS/Three groups, two sighted and one blind, were involved in the study. The ages ranged from Stage I, two to four years, Stage II, four to six years, to Stage III, six to eight years. Each group comprised 15 children with five at each stage level. Sighted subjects were asked to examine objects haptically. 'Sighted Group A were to respond visually by selecting, from four objects in a visual display, one that had originally been felt. Both sighted group B and blind group C responded tactually by identifying without the use of vision one object previously felt among those handed them.'

METHOD/The general shapes used in Gottesman's study were patterned after Page (1959, p. 114) and Pinard and Laurendeau (1966, p. 244) investigations. The various objects for recognition were classified in three groups: (a) familiar solids; (b) flat geometrical shapes; and (c) topological forms.

The instructions to group A at all stages were as follows: 'I will now hand you something to feel. See if you know what it is.' At stage I the subjects were only asked to recognize familiar solids visually. Further questions were: 'I am now going to place four objects in front of you, one of which has the same shape as you just felt. I want you to point to that object.' Subsequently, flat geometric shapes and topological items were introduced, with identical instructions as before.

Groups B and C received the following instructions at all stages. At stage I, children in Groups B and C were asked to explore, recognize and identify familiar solids. 'I will now hand you an object. Feel it and see if you know its shape. Then I want you to try to remember it.' These subjects were only permitted to use 'touch' to complete the presented task. 'I am now going to hand you four objects one right after the other. From these four objects, I want you to pick the one that has the same shape as the first you felt.' This was followed by geometric shapes and topological forms. Questioning was identical to that for Stage I.

RESULTS/Gottesman's findings demonstrated that the

ability of blind and sighted children was very much similar on Piagetian-type tasks of haptic perception. The levels of operativity achieved by these blind and sighted subjects substantiated the Piagetian developmental stages. However, Gottesman's blind subjects were not randomly selected and a generalization of the results may not be appropriate to all blind children. The author further points out: 'The blind and the sighted subjects not using vision had the disadvantage of exploring each object successively; the sighted were able to select appropriate objects from a visual array simultaneously. A further disadvantage of having the subjects choose the same object haptically could be one of short-term memory.' He draws attention to the relevance of Piaget-type findings to the comprehension and development of spatial operativity for blind children.

III *Hearing Impairment*

Furth (1970) maintains, 'Piaget's theoretical model of cognitive development and his basic biological position on intelligence as being rooted in overt action would suggest that the growth of intelligent, logical operation is not dependent on but rather reflected in language behaviour. In line with this reasoning, it could be predicted that the deaf would not differ from hearing children with respect to the age of which logical operations emerge.' Borelli (1951) concluded that deaf children between five and eight years showed no fundamental difference in logical capacities and that the beginnings of logical operations are largely independent of language. She suggested that this may not be applicable at the formal level.

Oléron and Herren (1961), in an investigation involving training in the conservation of weight and volume, found a retardation of six years among the deaf subjects when compared with hearing subjects. The authors suggested that Piaget's theory does not sufficiently emphasize the role of language. In a modification of Oléron and Herren's training procedure, Furth (1964, 1966) supports the view that the '... kind of experience with the physical world rather than language or formal training determines, in part, the age at which children pass from a perceptual to a logical judgement on many Piaget type experiments'.

In a further study involving six- and eight-year-old hearing and deaf children, Bradshaw (1964) demonstrated that the older hearing children performed at a higher level of operativity than the younger children. However, the eight-year-old deaf children performed more like the six-year-old hearing children on the 'sequential' but were equal to the eight-year-old hearing children on the 'simultaneous operational task'

CHAPTER EIGHT
CROSS CULTURAL RESEARCH

Piaget's views are that 'Cross-cultural research which is most important does not only concern child development but development in general including the final adult stages', (1966). However, with the evidence available so far, it is difficult to make any sweeping statements about the cross-cultural replication of Piaget's findings. Perhaps in no other area of psychology is there so much cross-cultural and cross-social-class empirical research data available as on the Piagetian tasks. For example, conservation problems have been given to subjects in Algeria (Bovet, 1972), Arabia (Hyde, 1959), Australia (De Lemos, 1969; Dasen, 1972), Canada (Dodwell, 1960, 1961; Laurendeau and Pinard, 1962), Central Africa (Heron and Simonsson, 1969), China (Cheng and Lee, 1964), England (Lovell and Ogilvie, 1961), Hong Kong (Goodnow and Bethon, 1962), Iran (Mohseni, 1966), Italy (Peluffo, 1962), Jamaica (Vernon, 1965), Japan (Noro, 1961; Fujinaga, Saiga and Hosoya, 1963), Lebanon (Za'rour, 1971), Mexico (Price-Williams, 1968), New Guinea (Prince, 1968; Weddell, 1968), Senegal (Greenfield, 1966), USA (Mermelstein and Shulman, 1967), and West Africa (Price-Williams, 1961; Lloyd, 1971; Piller, 1971).

There are problems in interpreting results from cross-cultural studies, partly because of the differences in language and partly due to experience and cultural values. If differences are observed, it is not easy to interpret or account for the cause of the differences.

Among the early attempts to replicate Piaget's contentions on a cross-cultural basis, is Hyde's (1959) study. She repeated many of Piaget's tasks with a multi-racial group of children in Aden. The results described by Piaget were generally confirmed. In her study there was some indication that quantity (substance and liquid) was easier than weight and volume, but the results of individual subjects suggested that the sequence was not invariable. There was therefore no support for the theory that the concepts of substance, weight and volume were invariably acquired in that order. (Fuller details appear in Hyde, 1959; Lunzer, 1960 and Flavell, 1963, pp. 383, 387.)

226

Noro (1961) with a group of Japanese children administered tasks from Piaget's 'The Child's Conception of Number' (1952b) and results indicated identical stages to those of the Swiss children. However, another inquiry (Fujinaga, Saiga and Hosoya, 1963) suggests that 'too much attention is paid to the natural sequence of developmental stages and not enough to the role of learning'. An investigation with completely contradictory results to those of Piaget is that of Cheng and Lee (1964), which involved Chinese children. However, the authors have not published full details of the subjects, nor of methodology or the analytic procedure of the children's behavioural responses. They state that the results of 'an experiment' are in violation of the contention of the 'bourgeois scholar Piaget' and further maintain that 'children's conception of number is completely determined by age'.

Beard's (1963) study (Part One) drew a sample of Ghanaian children ranging in age from eight to 11 years. A comparison was made with a sample of English children. She points out that the ages of the English children were somewhat younger than those of the Ghanaians. She argues, 'if maturity rather than schooling or experience, was an important factor in the acquisition of mathematical concepts we would expect the Ghanaian sample to excel'. The results indicated that in tests of concepts of number, quantity and of mechanical arithmetic, the range of mean scores for the schools in the two samples was roughly the same. However, the mean for all the English sample significantly exceeded the mean for all the Ghanaian sample. The increase in score with age was significantly greater for the English than for the Ghanaian sample. In tests of spatial concepts, the English sample greatly excelled the Ghanaian children and it was suggested that the environment of English children favoured the development of spatial concepts. Similarly, Vernon's (1966) Eskimo subjects performed at higher levels of perceptual-spatial operativity in relation to West Indians and Canadian Indians. Vernon argues that the training that the Eskimo children have in tracking and in locating objects may have been a contributory factor in this respect. This kind of result may suggest that good spatial performances may occur without a high level of schooling. Such a finding gives impetus to the question as to the kinds of experiences which contribute to the particular kinds of skills. This lends credence to Piaget and Inhelder's statement (1967, p.296), 'the child who is familiar with folding and unfolding paper shapes through his work at school is two or three years in advance of children who lack this experience'. (See also Vernon, 1969 whose study is described later in this chapter and for fuller details refer to 'Intelligence and Cultural Environment', 1969.)

Price-Williams' (1961) study with West African Bush children of the Tiv tribe is another such investigation. Five groups each of nine illiterate children were tested on the question of conservation of continuous and dis-continuous quantities. Price-Williams admits some difficulties in ascertaining the child's exact chronological age. He stresses too, that mastery of the language was not sufficient to allow follow-up questions of the type which the Piagetian tasks demand, other than the question 'Why?' Results indicated that the progression of the idea of conservation paralleled that found in European and other Western children. However, Furby (1971, p.244) maintains that, 'there is a very common game among the Tiv children which seems very much like a conservation task — in fact, the child may learn task-specific responses that allow him to perform well in the conservation task since it is so similar'. Okonji (1971a p.127) elaborates on this common game and maintains 'Price-Williams (1961) might not have claimed that as Tiv children had no formal instruction in concepts of abstract numbers, there is much to be said for the neurophysiological interpretation of readiness for dealing with such concepts if he had taken into account the possible effect of engaging in a game involving the placing of seeds in rows of six holes which is common in most parts of Africa (it is called Omweso or Ekyeso in Uganda, Owar in Ghana and Okwe in Iboland). Such a game enjoyed by both adults and children requires some understanding of number concepts.' Uzgiris (1964, described in Chapter Three) found that there were appreciable differences in the ability to conserve when the tasks dealt with different materials and that these differences were not constant across individuals and materials. Lloyd (1971, described below) argues that in Price-Williams' study standard western materials were not employed as a control in investigating conservation of quantity. (Price-Williams' (1961) study is described more fully in 'Cross-Cultural Studies' Edited by Price-Williams (1969).)

In another investigation, Price-Williams (1962) found moderate differences due to length of schooling in tasks requiring classificatory strategies. He stresses familiarity of materials as influencing level of performance. Nigerian children performed at a higher level of operativity relative to English children in classifying and abstracting the common features of indigenous plants. However, the Nigerian subjects performed at a lower level of Piagetian operativity with animals which were considered to play a less meaningful role in everyday living. Okonji (1971) comments 'Price-Williams (1962) used familiar indigenous objects for studying classification among the Tiv of Northern Nigeria. Following this example, Kellaghan (1965) used local materials for the investigation of classificatory behaviour among some western Nigerian Yoruba children. These studies showed for the first time that when appropriate test materials are used the African children involved were not qualitatively different from their European counterparts in their abstract attitude. Although the results of these studies are important they do not throw any light on the nature of the effect of familiarity on test performance in different cultural groups.' (Okonji's 1971 study, discussed below, attempted to fulfil such an objective.)

A study of the effects of familiarity on classificatory behaviour was undertaken by Okonji. Two hundred and forty-three Ibusa and Glasgow children (CA six to 12 years) were administered two classificatory tasks. Although the degrees of familiarity influenced classificatory behaviour in some aspects, the overall developmental trends in both the tasks were similar in both samples. (Details of this study and two other studies by the same author, 1970 and 1971a, are described later in this Section.)

The finding of no differences between Western and non-Western samples in classificatory behaviour in Okonji's study led to another partly-related study. Deregowski and Serpell (1972, in preparation) demonstrated that Zambian children did not differ significantly from the Scots on re-sorting of toys. However, the Zambian subjects performed at lower levels of classification than the Scots, when re-sorting colour or black-and-white photographs of these toys.

The developmental ability of 224 Lebanese children to conserve number and liquid was examined with regard to the effect of age, sex, religion, socio-economic status, scholastic level and mother's literacy (Za'rour, 1971). Such an ability increased significantly with age. Sex was the only other variable which yielded a difference significant at the .05 level in number conservation. This contradicted Dodwell's (1961) study (described in Chapter Three) and the Almy et al. (1966) study (described in Chapter Nine) but confirmed Goldschmid's (1967) possible explanation that '... boys in their play activities have more opportunity to manipulate objects and perceive them after different transformations than girls do'. (Full details of Goldschmid's 1967 study are described in Chapter Eleven, and Za'rour's study later in this chapter.)

In continuation, Za'rour's (1971a) study was designed to investigate the effects of materials, age, sex, scholastic level and mother's literacy on weight conservation behaviour of Lebanese children. The results indicated that for the seven- to nine-year-old children, it was easier to conserve weight on plasticine rather than on a rubber band or on alcohol in a thermometer. (Full details appear later in this chapter.)

Issues concerning the effect of familiar and alien materials, age and culture on conservation behaviour of Yoruba children were investigated by Lloyd (1971). Conservation operativity among Yoruba subjects was observed at the same age as their counterparts in other cultures. Performance was similar with familiar and with alien materials, 'although it improved with practice'. (Details appear later in this Chapter.)

Mermelstein and Shulman's (1967) study dealt with the performance of Piagetian conservation tasks by children who had been without schooling for four years. Findings revealed generally no significant differences attributable to the effects of non-schooling. (Details of the study are given later in this chapter.) Okonji (1971a, p.127) argues: 'Mermelstein's evidence does not seem to be very convincing as some of his subjects have had some brief or irregular schooling experience and there was no way to show that some did not continue to get some sort of formal teaching at home when the public schools were closed'.

The Harvard Centre for Cognitive Studies (Bruner, Olver and Greenfield, 1966) have gathered results from a wide variety of cultures — Boston, Senegal, Alaska, and urban and rural Mexico.

In Greenfield's (1966) study of the conservation of liquid in Senegal, the results indicated that the unschooled children showed apparent arrest in any qualitative change in intellectual development (conservation task) after the age of eight or nine years, with also differences between the younger children. Further, a lack of schooling was clearly more relevant than rural vs. urban environment. (Details of the study appear later in this chapter.)

Goodnow and Bethon (1966) in their study attempted to elucidate results with schooled and unschooled children in Hong Kong with respect to Piaget's conservation tasks and found that the only task on which the unschooled Chinese children operated below the 'average' American schooled child was the task of combinatorial reasoning. No differences in the American children and the unschooled Chinese subjects in the conservation operativity of the concepts of substance, weight, volume and area were observed. The strategy employed by the unschooled group did not follow any consistent pattern in a combinatorial reasoning task — a finding reported by Peluffo (1964). Peluffo's subjects found the combinatorial task harder than conservation of displacement volume for rural, but not for urban school children in Sardinia. It is interesting to point out here that full operativity in tasks requiring combinatorial strategies is regarded by Piaget as most pertinent to formal reasoning. Peluffo concluded from his results that 'low-cultural level' or an 'underdeveloped milieu' does not stimulate the development of operational thinking, though transfer to a more favourable milieu may do so.

Variations in the rate of conservation acquisition among several cultural groups were attributed to specific environmental differences (e.g. schooling) in a study by Goldschmid, Bentler, Kohnstamm, Modgil, et al. (1973). The Conservation Assessment kit Scale A, described more fully in Chapter Twelve was administered to 25 boys and 25 girls at each age level from four to eight years, comprising a total sample of 250 children in each of eight countries. Overall, the results indicated that the sequence of Piagetian conservation development in both males and females is fairly consistent from culture to culture.

Dasen (1972) reports, 'Thus more important than schooling itself seems to be the contact with Western Cognitive values and stimulation which schooling brings with it. European contact ... is difficult to define precisely (de Lacey, 1970); it is usually linked to the urban/rural difference (Mohseni, 1966; Greenfield, 1966; Peluffo, 1967; Poole, 1968; Vernon, 1969), to linguistic difference, either in the richness of the Vernacular (Greenfield, 1966), or in the fluency of the acquired European language (Vernon, 1969) or to social class (Lloyd, 1971).'

In his 1970 study, de Lacey demonstrated that in the development of operational thinking as assessed by a battery of classification tasks, although both of the European samples were generally superior to the Aboriginal samples, a small sample of high-contact Aboriginals was found to perform as well as the low-socio-economic Europeans. However, the number of children involved was small (N = 34). (Details of the study appear below.)

In extending his above study, de Lacey (1971), alongside with two tests of Piagetian classificatory tasks, administered the Peabody Picture Vocabulary Test to 40 full-blood urban Aboriginal children and 80 white subjects. 'A trend in an earlier study for high-contact Aboriginals to perform on classification tests at about the same level as white children in a similar environment was confirmed, despite the markedly lower verbal IO scores of Aboriginal children.' (Full details of the study appear later in this chapter.)

In continuing his 1970 and 1971 studies, de Lacey (1971a) attempted to establish whether there were any differences in cognitive organization between reserve and town-dwelling part-Aboriginals, in terms of both verbal intelligence and Piagetian operational thinking. The European subjects performed at the higher levels on the Peabody Picture Vocabulary Test and the Nixon Test (1967), than the reserve part-Aboriginals. 'Rural part-Aboriginals are, therefore, too heterogeneous to be considered as a single population in studies of cognitive development. Correlations between scores on the two tests were low.' (Full details appear below.)

De Lemos (1969)[1] demonstrated that the conservation performance of full-blooded Australian Aboriginal children was significantly lower than for part-blooded Aboriginals. She concluded that the significant differences found may be due partly to linguistic factors (and cites the work of Luria, 1961, and Bernstein, 1961), but mainly to genetic factors which could have contributed to retarded development of conservation in these children, since she found no 'apparent differences in the environment of the two groups' (p.265).[2] (Cf. recent controversial research evidence of Jensen (1969,[3] 1972). (De Lemos' study is described below.) Tuddenham (1968, 1969) (described fully in Chapter Twelve) demonstrated that Negro children performed at lower levels of conservation operativity than whites and orientals. Vernon (1965) in finding a large 'g' loading in Piagetian tasks, concluded that the performance of West Indian Negro children was substantially lower than a comparable group of English children. (See also Bat-Haee (1972) described later in this chapter, who concluded that '... the traditional intelligence tests and the ... Piagetian tasks ... appear to be sampling cognitive processes which are highly correlated and presumably rest on some fundamental construct, like Spearman's "g" factor'. However, in a study of Zambian primary school children Heron (1971) reported no correlation between conservation of weight and measures of non-verbal 'reasoning' ability ('induction' and 'matrices') or objective measures of School performance. The study is described below.)

A comparison of the performance in conservation operativity of three racial groups (Indians, Negro and white subjects) when contrasted with the results of a 'norming study' revealed the following results. The Negro sample showed a one year deficit in the acquisition of conservation, with a more pronounced retardation as a function of age. There were significant correlations between conservation, age and intelligence within all groups. This was true of each of the three age levels (Gaudia, 1972. Full details are given later in this Chapter.) Cf. Siegel and Kresh, 1971, who demonstrated that the classificatory performance of white children was slightly, but not significantly, superior to that of Negro children at ages four, five, six, seven and eight. Also, Overton, Wagner and Dolinsky (1971) who showed that at age eight to nine years the lower-class Negro group performed at the lower levels of classificatory operativity in contrast to the middle-class white group. However, no such superiority in multiplicative classification tasks was observed at ages four to seven inclusive. (Details of both the studies are more appropriately described in Chapter Five.)

Intelligence and cultural environment.
P. Vernon, 1969.

AIM/Vernon attempted to assess the relative performance of various culturally deprived groups against norms established with English children and to identify environmental variables which impair cognitive development.

SUBJECTS/The study included Scottish, Ugandan, Eskimo, Canadian, Indian, Jamaican and English boys, CA 11 years. N=375.

TESTS/I. Verbal and Educational Tests: Arithmetic, English, spelling, vocabulary and word and information learning. II. Induction Tests: included abstraction and matrices (patterned after Shipley). III. Concept Development: included sorting. IV. Piagetian Battery: included conservation, classification and spatial tasks. V. Creativity Tests: included Rorschach Inkblots and Torrance Incomplete Drawings. VI. Perceptual and Spatial Tests: included Porteus Drawings. VI. Perceptual and Spatial Tests: included Portus Mazes, Picture Recognition, Gottschaldt Embedded Figures Test, Bender-Gestalt, Kohs Block Designs, Goodenough Draw-a-Man Test and Vernon Formboard.

Additionally, Vernon utilized interviewing schedules designed to obtain home background variables as follows: (a) regularity of schooling; (b) health and general physical development: (c) unbroken home; (d) socio-economic status; (e) cultural stimulus; (f) linguistic background; (g) initiative; (h) planfulness; and (i) male dominance.

RESULTS/In comparison to the English performance where 14 per cent of the boys failed conservation, with the exception of the Gaelic group, all groups showed some retardation – 50 per cent of the Ugandan group being non-conservers on every item. 'Hostel' Eskimos failed 40 per cent, 'town' Eskimos 51 per cent and Indians 56 per cent. The median scores on Piagetian performance for the Gaelic- and English-speaking Hebrideans, Jamaicans, Ugandans, Indians, Tuktoyaktuk Eskimos and 'Hostel' Eskimos were 86, 102, 90, 73, 73, 73 and 85 respectively. Overall, most adversely affected were Piagetian conservation tasks with rote-learning-type tests being least affected.

On culture and conservation
P. Greenfield, 1966

SUBJECTS/Greenfield's subjects were Wolof children in Senegal. There were three groups of children differing in both level of education and degree of urbanization: (a) bush unschooled children from a rural village, (b) bush schooled children from the same village and (c) city schooled children.

METHOD/A Piagetian conservation of liquid task involved a pre-test, screening, unscreening and post-tests.

RESULTS/Greenfield's results indicated that there were differences between the younger children (six to nine years) in the three groups, but the unschooled children showed apparent arrest in any qualitative change in intellectual development (conservation task) after the age of eight or nine years. The results further suggested that a lack of schooling was clearly more relevant than rural vs. urban environments. In an attempt to explain the early inferiority of the urban schooled children in comparison to the bush schooled children, Greenfield classified the conservation and non-conservation responses into (a) 'perceptual' (b) 'direct action' and (c) 'transformational'. Furby (1971) sums up Green-field's results in this respect, as follows. 'A comparison of the three groups of subjects according to types of reasons used to support their judgements showed the following pattern. For the bush-schooled children, as age increased there was a very significant decrease in the percentage of their reasons that were perceptual (from nearly 80 per cent for the youngest to slightly over 25 per cent for the oldest). On the other hand, the bush unschooled group showed an increase in perceptual reasons from slightly over 40 per cent for the first-graders (much less than the bush-schooled group) to about 60 per cent for the sixth-graders (much more than their schooled counterparts). The city schooled subjects were intermediate between the two bush groups at the youngest age level (over 60 per cent) but they showed a significant decrease in perceptual reasons and by the sixth grade were identical to the bush-schooled children (over 25 per cent perceptual reasons).' She finally concludes that 'if these experiments indicate one thing of special importance, it is the way in which different modes of thought can lead to the same results: it has too often been assumed that different intellectual means must of necessity lead to different cognitive ends. This might occur in the case of problems which have no objectively definable "right" answer. But where there are action constraints and consequences for behaviour (as with the phenomena of conservation), a disparity in results is not necessarily the case.'

The 'action aspect' of Greenfield's study is what Bovet (1968) terms 'the initial act of fair distribution' — the inadequate analysis of figural aspects was evident as the cause of the deviant type of conservation of Bovet's seven- to eight-year-old subjects.

The formation of logical structures in six- to seven-year-old children
K. H. M. Teplenkaya, 1966

AIM/Teplenkaya in Moscow (1966) undertook '. . . the task of forming in six- to seven-year-old children the following logical structures: class membership and the relationships between classes and sub-classes'. The procedure of the experiment was constructed in accordance with principles 'of the stage-by-stage formation of mental actions'.

SUBJECTS/Very limited information is available about the subjects who took part in the study and no data about other variables are published. However, the author states that 'the children were unable to read or write'.

METHOD/Tests/Three series of experiments were administered individually to each child. The first series of experiments was preparatory; its task consisted of differentiating features in objects and of characterizing the object according to each feature identified. The ability to use the names of categories of identified features was consolidated. Play activities, lasting 20-25 minutes each, were encouraged and symbols were employed, 'since the children were unable to read or write'. The task of the second series of experiments consisted of learning the action involved in determining the class membership (Piaget's 'the including membership'). This was accomplished by three means: (a) identification of the properties and characteristics in the content of the concept; (b) the relationships between each of such characteristics of the object and features of the concept; (c) a judgement of the membership of the object to the class of the given concept. The third series of experiments was aimed at teaching the children to classify, that is to distribute objects into hierarchically connected classes (Piaget's 'inclusions'). This involved two actions: firstly, the division of the class into sub-classes; and secondly, the combination of sub-classes into the class. The learning of actions took place in the process of their performance. Each action was comprehended by practice within 'the main parameters according to the plan'. This further involved generalization, assimilation and completeness of operations.

RESULTS/The investigation substantiated the hypothesis 'that the usually observed level of formed concepts and logical actions in senior school children, as well as the development of those actions and concepts by usual stages, reflect only the course of the process of learning in concrete historical conditions of teaching, rather than the age potentialities of children and the necessary logic of the process of learning'. The author further maintains that results in all the three series of experiments indicated that six- to seven-year-old children could be taught true logical actions of determining the 'class membership' and 'the relationships between classes and sub-classes'. Data obtained may be accounted for by the fact that 'our method permits the formation of mental actions and concepts with the set features, including those qualities which are characteristic of the level of "formal operations", (according to Piaget)'.

Lack of formal schooling and acquisition of conservation
E. Mermelstein and L. S. Shulman, 1967

AIMS/To investigate: (a) the influence on the conservation concept of the effects of a period of non-schooling; (b) the differences between verbal and non-verbal assessment of identical cognitive schemata; and (c) whether a systematic variation of the types of questioning utilized in verbal tasks of conservation would indicate differential effects.

SUBJECTS/The possible effects of non-schooling on conservation were investigated on a total sample of 120 children: 60 six- to nine-year-old Negro children from each of 'schooled' and 'non-schooled' criteria. The two groups were equated for CA and sex.

METHOD/Each child was presented with Tasks 1 to 5 and the sequence in which the experiments were administered was counter-balanced to control for any order effects. The various tasks employed were as follows: (a) Task One: The Conservation of Continuous Quantities (non-verbal). The details of the 'Magic Experiment' are reported by Mermelstein and Shulman (1967) and again in Mermelstein, Carr, Mills and Schwartz (1966-1967). (b) Task Two: The Conservation of Continuous Quantities (Verbal) I (c) Task Three: The conservation of Continuous Quantities (Verbal) II. (d) Task Four: The Conservation of Discontinuous Quantities and its relation to one-to-one correspondence (Verbal) I. (e) Task Five: The conservation of Discontinuous Quantities and its relation to one-to-one correspondence (Verbal) II.

In order to examine the effects of the variation of questions, children were asked: 'Is the amount of water the same, more, or less?' — Type A question; 'Does one glass have more water? Why do you think that?' — Type B question; 'If you were thirsty, which glass would you drink?' 'Why do you think that?' or 'If you could have the gum-balls to keep, which glass would you want?' — Type C question.

The authors state that for any one child, a given type of question (A), (B), or (C) was consistently employed across all tasks.

RESULTS/Findings revealed generally no significant differences attributable to the effects of non-schooling, except within one questioning condition. Differences between verbal and non-verbal tasks were found to be highly significant.

The development of conservation in aboriginal children
M. M. De Lemos, 1969

AIM/De Lemos investigated the development of the concept of conservation among Australian Aboriginal children.

SUBJECTS/One hundred and forty-five children from Elcho Island and Hermannsburg in North Australia, with a CA range from eight to 15 years took part in the investigation. All children attended the mission schools, which provided only a primary level of education.

METHOD/The general experimental procedure, scoring techniques and the apparatus used were identical to those of the Geneva Centre. All children were seen individually and all responses were recorded verbatim. Justifications for judgements made were also observed and noted. However, some modifications were made to material used.

The tests dealt with the conservation of continuous quantity, weight, volume, length, area and number. (Fuller details appear in Piaget, 1956; Piaget and Inhelder, 1962; Piaget, Inhelder and Szeminska, 1960.)

RESULTS/The overall results of De Lemos' study verified the Piagetian stages of development. The behavioural responses in respect to conservation operativity and non-operativity involved the understanding or failure to grasp such acts as those of Reversibility, Compensation, Identity, Addition/Subtraction, Factual or Counter-Suggestion. However, De Lemos' evidence also indicated that conservation of area was not acquired at the same age as conservation of quantity and length, which was a later achievement. Moreover, the order of achievement for the conservation of quantity and weight did not follow the sequence as postulated by Piaget and Inhelder. In De Lemos' study more children performed at a much higher level on weight conservation than on quantity. The author argues that 'it is possible that the reversal of order found . . . may have been . . . due to the effects of experience on the tests. The tests were administered in a standard order such that the tests of quantity and length always preceded the test of weight . . . It is probable that the effects of experience would be more marked in Aboriginal children than in European, since these children are facing problems and situations that are quite new and unfamiliar to them.' The second reason advanced by De Lemos is the change of materials in the tests of quantity and weight and she cites the evidence of Uzgiris (1964), De Lemos (1968) and Boonsong (1968).

Generally, the study indicated that the concept of conservation developed later in Aboriginal than in European children. De Lemos attributes this to a lack of activity methods in schools, little provision for varied experience and language factors. The work of Goodnow (1962), Greenfield (1964), Luria (1961), Furth (1966), Sinclair (1967) and Bernstein (1961) are cited in her arguments and interpretations. Finally, the author suggests that 'it is likely that environmental and cultural factors play an important role in the development of concepts such as conservation'.

The influence of some task variables and of socio-economic class upon the manifestation of conservation of number
N. E. Baker and E. V. Sullivan, 1970

AIM/To test the hypothesis that conservation of number would be manifested to a greater extent by kindergarten children from the middle-classes than children of the same age and schooling from lower socio-economic classes among the Italian and Portuguese immigrant population in Toronto.

METHOD/Experiment One/(administered to 96 children). The tests involved a pre-test patterned after Gruen (1965), designed to exclude children who demonstrated a lack of the comprehension of verbal terms, 'same', 'more', and 'less'; conservation tasks modelled after Piaget (1952b); and a counting test designed to exclude children who could not enumerate.
Experiment Two/(administered to 60 children) involved the same general procedure but with varied materials termed as 'high interest' and 'low interest' objects.

RESULTS/Subjects who showed operativity in all conservation tasks belonged to the middle-class population. However, the significant difference was only upheld for females ($\chi^2 = 5.95$, df = 2, p<.05), not for males ($\chi^2 = 3.04$, df. = 2, p<.15). Likewise, in Experiment Two, significant socio-economic class differences were evidenced with the overall sample; and female subjects' comparisons ($\chi^2 = 5.22$, df = 2, p<.05 and $\chi^2 = 5.17$, df = 2, p<.05, respectively), but not with the male Ss' comparisons ($\chi^2 = .21$, df = 2, p<.45).

The authors conclude that conservation ability was manifested significantly more often by middle-class than by lower-class children, drawn from the Toronto schools with an Italian and Portuguese immigrant population.

A cross-cultural study of classificatory ability in Australia
P. R. De Lacey, 1970

AIMS/The study attempted to elucidate whether operativity in classificatory tasks and milieu are associated in each of the main ethnic groups in Australia. Further, to compare the performances of Aboriginal and white Australian children resident in similar environments.

SUBJECTS/Children were drawn from two European populations, with 'high socio-economic and low-economic status' and two Aboriginal populations described as 'high- or low-contact' in Sydney. From each of the populations, 10 children at each age range from six to 10 years were randomly selected. ('The index of contact was designed to express compositely the effect of 17 variables considered to contribute to contact with Europeans', De Lacey, 1970.)

METHOD/The battery consisted of four tests.
Test One/This test examined the children's ability to use the quantifiers 'some' and 'all' appropriately, implying a comprehension of the relationship between a part and the whole of which it is a part.
Test Two/Five questions on hierarchical classification were used. The material used comprised a four-tier hierarchy: all objects in a basket, food and other objects, fruit and other food, and bananas and oranges.
Test Three/This test was a multiple-classification task similar in pattern to Raven's Progressive Matrices (1938). The general experimental procedure for Tests One to Three was identical to that of Inhelder and Piaget (1964).
Test Four/This test was Nixon's reclassification test 'which required subjects to perform six reclassifications according to new

criteria defined each time by two exemplars'. (Fuller details are given in De Lacey, 1971a page 298.)

RESULTS/De Lacey's research substantiated Inhelder and Piaget's (1964, page 289) contention that between additive and multiple classification operativity there is a parallel development. However, certain qualifications were noted by De Lacey, e.g. that such results may only be evidenced where the child's environment provides a favourable opportunity for cognitive development. The author finally concludes that the overall results indicate a marked relationship 'between the degree of enrichment in children's environments and the particular area of mental growth manifested in the ability to classify . . . this relationship is to be found in both Aboriginal and European children . . . the variety and nature of a child's life experiences are crucial determinants of his level of cognitive functioning.'

The implications of the study for the welfare of the Aboriginal children are discussed.

The effect of special training on the classificatory behaviour of some Nigerian Ibo children
M. O. Okonji, 1970

AIMS/An examination of the effect of special training on classificatory behaviour was undertaken by Okonji with a group of Ibo children. The specific hypotheses were: (1) that the experimental group would perform at a higher level of operativity 'make more shifts in the sorting task' than the control group; (2) that more children showing such operativity would utilize superordinate concepts to verbalize their bases of sorting; and (3) that any acquired concepts would be transferable to hierarchical and related sub-concepts involving abstract behaviour.

SUBJECTS/Forty boys with CA 11 and 12 were selected from rural schools. The experimental and control groups each consisted of 20 boys and were pre-tested on the animal-sorting task. This test also served as the principal transfer task. Subjects were matched for CA, length of time at school, SES.

METHOD/Two sorting tasks and Kohs Blocks were used. These sorting tasks involved such models of animals as goat, dog, sheep, snake, bird, crocodile, etc. These could be classified on the bases of: 'domesticity/non-domesticity, carnivorous/non-carnivorous, reptile/non-reptile, edibility/non-edibility'. The training task involved a 'colour-form-size' sorting of pieces of wood.

TRAINING/Two weeks following the pre-test, the experimental group were trained in small groups of four children each. The training sessions lasted two-and-a-half hours each week, for four weeks. The training was given by various examples of their daily experiences, e.g. 'of the farmer's arrangement and organization of his yams in the barn as one of the many instances of classificatory behaviour which helps to reduce chaos in man's daily activities'. Likewise, the child was trained to group objects and to verbalize the basis of his grouping. In each session three new bases of groupings were introduced, from additive classes to multiplicative classes. They were also encouraged to analyse the objects conceptually and to see the reasons for the justifications advanced both by the E and S. 'At the end of the training the average number of shifts had increased from 2.7 in the first session to 8.42 in the final session . . .'. (Fuller details are given elsewhere, Okonji (1970) pp. 22-24.) Four weeks following the training session, both groups were retested on animal sorting test and the Kohs Blocks. All responses were analysed and classified in terms of performance and verbalization.

RESULTS/In summary, the study indicated that, although training facilitated classification operativity, no positive transfer was noted on Kohs Blocks. Finally, 'the results highlight the need for a taxonomy of tasks requiring ability for abstraction. It seems no longer useful to write about the abstract behaviour of non-Western peoples on the basis of conventional tests used in Western cultures, for while in Western societies all such tests may inter-correlate, they seem not to do so in some non-Western societies . . . most of the tests which led to the earlier assumptions and conclusions about the abstract behaviour of Africans were orientated towards spatial perceptual analyses which are not the same as analyses by means of concepts.'

Verbal intelligence, operational thinking and environment in part-Aboriginal children
P. R. De Lacey, 1971a

AIM/The aim was to investigate any differences in the level of cognitive functioning between reserve and town-dwelling part-Aboriginals, both in terms of verbal intelligence and of operational thinking as conceived by Piaget. Further, to determine any patterning between a Piagetian test and a test of verbal intelligence.

SUBJECTS/Forty-six children in a first-year (school kinder-

241

garten) were examined. The part-Aboriginal children were assessed individually, together with a random sample of low socio-economic European children. The parental occupation for all children was either semi-skilled or unskilled manual worker.

Three groups of children were identified: reserve part-Aboriginals; town part-Aboriginals; and low socio-economic Europeans.

METHOD/Tests/The Peabody Picture Vocabulary Test (PPVT) (Form B) was administered as the test of verbal intelligence. This was 'ideal for Aboriginal children who tend to be reluctant to respond verbally'. The general procedure of administration was patterned after the PPVT manual.

The Nixon Test (Nixon, 1967) is an individual test of classificatory ability. This was employed as the test of operational thinking, 'since it has been shown to discriminate best of four Piagetian classificatory tests between children aged five to seven years from environments differing in enrichment, and to yield results in good agreement with Piagetian tests of additive and multiple classification (De Lacey, 1970a)'. The general experimental procedure was followed as described by Nixon (1967).

RESULTS/A 'depressed' verbal intelligence was noted with the PPVT IQ scores for all three samples. However, the low socio-economic European children performed better than the town part-Aboriginal on both PPVT and Nixon Test (p<.001); the town part-Aboriginals gained higher scores than the reserve part-Aboriginals on the Nixon Test (p<.001) and on the PPVT; although the latter difference was not significant (.1>p>.05).

Further, the correlation between Nixon Test scores and raw PPVT scores was .12 (ns) for all part-Aboriginal children, .45 for the European children, and .42 for all children.

DISCUSSION/The author maintains that progressively lower levels of verbal intelligence and operational thinking were demonstrated for low socio-economic European, town part-Aboriginal and reserve part-Aboriginal subjects. Some of these results substantiate De Lacey's (1970) study (op.cit.). Partial confirmation was also noted of the findings of Dodwell (1961) and Goodnow (1962) which had cast doubts on a positive relationship between intelligence test scores and operativity levels on tests involving operational thinking.

Classificatory ability and verbal intelligence among high-contact Aboriginal and low socio-economic white Australian children
P. R. De Lacey, 1971

AIM/This study is a natural extension of the author's previous study (De Lacey, 1970), described above. The main objectives of the present investigation were as follows:
(a) De Lacey's (1970) study demonstrated that high-contact Aboriginals performed classificatory tasks at the same operativity levels as the white children with low socio-economic background. The present study set out to prove this contention with a larger sample of Aboriginal subjects. (b) If the author's present results lent support to the 1970 study, what relevance, if any, would this have for measures of general intelligence?

SUBJECTS/Forty 'full-blood' Aboriginal children, with a CA range of six to 12 years were involved in the study from Northern Australia — Alice Springs and Darwin. The sample of 40 children varied in numbers at each age level from six to 12 i.e. three, 10, four, 10, six, four, and three respectively.

METHOD/Each child was seen individually and two main tests were administered. These were the multiple classification test (matrix) and reclassification tasks. Both were patterned after Inhelder and Piaget (1964).
The Peabody Picture Vocabulary Test (PPVT) (Dunn, 1965) was also administered to the 40 Aboriginal children and 25 white children with an identical age range. All subjects attended the same school. De Lacey also administered the PPVT to 80 white low socio-economic children in Wollongong, New South Wales — 10 at each age level from six to twelve.

RESULTS/Mean PPVT IQ for the 40 Northern Australian Aboriginals was 63.55 (SD 12.30), and for the 80 Wollongong low socio-economic white children the mean was 94.11 (SD 12.59). The difference of 30.56 was significant by a t-test well beyond the .01 level of probability.

DISCUSSION/De Lacey points out the small samples of children involved, and the even smaller sub-samples at each of seven age levels. However, the two populations were heterogeneous in terms of SES, urban environments and schooling. The overall results corroborated De Lacey's (1970) study that 'full-blood' Aboriginal subjects demonstrated classificatory operativity at the same level as white subjects in a similar low socio-economic urban environment. However, no such trends were observed in respect to the PPVT. 'To the extent that a well-developed system of linguistic symbols is a desirable condition for the development of classification operations (Inhelder and Piaget, 1964, p.4), then whatever the symbolic mode these Aboriginal children use, it finds little expression in either English as used in school, or in native tongues such as may be used at home . . . whether there are any other ethnic or social groups revealing this kind of disparity between operational level and verbal functioning, and if so to discover the linguistic symbols in fact employed in carrying out the Piagetian operations of classification.'

Concrete operations, 'g' and achievement in Zambian children
A. Heron, 1971

AIM/The author maintains that Hunt (1961) made clear 'the relation between what may be described as the "individual differences" approach to the study of human intelligence and that of Piaget was in need of closer attention . . . The purpose of this paper is to use some data obtained in a study of primary school children in Zambia as the basis for reopening this question . . . '.

A non-verbal (miming) Piagetian test of weight conservation was administered, patterned after Furth (1966). Heron and Simonsson (1969) have reported the results of this test elsewhere. Generally, the control group of 105 children of European background, verified the Piagetian stages of development. Likewise, the 200 Zambian African children demonstrated an identical developmental sequence, establishing further the reliability of the non-verbal method of assessment. However, Heron observed that the weight operational children 'did not continue to rise in the usual linear fashion, but reached a near-asymptote of 55-60 per cent after the age of about 11 years'. A similar finding has been reported by Goodnow (1962).

REASONING TESTS/The 'induction' and 'matrices' sections of the new British Intelligence Scale were used. (In preparation, Manchester University School of Education: details given in Chapter 12.) Data on African children in Piagetian concept of weight conservation were available to the author. In all, 66 children were involved as follows: 18 from Grade 2, 17 from Grade 4 and 31 from Grade 7. Grade 7 children had also participated in the Secondary School Selection Examination consisting of performance in Arithmetic, English, Verbal and Non-verbal Reasoning. The results were also accessible.

METHOD/The 'induction' test was preceded by an 18-item

peg-board training series. The actual test items incorporate the principles underlying the first six items of the training phase followed by nine more items in ascending order of difficulty. The 'matrices' test comprises 48 items and is preceded by a 12 item pre-test and training series. The progression is from 'symmetry' (or 'perceptual-solution') to multiple-classification (or 'operational-solution') type of items. (Fuller details, including diagrams, of these tests are given in 'The British Intelligence Scale', Manchester University School of Education, and Heron, 1971, pp. 326-7.)

RESULTS/Data gathered were subjected to several statistical techniques in order to establish the relation between performance on the reasoning tests and weight conservation operativity or non-operativity. Heron reported the following results:

(a) Zambian children exhibited individual differences on tests of non-verbal performance which involved 'induction' and the 'education of relations and correlates', which forms the basis of Spearman's 'g'.

(b) Likewise, Grade Seven subjects demonstrated a great degree of individual differences on objective tests of verbal and non-verbal reasoning and arithmetic.

(c) A highly significant relation existed between tests in (a) above and arithmetic. However, this was only true with older children (of Grade Seven).

(d) No significant differences were observed between Piagetian weight conservation operativity/non-operativity and children's performance in (a) and (b) above.

Heron finally concluded 'very little connection is found between the conservation-status of the subjects and their performance on these variables'. The observed discrepancies between the Piagetian and psychometric aspects, as related to human intelligence are elucidated and argued, in the light of cultural factors. In this discussion Heron draws on Goodnow and Bethon (1966), Heron and Simonsson (1969), Furth (1969), Piaget (1952, 1964), Kohlberg (1968), Halpern (1965), Cattell (1963), Jensen (1969), Vernon (1969) and Wohlwill (1968).

Studies of conservation with Yoruba children of differing ages and experience
B. Lloyd, 1971

Lloyd's study had a three-fold aim: (a) To investigate familiar and unfamiliar materials and their effect on conservation performance; (b) to compare the conservation performance involving Yoruba and American subjects; and (c) to analyse the justifications advanced by Yoruba subjects.

SUBJECTS/Eighty subjects were involved in the study drawn from élite and Oje homes in Nigeria, with an age range of three years five months to eight years. Equal numbers of either sex were investigated at five age levels and each age level included a range of six months and was separated from the next group by half a year. The parents of élite children had all received secondary school education. In contrast, Oje mothers were illiterate and the fathers had little formal schooling. The groups were therefore essentially different in respect to parental education, living standards and the educational opportunities that existed within the home setting.

METHOD/Each child was tested on Piagetian tasks; a learning problem; and the Stanford-Binet Intelligence Scale (with certain modifications). Two Yoruba University students conducted the testing in the Yoruba language under the guidance of Lloyd.

Three Conservation tasks were employed. Task A was concerned with provoked correspondence and equivalence of corresponding sets of discrete objects (Piaget, 1952b). Task B was a simple test of number conservation, while task C assessed the conservation of continous quantity. The general experimental procedure, including the recording and scoring of verbatim protocols were patterned after Almy, Chittenden and Miller (1966, pp. 51-58).

RESULTS/Lloyd examines the nature of the justifications advanced by the Yoruba children. Reasons offered by non-conservers in the study differed only to a small degree from the Wolof and Tiv non-conservers. However, the Yoruba children who demonstrated operativity justified conservation in terms unlike those observed either in Price-Williams' (1961, op. cit.) or Greenfield's (1966, op. cit.) studies. The Yoruba conservers relied on direct action to justify operativity and offered comparatively fewer perceptual explanations.

Lloyd finally concludes that Yoruba children show conservation operativity at the same age as American and African subjects, and that performance is a linear function of CA. Identical performance was observed with familiar and unfamiliar materials, although an improvement was noted with practice. She discusses her results with the findings of Price-Williams (1961) and Greenfield's (1966) studies. She casts doubt on Greenfield's hypothesis, that Wolof subjects achieved operativity through direct action and suggests a reanalysis of the phenomenon 'in terms of a competence-performance distinction'. She finally notes that 'Further progress in understanding cognitive development both within and across cultures may come from a combined programme of research in which the formal and functional aspects of phenomena will be more carefully delineated and these insights employed in seeking further cross-cultural comparisons'.

Culture and children's understanding of geometry
M. O. Okonji, 1971a

AIM/The author replicated Piagetian concepts of the development of geometric development among children in Ankole, Uganda, where 'there are no traditional precision measuring instruments either geometric or others, with a view to throwing some light on the extent to which schooling experience affected this development'.

SUBJECTS/As many as 358 children from 25 schools were involved in the study. One group with an age-range from six to 11 years were all school attenders and the 'Government of Uganda Primary School Syllabus' Ministry of Education (1965) encourages 'Geometric work, folding and arranging of shapes to form patterns, extensive measurement exercises involving the properties of geometric figures and the use of various measuring instruments including protractors'. The other group, ranging in age from six to 16, were all non-school going, their 'mensurational skills are often brought into play when they build houses or map out plots of land . . . measuring techniques are rudimentary . . . and the limbs and whole body length are used as units of measurement'.

METHOD/All children were tested individually in their native language. Responses were recorded verbatim, together with any movements made and questions asked: any vague behavioural responses were elucidated by further questioning. The order of presentation of the tests was the same for all subjects: length conservation; angular measurement; and the location of a point on a rectangular sheet of paper. Testing was conducted either in schools, community centres or 'in the house of a Chief'. All the tests were administered in accordance with the general experimental procedures of the Geneva Centre. Full details of these experiments appear in Piaget, Inhelder and Szeminska (1960).

RESULTS/Overall, the results verified the Piagetian stages of development 'with some evidence of the usually observed developmental lag among non-Western children relative to their Western Counterparts'. Okonji's non-schooling subjects revealed an unusual degree of stagnation in the acquisition of length conservation. Other studies which have promoted similar contentions are those of Greenfield (1966) and Prince (1968). However, some studies have parted from such evidence in their investigations — Goodnow et al. (1966); Mermelstein et al. (1967); and De Lemos (1969). (These studies have been discussed elsewhere.)

Okonji points out two inadequacies of his investigation — 'linguistic handicap and the consequent use of a research assistant'. The need for more research is indicated, which will employ variables of schooling, non-schooling and the quality of the relevant school geometry lessons. 'When enough convincing evidence is available it may become clear that what we need is a two-tier, Piaget-Bruner theory to explain children's understanding of geometry. For our present findings concerning the understanding of angular separation and coordinate reference system by Banyankole children make more sense when examined in the light of Bruner's (1966) view "that mental growth is in very considerable measure dependent upon growth from the outside in, a mastering of the techniques that are embodied in the culture . . . ".'

A cross-cultural study of the effects of familiarity on classificatory behaviour
M. O. Okonji, 1971

AIM/'The effect of familiarity with test materials on equivalence grouping was investigated by using two sets of materials that differed in the degree to which they were familiar to two different groups.'

SUBJECTS/A total of 243 children — 138 from Ibusa (Nigeria) and 105 from Glasgow — were involved in the study with a CA range from six to 12 years.

METHOD/Tests/Two sorting tests were administered. One set of materials was more familiar to the Ibusa subjects. The other set was equally familiar to both the Glasgow and Ibusa children. Examples of the first set (animals) included models of a snake, a crocodile, an elephant and a springbok. Examples of the second set (objects) included a metal gong, a red leather bag, a needle and a wooden spoon.

It was postulated by Okonji that familiarity with the sorting of the objects would enable Ibusa children to perform at a higher level of operativity than the Glasgow subjects. Also 'to be more accurate in their classification where accuracy means a correspondence between the "intension" and "extension" of the classes

248

formed in all age groups'. In respect to the sorting of the animals no difference in operational performance was predicted due to familiarity and finally, the overall developmental pattern was expected to be similar for both the groups of Ibusa and Glasgow children.

The tests were given in English to the Glasgow children and in Ibo to the Ibusa subjects. All children were seen individually and a full record kept of all the responses. With the Object sorting task, the child was familiarized with the names of each of the objects placed before him. 'A stimulus object around which sorting was done was brought out and S was requested to collect all other objects that were like it in some way or that went together with it.'

The procedure for animal sorting was similar to the object sorting. However, after the child had put together all the animals that went together or were like one another, he was requested for other ways of sorting. New groupings were encouraged until the child demonstrated that he could no longer do so. A second phase of this test consisted of the verbalization of E's sorting which was as follows: (a) Domestic/Nondomestic (b) Carnivorous/Noncarnivorous (c) Birds/Nonbirds (d) Reptiles/Nonreptiles

The child was asked to verbalize the bases of E's groupings.

RESULTS/Generally, the results revealed that familiarity has only a moderate influence on classification operativity. 'If, however, we take into account the fact that the degree of unfamiliarity of the task to the Glasgow group was not high, the importance of the result increases. It seems, therefore, that the obtained level of significance constitutes quite a weighty evidence in support of the view that familiarity with objects to be classified does affect a child's efficiency in classification.' Okonji has argued that Ibusa children are most influenced by schooling at ages 11 −12.

Further, examination of the results revealed that 'all that familiarity does to aid classification is to facilitate in a given context the availability of appropriate verbal templates and provide some visual cues for defining classes'.

Another feature of Okonji's study was the fact that 25 per cent of the six- to eight-year age group of the Ibusa sample classified the animals on the basis of colour. No such proportion of Glasgow children produced such a result. The author maintains: 'It is not clear why colour concepts are so salient for Africans even among adults, but cease to be so among Euro-Americans relatively early, probably before school age (Lee, 1965). It may be a case of "systematic preference" for colour cues. This preference is obviously not innate since it dwindles not only with age, but also with amount of schooling experience.'

Classification patterns of underprivileged children in Israel
S. Sharan (Singer) and L. Weller, 1971

The authors' main hypotheses were: (a) that lower-class and Middle Eastern children together will demonstrate a lower object-grouping ability than middle-class and Western children respectively; (b) that varied criteria for object-grouping would be utilized by lower-class and Middle Eastern children than by middle-class Western children, respectively; and (c) that lower-class and Middle Eastern children will be less able to inhibit motor performance than will middle-class and Western children, respectively.

They also set out to establish: (d) what sex differences in grouping behaviour and style are common to young children in Israel and (e) whether a correlation exists between motor inhibition and categorizing.

SUBJECTS/Three hundred and fifty-seven first grade lower- and middle-class Jewish children of Middle Eastern and Western ethnic backgrounds were investigated. Categorizing behaviour was assessed with a series of sorting tasks, patterned after Sigel et al. (1967).

METHOD/Briefly, the task consisted of an Active and Passive Condition. Under the Active condition, 12 objects were placed in front of the child. E selected one object from the array. 'Look at all these things and put over here the ones that are like this one or go with it.' The same procedure was used with each of the 12 objects. Reasons for selection were requested and all justifications recorded verbatim. Under Passive condition a selected grouping was shown to the child. There were 10 groupings with three objects, two groupings with two objects. Again all justifications were noted and responses scored on Grouping Ability and Categorization Style.

Grouping Ability/1. Grouping responses: The child in the active condition adds one object at a time in the formation of a group. This is in response to the object selected by the E. Verbal justifications are requested in the Passive Condition for the group as assembled by E. 2. Non-grouping responses: The child does not meet the task requirements. 3. Non-scorable responses: No verbal justifications are advanced.

Style Of Categorization/ A second scoring was used for style of categorization over and above the general grouping ability. The style of categorization was patterned after Kagan, Moss and Sigel (1963); Sigel, Jarman and Hanesian (1967). The categories were: Categorical — Inferential (CI); and Relational — Contextual (R).

Motor inhibition was evaluated by requesting the child to draw a line as slowly as he could from the top of an 8½- by 11-inch sheet of paper to a line drawn across the centre of the sheet (Kagan et al., 1964).

RESULTS/The authors concluded that varied configurations of grouping behaviour were positively associated with the background variables. The most abstract grouping style was less frequently employed by lower-class children than was the case with the middle-class children. Children of Middle Eastern ethnic background advanced fewer descriptive behavioural responses. Likewise, they also demonstrated more non-operational behaviour in the grouping tasks, than did the Western ethnic background subjects. Moreover, consistent sex differences were observed in favour of the girls who performed at a much higher level of operativity. 'Further research is needed to explore the possible adjustment.' The overall results are discussed in relation to the findings and contentions of Inhelder and Piaget (1964), Wallach and Kogan (1965), Witkin, Dyk, Paterson, Goodenough and Karp (1962) and Sigel and McBane (1967).

The conservation of number and liquid by Lebanese school children in Beirut
G. I. Za'rour, 1971

AIMS/The author was concerned to establish: (a) whether the Piagetian stages of development could be identified in Lebanese children; (b) a developmental comparison of Lebanese and American children in respect to number and liquid conservation; (c) any possible sequential relationships between conservation operativity of number and liquid; and (d) any relationship which may exist between conservation ability and variables of sex, socio-economic status, religion, scholastic level and mother's literacy.

SUBJECTS/One hundred and nine Christians and 115 Moslems, comprising a total sample of 224 Lebanese children were involved in the study, with CA ranging from five to nine years. The subjects were assigned in the top, middle or bottom one-third in respect to scholastic level by their respective teachers. Forty-six per cent of the Ss had illiterate mothers and belonged 'to the low and middle class background. However, they were classified into

251

three socio-economic groups.'

METHOD/The general experimental procedure was patterned after Almy's et al. (1966) cross-sectional study, and their results were used as a frame of reference in the cross-cultural comparison. (Almy's 1966 study has received detailed treatment elsewhere in this book.)

Three tests were administered prior to some practice items. These items were intended to assess the child's comprehension of relational terms and to familiarize him with the mode of questioning.

Test One/Briefly, 12 yellow and 12 red wooden cubes were aligned in two parallel rows. E makes sure that child recognizes equality before changing the red cubes by grouping them together. 'How about now? Is the number of yellow and red cubes the same or is one greater than the other?' All responses were recorded and justifications were asked.

Test Two/The original row of yellow cubes was spread even more and questions as in Test One were asked.

Test Three/Briefly, the liquid is poured from one of the two identical bottles into a graduated cylinder, and asked 'How about now? Is the amount of liquid in the cylinder equal to that in the other bottle, more or less?' All responses were recorded and justifications were requested.

RESULTS/The 75 per cent criterion of conservation was achieved by children in the fourth grade in liquid, but not in number. 'However, conservation was attained by 81 subjects in number and by 73 in liquid. Of these, 51 conserved both quantities – 30 conserved number only and 22, liquid only.' A chi-square test analysing the frequencies with which the children at various age levels fell under the three categories was significant beyond the .001 level in both number and liquid tasks.

Za'rour further examined the types of explanation advanced by children performing at a higher level of conservation operativity. These included the acts of Reversibility, Addition/ Subtraction, Action and Identity. On the other hand, non-conservers responded mostly on perceptual dimensions or were unable to advance any explanations at all. Further, the relation of sex and conservation categories was observed to be significant at the .05 level only for the number tasks (χ^2 = 6.83, df = 2). However, the effect of religion, scholastic level, socio-economic status and mother's literacy demonstrated no significance at .05 level for any of these variables in any of the tasks. Likewise, the differences among various socio-economic groups were not significant.

A Lebanese-American Comparison/The results of the Lebanese children corresponded, at least in part, to those of Hyde (1959, op. cit.) who found that British children were developmentally ahead of their non-European (Arab, Somali and Indian) counterparts in conservation abilities. However, children in Almy's (1966) study performed at a much higher level of conservation operativity than did the Lebanese subjects, both in number and liquid conservation tasks. Za'rour argues that these discrepancies are due to modes of parent-child interaction and child-rearing practices which affect cognitive development and cites the work of Bing (1963) and Prothro (1961). Educational experiences, culture and environment appear to influence the development of these abilities.

Further, Za'rour's present study indicated a significant difference (p<.05) in favour of the boys for number conservation ability only. This finding supports Goldschmid's (1967) results but not those of Dodwell (1961) and Almy et al. (1966, page 82), who reported no such sex differences. The results of Za'rour's study also revealed that number was conserved more easily than liquid, but no general patterns emerged to lend credence to the contention that the ability to conserve number necessarily precedes that of liquid.

Conservation of weight across different materials by Lebanese school children in Beirut
G. I. Za'rour, 1971a

AIMS/The main aims of Za'rour's study were to examine: (a) the development of the concept of conservation of weight among Lebanese and American children; (b) the effect-of varying the materials used in the acquisition of weight conservation; and (c) the relationship of the variables of sex, socio-economic status, scholastic level, mother's literacy to the acquisition of weight conservation.

SUBJECTS/Twelve schools were involved with a total sample of 132 Lebanese — 69 boys and 63 girls. The CA ranged from seven years to nine years eight months and all spoke Arabic as their mother tongue. The subjects were identified as belonging to the top, middle or bottom of scholastic levels as well as to three socio-economic groups — the latter being identified mainly through parental occupation.

METHOD/Materials: (a) five balls of red plasticine, two of them equal in weight; (b) a rubber band; (c) a thermometer with

253

the alcohol dyed blue.

The weight experiment consisted of a child's identification of the equality of the two plasticine balls which preceded the transformation of one of them into a sausage by E. The rubber band was stretched to about twice its length. In respect to the thermometer experiment, the application of heat resulted in a four centimetre rise of the alcohol level. Questions were asked regarding the weight of the object after transformation – whether it had remained the same or increased, or decreased. (Fuller details appear in Za'rour, 1971a, page 388.)

RESULTS/Children with CA seven to nine performed at a higher level of weight conservation operativity on plasticine than they did either on a rubber band or on alcohol in a thermometer. For each of the materials, boys demonstrated higher levels of operativity than did the girls.

A comparison of operational children in the plasticine task with those of Elkind (1961) and Uzgiris (1964), demonstrated no age difference between the performance of Lebanese and American children. Za'rour's study also observed 'that the conservation of a quantity as weight is not necessarily an all or none phenomenon. Even within a quantity, whether one conserves or not depends upon the type of material used . . . The difficulties seem to be inherent in the experiments or materials themselves rather than being produced by individual differences'. Za'rour's present findings in this respect lend further credence, at least in part, to the findings of Uzgiris (1964) and those of Lovell and Ogilvie (1961). Za'rour puts forward the following arguments as contributing to the observed discrepancies in weight conservation across different materials:

(a) 'Compensatory relations are relatively easy to observe in the plasticine experiment. They are harder to perceive in rubber band and they are empirically absent in the thermometer experiment as the alcohol actually increases both in volume and in height without diminishing in width.'

(b) 'In the plasticine experiment the S had to admit the equality in weight of the two balls before the transformation. The rubber band and thermometer experiments did not involve such a reference to equality prior to testing.'

(c) 'In the rubber band and thermometer experiments the initial state of the rubber band and of the alcohol had to be reconstructed abstractly by the child before answering the questions. In the plasticine experiment, the standard was exposed along with the transformed object. In addition, the rubber band and thermometer experiments provided a direct test of identity while plasticine was a test of equivalence.'

The correlation between Piaget's conservation of quantity tasks and three measures of intelligence in a select group of children in Iran
M. A. Bat-Haee, A. H. Mehryar and V. Sabharwal, 1972

AIMS/The authors attempted an investigation into the relationships between Piagetian tests of conservation and certain standard tests of intelligence.

SUBJECTS/The total sample of 65 children (35 boys and 30 girls) from a community school in Southern Iran participated in the study. The CA ranged from six to 11 years and the 'national origins' of parents were: both parents Iranian 46 per cent; both parents western 28 per cent; one parent Iranian and one western 26 per cent. Subjects involved came from 'higher professional' and 'administrative echelons'.

METHOD/The following tests were administered: 1. Piaget's Test of Conservation of Quantity, patterned after Elkind (1967); 2. Raven's Coloured Progressive Matrices (CPM); 3. Vocabulary and Arithmetic Scales of the WISC.
'The guiding principle in the choice of the tests of intelligence was inclusion of representative measures of both "g" and the more educationally determined verbal and numerical dimensions of intelligence.'
All tests were administered individually and all behavioural responses recorded verbatim.

RESULTS/The results indicated Iranian Ss' high performance on the intelligence scales. However, children in grades 1 and 2 performed at a much lower level of Piagetian conservation. The authors argue that this discrepancy is contrary to their own previous studies (Bat-Haee and Hosseini, 1971) and 'may have arisen out of a failure on the part of the tester'.
Furthermore, the two subscales of the WISC were highly correlated (r = .75). The CPM, likewise, also correlated significantly with the WISC vocabulary and Arithmetic subtests (r = .68 and r = .72, respectively). Similarly, the highest correlation computed was with the conservation score (r = .45).
The authors conclude the results of their study as follows: '. . . the present findings seem to support the contention that in spite of the different orientations and origins of the traditional intelligence tests and the currently popular Piagetian tasks, they both appear to be sampling cognitive processes which are highly correlated and presumably rest on some fundamental construct, like Spearman's "g" factor.'

Race, social class, and age of achievement of conservation on Piaget's tasks
G. Gaudia, 1972

AIM/An investigation into the conservation acquisition across sub-cultural groups formed the main theme of the present study.

SUBJECTS/The total sample of 126 American Indian, Negro and white subjects comprised seven boys and seven girls in each group from each of the first three grades. The Indian children were drawn from seven schools, Negro children from 24 schools and white children from 19 schools all from four counties in Western New York State. The subjects came from the lowest social class (Warner, Meeker and Eells, 1949).

'It was planned to examine the data for social class effects by comparing the performance of the total research sample with the norming group data obtained by the authors' tests on large samples of children who represented all strata of society.'

METHOD/Form A of the Conservation Concept Assessment Kit (Goldschmid and Bentler, 1968b) was administered. The six tasks were: Two-dimensional space; Number; Substance; Continuous Quantity; Discontinuous Quantity and Weight.

RESULTS/Overall, the study provided evidence of major differences in rates of acquisition of conservation between children of different racial and social class backgrounds. In the rate of acquisition, Negro children (especially older Negro children) performed at a lower level of conservation operativity than Indian and white children. Gaudia argues: 'This increasing difference between racial groups with increasing CA suggests that lower-class environments may be entirely different among different races. When the lower-class children in the research sample were compared with the more heterogeneous norming groups, the lower-class children were later in acquiring conservation than the more advantaged social class groups. There was also a tendency for the Negro IQs . . . to decrease with age . . . Piaget (1964), page 10 claims that environment is a factor in cognitive development, but a relatively minor one, and then only when the cultures are widely divergent . . . He also maintains that nervous maturation is a necessary factor, and that there is evidence of racial and social class differences in rate of physical maturation. If these are the factors separating the groups in the present study, and if they are cultural, rather than, or in addition to, intrinsic developmental factors, they have as yet to be identified specifically.'

[1] Dasen (1972a) attempted to replicate De Lemos' (1969) study and reports: 'We have envisaged a variety of explanations of the disagreement in results concerning the possible differences in cognitive development between part-blood and full-blood Aborigines living in apparently identical conditions. None could be sufficiently substantiated and the problem remains open to discussion and further investigation.'

[2] Dasen (1972a) argues: 'additional support for the interpretation that differences in the rate of attainment of concrete operations are mainly environmental, comes from a study of Australian Aboriginal children who have been fostered or adopted early in life by European families (Dasen et al., 1972b). The rate of cognitive development of these children was very different from that found at Hermannsburg, and was almost identical to the development found in middle-class European children. Our results cannot, of course, be taken as conclusive until their contradiction with those obtained by de Lemos (1969) has been resolved. However, until this can be done, de Lemos' results should no longer be used to support the argument for genetic differences in mental functioning.'

[3] Jensen points out: ' . . . the value of heritability index (h) is jointly a function of genetic and environmental variability in the population . . . Values of h reported in the literature do not represent what the heritability might be under any environmental condition . . . ' (p. 43). (See also Tizard 1974, p. 73).

CHAPTER NINE
COGNITIVE DEVELOPMENT RESEARCHES AND THE SCHOOL CURRICULUM

Among the early attempts to illustrate the significance of Piaget's work for curriculum development is that of Banks (1958). He examined formal reasoning in students using experimental situations drawn from Piaget's 'The Child's Conception of Physical Causality' (1930). The author concluded that secondary modern school pupils should be inspired to analyse and reason concerning scientific phenomena as opposed to formal presentation of scientific principles. (Fuller details appear in Banks, 1958, and Lunzer, 1960.)

Peel (1959) reviews studies by his students. Lodwick studied inferences drawn from reading historical passages and the responses advanced by children. He contends that the reasoning inherent in Piagetian tasks may be appropriately transferred to other areas of the curriculum. He identified three stages corresponding to the three Piagetian levels. However, Peel (1959) states '. . . the form of the questions and their relation to the passages, all vary and may limit some replies to certain parts of the range of reasoning. Also different passages and questions may motivate a child to varying degrees.' (Fuller details appear in Peel, 1959, and Lunzer, 1960.)

A study by Ross (1959) involved children drawn from two junior schools and one secondary modern school. He employed a demonstration method to explore the principles of sound involving relations between sound and movement of the vibrating body; frequency and length; length and pitch; conduction of sound; and interrelated topics. Through experimental demonstrations, children were asked to predict the results following procedural variations. The majority could not comprehend sound, detecting only its relationship with movement. (Fuller details appear in Ross, 1959, and Lunzer, 1960.)

'The Place of Maps in the Junior School', an investigation undertaken by Prior (1959) draws its experimental tasks from the later experiments reported in 'The Child's Conception of Space'

258

(Piaget and Inhelder, 1956). Prior was intent to obtain guidance for appropriate curriculum content. Prior concludes that '... while experiences using actual models and simple maps provide the necessary material on which to base true concepts, they should enter only incidentally in the junior school programme'. However, it must be stressed that Prior's presentation of results lacks the clinical Piagetian depth. (Fuller details appear in Prior, 1959, and Lunzer, 1960.)

(More recently, Peel, 1971, has assembled and extended his own investigations and those of his research students, in relation to the psychological nature and development of judgement in adolescence. The monograph is summarized at the end of this Chapter.)

'The Process of Education' (Bruner, 1960) drew attention to the relevance of Piaget's ideas of curriculum revision. Lovell's 'The Growth of Basic Mathematical and Scientific Concepts in Children' (1961), Churchill's 'Counting and Measuring' (1961), Goldman's 'Religious Thinking from Childhood to Adolescence' (1964) and the work of the Nuffield Foundation (Matthews, 1968) were the pioneers in relating the Piagetian theory to the development of curriculum organization in England. The Nuffield Foundation has published two volumes of 'Check Ups', devised in Geneva, which are currently used by some teachers in schools to find out, 'how far (the children's) thinking has progressed'. (Fuller details and evaluation are given in Harlen, 1968). Piaget observes the often illogical thinking of the younger child and the more mobile and systematic thought of the older child in his works on quantity (Piaget, 1941), number (1952b), classification and seriation (Inhelder and Piaget, 1964), space (Piaget and Inhelder, 1956), movement and speed (Piaget, 1970), physics and chemistry (Inhelder and Piaget, 1958) and geometry (Piaget, Inhelder and Szeminska 1960).

Kessen and Kuhlman (1962) addressed the first of their conferences entirely to the work of Piaget concerning cognitive processes in children and Flavell (1963) has summarized both Piaget's psychological and epistemological views. In 1964 Piaget elaborated his views at the Cornell and California conferences which addressed their inquiry to the implications of current cognitive development researches for the mathematics and science curriculum (Ripple and Rockcastle, 1964). Various issues were discussed: for example, the appropriate sequence of the presentation of specific concepts in curricula; relative usefulness of direct instruction, as opposed to self-discovery in the formation of concepts; and the role of language in such formation.

Kilpatrick (1964) describes the curriculum programme of the School Mathematics Study Group. He discussed the issue of spontaneous development in children's thinking versus acceleration of this development through formal instruction and

259

experience. However, it is essential to point out that the features of this curriculum scheme are not entirely compatible with the findings of Piaget's studies. Kilpatrick speculates that the child's ability to understand may be changed by new curricula, and that the issue of stages, therefore, remains an open one. Bruner (op. cit.) has provided a psychological rationale for the major ideas of this new mathematics curricula and the work of Dienes (1959) is especially relevant in this respect. Similar research efforts have been undertaken by Fischer (1964). He maintains that Piagetian work has indicated 'the need for following a plan designed in accordance with the child's developing thought structures. Providing the requisite concrete experiences which undergird abstract and symbolic learning presents a challenge to the teacher, and calls for changes in much of the traditional curriculum.' (See Piaget, 1973.)

Collis (1971), attempted to distinguish mathematical material most suited to the abilities of concrete operational and formal operational level pupils, respectively. He concluded that educationalists should be familiar with the characteristics of the mental strategies manifest at the various Piagetian stages and that curriculum content should be adjusted accordingly. (Details appear later in this chapter.) Cathcart (1971), in an investigation into the relationship between conservation and mathematical achievement with primary school children, emphasizes that for success in mathematics the child should be able to analyse a problem from different points of view. The implication for teaching is that there should be a more general problem-solving approach, rather than the teaching of particular rules for particular types of problems. (Details of the study appear later in this chapter. Cf. Wang, Resnick and Boozer, 1971.)

Karplus (1964) developed the 'Science Curriculum Improvement Scheme'. The aim of the scheme is described as 'that of enhancing the development of thinking to the formal operational level' — an aim which lends itself to the use of Piagetian concepts. Karplus argues that in his experience with teachers and children, there are some who enter adulthood without reaching the formal level (cf. Hughes, 1965, Tomlinson-Keasey, 1972). If and when this is achieved, the areas of acquisition are restricted. The author specifically mentions Piaget's experiments on the concept of conservation of volume, as an instance.

Cole (1968) hypothesized that 'educators are aware of the necessity for negative instances in teaching new concepts to students, but are probably less aware of the need in problem-solving to learn the technique of rejecting the more obvious e.xplanations which, for children, are often the perceptually dominant feature of the situation'. Cole's study (described later) is of special interest to science teachers, and may well suggest new ways of introducing scientific principles in the classroom.

Field and Cropley (1969) attempted to clarify the relationship between science achievement and four cognitive style variables—mental operations, originality and flexibility and category width — among 178 subjects, aged 16 to 18 years, all following Science courses. The questionnaire developed by Tisher (1971, described in Chapter Five) was employed to measure the stage of mental operations. A highly significant relationship existed between operations classifications and level of science achievement for each sex. High science achievement was therefore associated with the ability to apply formal operations in processing science information. The boys' performance was superior to that of the girls on all variables. The superiority of the boys with regard to the development of formal operations was considered by the authors to be of interest, particularly as little has been attempted to date in this area with pupils beyond 15 years. No sex differences were reported by Inhelder and Piaget (1958) and Tisher (1971). Field and Cropley comment that the apparently slower development of formal operations by the girls is perhaps, 'a contributing factor to their general inferiority to boys in handling science information at this stage of schooling and in later stages also'. The study implies that 'teachers should become better informed of their pupils' abilities or modes of cognitive functioning and endeavour to programme the class work both to capitalize on and extend these'. Furthermore, that 'a multidimensional view of intellectual functioning might provide more useful information about interpupil differences in science achievement than any univariate approaches'.

An active attempt towards the fulfilment of the Cornell Conference issues (op. cit.) was made by Almy and associates (1971). The authors' aim was to investigate the effects of instruction in the basic concepts of mathematics and science on the logical thinking abilities of second grade children. They argue that the group of children who had no prescribed lessons in either kindergarten or first grade operated equally well in the Piagetian tasks as did the groups who had prescribed lessons beginning in kindergarten. But the latter groups performed better than did the groups whose prescribed lessons began only in the first grade. However, Almy and associates conclude: 'The ambiguity of the findings precludes the drawing of final conclusions, either as to the major questions of the study, or as to the more subsidiary questions having to do with the relative efficacy of different ways of presenting science concepts to children and also with the relative effectiveness of different kinds of teaching strategies.' Nevertheless, the study provides evidence as to the nature of the children's thinking at this age and illuminates the complex interactions that are involved when early instruction is undertaken. The authors conclude their investigation with a full discussion on curricula content and its timing together with instruction and the assessment of the individual. Almy, Chittenden and Miller (1966, p.121, and described more fully later in this chapter) maintain: 'Of most importance, there are indications of the different ways that children in the same grade view phenomena and problems that the adult regards as similar or even identical. The significance of such diversity for the early childhood curriculum and for the instruction of the child remains to be explored.' (Criticism of the methodology of this study has, however, been advanced by Gaudia, 1972 — see abstract Almy, Chittenden and Miller cf. Figurelli and Keller, 1972, Little, 1972.)

Kohlberg (1968a) examines the Piagetian contributions to preschool programmes with specific reference to academic and linguistic training. Kohlberg attempted to demonstrate how Piagetian theory leads to the conclusion that it is futile to teach cognitive skills. 'The conception of the preschool period as a critical period for the environmental stimulation of general intelligence is examined, considering general intelligence in both psychometric and Piagetian terms.' Kohlberg further recalls the contributions of Piaget and associates in the 'development of preschool children's play, their conversations with one another, their conceptions of life, of death, of reality, of sexual identity, of good and evil. The implications of these and other themes for the broader definition of preschool objectives are taken up elsewhere'. (Kohlberg and Lesser, in preparation.)

However, Bereiter (1970, pp. 25-31) responded critically to Kohlberg's conclusion against specific instruction. Bereiter accuses Kohlberg of treating instruction as if it were an alternative to experience when the issue concerns only a half-hour per day of structured interaction between teacher and child within the day of free activity. Kamii (1970, pp. 33-39) argues that Bereiter did not succeed in making a convincing case in support of specific instruction, but at the same time Kamii considered that the educational implications that Kohlberg drew from Piaget's theory were too general. She maintains that 'the two schools of thought converge with regard to the teaching of social knowledge, but not with regard to logico-mathematical knowledge ... The relative merits of the two approaches can be determined only through long-term longitudinal comparisons'. However, Kohlberg (1970 pp. 40-48) reiterates the points of his 1968a article, which he directs to the criticisms of Bereiter and Kamii. (For the full dialogue among Kohlberg, Bereiter and Kamii, refer to 'Interchange', A Journal of Educational Studies, I, 1, 1970.)

Sullivan (1967, p.23) maintains that the controversy is continued by several other authors who concluded that Piaget can make no contribution to education concerning the concept of, for example, readiness in mathematics (Aebli, 1966; Gagné, 1966; Kohnstamm, 1966). Aebli (quoted in Kohnstamm, 1966 p. 3) notes that 'If Piaget in his developmental experiments demonstrates that at a certain age a certain operation exists, it does not have to be taught anymore. However, if the child does not yet have the operation at his disposal, it cannot be taught.' Kohnstamm (1966) recognizes this as the basic problem in Piaget's theory for several reasons, the first being that Piaget believes that experience in daily life is necessary for development and that the child learns gradually from his own spontaneous experiences. There is, according to Kohnstamm, no place in the theory for the systematic teaching of thought strategies. The second reason is inherent in the fact that, for Piaget, the child's activity rather than his language, is the main factor in cognitive development.

'In Piaget's view the social transmission of spoken language is not essential for the formation of operational structures. Therefore all the words a teacher might use in trying to explain a certain Piagetian problem to the child are considered useless. If the child has had the necessary experience he will discover the insight into the problems all in due time; if he has not, the only thing a teacher can do is to teach the child to recite the rules parrot-wise without real understanding.' (Fuller details of this critical appraisal can be found in Sullivan E. A. (1967) 'Piaget and the School Curriculum'.)

Young children's thinking: studies of some aspects of Piaget's theory
M. Almy, E. Chittenden, P. Miller, 1966.

SUBJECTS/The 330 kindergarten children were selected from two schools, one located in a middle-class the other in a lower-class area.

TESTS/(a) The child's ability to conserve number (Piaget 1952b), and quantity (Piaget 1941) were assessed together with an experiment dealing with floating and sinking of objects. (b) The Pintner-Cunningham Primary Test; (c) The New York Test of Reading Readiness and Growth in Reading; (d) The New York Inventory of Mathematical Concepts; (e) The Arthur Stencil Design Test; (f) The WISC.

RESULTS/The patterning of children's performances lent

263

further credence to Piaget and Inhelder's contentions, with certain reservations. e.g. the sequence of development portrayed that school children from the lower-class neighbourhood made slower progress, from which the authors conclude that for the child to be fully operational and for the mobility of his acquired strategies, in so far as they are related to the development of logical abilities, must be accompanied by the role that maturation plays. Almy's findings also suggest, in accordance with Piaget's contentions, that maturational factors must be upheld by experiential factors. 'Of most importance, there are indications of the different ways that children in the same grade view phenomena and problems that the adult regards as similar or even identical. The significance of such diversity for the early childhood curriculum and for the instruction of the child remains to be explored' (Almy, et al., (1966, p. 121).

Figurelli and Keller, 1972, p. 296 report, 'On conservation test performance, middle-class children scored significantly higher than lower-class children of the same age on both the pre-test and the transfer test. This is in close agreement with the data of Almy, 1966, who did not employ training procedures.'

Little, (1972) with a middle-class sample categorized into 'average' and 'superior' children showed more mature responses on Piaget tasks than children of the same age with 'average' intelligence. She focuses on the differences in IQ between Almy's (1966) middle-class sample (mean IQ, 120.80) and the lower-class sample (Mean IQ,106.52) and concludes that 'the influence of "mental" maturity seems to be clearly evident'.

However, Gaudia (1972, discussed in Chapter Eight) draws attention to some serious inadequacies of Almy's 1966 study, '... otherwise an excellent cross-sectional and longitudinal investigation of conservation in lower and middle-class children, exemplified the typical design failure in this type of research. Two schools were identified as a "middle-class" and a "lower-class" school and performances of the children from the two schools were than compared for social class effects. The assumption that every child attending each of the schools was in the same social class was untenable and allowed for no meaningful social class comparisons (see Sigel and Parry, 1968 for further discussion of global measures of socio-economic status).'

An analysis of the effects of a structured teaching approach developed from the work of Piaget, Bruner and others
H. Cole, 1968

AIMS/Cole hypothesized that 'educators are aware of the

264

necessity for negative instances in teaching new concepts to students, but are probably less aware of the need in problem solving to learn the technique of rejecting the more obvious explanations which, for children, are often the perceptually dominant feature of the situation'. Cole utilized Piaget's (1958) problem of floating bodies. He argues that the results of such concept developments would aid science teachers who are mainly interested in teaching the correct principle.

SUBJECTS/The study involved three samples of students. Sample one comprised 97 junior high school students with a middle-class background. Sample two comprised 259 junior high school students also with middle-class backgrounds. In sample three 38 college students participated. All subjects were randomly assigned to various treatment conditions.

METHOD/There were five such conditions: I-A no-treatment or control condition; IIA and IIB — Instruction in only the correct principle; III and IV — Instruction in both the exclusion of the four common false principles together with the correct principle. Details of the four irrelevant principles in respect to why objects float or sink are given by Inhelder and Piaget (1958). Cole established a concept-criterion test which was drawn from the work of Smedslund (1961) relating to the 'trick' test in his conservation weight studies.

A development of an instructional sequence, patterned after Piagetian thinking, was evolved. A 72-minute instructional sequence, comprising 35mm colour slides, tape recorded verbal statements and student response booklets, was compiled. The underlying principles were consistent with those of the sequence Inhelder and Piaget reported using with their operational subjects involved in the floating bodies tasks. The student was required to progress through the same logical sequence as that postulated by Piaget. Part I aimed at the exclusion of the four common false principles, and Part II was designed to develop the correct principle.

RESULTS/Cole utilized two statistical techniques. A three-way fixed analysis of covariance and a two-way fixed analysis of covariance. Early utilization of the criterion instrument indicated that the conventional instruction did not assist in the acquisition of the concept of the principle of 'specific gravity'. This was true with all three samples, particularly so with the 31 college students registered for a physical science course. The overall results also indicated evidence that at least, in part, the effectiveness of the instructional sequence may be related to the effort made to teach students to reject the common false principles before the correct principle may be introduced.

The musical development of children aged seven to eleven
S. Taylor, 1969

AIMS/The research was concerned with the melodic, rhythmic and harmonic aspects of children's musical development, together with certain aspects of the formation of musical taste. The trends selected for investigation and statistical treatment included (a) development with age, (b) difference between girls and boys in this field of auditory discrimination, (c) the relationship of these particular aspects chosen to verbal reasoning ability, (d) the influence of instrumental experience and (e) the influence of special choral experience, e.g. membership of a church choir or school choir.

SUBJECTS/Three thousand children were tested altogether, between the ages of seven and 11, but there was very little overlap between the samples of children constituting the three testing programmes, which were carried out over a period of three years.

METHOD/Three short group-tests, each of twenty to twenty-five minutes duration, were constructed and recorded on tape by the writer, specifically for the purposes of this study. Each test formed its own separate programme. 'The Music Responsiveness Test' was in the form of a Battery of three sub-tests: melody, rhythm and harmony. It was designed to measure simple sensory discrimination in a musical setting and a variety of instruments was used to help maintain interest through the test procedure. 'The Music Discrimination Test' was constructed to measure children's ability to discriminate between correct and distorted versions of the researcher's own brief original compositions — discrimination in a complex musical setting. 'The Music Preference Test' examined children's relative preferences for the musical idiom of six stylistic periods ranging from late Renaissance to contemporary; work of an orchestral nature only was presented, in the form of brief excerpts.

RESULTS/Results showed that the selected aspects of musical ability developed with age; there were consistent increases in scores through the age groups tested. For the majority of children there was strong harmonic development around the age of nine.
Girls were significantly superior to boys where the musical

setting was simple, as in the tasks set by the Music Responsiveness Test. In the complex musical situation provided by the Music Discrimination Test, boys scored as well as girls. Only a moderately low correlation was revealed between test scores and the corresponding verbal reasoning quotients.

The category of instrumentalist was defined as that where there was evidence of regular lessons leading to instrumental techniques and mastery of musical notation. Surprisingly, two-fifths of the extensive sample qualified for the instrumentalist category spread through the entire age range. That this instrumental experience was beneficial to all aspects of musical ability tested was demonstrated by the superiority of scores, usually at a marked level of significance. Choral experience led to enhanced development of the melodic aspect of musical ability.

Stronger musical preferences for particular stylistic periods emerged with increasing age. Boys and girls differed widely in their musical tastes. The preferences of the instrumental category were much stronger than those of non-players. Musical development seemed to be related to the quality of early musical experience, especially to instrumental experience.

The relationship between primary students' rationalization of conservation and their mathematical achievement
W. G. Cathcart, 1971

AIMS/Cathcart argues that an understanding of identity, reversibility and compensation are necessary for conservation operativity. These modes of rationalization in turn may have some relationship to achievement in mathematics. Two other hypotheses were advanced: (a) to establish the frequency with which the varied kinds of rationalizations are utilized; and (b) 'to investigate differences in social and personal characteristics of subjects who preferred different kinds of rationalizations for conservation'.

SUBJECTS/One hundred and twenty subjects of middle-class background were drawn from 12 schools. The children were selected from second and third grades.

METHOD/Conservation Test/The main test comprised eight items related to conservation operativity. These were typical Piagetian situations. (Fuller details appear in Cathcart (1971) pp. 757-759.) Responses were categorized into one of the following: (a) Operational Identity; (b) Substantive Identity; (c) Reversibility; (d) Compensation; (e) Other Rational Responses; (f) Non-classifiable Responses; (g) No Response.

In addition to the eight Piagetian situations, Cathcart also administered tests of mathematical achievement, vocabulary, intelligence and listening ability.

RESULTS/The results demonstrated that the children in Cathcart's study preferred the act of identity as the mode of rationalization. This was found to be true of children in both grades two and three.

However, a further χ^2 analysis indicated that while the act of identity was most commonly employed for justification, partial conservers (Transitional children) tended to employ the act of compensation more than total conservers, who in turn used reversibility justifications to a greater extent than partial conservers.

'The reversibility group had the highest mean score on the conservation test (7.44) followed by the operational identity group (6.71), the substantive identity group (5.79), and finally the compensation group (5.20).'

A possible relationship between social and personal characteristics of subjects and the preferred mode of rationalization for operativity, revealed no significant trends. The chi-square test demonstrated no relationship between mode of rationalization and intelligence, socio-economic status, vocabulary and listening ability.

Lastly, the kind of verbalization advanced to justify conservation operativity was shown not to be an indicator of success in mathematics. None of the five aspects of achievement was significantly related to the mode of rationalization employed.

DISCUSSION/Finally, Cathcart argues that there may be two reasons as to why the act of identity was most frequently advanced by the subjects in the study: identity rationalizations may be the easiest to voice quickly and such an act calls for less abstraction than, perhaps, the acts of reversibility or compensation. Another important feature of the study was that mathematics achievement was higher for subjects who employed varied rationalizations for conservation operativity than for those who could advance only one. 'This result may indicate that for success in mathematics the child should be able to analyse a problem from different points of view ... The implication for teaching is that we should not teach particular rules for particular types of problems ... a more general problem solving approach ... (will be) able to draw upon all his relevant background knowledge.'

A study of concrete and formal reasoning in school mathematics
K. F. Collis, 1971

AIMS/Collis defines the main object as follows: 'The present study focuses on mathematics as the material of thought and sets out to distinguish between kinds of material in this field which can be processed by concrete operational level pupils and kinds of material which need formal operational level thinking.'

SUBJECTS/The total of 101 girls was selected as follows: 35 from each of primary, junior secondary and senior secondary schools, respectively. The subjects ranged in CA from eight years nine months to 17 years. The assumption was made that the primary school Ss would be at the concrete level and the senior secondary Ss at the formal level, with the junior secondary group at the transitional level.

METHOD/Nine group tests were administered. The items were such that (a) 'they were directly related to the kinds of mathematical stimuli with which the children would be familiar from the classroom and (b) they could be logically related to Piagetian concepts'. (Fuller details of the Tests, the experimental procedure and an analysis of the structure of the items are described elsewhere, Collis (1971) pp. 291-293.)

RESULTS/Collis summarizes the findings as follows: '... items with both concrete elements and structure were successfully handled by all age groups; as either structures or elements were made more abstract the younger age groups began to fail and only the oldest group had any success when both structures and elements were made more abstract'.
Further: 'Curriculum planners and teachers should be aware of the kinds of thinking implied by the various stages delineated in the Piagetian model and of the age ranges over which these apply before they can adjust their material and methods of presentation suitably'.

The nature of adolescent judgement
E. A. Peel, 1971

The justification for including a summary of this book is that Peel attributes his work at a fundamental level to the investigations of Inhelder and Piaget (1958) into the growth of logical thinking in adolescence. He emphasizes, however, that whereas Inhelder and Piaget used practical science situations, he has constructed verbal situations for assessing the maturity of judgement. 'The substantive part of the book is concerned with the elaboration of a theory about the psychological nature and development of judgement and with attempts to materialise this theory by devising measures to investigate the conditions under which adolescents make judgement.'

Peel asserts: 'Above all else the adolescent and young adult apprehend the inconsistencies between the actual and the possible. They are impelled to the opinion and action which characterizes their lives by a drive to reconcile this actuality of their existence with the possibilities they themselves envisage. Usually they strive to modify the actual. This going forward and outward to conceive of possibilities beyond the limits of their environment is the central feature of their intellectual life.' He acknowledges that this view of adolescent thinking emerges from a speculation by Piaget and Inhelder (1958) and has been implied in the writings of many educationists, but has received no empirical investigation. Further, that there have been 'few systematic investigations into the growth of thinking during adolescence, despite the fact that learning during the secondary . . . years is most important and formative for real understanding in the upper school and higher education'. He emphasizes, however, that understanding is not sufficient; the ability to make effective judgements for appropriate action is also needed. He defines judging in relation to thinking as 'a form of thinking and is therefore invoked whenever we are in a situation for which we have no ready-made answer learned off pat'.

The test material designed to assess the developmental changes in adolescent thinking consisted of passages relating to topical, social or intellectual problems followed by a question demanding more for its answer than the information given in the passage. A second question 'Why do you think so?' provided the insight into the maturity of the judgement. The resulting answers were grouped into three main categories: 'Restricted', which were 'tautological, premise-delaying and irrelevant'; 'Circumstantial', which were 'bound solely by the content of the passage, often taking account at first of only one element'; and 'Imaginative — Comprehensive', answers which involved the 'invocation of independent ideas and the consideration of the problem in their terms'. These three categories were subdivided into finer divisions where necessary, in the various investigations carried out by Peel and his students. He considers that the distinction between 'content-dominated' answers and imaginative answers, involving explanation, is crucial.

Peel (1966), in an investigation with pupils nine-plus to 15-plus in New Jersey, confirmed that answers involving thinking beyond the evidence given in the passage are not prevalent before

13½-14½ years. 'Circumstantial' answers were associated with the ages of 12-13½ and there was little evidence of restricted answers. A number of Birmingham University students have supported Peel in his investigations. Rhys (1964) investigated adolescent thinking in terms of geographical material. On the premise that 'the understanding of geographical material at the secondary stage compels the adolescent to place a person other than himself in an environment other than his own and furthermore, he must take into account the complex interplay of a miscellany of factors within that foreign environment', Rhys obtained four main categories of answers ranging from the tautological to the imaginative. The highest level of mature judgement occurred at CA 15 years and MA 16 years.

Davies (1964) found that average mid-adolescents have difficulty in dealing with problems involving the selecting and eliminating of hypotheses, even when the hypotheses and the supporting evidence is provided. Similarly, Mealings (1961; 1963), revealed the difficulties in choice and rejection of hypotheses in practical science problems. Peel comments: 'Teachers at all levels tend to streamline the learning process by presenting the most acceptable hypothesis and neglecting to eliminate the remainder . . . teachers should not forget that it is part of their task to promote thinking and that the complete act of selecting a best judgement entails rejecting the others. To this end they might more often draw attention to alternate explanations in order that the pupils may themselves reject them.'

The results of a study by Thomas (1967), indicated that 'we may expect immature causal judgements from pupils as old as 15 years of age in relatively non-technical situations where a multiplicity of factors operate over a long period of time'. Peel draws attention to the necessity of understanding in many fields of knowledge of the 'wide class of changes which appear to be dominated by a process of transforming random elements into ordered structure and the reverse process of going from order to disintegration'. In considering this 'Order-Disorder' change Peel comments that test situations are needed where ordered material can be presented and where the equivalent of a spontaneous change can be carried out, with the request for predictions of the outcome. He envisages these tests being concerned with a wide field including human affairs.

With respect to the promotion of mature judgement, Peel cites the work of Suchman (1961, 1964), who investigated the classroom conditions necessary to develop the inquiring mind. He initiated 'learning to think' sessions in which pupils were encouraged to inquire and discover concepts autonomously. Biran (1968) constructed a successful learning programme which

271

demonstrated to pupils how to design experiments, to test hypotheses and to draw conclusions. Gray (1970) found that adolescents subjected to programmed texts for training judgement obtained higher scores on thinking problems. Anderson (1967) administered instruction in thinking to pupils and the results showed a considerable influence on the maturity of judgement. Stones (1965) gave programmed instruction in relevant historical concepts and increased the maturity of historical judgements in a group of secondary pupils. Peel (1967) discusses the possibility of using the actual responses obtained in the investigations of persons' judgements as a means of teaching individuals how to judge.

Piaget and the School Curriculum

Piaget (1972), in a recent article written for a series of studies prepared for the International Commission on the Development of Education, at Unesco, draws attention to the proportionally small number of students choosing a scientific, as opposed to a liberal arts, career. Piaget considers that, in order to bring education into line with the needs of society, it is necessary to undertake a complete revision of the methods and aims of education. Piaget proposes that this reorganization would involve the question of the role of pre-school education; the true significance of active methods ('which everyone talks about but which few educators effectively apply'); the application of child and adolescent psychology and 'that of the necessarily inter-disciplinary nature at every level of the subjects taught as opposed to the compartmentalization still so widely prevalent both in the universities and secondary schools.'

Piaget comments that in his investigation of the development of physical causality, he found no evidence of the existence of special aptitudes. 'Consequently our hypothesis is that the so-called aptitudes of "good" students in mathematics or physics, etc., consist above all in their being able to adapt to the type of instruction offered them, whereas students who are"bad" in these fields, but successful in others, are actually able to master the problems they appear not to understand — on condition that they approach them by another route. What they do not understand are the "lessons" and not the subject. Thus it may be — and we have verified it in many cases — that a student's incapacity in a particular subject is owing to a too-rapid passage from the qualitative structure of the problems (by simple logical reasoning but without the immediate introduction of numerical relations and metric laws) to the quantitative or mathematical formulation (in the sense of previously worked-out equations) normally employed by the physicist. Nevertheless, we willingly admit certain aptitudes (once sufficient maturity is attained) which distinguish strictly deductive from empirical and factual minds, but even in mathematics many failures in school are owing to this excessively rapid passage from the qualitative (logical) to the quantitative (numerical).'

Piaget emphasizes that the use of active methods giving broad scope to the spontaneous research of the child or adolescent requires that the teacher be far from dispensable; the teacher will be involved in creating situations and constructing initial devices in order to present problems to the child. Further, to 'provide counter-examples which compel reflection and reconsideration of over-hasty solutions'.

With respect to the teaching of mathematics Piaget states 'if mathematics teachers would only take the trouble to learn about the "natural" psychogenetic development of the logico-mathematical operations, they would see that there exists a much greater similarity than one would expect between the principal operations spontaneously employed by the child and the notions they attempt to instil into him abstractly'. (For further details see Piaget 1972, p.19.) In connection with science, Piaget's views again centre round the importance of active methods. If an experiment is not carried out by the individual himself with complete freedom of initiative it will no longer fall within the category of an experiment but will be mere drill with no educational value.

At the pre-school level Piaget considers that it appears possible to provide a 'kind of propaedeutic to scientific instruction' consisting of exercising the powers of observation. Piaget elaborates that certain actions can be successfully executed at age 4-5, but good descriptions cannot be given before 9-11 years: therefore practice in observation would be very useful. He cites Karplus, who 'considers these observation exercises to be so useful, even at the pre-school age, that he has devised situations with two observers in order to instil at a very early age an understanding of the relativity of observation'.

Piaget further draws attention to the increasing interdisciplinary nature of research in every field and the lack of preparation for this on the part of the researchers. Teaching should stress structuralism which 'with its interdisciplinary vision is gaining more and more acceptance and support' (Piaget elaborates on structuralism on p. 23). 'What is needed at both the university and secondary level are teachers who indeed know their subject but who approach it from a constantly interdisciplinary point of view, i.e. knowing how to give general significance to the structures they use and to reintegrate them into over-all systems embracing the other disciplines.' Further, there is a need to look closely at the future relations between the human and natural sciences and for students to be encouraged to pass freely from one section to another and be given a choice of many combinations.

With respect to teacher training Piaget recommends that the teaching profession should be upgraded at all levels: that there should be full university training for all teachers at every level ('for the younger students are the more difficult the teacher's task if it is taken seriously') and that such training is necessary for full psychological knowledge.

Piaget finally recommends 'a close union of training and research, the students being associated with the latter right from the start. Team research which is not supervised by a single professor but by representatives of neighbouring fields working closely together . . . (in spite of the difficulties attendant on such collaboration). These are not insurmountable as our experiments in Geneva have shown.'

CHAPTER TEN
PIAGET'S COGNITIVE-DEVELOPMENTAL APPROACH TO MORALITY
(This chapter is contributed by Celia Scaplehorn, Goldsmiths' College, London University)

Theoretically and methodologically, investigations of children's moral development are polarized in either behavioural or cognitive systems incorporating psychoanalytical, learning and cognitive-developmental approaches. Hoffman (1970) traces this diversity historically to three philosophical doctrines. The doctrine of 'original sin', resting on the importance of the intervention by adults and being represented in modified form by Freudian theory, has led to the research interest in the production of guilt when moral standards are violated. The doctrine of 'tabula rasa' assumed that the child is neither corrupt nor pure and also put stress on the importance of intervention by adults. These principles are embodied in the learning theory approach which regards morality in terms of specific acts learned on the basis of rewards and punishments with little accompanying rationale. The third doctrine, 'innate purity', stressing the corrupting influence of society (especially adult society), can be associated with Piaget's insight into the development of morality. He writes of the heteronomous nature of adult-child relations and stresses the importance of social interaction among peers, together with the development of cognitive processes for moral maturity.

Having associated Piaget with an early doctrine, attention must be drawn to his lack of allegiance to any school of psychology, together with his rejection of 'a priori' moralizing about the child's notions of right and wrong. Arising mainly from his general theory of the development of the child's conception of the world (Piaget, 1928), his objective was to study the mental processes and thought structures underlying judgements concerning a variety of problematical situations.

The first part of Piaget's investigation 'The Moral Judgement of the Child' (1932) was into the attitudes of different-aged children toward the origin, legitimacy, and alterability of rules, based upon a game of marbles: a situation natural and familiar to his Genevan subjects. Piaget's approach was to conceal his

275

knowledge of the rules and to probe the child's understanding while the game was played. As a result, Piaget distinguished a tendency in young children to regard rules as being sacred and to be obeyed without question, even though during the course of play there was an inclination for rules to be bent for self-advantage, together with little concern if both players were declared to have won. This 'moral realism' gradually becomes more flexible and Piaget attributed the establishment of 'co-operation and the development of the idea of justice' to intellectual growth and experiences of role-taking in the peer group. Piaget states that children require nothing more for this development than 'the mutual respect and solidarity which holds among children themselves'. Additionally: 'The collective rule is at first something external to the individual and consequently sacred to him; then as he gradually makes it his own, it comes to that extent to be felt as a free product of mutual agreement and an autonomous conscience.'

In alignment with his general cognitive-developmental stage sequence approach, Piaget outlined four successive stages in the marble play. In the 'motor' stage, (that is, up to about three years of age) the child plays individually and rules are irrelevant. Characteristic of the following 'egocentric' stage (approximately between the ages of three and seven years), play is to a certain extent individual, although parallel, and rules are followed to the extent that they can be recognized. 'Towards the age of 7-8 appears the desire for mutual understanding in the sphere of play.' Piaget continues: 'As a criterion of the appearance of this stage we shall take the moment when by "winning" the child refers to the fact of getting the better of the others, therefore of gaining more marbles than the others and when he no longer says he has won when he has done no more than knock a marble out of the square, regardless of what his partners have done . . . In seeking to win the child is trying above all to contend with his partners while observing common rules.' However, Piaget elaborates by indicating that the children of this stage do not yet know the rules in detail and different children within the same group may give contradictory accounts. 'Children of the fourth stage, on the contrary have thoroughly mastered their code and even take pleasure in juridical discussions, whether of principle or merely of procedure, which may at times arise out of the points in dispute.' Piaget gives 11 or 12 as the average age at which the fourth stage develops.

Within the consciousness of rules, Piaget outlines three stages: the first stage corresponds to the purely individualistic stage referred to in connection with the practice of rules, the child seeking merely to satisfy his motor interests. However, Piaget believes that the origins of the consciousness of rules, even in so restricted a field as that of the game of marbles, are conditioned by the child's moral life as a whole; 'even if it has never seen marbles before, it is already permeated with rules and regulations due to the environment'. A second stage 'sets in from the moment when the child, either through imitation or as the result of verbal exchange, begins to want to play in conformity with certain rules received from outside'. He then 'regards the rules of the game as sacred and untouchable; he refuses to alter these rules and claims that any modification, even if accepted by general opinion would be wrong.' It is not until about the age of six that this attitude appears clearly and explicitly. Piaget characterizes the third stage (after the age of 10 on average) as 'autonomy follows upon heteronomy: the rule of a game appears to the child no longer as an external law, sacred in so far as it has been laid down by adults; but as the outcome of a free decision and worthy of respect in the measure that it has enlisted mutual consent.'

Piaget therefore describes three kinds of rule: the motor rule, 'relatively independent of any social contact'; the coercive rule, 'due to unilateral respect' and the rational rule, 'due to mutual respect'. However, Piaget discusses the coercive rule in the following terms: 'On the one hand, the child knows that there are rules, the 'real rules', and that they must be obeyed because they are obligatory and sacred; but on the other hand, although the child vaguely takes note of the general scheme of these rules . . . he still plays more or less as he did during the previous stage, i.e. he plays more or less for himself, regardless of his partners, and takes more pleasure in his own movements than in the observance of the rules themselves, thus confusing his own wishes with universality.' In connection with rational rules, Piaget explains that the moment children really begin to submit to rules and to apply them in a spirit of genuine co-operation, they acquire a new conception of rules. They become something that can be changed if it is agreed that they should be, for the truth of a rule rests on mutual agreement and reciprocity. Piaget adds that mutual respect and co-operation are never completely realized. 'Even the most rational of adults does not subject to his 'moral experience' more than an infinitesimal proportion of the rules that hedge him round.' It is upon the distinction between constraint and co-operation that Piaget's whole theory of moral development rests.

In the second section of 'The Moral Judgement of the Child', Piaget presented children with hypothetical situations in the form of stories and attempted to examine the criteria upon which the child made moral judgements. Within the chapter entitled 'Adult constraint and Moral Realism', Piaget examines objective responsibility incorporating clumsiness, stealing and lying. The chapter

'Co-operation and the Development of the Idea of Justice' includes experiment and discussion concerning the problem of punishment, collective and communicable responsibility, three forms of justice (immanent, retributive and distributive), together with equality and authority. In the final chapter Piaget discusses the two moralities of the child and types of social relations, reviewing his own conclusions in the light of the theories of Durkheim, Fauconnet, M. Pierre Bovet and J. M. Baldwin.

Piaget refers to moral realism as 'the tendency which the child has to regard duty and the value attaching to it as self-subsistent and independent of the mind, as imposing itself regardless of the circumstances in which the individual may find himself'. Moral realism possesses three features: duty as viewed by moral realism is essentially heteronomous; secondly it demands that the letter rather than the spirit of the law shall be observed and thirdly, it induces an objective conception of responsibility.

Piaget encouraged children to compare stories involving two kinds of clumsiness, 'one entirely fortuitous or even the result of a well-intentioned act, but involving considerable material damage, the other, negligible as regards the damage done but happening as the result of an ill-intentioned act'. When studying problems related to stealing, the aim was to discover whether the child paid more attention to the motive or to the material results; consequently, the problems were confined to the comparison of selfishly-motivated acts with those that are well-intentioned. Concerning lying, Piaget's investigation included the definition of a lie: 'responsibility as a function of the lie's content and responsibility as a function of its material consequences'. Additionally, he questioned the children with regard to the acceptability of children lying to one another. Piaget found that the child's judgements tended to be centred on the amount of damage done by the action, but that this 'objective responsibility' diminished as the child reached the age of 10 years. Piaget felt that adult constraint is to a certain extent responsible for this 'objective' response: 'It is very easy to notice — especially in very young children, under 6-7 years of age — how frequently the sense of guilt on the occasion of clumsiness is proportional to the extent of the material disaster instead of remaining subordinate to the intentions in question.' He continues, 'there is no doubt that by adopting a certain technique with their children, parents can succeed in making them attach more importance to intentions than to rules conceived as a system of ritual interdictions'. With regard to lying, the child's judgements were objective in the sense that he evaluated the lies, not according to the intentions of the liar, but according to the greater or lesser likelihood of the lying statement — 'the more a statement departed from the truth, the

278

more it would seem to the child to be a lie'. It was noticeable that judgements in terms of intentions became more frequent at approximately nine years of age. Piaget detected three stages in the attitude to lying: in the first stage it is regarded as wrong because it is punished; secondly, it is seen as a fault in itself and would remain so even if it were not punished; and eventually (at about 10 to 12 years) because 'truthfulness is necessary to reciprocity and mutual agreement'. Younger children considered that lies between children are allowed but lying to adults is worse than lying to peers. Piaget concludes that 'the consciousness of lying gradually becomes interiorized and the hypothesis may be hazarded that it does so under the influence of co-operation'. He continues: 'If we attribute the advance to the child's intelligence alone, which is constantly improving his understanding of what he originally took in a purely realistic sense, we are only shifting the question. For how does psychological intelligence advance with age if not by means of increased co-operation?'

In the section dealing with the child's ideas about punishment and justice, Piaget used essentially the same techniques, except that, in the stories concerning punishment, three alternative forms of punishment were given in connection with the wrongdoer. The child was requested to say which was the fairest punishment and then the most severe in order to determine whether the child evaluated the punishment in terms of its severity or in accordance with some other criterion of retribution. The suggested punishments were either 'expiatory' (i.e. no relation between the content of the guilty act and the nature of its punishment) or 'punishments by reciprocity' (misdeed and punishment are related both in content and nature). Piaget found a marked development from expiation responses to reciprocity responses as age increased and he finally concludes this section by emphasizing: 'the law of reciprocity implies certain positive obligations in virtue of its very form. And this is why the child, once he has admitted the principle of punishment by reciprocity in the sphere of justice, often comes to feel that any material punitive element is unnecessary, even if it is "motivated", the essential thing being to make the offender realize that his action was wrong, in so far as it was contrary to the rules of co-operation.'

Relating to the question of 'collective' (or 'communicable') responsibility ('collective punishment has long been resorted to in the classroom and in spite of the many protests that have been raised against this practice'), Piaget administered stories involving situations in which the adult punishes the whole group for the offence committed by one or two of its members; secondly, where the adult attempts to discover the transgressor who is not owning up and the group refuses to reveal his identity; and finally, where the adult is attempting to discover the transgressor, who is not prepared to own up, while the group is ignorant of his identity. In each of the three cases the child was asked whether it is fair to punish the whole group and why. In the first instance even the younger children showed no trace of collective responsibility. To the second situation the reactions were indeterminate. There was however, a tendency for the younger children to say that everyone should be punished as each individual is guilty because of the failure to reveal the transgressor. The older children tended to offer the response that everyone should be punished because of the solidarity of the group in deciding not to reveal the offender. Children of approximately an intermediate age felt that 'no one should be punished; partly because it is right not to "tell" and partly because the guilty one is not known'. In the third situation, the younger children accepted collective punishment, because the guilty one is unknown and 'there must be a punishment at all costs'. (The necessity of punishment is the fundamental fact.) The older children considered general punishment as a greater injustice than the impunity of the guilty. In conclusion, Piaget discusses that in none of the three situations is any judgement found comparable to the classical notion of collective responsibility, but in situations two and three, the reactions can be regarded as bearing upon communicable responsibility.

A problem connected with that of punishment is immanent justice. Piaget hypothesized that during the early years of his life, the child would affirm the existence of automatic punishments which emanate from things themselves, while later, under the influence of factors affecting his moral growth he is likely to abandon this belief. Piaget's hypothesis was confirmed and he found belief in immanent justice to decline with age.

Piaget then approached the analysis of the conflicts that can take place between distributive or equalitarian justice and retributive justice. Three stories were administered, asking each time whether or not it was fair to favour the well-behaved child. The first situation mentioned no special fault and established the conflict between retributive and distributive justice in the abstract; the second introduced only negligible faults and minor punishment; the third, brought in a punishment which might strike the child as very severe. The younger children reacted in the form of punishment outweighing equality, whereas the opposite was the case for the older children. Concerning the relation between equality and authority, Piaget was intent to discover whether the subjects would place the adult in the right, out of respect for authority or whether they would defend equality out of respect for an inner ideal, even if the latter was in opposition with obedience. As expected, there was a predominance of the first solution among the younger children and as the age of the subjects increased (about 11 to 12 years) there was a definite progression in the direction of the latter. Piaget was able to distinguish three broad stages in the development of distributive justice in relation to adult authority. In the first stage, justice is not distinguished from the authority of the law; during the second stage, equalitarianism grows in strength and comes to outweigh any other consideration; and during the third stage, equalitarianism makes way for a more subtle conception of justice which 'we may call "equity" and which consists in never defining equality without taking account of the way in which each individual is situated'. In the domain of retributive justice, equity consists in 'determining what are the attenuating circumstances'. In the domain of distributive justice, equity consists 'in taking account of age, of previous services rendered etc.'. With respect to adults and children being served in shops, even the majority of the six-year-old children responded that each should be served in turn. Responding to questions in connection with cheating and tale-telling, there was again a gradual diminution in the preoccupation with authority and an increase in the desire for equality.

In summary, Piaget views moral development as the result of a process involving the development of cognitive processes in conjunction with experiences of role-taking in the peer group, allowing the movement from moral realism to autonomy. In connection with the sense of justice, Piaget concludes that 'though naturally capable of being reinforced by the precepts and the practical example of the adult (it) is largely independent of these influences and requires nothing more for its development than the mutual respect and solidarity which holds among children themselves. It is often at the expense of the adult and not because of him that the notions of the just and unjust find their way into the youthful mind.'

I Replications of Piaget's Investigations

Although not falling strictly under the designation of this section it is perhaps pertinent to draw attention to a number of early studies described by Johnson (1962) as 'adding force in their buttressing of Piaget's position'. Taking into account that the studies were carried out nearly 40 years before Piaget's work, they yield similar results and, as they apparently took place independently, they can be considered to support Piaget. Johnson cites three main studies — Barnes (1894, 1902) and Schallenberger (1894) — all of which obtained 'written responses to questions from extremely large samples of children at various ages.' From the responses of children aged 7-16 years, to questions asking for descriptions of just and unjust punishments, Barnes (1894) concluded that punishments are usually considered to be just, since they come from adults. Further, children believe that offences can be paid for with pain. This view was found to decrease with age. Schallenberger (1894) after analysing the written responses of children aged six to 16 years, to a story involving a child painting 'all the chairs in the parlour, so as to make them look nice for her mother', found that the younger children most frequently said that the mother should punish the child harshly. At the older level there was an emphasis on explanation as to why the chairs should not have been painted. Schallenberger concluded: 'Younger children judge actions by their results, older children look at the motives that prompt them'. Barnes (1902) replicated Schallenberger's work with English children as opposed to American, and again revealed that punitive measures were most often suggested at younger age levels. Expiatory punishment was found to occur before restitutive, and older children often emphasized the importance of explanation as to why the deed was wrong. He described a correlation between the 'explanation' responses and the highest intelligence levels. English children were found to be more mature in their earlier rejection of punitive punishment but not differing in the more mature forms of response. These studies can therefore be said to add support to Piaget's work in that they illustrated the young child's moral realism and the increasing concern for motives with increasing age; they reveal the younger child's belief in the justness of adult punishment and the expiatory value, together with the younger child's belief in severe punishment. The major changes in age also occurred at about 12 years of age.

Among early studies which can be considered as replicating Piaget's work is Harrower's (1934) investigation. As a result of responses obtained from working-class and upper-middle-class children, Harrower queried the existence of stages and considered that the children were merely reflecting different kinds of experiences. She suggested that mature responses are learnt from parents. Attention is drawn to a comprehensive review by Medinnus (1959) of the early literature relating to the development of immanent justice, in children, namely, Lerner, Abel, Dennis, Lin, Havighurst and Neugarten and MacRae.

Lerner (1937) investigated the relationship between social status, parental authority and moral realism. With a sample of children between the ages of six and 12 years, belonging to two contrasted status groups, Lerner showed that high-status parents used fewer coercive techniques in child-rearing and that there was less tendency in their children (as compared with the low status children) to see principles as external and unvarying. The findings agreed with Piaget's in showing a decrease with age in the number of children expressing a belief in immanent justice. Lerner considered that middle-class children passed through the earlier stage more quickly. Abel (1941) adopted Piaget's approach to study the moral judgements of mentally retarded girls. The subjects were 94 subnormal girls, CA 15-21 years, with mental ages of six to 11. Comparing the institutionalized girls with those living in the community, it was found that approximately twice as many of the former gave responses which indicated a belief in immanent justice. Dennis (1943), in his work with Hopi Indian children, although mainly concerned with the concept of animism, also investigated immanent justice. In his sample of 98 subjects, aged 12-18 years, Dennis found that 64 per cent of his youngest subjects indicated a belief in the immanence of punishment. This figure decreased markedly with age and among the 16-year-old and 17-year-old subjects was only nine per cent. Dennis attributed the differences in the findings of these early investigators to a variety of cultural factors specifically unidentifiable, but contended that development was universal in all societies.

In connection with immanent justice, Liu (1950) found a decrease in belief in immanent justice responses at the ages of six to 12 years, but at each level, more non-Chinese children than Chinese revealed a belief in immanent justice. Liu concluded that decreasing moral realism is not due to age maturity alone. Havighurst and Neugarten (1955), in a large investigation involving 902 Indian children from six Indian tribes and aged from six to 18 years, showed that there was either an increase or no change with age in the children's belief in immanent justice for most of the groups studied. Except for one group, 85 per cent of the 12- to 18-year-old subjects indicated a belief in immanent justice. Within the younger age groups the percentage tended to be smaller. It was considered that these findings supported Piaget's hypothesis that children in primitive societies become more rigid in their moral development as they increase in age, due to constraints being placed on them. There is, however, a discrepancy with the findings of Dennis in which he found a decrease with age in belief in immanent justice in his Hopi Indian subjects. When comparing differing degrees of acculturation, Havighurst and Neugarten found that there were no significant differences in immanent justice responses and they concluded that rather than measuring the degree of influence from modern societies, environmental factors within each cultural group must be investigated in depth. Medinnus (1959) draws attention to Thompson's (1948) view that the basic orientation of primitive people is deeply rooted in the tribal past and it persists regardless of changes in the group's economy or exposure to white cultures. This can be considered as accounting for the lack of relationship between the degree of acculturation and belief in immanent justice. In a study of immanent justice among West African children, Jahoda (1958) aimed to replicate the work of Havighurst and Neugarten and confirmed the prevalence of immanent justice responses among young African children but questioned the inclusion of 'acts of God' in the category of immanent justice responses. He emphasized that this inclusion leads to a much less marked decrease among older children. (See Investigations within different Cultures.) In a study among Lebanese children and adults, Najarian-Svajian (1966) confirmed his hypothesis that the Lebanese culture would reinforce the belief in immanent justice in adults of little education. He concluded that educational and social factors were effective in changing thinking connected with immanent justice. (See IIIf below.)

MacRae (1954) found in general 'a decrease over the age range in the children's belief in immanent justice, the trend was not consistent. For both stories a smaller percentage of the five- and six-year-olds gave responses which were scored as indicating a belief in immanent punishment than the nine- and 10-year-olds,' (Medinnus 1959). The latter, considering that research findings of the various studies on the whole support Piaget's conclussions that there is a decrease with age of children's belief in immanent justice, was intent to further replicate this area of Piaget's theory, (Details are given later in this chapter.) In discussing his findings, he drew attention to the importance of the context and content of the story. Grinder (1964), in his investigation into behavioural and cognitive dimensions of conscience, also found that the influence of the morality of constraint on children's moral judgements decreased with age. (See IIIe below.) Brennan (1962) confirmed 'movement away from moral realism' but found that CA and MA were significantly related to moral judgment only up to 9.5 years. (See IIIa below.)

Turning to punishment, Durkin's (1959a) subjects substantiated Piaget's contention of a relationship existing between age and concepts of justice but also found, contrary to Piaget, that only between the years seven and 10 was there evidence of an increasing acceptance of reciprocity: even the 13-year-old subjects tended to seek justice in the authority person. However, it was evident that older children were more aware of the complexity of the situation. (Details are given later in this chapter.)

Results essentially in agreement with Piaget's with respect to the child's conception of lying were obtained from Medinnus (1962) questionnaire consisting of stories drawn from Piaget. (Details are given below.) Again modelled on Piaget's approach,

Kane (1970) also investigated children's attitudes to lying. (Details are given later in this chapter.)

Bobroff (1960) observed and assessed the practice and consciousness of rules during a game of marbles, following Piaget's approach. His results were generally consistent with the findings of Piaget. The group of mentally retarded children were found to follow the same sequence of developmental stages as normal children. (Details are given below.) Piaget's contention that, by the age of 12 years, children judge behaviour according to interiorized rules rather than mere conformity to rules was not supported by Medinnus (1966) in his behavioural and cognitive measures of conscience development enquiry. (See IIIe below.)

Children's concepts of justice: a comparison with the Piaget data
D. Durkin, 1959a

AIM/The investigation was designed to examine developmental trends with age in relation to the concept of justice — particularly justice regarding one's person — and to compare the trends with those described by Piaget. In addition, it aimed to examine the relationship between the intelligence of children and their justice-concepts. The experimenter was also intent on carrying out the investigation with children of different nationality and economic status from those included in the Piaget study (but similar in terms of chronological age), in order to determine whether Piaget has made 'too sweeping generalizations about children in general'.

SUBJECTS/N = 101 children. The mean ages of the three groups were seven years, eight months; 10 years, nine months; and 13 years, nine months respectively. (The chronological ages of 7, 10 and 13 years were those designated by Piaget as 'three great periods in the development of the sense of justice in the child'.) The majority of the subjects were rated as 'average', middle-class in terms of economic status and were therefore assumed to be different from Piaget's 'poor' subjects.

METHOD/Following Piaget's procedure, an attempt was made to arrive at children's concepts of justice regarding one's person through their responses to questions about story-situations which depicted possible violations of justice.

The Kuhlmann-Anderson Intelligence Test was administered. The mean scores for the three groups were 103.4, 101.6 and 103.4, respectively.

RESULTS AND DISCUSSION/While subjects' responses

substantiated Piaget's contention of a relationship existing between CA and concepts of justice, they did not substantiate his more specific proposal that 'children maintain with a conviction that grows with their years that it is strictly fair to give back the blows one has received'. Only between the years of seven and 10 was there evidence of an increasing acceptance of reciprocity; the 13-year-old subjects, like the seven-year-olds, tended to seek justice in the authority person. However, it cannot be said that the similarity of responses between the younger and older children reflected similarity in their disposition toward such a proposal; older children were more aware of the complexity of the situation. In no instance did acceptance of reciprocity include approval of returning aggression that was different from the aggression received. This unanimous reaction duplicated Piaget's finding that children who approve of reciprocity do not accept 'a sort of arbitrary punishment whose content bears no relationship to the punishable act'. The role of intelligence in moral-judgement development remained undefined. Data concerning the relationship of intelligence and kind of justice were conflicting.

Immanent justice in children: a review of literature and additional data
G. R. Medinnus, 1959

AIM/The author reviews the early literature concerning Piaget's notion of immanent justice and emphasizes that the findings support Piaget's conclusions of a decrease with age in belief in immanent justice among children. The author was intent to further replicate this area of Piaget's theory.

SUBJECTS/ N = 240. Thirty boys and 30 girls, at each of the age levels of 6, 8, 10 and 12 years. The subjects were selected from the lower socio-economic groups in order to make comparisons with Piaget's sample from 'the poorer parts of Geneva'.

METHOD/A total of 18 story-situations and questions drawn from Piaget were administered to each subject individually, but only the two stories relating to belief in immanent justice were specifically dealt with under the terms of reference of this Paper.

RESULTS/Although the number of subjects revealing a belief in immanent justice decreased with age for Story 1, the opposite trend was indicated for Story 2. The chi-squares for the two stories were not however, significant; nor were those for sex differences.

DISCUSSION/Whereas Piaget found that 86 per cent of the six-year-olds whom he questioned affirmed a belief in immanent justice, only 62 per cent of the six-year-olds in this study gave immanent justice responses to Story 1.

A smaller percentage of children at each age level indicated belief in immanent justice for Story 2 than for Story 1 and this could be explained by the presence in Story 2 of information accounting for the incident. Mention is made of the fact that the bridge on which the culprit crossed the river was rotten and there is no need for the subject to resort to an explanation of the punishment inflicted. In Story 1 however, no rational explanation is provided to account for the boy's misfortune which occurred while he was cutting up paper. The study indicates that the point of view which a child expresses varies depending on the story used and attention is drawn to the failure of Piaget and other investigators to tabulate separately the results obtained from the different stories.

The author summarizes: 'the present findings indicate that a child's expressed belief in immanent justice is dependent upon a number of such factors as the meaningfulness of the situation to him, the presence or absence of rational alternative explanations, the range of his experiences, the concreteness of the young child's thought and so forth'. The author also mentions the importance of 'specific parental teachings.'

The stages of maturation in socialized thinking and in the ego development of two groups of children
A. Bobroff, 1960

AIM/'The study was designed to investigate the levels of thought and behaviour associated with the development of socialization in two groups of children.' In addition to examining phases of ego development by analysing their TAT protocols, the children were evaluated in terms of Piaget's categories of the practice and the consciousness of rules. Comparisons were made between the stages of maturation of normal and mentally retarded subjects. The aim was to interrelate two theories of development on an empirical level: the theory of 'genetic mental development as set forth by Piaget' and the psychoanalytical description of ego development. The author hypothesized that 'since the two viewpoints converge in the roles they each assign to genetic and sociocultural factors in influencing maturation processes, one would expect to find their stages of development proceeding concurrently'.

SUBJECTS/N = 64 boys. Thirty-two boys, IQ 90+, (8 boys from each of ages 6, 8, 10, 12); and 32 boys, mentally retarded, IQ 60-80, (8 boys from each of ages 8, 10, 12, 14) were involved.

METHOD/The practice of rules and the consciousness of rules were assessed by observation and questioning. Each child played marbles, first with himself and then with the investigator. The child was questioned concerning his conceptions of the game. The children were classified into stages of development on the basis of criteria established by the investigator according to the descriptions of behaviour given by Piaget at the various successive stages. TAT was also administered and four successive levels of ego development were defined by the investigator within each of the categories formulated by Henry (1956).

RESULTS/The stages of development concerning maturation in the areas of the practice of rules were generally consistent with the findings of Piaget. It was found that the groups of children proceeded through concomitant stages in both the areas studied. A full discussion of the five stages of marble play and the four levels of ego development within each of the categories can be found in Bobroff (1960). Generalizing from the data, the investigator was able to formulate sets of characteristics typical of four stages of child development. The mentally retarded children were found to follow the same sequence of developmental stages as normal children.

DISCUSSION/To the extent that the present study was a replication of the marble game experiment conducted by Piaget, comparisons between the Swiss and the American data can be made. The children in both studies progressed through a similar sequence of stages but while Piaget found that his subjects made advances in the practice of rules before they progressed in the consciousness of rules, the present investigator found this to be true only for his older subjects. The younger boy who was at a different level of development in the practice of rules than in the consciousness of rules, tended to be more advanced in this latter respect than in the practice of rules. Taken as a whole however, the children were found to be in concomitant stages of progress in the practice of rules, consciousness of rules and ego development. Although many children were classified into a more advanced stage of development in one area than in another, the statistical results indicated concomitant progress in the three areas for the groups as a whole.

Objective responsibility in children: a comparison with the Piaget data
G. R. Medinnus, 1960

AIM/The study was concerned with 'the shift from subjective to objective responsibility as it is reflected in children's attitudes toward lying.'

SUBJECTS/N = 240. Thirty boys and 30 girls, at each of the age levels, 6, 8, 10 and 12 years were involved. The subjects were selected from the lower socio-economic groups according to the Minnesota Scale for Paternal Occupations. It was intended that the sample would be as comparable as possible to Piaget's subjects from 'the poorer parts of Geneva'.

METHOD/Eighteen story situations and questions drawn from Piaget were administered. Responses were classified by judges according to the stages described by Piaget.

RESULTS AND DISCUSSION/High inter-judge agreement was shown in the judges' categorizations of the responses.
There was a significant change with age in the Subjects responses and a tendency toward a greater number of mature responses with increasing age. However, 162 of the 214 classifiable responses were assigned to Stage II: i.e. 'a lie becomes something that is wrong in itself and would remain so even if the punishment were removed'. Only 16.6 per cent of the responses of the six-year-olds fell into Stage I: i.e. 'a lie is wrong because it is an object of punishment − if the punishment were removed it would be allowed'. Twenty-five per cent of the 12-year-olds' responses were classified as belonging to Stage III: i.e. 'a lie is wrong because it is in conflict with mutual trust and affection'. The sex difference was not statistically significant.
When the responses to the question, 'Why is it naughty (wrong) to tell a lie?' were more closely examined, a number of meaningful themes were revealed: '(a) you get punished; (b) it is naughty; it isn't right; God, Jesus or parents don't like it; (c) you get into trouble; (d) you hurt others; (e) you don't get any place; it just leads to more lies; (f) you always get found out anyway'. When the responses were classified into these six categories, it was found that in general the number of responses falling into the first two categories decreased from age six to age 12 'while the opposite was true for the remaining categories'. When the six themes are interpreted in terms of Piaget's discussion of moral realism and objective responsibility, 'it would seem appropriate to group together the first two themes on the basis of their

explanation of lying as wrong because it is forbidden and because it results in punishment. The last four themes, on the other hand, seem to reflect the child's concern with possible consequences which might arise from lying.' Eighty-five per cent of the responses at both ages six and eight fell into the first category, the 10-year-olds responses were divided almost equally between the two types, while a greater number of the 12-year-olds indicated a concern with the consequences of a lie.

The author suggests that future investigators attempting to replicate Piaget's investigations should not adhere too rigidly to Piaget's schemes for the classification of responses and would be advised to devise their own definitions.

A study of children's concepts of lies
K. R. Kane, 1970

AIM/The purpose of the study was to record developmental progressions in children's concepts of lies patterned after the investigations of Piaget.

SUBJECTS/N = 60 girls ages six, nine and 12 years from an upper middle-class suburban school.

METHOD/The child's moral knowledge of lies was investigated by inquiries into the definition of lies and the wrongness of lies.

Four pairs of Piaget's stories involving lies were slightly revised and each child was asked to choose the story which contained the worse lie.

In an effort to investigate more thoroughly factors which influence children's moral judgements of lies, further stories were administered and the child was asked to indicate if the lies in the stories were the same or if one lie was worse and to substantiate the judgement with reasons.

RESULTS/In the definition of lies the following hypothesized progression was supported: 'a lie is (a) something that is wrong, (b) something described by specific, concrete examples, (c) a falsehood, (d) an intentional falsehood'. Children's ideas about why lies are wrong were assumed to follow the following progression: 'concern with (a) punishment or censure, (b) an absolute rule, (c) distress caused others, (d) breach of mutual trust or violation of personal integrity. Analyses found increments in scores with age and significant differences among age groups.'

Relating to the Piaget stories, the results supported Piaget's contention of developmental change in children's moral judgements.

'The four factors which influenced children's moral judgements of lies were: (a) the one relevant factor of intent and these three irrelevant factors; concern with (b) if the lie was believed or not, (c) if the amount of damage in the situation was great or small, and (d) if the lie was believable or unbelievable. The significant differences among age groups on these four factors support the contention of developmental progression within each factor and the contention that these are factors which do influence maturity of moral judgement of lies.'

II Developments from Piaget's Approach

Strauss (1954) studied the growth of the awareness of rules governing transactions, particularly purchasing, and disregarded the importance placed by Piaget on 'special kinds of' social relations (i.e. parent/child, child/peers) concerning the conceptions of rules, viewing rules rather in terms of sets of relations that exist among general roles. (Details are given later in this chapter.)

Armsby (1971) emphasizes that 'the story-pairs used by Piaget to test the shift in moral judgement reveal that they do not clearly differentiate accidental from purposive behaviour. For example, in Piaget's cup-breaking story pair, one boy accidentally breaks 15 cups while the other boy breaks one cup while attempting to get some jam.' Armsby points out that in both stories the damage done is accidental and in order to make a valid assessment of the development of intentionality it is surely necessary to devise moral judgement stories that contrast an accidental act with a purposive act. He also thought it important to provide written copies of the stories to reduce the confounding factor of memory ability. As a result of these innovations, Armsby concluded that children make moral judgements based on intentionality at an earlier age than Piaget and other experimenters have suggested and, although there is an age progression, there is no clear age level at which the morality of constraint ceases to operate. (Details are given below.) Breznitz and Kugelmass (1967), when attempting to contrast a more adequate measure to assess the sequential structure of the principle of intentionality through adolescence, considered: 'what is it in the use of intentionality that would characteristically be acquired in the later years of childhood and adolescence'. They hypothesized that 'as the child matures and broadens his range of experience, it is possible for him to respond to a wider range of situations' and that 'an intentionality-oriented response might be the predominant type of response in increasingly more spheres of life.' Thus development would tend to be a quantitative change. Secondly, when the range of stimuli to which the same type of response is given is sufficiently broad, a cognitive principle to abstract all specific relations may need to be developed. Breznitz and Kugelmass considered that the interrelation of these two processes was highly complex and they therefore concentrated solely on the cognitive principle. The analysis following the administering of the final construction of the measure indicated that the emergence of a cognitive principle underlying the use of intentionality in moral judgement goes through four successive stages. Breznitz and Kugelmass comment that a highly developed principle of intentionality could be termed essentially similar to Inhelder and Piaget's 'formal operations'. (Details are given later in this chapter.) McKechnie (1971) found in a pilot study that, if the structure of Piaget's stories were reversed and the ill-intentioned act led to greater material damage, then the frequency of 'subjective responsibility' responses increased. The study also suggested that the size of consequence may influence the judgement and that it might be expedient to look at 'good' and 'bad' intentions separately. He also noted that Durkin (1959b, 1961) and Boehm and Nass (1964) drew attention to children making different judgements depending on the characteristics of the situations described in the stories. He therefore designed a study to investigate further the influence of story structure and context on the moral judgement of the child. He confirmed his further hypothesis that the structure of Piaget's stories masked the development taking place between the two extremes Piaget detected: 'the two moralities are only end-points of a developmental process in which consequences originally dominate the complex of factors and eventually give way to the increasing importance of intentions in the mind of the child'. (Details are given below.) Irwin & Moore (1971) attempted to measure the degree to which pre-school children make conventional judgements concerning, among other aspects, accidental and intentional misdeeds. The outstanding feature of this study was the use of illustrated material, thus reducing the necessity for a verbal response. The older pre-school children understood notions of justice better than the younger ones. The understanding of guilt, innocence, apology and restitution was clearer than intentionality. The data were consistent with Piaget's theory that the concept of intentionality is slow to develop compared with the notion of restitution. (Details are given later in this chapter.)

Durkin (1959b) questioned her subjects about violations of justice other than physical aggression in order to evaluate still further the applicability of Piaget's theory concerning 'the increasing acceptance with age, of reciprocity as a justice-principle'. The results indicated that, when justice-violations were described in terms of violations of property and character rights, the acceptance of reciprocity was negatively related to CA. Contrary to Piaget's suggestion, it was the seven-year-old children rather than the children of 13 years who saw restoration of justice in terms of reciprocity. Specificity of judgement was indicated in that only four subjects out of a total of 101, consistently gave reciprocity responses for all four stories. This suggests a further weakness in Piaget's theory in that his investigation in this respect was based on responses to only one kind of violation. She emphasizes the complexity involved in arriving at a reliable theory of the development of justice in children. In a further study (1961), Durkin systematically examined the specificity of the judgements given by the subjects in the previous study and examined the reasons they gave for their judgements as an attempt to explain the specificity. The 'findings indicated that a child's judgements about the restoration of "right order" in various situations was affected by the particulars of each situation.' She reported that the 'phenomenon of specificity can be said to place limitations on the general applicability of Piaget's theory of the development of concepts of justice in children.' Closer analysis of responses revealed that apparently identical responses were fundamentally different when further details were sought. (Details are given later in this chapter.)

Morris (1958) attempted to gain further insight into the behaviour which young people expect of their contemporaries by devising, 'Piaget-style', a number of everyday problem situations. There was also an attempt to assess any differences between what adolescents thought should be done in the problem situations and what they thought would actually be done. Although there was a tendency to greater reciprocity and equity with increasing age, the study drew attention to individual differences in moral development and the social influences. (Details are given below.)

A wide survey by Johnson (1962) attempted to determine the degree of interrelation within and between areas of moral judgement together with the investigation of the relation of various antecedent conditions to moral judgement. The stories were modelled closely to those of Piaget, but new questions were devised to suit the adolescent subjects and to allow the test to be administered in pencil and paper form. The results indicated some consistency of response between areas of moral judgement and the experimenter considered that a general factor of moral judgement could be said to exist (Details are given later in this chapter.)

The development of conceptions of rules in children
A. L. Strauss, 1954

This paper reports a study of the growth of awareness of rules governing transactions, particularly purchasing, and discusses the findings in relation to the development of moral rules in general and the theories accounting for this development.

The author disregards both the importance placed by Piaget on 'special kinds of' (i.e. parent/child, child/peers), social relations concerning the conceptions of rules, and Piaget's recourse for the explanation of the growth of moral conceptions to such 'dubious, or, at any rate, such oversimplified, principles as reward and punishment, pleasure and pain and learning from specific direct experience to "recognize a common element in a variety of situations" '.

The author sees rules in terms of sets of relations that exist among general roles; all these roles are systematically related to one another. The more advanced the child's conceptions of these roles, the closer his systematization approaches that of the adult. 'Conception of role' denotes a conceptualization of a set of activities seen in relationship to other sets of activities. Built into role conceptions are the justifications of motivations for behaviour appropriate or inappropriate to the enactment of roles.

The development of moral values in children
J. F. Morris, 1958

AIM/The author attempted to illumine the relationship between age and moral development in Britain in the period of adolescence. By studying the value-judgements made by Grammar School pupils he was also intent to gain insight into the behaviour which young people expect of their contemporaries in a number of everyday problem-situations.

SUBJECTS/N = 94 boys and girls selected at random from the total population of the school.

METHOD/The interviews centred around responses to 14 problem-situations of the following type.

'Someone in J's class at school has broken the school rules and the form teacher wants to find out who did it. He asks the pupils to own up; but no one does. Then he asks anyone who knows anything about it to come and see him afterwards. J knows who did it. What should he do?'

'J wants to take a girl that he knows to the pictures, but his parents refuse to let him have the money because they think that he is too young to go to the pictures with girls. He borrows the money from a friend and then after he has been, the friend wants the money back urgently. What should J do?'

'J' (or 'K' for girls) was identified as being the same age as the subject being interviewed and after saying what he thought should be done, he was asked to go through the situations again saying what he thought 'J' would actually do.

The material was then analysed into the direction of choice in each situation and allocated to one of the following six categories: (i) normative (referring to a principle of assumed general validity); (ii) authority (use of an authoritative edict, emanating from teachers, parents etc., to justify a course of action); (iii) reciprocity; (iv) self-interest (a desire for self-gratification and avoidance of punishment); (v) independence (emphasis upon making up one's own mind, whatever the course of action decided upon); (vi) conformity (emphasis upon doing what 'others', particularly in one's age group, do). There was some similarity to the categories of Piaget.

RESULTS/'The conclusions reached on the basis of the detailed analysis were: (i) there were marked discrepancies between what adolescents thought should be done in the problem-situations and what they thought would actually be done. On the normative level these tend to increase with age; (ii) a relatively rapid growth of "normative" elements occurred in judgements of what should be done in the situations, together with a much slower growth of such elements on the level of actually expected behaviour; (iii) there was a slow decline with age in value-judgements based upon self-interest, most marked on the level of actually expected behaviour; (iv) there was a decline in moral dependence upon authority and an increase in independence, both subject to marked fluctuations around puberty; (v) the complexity of value-judgements increased with age; (vi) marked situational differences occurred in value-judgements (but these differences did not necessarily imply subjective inconsistency on the part of the respondent); (vii) there were no striking differences between boys' and girls' responses to the problem-situations.' Two slight differences were observed; girls' values tended to be slightly ahead of those of boys and the discrepancy between 'should' and 'would' was somewhat greater for girls.

AN EXTENSION OF THE RESEARCH/Comparisons were made in a Grammar School and a Secondary School in the Manchester area. The investigation was considerably shortened and written responses had to be made instead of verbal. An additional finding emanating from this second research was that there seemed to be differences between Grammar School and Secondary Modern School pupils in attitudes to peer-group conformity. There was a tendency for the Grammar School pupils to show less conformity to friends. In the previous data, conformity declined sharply with age on the 'should' level but remained relatively constant (with increase at puberty) on the 'would' level.

DISCUSSION/The author concludes that further studies are needed to determine the nature of individual differences in moral development in view of the marked degree of individuality of response: general agreement upon morally relevant issues cannot be expected. Social factors influencing judgements also need further investigation.

Children's acceptance of reciprocity as a justice-principle
D. Durkin, 1959b

AIM/This study formed an extension of a previous investigation by the author (Durkin, 1959a), the major purpose being to question the same subjects about violations of justice other than the one of physical aggression and to assess the developmental trend in association with the one described by Piaget. By enlarging the violations about which the subjects are questioned, the investigator hoped to evaluate still further, the general applicability of Piaget's theory concerning 'the increasing acceptance, with age, of reciprocity as a justice-principle'.

SUBJECTS/N = 101. The mean chronological age for the three groups was seven years eight months, 10 years nine months, and 13 years nine months respectively.

METHOD/Justice was defined in terms of (a) the rendering of rights regarding one's property and (b) the rendering of rights regarding one's character. Possible violations of these two kinds of rights were depicted in four story situations and subjects were questioned concerning appropriate justice behaviour.
The Kuhlmann-Anderson Intelligence Test was administered and the mean scores for the three groups were found to be 103.4 101.6 and 103.4 respectively.

RESULTS/'Acceptance of reciprocity as a justice-principle, contrary to Piaget's proposal, decreased as the chronological age of subjects increased.'

'Acceptance of reciprocity did not appear to be related to a child's level of intelligence. This relationship was consistent throughout the different age levels.'

DISCUSSION/When justice-violations were described in terms of violations of property and character rights, the tendency for subjects to accept reciprocity as a principle of justice was negatively related to CA. Contrary to Piaget's suggestion, it was the seven-year-old children rather than the children of 13 years who tended to see restoration of justice in terms of reciprocity.

It is interesting to note that only four subjects out of the total group of 101 consistently gave reciprocity responses for all four stories. This could suggest a further weakness in Piaget's theory that it is based entirely on judgement responses to only one kind of violation, namely physical aggression.

The author concludes in summary 'all of these various kinds of comparisons would tend to indicate that the factors affecting a child's understanding of justice are sufficiently multiple and that justice, operationally defined, is sufficiently complex that any theory which attempts to explain "The Development of the Idea of Justice in Children" is from the start, doomed to inevitable over-generalization and consequent error'.

The specificity of children's moral judgements
D. Durkin, 1961

AIM/In a previous study Durkin (1959b), reported findings which failed to substantiate Piaget's proposal concerning the child's increasing acceptance, with age, of reciprocity as a justice principle. Also noted, was the exposition that the subjects made quite different kinds of judgements about the varying justice-violations introduced into the investigation. The author comments that this phenomenon of specificity tends to suggest a further weakness in Piaget's theory, in that Piaget describes the development of children's attitudes toward reciprocity on the basis of their judgements about a single kind of justice-violation, that of physical aggression. The present study was therefore designed to (a) examine systematically the specificity of the judgements made by the previous group of subjects and (b) to examine the reasons they gave for their judgements as an attempt to explain the specificity.

SUBJECTS/N = 101. The mean ages of the three groups were seven years eight months, 10 years nine months and 13 years nine months: age groups corresponding to Piaget's designation of the 'three great periods in the development of the sense of justice in the child'.

METHOD/The four story situations presented were described in Durkin (1959b).

RESULTS/1'. Considered as a group, subjects' responses to the four stories were with one exception, significantly different in kind.
2. Considered as individuals, their responses to the four stories were found to be consistently independent of each other.
3. Reasons given by subjects for their responses were found, in some instances, to alter the apparent nature of such responses. It was thus demonstrated that responses overtly identical can, when analysed through the reasons given for them, be essentially different in kind.
4. Reasons given by subjects for their responses also suggested, in some instances, the possibility that a definition of reciprocity as being a return of identical behaviour is too narrow in that it fails to include the more subtle forms of reciprocity.'

A study of children's moral judgements
R. C. Johnson, 1962

AIM/This study was concerned to 'attempt to determine the degree of interrelation within and between areas of moral judgement.' Additionally, it sought to investigate the relation of various antecedent conditions to moral judgement.' 'There was an attempt to discover the relation of adult constraint, egocentricity, age, sex, IQ and parental occupational level to moral judgement.' To measure peer group co-operation was considered to be incompatible with the large sample designed to give a reliable interpretation to the main problems under investigation.

SUBJECTS/N = 807. The distribution of the sample was as follows: grade 5, 93 boys, 97 girls; grade 7, 97 boys, 76 girls; grade 9, 125 boys, 143 girls and grade 11, 84 boys and 92 girls. Relating to socio-economic status, 'the sample was a very close approximation of the general population, as measured by the Minnesota Occupational Scale'. The mean IQ was 105.9.

METHOD/The author was intent to devise a test of moral judgement within which a number of questions could be found having to do with each of the areas of immanent justice, moral realism, retribution and expiation *vs.* restitution and reciprocity, the efficacy of severe punishment and communicable respon-

298

sibility. The stories were modelled quite closely to those of Piaget but new questions were devised to suit the older sample and to allow the test to be administered as a paper and pencil test. Since Medinnus believed 'that differences in the "level of abstraction" in the stories might account for differences in the type of response obtained, items were eliminated and revised until they seemed of approximately equal difficulty to this writer and to Medinnus, who helped in their selection'. Full details of the stories devised can be found in Johnson (1962). Successful categorization by judges indicated that the items were directed toward the five areas of moral judgement to be studied and the judges reached a high level of agreement concerning the degree of difficulty of the questioning. (Only three questions were considered most difficult by over 10 per cent of the judges, the percentages being 12, 14, and 17, together with no single question being chosen as the easiest by more than 10 per cent of the judges.)

.   Shoben's (1949) Parental Attitude Test was used to categorize parental attitudes into 'dominativeness, ignoringness and possessiveness'.

Gorham's Proverbs Test (1956) designed to measure concreteness and abstractness of thought was used to measure for the degree of egocentricity. 'The stage of concreteness for Piaget is a late portion of the egocentric period of the child's development' and is followed by a 'reflective thought' period. This test was therefore considered to be related to Piaget's concept of egocentricity.

Fifty-one children in Grade 7, 61 children in Grade 9 and 55 students in Grade 11 were tested on the Gorham Proverbs Test.

One hundred and twenty-eight sets of parents were involved in the parent attitude study, 96 sets returned the completed questionnaires and were found to be representative of the subject population.

RESULTS/The reliability of the moral judgement test and also of the subscales were not as high as that usually attained in educational tests, the reliability figures for the total test being .61 for Grade 5, .59 for Grade 7, .55 for Grade 9 and .56 for Grade 11.

Correlations between moral judgement responses revealed far more positive and significant correlations than might be expected by chance. (From a total of 760 correlations, there were 294 positive correlations and 79 negative correlations significant at or beyond the .05 level of confidence.) Responses within moral judgement areas were nearly always positively and significantly correlated. 'Correlations of the number of mature responses in the various areas of moral judgement showed response tendencies in the areas of moral realism, retribution versus restitution and the efficacy of severe punishment to be rather closely related. Responses to immanent justice questions were less closely related, while responses to questions involving communicable responsibility were essentially unrelated to other response tendencies.'

Abstractness and concreteness were only slightly related to moral judgement responses. Out of 45 correlations of abstractness with moral judgement, six were significant. 'If abstractness is indicative of a freedom from egocentricity, one would expect high abstractness scores to be positively related to mature moral judgement.' Five of the six significant correlations were in this direction. Only three of the 45 correlations of concreteness with moral judgement were significant. 'If concreteness is a manifestation of egocentricity, concreteness should be negatively correlated with mature moral judgement. The reverse held true in two of the three significant correlations.'

Of the 45 correlations of the parent attitudes of expressed dominativeness, possessiveness and 'ignoringness' with the level of the child's moral judgement, eight were significant, seven of them in the predicted direction, i.e. possessiveness and dominativeness positively correlated and 'ignoringness' negatively correlated with the acceptance of the beliefs of immanent justice, moral realism, retribution and expiation and in the efficacy of severe punishment. The most significant correlations were in the areas of immanent justice and communicable responsibility.

IQ and to a lesser extent, parental occupation were positively and significantly correlated with mature moral judgement in all areas.

Intentionality in moral judgement: developmental stages
S. Breznitz, and S. Kugelmass, 1967

AIM/The aim was to construct a measure to assess the possible sequential structure of the principle of intentionality in moral judgement and to examine the possible emergence of a cognitive principle underlying the use of intentionality through adolescence.

SUBJECTS/N = 1,014. The sample was obtained from five Israeli urban public schools and the children, aged from 11-17 years, represented a broad range of economic, ethnic and social backgrounds.

METHOD/Facet analysis suggested by Guttman (1958) was employed. An attempt was made to concentrate on three facets of the development of intentionality: V: usage/verbalization to test the subject's ability to verbalize his use of the principle of intentionality; R: recognition/recall, attempting to test the subject's ability to express spontaneously the principle of intentionality; and Q: crude/refined, which relates to the testing of the subject's competence in using the principle of intentionality as criteria in moral judgement.

The authors state: 'Following Guttman's procedure (1954-55, 1958, 1959), we may now define our questionnaire as: "A measure of S's ability to (verbalize/use) (recall/recognize) the principle of intentionality in a (refined/crude) manner".' From the three facets, eight-item possibilities were derived for the questionnaire although three were discarded. Full details of the questionnaire and the definition of the mature response for each of its parts can be obtained from Breznitz and Kugelmass (1967).

RESULTS/The psychometric analysis suggested that the emergence of a cognitive principle underlying the use of intentionality in moral judgement goes through four successive stages. 'Starting with the preverbalized usage of the principle, the development moves through the stage of verbalization, then to the ability to recall the principle spontaneously until eventually the refined use of the principle is possible:' 'a person in this stage would be using a more highly differentiated dimension of intentionality in his moral judgements.'

DISCUSSION/The authors comment that, although their analysis focuses on the qualitative changes, it is possible to hypothesize that, as the individual passes through each stage, there should be a positive change in the acceleration of the rate of increasing probability of using the principle. The psychological advantages of a highly developed principle of intentionality to the individual could be said to be to help him draw systematically on his past experience, select and organize the elements most relevant to the problem arising and 'serve as a guide in generating hypothetical meaningful instances for comparison'. Such a highly developed principle could allow even abstract activity and this characteristic could be said to be essentially similar to Inhelder and Piaget's theoretical construct of 'formal operations'.

Moral judgement from childhood to adolescence
N. Bull, 1969

AIM/Bull, together with his students, was intent to investigate the moral judgement of children over a wide age-range and with a diversified battery of tests. The aim was to assess moral judgmental development in terms of a four-stage scale: anomy, heteronomy, socionomy and autonomy, taking into account the relationship with the main individual variables of chronological age, sex, intelligence, socio-economic class and religious background.

SUBJECTS/Sixty subjects, 30 of each sex from each of ages seven, nine, 11, 13, 15 and 17 years from urban schools in the south-west of England were involved.

METHOD/Five visual projection tests were devised, aiming to be inductive rather than deductive, empirical as opposed to theoretical and to limit subjectivity by standardized structuring developed during pre-testing. The visual projection tests covered the areas of the value of life, reciprocity and conscience, cheating, stealing, and lying.

Written tests to obtain ancillary evidence were adapted from tests used in previous studies and included: 'the ideal person test'; 'virtues and vices' (including 'good deeds and bad deeds' and 'right or wrong stories'); 'choosing reasons'; 'concepts of justice'; and sentence completion tests.

RESULTS/Development was traced in moral judgement based on anomous, heteronomous, socionomous and autonomous responses between the ages of seven to 17 years in all the areas tested.

Intelligence appeared as the most significant variable, socio-economic class as of less significance and 'religious class' as the least significant. Associations with intelligence were more noticeable for girls and with socio-economic class for boys: particularly in the verbal tests. Associations with religious class 'were not impressive', but were stronger for girls, again with respect to the verbal tests.

With respect to the comparison of the written tests with the verbal tests: intelligence was more clearly apparent in the verbal tests and associations with socio-economic class were broadly similar. Associations with 'religious class' were more apparent in the written tests. (Detailed results and discussion can be found in Bull, 1969.)

The Farmington Trust Research Unit, Oxford.

The Farmington Trust Research Unit team, as part of the Trust's general research on moral education studied moral development involving 790 children representing each year group from four years to 18 years. From responses to an Interview Guide involving seven areas of moral thinking, namely the child's ideas of good, ought, bad or naughty, fair, stealing, lying and bullying, four modes of thought were obtained. The modes have been designated 'other-obeying', 'self-obeying', 'self-considering', together with 'other-considering'. Notably, the interview guide was concerned with the child's reasons for the moral attitudes displayed and did not employ 'anecdotes featuring situations of moral conflict'. Williams (1969) reports 'evidence of some specificity of response': older subjects tend to give a wider variety of responses to the same stimulus. 'These findings may be accounted for by postulating concurrent development in two different directions – an overall increase in the sophistication of the child's response, running parallel to his general intellectual development: and a generalization effect, by which any given mode of thought, starting from highly specific situations becomes more and more generally applied.'

A re-examination of the development of moral judgements in children
R. E. Armsby, 1971

AIM/The investigator was intent on a threefold aim: (a) to administer new moral judgement stories that contrast an accidental act with a purposive act in order to extend from Piaget's investigation in which the stories did not clearly differentiate accidental from purposive behaviour; (b) to assess the presence of intentionality judgements when the consequences resulting from the accidental act in each story-pair received manipulation, together with an increase in the severity of the consequences; and (c) to explore the relationship between religious training and the maturity of moral judgements.

SUBJECTS AND PROCEDURES/N =240. Social class and IQ were controlled (IQ was within the average range). The ratio of boys to girls was equal. Half of the sample were from a public school (non-Catholic) and the other half from a Catholic school. In each school, 20 children from each of the age groups, 6, 8, and 10 years respectively were read, and asked to respond to, the three standard Piaget story-pairs. Those who made intentionality judgements in response to at least two story-pairs were considered to be judging in terms of intentionality. Twenty additional students at each of the ages responded to the four revised story-pairs, one at each of the four levels of accidental consequences. These children were given written copies of the stories for constant reference.

303

METHOD/A battery of four 'story-pair' situations revised from those of Piaget that clearly pair an accidental act against a purposive act. Each of these story-pairs had four different levels of accidental consequence.

Three of Piaget's standard story-pairs were also administered for comparative purposes.

RESULTS/The Hoel Test (1962) was used to compare the percentage of children making intentionality judgements at the three different ages and in the two different schools.

CONCLUSIONS/(1) Children make moral judgements based on intentionality at an earlier age than Piaget and other experimenters have suggested. (2) 'Although there is an age progression in the internalization of intentionality (as Piaget postulates), there is no clear age level at which the morality of constraint ceases to operate and the child moves into the more mature stage of the morality of co-operation.' Seventy-five per cent of all six-year-old children made intentionality judgements compared with 95 per cent of all eight- and 10-year-old children. (3) When the distinction between purposive and accidental behaviour is clarified by the use of the revised stories, the percentage of Catholic children who make intentionality judgements is no higher than the percentage of public school children.

DISCUSSION/Although a higher percentage of Catholic children made intentionality judgements in response to the Piaget stories (a result obtained previously by Boehm, 1962b; 1963 — see Religious Influences) there was no significant difference between Catholic and Public School children's intentionality responses to the revised stories. The offered explanation for this phenomenon is that the standard Piaget stories were in the context of accidental damage occurring while a child was disobeying his mother. The revised stories did not stress obedience. It is suggested that Catholic schooling sensitizes children towards obedience and it can therefore be concluded that Catholic orientation does not encourage an earlier internalization of intentionality or enhance earlier mature moral judgement but arouses a greater sense of obedience.

The young child's understanding of social justice
D. M. Irwin, and S. G. Moore, 1971

AIM/'There have been few attempts to investigate the extent

to which children under six years possess mature notions of justice and the present study was designed to measure the degree to which pre-school age children make conventional moral judgements concerning guilt and innocence, apology and restitution and accidental and intentional misdeeds.'

SUBJECTS/The study was originally carried out in 1967 and replicated in 1969. The 1967 sample consisted of 31 children; Group 1 including eight girls and eight boys, age range three years nine months to four years ten months and Group 2 comprising eight girls and seven boys, age range four years eight months to five years six months. The 1969 sample included 34 children with similar grouping. Socio-economic background was classified as middle-class.

METHOD/A 'forced-choice, story-completion instrument was developed in which children were asked to select, from among well-behaved and ill-behaved story characters, those whose behaviour they regarded as worthy of criticism and punishment. Twenty-one stories were used to assess the level of the child's conceptions of justice. Three training stories were employed and 18 test stories. There were six test stories for each of three categories of social justice: guilt-innocence, apology-restitution and intent-accidental. The interviewer presented the child with two possible endings for each test story and the child was asked to indicate the preferred ending.' In each case, one story ending conveyed a just resolution and the other a non-just resolution. The format differed from that used by Piaget, in that the child was only presented with one story at a time, the stories were illustrated and the child could indicate his response by pointing, thus reducing the necessity for a verbal response.

RESULTS/Both younger and older pre-school children were significantly more just, than unjust. The 1967 confidence level was .01 for boys and .001 for girls. The 1969 data revealed a .001 confidence level for both sexes. A Mann-Whitney U Test for independent samples indicated that boys and girls did not differ significantly from each other in total justice.

The older children understood notions of justice better than the younger ones. Understanding of guilt and innocence and apology and restitution was clearer than understanding of intentionality. Restitution emerged before apology.

DISCUSSION/It can be reflected that restitution develops before apology, due to the former being a physical, observable act, whereas the latter is verbal and perhaps not fully understood.

Additionally, restitution may be more effective in the child's experience. Age and category differences can be said to be due to changes in the ability to form concepts and changes in egocentrism, together with greater experience in forming reciprocal peer relations. The data are consistent with Piaget's theory that the concept of intentionality is slow to develop compared with the notion of restitution.

Between Piaget's stages: a study in moral development
R. J. McKechnie, 1971

AIM/The investigator comments that Piaget's moral judgement stories make accessible the extremes of moral development but that it is possible that the material obscures what is happening between those extremes. He found in a pilot study that if the structure of Piaget's stories were reversed and the ill-intentioned act led to great material damage, then the frequency of 'subjective responsibility' responses increased. The pilot study also suggested that the size of consequence may influence the judgement and that it might be expedient to look at 'good' and 'bad' intentions separately. It was noted that children made different judgements depending on the characteristics of the situations described in the stories (Durkin, 1959b; 1961) and that this was confirmed by Nass (1964).

The present study was designed to investigate further the influence of story structure and behavioural area on the moral judgement of the child.

SUBJECTS/N = 60. Twenty subjects at each age level, mean ages six years four months, nine years four months, 12 years four months were selected from a primary and a secondary school within the same catchment area. Mean IQ at age nine was 97.8 and at age 12, 99.7. IQ scores were not available for the youngest group but the mean was estimated to be within the same range. The groups were drawn from skilled and semi-skilled working class families.

METHOD/Pairs of stories were produced using as far as possible those occurring in the literature and those that had been useful in the pilot study. Four areas of behaviour were chosen in accordance with Piaget and included lying, stealing, aggression and obedience. The characteristics of the story-pair structure were as follows:

'Structure	Actor	Intention	Consequence
A	1st	Good	Small
	2nd	Bad	Small
B	1st	Good	Large
	2nd	Bad	Large
C	1st	Good	Small
	2nd	Good	Large
D	1st	Bad	Small
	2nd	Bad	Large'

The children were interviewed using Piaget's approach and the protocols were scored in terms of whether the child had judged according to intentions or consequences.

RESULTS/The results indicated that the development of moral judgement is related to age and 'with the hypothesis of specificity of moral judgement as a function of behavioural area'. Differences due to the structure of the story-pair were also shown.

DISCUSSION/The results supported the hypothesis that the structure of Piaget's stories masked the development taking place between the two extremes Piaget detected. 'Far from ignoring the intentions of the actor, the child does appear to consider them, although this is not always obvious from his verbal response. This finding emphasizes that the "two moralities" are only end-points of a developmental process in which consequences originally dominate the complex of factors and eventually give way to the increasing importance of intentions in the mind of the child.'

Story structure appeared to be as important as age. 'The order of achievement of success on the different structures is consistent over the age levels and suggests that the child is able to use intention as a criterion if the consequences of the acts are the same, before he learns to use it in other circumstances.'

'Although there is little difference between structures A and B there is a consistent tendency for structure A, where consequences are small, to elicit a larger number of mature responses. It is thus possible that the child will use intention as a criterion where the consequences are relatively unimportant but returns to the use of consequences if they are large enough to be seen as important. A parallel can be seen here with the development of conservation of area and volume where the maturing child who once attended to only one dimension will return to the use of that dimension if the differences on the other dimensions become too great. It may be profitable to follow this line of investigation and establish links with the work of Lerner (1937) and Stuart (1967) who have shown that it is the ability of the child to "decentre" which enables him to make mature judgements.'

It was also revealed from the different story structure that the child learns to evaluate bad behaviour before good and this can be explained in terms of the disciplinary approaches used by parents and teachers. Piaget claimed that the concept of 'good' does not develop until fairly late and Kohlberg (1964) describes the elementary stage of development as being punishment-oriented.

Consistent with Piaget's findings was the exposure of lying as the first area in which the child reveals mature responses. Durkin (1961) was supported in her contention that the behavioural area influences the judgement of the child.

It was felt that this study indicates a method of assessing moral development with greater accuracy than that used by Piaget and that it could have important implications for programmes of moral education.

III Associated Factors

(a) Relations with other cognitive measures

Generally, research indicates that intelligence is associated with mature moral judgement. However, Durkin (1959a, 1959b) found the relationship of intelligence and kind of justice response conflicting throughout different age levels (see II above). Boehm (1962: see IIIb below) observed that academically gifted children mature earlier in their moral judgements concerning distinctions between intention and outcome of an action, than children of average intelligence. In a later analysis Boehm (1962b), in relation to recognizing the distinction between motivation and results of an action, found that gifted upper middle-class children, irrespective of type of school, scored higher at an earlier age than their counterparts of average intelligence. Gifted working-class children also scored higher than their peers. With respect to independence from adults and peer reciprocity, gifted working-class children and upper middle-class children scored higher than their counterparts of average intelligence (see IIId below). Johnson (1962) found IQ to be positively correlated with mature moral judgement in all the aspects investigated (see II above). Whiteman and Kosier (1964) revealed 'systematic increases in mature responses in association with increases in age and with IQ at each age'. (Details are given later in this Section.) Combining the verbal and numerical raw scores of the Differential Aptitude Test to represent the intelligence level, Porteus and Johnson's (1965) investigation indicated that intelligence seemed to be the most important variable for measures of both 'cognitive and affective zones' of conscience development (see IIIe below). The hypothesis that the more intellectually able children, as measured by the WISC vocabulary, are also more mature in moral attitudes was supported in Harris (1970: see IIIf below).

MacRae (1954) reported that children of above-average intelligence respond more maturely to cognitive aspects of moral development. He maintains that cognitive responses are based on knowledge of adult expectations and are due to 'cultural indoctrination and learning of norms.' He believes that the bright child and the child of the upper social class internalizes parental rules more strongly and remains dependent upon parents longer than children of average intelligence and lower class. However, Boehm's findings (op.cit.) did not bear out MacRae's study. Bull (1969: see II above), concludes that 'intelligence is a leading constituent factor in moral judgement; and that, as such, it facilitates development in moral judgement. But is not by any means the only factor. Intelligence "per se" does not guarantee higher levels of moral insight and action'. Although finding significant association between moral judgement and intelligence at earlier ages Bull reports no positive associations at 17 years.

Ugurel-Semin (1952) concluded that the progress of moral thought is characterized by five different tendencies whose common trait is found in the change from centralization to decentralization (see IIIe below). Likewise, Stuart (1967) drew attention to the importance of the ability to 'decenter' in the development of moral judgement. When the moral and causal judgements of high and low decentering subjects were contrasted, high decenterers were significantly superior. A traditional measure of IQ was found to be a significant influence in the two moral judgement areas and decentration. (Details are given later in this Section.)

Breznitz and Kugelmass (1967) suggested that there was a cognitive principle underlying the use of intentionality in moral judgement through four successive stages. A highly-developed principle of intentionality could allow abstract activity which can be seen to be synonymous with Inhelder and Piaget's 'formal operations' (see II above). Johnson (1962), however, found concreteness and abstractness to be only slightly related to moral judgement responses. It should perhaps be pointed out that the measure used was Gorham's Proverbs Test. (See II above; and also Stephens, Miller and McLaughlin 1969 in Chapt.7 'The Development of Reasoning among Handicapped Children'.)

Seltzer (1969) addressed his inquiry to the development of the child's ability to conceptualize time, and its relationship to the development of his ability to make mature moral judgements.

Furthermore, he investigated the hypothesis that the child's moral conduct is significantly related to his ability to accurately perceive the passage of time. Both hypotheses were substantiated. (Details are given later in this Section.) In Brennan's (1962) research (details given below) high perspective (the cognitive aspect of social adaptation) was associated with low 'moral realism', though this was significant only at the nine-and-a-half year level.

(Details of the approach of Kohlberg and his colleagues to cognitive aspects of moral development are given in IV below.)[1]

The relation of social adaptation, emotional adjustment and moral judgement to intelligence in primary school children
W. K. Brennan, 1962

AIM/'The main aim of the research was to study the relation of social adaptation to different levels of intelligence and to age,' together with 'the relation of social adaptation to moral judgement and the relation of both to emotional adjustment.'

SUBJECTS/N = 548 primary school children. Following the administration of the Cornwell Intelligence Test, seven experimental groups of 20 children were selected, all matched for size of family and occupation of father, but with controlled contrasts in age and intelligence.

METHOD/The Cornwell Orally Presented Group Test of Intelligence for Juniors (Cornwell 1950), the Vineland-Manchester Scales of Social Adaptation (Lunzer 1959) and a test of moral judgement based on the work of Piaget (1932) were administered to each child individually; and for each child, teachers completed a schedule of the Bristol Social Adjustment Guides (Stott 1958) as a measure of emotional adjustment.

Guttman's (1950) Scalogram technique was used to establish the scalability of the moral judgement questions and two separate analyses of variance were applied to scores from the Vineland-Manchester and moral judgement tests.

RESULTS/Concerning moral judgement the following results were obtained.

(a) 'Seven moral judgement questions are scalable and increasing total score indicated movement away from 'moral realism' as defined by Piaget (1932).'

(b) Chronological Age and Mental Age were significantly related to moral judgement up to nine-and-a-half to 11 years; when the significance of MA was reduced and CA became insignificant.

(c) High perspective (the cognitive aspect of social adaptation) was associated with low 'moral realism', though significant only at nine-and-a-half years.

(d) Where age and intelligence did not differ significantly, moral judgement was not correlated with responsibility or emotional adjustment.

Other results indicated positive associations between perspective and MA; responsibility and CA; IQ and level of adjustment (significant only at the nine-and-a-half year level); and a negative relation of perspective and responsibility to emotional adjustment.

Development of children's moralistic judgements: age, sex, IQ, and certain personal-experiential variables
P. H. Whiteman and K. P. Kosier, 1964

AIM/The purpose of the study was systematically to consider the influence of a number of 'personal-experiential' variables upon the development of children's moral judgements. It was hypothesized 'that the ability to formulate mature judgements about behaviour (i.e. judgements based upon intent rather than consequences): (a) increases with advances in age at each level between the ages of seven and twelve years, (b) increases with level of intelligence at each level of age, (c) is more advanced among girls than among boys of the same age, (d) is more advanced among children who attend Church Sunday Schools than among children who do not, (e) is more advanced among children who are members of boy or girl scout organizations than among children who are non-members, (f) is more advanced among children who attend combined-grades classrooms than among children attending conventionally graded classrooms, (g) is negatively correlated with personality problems as rated by teachers."

SUBJECTS/N = 173 children from 7 to 12 years. Three age groupings were formed: 7-8, 9-10, and 11-12. The children were from a public elementary school in a lower-middle socio-economic area of a city. Level of IQ was based upon the California Test of Mental Maturity, Form S, and each age group included three levels of IQ: 70-90, 100-110 and 120-145.

METHOD/Children's conceptualizations and judgements of behaviour were obtained from stories revised from those of Piaget relating to intentionality. Teachers were asked to complete Griffith's questionnaire for purposes of assessing problem behaviour.

RESULTS/The analysis of variance supported the hypothesis that the development of the ability to make mature judgements regarding behaviour will increase with IQ, within each of the age groups to be studied, as well as with advancing chronological age (the F ratios for both age and IQ were significant at the .01 level).

The data provided support for Piaget's contentions regarding the influence of advances in age on moral judgement, 'but they did not support his observation that objective (immature) approaches are found only in children of less than ten years . . .'.

The ratio for the main effect of sex was not significant, but there was a consistent trend in the hypothesized direction: i.e. that girls would show superior ability in making moral judgements.

The differences between members and non-members of Sunday Schools and Scout groups were not statistically significant.

Children in the combined-grades situation were more mature in their moral judgements than children 'in a conventionally graded programme'. This hypothesis was supported at the .05 level of significance.

The hypothesis of a relation between teachers' ratings of children's personal characteristics and children's maturity of moralistic judgements was not substantiated.

Decentration, age and intelligence in the development of children's moral judgement
R. B. Stuart, 1967

AIM/An attempt was made to assess the influence of age, intelligence and decentration upon the development of moral and causal thought.

SUBJECTS/N = 120. The children studied were drawn from the second, fourth, sixth and eighth grades. Each grade had balanced age and intelligence distribution.

METHOD/Decentration was measured by social and perceptual decentration items as well as by items testing lateral discrimination. Many of these items were adapted from the work of Piaget as were the moral and causal judgement items.

RESULTS/Following factor analysis of the 23 item instrument, discriminating items were considered. Two moral judgement areas (immanent justice and objective responsibility), two decentration areas (social decentration and lateral discrimination) and a physical causality area appeared.

When the components of the decentration area were

investigated it was seen that they had sufficient reliability to warrant experimental use.

When the moral and causal judgement of high and low decentering subjects was contrasted, high decenterers were significantly superior. 'This relationship held, although not always at a significant level, when age and intelligence were controlled.' When the effects of age, intelligence and sex were evaluated, it was seen that age was the most powerful influence upon development in the two judgement areas and decentration; that intelligence was a significant influence in all three areas and that sex was a significant influence only in the area of causal judgement.

DISCUSSION/It was speculated that it may be possible to train children in the ability to decenter and in that way, materially to alter moral judgement behaviour.

The relationship between moral development and the development of time perception and time conceptualization in lower-class negro children
A. Seltzer, 1969

AIM/The author addressed herself to the following inquiries: (1) the development of the child's ability to conceptualize time is closely related to the development of his ability to make mature moral judgements; (2) the child's moral conduct is significantly related to his ability to accurately perceive the passage of time; and (3) there is a significant relationship between moral conduct and moral judgement.

SUBJECTS/N = 144 Negro children. The children were drawn from three schools located in an urban area inhabited almost entirely by lower-class Negro families, and were selected by their teachers from the kindergarten grade two, grade four, and grade six on the basis of their moral conduct.

METHOD/The children were judged to be high or low in moral conduct on the basis of certain uniform criteria which were used by all judges.

The measure of moral judgement consisted of eighteen story inquiries adapted from Piaget's work on moral development.

The conceptual time scale consisted of 18 questions which were chosen to reveal the child's ability to order events in chronological sequence and to use objective measures of time. The child's perception of time was determined by his accuracy in reproducing three 10-, three 20-, and three 30-second intervals which were bounded by a visual and auditory stimulus.

RESULTS/Developmental trends emerged clearly. There was an increase in mature moral judgement from kindergarten to fourth grade. The concept of time improved with each successive grade level. Analysis of variance showed that these trends were significant (p<.01). In each case an apparent plateau was reached at grade four with little apparent improvement at grade six. No significant sex differences were found.

Hypothesis 1 was clearly supported by the data. Moreover, these two variables were significantly correlated with each other at every grade level. As predicted in Hypothesis 2, the child's ability to accurately perceive the passage of time was significantly related to his moral conduct and not to his moral judgement.

(b) *Social Factors*

Boehm and Nass (1962) failed to confirm their hypothesis that middle-class children will be more concerned with underlying motives and working-class children with the amount of physical injury in response to a physically aggressive situation. However, the authors cast doubt on the assigned socio-economic status of the children in the sample. (Details are given later in this Section.) Boehm, in her 1962 study, revealed class differences to the extent that working-class children (at two intelligence levels) showed earlier peer reciprocity and adult independence than upper middle-class children. However, with respect to distinctions between intention and outcome of an action, upper middle-class children develop earlier than those of working class background. (Details are given later in this Section.) Harris (1970) concluded that both White and Negro children of higher social class groups were more mature in moral attitudes than children of lower social class groups (see IIIf below). When subjects were classified into rich, middle-class and poor groups, Ugurel-Semin (1952) found that the poorer children were generous as often as the rich, more often equalitarian and less often selfish (see IIIe below). Bull (1969) found throughout his research with children aged seven to 17 years that for boys, socio-economic class had a close association with moral judgements.

Ugurel-Semin (op.cit.) also demonstrated that the child of the larger family was moderately more often generous than the only child. With respect to peer group conformity, Morris (1958) revealed differences between Grammar School and Secondary Modern pupils: Grammar School pupils indicated less conformity to friends (see II above).

The results of the Boehm (1962) research did not support

314

Piaget's belief that maturity of moral judgement increases as the child becomes independent of adults and achieves peer reciprocity. There was little relation between responses involving right and wrong and responses revealing adult independence. (Details are given later in this Section.) Bandura and McDonald (1963) report the influence of the adult on the child: children's judgements were modifiable through cues given by the adult models (see IIIg below). McKechnie (1971) interprets his findings that the child learns to evaluate bad behaviour before good, in terms of the disciplinary approaches used by parents and teachers (see II above). Similar contentions were expressed by Piaget. From 45 correlations of dominating, possessive and ignoring parental attitudes with maturity of moral judgements, Johnson (1962) reports significant findings for only eight (see II above). MacRae (1954), did not generally find retardation in moral development in children whose parents were authoritarian but he reports associations between parental authority and 'violation of norms regarding lying and stealing'. Piaget's contention that the authoritarianism of the adult retards moral development was therefore not entirely upheld by MacRae and Johnson.

A reflection on the possible differences in social development between American and Swiss children is offered by Boehm (1957). She reports that the American child becomes less parent-dependent and more peer-dependent at an earlier age. As a result, 'the American child's conscience becomes less egocentric and interiorizes earlier than does that of the Swiss child' (see IIIf below). Also worthy of note in this section are Najarian-Svajian (1966) and Jahoda (1958: see IIIf below).

Kohlberg (1958, 1964) reports that children involved in more extensive social participation (middle-class and popular children) tended to be more mature in moral judgement (see IV below).

The development of conscience: a comparison of American children of different mental and socio-economic levels
L. Boehm, 1962

AIM/In this study, the author was interested in investigating at what age different groups of American children learn to distinguish between intention and result of an action, together with testing Piaget's belief 'that the child cannot attain "morality" until he becomes independent of adults and achieves peer reciprocity'.

The author formulated the hypotheses that, in answer to questions concerning intention versus result, (1) academically gifted children might respond with earlier maturity than children

315

of average intelligence; (2) that upper middle-class children might respond with earlier maturity than children of working-class parents; but that, 'in answer to questions regarding independence from adult versus peer reciprocity, (a) gifted children might be less mature than children of average intelligence and (b) upper middle-class children might be less mature than working-class children'.

SUBJECTS/N = 237. Boys and girls of two intelligence levels in the upper middle class and working class, aged six to nine years attending Public, Jewish and Catholic Schools.

METHOD/Of the four stories administered, two were drawn from Piaget, the others being devised by the author and Szeminska. Responses to each story by each child were classified according to Piaget's three levels of morality: (a) 'morality of constraint, (b) an intermediary stage and (c) "morality of co-operation" '.

RESULTS/'1. Academically gifted children mature earlier in their moral judgements concerning distinctions between intention and outcome of an action than children of average intelligence. 2. Upper middle-class children develop earlier in this aspect than working-class children. 3. There is a greater difference between responses of academically gifted children and children of average intelligence of the upper middle class than between gifted children and those of average intelligence in the working class. 4. Working-class children at both intelligence levels show earlier peer reciprocity and adult independence than upper middle-class children.'

DISCUSSION/The results generally confirmed the hypothesis of a difference between gifted children and those of average intelligence with regard to maturity of moral judgement. The author attributes this finding being at variance with other researches (Kohlberg, 1958; Durkin, 1959a, 1959b, 1959c; MacRae, 1950) to her larger sample, differences in range of age groups, differences in range of IQs in the gifted and average categories and in the specific aspect within the area of moral development being investigated.

The author concludes: 'Contrary to Piaget, our data do not show that "maturity of moral judgement" increases as the child becomes independent of adults and achieves peer reciprocity. In the present study there seemed to be no connection between "mature" responses concerning right and wrong and responses indicating adult independence. Rather, working-class children who

316

gave early "c level" responses to the stories concerning adult independence, scored more lower level responses at the same age when distinguishing right from wrong in considering intention and result of actions. Upper middle-class subjects, who were more discerning at an earlier age than working-class children with regard to intention and consequence, scored more lower level responses at the same age regarding issues of adult independence and peer reciprocity.'

Social class differences in conscience development
L. Boehm, and M. L. Nass, 1962

AIM/The investigation was designed to study the influence of social class on children's responses to stories involving moral judgements.

SUBJECTS/N = 160 children aged six to 12 years. Fifty-four of the group were of upper-lower socio-economic class and 48 were of the upper middle class according to parent occupation. IQ was of average level throughout and all the children were well-adjusted and had older siblings (Sears Maccoby and Levin 1957, had found a more strongly developed conscience in only and eldest children). The groups contained an equal number of boys and girls. The sampling was extended to include a group of 58 intellectually gifted children: 27 working class and 31 upper middle class. 'Since the responses of this group failed to show statistical differences from the original population, these data were combined with the average group.'

METHOD/The four stories employed were designed to test the hypotheses that (a) middle-class children will concern themselves more with the underlying motive for a physically aggressive act than with the aggressive act itself, in contrast with working-class children who will still be primarily oriented to the amount of physical injury involved; (b) that working-class children will concern themselves more with material values than with the underlying motives, the middle-class group being more concerned with motivation; (c) that the groups will show no significant differences in their attitude towards lying and (d) that the groups will show no significant difference in a situation involving a choice between peers and authority. Two stories were taken from Piaget and two were constructed by Boehm with the assistance of Szeminska. Additionally, the study hypothesized that girls' responses would indicate earlier maturity of moral evaluations than would boys' and that the child's sense of morality is

317

dependent upon the specific situation and does not represent a common level in all situations. Responses were classified according to Piaget's three stages of morality: (a) 'morality of constraint'; (b) an intermediate stage in which the child internalizes rules without evaluating them or alternates his responses to the situations; (c) 'morality of co-operation'.

RESULTS/The results indicated that age was the only significant variable in three of the four stories. The age of nine years was a critical turning point toward greater maturity. Therefore, with reference to the major hypotheses, two of the four were supported, while two were refuted. The lack of class difference in (c) and (d) supports the predictions, and, in hypothesis (b), although there was a trend in the predicted direction, it failed to be significant, the p value falling between the 10 and 5 per cent levels. With respect to hypothesis (a), no trend was evident. The comparison of the sexes failed to show that girls are more advanced in their conscience development than boys. The hypothesis that the child's response is specific to the situation was tested by computing a Friedman two-way analysis of variance by ranks (Siegel 1956). A χ^2 of 16.92 was obtained, with a corresponding p value of .001.

(c) *Sex differences*

Durkin (1960) addressed her inquiry specifically to investigating sex differences in children's concepts of justice, but statistically significant differences were not revealed. She concluded that, unlike other aspects of socialization, moral training pressures are not exerted differently towards boys and girls. (Details are given later in this Section.) Whiteman and Kosier (1964), in their investigation relating to age, sex, IQ and personal-experiential variables and the development of children's moral judgements, hypothesized that 'girls because of maturational advantages during later childhood and parental and social pressures relating to impulse control, would manifest superior ability to formulate mature judgements when compared with boys of the same age'. The authors report a trend in the hypothesized direction but it was not significantly supported (see IIIa above). Boehm and Nass (1962: see IIIb above); Irwin and Moore (1971: see II above); Jensen and Hughston (1971: see IIIg below); Medinnus (1962: see I above); and Ugurel-Semin (1952: see IIIe below) all report no highly significant differences between responses from boys and girls, although some trends in favour of girls were found. Morris (1958) reported generally no differences between boys' and girls' responses to problem-situations. However, some tendency for girls' values to be slightly more developed than boys', and a greater discrepancy between 'should' and 'would' were noted (see II above). Grinder (1964) found some greater sophistication for girls with respect to resistance to temptation at early ages, but these differences were eliminated by 11 or 12 years. Grinder elaborates: 'behavioural and cognitive characteristics of the mature conscience especially in boys may develop independently of one another' (see IIIe below). Girls showed greater moral maturity than boys in a study reported by Porteus and Johnson (1965); their responses also revealed less consistency with respect to the 'cognitive' and 'affective' stories (see IIIe below). Bull (1969) found girls in advance of boys in all the areas of moral judgement studied (see II above).

Magowan and Lee (1970) consider that differences found by investigators between the sexes 'may be an artifact of the measuring instrument' (see IIIh below). (See also IV below — esp. Kohlberg, 1964b; and Keasey, 1972.)

Sex differences in children's concepts of justice
D. Durkin, 1960

AIM/The study was designed to examine sex differences in children's concepts of justice.

SUBJECTS/N = 190. The middle-class group of 39 girls and 62 boys, together with the lower class group of 51 girls and 38 boys, were from the second, fifth and eighth Grades.

METHOD/Two stories were administered, designed to examine understanding of rights regarding one's person, together with two stories designed to measure understanding of rights regarding one's property. A fifth story was devised for examining the subjects' understanding of rights regarding one's character-reputation. Each of the five stories provided an opportunity for subjects to accept or reject, directly or indirectly, the 'eye for an eye' concept of justice described by Piaget as being related to CA.

RESULTS/No statistically significant sex differences in children's concepts of justice were found in this study.

DISCUSSION/The author considered that the reasons for this lack of difference could lie in the nature of the stories used and could be related to the nature of the subjects' moral training.

Even for stories depicting physical aggression, traditionally masculine behaviour and verbal aggression, usually seen as being feminine behaviour, no significant sex differences in response were found.

The author concluded: 'It is therefore hypothesized that these boy-girl responses were similar because the kind of moral training given to children is not affected by the sex of the child. It is also hypothesized that studies which have described differences in the actual behaviour of boys and girls (Fite, 1940; Jones, 1946; Sears, 1951; Terman, 1946) were noting the end-result, not of differences in their training, but rather of important differences in the pressures exerted on boys and on girls, by parents, teachers, and peers, to adhere to the various precepts and values defined in this training process.'

(d) *Religious influences*

With respect to recognizing the distinction between the motivation and the results of an action Boehm (1962b) confirmed that 'Catholic children, regardless of socio-economic class or intelligence level, scored higher at an earlier age than public school children'. She concludes that this difference can be explained by the encouragement given to Catholic children towards confession and the insight gained into the motivation of actions. Some superiority was shown by Jewish children compared to Catholic children in response to the 'Fight' story in Boehm's 1963 study. Boehm explained this in terms of the greater emphasis on guilt made by exponents of Catholicism. The immature responses of the Jewish children to the 'Scout' story were attributed to the strong traditional belief in authority and the Jewish child therefore chose to follow the advice of a teacher. (Details are given later in this Section.)

While a higher percentage of Catholic children made intentionality judgements to the standard Piaget stories in Armsby's (1971) study, there was no significant difference between the percentage of Catholic and public school children who made intentionality judgements in response to the revised stories (see II above). Armsby offers the explanation that in the standard Piaget stories, the supposedly purposive act was often accidental damage resulting while a child was disobeying his mother. The revised stories, on the other hand, compare clear accidental behaviour with clear intentional behaviour; obedience is therefore not an intervening factor. Armsby hypothesizes that the greater emphasis on obedience and the more authoritarian approach to education in the Catholic schools sensitized the Catholic school children to make judgements in terms of whether a child was obeying his mother or not. Obedience was not so important to the Public school children, so when obedience factors were minimized there were no differences. Armsby concludes that Catholic training does not foster earlier mature moral judgement although it may more successfully train obedience. Armsby also criticizes Boehm's samples in that the Catholic and Public school samples were drawn from two distinctly different areas. MacRae's (1954) sample of Parochial school children showed more moral realism with regard to authority, a more extended belief in immanent justice and selected more severe punishment for breaking of norms and rules. (Kohlberg, 1964, found no differences in the development of moral judgement between Protestants and Catholics — see IV below.)

Whiteman and Kosier (1964) found slight trends in favour of members of Sunday Schools and Scout groups relating to moral judgements, but they were not statistically creditable (see IIIa above). Bull (1969) found 'scattered, unpatterned and inconsistent' associations between moral judgements and church affiliation. The 'lying' situation and the 'value of life' test elicited the strongest associations.

The development of conscience: a comparison of students in Catholic parochial schools and in public schools
L. Boehm, 1962b

AIM/The author compared children attending Catholic parochial schools and children attending public schools in relation to the development of conscience.

SUBJECTS/N = 222. One hundred and ten Catholic children of semi-rural and urban background attending New York and Massachusetts parochial schools and 112 children attending New York public schools were involved. The children from both types of school were divided into groups on the basis of social class and IQ.

METHOD/Procedures, criteria and the stories used in this investigation have been described in Boehm and Nass (1962) and Boehm (1962).

RESULTS/'With regard to recognizing the distinction between motivation and results of an action, it was found that:
1. Catholic children, regardless of socio-economic class or intelligence level, scored higher at an earlier age than public school children.
2. Academically gifted upper middle-class children in both

types of schools scored higher at an earlier age than their counterparts of average intelligence or than working-class children of either level of intelligence.

3. In Public schools academically gifted working-class children scored higher than their counterparts of average intelligence. In Catholic parochial schools this was not so. Differences due to levels of intelligence among the working-class group, although insignificant, favoured the working-class child of average intelligence.

With regard to independence from adults and peer reciprocity, it was found that:

1. In Catholic parochial schools children scored higher and at earlier ages in one of the two stories and scored the same in the other story as children in public schools.

2. In both types of school, working-class children scored higher and at earlier ages than upper middle-class children. Parochial school students scored much higher in one of the two stories than public school students and somewhat lower in the other story.

3. In public schools the academically gifted working-class children scored higher than their counterparts of average intelligence. In Catholic parochial schools, this was so for one story but not for the other.

4. Academically gifted upper middle-class children scored higher than children of average intelligence in both kinds of school.'

DISCUSSION/The author comments: 'We might have expected to find what we did find, namely that the Catholic parochial school students obtained more "morality of co-operation" than public school students at earlier ages to the two stories concerned with motivation and consequence'. This is explained in terms of Catholic schools emphasizing the distinction between accident, misdeed and sin; seven-year-old Catholic children are considered to be at the age of reason and to be ready for confession and communion. Catholicism involves discriminating in relation to confession and gaining insight into the motivation of actions. Parochial school children were not found to be as dependent upon persons in authority as was expected.

*The development of conscience: a comparison of upper middle
class academically gifted children attending Catholic and Jewish
parochial schools*
L. Boehm, 1963

AIM/The purpose of the study was to investigate whether
children at religious schools other than Catholic also learn to
distinguish right from wrong at an earlier age than public school
students because of daily emphasis upon ethical principles.

SUBJECTS/Upper-middle class and academically gifted
subjects were selected from a modern Jewish parochial school.
Fifteen children were involved: two boys and two girls at each age
level, from six to nine years. IQ = 110+. (One child was later
excluded from the study.)

METHOD/Four stories were administered, two devised by
Piaget and two devised in collaboration with Szeminska. The
stories were directed towards the evaluation of an act as to intent
or result and peer reciprocity versus authority dependence.
     Responses to each story were classified according to Piaget's
three levels of morality: 'morality of constraint'; intermediary
stage; and 'morality of co-operation'.
     To make the statistical analysis, this group, owing to its small
size, was compared with other cohorts of gifted, upper-middle-
class children (Boehm 1962), including those from Catholic and
public schools.

RESULTS/The findings were not of statistical significance,
due to the small Jewish sample. Analysis of responses to the two
stories concerned with authority independence and peer relationship indicated a wide divergence. In Boehm and Szeminska's
'Fight' story, the Jewish group was superior to the children in the
Catholic and public schools. For the 'Scout' story, the Jewish
group had the lowest response.
     Resulting from Piaget's stories, which were concerned with
the problem of distinguishing between motivation and the
consequence of an act, the Jewish children scored at a point
between the Catholic and public school children.

DISCUSSION/Religious differences were offered as explanations for the superior response from the Jewish children to
the 'Fight' story for, unlike the Catholic children, they were
concerned solely with the friend, rather than being preoccupied
with possible guilt or self-centredness. Catholicism is more
concerned with guilt and expiation. The immature responses of

the Jewish children to the 'Scout' story were attributed to the strong traditional group belief in authority and the Jewish child therefore chose to follow the advice of a teacher. 'To the Jewish family the teacher is to a large extent omniscient in a tradition of Jewish regard for learning.'

(e) *Consistency across moral attributes*

Piaget speculated about the developmental relation between children's behavioural resolutions of actual moral conflicts and cognitive processes and regarded further research into the question as of 'fundamental importance in human psychology'. Attention has frequently been drawn to the necessity for evidence concerning the relation of judgements upon hypothetical moral situations and actual behaviour in concrete moral situations (Aronfreed, 1961; Bull, 1969; Grinder, 1964; Medinnus, 1966; Pittel and Mendelsohn, 1966; Uğurel-Semin, 1952; Wright, 1971). An extensive early study by Hartshorne and May (1928-30) involved the devising of ingenious tests to measure actual moral conduct in concrete situations together with tests to assess moral conduct. There was considerable doubt expressed at the time of the analysis concerning a general factor in moral development, but Burton (1963) in a re-analysis of the data has reported more generality than was first indicated. Peck and Havighurst (1960), in a longitudinal study involving the population of 'Prairie City', produced evidence for generality rather than specificity in moral behaviour. Basing the study upon a 'motivational definition of character', it was found that inconsistency was characteristic of all subjects but that, nevertheless, there was a consistent pattern of behaviour which was maintained throughout maturation. However, there have generally been few studies investigating an individual's theoretical morality and the way he actually behaves in moral conflict situations. It is obvious that feasibility and reliability are the inhibiting factors. Uğurel-Semin (1952) was interested in Piaget's hypothesis that the child would demonstrate moral judgement in action far earlier than in speech and devised his 'sharing' investigation, designed, among other purposes, to assess the relationship between moral behaviour and moral judgement. Among the children who shared equally and children classified as generous, some consistency between moral conduct and moral judgement was apparent. (Details are given later in this Section.) Grinder (1964) concluded that children's resistance to temptation occurs more as a result of social-learning experiences than from changes in the cognitive structure and that maturation of the cognitive processes does not guarantee alteration of behavioural habits established by social reinforcement. He therefore considers 'that behavioural and cognitive characteristics . . . may develop independently of one another'. (Details are given later in this Section.) Medinnus (1966 details below) reported results indicating little association between behaviour and verbal responses. (See also Stephens, Miller and McLaughlin, 1969 in Chapter 7, 'The Development of Reasoning among Handicapped Children'). Porteus and Johnson (1965), using stories to measure cognitive and affective aspects of moral development, together with sociometric ratings to assess behaviour, found a significant relation between responses to cognitive and affective measures, especially for boys, although these were 'not of any great magnitude'. The relation between the affective measure and nominations for moral behaviour was insignificant. It was concluded that popularity was a major factor in determining moral nominations. The authors drew attention to the need to develop reliable measures of actual behaviour and cited the contribution of Grinder (op. cit). (Details are given later in this section.) Ward (1965) found small positive correlations between moral judgement and moral knowledge. (Details are given later in this Section. See also IV below.)

Moral behaviour and moral judgement of children
R. Uğurel-Semin, 1952,

AIM/The author was interested in Piaget's hypothesis that the child would demonstrate moral judgement in action far earlier than in speech, and he was intent to investigate this proposition by experimentally placing the child in a moral situation less delicate than either lying or stealing. An attempt was made to determine the following in regard to generosity: the types of moral behaviour as related to age; a difference in moral conduct according to sex; the effect of socio-economic status upon moral behaviour; the effect of family size; the relationship between moral behaviour and moral judgement; the types of moral judgement and their evolutionary process; and finally, the similarity between the adaptation of the mind to the physical environment and to the social environment.

SUBJECTS/N = 291. The children, attending schools in Istanbul, were aged between four and 16 years. The subjects could be classified into three socio-economic groups: 'rich, middle-class and poor'.

METHOD/The experiment required a child to divide an unequal number of nuts between himself and another child.

Different pairs of children divided from five to 15 nuts. 'The nuts were placed on the table and subject A was told that he was to share them with subject B. But, before A began to speak, subject B was requested to leave the room and wait outside until called. Subject A was then asked how he was going to share the nuts with B, upon the latter's return. Subject B was then called in and A was made to perform the sharing act and be questioned in front of B.'

RESULTS/Considering moral behaviour (related to generosity), 14 per cent were classified as selfish, 42 per cent as sharing equally and 44 per cent as generous, (giving more). The selfish tendency diminished with age. Between the ages of four and six years, the tendency to be selfish was at its highest (66-67 per cent), diminishing noticeably until it completely disappeared at 12 years. Generosity increased after five to six years and reached 63 per cent at seven to eight years. After this the tendency fluctuated. The author commented on the coincidence of the age of generosity with the decline in egocentrism. The tendency to give an equal share evolved progressively until 11 to 12 years where it reached 68 per cent. It dominated all other tendencies at most ages beyond eight. From the age of 11 to 12 years onward, the tendency toward equality and generosity in sharing, alternate constantly: sometimes generosity was of a high percentage and at other times the tendency to share equally predominated.

No difference in moral behaviour between the sexes could be found.

When 167 of the subjects were classified into three socio-economic groups, rich, middle-class and poor (the younger children, aged four to six years, were not included as all children attending the kindergartens were those whose parents could afford to pay for them) it was found that the socio-economic level of the family affected the behaviour of the children. In general, 'the poorer children were generous as often as the rich, more often equalitarian, and less often selfish' ($\chi^2 = 20.5$, $df = 4$, sig. .01).

The child of the larger family was slightly more often generous than the only child. It was concluded that the moral behaviour of children in the experiment was determined by the age of the child, the socio-economic conditions in which the child was living and the number of children in the family.

Among the children who shared equally and those who were generous some consistency between moral conduct and moral judgement was apparent. However, among those who were classified as selfish, two types of moral judgement were distinguished: approval of the selfish behaviour and disapproval (within which there were a variety of sub-categories – for a detailed description see Uğurel-Semin (1952).

When the moral judgements were classified according to type, without consideration of the action involved, a distinct curve in the evolution of moral judgement was observed. The types of judgement were classified into 32 subgroups within the categories of Egocentrism, Sociocentrism (obedience to moral and religious rules and customs), Awareness of Social Reaction, Superficial reciprocity, Deeper and Enlarged Reciprocity, Altruism and Justice. (The types of moral judgement are fully examined in Uğurel-Semin, 1952.)

Uğurel-Semin concludes that the progress of moral thought is characterized 'by five different tendencies whose common trait is found in the change from centralization to decentralization. Moral thought moves (a) from external consideration of the moral situation at hand toward internalization of moral understanding, (b) from being linked to the present moment toward consideration of life as a whole, (c) from a consideration of a specific connection to a linking up of various connections, (d) from an individual and personal consideration of the moral action toward reciprocity and co-operation, and (e) from unilateral consideration of the moral rule toward its mutual understanding. (The latter two traits have been clearly explained by Piaget.)' Uğurel-Semin continues to expound on the underlying common trend from centralization to decentralization (see Uğurel-Semin 1952). He concludes that 'the internalization of the motives of moral thought and the freeing of the individual from the immediate state of the moral situation are decisive moments in the decentralization of the self. As a result, moral judgement follows from an integration of different viewpoints.'

While comparing the results of his investigation with Piaget's stages of cognitive development, the author differs with the latter 'according to Piaget, the climax of egocentrism coincides in development with that of social constraint and the opinion of society. However, according to the results of the present study, the climax of social pressure shows itself much later (9 years 2 months).' Uğurel-Semin attributes the difference to the use by Piaget of theoretical judgements whereas his study was concerned with practical judgements. Piaget's period of concrete operations was compared with superficial reciprocity and it was considered that abstract idealism revealed the qualities of Piaget's formal operations. The child, reaching complete detachment from the momentary state was able to judge the moral situation from an abstract viewpoint and the moral conscience was constituted.

When considering the relationship between action and moral thought, the author refers to 'a movement of liberation'. In the beginning, egocentric action prevails and judgement is subordinate to its exigency. Secondly the child's moral thoughts are more egotistical than egocentric and he is not free to direct his action by them. He understands the value of the moral rule but does not obey it. In the third phase the child is not yet free to direct his action, because the moral rule understood in a unilateral sense has the upper hand. 'It is here that the climax of social pressures should be placed. In this case, moral thought directs conduct, but only by way of social constraint.' In the fourth phase, the child begins to direct his action himself. 'Owing to an ever increasing exchange of moral and intellectual values, he becomes capable of ridding himself of centralizations on the self, on a particular state of the object and on the moral rule in its unilateral understanding. Thus from this moment, the child is able to envisage in a harmonious whole what emanates from the self, from the physical and from the social. In other words, the child can place himself among other individuals and other points of view. Society no longer exercises deforming constraint upon the individual but stimulates the freedom of his activities. This work of the freeing of moral thought is completed with the internalization of moral appreciation detachment from the momentary state, reciprocity, and a connecting up of view points. Thus moral autonomy is constituted.'

Relations between behavioural and cognitive dimensions of conscience in middle childhood
R. E. Grinder, 1964

AIM/With the recognition that many previous researches were polarized in either behavioural or cognitive systems, the investigator was intent to investigate the relations between behavioural and moral judgement processes. The study aimed therefore, to test the hypotheses that (a) the strength of children's resistance to temptation will increase with age; (b) the influence of the morality of constraint on children's moral judgements will decrease with age; and (c) the strength of children's resistance to temptation will be negatively associated across age groups with the immaturity of their moral judgements. Comparisons were also made by sex.

SUBJECTS/N = 106 boys and girls: 20 boys and 15 girls, average age seven years, five months; 18 boys and 16 girls, average age nine years, six months and 18 boys and 16 girls, average age 11 years seven months.

METHOD/The 'ray-gun' shooting gallery game described in

Grinder (1961) was employed for the assessment of resistance to temptation. Four story-completion items patterned after those developed by Piaget were used to deduce the degree to which both moral realism and immanent justice were present in the subject's thinking. The 'breaking of cups' and 'stealing food for a friend' were used to assess moral realism and two variations of the 'rotten-bridge' story were employed to test belief in immanent justice. Subjects were helped to complete the story items by a multiple-choice approach, the six alternatives ranging from relatively immature to mature outcomes.

RESULTS/Differences in subjects' strength of resistance to temptation were compared by two methods: focusing on 'the resist-yield dichotomy' in relation to incentive; and the number of shots taken, relating to the degree to which the instructions of the game were actually followed.

Hypothesis (a), 'that the strength of children's resistance to temptation will increase with age', was partially confirmed for girls (on the basis of conformity to the rules of the ray-gun game only). Hypothesis (b), 'the influence of the morality of constraint on children's moral judgements will decrease with age', was confirmed for both boys and girls. The expected negative association between strength of resistance to temptation and moral realism was unsupported.

DISCUSSION/The positive association between age and degree of conformity to the rules of the ray-gun game for girls suggested that the antecedents affecting development of self-control are more effective for girls. However, both boys and girls appear to have developed equally strong consciences by 11 or 12. The association between age and changes in cognitive moral judgements corroborates Piaget's theory, together with studies substantiating his conclusions: Boehm and Nass (1962); Durkin (1959a) and Johnson (1962). Homogeneity in the maturity of children's moral judgememts within each of the age groups leads to the prediction that such similarity is more likely to be based on changes in cognitive structure rather than on social-learning, given the complexity and variety of children's socialization experiences. Non-significant sex differences are consistent with Boehm and Nass, (op. cit.) Durkin (1960) and Medinnus (1959).

The failure to support the hypothesis that there is a negative association between strength of resistance to temptation and adherence to the morality of constraint is contrary to the expectations of Piaget. From his investigation in connection with playing marbles Piaget found 'a certain correspondence (not simple but yet quite definable) between children's judgements about rules and their practice of these same rules'. His findings led him to hypothesize that 'the verbal and theoretical judgement of the child corresponds, broadly speaking, with the concrete and practical judgements which the child may have made on the occasion of his own actions during the year preceding the interrogatory'. This is in connection with Piaget's assumption that children progressively develop cognitive schemata out of their concrete experiences. However, Piaget may have underestimated the affective components.

The empirical evidence therefore indicated 'that behavioural and cognitive characteristics of the mature conscience, especially in boys, may develop independently of one another. Children's compliance with social standards in the face of temptation probably occurs more as a function of social-learning experiences than as a result of changes in the cognitive structure; conversely, maturation of the conceptual schemata necessary for mature moral judgement, although dependent upon interaction with the social environment, does not guarantee significant alteration of habits previously established by reinforcement contingencies'.

Children's responses to two measures of conscience development and their relation to sociometric nomination
B. D. Porteus and R. C. Johnson, 1965

AIM/Piaget's cognitive measure and an affective measure were aimed to gain information regarding (a) sex differences; (b) the relation between responses to cognitive and affective measures; and (c) to determine the relation between responses to cognitive and affective measures and behaviour as measured by sociometric ratings.

SUBJECTS/The subjects were 235 students (113 boys and 122 girls) comprising the ninth grade of a public school in Honolulu.

METHOD/In the consequent groupings, intelligence was not balanced between the main variables and was considered to be a possible confounding variable. The combined verbal and numerical raw scores of the Differential Aptitude Test (DAT) were available and used to represent the intelligence level of each subject.

Four stories were used to measure the 'affective zones,' modelled closely after those of Allinsmith (1960) and Aronfreed (1960). Eight stories adapted from Johnson (1962) were employed to measure the cognitive areas. Each of the stories appeared in two parallel forms, one with a female and one with a male central figure.

The sociometric test included ten items, each of which required the nomination of a male and of a female subject e.g. 'He/She is a very trustworthy and honest person'.

RESULTS/Intelligence seemed to be a most important variable for measures of both cognitive and 'affective zones.' Sex differences were also significant with girls showing greater moral maturity on both measures. Although girls were more mature in both types of judgement, they were less consistent than boys in responding to the two types of stories. Even for boys, the relation between responses to cognitive and affective measures was not of any great magnitude although it was significant. The relation between story completions (the affective measure) and nominations for moral behaviour was insignificant; it is likely that popularity was a major factor in determining moral nomination.

The author concludes: 'It would appear that a major need in this particular area of research is to continue the development of reliable measures of actual behaviour, as has been done by Grinder (1961, 1962, 1964) and to pursue still further the relation of story responses to rated behaviour as done herein, but perhaps using raters other than peers.'

An investigation into the attitudes of pupils in a girls' grammar school to the moral aspects of historical events
L. O. Ward, 1965

AIM/'This investigation was concerned to examine the nature of the moral judgements of selected grammar school girls on specific historical events and to ascertain whether they could be classified at levels defined by Piaget.' The influence of chronological and mental age on the levels of judgement was to be explored, together with the relationship between judgements on specific situations and abstract principles.

SUBJECTS/N = 94 Grammar School girls, aged 13 years 11 months to 16 years five months.

METHOD/Two questionnaires of moral judgement were administered together with one of moral knowledge. The subjects of the narratives for the moral judgement questionnaires included such subjects as 'the use of force to further ambition,' 'the various reasons for marriage, political morality and filial obligations.' Three Judges assessed the responses according to Piaget's schema: the Authority judgement to 'show the acceptance of an ethic imposed by parent or teacher;' the Equality judgement stressing the 'individual's right to do what he chooses' and the Equity stage of judgement to 'reveal an ability to assess personal and social obligations in relation to individual rights.'

A test of moral knowledge used a list of abstract principles reflected in the narratives. The girls were required to indicate the extent of their agreement or disagreement according to a Likert-type scale. A score of moral knowledge was obtained 'by interpreting the answers in the light of the Piaget schema.'

The Otis Self-Administering Test of Mental Ability, Higher Examination: Form A was also used. Its highly verbal content and simple logical arguments closely resembled the activity involved in the questionnaires.

RESULTS/Authority judgements were common to all, but especially those with a low mental age. Correspondingly the older and more intelligent tended to pass more Equity judgements. The Equality stage predominated. 'All the correlations between moral judgement, moral knowledge, chronological age and mental age were positive but small.'

Behavioural and cognitive measures of conscience development
G. R. Medinnus, 1966

AIM/The purpose of the study was to explore the relation between a behavioural measure of conscience and a cognitive measure designed to assess the child's attitude toward a temptation situation. It was predicted 'that children who resist temptation behaviourally when no external control is present will express attitudes indicating an internalized understanding of compliance with rules'.

SUBJECTS/Thirty-eight boys and 36 girls comprising three sixth-grade classes of a suburban school were involved. Socio-economic status included upper-lower and lower-middle class.

METHOD/Grinder's (1961) ray-gun game was used as the behavioural measure of resistance to temptation.

'A questionnaire essay was administered to assess the subjects' attitudes toward a temptation situation.' The contents of the questions were related to 'a current newsworthy incident at a nearby military establishment.'

Answers were categorized 'according to whether control of behaviour appeared to rest in sources external to the individual or whether controls were internalized. Examples of the former type of response were as follows: parents have always forbidden cheating; the code forbids cheating; you might get caught and get into trouble. Indications of internalized control were mentions of conscience, honesty, being honourable, fairness, not taking unfair advantage over others'

RESULTS/The chi-square for the relation between the behavioural measure and the essay responses categorized according to externalized vs. internalized was not statistically significant. It was evident that a majority of children at this age level 'gave responses suggesting externalized control.'

DISCUSSION/The findings did not support Piaget's contention that by the age of 12 years, children judge behaviour according to interiorized rules rather than mere conformity to rules.

The results supported those of previous investigators revealing little association between a child's actual behaviour and his verbal responses. The author suggested that motivation was the crucial factor, a strong incentive for falsifying scores was present in the behavioural situation: 'at any age level children's behaviour in a temptation situation certainly is a function of the strength of motivation'. The cognitive measure was assessing the child's moral knowledge removed from pressures. Support was provided for the distinction between moral conduct and moral knowledge.

(f) *Investigations within different cultures*

Dennis (1943) contended that moral development with respect to immanent justice was universal in all societies but that differences in ages at which moral maturity is reached are due to a specifically unidentifiable variety of cultural factors. Liu (1950) in an investigation involving Chinese and non-Chinese children concluded that decreasing moral realism is not due entirely to increase in age. Havighurst and Neugarten (1955) considered that their findings, from the responses given by children from six Indian tribes, supported Piaget's hypothesis that children in primitive societies become more rigid in their moral development as they increase in age, due to greater constraints being placed upon them. However, when investigating differing degrees of acculturation, Havighurst and Neugarten found no significant differences in immanent justice responses and they concluded that environmental factors within each culture should be investigated in depth rather than measuring the degree of influence from modern societies (see I above). Dennis (op. cit.) found a decrease with age in belief in immanent justice in his Hopi Indian subjects, and Jahoda (1958: details are given later in this Section) confirms the prevalence of immanent justice responses among young African children but states that if 'acts of God' are included as immanent justice responses (Piaget is rather ambiguous in this respect) then the decrease among older children is less marked. He considers that neither his African sample nor Havighurst and Neugarten's Indian subjects were entirely representative of a primitive population, and further, that Havighurst and Neugarten's claim to have confirmed Piaget's hypothesis was due to a faulty methodology and their evidence must therefore be discounted. Njarian-Svajian (1966) reports cultural influences affecting the development of moral realism. (Details are given later in this Section.)

Although all studies carried out other than in Geneva can be considered within the category of investigations within different cultures, mention is made of Boehm (1957) as she specifically addressed her inquiry to a comparison between American and Swiss children in 'content of conscience' according to differences in the cultural pattern. (Details are given in this Section.) Harris (1970), in her comparison between White and Negro boys, concluded that social class had a slightly greater and more consistent influence on maturity of moral attitudes than race. (Details are given later in this Section.) Attention should also be drawn to Seltzer's 1969 study (see IIIa above) involving a Negro sample.

Evidence for or against cultural factors stimulating or retarding age trends of development on the Piaget dimensions remains inconclusive. (For Kohlberg's approach to cultural problems see IV below).

The development of independence: a comparative study
L. Boehm, 1957

AIM/While engaged in other research the author became interested to determine differences in the rate of social development and in content of conscience between American and Swiss children according to differences in the cultural pattern.

SUBJECTS/Twenty-nine French-speaking Swiss children attending elementary school in a 'rather run-down neighbourhood' in Geneva, together with 40 American children attending elementary school in 'a well-to-do' suburb of Chicago were involved in the study. The children were aged from six to 15 years. Boehm elaborates: 'One might wonder whether the results of this study were influenced by the difference in socio-economic background between the children living in the US and those in Geneva. However, results obtained, with the same stories, from 10 upper middle class German children living in Berlin were quite similar to those obtained from the Swiss children. This would seem to indicate that the phenomenon we are studying here is due more to the cultural structure of the society in which a child grows than it is to his socio-economic class.'

METHOD/Two stories, 'The Scoutleader's Birthday Party' and 'Fight' were administered. (For full details, see Boehm, 1957.)

RESULTS/For the first story 69.5 per cent of the Swiss children (all at least 10 years three months old) insisted that teachers and parents always give the best advice. They explained that adults know better because they have more experience. In the United States, 7.5 per cent preferred the teacher's advice to that of the gifted child and all three of these were six years of age. Whereas 91 per cent of the Swiss children imagined that the teacher would be angry if his advice was not followed, only 15 per cent of the United States children believed so, these being younger children.

In the second story, only 17.5 per cent of the American children showed 'egocentricity' of conscience as compared to 69 per cent of the Swiss children.

DISCUSSION/The author concluded that in certain areas of social development, the American child matures earlier than the Swiss child. The American child seems to transfer his parent dependence to a peer dependence at an earlier age. 'One result of this earlier transferring appears to be that the American child's conscience becomes less egocentric and interiorized earlier than does that of the Swiss child.'

'Within the age range studied, this study seems to support the following conclusions: (1) American children are emancipated from their own adults at an earlier age than are their Swiss counterparts. (2) They are less subjugated to adults. (3) They are, rather, more dependent on their peers. (4) They enjoy freedom of thought and independence of judgement at an earlier age. (5) They develop earlier a more highly autonomous, though less complex, conscience.'

Immanent justice among West African children
G. Jahoda, 1958

AIM/The study had as its aim the replication of the work of

Havighurst and Neugarten (1955) in a different culture.

SUBJECTS/N = 120. Half the subjects were boys and half girls. It was difficult to ascertain ages with any accuracy and the sample was divided into the age ranges six to 12 and 12 to 18 years. About one fifth of the sample had totally illiterate parents, the remainder being divided between those where only the father was literate and, those where both parents had experienced some schooling. Over a third of the families were polygamous. The sample was not representative of the population at large: it was biased in the direction of the higher educational and occupational strata.

METHOD/The story used for investigating immanent justice was one originated by Piaget with modifications by Havighurst and Neugarten. This was further adapted to make it suitable for the African children. (The story can be found in full in Jahoda, 1958.)

RESULTS AND DISCUSSION/When the material was examined it became apparent that it was essential to acknowledge five categories of response: pure immanence, act of God, inconsistent, (partly immanent and partly naturalistic) magical causation, and naturalistic (including causal guilt and pure accident). (Examples of these different responses can be found in Jahoda, 1958.)

The main age changes were both highly significant: a decrease in pure immanence and the emergence of a naturalistic type of explanation. (Ages six to 12 years – pure immanence responses: 45 per cent; act of God: 33 per cent; inconsistent: 15 per cent; magical causation: seven per cent. Ages 12 to 18 years – pure immanence: eight per cent; act of God: 47 per cent; inconsistent: 17 per cent; magical causation: eight per cent; naturalistic (causal guilt): 10 per cent; naturalistic (pure accident): 10 per cent.)

These findings clearly confirmed the prevalence of 'immanent justice' responses among young African children, not one of whom gave a purely naturalistic answer. However, if 'Acts of God' are considered as immanent justice responses, (Piaget is rather ambiguous in this respect), then immanent justice is present in a much higher proportion of young children and the decrease among older children much less marked.

Further, Jahoda draws attention to Piaget's suggestion that immanent justice should not be expected to 'decline' in 'primitive' societies, due to adolescent initiation rites placing children under severe constraint from adults who 'themselves are subject to the wills of spirits and ancestors.' However, it was suggested that neither the present sample nor Havighurst and Neugarten's was entirely representative of a primitive population.

It was considered that Havighurst and Neugarten's claim to have confirmed Piaget's hypothesis was due to a faulty methodology and that their evidence must be discounted. (Full discussion can be found in Jahoda, 1958.)

The idea of immanent justice among Lebanese children, and adults
P. H. Najarian-Svajian, 1966

The study started with the hypothesis that in Lebanese culture, two related factors would reinforce the continuation of immanent justice responses in adults of limited education. These factors are religious-moral teaching and child-rearing practices. Statements such as 'It serves you right, you deserve it' or 'You see how God punished you' are common, together with Middle Eastern thinking which supports destiny and fate. The main purpose was therefore to investigate the frequency of ideas of immanent justice among Lebanese children and adults in comparison with the data reported by Piaget and others.

SUBJECTS/Group 1 consisted of students aged six to 25 years, in elementary and secondary schools and College.

Group 2 were adults aged 18-45 years. (Some of these were illiterates, while others had completed high school.)

METHOD/Elementary and secondary school subjects were given one or more of Piaget's three stories regarding immanent justice in Arabic to which their responses were requested.

For subjects above 17 years, stories more pertinent to adult activities were devised.

RESULTS/The responses were grouped under four categories: immanent justice, mixed (immanent and naturalistic), destiny and naturalistic.

The incidence of the idea of immanent justice in the subjects below eight years of age was comparable to the results obtained by Piaget. While Piaget's group showed a considerable drop beginning with age nine, the present group showed no such decrease, suggesting that at this age level, cultural influences became important, and that an increase in mental age alone did not diminish moral realism.

Among the subjects in school, the decrease in the idea of immanent justice began in High School and became marked with the subjects aged 15-17 years.

Reduction in the frequency of immanent justice responses was not immediately accompanied by a proportionate rise in naturalistic thinking.

337

On the College level, naturalistic thinking was prominent. The striking differences between the responses of illiterate 18- to 25-year-olds and College students showed that educational and social factors were effective in changing thinking connected with immanent justice.

Development of moral attitudes in White and Negro boys
H. Harris 1970

AIM/In the light of the findings that Negro children of all social classes showed somewhat lower IQ scores than White children of comparable social classes (Anastasi, 1958; Deutsch and Brown, 1964;) and that Negro middle-class children were superior in general conceptual ability to Negro children from depressed urban areas (John 1963), together with findings among White children establishing a positive relationship between moral attitudes and both social class and psychometric intelligence, the following three hypotheses were suggested. (1) White children are more mature in moral attitudes than Negro children of similar social class. (2) Both White and Negro children of higher social class groups are more mature in moral attitudes than children of lower social class groups. (3) There is a positive relationship between maturity of moral attitudes and intellectual functioning.

SUBJECTS/N = 200. One hundred American born White and 100 Negro boys between the ages of 9½ and 11½ years. The complete sample was distributed equally in four SES groups established on the basis of the father's occupation. Therefore there were eight racial socio-economic groups.

METHOD/The study focused on a developmentally intermediate age level in the maturity of moral attitudes. The age range investigated was one which previous research has indicated can be regarded as representing a developmental level occurring approximately between the immature and mature. It was assumed that children of approximately the same age whose social and cultural backgrounds differed in racial membership and socio-economic status would vary in level of response.

The level of IQ was determined by the WISC Vocabulary test.

The structured interview for measuring moral items consisted of 13 items, many of which were identical to those used by Piaget. Based on the inquiry associated with the 13 items, each subject received a score on five moral attitude subtests as follows: consequences versus intentions (CI) Immanent Punishment (IP); Solutions to Transgression: Nonpunitive Solutions (NP); Solutions to Transgression: Physical Punishment (PP) and Meaning of Rules (RU).

RESULTS/Hypothesis I was supported on only two of the five moral attitude subtests. It was concluded that White children are more mature than Negro children only on (IP) and (PP). (IP:F = 6.1, p < .05; PP:F = 3.9, p < .05.)

Hypothesis 2 was supported on all five moral attitude subtests. It was therefore concluded that both White and Negro children of higher social class groups are more mature in moral attitudes than children of lower social class groups (four subtests: p < .01; one subtest: p < .05).

Hypothesis 3 was supported. The multiple correlation coefficient of the five moral attitude subtests to the WISC Vocabulary was .49 (p < .01, using the F test). The conclusion that the more intellectually able children as measured by the WISC Vocabulary are also more mature in moral attitudes was supported. The relationships were further explored by other statistical methods: see Harris (1970) for further details.

DISCUSSION/Social class appeared to have a slightly greater and more consistent influence on maturity of moral attitudes, than race.

The author comments: 'In general, the behaviour of the two racial groups on the two Solutions to Transgression subtests, (NP) and (PP), constituted the most interesting finding of the present research. Both racial groups followed the pattern that might have been expected from both Piaget's formulations and Piaget-derived research on the other three subtests. While the White children followed the predicted pattern on (NP) and (PP) insofar as the higher SES groups were more mature in moral attitudes than the lower SES groups, this trend was not observed among the Negro children on these two subtests.' Differences in techniques of parental discipline were contemplated, together with the issue of the racial background of the interviewer.

(g) *Training techniques in the inducement of moral concepts*

Piaget has shown that age changes in moral judgement occur but he has not indicated exactly what influence various factors have in producing this change. Various training studies have attempted to accelerate or change the orientation of the developmental sequence, thereby aiming to determine the crucial factors involved in maturation.

Bandura and MacDonald (1963) predicted that children's moral orientations can be altered and even reversed by 'the manipulation of response-reinforcement contingencies and by the provision of appropriate social models'. The experimental conditions utilizing adult modelling procedures alone were the most effective in modifying children's judgements as opposed to a combination of modelling/reinforcement and conditioning alone. (Details are given later in this Section.) In a replication of Bandura and MacDonald could be used to affirm or deny Piaget's extent of the modelling effects depended on a number of other variables: 'subjects' pre-test scores, the particular measure used . . . , the time between the conditioning and post-test, the type of item and the direction of conditioning (up or down)'. Cowan et al. concluded that neither their study nor that of Bandwa and MacDonald could be used to affirm or deny Piaget's sequential stages of moral development. (Details are given later in this Section.) Dworkin (1968), in a comparison of training techniques involving imitation, imitation/reinforcement and cognitive information, found that cognitive information was the most successful in promoting an intentional moral orientation. Further, although imitation and reinforcement were successful for younger children, the effectiveness was lost as the child gains understanding of the concept being taught. (Details are given later in this Section.) Crowley (1968) gave evidence to the effect that training which employed stories with moral content proved to be more effective than training using non-moral stories, but all the training situations used were effective in the acquisition of mature moral judgement. (Details are given later in this Section.) However, attention is drawn by the author to Turiel's explanation (1966: see IV below) for the success: that it is dealing with a specific response; and further, that changes resulting from training must be interpreted as an isolated change rather than in a mental structure or stage. The failure of the discussion method to produce better results than mere labelling is explained in Piaget's terms: that assimilation of information can only take place if the relevant cognitive schemata are available.

However, Jensen and Larm (1970), in a study with kindergarten children, designed to train the concept of intentionality, asserted that 'a brief training programme can immediately produce more mature moral judgements'. They report that a discussion-type training was superior when an understanding of the underlying principle is required, and, due to the necessity for trained subjects to state verbal explanations, it seemed that the concepts were understood. (Details are given later in this Section.) Jensen and Hughston (1971), working with four- and five-year-old children, who patterned their inquiry after the programmes used by Crowley, and Jensen and Larm and related the training to independence of sanctions, report training to be more effective for the older children. It was considered that older children are closer to moving towards higher levels of thought and are therefore more able to benefit from training. It was further acknowledged that training produced changes in moral reasoning only about the moral issues introduced. (Details are given later in this Section.) In a study by Le Furgy and Woloshin (1969) it was found that adolescents of both sexes and varying moral orientation will respond to immediate, face-to-face peer pressures with dramatic shifts away from their initial orientations. The authors emphasize that this does not imply long-term changes. (Details are given later in this Section: see also IV below.)[2]

The influence of social reinforcement and the behaviour of models in shaping children's moral judgements
A. Bandura, and F. J. Macdonald, 1963

AIM/The purpose of the present investigation was to demonstrate that moral judgement responses are less age-specific than implied by Piaget and that children's moral orientations can be altered and even reversed by 'the manipulation of response-reinforcement contingencies and by the provision of appropriate social models'. It was predicted that the combined use of models and social reinforcement would have the most powerful effect on altering the children's behaviour and that social reinforcement alone would be the least effective of the three treatments administered.

SUBJECTS/A total of 78 boys and 87 girls ranging in age from five to 11 years, drawn from schools serving predominantly middle class areas were involved.

METHOD/Children who revealed predominantly objective and subjective moral orientations according to responses to stories which contrasted intentionality with serious consequences (identical to or patterned after those devised by Piaget) were assigned at random to one of three experimental conditions. In the first condition, the children observed adult models who gave moral judgements counter to the group's orientation and the children were positively reinforced for adopting the same judgements. The second group observed the models but the children received no reinforcement for matching the models' behaviour. The third group had no contact with models but each child was reinforced whenever he expressed moral judgements that 'ran counter to his dominant evaluative consequences'.
Following the treatment procedure, further stories were

presented to each child to assess the stability of changes in judgements when models and social reinforcement were absent. The experiment was concluded with a brief interview designed to assess the child's awareness of the behaviour exhibited by the model and the social reinforcements.

RESULTS/Evidence was provided for subjective morality increasing with age, but there was a failure to substantiate Piaget's theory of sequential stages of moral development. Children at all levels gave credence to the theory of the concurrent existence of stages of objective and subjective responsibility. Durkin (1961) gave further support to the condition of specificity. Limitations to Piaget's stage theory are suggested from the finding that children's judgements are modifiable through cues given by adult models. The experimental conditions utilizing modelling procedures proved to be considerably more effective than conditioning alone, which did not produce statistically significant increases in objective judgemental responses. Only nine per cent of the children who were exposed to the objective models failed to produce a single objective response; in contrast, 38 per cent of the subjects in the conditioning group did not give a single objective response despite obtaining twice as many trials.

The results failed to confirm the hypothesis that a combination of reinforcement and modelling procedures constitutes a more powerful learning condition than modelling alone.

Effect of training upon objectivity of moral judgement in grade school children
P. M. Crowley 1968

AIM/The author predicted that children trained by techniques which helped them to focus on intentionality, while minimizing the influence of prominent, but irrelevant cues, would make more mature moral judgements than children who received no training.

With the structure of training material held constant it was anticipated that training which employed material specifically moral in content would be more effective than training which employed material of non-moral content. (This hypothesis was based on the literature concerning transfer and generalization e.g. Deese, 1958.)

It was also hypothesized that training which encouraged 'discovery and verbalization of a principle would be more effective than training which merely provided a verbal discrimination response.' (See Beilin, 1965 and Gagné and Smith, 1962.)

SUBJECTS/First-grade Parochial school boys and girls of middle-class socio-economic status, as measured by father's occupation and cost of housing in the area.

METHOD/The experimental design comprised three phases: (a) a pretraining session in which subjects were selected who consistently made immature moral judgements, these subjects were distributed among four experimental groups and one control group; (b) a series of three small group training sessions, in which the four experimental groups received training appropriate to their respective treatment conditions; (c) a post-training session, in which all the subjects were individually retested on a new set of moral judgement stories similar in style to the pre-training stories.

The five groups were equated for age, IQ and ratio of boys to girls.

The children were trained by means of pairs of stories in which the size of the damage was kept constant so that attention was directed solely to intentionality. The training groups were based on a two-fold combination of story content (moral and non-moral) and method of administration (merely labelling the correct answer or providing discussion as well as labelling.) The training period averaged from two-and-a-quarter to three hours. Following a lapse of 18 to 19 days, the subjects from the five groups were individually tested on 12 items.

RESULTS/All four training situations provided support for the proposition that training aids the acquisition of mature moral judgement. A two-way analysis of variance indicated that the moral content versus the non-moral was highly significant ($F = 118.81$; $p < .01$) but that the method of presentation (i.e. labelling versus labelling accompanied by discussion) was not significant. Therefore, training which employed stories with moral content proved to be far more effective than training which used non-moral stories, but the experiment did not indicate that 'verbalization of a principle was more effective as a means of training than the provision of a verbal discrimination response.'

DISCUSSION/The effectiveness of a brief training phase could be taken as evidence that Piaget's theory of slowly maturing cognitive processes is unwarranted, since moral judgement was so quickly trained. Turiel's (1966) explanation for the success of training was that it has effect because it is dealing with a relatively specific response. Any change resulting from training must be interpreted as a change in an isolated social response rather than in a mental structure or stage. The author notes that refinement of a measuring instrument consequently leads to more restricted theoretical implications.

Piaget's theory readily accommodates an explanation for the. failure of the discussion method to produce better results than mere labelling. He stressed that cognitive input must be congruent with the available cognitive schemata if assimilation of information is to occur. This has been shown in studies such as Gagné and Smith (1962).

The author concludes: 'The subjects' uniformly excellent performance on the training task indicates that objectivity does not betoken inability to group intention, but rather failure to focus on intention when a competing cue (size of damage) is introduced. Centration thus appears to be a major factor in objective moral judgements.'

The effects of imitation, reinforcement and cognitive information on the moral judgements of children
E. S. Dworkin, 1968

AIM/The investigation was undertaken to test the effects of three different training procedures on the moral judgements of young children. The training procedures were imitation, imitation plus reinforcement and cognitive information.

SUBJECTS/Eighty girls between the ages of six years, four months and nine years, 11 months.

METHOD/The subjects were divided equally into two groups, one decidedly 'objective' in their initial moral orientation, the other 'intermediate'. The subjects were individually presented with pairs of stories, each of which described a well-intentioned or accidental act which resulted in considerable material damage, compared to a selfishly motivated act resulting in minor damage. The subjects were asked to specify the naughtier of the two and the reason for their choice.

There were three phases to the study: a pre-test, an experimental phase and a post-test. In the experimental phase the children were exposed to an adult model in one of the following conditions (i) pure imitation, the subject and the model receiving alternate stories and the model always specifying the intentional child as naughtier; (ii) imitation plus reinforcement, as in the previous condition but the model and subject receiving verbal approval from the experimenter and (iii) cognitive information, when the model justified her answer by appealing to the notion of intentionality. The post-test was held one month after the experiment with a new set of stories administered in the absence of the model.

RESULTS/'(1) There was a highly significant shift towards greater intentionality from the pre- to the experimental phase. This shift was maintained during post-testing, i.e. there was no regression to pre-test levels.

(2) There were significant differences in effectiveness between the three treatment procedures. The experimental treatment utilizing cognitive information was more effective in producing an intentional orientation than were the other procedures.

(3) Cognitive information resulted in a significantly greater understanding of the concept of intention.'

DISCUSSION/It was concluded that the results failed clearly to substantiate either a Piagetian or social learning theory explanation of the acquisition of moral judgemental responses in children.

The results clearly showed that cognitive information was more effective than both imitation and imitation plus reinforcement in promoting an intentional moral orientation.

It was further suggested, that the latter two techniques, while effective for the younger and 'cognitively naive' child, lose their effectiveness as the child gains a partial understanding of the concept being taught. When children begin to gain some cognitive grasp of what they are learning, 'the communication of the relevant cognitive dimensions is necessary to promote acquisition.'

It was concluded that training must concentrate on cognitive mediating processes.[3]

Social learning and Piaget's cognitive theory of moral development
P. A. Cowan, J. Langer, J. Heavenrich and M. Nathanson, 1969

'The study provides a replication, with extended analyses of a previous study of moral judgement by Bandura and MacDonald. In a pre-test using Piaget-type pairs of moral judgement stories, 77 five-to 12-year-olds indicated which of two children in the stories was naughtier (names) and then justified their judgements (explanations). Thirty-two of these subjects, half with a majority of high level judgements and half with a majority of low, were exposed to an adult model responding at the opposite level. A post-test with six repeated items, six new items and six somewhat unusual items was given either immediately or two weeks after the modelling ("conditioning") session. Bandura and MacDonald's results were replicated with additional support, but it was found that the extent of the modelling effects depended upon a number of variables either singly or in inter-action: subjects' pre-test scores, the particular measure (names versus explanations), time between conditioning and post-test, type of item and direction of conditioning (up or down). A theoretical analysis showed that neither the present study nor that of Bandura and MacDonald could be used directly to affirm or deny Piaget's hypotheses. Most of the present results serve as a basis for more differentiated statements concerning the models' effects, but some of the findings raise questions which cannot yet be answered within the social learning framework.'

Immediate and long-term effects of experimentally induced social influence in the modification of adolescents' moral judgements
W. G. Le Furgy and G. W. Woloshin, 1969

'The experiment sought to specify the relationships of peer influence to immediate and long-term modifications of adolescents' styles of moral judgement. Twenty-four morally realistic and 29 morally relativistic 13-year-old children were exposed to classical social influence procedures. Children of both sexes and moral orientations evidenced significant yielding to peer influence in their responses to a series of moral dilemmas that were designed to tap various aspects of Piaget's (1932) autonomous and heteronomous stages of moral development. Morally relativistic subjects, while evidencing short-term responsiveness to social influence, showed a significant diminution of these effects over the 100 days of the experiment. Long-term changes in judgemental style were found to be a direct, decreasing, monotonic function of initial yielding to social influence. Results were discussed in terms of the differential long-term effectiveness of social influence in promoting progressive versus retrogressive changes in moral development.'

The effects of two training procedures on intentionality in moral judgements among children
L. C. Jensen and C. Larm, 1970

AIM/'This experiment was designed to demonstrate that a short training programme can produce understanding and/or verbalization of the concept of intentionality among children who had not previously acquired the concept.' It was hypothesized that 'a discussion-type training programme would be more effective.'

SUBJECTS/Thirty-five kindergarten children were randomly assigned into either a discussion, reinforcement (verbal discrimination) or control group.

METHOD/'The verbal discrimination group received nine pairs of Crowley's intentionality stories on each of five consecutive days. After hearing the stories twice, the subjects were asked which child was naughtier and reinforced with a poker chip if they made a more mature response. In the discussion group, the experimenter elicited a discussion about intentionality after presenting five pairs of stories on each of five consecutive days. The control group received stories without a moral emphasis.' During the post-test (10 days later): '12 pairs of stories were presented and each subject selected the character who was "naughtier" and received a (+) if intentionality rather than consequences served as the basis for the choice. Each child was also required to give a verbal explanation for his choice.'

RESULTS/'Planned comparisons between the combined experimental groups and the control group showed that the training groups made choices and verbal explanations requiring an understanding of intentionality (t = 6.31, 4.27, p < .001). The second prediction stated that the discussion group would be superior to the verbal discrimination group. The discussion group made more correct choices (t = 1.56, p < .1) and also gave more mature explanations for their choices (t = 1.89, p < .05).'

DISCUSSION/'The results are interpreted as demonstrating that a brief training programme can immediately produce more mature moral judgements. The superiority of the trained subjects in stating verbal explanations for their choices indicates that they understood the concept and are not simply making an isolated social response. It also appears that a discussion-type training procedure is superior to a reinforced discrimination procedure when a statement of the underlying principle is required.'

The effects of training children to make moral judgements that are independent of sanctions
L. Jensen, and K. Hughston, 1971

AIM/Within the specific dimension of independence of sanctions there has been little research; consequently this experiment was designed to determine if pre-school children could be trained 'to disregard the sanction following an act when they evaluated the act on a good/bad dimension'.

SUBJECTS/N = 72. The subjects were randomly selected

from an initial population of 90 to form three groups of six boys and six girls at age four and age five years. The socio-economic class was described as middle-class.

METHOD/Two types of training were employed, patterned after the programmes used by Crowley (1958) and Jensen and Larm (1970). (These researchers predicted that training that encouraged discovery and verbalization of a principle would be more effective than training that focused primarily on choosing the more correct of two responses.)

Stories depicted a child's act followed by a sanction. The two types of stories included a good act followed by punishment and a bad act followed by punishment.

The experimental design had three phases: (a) a pre-testing session in which the 10 pre-test stories were told to the subjects and they were then asked whether the actions of the children in the story were good or bad; (b) a 10- to 15-minute training session in which 10 stories were presented each day for eight days; and (c) the post-testing session.

In the training sessions the subjects were randomly assigned to three groups: the discussion group, the verbal discrimination group and the control group. The verbal discrimination group received poker chips and eventually prizes for giving the correct 'good' or 'bad' response. However, in the discussion group only verbal responses reinforced correct 'good' or 'bad' judgements. After the response was made, a group discussion followed focusing on why the answer was good or bad; additionally, why the child in the story was punished. It was pointed out that not everything that is punished is bad. The subjects in the control group participated in question and answer activities not having anything to do with moral training.

Between three and eight days after the administration of the last training session, all subjects were individually post-tested using different stories and pictures.

RESULTS AND DISCUSSION/Older children more frequently said a good act was good even when it was followed by punishment and this supports the Piagetian belief that judgements made independent of sanctions are typical of more mature children. Training was more effective for the older children. This could be explained by acknowledging that older children are closer to the time when they would move towards a higher level of thought or alternatively, that older children are more intelligent and socialized, thus being able to benefit more from any kind of training programme. Failure to find differences between the sexes is compatible with other researches in the area of moral judgement. The authors conclude, 'The superiority of the two training groups relative to the controls presents a difficult interpretation problem from the Piagetian theory, which maintains that slow natural changes of the thought processes underlie the developmental changes observed in responding to the moral dilemma such as these used in this experiment. Obviously, since no attempt was made in the two weeks of training to influence unrelated and underlying thought processes and because important maturation changes are unlikely to occur within two weeks, it is concluded that the training produced changes in the children's moral reasoning about these moral issues.'

The authors draw attention to Turiel (1966), when discussing the Bandura and McDonald study, who explained that the changes found following the brief training programme represent only surface changes and the underlying thought processes are unaffected.

It was concluded by the authors that the training programme on independence of sanctions changed the subjects' reasoning about these and perhaps even other related kinds of moral questions.

(h) *Methodological issues*

Pittel and Mendelsohn (1966), in a review and critique relating to the measurement of moral values, enumerate conceptual and methodological weaknesses. The authors consider that a number of instruments assess knowledge of 'legal, moral or ethical standards rather than the individual's attitude toward these standards'. With this emphasis on information it can be speculated that this may account for the correlations with measures of intelligence and the increase of scores with age. The scoring of some measures is based on 'normative or other evaluative standards of "correctness" determined by societally defined criteria'. The tendency is therefore to assign high scores to those responses in agreement with the norms established by the investigators. Pittel and Mendelsohn further perpend that 'subjects are asked to evaluate abstract acts independent of the setting in which such acts occur and in which contextual factors may serve to mitigate or justify their wrongness'. Subjects are often asked to respond to situations in the test context which are unlikely to be met in 'real life'. The specificity of the investigations is also queried by the authors: 'The content typically sampled is based on categories of conventional morality or on the author's theoretical preoccupation. Many dimensions of behaviour which are potentially morally salient are thereby excluded.' The standardization, validity and reliability of the majority of the instruments can also be questioned. The authors in conclusion state that the problems seem to be the result of an 'insufficient effort to conceptualize the nature of moral values and their relation to behaviour. Perhaps the greatest single shortcoming underlying each of the specific criticisms discussed is the failure to view evaluative attitudes as subjective phenomena whose measurement is best achieved independent of a concern with the relationship of these attitudes to conventional and normative standards of moral valuation. It is important to assess at an individual level the content, strength and patterning of subjective attitudes of evaluation per se. Whether these attitudes would be approved or disapproved by society is a subsequent question which need not be considered in the construction of measures of evaluative attitudes.'

Purcell (1958), in a critique related to projective tests in general, also considers that defects in the experimental conceptualization of the problem can be causal to the inadequacies of the results.

Magowan and Lee (1970) in an investigation involving three story variables, conclude that 'the projective method is liable to serious imperfections and more stringent controls are urged for its future use' (details appear below).

Some sources of error in the use of the projective method for the measurement of moral judgement
S. A. Magowan, and T. Lee, 1970

AIM/The study was designed to investigate the effects of varying approaches to the measurement of moral judgement. Comparisons were made relating to 'open-ended v. forced-choice instruments; unfamiliar v. familiar type stories; the sex of the identification figure and the degree of projective facility'. The effects upon the dependent variables of moral judgement by age and sex were also analysed.

SUBJECTS/Initially, (N = 98) the subjects included all the children aged 9-12 years from three rural primary schools. Fifty-six children were divided into two age groups, nine to 10 years and 11-12 years, subdivided by sex to form four groups of 14, precision-matched by projective facility.

METHOD/The projective facility was measured by a specially devised test administered in pictorial form to minimize transfer to the experimental session. Three meaningful and three abstract outline drawings were used and subjects were asked to write about the pictures for 20 minutes. The total number of 'distinguishable statements' were scored and there was 100 per cent reliability between judges.

A total of 12 stories was administered to each child, including the variables: familiar/unfamiliar and open-ended/ multiple choice.

Of the familiar stories, two had a strongly masculine central theme, two strongly feminine and two neutral (the central figure in the 'neutral' stories was given a name of the subject's own sex).

A number of alternative endings were composed for the multiple-choice stories and three judges rated them as immanent justice, moral anxiety, restitution or 'pleasant but unconnected' type endings. A similar approach was employed for the 'open-ended' responses and there was high inter-judge agreement for both story types.

The number of immanent justice responses was used as an inverse measure of moral maturity.

RESULTS/In the first analysis of story familiarity, ($F = 7.7$; d.f. $= 1,91$; $p < 0.01$) and age ($F = 8.4$; d.f. $= 1,91$; $p < 0.01$) were significant. Fewer immanent justice type endings were given to the familiar stories than to the unfamiliar ones and older children gave fewer immature endings to either story type. Sex was not significant.

Relating to familiar stories and open-ended v forced choice, together with sex and age, the significant factors were type of ending ($F = 42.7$; d.f. $= 1,91$; $P < 0.001$) and age ($F = 5.0$; d.f. $= 1,91$; $P < 0.05$) 'These were in the direction of more immanent justice type responses to the open-ended stories and again older children gave fewer such responses to the stories with either type of ending.' Sex was not significant. The authors comment that the children tended to accept the 'rational' alternatives in the forced-choice measure and therefore gave fewer immanent justice responses than in the open-ended test.

More immanent justice responses were provided where the central figure of the story was male and this was found for both boys ($X^2 = 7.76$; d.f. $= 1$; $P < 0.01$) and girls ($X^2 = 8.72$; d.f. $= 1$; $P < 0.01$).

When the moral maturity of boys and girls was compared on the basis of the 'same sex as subject' stories, the shortcomings of this approach were revealed, for their level of maturity emerged as different from the earlier comparison based on a range of identification figures ($X^2 = 23.91$; d.f. $= 1$; $P < 0.001$), the difference being in the direction of greater maturity for girls.

The neutral stories were no more adequate as a basis for sex comparison than were the same sex stories.

The authors conclude '... in the absence of more infor-

351

mation it would be preferable to use settings with both male and female figures to yield an equally weighted composite score. Methodologically, perhaps the most practical recommendation arising from the study is that forced-choice instruments should be used whenever possible. They offer the advantage of control over differences in projective facility, in acquiescence set, in comprehension and in response fluency. The non-methodological findings are limited by the somewhat narrow criterion of moral maturity that was adopted, but it is noteworthy that they confirm previous findings of a marked advance of moral maturity with age at this stage. They also imply that the differences previously found by some authors between the sexes may be an artifact of the measuring instrument. These differences have invariably been in the direction of greater maturity for girls, and this is precisely the effect that is obtained by using "same sex as respondent" control figure.'

IV *Lawrence Kohlberg's Extension of Piaget's Schema*

Kohlberg, using an elaborate and detailed set of hypothetical moral dilemmas has made even more refined distinctions within an extended sequence of moral developmental stages. For 15 years, Kohlberg and his colleagues have studied the same group of 75 boys, following their development at three-year intervals from early adolescence (10-16 years), through early manhood (22-28 years). (cf. Kohlberg, 1958, 1963, 1968, 1971b, Kohlberg and Kramer, 1969; Turiel, 1966.) Together with a variety of other studies carried out by Kohlberg and his colleagues (many of which are listed later in this section), Kohlberg has investigated developmental morality in other cultures: namely, Great Britain, Canada, Taiwan, Mexico and Turkey.

Inspired by Piaget's pioneering efforts, Kohlberg over the years has elaborated his 'typology of definite and universal levels' on the basis of subjects' reasoning concerning the hypothetical moral dilemmas in which obedience to laws, rules or authority conflict with the needs and welfare of other people. Intent to acquire moral evaluations in addition to moral judgements, Kohlberg probed the thinking underlying the choices of action with a series of questions. Kohlberg's 'typology' contains three distinct levels of moral thinking and each of the levels distinguishes two related stages. He termed the scheme a 'typology' following the indication that about 50 per cent of most people's thinking is at a single stage, regardless of the moral dilemma involved. 'Stages' imply an 'invariant developmental sequence'.

At the 'Pre-conventional level', the child is responsive to

'cultural rules and labels of good and bad, right or wrong', but responds to them in terms of the consequences of the action; i.e. punishment, reward or exchange of favours, or in terms of the physical power of those defining the rules and labels. Stage-1 is termed by Kohlberg as the 'punishment and obedience' orientation and Stage-2, as 'the instrumental relativist orientation': 'right action consists of that which instrumentally satisfies one's own needs and occasionally the needs of others.' The second level, 'The Conventional level', is characterized by not only conforming to personal expectations and social order but of 'actively maintaining, supporting and justifying the order and of identifying with the persons or the group involved in it'. At this level, there are the stages of (3), 'the interpersonal concordance of "good boy — nice girl" orientation', involving such intention judgements as 'he means well' and earning approval by being 'nice'; together with Stage-4, 'the "law and order" orientation', right behaviour consisting of doing one's duty, showing respect for authority, and maintaining the given social order for its own sake.' At the level of 'Post conventional, autonomous or principled . . .', there is a definite 'effort to define moral values and principles which have validity and application apart from the authority of the groups or persons holding these principles and apart from the individual's own identification with these groups.' Stage-5 characteristically has 'utilitarian over-tones' and is termed 'the social-contract legalistic orientation'. Stage-6: 'the universal ethical principle orientation' defines right as 'the decision of conscience in accord with self-chosen ethical principles appealing to logical comprehensiveness, universality and consistency. These principles are abstract and ethical . . .; they are not concrete moral rules like the Ten Commandments. At heart, these are universal principles of justice, of the reciprocity and equality of human rights and of respect for the dignity of human beings as individual persons.' Kohlberg lists 26 aspects of moral judgement (Kohlberg 1971b), covering the categories of 'modes of judgement of obligation and value'; 'elements of obligation and value' and 'the issues or institutions'. Each aspect is allocated six levels corresponding to the six stages of development.

Kohlberg emphasizes that the concept of stages has greater implications than mere age trends. It implies an invariant sequence with the possibility for a child to move at varying speeds, becoming fixated at any level of development. If, however, the child moves upward, he moves in accordance with the defined steps. Kohlberg cites his longitudinal study (1963, 1969) as providing evidence for this. 'Tommy is Stage-1 at age 10, Stage-2 at age 13 and Stage-3 at age 16. Jim is Stage-4 at age 16, Stage-5 at age 20 and Stage-6 at age 24.' Additionally, stages define 'structured wholes, total ways of thinking, not attitudes toward particular situations'. Further, a stage 'illustrates the distinction between moral form and moral content'. Correlational analyses 'indicate a general factor of moral level which cross-cuts aspect'. By way of illustration: 'An individual at Stage-6 on a "cognitive" aspect (universalized value of life) is also likely to be Stage-6 on a "motive" aspect (motive for difficult moral action in terms of internal self-condemnations).' However, it should be noted that any individual is usually not entirely at one stage. Finally, a stage concept 'implies universality of sequence under varying cultural conditions. It implies that moral development is not merely a matter of learning the verbal values or rules of the child's culture, but reflects something more universal in development, something which would occur in any culture.' Kohlberg's cultural investigations suggest that the same basic ways of moral valuing are found in every culture investigated and development follows the same sequence. Religious values, although elaborating particular aspects of moral attitudes are not solely responsible for the development of basic moral values.

Kohlberg (1971b), emphasizing the importance of the cognitive component in moral development, cites Kohlberg and De Vries 1969, Selman 1971, and Kuhn, Langer and Kohlberg 1971, as indicating that a high level of cognitive development is necessary for the upper stages of moral development, but, as would be expected, higher levels of cognitive ability do not automatically imply mature moral reasoning. Strong affective components of moral judgement do not reduce the cognitive component, though there may be a different functioning of the 'cognitive component than is implied in more neutral areas', Generally, 'the quality (as opposed to the quantity) of affects involved in moral judgement is determined by its cognitive-structural development and is part and parcel of the general development of the child's conceptions of moral order'.

Kohlberg supports Piaget's stress on the importance of peer-group participation as a source of moral role-taking but suggests that role-taking stimulates moral development rather than producing a particular value system. He refers to Holstein (1971) for indications that opportunities for role-taking within the family work together with and have an effect on peer relationships. Kohlberg elaborates by stating that the central mechanisms of role-taking are justice structures of reciprocity and equality and contexts which are better organized in terms of justice, therefore provide greater opportunities for role-taking. Experience of conflict results from opportunites for role-taking and Kohlberg draws attention to Turiel's (1969) postulation that 'cognitive conflict is the central "motor" for development'. Pertinent to this present discussion is perhaps Kohlberg's insistence that the levels and stages of development may be considered 'separate moral philosophies, distinct views of the social-moral world'. He elaborates: 'We can speak of the child as having his own morality or series of moralities. Adults seldom listen to children's moralizing. If a child throws back a few adult clichés and behaves himself, most parents — and many anthropologists and psychologists as well — think that the child has adopted or internalized the appropriate parental standards. Actually, as soon as we talk with children about morality, we find that they have many ways of making judgements which are not internalized from the outside and which do not come in any direct and obvious way from parents, teachers or even peers.'

In summary, Kohlberg (1971b) writes: 'We have presented evidence of a culturally universal, invariant moral sequence, as well as evidence that this sequence represents a cumulative hierarchy of cognitive complexity perceived as successively more adequate by non-philosopher subjects. We then outlined the logical structure of each stage, showing the way in which each higher stage (a) had new logical features, (b) incorporated the logical features of lower stages and (c) addressed problems unrecognized by, or unresolved by, lower stages. We have attempted to show that a justice structure organizing patterns of role-taking in moral-conflict situations is the common core at every stage, culminating in the stage-6 capacity to consistently derive moral decisions from the generalized principle of justice, that is, to use it as a consistent guide to situational role-taking independent of the arbitrary specification of the particular cultural order of the moral judge. These ideas outline our psychological theory of moral judgement, a theory which assumes certain philosophical postulates for the sake of psychological explanation.' Kohlberg further claims that moral psychology and moral philosophy should work together.

Concerning the relation between moral judgement and moral action, Kohlberg feels that maturity of moral thought should predict maturity of moral action. Kohlberg (1965, 1967, 1969a) discusses some attempts to investigate this relationship and concludes that the correspondence of judgement and action is not one of conformity of behaviour to cultural rules but of responsible decision-making in conflict situations, leading to self-accepted principles of judgement. Later Kohlberg (1971b) reflects on the psychological assumption that action is determined by emotional and social forces, that the relation of belief to action is independent of the cognitive adequacy of the belief. He believes that theorizing about thought and action must be approached in a new way: that the relation of social cognitive structures to social action is similar to physical cognitive structures and physical

355

action. Further, as morality involves basic sacrifice 'We are faced with a conception of the rational and of cognitive structure which has no parallel in the realm of scientific and logical thought'.

Kohlberg therefore elaborates on Piaget's explanation of heteronomy and autonomy as an account of moral development and sees it as more extended in developmental time and more cognitively complex than internalization of external values. Kohlberg found elements of Piaget's heteronomy in his stages 1-4, and elements of Piaget's autonomy in stages 2-6. He puts greater emphasis on the cognitive-developmental approach to stages than Piaget and considers that cognitive factors predominate whereas Piaget stressed the social determinants. Although both Piaget (see IIIe above) and Kohlberg are aware of the problem of the relation between moral judgement and moral behaviour together with the affective component, it is evident that a great deal more research is needed in these respects. However, Kohlberg is relating his work in the area of morality to curriculum development.

Peters (1971) argues: 'His (Kohlberg) findings are of unquestionable importance, but there is a grave danger that they may become exalted into a general theory of moral development. Any such general theory presupposes a general ethical theory, and Kohlberg himself surely would be the first to admit that he has done little to develop the details of such a general ethical theory. Yet without such a theory the notion of "moral development" is pretty insubstantial', (Peters, 1972, reiterates these views, pp 509-10). Alston (1971) also evaluates Kohlberg's work and comments on Peters' critique (pp 269-84).

(a) *Kohlberg's published work*

1958. 'The development of modes of moral thinking and choice in the years ten to sixteen'. Unpublished doctoral dissertation, University of Chicago.

1963(a). 'Moral development and identification', in Stevenson, H., (Ed.), 'Child Psychology'. 62nd. Yearbook of the National Society for the Study of Education. Chicago, Illinois: University of Chicago Press.

1963(b). 'The development of children's orientations toward a moral order: I Sequence in the development of moral thought', 'Vita Humana', 6, 11-33.

1964. 'The development of moral character and moral ideology', in Hoffman, M. L. and Hoffman, L. W., (Eds.), 'Review of Child Development Research'. Volume 1. New York: Russell Sage Foundation.

Kohlberg discusses the varying approaches to the study of children's morality together with the concepts of 'moral character' and 'moral conduct'. The discussion is developed to consider the development of moral ideology and judgement including Piaget's investigations and Kohlberg's extensions. Moral factors in delinquency and neurosis, personality integration and its relation to moral ideologies and implications for moral education also receive attention.

1964(b). 'Sex differences in morality', in MacCoby, E. E. (Ed.) 'Sex Role Development'. New York: SSRC.

1965. 'Relationships between the development of moral judgement and moral conduct'. Paper presented at Symposium on Behavioural and Cognitive Concepts in the Study of Internalization at the Society for Research in Child Development, Minneapolis, Minnesota, March 26th 1965.

In this paper Kohlberg presents the results of several studies showing some empirical relationships between moral behaviour and moral judgement. He argues that these relationships between verbal moral values and moral behaviour make most sense from a cognitive-developmental viewpoint. More specifically, judgement-action relationships may be best thought of, not as the direct conformity of action to verbal moral values, nor as conformity of action to anticipated self-judgements of guilt, but rather as the correspondence between the general maturity of an individual's moral judgement and the maturity of moral action. He argues that both maturity of moral judgement and maturity of moral action have heavy cognitive components. Finally, he attempts to show how a consideration of the correspondence between judgement and action allow an elaboration of a broader developmental notion of moral action than that represented by resistance to temptation concepts.

1966. 'Moral education in the schools: a developmental view', 'The School Review', 74, 1-30.

Kohlberg discusses research findings relating to the development of moral character and their relevance to moral education in the schools, particularly Hartshorne & May (1928-30) and Kohlberg (1963), together with a developmental conception of the aims and nature of moral education.

1967. 'Moral education, religious education and the public schools: a developmental view', in Sizer, T., (Ed), 'Religion and the Public Schools'. Houghton Mifflin.

1968. 'The child as a moral philosopher', 'Psychology Today', 2, (4), 27.

1969(a). 'The relations between moral judgement and moral

action: a developmental view'. Paper presented at colloquium at the Institute of Human Development, University of California, Berkeley, March, 1969.

This paper is reminiscent of Kohlberg (1965) but discusses more recent findings relating to moral judgement and moral behaviour, e.g. Haan, Smith and Block (1968), Lehrer (1967) and Grim, Kohlberg & White (1968). Again there is the emphasis that judgement-action relationships may be best thought of as the correspondence between the general maturity of an individual's moral judgement and the maturity of his moral action. Kohlberg begins to formulate his position regarding the affective components of moral judgement and action. (This is later expanded in Kohlberg, 1971b.)

1969(b). 'Stage and sequence: the cognitive-developmental approach to socialization', in Goslin, D., (Ed.), 'Handbook of Socialization Theory and Research'. New York: Rand McNally.

1969. Kohlberg, L. and De Vries, R. 'Relations between Piaget and psychometric assessments of intelligence'. Paper presented at the Conference on the National Curriculum, Urbana, Illinois' In Lavatelli, C., (1971) 'The Natural Curriculum', University of Illinois Press.

'Almost all (93 per cent) children aged five to seven who passed a moral reasoning task at Stage-2 passed a corresponding task of logical reciprocity or reversibility. However, many (52 per cent) children who passed the logical task did not pass the moral task.' (Cited in Kohlberg, 1971b, p. 187.)

1969. Kohlberg, L. & Kramer, R. 'Continuities and discontinuities in childhood and adult moral development', 'Human Development', 12, 93-120.

Kohlberg and Kramer report the findings on longitudinal subjects as they progressed from age 16 to 25, and on their middle-aged fathers (Kramer's continuation from Kohlberg's longitudinal study). Kramer found that there was no further age increase in moral maturity after age 25, and that high school scores on moral judgement maturity were highly predictive of adult scores on moral maturity.

1970(a). 'Stages of moral development as a basis for moral education', in Beck, C. and Sullivan, E., (Eds.) 'Moral Education'. Toronto: University of Toronto Press.

Kohlberg claims that in this and other papers (particularly 1971b — Conference Paper, 'From is to ought') he defines an approach to moral education which unites philosophic and psychological considerations and therefore implies a base of psychological and sociological facts of moral development, an involvement of educational methods stimulating moral change, a philosophically defensible concept of morality and 'being in accord with a constitutional system guaranteeing freedom from belief.' Kohlberg was intent to set out the philosophic basis for his definition of moral maturity and proposes that his conception of moral maturity be criticized concerning its adequacy as a starting point for planned moral education in schools. He considers two alternative approaches to his own 'culturally and historically universal pattern of mature moral thought and action': the 'hidden curriculum' approach dominant in the United States and the more explicit 'bag of virtues' approach.

1970(b). 'Education for justice: A modern statement of the Platonic view', in Sizer, T., (Ed.) 'Moral Education'. Cambridge, Massachusetts: Harvard University Press.

1970(c). 'The moral atmosphere of the school'. Paper delivered at the Association for Supervision and Curriculum Development Conference on the 'Unstudied Curriculum', Washington D.C. January 9th 1969. Printed in the AASC. Yearbook.

Kohlberg contends that the only integrated way of thinking about the 'hidden curriculum' is to think of it as moral education. He argues that whether the 'hidden curriculum' educates or miseducates depends upon a viable conception of moral development. 'Hidden curriculum' indicates that children are learning much in school which is not formal curriculum and poses the question as to whether this learning is truly educative. Kohlberg leads his considerations to the view that there is a need to make the 'hidden curriculum' an atmosphere of justice and for it to become explicit in intellectual and verbal discussions of justice and morality.

1971(a). 'Moral Judgement Interview and Procedures for Scoring'. University of Harvard.

Kohlberg's developmental stages were determined by a moral judgement questionnaire containing nine hypothetical conflict stories and corresponding sets of probing questions. Kohlberg has developed a total weighted developmental score together with a 'pure-type' measure in which the 'modal' or 'dominant' stage is considered to be the most representative.

1971(b). 'From is to ought: how to commit the naturalistic fallacy and get away with it in the study of development', in Mischel, T., (Ed.), 'Cognitive Development and Epistemology'. New York and London: Academic Press.

A conference Paper, revised following comments and discussion, providing a comprehensive account of Kohlberg's approach (together with his colleagues') to the complexities of moral development.

1971. Kohlberg, L. and Turiel, E. Moral development and moral education', in Lesser, G., (Ed.) 'Psychology and the

Educational Process'. Chicago: Scott, Foresman.
(To be published). Kohlberg, L. and Turiel, E. 'Recent Research in Moral Development'. New York: Holt.

(b) *Further developments from Kohlberg's work*

Bar-Yam, M. and Kohlberg, L., (To be published). 'Development of moral judgement in the Kibbutz', in Kohlberg, L. and Turiel, E., (Eds.) 'Recent Research in Moral Development'. New York: Holt.

Blatt, M., (1969). 'The effects of classroom discussion on the development of moral judgement'. Unpublished doctoral dissertation, University of Chicago.

Blatt, M. and Kohlberg, L., (To be published) 'The effects of classroom discussion on the development of moral judgement', in Kohlberg, L. and Turiel, E. (Eds.). 'Recent Research in Moral Development'.

Blatt's findings suggest that the effects on moral judgement of naturally occurring moral discussions induce cognitive conflict in the child and he subsequently reorganizes his thinking to the next level. Blatt conducted moral discussion classes, presenting 'dilemmas and focus arguments between adjacent stages (that is Stage-2, versus Stage-3 etc.) This led most of the children to move up one stage, an advance retained over the control groups one year later. In other classes, children simply discussed moral dilemmas without teacher direction. Arguments between adjacent stages often developed naturally and there was considerable change, varying with the class ability and interest in free discussion. (In the leaderless groups with high interest in discussion, upward change was about as great as it was in the teacher-led groups)' (Cited in Kohlberg 1971b, p 195.)

Brown, M., Feldman, K., Schwartz, S. and Heingartner, A., (1969), 'Some personality correlates of conduct in two situations of moral conflict', 'J. of Pers', 37, 1.

'This study examined the value of distinguishing between personality characteristics uniquely responsive to the moral aspects of decisions and those responsive to non-morally relevant cues in decision-making situations. Subjects who participated in two experimental situations intended to arouse moral conflict: (a) a group-administered vocabulary test providing a temptation to cheat: (b) a puzzle task in the company of an accomplice who varied pressure to be helpful. Level of moral thought, which represented morally relevant characteristics, was associated with morally desirable conduct in both situations, as predicted. As the analysis of the achievement and affiliation cues and possibilities in two situations led us to expect; achievement related positively to not cheating but negatively to helpfulness, and affiliation was associated positively with helpfulness but unrelated to cheating.' Implications for the moral consistency of behaviour across situations are discussed.

Fodor, E. M., (1969), 'Moral judgement in negro and white adolescents', 'J. Soc. Psych.', 79, 289-91.

The aim of the study was to compare negro and white male adolescents in moral judgement in accordance with the Kohlberg interview. The subjects consisted of 25 socially disadvantaged negro boys together with 25 white boys aged 14-17 years. The Cornell Parent Behaviour Description was also administered. The difference between the moral judgement scores for white and negro boys was non-significant. There was a statistically significant difference on moral judgement scores between boys whose mothers had graduated from high school and boys whose mothers lacked this experience.

Fodor, E. M., (1972). 'Delinquency and susceptibility to social influence among adolescents as a function of level of moral development', 'J. Soc. Psych.', 86, 257-60.

Assessed by the Kohlberg Interview, delinquents (as predicted), obtained lower Moral Judgement scores than nondelinquents. Delinquents who yielded to attempts to dissuade them from moral decisions they had made, received lower scores than delinquents who resisted this influence. The findings were viewed as increasing the validity of Kohlberg's schema of moral development.

Gilligan, C., Kohlberg, L., Lerner, J., and Belensky, M., (1971), 'Moral Reasoning About Sexual Dilemmas: An Interview and Scoring System'. Technical Report of the Commission on Obscenity and Pornography, 141-174.

Grim, P., Kohlberg, L. and White, S., (1968). 'Some relationships between conscience and attentional processes,' 'J. Pers. Soc. Psych.', 8, 3, Part 1, 239-52.

'Twenty-two 1st-grade and 22 6th-grade children were administered measures of attention based on a reaction time (RT) task involving varying preparatory intervals with associated GSR measures and experimental and teacher-rating measures of resistance to temptation (RTT) to cheating. In both groups significant correlations were found between good performance on attention measures and RTT. The highest correlation (r's = .61, .59) was between high variability (SD) of RT and high cheating. Orthogonally rotated factor analysis indicated three similar factors at each grade. The first factor, task conformity, included psychomotor efficiency and teacher RTT rating variables. The second factor, inner stability, included experimental RTT and psychomotor stability variables. The third factor, restlessness, included nonspecific GSR and RTT rating variables. It is noteworthy that attention (psychomotor) and moral variables loaded on each factor rather than being separated by the factor analysis. The relations of the psychomotor to the moral variables at the two ages seemed to depend on the age developmental course of the former, relations being best when the variables represented attention rather than maturation of the psychomotor skill. An ego-strength rather than a super-ego strength interpretation of moral behaviour is advanced to fit the findings. It is suggested that moral temptation distractors from task performance are psychologically related to the ordinary distractors of task performance. The interpretation advanced is James' (1890) notion that "the essential achievement of will is to attend to a difficult object . . ." (p 549).'

Haan, N., Smith, M.B., and Block, J., (1968). 'Moral reasoning of young adults: political-social behaviour, family background and personality correlates', 'J. Pers. Soc. Psych.', 10, 183-201.

'College students and Peace Corps volunteers were assigned to a typology of moral reasoning according to their responses to the Kohlberg Moral Judgement Scale. Differences among five moral types in family-social background, self- and ideal descriptions and descriptions of mother and father were analysed. In general, S's of principled moral reasoning as contrasted with the conventionally moral, were more active in political-social matters, particularly in protest; their views on current issues were more discrepant from their parents who themselves were politically liberal; their self and ideal conceptualizations emphasized interpersonal reactivity and obligation, self-expressiveness and a willingness to live in opposition. Perceptions of parental relationships suggest that little conflict or separation occurred in the families of the conventionally moral with more in those of the principled.'

Holstein, C., (To be published). 'Parental determinants of the development of moral judgement', in Kohlberg, L. and Turiel, E. (Eds.) 'Recent Research in Moral Development'. New York: Holt.

'The amount of parental encouragement of the child's participation in discussion (in a taped 'revealed differences' mother-father-child discussion of moral conflict situations) was a powerful correlate of moral advance in the child.' (Cited in Kohlberg, 1971b, p 191.)

Keasey, C.B., (1971). 'Social participation as a factor in the moral development of preadolescents', 'Dev. Psych.', 5, 2, 216-20.

The study was designed to examine the relation between moral development and a number of indexes of social participation. It was hypothesized that higher stages of moral development are positively associated with greater social participation.

Seventy-five boys and 69 girls from fifth and sixth grade, of average intelligence and predominantly lower-middle class background were administered the Moral Judgement Interview. The quantity and quality of social participation was assessed by the number of clubs and societies attended and the leadership positions held. Peers and teachers were asked to rate each child in leadership and popularity. The hypothesis received strong support from all three sources of data: self-reports, peer ratings and teacher ratings; 't' tests indicated that boys rated as popular and as leaders by teachers and who themselves reported being members of a large number of clubs had higher moral judgement scores than the comparable group of girls. The author concluded that both the quality and the quantity of a child's social participation facilitates moral development.

Keasey, C. B., (1972). 'The lack of sex differences in the moral judgments of preadolescents', 'J. Soc. Psych.' 86, 157-8.

The findings were consistent with cognitive-developmental theory and suggested that during preadolescence, males and females do not differ in their moral judgements. Freudian theory, which suggests that females have a weaker superego than males was not directly refuted, 'since the Freudian concept of the superego focuses upon rules and prohibitions rather than their underlying reasoning'.

Kramer, R., (1969), 'Progression and regression in adolescent moral development', Soc. Res. Child Dev., Santa Monica, March 26th 1969. (See Kohlberg and Kramer, 1969).

Krebs, R. L., (1967). 'Some relationships between moral judgement, attention and resistance to temptation.' Unpublished doctoral dissertation. Univ. of Chicago.

Krebs found that sixth-grade children at stages five and six resisted temptation to a greater extent than children at stages three and four. (Cited in Kohlberg, 1971b, p 229.)

Kuhn, D., Langer, J. and Kohlberg, L. (to be published) 'Relations between logical and moral development', in Kohlberg, L. and Turiel, E. (Eds.) 'Recent Research in Moral Development'.

'All adolescents and adults using Stage 5 or 6 reasoning are capable of formal reasoning on the Inhelder and Piaget pendulum and correlation problems. Many adolescents and adults capable of the latter show no Stage 5 or 6 moral reasoning.' (Cited in Kohlberg, 1971b, p 188.)

Lehrer, L., (1967). 'Sex differences in moral behaviour and attitudes'. Unpublished doctoral dissertation, Univ. of Chicago.

Lehrer built a ray gun test improving on Grinder (1962) to induce greater temptation and lead the children to the brink of success in a realistic but random fashion. Only 15 per cent cheated, but it was concluded that this was hardly a decision of conscience; the machine evidently appeared to the children as a computer keeping its own score, unlike the Grinder machine. (Cited in Kohlberg, 1971b, p 227).

Podd, M. H., (1972) 'Ego identity status and morality: the relationship between two developmental constructs?'

'Ego identity status and "level of moral judgement" were independently assessed and examined in relation to each other and to a measure of moral conduct. Subjects who achieved an ego identity were generally characterized by the most mature level of moral judgement, while those with a relative lack of ego identity were generally characterized by either the least mature level of moral judgement or a transitional period between moderate and highly mature moral judgement. People undergoing an identity crisis were found to be unstable and inconsistent in their moral reasoning. Motives but not behaviour on the moral conduct task differed according to identity status and level of moral development. The results were discussed in terms of moral ideology as a factor in ego identity formation.'

Rest, J., (1968). 'Developmental hierarchy in preference and comprehension of moral judgement'. Unpublished doctoral dissertation. Univ. of Chicago.

Rest, J., (to be published), 'Comprehension preference and spontaneous usage in moral judgement', in Kohlberg, L. and Turiel, E. (Eds) 'Recent Research in Moral Development'.

Rest, J., Turiel, E. and Kohlberg, L., (1969). 'Relations between level of moral judgement and preference and comprehension of the moral judgement of others', 'J. Pers,' 37, 225-52.

'On the basis of Kohlberg's developmental hierarchy of moral judgement, it was hypothesized that modes of moral thought above an individual's own stage would be preferred to modes below, and that modes of thinking above are increasingly more difficult to comprehend than stages below. After determining each subject's dominant moral stage in a pretest, the subjects were presented with a series of statements corresponding to the stages one below, one above and two above their own. Measures of preference, comprehension and assimilation of these statements were then obtained. It was found that children generally prefer concepts above their own stage to concepts below. Thinking two stages above was more difficult for subjects to comprehend than thinking one stage above, which in turn was more difficult than thinking one stage below. Further analyses showed that assimilation effects were a function of both the S's preference and the highest level of thinking comprehended. The results were also discussed in relation to social leadership and developmental change.'

Scaplehorn, C., (1971) 'The patterning of reasoning, moral judgement and moral behaviour in adolescents.' M. Phil (in preparation), University of Surrey.

It is proposed to relate measured intelligence to stages of concrete and formal thought operations (to be measured through Piaget-oriented tasks devised by Tisher, 1971, described in Chapter Five), which in turn will be related to modes of moral judgement assessed by the Kohlberg Moral Judgement Interview Schedules (described earlier in the Chapter). Further verification will be sought for findings reported by Kuhn, Langer and Kohlberg (to be published; described earlier in this Section).

Selman, R. L., (1971) 'The relation of role taking to the development of moral judgement in children', 'Child Dev.', 42, 79-91.

'In order to explore the relationship in middle childhood between two social-cognitive processes, role-taking ability and moral reasoning, 60 middle-class children (10 boys and 10 girls each at ages 8, 9, 10,) were administered Kohlberg's (1963) moral-judgement measure, two role-taking tasks and the Peabody Picture Vocabulary Test, a conventional measure of intelligence. Results indicated that at this age range, with intelligence controlled, the development of reciprocal role-taking skills related to the development of conventional moral judgement. Results of a re-examination one year later of 10 subjects whose role-taking and moral-judgement levels were low in the original study supported the hypothesis that the development of the ability to understand the reciprocal nature of interpersonal relations is a necessary but not sufficient condition for the development of conventional moral thought.'

Selman, R. L., (to be published). 'The importance of reciprocal role-taking for the development of conventional moral thought' in Kohlberg, L. and Turiel, E. (Eds). 'Recent Research in Moral Development'.

Sullivan, E. V., McCullough, G., and Stager, M., (1970) 'A developmental study of the relationship between conceptual, ego and moral development', 'Child Dev.', 41, 399-411.

The study 'explored the relationships between "ego", "conceptual systems" and moral developmental theories. The age-developmental trends on all three measures were consistent with the stage formulations of all three theorists. (Loevinger 1966; Harvey, Hunt and Schroder 1961 and Kohlberg 1958). Low to moderate correlations were reported between all of the measures, after age was partialled out of the correlation coefficients, suggesting that further, more precise investigation into common aspects of the personality dimensions involved and transition rules in stage development would be worthwhile.'

Thrower, J., (to be published). 'Effects of orphanage and foster home care on development of moral judgement', in

Kohlberg, L. and Turiel, E. (Eds.) 'Recent Research in Moral Development'.

'In traditional orphanages a large majority of children are still at the preconventional level (Stages 1 and 2) at age 16.' (Cited in Kohlberg, 1971b, p.191.)

Turiel, E., (1966). 'An experimental test of the sequentiality of developmental stages in the child's moral judgement,' 'J. Pers. Soc. Psych.', 3, 6, 611-18.

'Two developmental propositions of Kohlberg's theory of moral judgements were tested: a) that the stages form an invariant sequence, and thus, more learning results from exposure to the stage directly above one's level than to stages further above; b) that passage from one stage to the next involves integration of the previous stages and thus, more learning results from exposure to the stage directly above than to the stage one below. First S's stages were determined in a pretest. Forty-four S's of Kohlberg's Stages 2, 3 and 4 were equally distributed among three experimental groups and one control group. In the treatment conditions, S's were exposed to either the Stage one below, one above or two above the initial dominant stage. The control group was not administered a treatment condition. In a post test the influence of the treatment conditions was assessed. The results confirmed the hypothesis since exposure to the stage directly above was the most effective treatment.'

Turiel, E., (1969). 'Developmental processes in the child's moral thinking', in Mussen, P., Langer, J. and Covington, M. (Eds) 'New Directions in Developmental Psychology'. New York: Holt.

Following cognitive-developmental theory, Turiel postulates that 'cognitive conflict is the central "motor" for reorganization or upward movement'. To test this, Turiel is conducting a series of experiments presenting children with varying combinations of contradictory arguments flowing from the same stage structure. 'The studies should provide concrete evidence for the general notion that stage change depends upon conflict — induced reorganization.' What Turiel hopes to show is 'that exposure to the next stage up effects change not through the assimilation of specific messages, but by providing awareness that there are other, better or more consistent solutions than the child's own, forcing him to rethink his own solution.'

Turiel, E., (1973). 'Stage transition in moral development', in Travers, R. M. (Ed). 'Second Handbook of Research on Teaching'. Chicago: Rand McNally.

Turiel, E. and Rothman, G. R. (1972). 'The influence of reasoning on behavioural choices at different stages of moral development', 'Child Dev.', 43, 741-756. 'This study examined the effects of exposure to moral reasoning on behaviour. 43 seventh -

366

and eighth grade boys were pre-tested using Kohlberg's moral-judgement interview to determine their moral-development stages. The experimental condition required Ss to choose between two actions. Before choosing, Ss were exposed to reasoning; One behavioural choice was supported by reasoning at the stage above their own and the other by reasoning at the stage below. Ss made a choice and reasoned about it. A post-test was administered. Compared with control Ss, the reasoning presented did not effect a shift in behavioural choice for stage 2 and stage 3 Ss; reasoning at the stage above led to a shift for stage 4 Ss. The post-test showed no significant stage changes'.

Weisbroth, S. P., (1970). 'Moral judgement, sex and parental identification in adults', 'Dev. Psych.' 2, 3, 396-402.

'The relationship of moral judgement with both sex and parental identification was studied in 37 males and 41 female adults, all white, middle-class college graduates, aged 21-39 years. Two hypotheses were proposed: a) that the women attain a higher level of moral judgement than men and b) that, within each sex group, individuals with a close parental identification attain a higher level of moral judgement than individuals with a more distant parental identification. Moral judgement was defined in terms of Kohlberg's developmental analysis and measured by his moral judgement test. Parental identification was measured by means of the semantic differential. Results indicate that there is no significant difference in moral judgement between the sexes. Identification with both parents is significantly related to high moral judgement in males, while identification with the father is significantly related to high moral judgement in females. Freud's statements regarding the relationship between morality, sex and parental identification are evaluated in the light of the present data.'

[1] Another study (Lee, 1971), has come to the author's attention since the completion of this chapter. Lee was intent to investigate whether the development of cognitive strategies and the growth of moral judgement developed concomitantly. A battery of six Piagetian tasks was administered to children, from five to 17 years, inclusive. The Piagetian tasks were aimed to establish levels of cognitive functioning and the levels of moral judgement were identified by responses to nine morally conflicting story situations. The results were discussed in relation to children functioning at each of the three stages of preoperational, concrete-operational and formal-operational. Overall, the findings substantiated Piaget's contention of concomitant develop-

ment of the two modes of thought.

[2] See also Merchant and Rebelsky (1972) who were intent to show the effects of participation in rule formation on the moral judgement of children.

[3] See also Glassco, Milgram & Youniss (1970).

CHAPTER ELEVEN
PERSONALITY, SOCIALIZATION AND EMOTIONALITY RELATED TO PIAGET'S THEORY

No direct literature exists on this problem to date, apart from the related studies of Dudek (1972), Goldschmid (1967, 1968), Hamilton (1971, 1972), Modgil (1969, 1973), Modgil and Dudek (1973) and Modgil, Dudek and Strobel (1973) and Pimm (1974).[1]

In general, on the relation between affectivity and cognitive development, there is a Paper by Piaget which is not generally available — 'The Relation of Affectivity to Intelligence in the Mental Development of the Child'. Bulletin of the Menninger Clinic, May 1962, Volume 26 Number 3, pp. 129-37.[2] Piaget discusses the main contributions of authors like Odier, Wallon, Melrieux, Spitz, Tinbergen, Lorenz, Claparede, Janet and Lewin. Piaget concludes (page 131): 'All the authors agree that in all behaviour the structure is cognitive, and the force, or the economy, is affective. Therefore, affect cannot be the cause of a cognitive structure, any more than intelligence can be the cause of affect, because a structure is not the cause of this energy, this force and vice versa. Between the two is a relation of correspondence, and not of causality.' Piaget has promoted similar views in earlier and later works (1947, page 6; 1967, page 69; and 1969, pages 114-29).

Piaget's concern has been almost exclusively with cognitive structurs. However he accepts the relevance of affective factors in the child's intellectual development. Authors like Anthony (1956, 1957), Mehrabian (1968), Sigel (1968) and Wolff (1966) have attempted to relate Piaget's theory of cognitive development to theories of personality development, particularly to the psychoanalytic theory.

Currently Piaget (1972, Page 36) reflects: '. . . je crois que ces questions particulières relatives à l'inconscient cognitif sont parallèles à celles que soulève en psychanalyse le fonctionnement de l'inconscient affectif . . . je suis persuadé qu'il viendra un jour où la psychologie des fonctions cognitives et la psychanalyse seront obligées de se fusionner en une théorie générale qui les améliorera toutes deux en les corrigeant l'une et l'autre, et c'est cet avenir qu'il convient de préparer en montrant dès maintenant les rapports qui peuvent exister entre les deux.'

Piaget continues (page 51); 'Une série d'études ont déja été entreprises sur les relations entre nos analyses du développement cognitif durant la période sensorimotrice et les travaux de Freux, y compris les stades qu'il a distingues au cours de la même période. Je rappelle, par exemple, les analyses, de D. Rapport et la belle etude de Wolff, ainsi que l'appendice de Cobliner au dernier ouvrage de Spitz.'

Holmes (1973) has argued that Piaget's contribution to psychology can bring about a reconciliation between psychology and psychoanalysis. Piaget has by and large disregarded individual differences and has instead attempted to uncover universal sequences and laws governing the acquisition of knowledge. The intractable individuality of children continues to assert itself even in the face of Piaget's 'elegant normative theory' — a contention expressed by Tuddenham (1969, cited in Dockrell (Ed.) 1970). The time has come to relate Piagetian concepts to psycho-social and personality characteristics on a larger scale. There is reason to suspect that such a relation exists in 'personal conservation' (with respect to interpersonal relationship, stability of the home and environment, child-rearing and parental attitudes, and the child's own perception of himself — self image) and 'object conservation'. Geneva research seems uninterested in the total global growth of the child (that is the interaction between various facets of child development). Piaget himself has presented no data on the relationship between cognitive and affective development findings. When questioned by Hill regarding his interests in the connections between intellectual and emotional development, he replied ((1972), '. . . Emotional development is the driving force. Intelligence does not work without affective motivation. That's clear. By the affective aspect emotions are modified by the structures of intelligence. The energy factor is the driving force. Then there are the structural factors. It is the structure which interests me, not the driving force. . . . as an investigator the problem of knowledge has interested me.' Goldschmid (1970, 1971 in private communication) maintains; 'The Freudians and Neo-Freudians, the "social role" and "socialization" people have never produced a meaningful theory of thought development. Studies of the relationship between Piagetian concepts and other variables in child development are still very rare, yet most desirable, if one is to develop a "psychological" theory of child development as opposed to a "cognitive", or "social" or "emotional" theory of child development on an empirical basis. One ultimately seeks to comprehend the whole child, not just one facet of him. Such relationships may explain individual differences that many studies have demonstrated, not only within groups, but also between different groups of subjects of the same age.'

Piaget has remarked that '. . . experience is always necessary for intellectual development' and has specified the importance of physical activity and social interactions as ingredients of experience (1964, page 31). Despite this and despite his elaboration of his equilibration theory, Piaget has in Flavell's terms '. . . shed no or very little empirical hard-fact light on precisely how [the cognitive structures he demonstrated] work their way into the child's cognitive life' (1963, page 370).

There is very little empirical evidence on the inter-relationship between social, emotional and cognitive development. Goldschmid's (1967, 1968) studies suggest the existence of such meaningful relationships. His 1967 investigation demonstrated that emotionally disturbed children, who were on average two years older than the normal children, were at about the same level of conservation behaviour. This finding was not, however, clear-cut, because the emotionally disturbed children also had lower IQs, which could have been the crucial variable.

In another related study, Goldschmid (1968) administered the same battery of 10 Piagetian tasks and reported that children with a higher level of conservation tended to be more objective in their self-evaluation; less dominated by their mothers, and seen as more attractive and passive than children with a lower level of conservation. However, the problem of IQ is again a factor. (Goldschmid's 1967 and 1968 studies are described later in this chapter.) The study also demonstrated that children performing at a higher level of conservation operativity were preferred by their peers. Rardin and Moan (1971) attempted to establish a relationship between the development and affective quality of peer relations to physical concept development. The hypotheses were generally substantiated, but the results were only moderately significant (Details are given later in this chapter.)

Murray (1972) demonstrated that social interaction improved the child's ability to advance conservation judgements together with logical justifications. (Details are given later in this chapter.)

More recently, Lloyd and Burgess (1973) investigated the hypotheses of Piaget and others concerning the facilitating effects of peer interaction on cognitive development. The data are currently being analysed.

Lovell (1969) has lent support to Goldschmid's (1968) study. 'Children who are concerned about school are likely to be doing better in school work, are likely to be regarded by their teachers as better all around than pupils who are not. I agree, of course, whole heartedly that social and emotional factors are extremely important relative to cognitive development. But I would also like to see a longitudinal study, from the age of say, three or four years upwards, showing what kinds of personalities show early and late conservation instead of measuring the personality, assessing the personality, at the conservation stage.'

Pertinent here is a four-year longitudinal study by Dudek (1972) who hypothesized that an analysis of the personality of the child who shows a faster rate of intellectual maturation would show a more mature and better developed affectivity and egocentric structure. To test this hypothesis she employed the Cattell Early School Personality Questionnaire (Cattell and Coan, 1968) and the Rorschach test as measures of personality development. She concludes: 'children showing conceptually faster development on Piaget tests scored higher on WISC intelligence and higher on emotional maturity ... Rorschach analysis of personality characteristics of 16 children who showed instability of stage acquisition on Piaget tests revealed a characteristic pattern of responding suggestive of marked obsessive traits which exist over time.'

In continuation, Modgil and Dudek are collaborating in a three-year longitudinal study with children in the county of Surrey. The results of this study are expected in 1974. In passing it might be stated that Lovell (1961b) also pleads for a consideration of the effect of strong emotions on logical thinking.

Piaget (1972, op. cit.), in connection with his interest in education and child-rearing, maintains that: 'They are of great interest to me. But I believe that in the psychology of child development there is so much to be learnt, so many unknowns that this is the first work of a psychologist who is fortunate enough to be able to undertake experiments.'

Of some relevance is the study of Bell (1968, discussed more appropriately in Chapter Two), which includes in its findings the suggestion that the quality of a baby's interaction with his mother affects the development of object permanence at the sensori-motor stage of cognitive acquisition. Further, a study by Birns and Golden (1972) which involved 18- and 24-month-old infants, demonstrated that the amount of pleasure manifested by infants at an early age on the Cattell and Piaget Object Scales was predictive of intellectual performance (Stanford-Binet) at CA three years. The authors interpret the finding to indicate that pleasure in problem-solving facilitates cognitive development. While raising a number of issues requiring further investigation, they draw attention to the need to determine the kinds of maternal behaviours that foster or inhibit pleasures in problen solving. (Details are given in chapter 2.) The results of Lefevre (1970) and Dasen (1972b) suggest that inconsistent early mother-child relationships may contribute to difficulty in grasping the notion of object permanence necessary in handling conservation tasks.

The role of specifically maternal attitudes in the child's information processing skills is taken a step further by Hamilton (1971). The study presented evidence that children of rejecting mothers showed a lower level of operational conservation than the children of accepting mothers. Children of rejecting mothers also demonstrated limitations of the conserving skill when a stress factor (maternal participation) was present in a conservation task. This needs further verification in view of the small samples involved, (details are given later in this chapter). In order to synchronize Piagetan operativity and socialization, Hamilton (1973) submits an exploratory model to illustrate the inconstancy of information processing ability in respect to social-emotional forces.

Modgil's (1969) study attempted to determine what empirical links might be present among cognitive, affective and environmental factors in the child's development. More specifically, the author tested the hypothesis that there is a positive relationship between emotional and social order in a child's life and his development of invariance concepts. The results indicated that emotional stability and social 'order' have a facilitative effect on cognitive functioning (cf. Goldschmid, op.cit. and Dudek, op.cit.) Further, children who tend to score high on conservation tasks tend to possess parents with less dominating, ignoring and possessive attitudes. Over and above the association of low conservation with unfavourable parental attitudes, there is a specific association with high dominance: a finding also reported in the study by Goldschmid using a different experimental design.

However, Modgil's study did not establish whether operativity, as conceived by Piaget, is differentially affected by socialization as compared with scholastic performance as a whole and attempts are currently being made to substantiate such a hypothesis (Modgil, 1973, in progress).

Different types of conservation and their relation to age, sex, IQ, MA and vocabulary
M. Goldschmid, 1967

SUBJECTS/Goldschmid's study involved 102 children drawn from upper middle-class and lower middle-class families. The subjects were selected from three schools — a public school (22 boys, 21 girls) with a mean age of seven years, three months; a private school (16 boys, 22 girls) with a mean age of six years, 10 months; and a school for emotionally disturbed children (17 boys and four girls) with a mean age of nine years, one month.

METHOD/Tests The author administered a battery of 10 conservation tasks to normal children and to emotionally disturbed children. The tests were as follows: (a) Substance (patterned after Elkind, 1961a); (b) Weight (patterned after Elkind, 1961a); (c) Continuous Quantity (patterned after Elkind, 1961b); (d) Discontinuous Quantity (patterned after Elkind, 1961b); (e) Number (patterned after Dodwell, 1961 and Feigenbaum, 1963); (f) Area (patterned after Flavell, 1963, pp. 338); (g) Distance (patterned after Flavell, 1963, pp. 323 and 336); (h) Length (patterned after Beilin and Franklin, 1962); (i) Two-Dimensional Space (patterned after Flavell, 1963, pp. 338-9); (j) Three-Dimensional Space (patterned after Lovell and Ogilvie, 1961).

Each child was seen individually and all responses were recorded verbatim. The general procedure was identical to that of the Geneva School, apart from some flexibility where additional questions were necessary to elicit further information or to elucidate ambiguous behaviour.

Additional data were secured from the records of the participating school, especially IQ scores based on the Pintner-Cunningham, Otis and Stanford-Binet. The scores on these intelligence tests were not entirely comparable, and this necessitated the administration of the WISC Vocabulary subtest.

RESULTS/The results supported the differential growth rate of conservation of substance, weight and volume that other studies have shown. A significant relation existed among different tasks of conservation and the total conservation scores, substantiating a basic cognitive structure, that is, the schema of conservation. The study also demonstrated the presence of sex differences within this sample. Most pertinent of the results for our purpose was the fact that the emotionally disturbed children, who were on the average two years older than the normal children, were at about the same level of conservation behaviour. This finding was not clear-cut, however, because the emotionally disturbed children also had lower IQs which could have been the crucial variable.

The relation of conservation to emotional and environmental aspects of development
M. Goldschmid, 1968

Goldschmid administered the same battery of 10 Piagetian tasks, as he used for his 1967 study (op.cit.).

SUBJECTS/The 102 subjects were selected from predominantly upper middle-class and lower middle-class families. Three schools participated in the study — a public school (22 boys, 21 girls were selected with a mean age of 87.35 months); a private school (16 boys and 22 girls with a mean age of 82.16 months); and a school for emotionally disturbed children (17 boys and four girls with a mean age of 109.05 months).

METHOD/Tests/Amongst the affective and environmental variables Goldschmid utilized the following measures:

(a) Children's Manifest Anxiety Scale (patterned after Castaneda, McCandless and Palermo 1956 and Palermo 1959). This was administered individually to each child. Anxiety scale and the Lie Scale were analysed separately.

(b) Actual and ideal self-ratings. This was administered individually to each child and was modelled after Domino Goldschmid and Kaplan (1964), Goldschmid and Domino (1965) and Gough (1960). Three scores were derived from this measure: the total number of positive adjectives, and negative adjectives for the actual self, and the difference score between the actual self and ideal self.

(c) Teacher's rating. Each child was assessed on the same adjective check list (as in (b) above) by the respective teacher. The teacher's positive and negative adjectives were computed, as were the differences between the child's actual self-rating and the teacher's rating.

(d) Sociometric Choice. The general procedure as utilized by McCandless and Marshall (1951) and Moore and Updergraff (1964) was followed.

(e) The Parental Attitude Survey (Shoben 1949) was independently administered to both mother and father. The Survey purports to measure three parental/maternal paternal attitudes. These are Dominating, Possessive and Ignoring variables.

(f) IQ scores were obtained from participating school records, who had used the Pintner-Cunningham, the Otis and the Stanford-Binet.

RESULTS/Goldschmid reports: 'Children with a high level of conservation tend to be (i) more objective in their self-evaluation, (ii) described more favourably by their teachers, (iii) preferred by their peers, (iv) less dominated by their mothers and (v) seen as more attractive and passive, than children with a low level of conservation'.

The relation of emotional adjustment to the conservation of number
S. Modgil, 1969

AIM/To determine what empirical links might be present among cognitive, affective and environmental factors in the child's development. The study was an attempt to elucidate and establish how far the development of the concept of conservation of number might be impeded by lack of order and stability in a child's home life, that is, a lack of invariant 'conserved' entities in his personal social world; or, more specifically, to test the hypothesis that there is a positive relationship between emotional and social order in a child's life and his development of invariance concepts.

SUBJECTS/Variables controlled were (i) CA seven to eight years, (ii) children were selected from urban areas, (iii) IQs 90-110, (iv) socio-economic status (social class), (v) sex and (vi) verbal facility. Two groups each of 35 children were selected, all of whom satisfied criteria (i), (ii) and (iii) and were matched on criteria (iv), (v) and (vi). Group A consisted of emotionally unstable and Group B of emotionally stable children.

METHOD/Tests/Piaget's concept of conservation was chosen as the cognitive variable and was investigated in five simple situations similar to those used by Piaget. Affective variables consisted of: (i) the child's emotions as measured by The Bristol Social Adjustment Guides (Scott, 1958) and the Rutter (A and B Scales (1967-68)); (ii) anxiety as measured by the quesionnaire which was an adaptation of Sarason's GA and TA scales (1958); and (iii) the child's conceptualization of his actual self as measured by the adjective check-list modelled after those by Domino, Goldschmid and Kaplan (1964), Goldschmid and Domino (1965), Gough (1960) and Goldschmid (1968). Environmental factors included the child's attitudes to arithmetic, school and teacher, the teacher's view of the child and the parent's attitudes toward child-rearing as measured by the Parental Attitude Survey (Shoben, 1949).

RESULTS/Results on 29 variables were correlated and the resultant matrices subjected to factor analysis with the aid of the standard Atlas computer programme used in the Department of Education, Manchester University. The programme calculated principal components, varimax and promax rotations both on the original matrix and on the higher order matrices generated by successive promax rotations. Additional checks were made by the use of chi square to establish which tests differentiated most sharply between the two samples.

The results indicated that:

(a) Emotionally unstable or disturbed children develop conservation later than 'normal' stable children of the same mental age. Emotional stability and social 'order' have a facilitative effect on cognitive functioning. (Cf. Dudek, 1972, who established that children who attained the higher stages of causal and operational thinking were the most highly developed emotionally and intellectually.)

(b) Children with a high level of conservation tend to see themselves more objectively and may be described as being more reflective.

(c) Children who tend to score high on conservation tasks tend to possess parents with less dominating, ignoring and possessive attitudes.

(d) Over and above the association of low conservation with unfavourable parental attitudes, there is a specific association with high dominance, a finding also reported in a study by Goldschmid (1968, op.cit.) using a different experimental design.

Negative findings were:

(a) It has not been shown conclusively that conservation will be more affected than performance in mechanical arithmetic tests.

(b) There is little evidence from this sample that the child's positive attitudes to arithmetic, school and teacher have facilitative effects on conservation performance.

Effect of maternal attitude on development of logical operations
V. Hamilton, 1971

SUBJECTS/Hamilton's study drew children from two North Toronto schools in Grade 3. The children were matched for age, sex, socio-economic status, intelligence, immediate memory and educational attainment, and they ranged in age from six to eight years.

METHOD/The general procedure involved three phases — the measurement of conservation; the measurement of maternal attitude and the maternal participation in problem solving.

Modifications were made to the typical Piaget type conservation situations. Each problem purporting to measure conservation comprised 21 items. Briefly, the test involved either subdivision, or deformation of substance or the distribution of water into a large number of differently shaped containers. These problems were portrayed on cards and administered to each child individually. 'It took the form of two consecutively presented isometric drawings, indicating the first and last stage in the manipulation of material.' Fuller details are published elsewhere (Hamilton, 1970; 1971).

Four techniques were utilized in the measurement of maternal attitude. These are best described in Hamilton's own words. 'First, a questionnaire adapted from existing sources was devised to assess the range of maternal rejection. Second, two critical situations were extracted from two sub-scales of this questionnaire, which were reassessed in the context of the paired-comparison method. Thirteen hypothetical maternal responses to aggressive and nonconforming child behaviour were compared each with each, counterbalancing for order of presentation, left/right sequence, and severity of the pair of responses being compared. The third technique was projective: assessment of responses to four TAT cards (5, 7BM, 7GF, 13B) representing actual or inferable parent-child interactions. The fourth device for assessing maternal attitude was the mother's description of her children to the interviewer.' The two main attitudes extracted were 'accepting' and 'rejecting'.

The maternal participation in problem solving involved a playback of certain messages which the participating mothers offered to their children. Behavioural patterns and relationships were recorded for later assessments. Fuller details are published elsewhere (Hamilton, 1970; 1971).

RESULTS/The study presented evidence to support the hypothesis that 'sub-optimal mothering may be a causative factor in sub-optimal conservation.' Specifically, Hamilton's study demonstrated that children of rejecting mothers (as defined) showed a lower level of operational conservation than the children of accepting mothers (as defined). Children of rejecting mothers also demonstrated limitations of the conserving skill when a stress factor (maternal participation) was present in a conservation task. However, the empirical generality of Hamilton's study must be taken with some caution, particularly in view of the fact that the samples were very small and the sub-samples even smaller.

Peer interaction and cognitive development
D. R. Rardin and C. E. Moan, 1971

The study examined two hypotheses: (a) that there is a parallel relationship between the development of peer relations and interactions and that of physical concept development in young children; and (b) that 'the individual's progress in cognitive development, as reflected by two measures of physical concept development which assess the ability to classify and conserve, will vary directly with the affective quality of his peer relations'.

SUBJECTS/The total sample of 81 children (43 males and 38 females) consisted of 20 kindergarten, 19 first- 21 second- and 21 third-grade children from a school in Wyoming town.

METHOD/Each child was seen individually on cognitive and sociometric choice tasks. Responses were recorded verbatim and protocols examined for resultant patterns.

Cognitive Measures/This consisted of the following six tasks taken from Form A of the Goldschmid and Bentler Concept Assessment Kit (1968b). The tasks assessed conservation ability and comprised Number, Substances, Two-dimensional space, Weight Continuous Quantity and Discontinuous Quantity. A second cognitive measure included tasks involving inclusion or classification operativity. Three such tasks were administered and the general experimental procedure was patterned after Kofsky (1966).

Modified Sociogram/The sociometric choice task was patterned after McCandless (1957). However, certain modifications were made to the sociogram, but without violating the basic principles advanced by McCandless. (Details of the scoring techniques in respect to conservation, classification and the socio-metric choice tasks are described by Rardin and Moan, 1971, pp.1690-1.)

RESULTS/Overall, the results demonstrated that peer relations develop parallel to the development of physical concepts. Cognitive and social skills indicated progressive gains from kindergarten through to third grade. Furthermore, that a child's cognitive development would be affected by the quality of his peer relations (popularity) was shown to be closely related to social development. However, such relations to physical concept development were 'relatively minor'.

Finally, Rardin and Moan conclude: 'In the area of child development, there does appear to be a qualitative change at the second grade . . . in cognitive processes. This change demonstrates many of the qualities which Piaget described as grouping of structure . . . In the area of education . . . the best way to learn awareness of others is by having active exposure with them . . . highly structured, noninteractive classes during early ages would appear to discourage this type of growth . . . in the area of psychotherapy, it would appear that group therapy before age six would have few, if any, therapeutic advantages.'

Acquisition of conservation through social interaction
F. Murray, 1972

Murray contended that the young child's ability to advance conservation judgements together with logical justifications might improve when he was subjected to contrary arguments and viewpoints of other children.

SUBJECTS/Experiment One/The sample of 57 white children comprised 28 boys and 29 girls from a Minneapolis elementary school (mean age six years seven months).

Experiment Two/Twenty-eight boys and 23 girls were involved. The 51 white children in the sample were drawn from a parochial elementary school in Delaware (mean age six years seven months).

METHOD/In the first of three sessions of both experiments, Form A of the Concept Assessment Kit-Conservation was administered to all subjects (Goldschmid and Bentler, 1968b). The Kit consists of six conservation tasks: two-dimensional space, number, substance, continuous quantity, weight and discontinuous quantity. (Fuller details of the general experimental procedure including the scoring techniques, may be found in Goldschmid and Bentler, 1968b.)

In a second session the problems of Form A were administered again. 'In each group, subjects were told that they could not receive a score until all of them agreed on the answer to each problem. Subjects were given five minutes to solve each problem. The experimenter started with the lowest scorers on Form A, and asked each child in a group to answer a problem, and when there was disagreement between children, they were directed to discuss the problem, and explain to each other why they had said what they had. Subjects were allowed to manipulate the conservation stimuli, but the experimenter gave no information or reinforcement for correct or incorrect answers.'

Seven days after the group discussion and interaction, each child was seen again on problems from Form B, Form C and Form A respectively from the conservation Kit. (Fuller details of all Forms are described elsewhere: Goldschmid and Bentler, 1968b.)

RESULTS/Evidence produced demonstrated the facilitative value of social conflict (interaction) in cognitive acquisition, for both groups of children performing at the low and high levels of conservation performance. Murray further argues that 'performance on Post-tests A, B and C was significantly higher than that of the standardized children on these tests, and indicates that the training effect cannot be attributed to retesting or maturation effects, although the effects may have been due to modelling and not the communication interaction'.

Furthermore, the effectiveness of social interaction in conservation gains added credibility owing to the absence of organized instructional effort. The results of Murray's study differ, at least in part, from those reported by Brison (1966).

Finally, Murray cites the work of Smedslund (1966) who reported that 'the occurrence of communication conflicts is a necessary condition for intellectual decentration', and suggests that the interaction of an individual with his peers is more relevant to cognitive organization than the interaction between the individual and his physical environment. 'The present data support his hypothesis and emphasize, as Piaget has (Sigel, 1969), the educational role of social interaction in the transition from egocentrism to operational thought.'

[1] Immediately prior to publication, 1974, personal communication with Pimm revealed further activity in this research area. Pimm reviews cognitive/psychoanalytic reconciliation attempts, namely Anthony (1956), Wolff (1960)and Piaget (1972), together with studies comparing the performance of 'emotionally disturbed' children with 'normal' children on conservation tasks, (Goldschmid and Bentler, 1968; Lerner, Bie and Lehrer, 1972), classification tasks (Howell, 1972), perspective tasks (Anthony, 1966; Cowan, 1966 and Neale, 1966) and a Piagetian battery of nine tasks (Dudek, 1972). Further, investigations into the effects of anxiety (Goldschmid, 1968), a 'social order' Modgil, 1969) and egocentrism (Rubin, 1973). Pimm's investigation incorporated 'emotionally disturbed' children from special classes, those assessed as 'disturbed' and 'normals'. Three analyses compared the various performances of the subjects on tasks included in the Goldschmid and Bentler Concept Assessment Kit (1968b) together with the effects of training. The 'emotionally disturbed' children in all studies were less able than 'normals' to conserve and were considered to be more egocentric. Pimm concludes that the results provide support for Piaget's contention that cognitive and affective development occur simultaneously. Currently Pimm using an extensive battery of Piagetian tasks is attempting to identify the specific tasks which reveal depressed performances in 'emotionally disturbed' children as compared with 'normals'. Further, 'to explore possible antecedent variables in an effort to understand what developmental experiences are important to adequate emotional and cognitive development'.

[2] Based on a series of lectures delivered by Piaget at the Sorbonne in 1954.

CHAPTER TWELVE
TEST DEVELOPMENT

Pinard and Laurendeau's (1964) longitudinal project with a group of 700 French-Canadian subjects has two main objectives: to verify the existence of Piaget's stages of mental development, and to construct an ordinal scale of mental development applicable to children aged two to 12 years. A total of 57 sub-tests together with some 300 behavioural items, designed to elicit mental strategies, are included. The sub-tests comprise 24 tests of sensori-motor coordination, eight tests of verbal comprehension and 25 Piagetian tasks. Interim results confirm the existence of Piaget's stages. 'However, in certain cases it may well be necessary to eliminate certain levels which the test fails to justify, or perhaps more frequently, to add new ones in order to take into account some totally new answers which apparently cannot be integrated with Piaget's established stages, and which seem authentically to characterize new levels of development.' It is interesting to note that the various developmental stages are generally acquired at slightly later ages by French-Canadian children than by the Swiss children. (More recently, Dudek et al. 1969, administered nine tests from the battery devised by Pinard and Laurendeau in their investigation into the relationship of Piaget measures to standard intelligence and motor skills. The tests were found to be equally effective in predicting achievement in young children.)

Tuddenham (1968) is engaged in developing a cognitive scale based on Piaget's theoretical formulations. To date, they have made extensive explorations of 15 items on a sample of 350 children of Junior school age range with a wide spectrum of socio-economic levels. Piagetian concepts of quantity, area, number, length, spatial reversals, classification and the transitivity-of-length problem, as studied by Smedslund (1963) are included. Situations in which the child's reasoning may be inferred from what he does rather than from what he says are being established. Some attempt is also being made to develop easier methods of test administration and scoring. Some built-in checks upon the child's understanding of the relational terms 'more', 'less', 'the same', 'longer', 'shorter' are also being examined.

Tuddenham's provisional results indicate that it is possible to categorize children's behaviour patterns into the three Piagetian stages. Their data show some superiority of boys over girls, especially on transitivity, perspectives and most of the conservation items. Race and socio-economic status were correlated and Negroes did less well than Whites on every test and on certain tests, the difference is significant at the .01 level. The results also showed intercorrelations between items which, to date, are available only for the sample of 200 children. Although occasional values are as high as .4 and some conservation items intercorrelate .65, the values are generally around .25. 'Data strongly suggest that the attainment of concrete operations on one problem is no guarantee that the child will achieve a comparable level when another problem is posed.'

Tuddenham has partially succeeded in producing a standardized format. However, he states 'I must confess as a differential psychologist, that I am pleased rather than dismayed that the intractable individuality of human beings, which has plagued normative psychologists since Bessel tried to eliminate individual differences in reaction time, continues to assert itself, even in the face of Piaget's elegant normative theory' (Tuddenham, 1969, cited in Dockerll (Ed.) 1970p. 70).

The British Intelligence Scale (Warburton, cited in Dockrill (Ed.) 1970) hopes eventually to cover the age-range from two to 18 years. The Scale hopes to gather 12 sub-scales, giving scores for specialized abilities as follows:

    (i) R (Reasoning);
    (ii) V (Verbal);
    (iii) S (Spatial);
    (iv) N (Number);
    (v) M (Memory);
    (vi) F (Fluency).

The combined scores will provide an index of general mental ability.

Within each sub-scale there will be 25 items. The test will normally take 45 minutes to one hour to administer. Several of the Scales contain items based on the work of Piaget and others on the development of children's thinking. It will be possible to obtain scores showing the qualitative level of thinking, e.g. pre-logical concrete and propositional.

'The Concept Assessment Kit — Conservation' developed by Goldschmid and Bentler (1968b) was based on Piaget's systematic developmental theory of cognitive structure depicting a stage-by-stage progress of a child's thinking. The Kit measures the concept of conservation and is designed for administration with pre-school and early school-age children. The purpose of the Concept Assessment Kit is to provide a brief and practical assessment of a child's comprehension to the principle of conservation. The Kit consists of three Forms: A, B and C. Forms A and B are parallel forms including tasks measuring conservation of two-dimensional space, number, substance, quantity and weight and discontinuous quantity. Form C measures a slightly different dimension of conservation including conservation of area and length. These assessments could be employed in the classroom situation. The authors describe their scales as 'measures of a general concept of conservation – like a general factor of factor analysis'; and provide strong psychometric evidence to support their interpretation. The Conservation Assessment Kit is already receiving attention and has been administered in the investigations by Wasik and Wasik (1971) and Harasym, Boersma and Maguire (1971), both described in Chapter Three. Figurelli and Keller (1972 p.296) report: 'It should be noted that all mean scores, with the exception of the post-test scores for the middle-class trained group, were somewhat lower than those found in the preliminary norms of the Concept Assessment Kit – Conservation.' However, Fleck (1972) reports encouraging evidence in support of the Kit in an investigation of the relationship of field-independence – dependence and verbal mediation – nonmediation to Piagetian conservation behaviour. Likewise, Goldschmid, Bentler, Kohnstamm, Modgil et al. (1973) administered the Conservation Assessment Kit (Scale A) to 25 boys and 25 girls at each age level from four to eight, comprising a total sample of 250 children in each of eight countries. The Concept Assessment Kit appeared to be a reliable indicator of conservation across several cultural groups. (Details of the study appear in Chapter Eight.)

The aim of the Social Science Research Council Project (1971): 'The Development of Systematic Thinking' under the guidance of Lunzer at Nottingham University is to 'establish a firm body of data on how children progress from intuitive reasoning to systematic thought. One side of the work involves administering a fairly extensive number of individual tests to children at two ages, five and seven to eight. The results of these tests of logical thinking will be compared with various measures of scholastic performance. Particular attention will be paid to the effect of home and school environment, as well as the factor of language development.' A longitudinal follow-up is envisaged to measure the environmental effects on subsequent development. Furthermore, the results, 'should help to clarify the educational significance of laboratory studies on concept development and logical thought'. It is hoped that the data might assist in the construction of a standardized battery of Piagetian tests to assess the development of effective intelligence.

Yates and Richardson (1970) are engaged in an attempt to apply Piaget's theory of cognitive development to the assessment and training of children in a special care unit. The authors have drawn from the work of Woodward (1959, 1961, 1963) towards the construction of simple tests of sensori-motor intelligence 'that would allow a differential profile of cognitive abilities to be projected. The procedures are a mixture of structured tests and observations concerned with the development of operational intelligence, circular reactions, the construction of space and causality'. At present they are mainly concerned with a normal developmental age of about two years. The authors hope eventually to produce a complete developmental scale up to six years of age.

Tanaka, Campbell and Helmick (1966) are intent to develop a series of paper-and-pencil Piaget-oriented tasks. These are designed to give infant school teachers an estimate of a child's cognitive performance at the time of school entrance. Six areas were chosen: Shapes and Forms; Spatial Relations; Time Concepts; Communications Skills; Mathematical Understanding and Logical Reasoning. Each set of 'exercises' was administered to groups of 100 to 200 children. Pilot trials have been reported as being satisfactory and the final outcome is awaited with interest.

The Nuffield Foundation (1968) have devised 'Check Ups' based on Piaget research, the aim of which is stated as '. . . to try and show that children acquire concepts gradually and to point the difficulties that they are likely to encounter during their progress'. The Foundation maintain that the 'Check Ups' are not tests and that 'there is no question of 'right' or 'wrong' or marking. They are simply to be given to the children as and when the teacher feels the need to know how far their thinking has progressed.'

Burgess (1969) designed a group test for secondary school pupils to test their abilities to solve a problem, recognize the structure of the problem and extract relevant information in order to solve problems. Information was obtained with respect 'to the development of the schemata of inclusion and combination and on the relative complexity of abstract and concrete material'. (Details are given later in this chapter.)

Tisher (1971) devised a pencil-and-paper questionnaire based on Inhelder and Piaget's (1958) tasks designed to assess the development of formal operations, with a group of Australian subjects aged t12 to 16 years four months. In a comparison with the Piagetian conservation — interview method — there was 'a 77 per cent agreement in classification between the interview and questionnaire techniques'. Field and Cropley (1969) employed the Tisher questionnaire (unpub. 1962) in their investigation into cognitive style and science achievement and found a highly significant relationship between 'operations, classifications and level of science achievement'. The Australian Science Education Project has employed the Tisher questionnaire with encouraging results. (Private communication, 1973). Further use of the measure is being made on a sample of British children (Scaplehorn 1971). (See Chapter Five for the Tisher study.)

Bart (1972) (discussed more appropriately in Chapter Five) as a result of his construction and validation of a paper-and-pencil formal operational test considers that these, 'could be employed by educators to select students who are capable of abstract conceptualization and theoretically might profit from a curriculum emphasizing symbolic and verbal instruction and an abstract mode of learning' (p.663).

Kaufman (1971) maintains 'Analysis of the tasks used in Piaget's and Gesell's experiments provides one tangible method of learning more about their over-all systems — the interactionist theory of Piaget and the maturationist viewpoint of Gesell. A comparison of the inter-relationships among their independently conceived tasks, and an evaluation of the relationships of these tasks to other pertinent variables, might tell much about the psychological meaning of the tasks themselves and, hence, about the theories in which these tasks are rooted'. The data gathered were subjected to a correlation analysis with the following results: the Piaget test and the Gesell school readiness tests correlated fairly well with Lorge-Thorndike mental age and IQ, teething level, chronological age, and Warner's revised scale of Father's occupations. (Details of the study appear later in this chapter.) In continuation, Kaufman and Kaufman (1972) attempted to compare the effectiveness of tests derived from the Gesell and Piagetian tasks as predictors of First-grade achievement.

Inhelder (Sigel and Hooper, 1968) recently noted that 'the relationships between different tasks and substructures apparently requiring the same mental structures is still far from adequately explored' . . . (p. vii). Stephens, McLaughlin, Miller and Glass (1972) were intent to determine relationships which existed among 27 Piagetian variables and standard measures of intelligence and achievement. The data were taken from the first phase of the author's eight-year longitudinal study (still in progress) of the development of reasoning in normals and retardates. The data gathered were subjected to factor analytic techniques in order to determine relationships among the scores for the 150 subjects on 27 Piagetian reasoning variables and subscores from the Wide Range Achievement Test and the Wechsler Intelligence Scales, MA and CA. The author's report: 'Review of the factor matrix indicated that Piagetian reasoning tasks involve abilities separate from those measured by standard tests of intelligence and achievement.' (The longitudinal study is described in Chapter Seven and the details of the factor analytic study, later in this chapter.)

Vinh-Bang, in collaboration with Inhelder (1962), has arranged and determined a sequence of experiments and provisional percentages passing for various ages. 'It goes without saying that results obtained by such a flexible procedure do not lend themselves to statistical treatment. Because of this we have undertaken, with Vinh-Bang, the standardization of some of our procedures, adapting them to the diagnosis of the reasoning process. When we have once explored the whole range of reasoning exhibited by children of different ages, we then standardize the procedures of investigation.'

Alternate paths: an inquiry into the development of adult reasoning
J. W. Burgess, 1969

AIM/The aim of this investigation was to consider the data processing mechanism, considered a necessary part of structural change in the Piagetian sense. Such change is thought to be the result of the organism's attempt to adapt inadequate schemata in response to the external pull of the environment, and as a result of this adaptation new schemata develop.

METHOD/The method was to limit the inquiry to a systematic study of two kinds of cognitive activity, which Piaget claims to be characteristic of distinct developmental stages, namely the ability to conceptualize the relationship between a subcategory and the major category of which it is a part, known as 'inclusion', for the concrete stage; and operations based on combinatorial schemata for the formal stage. A group test was devised, which included abstract and concrete material. The test was designed to study three types of behaviour: the ability to solve a problem; the ability to recognize the structure of the problem, as indicated by being able to construct an item of the same type; and the ability to recognize what information was relevant to its solution. This test was given to 330 secondary school children.

RESULTS/The results give information on the development of the schemata of inclusion and combination, on the relative complexity of abstract and concrete material, and on the relative difficulty of the three tasks. The three types of behaviour were seen to be related and to affect one another. A group test, with some reservations, appeared to be a practicable method of gaining such information.

Three results which might be worthy of further investigation were the finding that this mechanism has the appearance of a balance similar to Festinger's model, in that there appeared to be an interaction between cognitive elements which resulted in the organism adapting its behaviour as if to balance incongruous cognitive elements; that production can result from a limited comprehension; and the limited extent to which formal thinking can be considered characteristic of the average adult.

Piaget and Gesell: a psychometric analysis of tests built from their tasks
A. Kaufman, 1971

AIMS/Kaufman was interested in the following issues: (a) the Psychometric properties of the Gesell School Readiness Tests and Piagetian tasks; (b) the relationship of the Gesell and Piagetian Battery to intelligence, teething level and to each other; and (c) the factor structures of the Piaget Battery and the Gesell School Readiness Tests.

SUBJECTS/A total sample of 103 Caucasian kindergarten children (59 girls and 44 boys) from New York was involved in the study, with a CA range from 60 to 74 months (mean age 66.6 months), and an IQ range from 75 to 145 (Lorge-Thorndike Intelligence Test). Mean IQ was 107.6. Subjects came from 'about-average' socio-economic environments (Warner, Meeker and Eells, 1960).

METHOD/Lorge-Thorndike Intelligence Test/The test purports to measure abstract thinking and consists of oral vocabulary, pictorial classification and pictorial pairing.

Gesell School Readiness Tests/This test (GSRT) has been fully described elsewhere (Ilg and Ames, 1965; and Kaufman, 1971).

Teething Level/Kaufman argues: 'A measure of teething level is the one physiological index obtained routinely when the GSRT is used to help determine school readiness.' Fuller details appear in Kaufman (1971, p. 1346) and Ames (1967, p. 53).

Piaget Battery/The tests were in the areas of number (based on Piaget 1952b), logic (Inhelder and Piaget 1964), geometry (Piaget, Inhelder and Szeminska 1960) and space (Piaget and

Inhelder 1956). Additional information on these tests was also drawn from the work of Almy, Chittenden and Miller (1966), Dodwell (1963), Elkind (1964) and Kofsky (1966). Other details, including scoring techniques, are described by Kaufman 1971, pp. 1349-50.

RESULTS/Girls performed at a higher level of operativity than boys on both the Piagetian Battery (PB) and Gesell School Readiness Test (GSRT). However, no sex differences were noted on any of the other variables.

Correlates of Piaget and Gesell Batteries
A high relationship between the two batteries was computed. The correlation between PB and GSRT total scores was .64. Furthermore, advanced teething was not associated with high scores on either PB or GSRT.

Moreover, almost identical correlations among the total scores of the PB, GSRT, and L-T (Lorge-Thorndike Intelligence Test), together with the reliability coefficients of each, were observed.

Factor Analysis of Piaget and Gesell Batteries
Three main factors were extracted. These were as follows:
(a) Number. Numeration, addition and subtraction, together with the two conservation of number tasks had the highest loadings on this factor.
(b) Logic. This factor included tasks based on seriation and classification, and all these tasks had meaningful loadings and are basic to cognitive organization.
(c) Cognition of size relationships. Insertion, seriation and length all had meaningful loadings (approaching .60 on this factor). The tasks deal with the conceptual understanding of size relationships.
'Essentially, the Piagetian factors were, in order, "number", "classes" and "relations". These three concepts, or operations, were developed as a trilogy by Piaget (1952) . . . the psychological as well as the logical, constitution of classes, relations, and numbers in a single development, whose respective changes are synchronic and interdependent' (p. 157) . . . 'the three Piagetian factors seem to correspond to three fundamental logico-mathematical operations that develop between the sensori-motor and concrete operational stages. To Piaget (Flavell, 1963), "Logico-mathematical structures . . . are conceived as models of cognitive structure", p. 169 . . . the resulting factors offer support not only to the existence of his three hypothesized operations, but also the structural basis of his theory of the development of intelligence.'

389

Kaufman finally concludes: 'To Piagetians, the separate PB and L-T factors suggest that the ability to think logically in a Piaget-type experimental situation is at least somewhat distinct from the ability to score high on conventional, empirically derived, intelligence tests . . . since Piaget's tasks and Gesell's tasks are developmental in nature, it certainly would make sense to evaluate the psychometric properties of these tests, their interrelationships and their relationships to other variables across a wider age span.'

Factorial structure of selected psycho-educational measures and Piagetian reasoning assessments
B. Stephens, J. McLaughlin, C. Miller and G. Glass, 1972

AIM/The authors attempted to establish relationships which might exist among 27 Piagetian assessments and standard measures of intelligence and achievement (based on the 1969 data).

SUBJECTS/The total sample of 150 children comprised 75 mentally retarded male and female subjects (IQ 50 − 75, WISC, or WAIS); and 75 normal male and female subjects (IQ 90 − 110, WISC or WAIS). The mean IQ for the retarded subjects was 66.2 and for the normals 100.5. The CA for all subjects ranged from six to 18 years and they were drawn from the Philadelphia area of upper-low to lower-middle class background.

METHOD A/The Reasoning Assessments included nine Piagetian conservation tasks, six classification tasks, four tasks designed to assess the relations between operativity and symbolic imagery and one formal operation measure. (Fuller details of these are described in Stephens, McLaughlin, Miller and Glass, 1972.)

B/Standard Measures of Intelligence, Achievement and Social Status
(a) Wechsler Intelligence Scale for Children (WISC);
(b) Wechsler Intelligence Scale for Adults (WAIS);
(c) Wide Range Achievement Test (Reading, Spelling, Arithmetic);
(d) Social Status (Warner's Index of Social Characteristics).

RESULTS AND DISCUSSION/Five main factors were identified. (Fuller details of these factors have been assembled in Tables 2 and 3, pages 346-7).
Evidence suggested that Piagetian operativity measured performance different from that measured by the WISC and WAIS

and the wide range Achievement Test. The authors summarize the main results as follows: 'Factor 1 is defined by major loadings from 13 Wechsler and 3 Wide Range Achievement Test variables. Only one Piagetian measure is represented by a loading of .25 or above. Only two of the factor's intercorrelations with other factors were above .25; these were .37 with Factor 2, a factor which also had loadings from CA as well as rotation of beads, and .25 with Factor 3, a factor defined by loadings from categorical sorting tasks. Factor 2, an operational thought factor reveals positive loadings from both CA and MA which serve to indicate developmental influences. Loadings of .25 or above were obtained from 23 Piagetian Tasks.[1] The factor inter correlated .38 with Factor 3, a factor defined by Piagetian measures of classificatory thought, and .39 with Factor 4 . . . defined by Piagetian measures of spatial operations.'

'When a task involving hierarchical class inclusion defined a separate factor, Factor 3, a basis was provided for Piaget's distinction between abilities in categorization, conservation, and spatial orientation. The factor had intercorrelations of .38 and .39 with the other two factors representative of 'thought in action'. The fact that factor 4 also had loadings from CA and MA serves to underscore the possible influence of maturation on the ability to anticipate the positions of objects as they are rotated in space . . . a separate Wechsler visual perceptual synthesis factor, Factor 5, had a low intercorrelation, .04, with Factor 1, which also was defined by loadings from Wechsler scales. Both perceptual organization and/or performance as measured by the Wechsler scales also had low intercorrelations with Piagetian measures; the highest intercorrelation, .19 was with Factor 2, an operational thought factor.'

[1] Berzonsky (1971) argues, in relation to Stephens et al. (1969 study, described more appropriately in Chapter Seven): 'The 150 subjects used in the study, however, were selected from a wide age range six to 18 years, which might have increased the intertask correlation due to general improvement with age.'

POSTSCRIPT

Research evidence has shown that the theory, initiated and so energetically pursued throughout many years by Piaget, has yet to reach fulfilment. Hunt's (1969) reflection is still more than relevant:

'Piaget's stature as the giant of developmental psychology, then, resides less in what he has completed, much as it is, than in the many beginnings his many observations and his theoretical interpretations provide'.

This book bears witness to the involvement and industry of hundreds of investigators anxious to elucidate this intriguing research into human development. Brief references have been included to research findings reported just before going to press: undoubtedly, further material will continue to be produced, and the publication of a follow-up volume will not be inappropriate. Accordingly, the author would like to invite readers who are engaged in Piagetian research to contribute abstracts of their investigations for possible inclusion in any sequel. The format of the abstracts should be similar to those reported in the present volume.

S. Modgil

ABBREVIATIONS USED IN THE BIBLIOGRAPHY

Acta Psychol. — Acta Psychologica (Holland)

Alberta J. Ed. Res. — Alberta Journal of Educational Research

Am. Ed. Res. Assoc. — American Educational Research Association

Am. J. Ment. Def. — American Journal of Mental Deficiency

Am. J. Orthopsych. — American Journal of Orthopsychiatry

Am J. Soc. — American Journal of Sociology

Am. Psych. — American Psychologist

Am. Psych. Assoc. — American Psychological Association

Am. Soc. Rev. — American Sociological Review

Ann. Rev. Psych. — Annual Review of Psychology

Arch. Dis. Child. — Archives of the Diseases of Childhood (UK)

Aust. J. Psych. — Australian Journal of Psychology

Aust. J. Soc. Issues — Australian Journal of Social Issues

Brit. J. Clin. & Soc. Psych. — British Journal of Clinical and Social Psychology

Brit. J. Ed. Psych. — British Journal of Educational Psychology

Brit. J. Psych. — British Journal of Psychology

Brit. J. Stat. Psych. — British Journal of Statistical Psychology

Brit. J. Psych. Stat. — British Journal of Psychology — Statistical Section

Brit. J. Soc. — British Journal of Sociology

Brit. Med. Bull. — British Medical Bulletin

Brit. J. Med. Psych. — British Journal of Medical Psychology

Bull. Danish Inst. for Ed. Res. — Bulletin of the Danish Institute for Educational Research

Calif. J. Ed. Res.	— Californian Journal of Educational Research
Can. Educ. Res. Dig.	— Canadian Educational and Research Digest
Can. J. Psych.	— Canadian Journal of Psychology
Child. Developm.	— Child Development (USA)
Childhood Psych.	— Childhood Psychology (UK)
Comtemp. Psych.	— Contemporary Psychology (USA)
Dev. Psych.	— Developmental Psychology (USA)
Diss. Abstr.	— Dissertation Abstracts (USA)
Educ. & Psych. Measmt.	— Educational and Psychological Measurement (USA)
Ed. Res.	— Educational Research (UK)
Ed. Rev.	— Educational Review (UK)
El. Sch. J.	— Elementary School Journal (USA)
Eug. Rev.	— Eugenics Review (UK)
Gen. Psych. Mon.	— Genetic Psychological Monographs (USA)
Harv. Ed. Rev.	— Harvard Educational Review
Human Developm.	— Human Development (Switzerland)
Inst. Child Welf. Monogr.	— Institute of Child Welfare Monographs
Int. J. Psych.	— International Journal of Psychology (France)
Int. Rev. Educ.	— International Review of Education (Germany)
Int. Soc. Sci. Bull.	— International Social Science Bulletin (France)
Jap. J. Ed. Psych.	— Japanese Journal of Educational Psychology
Jap. Psych. Res.	— Japanese Psychological Research
J. Abnorm. Soc. Psych.	— Journal of Abnormal and Social Psychology (USA)
J. Am. Stat. Assoc.	— Journal of American Statistical Association
J. App. Psych.	— Journal of Applied Psychology (USA)
J. Ed. Psych.	— Journal of Educational Psychology (USA)
J. Child Psych. Psychiatr.	— Journal of Child Psychology and Psychiatry

J. Clin. Psych.	— Journal of Clinical Psychology (USA)
J. Consult. Psych.	— Journal of Consultant Psychology (USA)
J. Cross. Cult. Psych.	— Journal of Cross-Cultural Psychology (USA)
J. Ed. Res.	— Journal of Educational Research (USA)
J. Ed. Stud.	— Journal of Educational Studies (USA)
J. Exp. Child Psych.	— Journal of Experimental Child Psychology (USA)
J. Gen. Psych.	— Journal of Genetic Psychology (USA)
J. Home Econ.	— Journal of Home Economics
J. Ment. Sub.	— Journal of Mental Subnormality
J. Negro Ed.	— Journal of Negro Education (USA)
J. Pers.	— Journal of Personality (USA)
J. Pers. Soc. Psych.	— Journal of Personality and Social Psychology (USA)
J. Pers. Assessm.	— Journal of Personality Assessment (USA)
J. Psych.	— Journal of Psychology (USA)
J. Res. Sci. Teach.	— Journal of Research in Science Teaching (USA)
J. Soc. Iss.	— Journal of Social Issues (USA)
J. Soc. Psych.	— Journal of Social Psychology (USA)
J. Soc. Res.	— Journal of Social Research
J. Spec. Ed.	— Journal of Special Education (USA)
J. Teach. Ed.	— Journal of Teacher Education (USA)
J. Verb. Learn. Verb. Behv.	— Journal of Verbal Learning and Verbal Behaviour (UK/USA)
Math. Teach.	— Mathematics Teacher (USA)
Merr.-Palm. Quart.	— Merrill-Palmer Quarterly (USA)
Mon. Soc. Res. Child. Dev.	— Monographs of the Society for Research in Child Development (USA)
Ped. Sem.	— Pedagocial Seminary
Percep. Mot. Skills	Perceptual and Motor Skills
Psych. Bull.	— Psychological Bulletin (USA)
Psych. Iss.	— Psychological Issues
Psych. Mon.	— Psychological Monographs (USA)
Psych. Mon. Gen. & Appl.	— Psychological Monographs: General and Applied (USA)

Psych. Rep.	— Psychological Reports (USA)
Psych. Rev.	— Psychological Review (USA)
Psych. Sci.	— Psychological Science (USA)
Publ. Opin. Quart.	— Public Opinion Quarterly (USA)
Quart. J. Exp. Psych.	— Quarterly Journal of Experimental Psychology (UK/USA)
R. belge de Ps. Ped	— Revue belge de psychologie et de pédagogie (Belgium)
Rev. Suisse Psych.	— Revue Suisse de psychologie (Switzerland)
Scan. J. Psych.	— Scandinavian Journal of Psychology
Sci. Ed.	— Science Education (USA)
Scot. Ed. Stud.	— Scottish Educational Studies
Soc. Psychi.	— Social Psychiatry
Teach. Coll. Contr. Ed.	— Teachers' College Contributions to Education (USA)
Times Ed. Supp.	— Times Educational Supplement
Train. Sch. Bull.	— Training School Bulletin
WHO Mon.	— World Health Organization Monographs
Wiener Arb. z. pad. Psychol.	— Wiener Arbeiten zur pädagogischen Psychologie (Austria)
Zeitschr. f. ang. Psychol.	— Zeitschrift für angewandte Psychologie und Charakterkunde (Germany)
Zeitschr. f. pad. Psychol.	— Zeitschrift für pädagogische Psychologie und Fugendkunde (Germany)

BIBLIOGRAPHY

ABEL, T. (1941) 'Moral judgements among subnormals', J. Abnorm. Soc. Psych., 36, 378-92.

ABRAVANEL, E. (1968) 'The development of intersensory patterning with regard to selected spatial dimensions', Mon. Soc. Res. Child Developm., 33 (2, Serial No. 118)

ACHENBACH, T. M. (1969) 'Conservation of illusion — distorted identity: its relation to MA and CA in normals and retardates', Child Developm., 40, 3, 950-6.

ACHENBACH, T. M. (1969) 'Conservation, below age three: fact or artifact?' Proceedings of the 77th Annual Convention of the Amerc. Psych. Ass., 4, 275-6.

ACHENBACH, T. and ZIGLER, E. (1968) 'Cue-learning and problem-learning strategies in normals and retardates', Child Developm., 39, 827-48.

ACKER, N. (1968) 'Conservation and co-ordination of relations in Piaget's liquid quantity problem', Predoctoral Thesis, Inst. of Child Development. Minnesota University.

ADLER, M. J. (1964) 'Some implications of the theories of Jean Piaget and J. S. Bruner for Education', Canadian Educ. and Res. Digest, 4, 291-305.

AEBLI, H. (1951) 'Didactique Psychologique: Application à la Didactique de la Psychologie de Jean Piaget'. Neuchatel: Delachaux et Niestlé.

AEBLI, H. (1970) 'Piaget and beyond', Interchange: J. Educational Studies. Published by the Ontario Institute for Studies in Education, 1, 1, 12-24.

AHR, P. R. and YOUNISS, J. (1970) 'Reasons for failure on the class inclusion problem', Child Developm., 41, 131-43.

AINSWORTH, M. D. S. and BELL, S. M. (1970) 'Attachment, exploration and separation: illustrated by the behaviour of one-year-olds in a strange situation', Child Developm., 41, 49-67.

AINSWORTH, M. D. S. and WITTIG, B. (1969) 'Attachment and exploratory behaviour of one-year-olds in a strange situation', in FOSS, B. (Ed.) 'Determinants of Infant Behaviour', IV. London: Methuen, 111-36.

AKUTAGAWA, D. and BENOIT, P. (1959) 'The effect of age and relative brightness on associative clustering in children', Child Developm., 30, 229-38.

ALLINSMITH, W. (1960) 'The learning of moral standards', in MILLER, D. and SWANSON, G. (Eds.) 'Inner Conflict and Defence'. New York: Holt.

ALMY, M. (1961) 'Wishful thinking about children's thinking', Teachers College Record, 5, 396-408.

ALMY, M. et al. (1966) 'Young Children's Thinking'. Studies of some aspects of Piaget's theory. Teacher's College, Columbia University.

ALMY, M. et al. (1971) 'Logical Thinking in Second Grade'. Teacher's College Press, Columbia University.

ALMY, M., DURITZ, J. L. and WHITE, M. A. (1970) (Eds.) 'The usefulness of Piagetian methods for studying primary school children in Uganda', in 'Studying School Children in Uganda'. New York: Teacher's College Press, Columbia University.

ALSTON, W. P. (1971) Comments on Kohberg's 'From is to ought'. Cited in MISCHEL, T. (Ed.) 'Cognitive Development and Epistemology' London: Academic Press.

ALTEMEYER, R. A., FULTON, D. and BERNEY, K. M. (1969) 'Long-term memory improvement: confirmation of a finding by Piaget', Child Developm., 40, 845-57.

AMERICAN ASSOCIATION for the Advancement of Science, Commission on Science Education. (1964) Newsletter 1, No. I.

ANASTASI, A. (1958) 'Differential Psychology'. 3rd Edn. New York: Macmillan.

ANDERSON, D. R. (1965) 'Can first graders learn an advanced problem-solving skill?' J. Educ. Psych., 56, 283-94.

ANDERSON, D. R. (1967) 'An investigation into the effects of instruction on the development of propositional thinking in children', Dip. Child. Psych., research, Birmingham University.

ANNETT, M. (1959) 'The classification of instances of four common class concepts by children and adults', Brit. J. Educ. Psych., 29, 223-33.

ANTHONY, E. J. (1956) 'Six applications de la théorie génétique de Piaget à la théorie et à la pratique psychodynamique'. Revue Suisse Psychologique, 15, 269-77.

ANTHONY, E. J. (1956) 'The significance of Jean Piaget for child psychiatry', Brit. J. Child Psych., 50, 255-69.

ANTHONY, E. J. (1957) 'The system makers: Piaget and Freud', Brit. J. Med. Psych., 50, 255-69.

ANTHONY, E. J. (1966) 'Piaget et le clinicien'. Thèmes Piagetian et Epistémologie Génétique. Paris

APPEL, K. J. and GRATCH, G. (1969) 'The cue value of objects: Piaget's stages IV and V', paper presented at the meeting of the Soc. for Res. in Child Developm., Santa Monica, California.

ARMSBY, R. E. (1971) 'A re-examination of the development of moral judgements in children', Child Dev., 42, 1241-8.

ARONFREED, J. (1961) 'The nature, variety and social patterning of moral responses to transgression', J. Abnorm. Soc. Psych., 63, 223-40.

ASSO, D. and WYKE, M. (1970) 'Visual discrimination and verbal comprehension of spatial relations by young children', Brit. J. Psych., 61, 1, 99-107.

ATHEY, I. J. and RUBADEAU, D. O. (1970) Educational Implications of Piaget's Theory. USA: Ginn-Blaisdell.

AUSUBEL, D. P. (1965) 'Neobehaviorism and Piaget's views on thought and symbolic functioning', Child Develop., 36, 1029-32.

398

AUSUBEL, D. P. (1965) 'Stages of intellectual development and their implications of early childhood education', in NEUBAUER, P. B. (Ed.), Concepts of development in early childhood education. Springfield, Illinois: Charles C. Thomas, 8-51.

AUSUBEL, D. P. (1968) 'Readings in the Psychology of Cognition'. New York: Holt, Rinehart and Winston.

AUSUBEL, D. P. (1968) 'Educational Psychology — A Cognitive View'. New York: Holt, Rinehart and Winston.

AUSUBEL, D. P. and SCHIFF, H. M. (1954) 'The effect of incidental and experimentally induced experience in the learning of relevant and irrelevant causal relationships by children', J. Gen. Psych., 84, 109-23.

AUSUBEL, D. P., SCHIFF, H. M. and GOLDMAN, M. (1953) 'Qualitative characteristics in the learning process associated with anxiety', J. Abnorm. Soc. Psych., 48, 537-47.

BABSKA, Z. (1965) 'The formation of the conception of identity of visual characteristics of objects seen successively', in MUSSEN, P. H. (Ed.), 'European Research in Cognitive Development'. Monogr. Soc. Res. Child Develop., 1965, Vol. 30, No. 2 (whole No. 100), 112-24.

BAKER, N. E. and SULLIVAN, E. V. (1970) 'The influence of some task variables and of socioeconomic class on the manifestation of conservation of number', J. Gen. Psych., 116, 21-30.

BANDURA, A. and MACDONALD, F. J. (1963) 'Influence of social reinforcement and the behaviour of models in shaping children's moral judgements', J. Abnorm. Soc. Psych., 67, 274-81.

BANKS, S. H. (1958) 'How students in a secondary modern school induce scientific principles from scientific experiments', unpub. PhD thesis, Birmingham University.

BARDECKE, A. (1959) 'The child's appreciation of the relation of part and whole', Psychologie Wychowaucza, 2, 385-99.

BARKER, M. C. (1969) 'An experimental study of the characteristics of logical thinking in children between the ages of 5 and 15', Dip. Ed. Thesis, Bristol University.

BARKER, N. (1967) 'The influence of some task and organismic variables on the manifestation of number', unpub. Master's thesis, University of Toronto.

BARNES, E. (1894) 'Punishment as seen by children', Ped. Sem., 3, 235-45.

BARNES, E. (1902) 'Growth of social judgement', Studies in Education, 2, 203-17.

BART, W. M. (1971) 'The factor structure of formal operations', Brit. J. Ed. Psych., 41, (I), 70-7.

BART, W. M. (1972) 'Construction and validation of formal reasoning instruments', Psychological Reports, 30, 663-70.

BAR-YAM, M. and KOHLBERG, L. (to be published) 'Development of moral judgement in the kibbutz', in KOHLBERG, L. and TURIEL, E. (Eds.) 'Recent Research in Moral Development'.

BAT-HAEE, M. A. and HOSSEINI, A. A. (1971) 'Conservation of quantity attained by Iranian elementary school children in Iran', Psych. Rep., 29, I, 282-8.

BAT-HAEE, M. A., MEHRYER, A. H. and SABHARWAL, V. (1972) 'The correlation between Piaget's conservation of quantity tasks and three measures of intelligence in a select group of children in Iran', J. Psych., 80, 197-201.

BEARD, R. M. (1957) 'An investigation of concept formation among infant school children', unpub. PhD thesis, University of London.

BEARD, R. M. (1960) 'The nature and development of concepts', Ed. Rev. (Birmingham) 13, 12-26.

BEARD, R. M. (1961) 'A study of number concepts in the infants' school.' Pre-publication draft of Report on behalf of ATCDE Math's Sec.

BEARD, R. M. (1962) 'Children's reasoning', Mathematics Teaching, 21, 33-9.

BEARD, R. M. (1963) 'The order of concept development studied in two fields. I. Number concepts in the infants' school', Ed. Rev., 15, 105-17.

BEARD, R. M. (1963-64) 'An investigation into mathematical concepts among Ghanaian children', Teacher Education in New Countries, 3-15 and 132-45.

BEARD, R. M. (1964) 'Further studies in concept development', Ed. Rev., 17, 41-58.

BEARD, R. M. (1969) 'An Outline of Piaget's Developmental Psychology'. London: Routledge & Kegan Paul.

BEAVER, A. P. (1932) 'The initiation of social contacts by pre-school children', Child Developm., Mon., No. 7.

BEILIN, H. (1959) 'Teachers' and clinicians' attitudes towards the behaviour problems of children: a reappraisal', Child Dev., 30, 9-12.

BEILIN, H. (1964) 'Perceptual—cognitive conflict in the development of an invariant area concept', J. Exp. Child Psych., 1, 208-26.

BEILIN, H. (1965) 'Learning and operational convergence in logical thought development', J. Exp. Child Psych., 2, 317-39.

BEILIN, H. (1968) 'Cognitive capacities of young children: A replication', Science, 162, 920-24

BEILIN, H. (1968) 'Stimulus and Cognitive Transformation in Conservation'. Festschrift in Honour of Piaget's 70th Birthday. NY: Oxford University Press.

BEILIN, H. (1969) Cited in 'The Role of Experience in the Rate and Sequence of Cognitive development', by M. L. Goldschmid. (Invited paper given at the Conference on Ordinal Scales of Cognitive Development, Monterey, California.)

BEILIN, H. (1971) 'On the development of physical concepts', in MISCHEL, T. (Ed.) 'Genetic Psychology and Epistemology'. New York: Academic Press.

BEILIN, H. and FRANKLIN, I. (1962) 'Logical operations in length and area measurement: age and training effects', Paper read at Soc. Res. Child Development. Pennsylvania State University.

BEILIN, H. and KAGAN, J. (1969) 'Pluralization rules and the conceptualization of number', Dev. Psych., I, 6, Am. Psychol. Assoc., Inc.

BEILIN, H., KAGAN, J. and RABINOWITZ, R. (1966) 'Effects of verbal and perceptual training on water level representation', Child Developm., 37, No. 2, 317-29.

BELL, S. M. (1968) 'The relationship of infant-mother attachment to the development of the concept of object-permanence', unpub. PhD thesis, Johns Hopkins University.

BELL, S. M. (1970) 'The development of the concept of object as related to infant-mother attachment', Child Developm., 41, 241-311.

BENE, E. (1957) 'The objective use of the projective technique, illustrated by a study of the difference in attitudes between pupils of grammar school and of secondary modern schools', Brit. J. Ed. Psych., 27, 89-100.

BENNETT, P. and MacKENZIE, E. (1969) 'Training procedures for conservation of number and length', MA thesis, Sussex University.

BENTLER, P. M. (1966) 'Multidimensional Homogeneity Scaling'. Paper presented at special meeting Psychometric Society, Chicago.

BEREITER, C. (1966) 'Contributions of psychology to pre-school education — suggestions for training', paper presented at the conference in Pre-school Education. (The Ontario Institute for Studies in Education, Toronto.)

BEREITER, C. (1970) 'Educational implications of Kohlberg's cognitive developmental view', Interchange, I, I, 25-33.

BEREITER, C. and ENGLEMANN, S. (1966) 'Teaching Disadvantaged Children in the Pre-school'. Englewood Cliffs, NJ: Prentice Hall.

BERG, T. J. C. and VAN DER WERF, D. (1966) 'A preliminary communication on experiences with a Dutch translation of the ESPQ'. Mimeo-graphed report from Int. for Child Therapy of the City of Amsterdam, Holland.

BERLYNE, D. E. (1957) 'Recent developments in Piaget's work', Brit. J. Educ. Psych., 27, 1-12.

BERLYNE, D. E. (1960) 'Conflict, Arousal and curiosity'. New York: McGraw-Hill.

BERLYNE, D. E. (1962) 'Comments on relations between Piaget's theory and S-R theory', in KESSEN and KUHLMAN (Eds.) 'Thought in the Young Child', Monogs. Soc. Res. in Child Developm., Serial No. 83, Vol. 27, No. 2, Yellow Springs, Ohio: The Antioch Press.

BERLYNE, D. E. (1965) 'Structure and Direction in Thinking'. New York: McGraw-Hill.

BERMAN, I. (1964) 'Wechsler scores vs. Piaget levels: A study of the cognitive efficiency of institutionalized retardates', Diss. Abstr., 25 (3), 2040.

BERNSTEIN, B. (1961) 'Social class and linguistic development: a theory of social learning', in HALSEY, A. H. FLOUD, J. and ANDERSON, C. A. (Eds.) 'Education, Economy and Society'. New York: Free Press.

BERRY, J. W. (1966) 'Temne and Eskimo perceptual skills', Int. J. Psych., I 207-29.

BERRY, J. W. (1969) 'On cross-cultural comparability', Int. J. Psych., 4, 119-28.

BERZONSKY, M. D. (1969) 'Factors influencing children's causal reasoning', unpub. PhD thesis, Toronto University.

BERZONSKY, M. D. (1971a) 'The role of familiarity in children's explanations of physical causality', Child Developm., 42, 705-15.

BERZONSKY, M. D. (1971) 'The interdependence of Inhelder and Piaget's model of logical thinking', Dev. Psych., 4, 469-76.

BERZONSKY, M. D. (1973) 'Some relationships between children's conceptions of psychological and physical causality', J. Soc. Psych., 90, 299-309.

BEVER, T. G., MEHLER, J. and EPSTEIN, J. (1968) 'What children do in spite of what they know', Science, 162, 921-4.

BIGGS, J. B. (1962) 'Anxiety, Motivation and Primary School Mathematics'. Slough, UK: NFER.

BIGGS, J. B. (1967) 'Mathematics and the Conditions of Learning'. Slough, UK: NFER.

BING, E. (1963) 'Effect of child-rearing practices on development of differential cognitive abilities', Child Developm., 34, (3), 631-48.

BIRAN, L. A. (1968) 'Do plants lose water?' Unpub. programmed learning text, Birmingham University.

BIRNS, B. and GOLDEN, M. (1972) 'Prediction of intellectual performance at three years from infant tests and personality measures', Merr. Palm. Quart., 18, 1, 53-58.

BITTNER, A. C. and SHINEDLING, M. M. (1968) 'A methodological investigation of Piaget's concept of conservation of substance', Gen. Psych. Mon., 77, 135-63.

BLANCHARD, E. B. and PRICE, K. A. (1971) 'A developmental study of cognitive style', Dev. Psych., 5, 2, 344-8.

BLATT, M. (1969) 'The effects of classroom discussion on the development of moral judgement', unpub. Doctoral Dissert., Univ. of Chicago.

BLATT, M. and KOHLBERG, L. (to be published) 'The effects of classroom discussion on the development of moral judgement', in KOHLBERG, L. and TURIEL, E. (Eds.) 'Recent Research in Moral Development'.

BLOOM, L. (1959) 'A reappraisal of Piaget's theory of moral judgement', J. Gen. Psych., 95, 3-12.

BOBROFF, A. (1960) 'The stages of maturation in socialized thinking and in the ego development of two groups of children', Child Developm., 31, 321-38.

BOEHM, L. (1957) 'The development of independence: a comparative study', Child Developm., 28, 85-92.

BOEHM, L. (1962) 'The development of conscience: a comparison of American children of different mental and socio-economic levels', Child Developm., 33, 575-90.

BOEHM, L. (1962b) 'The development of conscience: a comparison of students in Catholic parochial schools and in public schools', Child Developm., 33, 591-602.

BOEHM, L. (1963) 'The development of conscience: a comparison of upper middle class academically gifted children attending Catholic and Jewish parochial schools', J. Soc. Psych., 59, 101-10.

BOEHM, L. (1966) 'Moral judgement: a cultural and sub-cultural comparison with some of Piaget's research conclusions', Int J. Psych., I, 143-50.

BOEHM, L. and NASS, M. L. (1962) 'Social class differences in conscience development', Child Developm., 33, 565-74.

BOERSMA, F. J., O'BRYAN, K. G. and RYAN, B. A. (1970) 'Eye movements and horizontal décalage: some preliminary findings', Percep. Mot. Skills, 3 (3), 886.

BOOKER, D. (1969) 'Training in conservation of number: replication of Wallach and Sprott with six- and seven-year-old English children', MA thesis, Sussex University.

BOONSONG, S. (1968) 'The development of conservation of mass, weight and volume in Thai children', unpub. MEd thesis, College of Education, Bangkok.

BOOTE, D. W. (1967) 'An experimental study of concept attainment with reference to concrete and formal modes of thinking', MEd thesis, Manchester University.

BOOTH, M. B. (1967) 'A critical analysis of the secondary school history curriculum with particular reference to fourth year pupils: an empirical and statistical survey', MA (Ed) thesis, Southampton University.

BORELLI, M. (1951) 'La naissance des opérations logiques chez le sourd-muet', Enfance, 4, 222-38.

BOUSFIELD, W., ESTERSON, J. and WHITMARSH, G. (1958) 'A study of developmental changes in conceptual and perceptual associative cluster-ing', J. Gen. Psych., 92, 95-102.

BOVET, M. (1968) 'Piaget's theory of cognitive development — socio-cultural differences and mental retardation'. Private manuscript.

BOVET, M. (1974) 'Cognitive development in illiterate Algerians', in BERRY, J. W., DASEN, P. R. (Eds.) 'Culture and Cognition: Readings in Cross-cultural Psychology'. London: Methuen.

BOWEN, E. (1963) 'An investigation of Piaget's theories of the development of mathematical concepts among subnormal children', Univ. College, Swansea: thesis.

BOWER, E. (1957) 'A process for identifying disturbed children', Child, 4, 143-7.

BOWER, E. (1961) 'The Education of Emotionally Handicapped Children'. Sacramento: California State Dept. of Educ.

BOWER, E. (1963) 'An investigation of Piaget's theories of the development of mathematical concepts among sub-normal children', University College of Swansea, Ref. B2. 2.

BOWER, T. G. R. (1967) 'The development of object-permanence: some studies of existence constancy', Percept. Psychophys., 2, 411-8.

BOWER, T. G. R. and PATERSON, J. G. (1972) 'Stages in the development of the object concept', Cognition, 1/1 47-65.

BOWER, T. G. R. and PATERSON, J. G. (1972) 'The separation of place, movement and object in the world of the infant', J. Exp. Child Psych., 15, 161-68.

BOWLBY, J. (1951) 'Maternal care and mental health', WHO Mon., No. 2.

BOWLBY, J. (1969) 'Attachment and Loss: Vol. I Attachment'. London: Hogarth Press.

BOYLE, D. G. (1969) 'A Students' Guide to Piaget'. Oxford: Pergamon Press.

BRADSHAW, D. H. (1964) 'A study of inferred size relations using non-verbal methods', unpub. PhD Thesis, Catholic University.

BRAINE, M. D. S. (1959) 'The ontogeny of certain logical operations: Piaget's formulations examined by non-verbal methods', Psych. Mon. Gen. & Appl., 73, No. 5. (whole No. 475).

BRAINE, M. D. S. (1962) 'Piaget on reasoning: a methodological critique and alternative proposals', Mon. Soc. Res. Child Dev., 27, 41-61.

BRAINE, M. D. S. (1964) 'Development of a group of transitivity of length: a reply to Smedsland', Child Developm., 35, 799-810.

BRAINE, M. D. S. and SHANKS, B. L. (1965a) 'The conservation of a shape property and a proposal about the origin of the conservations', Can. J. Psych., 19, 197-207.

BRAINE, M. D. S. and SHANKS, B. L. (1965b) 'The development of conservation of size', J. Verb. Learn. Verb. Behv., 4, 227-42.

BRAINERD, C. J. (1970) 'Continuity and discontinuity hypotheses in studies of conservation', Dev. Psych., 3, 225-8.

BRAINERD, C. J. (1971) 'The development of the proportionality scheme in children and adolescents', Dev. Psych., 5, 3, 469-76.

BRAINERD, C. J. and ALLEN, T. W. (1971a) 'Training and generalization of

403

density conservation: effects of feedback and consecutive similar stimuli', Child Developm., 42, 693-704.

BRAINERD, C. J. and ALLEN, T. W. (1971) 'Experimental inductions of the conservation of 'first order' quantitative invariants', Psych. Bull., 75, 128-44.

BRENNAN, W. K. (1962) 'The relation of social adaptation, emotional adjustment and moral judgement to intelligence in primary school children', Brit. J. Ed. Psych., 32, 200-4.

BREZNITZ, S. and KUGELMASS, S. (1967) 'Intentionality in moral judgement: developmental stages', Child Developm., 38, 469-79.

BRIGHT, G. W. (1972) 'Conservation of volume: testing as a means of instruction', J. Psych., 82, 329-37.

BRISON, D. W. (1965) 'Acquisition of conservation of substance in group situation', unpub. PhD thesis. Illinois University.

BRISON, D. W. (1966) 'Acceleration of conservation of substance', J. Gen. Psych., 311-22, (109).

BRISON, D. W. and BEREITER, C. (1967) 'Acquisition of Conservation of Substance in Normal, Retarded and Gifted Children', The Education Research Series No.2, 53-72. Toronto: Ont. Institute for Studies in Education.

BRISON, D. W. and SULLIVAN, E. V. (Eds.) (1967) 'Recent Research on the Acquisition of Conservation of Substance', The Educational Research Series No. 2. Toronto: Ontario Inst. for Studies in Education.

BRITISH PSYCHOLOGICAL SOCIETY (1971) 'Symposium on Cognitive Development and Socialization', Easter Conference at Exeter University, April 9-11 incl.

BROADHURST, D. E. (1958) 'Perception and Communication'. London: Pergamon Press.

BRODLIE, J. (1966) 'An examination of the relevance of Piaget's theory of 'logical multiplication' to modern elementary school maths', unpub. PhD thesis, Teacher's College, Columbia University.

BRODZINSKY, D. M., JACKSON, J. P. and OVERTON, W. F. (1972) 'Effects of perceptual shielding in the development of spatial perspectives', Child Developm., 43, 3, 1014-6.

BROVERMAN, D. and LAZARUS, R. (1958) 'Individual differences in task performance and under conditions of cognitive interference', J. Pers., 26, 94-105.

BROWN, P. G. (1970) 'Tess of development in children's understanding of the laws of natural numbers', Brit. J. Ed. Psych., 40, 334-5.

BRUNER, J. S. (1959) 'The Viewpoint of a Psychologist'. Review of B. Inhelder and J. Piaget, "The Growth of Logical Thinking" ', Brit. J. Psych., 50, 363-70.

BRUNER, J. S. (1960) 'The Process of Education', Cambridge, Mass: Harvard Univ. Press.

BRUNER, J. S. (1964) 'The course of cognitive growth', Am. Psych., 19, (I), 1-15.

BRUNER, J. S. (1966) 'Toward a Theory of Instruction', Cambridge, Mass: Harvard Univ. Press.

BRUNER, J., GOODNOW, J. and AUSTIN, G. (1956) 'A Study of Thinking', New York: Wiley.

BRUNER, J. and OLVER, R. (1963) 'Development of equivalence transformations in children', Mon. Soc. Res. Child Dev., 28 (2, Serial No. 86), 125-41.

BRUNER J. S., OLVER and GREENFIELD (1966) 'Studies in Cognitive Growth', New York: Wiley.

BRYANT, P. E. (1971) 'Cognitive development', Brit. Med. Bull., Vol. 27, No.3, 200-5.

BRYANT, P. E. (1972) 'Bryant replies on Piaget', Times Ed. Supp., Page 4, Feb. 25th.

BRYANT, P. E. (1972) 'The understanding of invariance by very young children', Can. J. Psych., 26, (I), 78-95.

BULL, N. J. (1969) 'Moral Judgement from Childhood to Adolescence', London: Routledge and Kegan Paul.

BURGESS, J. W. (1968) 'Logical processes in some adolescents', unpub. Master's thesis, Edinburgh University.

BURGESS, J. W. (1969) 'Alternate paths: An inquiry into the development of adult reasoning', MEd thesis, Edinburgh University.

BURGESS, J. W. (1970) 'An inquiry into the development of adult reasoning', Scot. Ed. Stud., Vol. II, No.I.

BURT, C. (1915) 'The general and specific factors underlying the primary emotions', British Association, Annual Report, 84, 694-6.

BURTON, R. V. (1963) 'The generality of honesty reconsidered', Psychol. Rev., 70, 481-500.

BYNUM, T. W., THOMAS, J. A. and WEITZ, L. J. (1972) 'Truth — functional logic in formal operational thinking: Inhelder and Piaget's evidence', Dev. Psych., 7, 2, 129-33.

CALHOUN, L. G. (1971) 'Number conservation in very young children: the effect of age and mode of responding', Child Developm., 42, 561-72.

CANNING, M. (1957) 'Exploring the number concepts of blind children', unpub. dissertation, Birmingham University.

CARBONNEAU, M. (1965) 'Apprentissage de la notion de conservation de surfaces', unpub. PhD thesis, Montreal University.

CARLSON, J. S. (1967) 'Effects of instruction on the concept of conservation of substance', Sci. Ed., 4, 285-91.

CARMICHAEL, L. (1954) (Ed.) 'Manual of Child Psychology', (2nd ed.) New York: Wiley.

CARNEY, P. (1963) 'A study of the relations between home background, attainments and social adjustment among children in a junior school', MEd thesis, University of Manchester.

CARPENTER, T. E. (1955) 'A pilot study for a quantitative investigation of Piaget's original work on concept formation'; Ed. Rev., 7, 142-9.

CARUSO, J. L. and RESNICK, L. B. (1972) 'Task structure and transfer in children's learning of double classification skills', Child Developm., 43, 1297-308.

CASE, D. and COLLINSON, J. (1962) 'The development of formal thinking in verbal comprehension', Brit. J. Ed. Psych., 32, 103-11.

CASTANEDA, A., McCANDLESS, B. R. and PALERMO, D. (1956) 'The children's form of manifest anxiety scale', Child Developm., 27, 317-26.

CATHCART, W. G. (1971) 'The relationship between primary students' rationalization of conservation and their mathematical achievement', Child Developm., 42, 755-65.

CATTELL, R. B. and CATTELL, M. D. (1969) 'Handbook for the Jr. -Sr. High School Personality Questionnaire – HSPQ', Champaign, Illinois: Inst. for Person. and Ability Testing.

CATTELL, R. B. and COAN, R. W. (1957) 'Personality factors in middle childhood as revealed in parents' ratings', Child Developm., 28, 4, 439-58.

CATTELL, R. B. and COAN, R. W. (1958) 'Personality dimensions in the questionnaire responses of six- and seven-year-olds', Brit. J. Ed. Psych., 28, 232-42.

CATTELL, R. B. and COAN, R. W. (1966) 'Guidebook for the Early School Personality Questionnaire – ESPQ', Champaign, Illinois: Inst. for Personality and Ability Testing.

CATTELL, R. B. and COAN, R. W. (Oct. 1970) 'Guidebook Supplement – ESPQ', Champaign, Illinois: Inst. for Personality and Ability Testing.

CATTELL, R. B. and EBER, H. W. (1966) 'Handbook for the Sixteen Personality Factor Questionnaire', 3rd ed. Champaign, Illinois: Inst. for Personality and Ability Testing.

CATTELL, R. B., EBER, H. W. and TATSUOKA, M. M. (1970) 'Handbook for the Sixteen Personality Factor Questionnaire (16PF)', Champaign, Illinois: Inst. for Personality and Ability Testing.

CATTELL, R. B., KARSON, S. and NUTTALL, R. L. (1966) 'The High School Personality Questionnaire', Champaign, Illinois: Inst. for Personality and Ability Testing.

CHANCE, J. E. (1961) 'Independence training and first graders' achievement', J. Consult. Psych., 25, 149-54.

CHARLESWORTH, W. R. (1964) 'Development and assessment of cognitive structures', J. Res. Sci. Teach., 2, 214-9.

CHARLESWORTH, W. R. (1966) 'Development of the object concept: a methodological study', Paper read at Amer. Psychol. Assoc., New York.

CHARLESWORTH, W. R. (1968) 'Classification skills', in 'Cognitive Growth Pre-school Children', (Symposium presented at the meeting of the Am. Ed. Res. Ass, Chicago.)

CHENG TSU-HSIN and LEE MEI-KE (1960) 'An investigation into the scope of the conception of numbers among 6- to 7-year-old children', Acta Psychol., (Sinica), I, 28-35 (Psychol. Abstr., 35: 4710).

CHITTENDEN, E. A. (1964) 'The development of certain logical abilities and the child's concept of substance and weight: an examination of Piaget's theory.' Unpublished doctoral dissertation, Teacher's College, Columbia University.

CHURCHILL, E. M. (1958) 'The number concepts of young children', MEd thesis, Leicester University.

CHURCHILL, E. M. (1958a) 'The number concepts of the young child', Part I. Researches and Studies (Leeds University), 17, 34-39: 28-46.

CHURCHILL, E. (1961) 'Counting and Measuring', University of Toronto Press.

CHURCHILL, E. M. (1961) 'Piaget's Findings and the Teacher', London: National Froebel Foundation.

CLARKE, A. M. and COOPER, G. M. (1966) 'Age and perceptual motor transfer in imbeciles. Task complexity as variable', Brit. J. Psych., 57, 113-28.

CLARKE, A. M., COOPER, G. M. and CLARKE, A. D. B. (1967) 'Task complexity and transfer in the development of cognitive structures', J. Exp. Child Psych., 5, 562-76.

CLARKE, D. F. (1962) 'Some aspects of problem solving in older backward children', MEd thesis, Leicester University.

CLARKE, E. (1950) 'Number experiences of three-year-olds', Childhood Ed., 26, 247-50.

CLOUGH, F. (1973) 'Cognitive developmental theory and the hospitalization of children', Paper read at the British Psychological Society's Conference at Liverpool University, Easter.

COAN, R. W. and CATTELL, R. B. (1958) 'Reproducible personality factors in middle childhood', J. Clin. Psych., 14, 339-45.

COAN, R. W. and CATTELL, R. B. (1959) 'The development of the ESPQ', J. Exp. Ed., 28, 143-52.

COHEN, G. M. (1967) 'Conservation of quantity in children: the effect of vocabulary and participation', Quart. Exp. Psych., 19, 150-4.

COLE, H. P. (1968) 'An analysis of the effects of a structured teaching approach developed from the work of Piaget, Bruner and others', Paper presented at the American Educ. Res. Assoc., February 1968.

COLLIS, K. F. (1971) 'A study of concrete and formal reasoning in school mathematics', Aust. J. Psych., 23, 3, 289-96.

CONCANNON, J. (1966) 'An experimental study of the influence of individual vs. group instruction on spatial abilities in pre-school children', US Office of Education Project No.2885, Grant No.OE-5-10-228, Boston College, Chestnut Hill.

CONCANNON, J. (1970) 'A review of research on haptic perception', J. Ed. Res., 63, No.6, 250-2.

COOK, A. (1963) 'An investigation into space orientation concepts in children aged 12 to 15', MA thesis, Edinburgh University.

COOMBES, M. G. (1968) 'The effect of learning on the development of structures of formal reasoning', MEd thesis, Manchester University.

CORNWELL, J. (1950) 'The construction, standardization, and validation of an orally presented group test of intelligence for children between the ages of 8 and 11', unpub. MA thesis. Univ. of Birmingham.

COURT, S. R. (1920) 'Numbers, time, and space in the first five years of a child's life', Ped. Sem., 27, 71-89.

COWAN, P. A., LANGER, J., HEAVENRICH, J., and NATHANSON, M. (1969) 'Social learning and Piaget's cognitive theory of moral development', J. Pers. Soc. Psych., II, No.3, 261-74.

COWLEY, J. J. and MURRAY, M. (1962) 'Some aspects of the development of spatial concepts in Zulu children', J. Soc. Res., 13, 1-18.

COWRIE, L. E. (1962) 'A study of the development of the concept of volume in secondary school children', MA thesis, Edinburgh University.

COYLE, J., and CONCANNON, J. (1968) 'A Longitudinal Assessment of Pre-school Children in Haptic Learning', US Dept. of Health, Education and Welfare Project No.6-8429, Contract No.OEg-1-6-068429, Boston College, Chestnut Hill.

CRAWFORD, D. H. (1960) 'The work of Piaget as it relates to school mathematics', Alberta J. Ed. Res., 6, 125-36.

CROMER, R. F. (1973) 'Conservation by the congenitally blind', Brit. J. Psych., 64, 2, 241-250.

CROWLEY, P. M. (1968) 'Effect of training upon objectivity of moral judgement in grade school children', J. Pers. Soc. Psych., 8, No.3, part I, 228-32.

CURCIO, F., ROBBINS, O., and ELA, S. S. (1971) 'The role of body parts and readiness in acquisition of number conservation', Child Developm., 42, 1641-6.

CURCIO, F., KATTEF, E., LEVINE, D. and ROBBINS, O. (1972) 'Compensation and susceptibility to conservation training', Dev. Psych., 7, 3, 259-265.

DAEHLER, M. W. (1970) 'Children's manipulation of illusory and ambiguous stimuli, discriminative performance, and implications for conceptual development', Child Developm., 41, 225-41.

DANSET, A. and DUFOYER, J. P. (1968) 'Transitivité ou Inférence Prélogique Chez l'Enfant de Cinq Ans?' Travaux & Documents de Lab. de Psychol. Génétique de Paris, Sorbonne, III, No.1.

DART, F. E. and PRADHAN, P. L. (1967) 'Cross-cultural teaching of science', Science, 155, 649-56.

DASEN, P. R. (1970) 'Cognitive development in Aborigines of Central Australia: concrete operations and perceptual activities', unpub. PhD thesis, Australian National University.

DASEN, P. R. (1972) 'Cross-cultural Piagetian research: a summary', J. Cross-Cult. Psych., Vol. 3, No.I, 23-39.

DASEN, P. R. (1972, in press). 'The influence of ecology, culture and European contact on cognitive development in Australian Aborigines', in BERRY, J. W. and DASEN, P. R. (Eds.) 'Culture and Cognition: Readings in Cross-cultural Psychology', London: Methuen.

DASEN, P. R. (1972a) 'The development of conservation in Aboriginal children: a replication study', Int. J. Psych., 7, 2, 75-85.

DASEN, P. R., de LACEY, P. R. and SEAGRIM, G. N. (1972b) 'An investigation of reasoning ability in adopted and fostered Aboriginal children', in KEARNEY, G. E., de LACEY, P. R., and DAVIDSON (Eds.) 'The Psychology of Aboriginal Australians', Queensland University Press.

DAVIES, G. B. (1964) 'Concrete and formal thinking among adolescent children of average ability', unpub. MEd. thesis, Birmingham University.

DAVOL, S. H., CHITTENDEN, E. A., PLANTE, M. L. and TUZIK, J. A. (1967) 'Conservation of continuous quantity investigated as a scalable developmental concept', Merr. Palm. Quart., 13, 191-9.

DECARIE, T. G. (1965) 'Intelligence and Affectivity in Early Childhood'. New York: International Universities Press.

DEESE, J. (1958) 'The Psychology of Learning'. New York: McGraw-Hill.

DEESE, J. (1967) 'General Psychology'. Boston: Allyn and Bacon.

DeLACY, E. A. (1967) 'Some problems associated with a paper-and-pencil test of conservation of length', Child Developm., 869-75.

DeLACEY, P. R. (1970) 'A cross-cultural study of classificatory ability in Australia', J. Cross-cult. Psych., Vol. I. 4, 293-304.

DeLACEY, P. R. (1970a) 'An index for Aboriginal communities', Aust. J. Soc. Issues, 5, 219-23.

DeLACEY, P. R. (1971) 'Classificatory ability and verbal intelligence among high-contact Aboriginal and low socioeconomic white Australian children', Cross-Cult. Psych., 2, 4, 393-6.

DeLACEY, P. R. (1971) Verbal intelligence, operational thinking and environment in part-aboriginal children', Aust. J. Psych., 23, 2, 145-9.

DeLEMOS, M. M. (1966) 'The development of the concept of conservation in

Australian Aboriginal children', Unpub. PhD thesis, Australian National University, Canberra.

DeLEMOS, M. M. (1968) 'A study of the effects of experience and materials in a series of Piaget conservation tests', ACER Bull. for Psychology, 8, 1-4.

DeLEMOS, M. M. (1969) 'The development of conservation in aboriginal children', Int. J. Psych., Vol.4, 255-69.

DeLEMOS, M. M. (1972) 'The development of spatial concepts in Zulu children', in BERRY, J. W. and DASEN, P. R. 'Culture and Cognition: Readings in cross-cultural Psych.'. London: Methuen.

DeMELLO, S. and WILLEMSON, E. (1969) 'The development of the number concept: a scalogram analysis', Child Developm., 40, 681-8.

DEMPSEY, A. D. (1971) 'Time conservation across cultures', Int. J. Psych., 6, 115-20.

DENNEY, N. W. (1972) 'Free classification in pre-school children', Child Developm., 43, 1161-70.

DENNEY, D. R. and DENNEY, N. W. (1973) 'The use of classification for problem solving: a comparison of middle and old age'. Dev. Psych., 9, 2, 275-78.

DENNEY, N. W. and LENNON, M. L. (1972) Classification: 'A comparison of middle and old age', Develop. Psych., 7, 2, 210-14.

DENNIS, W. and RUSSELL, R. W. (1940) 'Piaget's questions applied to Zuni children', Child Develop., II, 181-7.

DENNIS, W. (1943) 'Animism and related tendencies in Hopi children', J. Abnorm. Soc. Psych., 38, 21-37.

DENNIS, W. (1957) 'A cross-cultural study of the reinforcement of child behaviour', Child Developm., 28, 431-8.

DEREGOWSKI, J. B. and SERPELL, R. (1972, in preparation). 'Performance on a sorting task with various modes of representation: a cross-cultural experiment'.

DEUTSCH, M. (1965) 'The role of social class in language development and cognition', Am. J. Orthopsychiatry, 35, (I), 78-88.

DEUTSCH, M. and BROWN, B. (1964) 'Facilitating development in the pre-school child: social and psychological perspectives', Merr. Plam. Quart., 10, 3, 149-63.

DEUTSCH, M. and BROWN, B. (1964) 'Social influences in Negro-white intelligence differences', J. Soc. Issues, 20, 24-35.

DIENES, Z. P. (1959) 'The growth of mathematical concepts in children through experience', Ed.Res., 2, 9-28

DOBSON, F. A. (1967) 'A study of the concept of time, movement and speed among primary school children', MA(Ed) thesis, Southampton University.

DOCKRELL, W. B. (Ed.) (1970) 'The Toronto Symposium on Intelligence'. London: Methuen.

DODWELL, P. C. (1960) 'Children's understanding of number and related concepts', Can. J. Psych., 14, 191-205.

DODWELL, P. C. (1961) 'Children's understanding of number concepts: characteristics of an individual and of a group test', Can. J. Psych., 15, (1) 29-36.

DODWELL, P. C. (1962) 'Relations between the understanding of the logic of classes and of cardinal number in children', Can. J. Psych., 16, (II), 152-60.

DODWELL, P. C. (1963) 'Children's understanding of spatial concepts', Can. J. Psych., 17, 141-61.

DOLLARD, J. and MILLER, N. (1950) 'Personality and Psychotherapy: An Analysis in Learning, Thinking and Culture', New York: McGraw-Hill.

DOMINO, G., GOLDSCHMID, M. L. and KAPLAN, M. (1964) 'Personality traits of institutionalized mongoloid girls', Amer. J. Mental Deficiency, 68, 498-502.

DONALDSON, M. (1964) 'A Study of Children's Thinking'. New York: Humanities Press.

DONALDSON, M. and BALFOUR, G. (1968) 'Less is more: a study of language comprehension in children', Brit. J. Psych., 59, 4, 461-71.

DONALDSON, M. and WALES, R. (1968) 'On the Acquisition of Some Relational Terms', (Edinburgh University), in: HAYES, M. J. R. (Ed.) 'Proceedings of the 4th Carnegie Symposium on Cognition'. New York: Wiley.

DOUGLAS, J. W. B. (1964) 'The Home and the School'. London: Mac-Gibbon & Kee.

DUCKWORTH, E. (1964) 'Piaget Rediscovered', in: RIPPLE, R. E. and ROCKCASTLE, V. N. (Eds.) 'Piaget Rediscovered'. Ithaca, New York: Cornell University Press Vol. 2, 172-175.

DUDEK, S. Z. (1972) 'A longitudinal study of Piaget's developmental stages and the concept of regression II', J. Pers. Assessm., 36, 5, 468-78.

DUDEK, S. Z. and DYER, G. B. (1972) 'A longitudinal study of Piaget's developmental stages and the concept of regression I', J. Pers. Assessm., 36, 4, 380-9.

DUDEK, S. Z., LESLIE, E. P., GOLDBERG, J. S. and DYER, G. B. (1969) 'Relationship of Piaget measures to standard intelligence and motor scales', Percep. Mot. Skills, 28, 351-62.

DUNN, L. M. (1965) 'Expanded Manual for the Peabody Picture Vocabulary Test', American Guidance Unit.

DUNNETT (1955) 'A multiple comparison procedure for comparing several treatments with a control', J. Am. Stat. Assoc., 50, 1096-121.

DUNNINGTON, M. V. (1954) 'An exploratory study of behavioural variables related to differences in sociometric status of nursery school children', unpub. Master's thesis, Cornell University.

DUNNINGTON, M. J. (1957) 'Behavioural differences of sociometric status groups in a nursery school', Child Developm., Vol.28, No.1.

DUNNINGTON, M. V. (1957) 'Investigation of areas of sociometric status groups in a nursery school', Child Developm., 28, 93-103.

DUNSDON, M. I. and ROBERTS, J. A. F. (1957) 'A study of the performance of 2,000 children on four vocabulary tests II', Brit. J. Stat. Psych., 10, 1-16.

DURKIN, D. (1959a) 'Children's concepts of justice: a comparison with the Piaget data', Child Developm., 30, 59-67.

DURKIN, D. (1959b) 'Children's acceptance of reciprocity as a justice principle', Child Developm., 30, 289-96.

DURKIN, D. (1960) 'Sex differences in children's concepts of justice', Child Developm., 31, 361-8.

DURKIN, D. (1961) 'The specificity of children's moral judgements', J. Gen. Psych., 98, 3-13.

DUSTIN, D. S. (1969) 'How Psychologists do Research — The Example of Anxiety'. New York: Prentice-Hall.

DWORKIN, E. S. (1968) 'The effects of imitation, reinforcement and cognitive information on the moral judgements of children', Diss. Abstr. 29B, 1-3, 365.

EASLEY, J. A. (1964) 'Comments on the INRC group', in: RIPPLE, R. E. and ROCKCASTLE, V. N. (Eds.) 'Piaget Rediscovered' (A report of the conference on cognitive studies and curriculum development.) Ithaca, NY: School of Education, Cornell University.

EDWARDS, A. L. (1957) 'Techniques of Attitude Scale Construction, New York: Appleton-Century-Crofts.

EDWARDS, A. L. (1968) 'Experimental Design in Psychological Research', (third edn.) New York: Holt, Rinehart and Winston.

EIFERMANN, R. R. and ETZION, D. (1964) 'Awareness of reversibility: its effect on performance of converse arithmetical operations', Br. J. Ed. Psych., 34, 2, 151-7.

ELITCHER, H. (1967) 'Children's causal thinking as a function of cognitive style and question wording', PhD thesis, New York University.

ELKIND, D. (1961) 'Quantity conceptions in junior and senior high school students', Child Developm., 32, 551-60.

ELKIND, D. (1961) 'Children's conceptions of right and left. Piaget replication study IV', J. Gen. Psych., 69, 269-76.

ELKIND, D. (1961a) 'Children's discovery of the conservation of mass, weight and volume: Piaget replication study II', J. Gen. Psych., 98, 279-87.

ELKIND, D. (1961b) 'The development of quantitative thinking: a systematic replication of Piaget's studies', J. Gen. Psych., 98, 37-46.

ELKIND, D. (1962) 'Children's conceptions of brother and sister: Piaget replication study V', J. Gen. Psych., 100, 129-36.

ELKIND, D. (1962) 'Quantity conceptions in college students', J. Soc. Psych., 57, 459-65.

ELKIND, D. (1967) 'Piaget's theory of perceptual development: its application to reading and special education', J. Spec. Ed., 4, 357-61.

ELKIND, D. (1967) 'Piaget's conservation problems'. Child Developm., 38, 15-27.

ELKIND, D. (1969) 'Piagetian and psychometric conceptions of intelligence', Harvard Educ. Rev., 39, 2, 319-37.

ELKIND, D. (1969) Cited in GOLDSCHMID, M. L. 'The Role of Experience in the Rate and Sequence of Cognitive Development', Invited paper given at the conference on Ordinal Scales of Cognitive Development, Monterey, California.

ELKIND, D. and FLAVELL, J. (Eds.) (1969) 'Studies in Cognitive Development'. London: Oxford University Press.

ELKIND, D. and SCHOENFELD, E. (1972) 'Identity and equivalence conservation at two age levels', Dev. Psych., Vol.6, No.3, 529-33.

ELKIND, D. and WEISS, J. (1969) 'Studies in perceptual development, Ill: perceptual exploration', Child. Developm., 551-61.

ELKIND, D., ANAGNOSTOPOULOU, R. and MALONE, S. (1970) 'Determinants of part-whole perception in children', Child Developm., 41, 391-7.

ELLIOTT, J. (1973) 'The Use of Orientation as a Cue for Discrimination in Young Children'. Paper read at The British Psychological Society Conference, Liverpool University, Easter.

411

ENDLER, N. S., BOULTER, L. R. and OSSER, H. (1968) 'Contemporary Issues in Developmental Psychology'. New York: Holt, Rinehart and Winston.

ERVIN, S. M. (1960) 'Transfer effects of learning a verbal generalization', Child Developm., 31, 537-54.

ERVIN, S. M. (1960) 'Training and a logical operation by children', Child Developm., 31, 555-63.

ESCALONA, S. (1953) 'Emotional development in the first year of life', in SENN, M. J. E. (Ed.) 'Problems of Infancy and Childhood': Transactions of the Sixth Conference New York: Josiah Macy, Jr., Foundation, 11-92.

ESCALONA, S. K. and CORMAN, H. M. (1967) 'The validation of Piaget's hypotheses concerning the development of sensorimotor intelligence: Methodological issues'. Paper presented at the meeting of the Society for Research in Child Development. New York.

ESTES, B. W. (1956) 'Some mathematical and logical concepts in children', J. Gen. Psych., 88, 219-32.

ESTES, B. W. (1961) 'Judgement of size in relation to geometric shape', Child Developm., 32, 277-86.

ESTES, B. and COMBS, A. (1966) 'Perception of quantity', J. Gen. Psych., 108, 333-6.

ETUK, E. (1967) 'The development of number concepts: an examination of Piaget's theory with Yoruba-speaking Nigerian children', unpub. DEd dissertation, Columbia University (order No.67-12. 685).

FANTZ, R. L. (1965) 'Ontogeny of perception', in SCHRIER, A., HARLOW, H. and STOLLNITZ, F. (Eds.) 'Behaviour of Nonhuman Primates'. New York: Academic Press.

FARBER, I. E. (1954) 'The role of motivation in verbal learning and performance', Psych. Bull., 52, 311-27.

FARMINGTON TRUST RESEARCH UNIT. WILLIAMS, N. 'Children's moral thought, parts I & II', Moral Education, 1, 1 & 2, (May and September 1969).

FARNHAM-DIGGORY, S. and BERMON, M. (1967) 'Verbal compensation, cognitive synthesis and conservation'. Paper read at Soc. Res. Child Developm., New York.

FEFFER, N. and GOUREVITCH, V. (1960) 'Cognitive aspects of role-taking in children', J. Pers., 28, 383-96.

FEIGENBAUM, K. D. (1963) 'Task complexity and IQ as variables in Piaget's problem of conservation', Child Developm., 34, 423-32.

FEIGENBAUM, K. D. (Contract OEC-3-7-068415-0428,Unpub. manuscript). 'A pilot investigation of some training techniques designed to acclerate the child's understanding of the concept of conservation'.

FEIGENBAUM, K. D. (1971) 'A pilot investigation of the effects of training techniques designed to accelerate children's acquisition of conservation of discontinuous quantity', J. Gen. Psych., 119, 13-23.

FEIGENBAUM, K. D. and SULKIN, H. (1964) 'Piaget's problem of conservation of discontinuous quantities: a teaching experience', J. Gen. Psych., 105, 91-7.

412

FERGUSON, G. (1954) 'On learning and human ability', Can. J. Psych., 8, 95-112.

FERGUSON, G. (1956) 'On transfer and the abilities of man', Can. J. Psych., 10, 121-31.

FERGUSON, G. A. (1966) 'Statistical Analysis in Psychology and Education'. New York: McGraw-Hill.

FERSTER, C. B. and DeMYER, M. K. (1961) 'The development of performances in autistic children in an automatically controlled environment', J. Chronic Diseases, 13, 312-45.

FERSTER, C. B. and DeMYER, M. K. (1962) 'A method for the experimental analysis of the behaviour of autistic children', Am. J. Orthopsych., 32, 89-98.

FESTINGER, L. (1947) 'The treatment of qualitative data by scale analysis', Psych. Bull., 44, 149-61.

FESTINGER, L. (1954) 'Motivations leading to social behaviour', in Nebraska Symposium on Motivation, University of Nebraska Press, Lincoln, Nebraska.

FESTINGER, L. (1957) 'A Theory of Cognitive Dissonance', Evanston. Illinois: Row, Peterson.

FIELD, T. W. and CROPLEY, A. J. (1969) 'Cognitive style and science achievement', J. Res. Sci. Teach., 6, 2-10.

FIGURELLI, J. C. and KELLER, H. R. (1972) 'The effects of training and socioeconomic class upon the acquisition of conservation concepts', Child Developm., 43, 293-8.

FINDLAY, A. D. (1971) 'An investigation of the emergence of ability for partial and complete multiplication of classes in young children', Brit. J. Ed. Psych., 91-8.

FINLAYSON, H. (1964) 'A study of maladjustment among the school children of an industrial small town', student thesis, Psychol Dept., Glasgow University.

FISCHER, H. (1964) 'The psychology of Piaget and its educational applications', Int. Rev. Ed., 10, 431-9.

FISHBEIN, H. D., LEWIS, S. and KEIFFER, K. (1972) 'Children's understanding of spatial relations: coordination of perspectives', Dev.Psych., 7, 1, 21-3.

FISHER, G. H. (1965) 'Developmental features of behaviour and perception', Brit. J. Ed. Psych., 35, 69-78.

FITE, M. D. (1940) 'Aggressive behaviour in young children and children's attitudes towards aggression', Gen. Psych., Mon., 22, No.2.

FITZGERALD, L. (1970) 'Cognitive development among Ga children: environmental correlates of cognitive growth rate within the Ga tribe', unpub. PhD thesis, California University.

FLAVELL, J. (1963) 'The Developmental Psychology of Jean Piaget', Princeton, NJ: Van Nostrand.

FLAVELL, J. H. (1963) 'Piaget's contributions to the study of cognitive development', Young Children, 21, 164-77.

FLAVELL, J. H. (1970) 'Historical and bibliographical note', in 'Cognitive Development in Children, Five Monog. and Soc. Res. in Child Developm.',

Univ. of Chicago Press, 3-17.

FLAVELL, J. H. (1970) 'Developmental studies of mediated memory', in LISPETT, L. and SPIKER, C. (Eds.) 'Advances in Child Development and Behaviour, Vol. 5'. New York: Academic Press.

FLAVELL, J. H. (1971) 'Concept Development', in 'Encyclopedia of Child Psychology', MUSSEN, P. (Ed.) 983-1059.

FLAVELL, J. H. (1972) 'An analysis of cognitive-developmental sequences', Gen. Psych. Mon., 86, 279-350.

FLAVELL, J. H. and WOHLWILL, J. F. (1969) 'Formal and functional aspects of cognitive development', in ELKIND, D and FLAVELL, J. H. (Eds.) 'Studies in Cognitive Development'. New York: OUP.

FLECK, J. R. (1972) 'Cognitive styles in children and performance on Piagetian conservation tasks', Percep. Mot. Skills, 35, 747-56.

FLEISCHMANN, B., GILMORE, S. and GINSBERG, H. (1966) 'The strength of non-conservation', J. Exp. Child Psych., 4, 353-68.

FLOUD, J. (1961) 'Social class factors in educational achievement', in HALSEY, A. H. (Ed.) 'Ability and Educational Opportunity'. NY: OECD, 91-109.

FODOR, E. M. (1969). 'Moral judgement in negro and white adolescents', J. Soc. Psych., 79, 289-91.

FODOR, E. M., (1972) 'Delinquency and susceptibility to social influence among adolescents as a function of level of moral development', J. Soc. Psych., 86, 257-60.

FOGELMAN, K. R. (1969) 'Difficulties in using Piagetian tests in the classroom, I, Ed. Res., 12, 1, 36-40.

FOGELMAN, K. R. (1970) 'Piagetian Tests and Sex differences, II', Ed. Res., 12, 154-6.

FOGELMAN, K. R. (1970) 'Piagetian Tests for the Primary School'. Slough, UK: NFER.

FORD, L. H. (1970) 'Predictive versus perceptual responses to Piaget's water-line task and their relation to distance conservation', Child Developm., 41, 205-13.

FORREST, G. M. (1961) 'An experimental study of concept attainment in children', MEd thesis, Manchester University.

FOURNIER, E. (1967) 'Un apprentissage de la conservation des quantités continues par une technique d'exercices opératoires', unpub. doctoral dissertation, Montreal University.

FOWLER, W. (1962) 'Cognitive learning in infancy and early childhood', Psych. Bull., 59, 2, 116-52.

FRANK, F. (1964) (Cited by J. S. Bruner.) 'The course of cognitive growth', Am. Psych., 19, 1-15.

FRANK, F. (1966) 'On the conservation of liquids', in BRUNER, J. S. et al. 'Studies in Cognitive Growth'. New York: Wiley.

FRASER, E. (1959) 'Home Environment and the School'. London: University of London Press.

FREEBERG, N. E. and PAYNE, D. T. (1965) 'A Survey of Parental Practices Related to Cognitive Development in Young Children'. Princeton, NJ: Inst. for Educ. Development.

FREEBERG, N. E. and PAYNE, D. T. (1967) 'Parental influence, on cognitive development in early childhood: a review'. Child Developm., 38, 65-87.

414

FUJINAGA, T., SAIGA, H. and HOSOYA, J. (1963) 'The developmental study of the children's number concept by the method of experimental education', Jap. J. Ed. Psych., 11, 18-26.

FULLERTON, T. J., and HALFORD, G. S. (1970) 'A discrimination task which induces conservation of number', Child Developm., 41, 205-13.

FURBY, L. (1971) 'A theoretical analysis of cross-cultural research in cognitive development: Piaget's conservation task', J. Cross-Cult. Psych., Vol.2, No.3, 241-55.

FURTH, H. G. (1961) 'Influence of language on the development of concept formation in deaf children', J. Abn. Soc. Psych., 63, 386-9.

FURTH, H. G. (1963a) 'Classification transfer with disjunctive concepts as a function of verbal training and set', J. Psych., 55, 477-85.

FURTH, H. G. (1963b) 'Conceptual discovery and control on a pictorial part-whole task as a function of age, intelligence and language', J. Ed. Psych., 54, 191-6.

FURTH, H. G. (1964a) 'Conceptual performance in deaf adults', J. Abn. Soc. Psych., 69. 676-81.

FURTH, H. G. (1964b) 'Conservation of weight in deaf and hearing children', Child Developm., 35, 143-50.

FURTH, H. G. (1966) 'Thinking Without Language. Psychological Implications of Deafness'. New York: Free Press.

FURTH, H. G. (1967) 'Concerning Piaget's view on thinking and symbol formation', Child Developm. (Sept.).

FURTH, H. G. (1969) 'Piaget and Knowledge – Theoretical Foundations'. Englewood Cliffs, NJ: Prentice Hall.

FURTH, H. G. (1970) 'Piaget for Teachers'. Englewood Cliffs, NJ: Prentice Hall.

FURTH, H. G. (1970) 'A review and perspective on the thinking of deaf people', Cited in HELMUTH, J. (Ed.) 'Cognitive Studies, Vol. I.'. Brunner/Mazel Publishers.

FURTH, H. G. and MILGRAM, N. A. (1965) 'The influence of language on classification: a theoretical model applied to normal retarded, and deaf children', Gen. Psych. Mon., 72, 317-51.

FURTH, H. G. and YOUNISS, J. (1964) 'Colour-object paired-associates in deaf and hearing children with and without response competition', J. Consult. Psych., 28, 224-7.

FURTH, H. G., YOUNISS, J. and ROSS, B. M. (1970) 'Children's utilization of logical symbols: an interpretation of conceptual behaviour on Piagetian theory', Dev. Psych., 3, 1. 36-57.

GAGNÉ, R. M. (1962) 'Military training and principles of learning', Am. Psych., 17, 83-91.

GAGNÉ, R. M. (1963) 'The learning requirements for inquiry', J. Res. Sci. Teach., 1, 144-53.

GAGNÉ, R. M. (1965) 'The Conditions of Learning'. New York: Holt, Rinehart and Winston.

GAGNÉ, R. M. (1966) 'Contributions of learning to human development'. Presidential address, Division I, AAAS, presented at AAAS Meeting, Washington, D.C.

GAGNÉ, R. M. (1966) 'The learning of principles', in KLAUSMEIER, H. J. and HARRIS, C. W. (Eds.) 'Analysis of Concept Learning'. New York: Academic Press.

GAGNÉ, R. M. (1968) 'Contributions of learning to human development', Psych. Rev., 3, 177-191.

GAGNÉ, R. M. and FOSTER, H. (1949) 'Transfer of training from practice on components in a motor skill', J. Exp. Psych., 39, 47-68.

GAGNÉ, R. M. and PARADISE, W. E. (1961) 'Abilities and learning sets in knowledge acquisition', Psych. Mon., 75, No.14 (whole No.518).

GAGNÉ, R. M., and SMITH, E. C. (1962) 'A study of the effects of verbalization on problem solving', J. Exp. Psych., 63, 12-18.

GARDNER, R. W., HOLZMAN, P. S., KLEIN, G. S., LINTON, H. B. and SPENCE, D. P. (1959) 'Cognitive control, a study of individual consistencies in cognitive behaviour', Psychol. Issues, 1, No.4.

GARRETT, H. H. (1953) 'Statistics in Psychology and Education'. London: Longmans.

GARRETTSON, J. (1971) 'Cognitive style and classification', J. Gen. Psych., 119, 79-87.

GARRISON, M. (1966) (Ed.) 'Cognitive models and development in mental retardation', Am. J. Mental Deficiency, 70, Monograph Supplement.

GAUDIA, G. (1972) 'Race, social class, and age of achievement of conservation on Piaget's tasks', Dev. Psych., 6, 1, 158-165.

GEACH, P. (1958) 'Mental Acts, Their Content and Their Objects'. London: Routledge and Kegan Paul.

GELMAN, R. (1967) 'Conservation, attention, and discrimination', unpub. doctoral dissertation, University of California, Los Angeles.

GELMAN, R. (1969) 'Conservation acquisition: A problem of learning to attend to relevant attributes', J. Exp. Child Psych., 7, 167-87.

GESELL INSTITUTE of Child Development (1965) 'Gesell Developmental Kit'. Lumberville, Pa: Programmes in Education.

GHENT, L. (1956) 'Perception of over-lapping and embedded figures by children of different ages', Am. J. Psych., 69, 575-87.

GIBSON, J. J. (1955) 'Perceptual learning: differentiation or enrichment', Psych. Rev., 62, 32-41.

GIBSON, J. J. (1962) 'Observations on active touch', Psych. Rev., 69, 477-91.

GILLIGAN, C., KOHLBERG, L., LERNER, J. and BELENSKY, M. (1971) 'Moral reasoning about sexual dilemmas: an interview and scoring system' (Technical Report of the Commission on Obscenity and Pornography, 141-74.

GILMORE, S. E. (1966) 'The effect of screening the visual cues in the classic conservation of liquid quantity experiment', unpub. Master's thesis, Cornell University.

GINSBURG, H. and OPPER, S. (1969) 'Piaget's Theory of Intellectual Development'. Englewood Cliffs, NJ: Prentice Hall.

GLADWIN, T. (1964) 'Culture and logical process', in GOODENOUGH, W. H. (Ed.) 'Explorations in Cultural Anthropology'. New York: McGraw-Hill, 167-77.

GLASSCO, J. A., MILGRAM, N. A. and YOUNISS, J. (1970) 'Stability of training effects on intentionality in moral judgement in children', J. Pers. Soc. Psych., 14, 4, 360-5.

GOLDEN, M. and BIRNS, B. (1967) 'Social class and cognitive development in infancy', Paper presented at the meeting of the Society for Research in Child Development, New York.

GOLDEN, M. and BIRNS, B. (1968) 'Social class and cognitive development in infancy', Merr. Palm. Quart., 14, 139-49.

GOLDEN, M. and BIRNS, B. (1971) 'Social class, intelligence and cognitive style in infancy', Child Developm., 41, 2114-6.

GOLDEN, M., BIRNS, B., BRIDGER, W. and MOSS, A. (1971) 'Social class differentiation in cognitive development among black pre-school children', Child Developm., 42, 37-45.

GOLDMAN, R. (1964) 'Religious Thinking from Childhood to Adolescence'. London: Routledge and Kegan Paul.

GOLDMAN, R. (1965) 'The application of Piaget's schema of operational thinking to religious story data by means of Guttman Scalogram', Brit. J. Ed. Psych., 35, 158-70.

GOLDMANN, L. (1953) 'Sciences Humaines et Philosophiques'. Paris: Paris University Press.

GOLDSCHMID, M. L. (1967) 'Different types of conservation and their relation to age, sex, IQ, MA and vocabulary', Child Developm., 38 1229-46.

GOLDSCHMID, M. L. (1968) 'The relation of conservation to emotional and environmental aspects of development', Child Developm., 39, 579-89.

GOLDSCHMID, M. L. (1968a) 'The role of experience in the acquisition of conservation', from the Proceedings, 76th Annual Convention, APA.

GOLDSCHMID, M. L. (1969) 'The role of experience in the rate and sequence of cognitive development', invited paper given at the Conference on Ordinal Scales of Cognitive Development: Monterey, California: Feb. 9-11.

GOLDSCHMID, M. L. (in press.) 'Cognitive development and pre-school education', Psychologia Wychowawcza.

GOLDSCHMID, M. L. and BENTLER, P.M. (1968) 'The dimensions and measurement of conservation', Child Developm., 39.

GOLDSCHMID, M. L. and BENTLER, P. M. (1968b) 'Manual: Concept Assessment Kit-conservation'. San Diego, California: Educational and Industrial Testing Service.

GOLDSCHMID, M. L. and BUXTON-PAYNE, G. (1968) 'Comprehension of relational terms and the development of conservation in young children', unpub. paper, McGill University.

GOLDSCHMID, M. L. and DOMINO, G. (1965) 'Some paradiagnostic implications of the IQ among mentally retarded patients', Training School Bulletin, 61, 178-83.

GOLDSCHMID, M. L. and MacFARLANE, B, (1968) 'The assessment of six Piagetian concepts in the same subjects: classification, conservation, perspective, probability, seriation and transitivity', unpub. paper, McGill University.

GOLDSCHMID, M. L. BENTLER, P., KOHNSTAMM, G., MODGIL, S. L. et al. (1973) 'A cross-cultural investigation of conservation', J. Cross-Cult. Psych., 4, 1, 49-75.

GOLDSCHMID, M. L., KASIMER, G., CAYNE, H. and BURCK, C. (1968) 'Accelerating the acquisition of conservation in mentally retarded and emotionally disturbed children', unpub. paper, McGill University.

GOLDSTEIN, K. and SEHEERER, M. (1941) 'Abstract and concrete behaviour: an experimental study with special tests', Psych. Mon., 53, 2, (whole No. 239).

417

GOODNOW, J. (1962) 'A test of milieu differences with some of Piaget's tasks', Psych. Mon., 76, No. 36 (whole No. 555).

GOODNOW, J. (1969) 'Problems in research on culture and thought', in FLAVELL, J. H. and ELKIND, D. (Eds.) 'Studies in Cognitive Development.' London: Oxford University Press.

GOODNOW, J. (1970) 'Cultural variations in cognitive skills', in HELLMUTH, J. (Ed.) 'Cognitive Studies, Vol. I.' Brunner/Mazel publishers,

GOODNOW, J. and BETHON, G. (1966) 'Piaget's tasks: the effects of schooling and intelligence', Child Developm., 37, 573-82.

GOODSTEIN, L. D. (1954) 'Interrelationships among several measures of anxiety and hostility', J. Consult., Psych., 18, 35-9.

GORHAM, D. R. (1956) 'Clinical Manual for the Proverbs Test'. Psychological Test Specialists.

GOTTESMAN, M. (1971) 'A comparative study of Piaget's developmental scheme of sighted children with that of a group of blind children'. Child Developm., 42, 573-80.

GOUGH, H. G. (1960) 'The adjective check list as a personality assessment research technique', Psych. Rep., 6, 107-22.

GRAHAM, D. (1972) 'Moral Learning and Development. Theory and Research'. London: Batsford.

GRATCH, G. and LANDERS, W. F. (1967) 'A partial replication of Piaget's study of infant's object concepts', paper presented at the meeting of the Society for Research in Child Development, N.Y., March.

GRATCH, G. and LANDERS, W. F. (1971) 'Stage IV of Piaget's theory of Infant's object concepts: a longitudinal study', Child Developm., 42, 359-72.

GRAVES, A. J. (1972) 'Attainment of conservation of mass, weight and volume in minimally educated adults', Dev. Psych., 7, 2, 223-4.

GRAY, K. (1970) 'Programmed cognitive development', MEd dissertation, Birmingham University.

GREATER CLEVELAND mathematics Programme (1962) 'Teachers' Guide for Kindergarten and First Grade'. Chicago, Science Research associates.

GREEN, D. R., FORD, M. P. and FLAMER, G. B. (1971) 'Measurement and Piaget'. New York: McGraw-Hill.

GREENFIELD, P. (1966) 'On culture and conservation', in BRUNER, J. S. et al. 'Studies in Cognitive Growth'. New York: Wiley, 225-56.

GREENFIELD, P. M. and BRUNER, J. S. (1966) 'Culture and cognitive growth', Int. J. Psych., 1, 80-107.

GRIEVE, R. (1967) 'Two experiments in logical thinking', MA thesis, Edinburgh University.

GRIFFITHS, E. J. (1964) 'A study of natural concepts of ESN children', Ref. No. B3. 8, University College of Swansea.

GRIFFITHS, J. A., SHANTZ, C. U. and SIGEL, I. E. (1967) 'A methodological problem in conservation studies, the use of relational terms', Child Developm., 38, 841-8.

GRIM, P., KOHLBERG, L., and WHITE, S., (1968) 'Some relationships between conscience and attentional processes', J. Pers. Soc. Psych., 8, 3, Part I, 239-52.

GRINDER, R. E. (1961) 'New techniques for research in children's temptation behaviour', Child Developm., 32, 679-83.

GRINDER, R. E. (1964) 'Relations between behavioural and cognitive dimensions of conscience in middle childhood', Child Developm., 35, 881-91.

GRUEN, G. E. (1965) 'Experiences affecting the development of number conservation in children', Child Developm., 36, 963-79.

GRUEN, G. E. (1966) 'Note on conservation: methodological and definitional considerations,' Child Developm., 37, 977-83.

GRUEN, G. E. and VORE, D. A. (1972) 'Development of conservation in normal and retarded children', Dev. Psych., 6, 1, 146-57;

GUTTMAN, L. (1950) 'Relation of Scalogram analysis to other techniques', in STOUFFER, S. A. 'Measurement and Predictions'. Studies in Soc. Psych. in World War II, 4, 172-212.

GUTTMAN, L. (1954-55) 'An outline of some new methodology for social research', Publ. Opin. Quart., 18, 395-404.

GUTTMAN, L. (1958) 'What lies ahead for factor analysis', Educ. & Psych. Measmt., 18, 497-515.

GUTTMAN, L. (1959) 'A structural theory for intergroup beliefs and action', Am. Soc. Rev., 24, 318-28.

GUTTMAN, L. and FOA, U. G. (1951) 'Social contact and an intergroup attitude', Publ. Opin. Quart., 15, 43-53.

GUYLER, K. R. (1966) 'The effects of variations in task contents and materials on conservation and transitivity', MEd thesis, Manchester University.

GUYLER, K. R. (1969) 'The effects of some task and subject variables on the accuracy and process of seriation and length; a comparison between infant and junior children based on Piaget's theory', MA thesis, London University.

GYR, J. W., BROWN, J. S. and CAFAGNA, A. C. (1967) 'Quasi-formal models of inductive behaviour and their relation to Piaget's theory of cognitive development', Psych. Rev., 74, 272-89.

HAAN, N., SMITH, M. B. and BLOCK, J. (1968) 'Moral reasoning of young adults; political-social behaviour, family background and personality correlates', J. Pers. Soc. Psych., 10, 183-201.

HALASA, O. (1967) 'A developmental study of the attainment of number conservation among economically and culturally disadvantaged children', Diss. Abstr., 28, 2606-7.

HALFORD, G. S. (1968) 'An experimental test of Piaget's notions concerning the conservation of quantity in children', J. Exp. Child Psych., 6, 33-43.

HALFORD, G. S. (1969) 'An experimental analysis of the criteria used by children to judge quantities', J. Exp. Child Psych., 8, 314-27.

HALFORD, G. S. (1970) 'A theory of the acquisition of conservation', Psychol. Rev., 77, 302-16.

HALFORD, G. S. (1971) 'Acquisition of conservation through learning a consistent classificatory system for quantities', Aust. J. Psych., 23, 2, 151-9.

HALFORD, G. S. and FULLERTON, T. J. (1970) 'A discrimination task which induces conservation of number', Child Developm., 41, 205-13.

HALL, V. C. and KINGSLEY, R. C. (1967) 'Problems in conservation research', paper read at Soc. Res. Child Developm., NY, March.

HALL, V. C. and KINGSLEY, R. C. (1968) 'Conservation and equilibration theory', J. Gen. Psych., 113, 195-213.

HALL, V. C. and SIMPSON, G. J. (1968) 'Factors influencing extinction of weight conservation', Merr. Palm. Quart., 14, 197-210.

HALLAM, R. N. (1966) 'An investigation into some aspects of historical thinking of children and adolescents', MEd thesis, Leeds University.

HALLAM, R. (1969) 'Piaget and the teaching of history', Ed. Res., 12, 3-12.

HALPERN, E. (1965) 'The effects of incompatibility between perception and logic in Piaget's stage of concrete operations,' Child Developm., 36, 491-7.

HAMILTON, V. (1970) 'Some effects of parent-child interaction on the child's cognitive development', final report on Res. Grant No. 67-0285, Canada Council.

HAMILTON, V. (1971) 'Effect of maternal attitude on development of logical operations', Percep. Mot. Skills, 33, 63-9.

HAMILTON, V. (1971) 'How parents affect a child's intellect', Medical News Tribune, 30th April, Page 9.

HAMILTON, V. (1973) 'An information-processing analysis of conservation', paper read at The British Psychological Society Conference, Liverpool University, Easter.

HANNAM, R. (1963) 'Concept formation in relation to the study of landforms among training college students', MEd thesis, Leeds University.

HARARI, H. and McDAVID, J. W. (1969) 'Situational influence on moral justice; a study of "finking",' J. Pers. Soc. Psych II, 3, 240-4.

HARASYM, C. R., BOERSMA, F. J. and MAGUIRE, T. O. (1971) 'Semantic differential analysis of relational terms used in conservation', Child Developm., 42, 767-79.

HARKER, W. H. (1960) 'Children's number concepts: ordination and cardination', unpub. MA thesis, Queen's University, Kingston, Ontario.

HARLEN, W. (1968) 'The development of scientific concepts in young children', Ed. Res., Vol. II, No. 1, 4-13.

HARMAN, H. (1967) 'Modern Factor Analysis'. Chicago and London: University of Chicago Press.

HARPER, A. C. H. (1964) 'The Cognitive Processes'. New York: Prentice Hall.

HARRIS, A. (1961) 'How to Increase Reading Ability'. New York: Longmans.

HARRIS, H. (1970) 'Development of moral attitudes in white and negro boys', Dev. Psych., 2, 3, 376-83.

HARROWER, M. R. (1934) 'Social status and the moral development of the child', Brit. J. Ed. Psych., 4, 75-95.

HARTSHORNE, H. and MAY, M. A. (1928-30) 'Studies in the Nature of Character'. (3 Vols.) New York): Macmillan.

HARVEY, O. J., HUNT, D. E. and SCHRODER, H. N. (1961) 'Conceptual Systems and Personality Organization'. New York: Wiley.

HATANO, G. and KUHARA, K. (1973) 'Training on class-inclusion problems', Jap. Psych. Res., 14, 2, 61-9.

HATWELL, Y. (1966) 'Privation Sensorielle et Intelligence. Paris: Presses Universitaries de France.

HAVIGHURST, R. J. and NEUGARTEN, B. L. (1955) 'American Indian and White Children: A Sociopsychological Investigation'. Chicago: Univ. of Chicago Press.

HAVIGHURST, R. J., GUNTHER, M. K. and PRATT, I. E. (1946) 'Environment and the Draw-a-Man Test: the performance of Indian children', J.

Abnorm. Soc. Psych., 41, 50-63.

HAYS, W. L. (1963) 'Statistics for Psychologists'. New York: Holt, Rinehart and Winston.

HAZLITT, V. (1930) 'Children's thinking', Brit. J. Psych., 20, 354-61.

HEBB, D. O. (1949) 'The Organization of Behaviour. A neuropsychological theory.' New York: Wiley.

HELD, R. (1965) 'Plasticity in sensori-motor systems', Scientific American, 213(5), 84-94.

HEMINGWAY, G. H. (1965) 'An investigation into the child's conception of death, and comparisons of findings indicated by answers to questions put to children between 4 and 7 years of age with those of Piaget's work in "The Child's Conception of the World" ', DipEd thesis, Bristol University.

HENDRICKSON, A. E. and WHITE, P. O. (1969) 'Promax: A quick method for rotation to oblique simple structure', Brit. J. Stat. Psych., 17, 65-70.

HENDRIKZ, E. (1966) 'A cross-cultural investigation of the number concepts and level of number development in 5-year-old urban Shona and European children in Southern Rhodesia', unpub. MA thesis, University of London.

HENRY, K. (1960) 'A study of the development of the concept of time in children', MA thesis, Liverpool University.

HENRY, K. (1969) 'The development of the concepts of speed, movement and time in children', PhD thesis, Liverpool University.

HENRY, W. (1956) 'An Analysis of Fantasy'. New York: Wiley.

HENSHAW, G. (1968) 'The development of analogical reasoning', MEd thesis, Leicester University.

HERMELIN, B. and O'CONNER, B. (1961) 'Recognition of shapes by normal and subnormal children', Brit. J. Psych., 281-4.

HERON, A. (1971) 'Concrete operations, 'g' and achievement in Zambian children', J. Cross-Cult. Psych., 2, 4, 325-6.

HERON, and SIMONSSON, M. (1969) 'Weight conservation in Zambian children; a non-verbal approach', Int. J. Psych., 4, 281-92.

HERRMAN, R. and CAMPBELL, S. (1973, in press) 'Piaget: Dictionary of Terms'. (To be published by Pergamon Press.)

HERTZIG, M., BIRCH, H., ALEXANDER, T., and MENDEZ, O. (1968) 'Class and ethnic differences in the responsiveness of pre-school children to cognitive demands', Mon. Soc. Res. Child Dev., I (Serial, No. 117).

HESS, R. D. (1965) 'Effects of maternal interaction on cognitions of pre-school children in several social strata', paper presented at the meetings of the American Psychological Association, Chicago.

HESS, R. D. and SHIPMAN, V. C. (1965) 'Early experience and the socialization of cognitive modes in children', Child Developm., 36, 4, 869-86.

HEWETT, I. V. (1965) 'The use of specially constructed apparatus for the understanding of the cardinal aspect of number', Dip Ed thesis, Bristol University.

HEWETT, I. V. (1969) 'An approach to number work in the infant school in the light of Piaget's theories', MEd thesis, Leicester University.

HILL, B. (1972) 'Review: Piaget', Parts One, Two and Three. Times Ed. Supp., pp 19-20, 11th Feb., 18th Feb. and 25th Feb. respectively.

HILL, S. A. (1960) 'A study of logical abilities of children', unpub. PhD thesis, Stanford University.

HOEL, P. G. (1962) 'Introduction to Mathematical Statistics'. New York: Wiley.

HOFFMAN, M. L. (1957) 'An interview method for obtaining descriptions of parent-child inter-action', Merr. Palm. Quart., 4, 76-83.

HOFFMAN, M. L. (1970) 'Moral development', in MUSSEN, P. (Ed.), 'Carmichael's Manual Of Child Development'.

HOFFMAN, M. L. and HOFFMAN, L. W. (Eds.) (1964) 'Review of Child Development Research'. I, New York: Russell Sage Foundation.

HOLLENSBERG, C. K. (1970) 'Functions of visual imagery in the learning and concept formation of children', Child Developm., 41, 1003-15.

HOLMES, R. (1973) 'Piaget and Psychoanalysis', paper read at the British Psychological Society Conference, Liverpool University, Easter.

HOLSTEIN, C. (to be published) 'Parental determinants of the development of moral judgement', in KOHLBERG, L. and TURIEL, E. (Eds.) 'Recent Research in Moral Development'.

HOLT, P. N. (1969) 'A study of children's responses to open-ended problems', PhD thesis, Southampton University.

HOOD, H. B. (1962) 'An experimental study of Piaget's theory of the development of number in children', Brit. J. Psych., 53, 273-86.

HOOPER, F. H. (1968) 'Piagetian research and education', in SIGEL and HOOPER (Eds.) 'Logical Thinking in Children'. New York: Holt, Rinehart and Winston. 423-35.

HOOPER, F. H. (1969a) 'The Appalachian child's intellectual capabilities — deprivation or diversity?' Chap. VI in The 1969 Yearbook of the Journal of Negro Education, 224-33.

HOOPER, F. H. (1969b) 'Piaget's conservation tasks: The logical and developmental priority of identity conservation', J. Exp. Child Psych., 8, 234-49.

HOOPER, F. H. and MARSHALL, W. H. (unpub. report). 'The initial phase of a pre-school curriculum development project.' final report, United States Dept. of Health, Education and Welfare, Office of Education Contract No. OEC-3-7-062902-3670.

HOUSSIDAS, L. (1965) 'Coordination of perspectives in children', Archiv. Fur Die Gesamte Psychologie., 117, 319-26.

HOWELL, R. W. (1972) 'Evaluation of cognitive abilities of emotionally disturbed children: an application of Piaget's theories', Unpub. thesis dissertation.

HUANG, I. (1943) 'Children's conceptions of physical causality: a critical summary', J. Gen. Psych., 63, 71-121.

HUGHES, G. B. (1969) 'An analysis, using Piagetian concepts of the responses of partially-sighted children of primary school age to the problem of representing their classroom by (a) using wooden blocks, (b) drawing, and their understanding of associated spatial relationships', DipEd thesis, Bristol University.

HUGHES, M. M. (1965) 'A four-year longitudinal study of the growth of logical thinking in a group of secondary modern schoolboys', MEd thesis, University of Leeds.

HULME, I. (1965) 'A comparative study of the play, language and reasoning of severely subnormal children and children of similar mental age', MEd thesis, Manchester University.

HUNT, E. B. (1962) 'Concept Learning'. New York: Wiley.

HUNT, J. McV. (1961) 'Intelligence and Experience'. New York: Ronald Press.

422

HUNT, J. McV. (1963) 'Intrinsic motivation and its role in psychological development', in LEVINE, D. (Ed.) 'Nebraska Symposium on Motivation'. Nebraska Press, 189-282.

HUNT, J. McV. (1969) 'The impact and limitations of the giant of developmental psychology', cited in 'Studies. in Cognitive Development', ELKIND, D. and FLAVELL, J. (Eds.) Oxford University Press, London.

HUNT, J. McV. and UZGIRIS, I. (1967) 'An instrument for assessing infant paychological development', paper presented at the International Congress of Psychology. New York, Mar. 29-April 1.

HUTTENLOCHER, J. (1964) 'Development of formal reasoning on concept formation problems', Child Developm., 35, 1233-42.

HUTTENLOCHER, J. (1967) 'Children's ability to order and orient objects', Child Developm., 38, 1169-76.

HYDE, D. M. (1959) 'An investigation of Piaget's theories of the development of the concept of number', unpub. doctoral thesis, University of London.

HYDE, D. M. (1970) 'Piaget and Conceptual Development'. London: Holt, Rinehart and Winston.

IMAI, S. and GARNER, W. R. (1965) 'Discriminability and preference for attributes in free and constrained classification', J. Exp. Psych., 69, 596-608.

INHELDER, B. (1936) 'Observation sur le principle de conservation dans la physique d l'enfant', Cahiers de Pedagogie Experimentale et de Psychologie de l'enfant, Université de Genève. 'Institut des sciences de l'education, No. 9, p 17.

INHELDER, B. (1940) 'Die Aufgaben der kantonalen Fursorgestelle für Anormale', Amtliches Schulblatt, St. Gallen, pp 46-61.

INHELDER, B. (1940) 'Schulpsychologie und Fursorge,' Schweizerische Lehrerinnen Zeitung, 10, pp 165-7.

INHELDER, B. (1940) 'Aus der Jugendfürsorgearbeit,' Schweizerische Lehrerinnen Zeitung, 10, pp 167-8.

INHELDER, B. (1943) 'The Diagnosis of Reasoning in the Mentally Retarded.' Translated by Will Stephens. 1968 New York: John Day, p 367.

INHELDER, B. (1944) Experimentelle Studien zur Kinderpsychologie im Genfer Institut,' Schweizerische Zeitschrift für Psychologie und ihre Anwendungen. Vol. 13, cahier 2, pp 128-38.

INHELDER, B. (1944) 'Le Diagnostic du Raisonnement chez les Débiles Mentaux.' Neuchâtel: Delachaux et Niestlé.

INHELDER, B. (1948-49) 'Contribution à l'étude de la formalisation spontanée chez l'enfant,' Synthèse, vol. 7, Np 1-2, pp 58-62.

INHELDER, B. (1949) 'Die spontane Geometrie des Kindes,' Schola. Mayence, 4, pp 622-28.

INHELDER, B. (1949) 'La representation de l'espace chez l'enfant', Atti del quinto congresso nazionale di nipiologia e delle prime giornate internazionali nipiologiche, Rapallo, Varello Sesia, Arti grafiche valsesiane Capelli, pp 216-224.

INHELDER, B. (1951) 'Le raisonnement experimental de l'adolescent,' proceedings and papers, 13th International Congress of Psychology, pp 153-54.

INHELDER, B. (1952) 'Jean Piaget. Biographien', Lexikon der Pädagogik,

423

(Berne, France), 3, 258-61.

INHELDER, B. (1953) 'La conduite experimentale de l'enfant,' lle congrès international de psychotechnique, Paris, 27 juillet — le août 1963.

INHELDER, B. (1953) 'Criteria of the stages of mental development', in TANNER, S. M. and INHELDER, B. (Eds.) 'Discussion on Child Development'. New York: 75-107.

INHELDER, B. (1954) 'Quelques reflexions a propos des 'études longitudinales aux Etats-Unis', Revue suisse de psychologie pure et appliquée. (Berne) 13, 4, 309-12.

INHELDER, B. (1954) 'Patterns of Inductive Thinking.' Proceedings 14th Int. Congr. Psychol., 217-48.

INHELDER, B. (1955) 'De la configuration perceptive à la structure operatoire', Bulletin de psychologie (Paris), 6-19. Also in Symposium de l'association psychologique scientifique de langue francaise: 'Le probleme des stades en psychologie de l'enfant,' Geneve. Paris. Paris, Presses universitaires de France, pp 137-62.

INHELDER, B. (1956) 'Die Affektive und kognitive Entwicklung des Kindes', Revue suisse de psychologie pure et appliquée (Berne), 15, 4, 251-68.

INHELDER, B. (1957) 'Developmental psychology,' Annual Review of Psychology, 8, 139-62.

INHELDER, B. (1957) 'La genèse de l'idée de hasard et la resistance du red aux operations,' Synthèse, (Amsterdam), 44-5C.

INHELDER, B. (1958) 'Ein Beitrag der Entwicklungspsychologie zum mathemathischen Unterricht', in DRENCKHAHN, (Ed.) Der mathemathische Unterricht. Göttingen: Imuk, 5, 67-80.

INHELDER, B. (1959) 'Die Stadientheorie Des Genfer Arbeitskreises', Psychologie und Pädagogik, 2, 139-60. Heidelberg: Quelle & Mayer.

INHELDER, B. and MATALON, B. (1960) 'The study of problem solving and thinking', in MUSSEN, P. (Ed.) 'Handbook of Research Methods in Childhood Development'. London: John Wiley, 421-56.

INHELDER, B. and NOELTING (1960) 'A pilot study of cognitive functions', in DAVID, H. P. and BRENGELMANN, C. (Eds.) 'Perspectives in Personality Research'. 8, 251-4. New York: Springer.
Also in Acta Psychologica (Amsterdam): Actes du 15e congres international de psychologie.

INHELDER, B. (1960) 'Le développement des activités intellectuelles de l'enfant au niveau de la crêche', Seminaire sur les crêches, Paris. 5, 6 et 7 decembre 1970. Centre intern. de l'enfance.

INHELDER, B. (1962) 'Les operations de classification dans la formation des concepts', Acta Psychologica (Amsterdam), 656-63. Actes du 16e congrès international de psychologie, Bonn.

INHELDER, B. (1962) 'A contribution of the genetic method of the study of various phenomena in the psychopathology of thinking', in OSTERGAARD, L. (Ed.) 'Clinical Psychology'. Copenhagen: Munksgaard. 154-67.

INHELDER, B. (1962) 'Some aspects of Piaget's genetic approach to cognition,' in KESSEN, W. and KUHLMAN, C. (Eds.) 'Thought in the Young Child.' Report of a conference on intellective development with particular attention to the work of Piaget. Monographs of the Society for Research in Child Development. 27, 2, serial 83, 19-34.

424

INHELDER, B. and PIAGET, J. (1958) 'The Growth of Logical Thinking'. London: Routledge and Kegan Paul.

INHELDER, B. (1963) Introduction à la seconde édition: 'Le diagnostic du raisonnement chez les débiles mentaux.' 1-32. Neuchätel: Delachaux and Niestlé.

INHELDER, B. (1963) 'Les operations de la pensée et leur symbolisme image', Cahiers de psychologie (édités par la Société de Psychologie du Sud-Est de France), 4, 143-71.

INHELDER, B. and SIOTIS, E. (1963) 'Observations sur les aspects opératifs et figuratifs de la pensée chez les enfants dysphasiques', in 'Problèmes de Psycholinguistique'. Symposium de l'Association de Psychologie Scientifique de langue Francaise, Neuchatel, 143-52. Paris: Presses universitaires de France.

INHELDER, B. (1964) Idem. Proceedings of the 27th international congress of psychology, symposium 5, 112-113, Amsterdam: North Holland. Published in résumé.

INHELDER, B. (1964) 'Zastosowanie Badan, genetycznich do oceny funkcji intelektualnych dzieciz zabukzeniami mowy,' Psychologia Wychowawcza, tom. 7 (11). Warsaw: Styczen-Luty.

INHELDER, B. (1964) 'Contributions des études génétiques a l'examen des fonctions intellectuelles et aux relations entre le langage et la pensée,' Table ronde: 'Troubles du langage et développement des fonctions intellectuelles et extralinguistiques.' Atti del 2° congresso europeo di pedopsichiatria, Roma, 1963, 1964, 396-398.

INHELDER, B. (1964) 'Battery of cognitive assessments', unpub. manuscript, Geneva University.

INHELDER, B. (1964) 'L'examen du symbolisme image et de certains deficits de la fonction symbolique'. Table ronde: 'Troubles du langage et developpement des fonctions intellectuelles et extralinguistiques.' Atti del 2° congresso europeo di pedopsichiatria, Roma, 1963, 1964, 396-98.

INHELDER, B. (1965) 'Operational thought and symbolic imagery', in MUSSEN, P. (Ed.) European research in cognitive development, Monographs of the society for research in child development, 30, serial 100, 4-18.

INHELDER, B. (1965) 'Contribution des études génétiques à l'examen des fonctions intellectuelles des enfants présentant des troubles du langage', Jahrbuch für Jugendpsychiatrie, 4, 11-22.

INHELDER, B. (1966) 'Cognitive development in relation to elementary science teaching', The Jennings Scholar Lectures, 1965-66, 12th lecture, 141-57. Educational Research Council of Greater Cleveland.

INHELDER B. (1966) 'Formation des concepts et action interiorisée', in 18e congrès international de psychologie, Moscou. Symposium 24: 'Psychologie de la formation du concept et des activites mentales.' Introduction, pp 3-5.

INHELDER, B. (1966) 'Développement et apprentissage,' in 18e congrès international de psychologie, Moscou. Symposium 24: 'Psychologie de la formation du concept et des activités mentales,' pp 27-37.

INHELDER, B. (1966) 'Psicologia genetica y psicopatologia', Revista de psicologia general y aplicada, (Madrid), pp 5-27.

INHELDER, B. (1966) 'Développement, régulation et apprentissage', in 'Psychologie et Epistémologie Génetiques, Thèmes Piagetiens', 177-88. Paris: Dunod.

INHELDER, B. (1966) 'Cognitive development and its contribution to the diagnosis of some phenomena of mental deficiency', Merr. Palm. Quart., 12, 4, 299-319.

INHELDER, B. (1966) 'Rapport sur le 18e congrès international de psychologie tenu à Mouscou du 4 au 11 août, Revue suisse de psychologie pure et appliquée. 24, 5, 336-42.

INHELDER, B., SINCLAIR, H. and BOVET, M. (1966) 'On cognitive development', Am. Psych., 21, 2, 160-4.

INHELDER, B., BOVET, M. and SINCLAIR, H. (1967) 'Développement et apprentissage', Revue suisse de psychologie pure et appliquée, 26, 1, 1-23.

INHELDER, B. (1967) 'Entwicklungs psychologische Studie über die intellektuellen Strukturen bei sprachgestörten Kindern', in BAUER, E. (Ed.) 'Ein Schulpsychologischer Dienst'. 86-96.

INHELDER, B. (1967) 'Contribution de la psychologie génétique à l'étude des cas d'encephalopathie chronique', Colloque sur les encephalopathies infantiles chroniques. La revue de pediatric, 1966-67, No. spécial, 209-13.

INHELDER, B. (1967) 'La formation des connaissances', in L'homme à la Découverte de Lui-même. Encyclopédie 'L'aventure humaine', 5, 108-22. Geneve et Paris: La Grange Batelière. In collaboration with BOVET, M. and SINCLAIR, H.

INHELDER, B. (1968) 'The Diagnosis of Reasoning in the Mentally Retarded'. New York: John Day. (French Edition, 1943).

INHELDER, B. (1968) 'Recent trends in Genevan research.' Paper presented at Temple University.

INHELDER, B. (1968) 'Apprentissage et développement chez l'enfant'. Attueli orientamenti della ricerca sull'apprendimento è la memoria. Academia dei Lincei, Roma, cahier 109, 283-91.

INHELDER, B. (1968) 'Rapport annuel de la Societé suisse de psychologie', Revue suisse de psychologie pure et appliquée, 27, 3-4, 324-6.

INHELDER, B. (1969) 'Preface to LONGEAT, F. 'Psychologie Différentielle et Théorie Opératoire de l'Intelligence' (thèse de doctorat). Paris: Dunod.

INHELDER, B. (1969) 'Memory and intelligence', in ELKIND, D. and FLAVELL, J. H. (Eds.) Studies in Cognitive Development. Essays in Honour of Jean Piaget. London: Oxford University Press.

INHELDER, B. (1969) 'Cognitive development and diagnostic procedures'. Paper read at the California Test Bureau Invitational Conference on 'Ordinal scales of cognitive development.' Monterey, Feb. 9th.

INHELDER, B. (1969) Cited in GOLDSCHMID, M. 'Experience in the Rate and Sequence of Cognitive Development.' Invited paper given at the Conference in Ordinal Scales of Cognitive Development, Monterey, California, Feb. 9-11.

INHELDER, B. (1970) 'The sensori-motor origins of knowledge'. Paper read at the symposium on 'Regulated mechanisms in early childhood', Pennsylvania State University, Jan. 12-15th.

INHELDER, B. (in press) Symposium de l'Association de Psychologie Scientifique de Langue Francaise. Paris: Presses universitaires de France.

INHELDER, B. and SINCLAIR, H. (1970) 'A propos des stades du développement. Notes sur le problème des transitions'. Revue suisse de psychologie pure et appliquée, 29, 1-2, 211.

IRWIN, D. M. and MOORE, S. G. (1971) 'The young child's understanding of social justice', Dev. Psych., 6, 3, 406-10.

ISAACS, N. (1961) 'Piaget's work and progressive education', in 'Some Aspects of Piaget's Work' (4th ed.) London: National Froebel Foundation, 32-46.

ITO, Y. and HATANO, G. (1963) 'An experimental education of number conservation', Jap. Psych. Res., 5, 161-70.

JACK, L. M. (1932) 'A device for the measurement of parent attitudes and practices', Univ. Iowa Studies. Child Welfare, 6, 135-49.

JACKSON, P. W. (1956) 'Verbal solutions to parent-child problems' Child Developm., 27, 339-51.

JACKSON, S. C. (1965) 'The growth of logical thinking in normal and subnormal children', Brit. J. Ed. Psych., 35, 255-8.

JACOBS, N. (1966) 'An investigation into the relationship between children's perception of form and their drawings of the real world', DipEd thesis, Bristol University.

JACOBS, P. I. (1966) 'Programmed progressive matrices', Proceedings of the 74th Annual Convention of the American Psychological Association, 2, 263-64. (Abstract.)

JACOBS, P. I. and VANDEVENTER, M. (1968) 'Progressive matrices: an experimental, developmental, nonfactorial analysis', Percep. Mot. Skills, 27, 759-66.

JACOBS, P. I. and VANDEVENTER, M. (1969) 'Evaluating the teaching of intelligence', Res. Bull. 69-20. Princeton, NJ: Educational Testing Service.

JACOBS, P. I. and VANDEVENTER, M. (1971) 'The learning and transfer of double-classification skills by first graders', Child Developm., 42, 149-59.

JACOBS, P. I. and VANDEVENTER, M. (1971a) 'The learning and transfer of double-classification skills: a replication and extension', J. Exp. Child Psychol., 12, 240-57.

JAHODA, G. (1958) 'Immanent justice among West African children', J. Soc. Psych., 47, 241-8.

JAHODA, G. (1962) 'Development of Scottish children's ideas and attitudes about other countries', J. Soc. Psych., 58, 91-108.

JAHODA, G. (1963) 'The development of children's ideas about country and nationality', Part I, Brit. J. Ed. Psych., 33, 47-60.

JAHODA, G. (1963) 'The development of children's ideas about country and nationality', Part II, Brit. J. Ed. Psych., 33, 143-53.

JAHODA, G. (1964) 'Children's concepts of nationality: a critical study of Piaget's stages', Child Developm., 35, 1081-92.

JAHODA, G. (1966) 'Geometric illusions and environment – a study in Ghana', Brit. J. Psych., 57, 193-9.

JAHODA, M. and WARREN, N. (Eds.) (1966) 'Attitudes'. Harmondsworth, UK: Penguin.

JAHODA, M., LAZARSFELD, P. F. and ZEISEL, H. (1972) Marienthal: the Sociography of an Unemployed Community. London: Tavistock.

JAMES, W. (1890) 'Principles of Psychology'. New York: Holt, Rinehart and Winston.

JENSEN, A. R. (1961) 'Learning abilities in Mexican-American and Anglo-American children', Calif. J. Ed. Res., 12, 147-59.

JENSEN, A. R. (1964) 'Social class and verbal learning', unpub. manuscript. Berkeley: University of California. (On file at Library, Educational Testing

Service, Princeton, NJ.)

JENSEN, A. R. (1969) 'How much can we boost IQ and scholastic achievement?', Harv. Ed. Rev., 39, 1-123.

JENSEN, A. R. (1972) 'Genetics and Education'. London: Methuen.

JENSEN, J. (1964) 'Lidt om Geneveskolens intelligensundersogelser', (About the research on intelligence according to the Geneva School). Skolepsykologi, 1, 24-41.

JENSEN, J. (1965) 'Nye veje i intelligensforskningen', (A new approach to the research on intelligence). The Danish Institute for educational research, 37-48.

JENSEN, J. (1965) 'Forskellige intelligensopfattelser og deres paedagogiske betydring', (Different conceptions of intelligence and their educational implications). The Danish Institute for Educational Research, 49-71.

JENSEN, J. A. (1969) 'Concrete transitivity of length: a method of assessment', Bulletin Danish Inst. for Ed. Res., Copenhagen.

JENSEN, J. A. (1969) 'Om muligheder for pavirkning af den kognitive udvikling', (On the possibilities of influencing cognitive development). Dansk Paedagogosk Tiddsskrift, 17, 99-117.

JENSEN, J. A. (1969) 'Learning Class Inclusion', in (Book review of KOHNSTAMM, G. A. 'Piaget's Analysis of Class Inclusion; Right or Wrong'.) New York: Humanities Press, 1967, In: Contemp. Psych., 14, 394-5.

JENSEN, J. A. (1970) Indlaering og deltagerforudsaetninger. (Learning and Capabilities). Et Bidrag til differentiel paedagogisk psykologi. Kobenhavn: Munksgaard, Arbejdstekster til psykologi og paedagogik.

JENSEN, J. et al. (1971) 'Egnethed og uddannelse. Egenskabsbegrebet i paedagogisk-psykologisk belysning'. (Fitness and education. An educational psychological analysis of the concept of faculties). Kobenhavn: Danmarks paedagogiske Institut, Publikation no. 73.

JENSEN, L. and HUGHSTON, K. (1971) 'The effects of training children to make moral judgements that are independent of sanctions', Dev. Psych., 5, 2, 367.

JENSEN, L. and LARM, C. (1970) 'The effects of two training procedures on intentionality in moral judgements among children', Dev. Psych., 2, 2, 310.

JESSOR, R. and HAMMOND, K. (1957) 'Construct validity and the Taylor anxiety scale', Psych. Bull., 54, 161-70.

JONES, E. D. (1961) 'The moral development of the child: A survey taking as its starting point 'Cooperation and the Idea of Justice'', Ch.III of "The Growth of Moral Judgment" by Jean Piaget', BEd thesis, Edinburgh University.

JOHN, V. P. (1963) 'The intellectual development of slum children: some preliminary findings', Am. J. Orthopsych., 33, 813-22.

JOHNSON, R. C., (1962) 'Early studies of children's moral judgements', Child Developm., 33, 603-5.

JOHNSON, R. C. (1962) 'A study of children's moral judgements', Child Developm., 33, 327-54.

JONES, H. E. (1954) 'The environment and mental development', in CARMICHAEL, L. (Ed.) 'Manual of Child Psychology'. New York: Wiley, 631-96.

JONES, P. A. (1972) 'Formal operational reasoning and the use of tentative statements', Cognitive Psych., 3, 467-71.

428

JONES, V. (1946) 'Character development in children – an objective approach', in CARMICHAEL, L. (Ed.) 'Manual of Child Psychology'. New York: Wiley.

KABANOVA-WELLER, Y. E. N. (1958) 'Formation of space perception and spatial concepts in children', in 'The Central Nervous System and Behaviour. Translations from the Russian Medical Literature'. Washington, US: Public Health Service.

KAGAN, J. and FREEMAN, M. (1963) 'The relation of childhood intelligence, maternal behaviours, and social class to behaviour during adolescence', Child Developm., 34, 899-911.

KAGAN, J. and LEMKIN, J. (1961) 'Form, colour, and size and children's conceptual behaviour', Child Developm., 32, 25-8.

KAGAN, J. and MOSS, H. (1962) 'Birth to Maturity, The Fels Study of Psychological Development'. New York: Wiley.

KAGAN, J., MOSS, H. and SIGEL, I. (1963) 'Psychological significance of styles of conceptualization', Monographs of the Society of Research in Child Developm., 28, 2, Serial No. 86, 73-112.

KAGAN, J., ROSMAN, B., DAY, D., ALBERT, J., and PHILLIPS, W. (1964) Information processing in the child. Psych., Mon. 78, (1, whole No.578)

KAMII, C. (1970) 'Piaget's theory and specific instruction: A response to Bereiter and Kohlberg', Interchange: J. Ed. Stud., Pub. by the Ontario Institute for Studies in Education, 1, 1, 33-9.

KANE, K. R. (1970) 'A study of children's concepts of lies', Diss. Abstr., 1971 A, 242.

KARPLUS, R. (1964) 'Relativity and Motion'. Science Curriculum Improvement Study, California University (mimeographed).

KARPLUS, R. (1964) 'The Science Curriculum Improvement Study – Report to the Piaget Conference', J. Res. Sci. Teach., 2, 236-40.

KATES, S. L., YUDIN, L. and TIFFANY, R. K. (1962) 'Concept attainment by deaf and hearing adolescents', J. Ed. Psych., 53, 119-26.

KAUFMAN, A. S. (1971) 'Piaget and Gesell: A Psychometric analysis of tests built from their tasks', Child Developm., 42, 1341-60. -

KAUFMAN, A. S. and KAUFMAN, N. L. (1972) 'Tests built from Piaget's and Gesell's Tasks as predictors of first-grade achievement', Child Developm , 43, 521-35.

KAUSLER, D. (1959) 'Intentional and incidental learning under high and low emotional drive levels', J. Exp. Psych., 58, 452-5.

KEASEY, C. B. (1971) 'Social participation as a factor in the moral development of pre-adolescents', Dev. Psych., 5, 2, 216-20.

KEASEY, C. B. (1972) 'The lack of sex differences in the moral judgements of pre-adolescents', J. Soc. Psych., 86, 157-8.

KEASEY, C. T. and CHARLES, D. C. (1967) 'Conservation of substance in normal and mentally retarded children', J. Gen. Psych., III, 271-9.

KEATS, J. A. (1955) 'Formal and concrete thought processes', Res. Bull., No.17, Princeton: Educ. Testing Service.

KELLAGHAN, T. P. (1965) 'The study of cognition in a non-Western society with special reference to the Yoruba of South Nigeria', unpub. PhD thesis, Belfast University.

KELLY, E. L. (1955) 'Consistency of the adult personality', Am. Psych., 10, 659-81.

429

KELLY, M. B. (1967) 'An inquiry into the ability of ESN children to handle money in practical situations in relation to their mathematical understanding', MEd thesis, Manchester University.

KELLY, M. R. (1971) 'Some aspects of conservation of quantity and length in Papua and New Guinea in relation to language, sex and years at school', Territory of Papua and New Guinea Journ. Educ., 55-60.

KELMAN, H. C. (1953) 'Attitude change as a function of response restriction', Human Relat., 6, 185-214.

KENDALL, E. (1954) 'The validity of Taylor's manifest anxiety scale', J. Consult. Psych., 18, 429-32.

KENDLER, H. and KENDLER, T. S. (1959) 'Reversal and non-reversal shifts in kindergarten children', J. Exp. Psych., 58, 56-60.

KENDLER, H. and KENDLER, T. S. (1962) 'Vertical processes in problem solving', Psych. Bull., 69, 1-16.

KENDLER, T. S. (1961) 'Concept formation', Ann. Rev. Psych., 13, 447-72.

KENNEDY, W. A. (1969) 'A follow-up normative study of Negro intelligence and achievement', Child Developm. Mon., 34, (3, whole No.126).

KEPHART, N. C. (1960) 'The Slow-Learner in the Classroom'. Columbus, Ohio: Merrill.

KERLINGER, F. N. (1964) 'Foundations of Behavioural Research'. New York: Holt, Rinehart and Winston.

KERRICK, J. S. (1955) 'Some correlates of the Taylor Manifest Anxiety Scale', J. Abnorm. Soc. Psych., 50, 75-97.

KERSHNER, J. R. (1971) 'Children's acquisition of visuo-spatial dimensionality: A conservation study', Developm. Psych., 5, 3, 454-62.

KESSEN, W. (1962) ' "Stage" and "Structure" in the Study of Children'. Monographs of the Society for Research in Child Development, 27, (2, whole No. 83), 65-82.

KESSEN, W. and KUHLMAN, C. (Eds.) (1962) 'Thought in the Young Child'. Monographs Soc. Res. Child Developm., 27, 2, whole No. 83).

KIELGAST, K. (1969) 'En experimentel vurdering af Piaget's spatiale egocentribegreb'. (An experimental assessment of Piaget's concept of spatial egocentricity). Copenhagen.

KIELGAST, K. (1969) 'Verbal og non-verbal opgaveanalyse. En experimentel undersogelse', (Verbal or non-verbal problem analysis). Copenhagen.

KILPATRICK, J. (1964) 'Cognitive theory and the SMSC programme', in RIPPLE, R. E. and ROCKCASTLE, V. N. (Eds.) 'Piaget Rediscovered: A Report of the Conference on Cognitive Development, 1964'. Ithaca, NY: School of Educ., Cornell University, 128-33.

KIMBALL, B. (1953) 'Case studies in educational failure during adolescence', Am. J. Orthopsychiatry, 23, 406-15.

KINGSLEY, R. C. and HALL, V. C. (1967) 'Training conservation through the use of learning sets', Child Developm., 38, 1111-25.

KIRK, R. E. (1968) 'Experimental Design: Procedures for the Behavioural Sciences'. Wordsworth Publishing Co., USA.

KITANO, H. H. L. (1960) 'Validity of the CMAS and the modified revised California Inventory', Child Developm., 31, 67-72.

KJOGE, K. (1970). Diagnostieering af kignitive funktionsmader. (Diagnosing cognitive function). Problemer i forbindelse med diagnostieering af konservation og transitivitet, Copenhagen.

KLAUSMEIER, H. J. et al. (1965) 'Concept learning and problem solving: a bibliography, 1950-64'. Technical Report No.1, Wisconsin University, Res. and Developm., Centre for Learning and Re-education.

KLEIN, S. D. (1963) 'A developmental study of tactual perception', unpub. PhD dissertation, Clark University, Massachusetts.

KNIGHT, C. A. and KOFSKY, E. (1973) 'Training comparison of the subset and the whole set: effects on inferences from negative instances', Child Developm., 44, 162-5.

KOCH, S. (Ed.) (1959) 'Psychology — A Study of a Science'. Vols. 1, 2, 3, Vol. 4, (1962), Vols. 5 and 6, (1963). New York: McGraw-Hill.

KOFSKY, E. (1966) 'A scalogram study of classificatory development', Child Developm., 37, 191-204.

KOFSKY, E. and OSLER, S. (1967) 'Free classification in children', Child Developm., 927-37.

KOHLBERG, L. (1956) 'The development of modes of moral thinking and choice in the years ten to sixteen', Unpub. doctoral dissertation, University of Chicago.

KOHLBERG, L. (1963a) 'Moral development and identification', in STEVENSON, H. (Ed.), Child Psych., 62nd Yearbook of the National Society for the Study of Education. Chicago, Illinois: University of Chicago Press.

KOHLBERG, L. (1963b) 'The development of children's orientations toward a moral order: I, sequence in the development of moral thought', Vita Humana, 6, 11-33.

KOHLBERG, L. (1964) 'The development of moral character and ideology', in HOFFMAN, M. and L. (Eds.) 'Review of Child Development Research'. Vol. I. New York: Russell Sage Foundation.

KOHLBERG, L. (1964b) 'Sex differences in morality', in MACCOBY, E. L. (Ed.) Sex Role Development. New York: SSRC.

KOHLBERG, L. (1965) 'Relationships between the development of moral judgement and moral conduct', Paper presented at Symposium on Behavioural and Cognitive Concepts in the Study of Internalization. (See KOHLBERG, 1967).

KOHLBERG, L. (1966) 'Moral education in the schools: a developmental view', The School Review, 74, 1-30.

KOHLBERG, L. (1967) 'Moral education, religious education and the public schools: a developmental view', in SIZER, T. (Ed.) 'Religion and the Public Schools'. Boston: Houghton Mifflin.

KOHLBERG, L. (1967) 'The Development of Children's Orientations Toward a Moral Order. II: Social Experience, Social Conduct and the Development of Moral Thought'. Unpub. Manuscript. Originally: 'Relationships between the development of moral judgement and moral conduct'. Paper presented at Symposium on Behavioural and Cognitive Concepts in the study of Internalization at the Society for Research in Child Development, Minneapolis, Minnesota, March 26th, 1965.

KOHLBERG, L. (1968) 'The child as a moral philosopher', Psychology Today, 2(4), 27.

KOHLBERG, L. (1968a) 'Early education: a cognitive-developmental view', Child Developm., 39, 1013-63.

KOHLBERG, L. (1969) 'The relations between moral judgement and moral action: a developmental view', Paper presented as colloquium at the Institute of Human Development, University of California, Berkeley.

431

KOHLBERG, L. (1969) 'Stage and sequence: the cognitive-developmental approach to socialization', in GOSLIN, D. (Ed.) 'Handbook of Socialization Theory and Research'. New York: Rand McNally.

KOHLBERG, L. (1970) 'Reply to Bereiter's statement on Kohlberg's cognitive-developmental view', Interchange, J.Ed.Stud. Vol. I. No.I, 40-9.

KOHLBERG, L. (1970a) 'Stages of moral development as a basis for moral education, in BECK, C. and SULLIVAN, E. (Eds.) 'Moral Education.' Toronto: University of Toronto Press.

KOHLBERG, L. (1970b) 'Education for justice: a modern statement of the Platonic view', in SIZER, T. (Ed.) 'Moral Education'. Cambridge, Mass: Harvard Univ. Press.

KOHLBERG, L. (1970c) 'The moral atmosphere of the school'. Paper delivered at the Association for Supervision and Curriculum Development Conference on the 'Unstudied Curriculum', Washington, DC, Jan. 9th 1969. Printed in the AASC Yearbook.

KOHLBERG, L. (1971) 'Moral Judgement Interview and Procedures for Scoring'.

KOHLBERG, L. (1971b) 'From is to ought: how to commit the naturalistic fallacy and get away with it in the study of moral development', in MISCHEL, T. (Ed.) 'Cognitive Development and Epistemology'. New York and London: Academic Press.

KOHLBERG, L. and DeVRIES, R. (1969) 'Relations between Piaget and psychometric assessments of intelligence', Paper presented at the Conference on the Natural Curriculum, Urbana, Illinois. In LAVATELLI, C. (Ed.) (1971) 'The Natural Curriculum'. University of Illinois Press.

KOHLBERG, L. and KRAMER, R. (1969) 'Continuities and discontinuities in childhood and adult moral development', Human Dev., 12, 93-120.

KOHLBERG, L. and TURIEL, E. (1971) 'Moral development and moral education', in LESSER, G. (Ed.) 'Psychology and the Educational Process'. Chicago: Scott, Foresman.

KOHLBERG, L. and TURIEL, E. (to be published), 'Recent Research in Moral Development', London and New York: Holt-Blond Ltd.

KOHN, N. (1972) 'The development of culturally disadvantaged and middle class Negro children on Piagetian tests of concrete operational thought', PhD thesis, University of Chicago, (in preparation).

KOHNSTAMM, G. A. (1963) 'An evaluation of part of Piaget's theory', Acta Psychol., 21.

KOHNSTAMM, G. A. (1965) 'Developmental psychology and the teaching of thought operations', 'Paedagogica Europaea, European Yearbook of Educational Research', Elsevier-Westermann.

KOHNSTAMM, G. A. (1966) 'Experiments on teaching Piagetian thought operations'. Paper read at the Conference on Guided Learning Educ. Res. Council of Greater Cleveland.

KOHNSTAMM, G. A. (1966b) 'The gap between the psychology of cognitive development and education seen from Europe'. Paper presented at the Jennings Lecture Series of the Educ. Res. Coun. of Greater Cleveland.

KOHNSTAMM, G. A. (1967) 'Piaget's Analysis of Class Inclusion: Right or Wrong?' The Hague and Paris: Mouton and Co.

KOHNSTAMM, G. A. (1968) 'Teaching Children to Solve a Piagetian Problem of Class Inclusion'. The Hague and Paris: Mouton and Co.

KOMISTAR, B. P. and MACMILLAN, C. B. J. (1967) (Eds.) 'Psychological

Concepts in Education'. New York: Rand McNally.

KOOISTRA, W. H. (1965) 'Developmental trends in the attainment of conservation, transitivity and relativism in the thinking of children: replication and extension of Piaget's ontogenetic formulation'. Ph.D. Dissertation in Cognitive Processes'. Wayne State Univ., 35pp (Abstract).

KOPP, C. B. (1973) 'Ordinality and sensori-motor series'. Child Developm., 44, 4, 821-23.

KOUSSY, A. A. H. EL. (1955) The Directions of Research in the Domain of Spatial Aptitudes. Paris: Centre National de la Récherche Scientifique.

KRAMER, C. Y. (1956) 'Extension of multiple range tests to group means with unequal numbers of replications', Biometrics, 12, 307-10.

KRAMER, R. (1969) 'Moral development in young adulthood', Unpub. Doctoral Dissertation. University of Chicago.

KREBS, R. L. (1967) 'Some relationships between moral judgement, attention and resistance to temptation'. Unpub. Doctoral Dissertation. Univ. of Chicago.

KUHN, D., LANGER, J. and KOHLBERG, L. (to be published). 'Relations between logical and moral development', in KOHLBERG, L. and TURIEL, E. (Eds.) 'Recent Research in Moral Development'. London and New York: Holt-Blond Ltd.

KURZWEIL, Z. E. (1968) 'Anxiety and Education'. London: Thomas Yoseloff.

L'ABATE, L. (1962) 'Consensus of choice among children: A test of Piaget's theory of cognitive development', J. Gen. Psych., 100, 143-9.

LALLY, V. M. (1968) 'The effects of supplementary verbal stimulation on the development of concepts of number', DipEd thesis, Bristol University.

LANDERS, W. F. (1971) 'Effects of differential experience on infants' performance in a Piagetian stage IV, object-concept task', Dev. Psych., 5, 48-54.

LANE, E. B. and KINDER, E. F. (1939) 'Relativism in the thinking of subnormal subjects as measured by certain of Piaget's tests', J. Genet. Psychol., 54, 107-18.

LANGER, J. (1964) 'Implications of Piaget's Talks for Curriculum', J. Res. Sci. Teach., 2, 208-13.

LANGER, J. (1969) 'Disequilibrium as a source of development', in MUSSEN, P., LANGER, J. and COVINGTON, M. (Eds.) 'Trends and Issues in Developmental Psychology'. New York: Holt, Rinehart and Winston.

LARSEN, G. Y. and ABRAVANEL, E. (1972) An examination of the developmental relations between certain spatial tasks', Merr. Palm. Quart., 18, 1, 39-51.

LARSEN, G. Y. and FLAVELL, J. H. (1970) 'Verbal factors in compensation performance and the relation between conservation and compensation', Child Developm., 41, 965-77.

LASRY, J. C. (1966) 'Enseignment operatoire de la notion d'inclusion', unpub. doctoral dissertation, Montreal University.

LAUBENGAYER, N. C. (1965) 'The effects of training on the spatial egocentrism of pre-schoolers', unpub. Master's thesis. Minnesota University.

LAURENDEAU, M. and PINARD, A. (1962) 'Causal Thinking in the Child'.

New York: Int. Universities Press.

LAURENDEAU, M. and PINARD, A. (1969) 'Les premiers notions spatiales chez l'enfant'. Neûchatel: Delachaux et Niestlé.

LAURENDEAU, M. and PINARD, A. (1970) 'The Development of the Concept of Space in the Child'. New York: International University Press.

LAVIN, D. E. (1965) 'The Prediction of Academic Performance'. New York: Russell Sage Foundation.

LAZARUS, R., DEESE, J. and OSLER, S. F. (1952) 'The effects of psychological stress on performance', Psych. Bull., 49, 293-317.

LeCOMPTE, G. K. and GRATCH, G. (1972) 'Violation of a rule as a method of diagnosing infants' levels of object concept', Child Developm., 43, 385-96.

LEE, L. C. (1965) 'Concept utilization in pre-school children', Child Developm., 36, I, 57-63.

LEE, L. C. (1971) 'The concomitant development of cognitive and moral modes of thought: a test of selected deductions from Piaget's theory', Gen. Psych. Mon., 83, 93-146.

LEE, L. C, KAGAN J. and RABSON, A. (1963) 'Influence of a preference for analytic categorization upon concept acquisition,' Child Developm., 34, 433-42.

LEE, M. (1965) 'Children's reactions to moral transgressions', MEd thesis, Univ. of Durham.

LEEPER, R. (1966) Cited in BRUNER, J. S., 'On cognitive growth', in BRUNER, J. S., OLVER, R. R., GREENFIELD, P. M. (Eds.) 'Studies in Cognitive Growth'. New York: Wiley, 20.

LEEPER, R. W. (1948) 'A motivational theory of emotion to replace "emotion as disorganized response" '. Psych. Bull., 55, 5-21.

LEFRANCOIS, G. R. (1966) 'The acquisition of concepts of conservation', PhD thesis, University of Alberta.

LeFURGY, W. G. and WOLOSHIN, G. W. (1969) 'Immediate and long-term effects of experimentally induced social influence in the modification of adolescents' moral judgements', J. Soc. Psych., 12, no.2, 104-10.

LEHRER, L. (1967) 'Sex differences in moral behaviour and attitudes', unpub. Doctoral Dissert. Univ. of Chicago.

LEIBMAN, O. B. (1953) 'The relationship of personal and social adjustment to academic achievement in the elementary school' unpub. PhD dissertation, Columbia University.

LERNER, E. (1937) 'The problem of perspective in moral reasoning', Am. J. Soc., 43, 249-69.

LERNER, S. and LEHRER, P. (1972) 'Concrete-Operational thinking in mentally ill adolescents', Merr. Palm. Quart., 287-91.

LESSER, G. S., FIFER, G. and CLARK, D. H. (1965) 'Mental abilities of children from different social groups and cultural groups', Mon. Soc. Res. Child Dev., 30, (whole No.102).

LeVINE, R. A. and PRICE-WILLIAMS, D. R. (1970) 'Children's kinship concepts: preliminary report on a Nigerian study'. Symposium presented at the American Anthropological Ass., San Diego.

LEVITT, E. E. (1968) 'The Psychology of Anxiety'. London: Staples Press.

LEVY, D. M. (1943) 'Maternal Over-Protection'. New York: Columbia Univ. Press.

LEWIS, A. and FISHBEIN, H. D. (1969) 'Space perception in children: a

434

disconfirmation of Piaget's developmental hypothesis'. Paper presented at the meeting of the Psychonomic Society, St. Louis.

LIGHT, R. (1969) 'Cognitive stages in dream concept development in English children'. Master's thesis, Sussex University.

LINDEN, J. (1972) 'The performance of schizophrenic children upon a series of Piagetian tasks', PhD thesis, Chicago University (in preparation).

LISTER, C. M. (1969) 'The development of a concept of weight conservation in ESN children', Brit. J. Ed. Psych., 245-52.

LISTER, C. M. (1970) 'The development of the concept of volume conservation in ESN children', Brit. J. Ed. Psych., 40, 55-64.

LISTER, C. M. (1972) 'The development of ESN children's understanding of conservation in a range of attribute situations', Brit. J. Ed. Psych., 42, 14-22.

LITTLE, A. (1972) 'A longitudinal study of cognitive development in young children', Child Developm., 43, 1024-34.

LIU, Ching-Ho, (1950) 'The influence of cultural background on the moral judgement of children', doctoral dissertation, Columbia University.

LLOYD, B. B. (1966) 'Education and family life in the development of class identification among the Yoruba', in LLOYD, P. C. (Ed.) 'The New Elites of Tropical Africa'. London: OUP.

LLOYD, B. B. (1969) 'Antecedents of personality and ability differences in Yoruba children', in JOLLY, R. (Ed.) Education in Africa: Research and Action. Nairobi: East Africa Univ. Press.

LLOYD, B. B. (1971) 'Studies of conservation with Yoruba children of differing ages and experience', Child Developm., 42, 415-28.

LLOYD, B. B. (1971a) 'The intellectual development of Yoruba children: a re-examination', J. Cross-Cult. Psych., 2, 29-38.

LLOYD, B. B. (1972, in press) 'Perception and Cognition from a Cross-Cultural Perspective'. Harmondsworth, UK: Penguin.

LLOYD, B. B. and BURGESS, J. W. (1973) 'Peer interaction and cognitive development in primary school children'. Paper read at The British Psychological Society Conference, Liverpool University, Easter.

LLOYD, B. B. and LIGHT, R. A. (1970) 'Cognitive stages in dream concept development in English children', J. Soc. Psych., 82, 271-2.

LODWICK, A. R. (1958) 'An investigation of the question whether the inferences that children draw in learning history correspond to the stages of Mental Development that Piaget postulates', Unpublished Diploma Thesis, University of Birmingham.

LOEVINGER, J. (1947) 'A systematic approach to the construction and evaluation of tests of ability', Psych. Mon., 61, 4, (whole No.185).

LOEVINGER, J. (1948) 'The technique of homogeneous tests compared with some aspects of "scale analysis" and factor analysis', Psych. Mon., 45, 507-29.

LOEVINGER, J. (1966) 'The meaning and measurement of ego development', Am. Psych., 21, 195-206.

LOOFT, W. R. (1973) 'Animistic thought in children: effects of two response modes'. Percep. Mot. Skills, 36, 59-62.

LOUGHRAN, R. (1964) 'A search for a pattern of development in the moral judgements made by adolescents', MEd thesis, Univ. of Birmingham.

LOVELL, K. (1959) 'A follow-up study of some aspects of the work of Piaget and Inhelder on the child's conception of space', Brit. J. Ed. Psych., 29, 104-17.

LOVELL, K. (1961a) 'The Growth of Basic Mathematical and Scientific Concepts in Children'. University of London Press.

LOVELL, K. (1961b) 'A follow-up study of Inhelder and Piaget's "The Growth of Logical Thinking" ', Brit. J. Ed. Psych., 52, 143-54.

LOVELL, K. (1966) 'The philosophy of Jean Piaget', New Society, 11th August, 222-6.

LOVELL, K. (1966) 'Concepts in mathematics', in KLAUSMEIER, H. J. and HARRIS, C. W. (Eds.) 'Analyses of Concept Learning'. New York: Academic Press.

LOVELL, K. (1968) 'Experimental Foundations', in 'Piaget in Perspective'. (Papers read at a conference of Sussex University, School of Education, pp.1-12, April 5-6.)

LOVELL, K. (1969) Cited in 'The Role of Experience in the Rate and Sequence of Cognitive Development' by M. GOLDSCHMID (Invited paper read at the Conference on Ordinal Scales of Cognitive Developm., Monterey, Calif., Feb. 9-11.)

LOVELL, K. (1971) Comments on Goldschmid's Paper 'The Role of Experience in the Rate and Sequence of Cognitive Development', in GREEN D. R. FORD M. P. and FLAMER, G. B. (Eds.) 'Piaget and Measurement'. New York: McGraw-Hill.

LOVELL, K. (1971a) 'Some problems associated with formal thought and its assessment', in GREEN D. R., FORD M. P. and FLAMER, G. B. (Eds.) 'Piaget and Measurement'. New York: McGraw-Hill.

LOVELL, K. and BUTTERWORTH, I. (1966) 'Abilities underlying the understanding of proportionality" Mathematics Teaching, 37, 5-9.

LOVELL, K., HEALEY, D. and ROWLAND, A. D. (1962) 'Growth of some geometrical concepts', Child Developm., 33, 751-67.

LOVELL, K., HOYLE, H. W. and SIDDALL, M. Q. (1968) 'A study of some aspects of the play and language of young children with delayed speech', J. Child Psych. Psychiat., 9, 41-50.

LOVELL, K., KELLETT, V. L. and MOORHOUSE, E. (1962) 'The growth of the concept of speed: a comparative study', J. Child Psychol. Psychiat., 3, 101-10.

LOVELL, K., MITCHELL, B. and EVERETT, I. (1962) 'An experimental study of the growth of some logical structures', Brit. J. Psych., 53, 175-88.

LOVELL, K. and OGILVIE, E. (1960) 'A study of the conservation of substance in the junior school child', Brit. J. Ed. Psych., 30, 109-18.

LOVELL, K. and OGILVIE, E. (1961) 'A study of the conservation of weight in the junior school child', Brit. J. Ed. Psych., 31, 138-44.

LOVELL, K. and OGILVIE, E. (1961) 'The growth of the concept of volume in junior school children', J. Child. Psychol. Psychiat., 2, 118-26.

LOVELL, K. and SHIELDS, J. B. (1967) 'Some aspects of a study of the gifted child', Brit. J. Ed. Psych., 201-9.

LOVELL, K. and SLATER, A. (1960) 'The growth of the concept of time: a comparative study', J. Child Psych. Psychiat., 2, 118-26, 179-90.

LOWE, G. and RANYARD, R. H. (1973) 'Intuitive statistical judgements in children: Estimates of proportion', Paper read at the British Psychological Society Conference, Liverpool University, Easter.

LUBINSKAYA, A. A. (1957) 'The development of children's speech and thought', in SIMON, B. (Ed.) 'Psychology in the Soviet Union'. London: Routledge and Kegan Paul.

LUBKER, B. J. (1969) 'The Role of between – and within – setting irrelevant dimensions in children's simultaneous discrimination learning', Child Developm., 40, 663-79.

LUNDBERG, G. A. (1937) 'Social attraction-patterns in a rural village', Sociometry, 1, 1.

LUNZER, E. A. (1959) 'Introduction to the Vineland – Manchester Scales of Social Adaptation', unpub. cyclostyle. Univ. of Manchester.

LUNZER, E. A. (1960) 'Recent Studies in Britain Based on the Work of Jean Piaget'. Slough: NFER. (New edit. 1973).

LUNZER, E. A. (1960a) 'Some points of Piagetian theory in the light of experimental criticism', J. Child Psych., Psychiat., 1, 191-202.

LUNZER, E. A. (1960b) 'Aggressive and withdrawing children in the normal school', Brit. J. Ed. Psych., 30, 1 and V.

LUNZER, E. A. (1965) 'Problems of formal reasoning in test situations', in 'European Research in Cognitive Development', Mon. Soc. Res. Child Dev., 30, 19-46.

LUNZER, E. A. (1965a) 'Les co-ordinations et les conservations dans le domaine de la géometrie', in BANG, V. and LUNZER, E. 'Études d'épistémologie génétique. Vol. XIX. Conservations Spatiales'. Paris University Press, 59-148.

LUNZER, E. A. (1968) 'Children's thinking', in: BUTCHER, H. 'Educational Research in Britain'. University of London Press, 69-101.

LUNZER, E. A. (1968a) 'The Regulation of Behaviour. (Development in Learning I)'. London: Staples Press.

LUNZER, E. A. (1970) 'Construction of a standardized battery of Piagetian tests to assess the development of effective intelligence', Research in Educ., 3, 53-72. Manchester University Press.

LUNZER, E. A. (1970) 'Problems of formal reasoning in test situations'. Cited in 'Cognitive Development in Children'. Five monographs of the Society for Research in Child Development. University of Chicago Press. (one volume edition).

LUNZER, E. A. (1971) 'The development of systematic thinking', in 'Report of the Social Science Research Council, April 1970-March 1971'. London: HMSO, 178-9.

LUNZER, E. A. (1972) 'The Piaget controversy', Times Ed. Supp., Feb. 11th., pp. 18-19.

LUNZER, E. A. and MORRIS, J. F. (Eds.) (1968) 'Development in Human Learning. (Development in Learning II)'. London: Staples Press.

LUNZER, E. A. and MORRIS, J. F. (Eds.) (1969) 'Contexts of Education. (Development in Learning III)'. London: Staples Press.

LUNZER, E. A. and PUMFREY, P. (1966) 'Understanding proportionality', Mathematics Teaching, 34, 7-13.

LURIA, A. R. (1957) 'The role of language in the formation of temporary connections' in SIMON, E. (Ed.) (1957) 'Psychology in the Soviet Union'. Stanford University Press, 116.

LURIA, A. R. (1959) 'The directive function of speech in development and dissolution, part I', Word, 15, 341-52.

LURIA, A. R. (1961) 'The Role of Speech in the Regulation of Normal and Abnormal Behaviour'. London: Pergamon Press.

LURIA, A. R. and YUDOVICH, F. La (1959) 'Speech and the Development of Mental Processes in the Child'. London: Staples Press.

LYNN, R. (1959) 'Two personality characteristics related to academic achievement', Brit. J. Ed. Psych., 29, 213-6.

MACCOBY, E. E. and RAU, L. (1962) 'Differential Cognitive Abilities'. Contract No.1040, USOE manuscript.

MACKAY, C. K., BRAZENDALE, A. H. and WILSON, L. F. (1972) 'Concepts of horizontal and vertical: a methodological note', Dev. Psych., 7, 3, 232-7.

MACKAY, C. K., FRASER, J. and ROSS, I. (1970) 'Matrices, three by three: classification and seriation', Child Developm., 41, 787-97.

MACKAY, M. J. (1972) 'An investigation into haptic perception among children', unpub. MSc thesis, London University.

MACKWORTH, N. H. (1967) 'A stand camera for line-of-sight recording', Perception and Psychophysics, 2, 119-27.

MACKWORTH, N. H. and BRUNER, J. S. (1970) 'How adults and children search and recognize pictures', Human Developm., in press, 13, 149-77.

MACRAE, D. (1954) 'A test of Piaget's theories of moral development', J. Abnorm. Soc. Psych., 49, 14-18.

MAGOWAN, S. A. (1966) 'A study of immanent justice in the moral development of the child', EdB thesis, University of St. Andrews.

MAGOWAN, S. A. and LEE, T. (1970) 'Some sources of error in the use of the projective method for the measurement of moral judgement', Brit. J. Psych., 61, 535-43.

MAIER, H. W. (1965) 'Three Theories of Child Development'. New York: Harper.

MANDLER, G. and COWEN, J. E. (1958) 'Test anxiety questionnaires', J. Consult. Psych., 22, 228-9.

MANDLER, G. and SARASON, S. B. (1952) 'A study of anxiety and learning', J. Abnorm. Soc. Psych., 47, 166-73.

MANNIX, J. B. (1960) 'The number concepts of a group of ESN children', Brit. J. Ed. Psych., 30, 80-1; also MEd thesis of same title, Manchester University.

MARATSOS, M. P. (1973) 'Decrease in the understanding of the word "Big" in pre-school children'. Child Developm., 44, 4, 747-52.

MASON, J. (1966) 'An investigation of the development of conservation of number in children', DipEd thesis, Bristol University.

MASON, J. (1969) 'A study of acceleration of concepts of number in young children through group treatment', MEd thesis, Bristol University.

MATHEMATICS TEACHING, (1963) 'Piaget's Researches into Mathematical Concepts'. Official bulletin of the Ass. of Teachers of Maths., 1-24.

MATTHEWS, G. (1968) 'The Nuffield Mathematics Teaching Project', The Arithmetic Teacher, 15, 101-2.

MAYS, J. B. (1963) 'The influence of environment', in 'Delinquency and Discipline'. London: Councils and Education Press.

McCANDLESS, B. R. and MARSHALL, H. R. (1957) 'A picture sociometric technique for pre-school children and its relation to teacher judgements of friendships', Child Developm., 28, 2.

McCANDLESS, J. and CASTANEDA, A. (1956) 'Anxiety in children, school achievement and intelligence', Child Developm., 27, 379-82.

McCARTHY, D. (1930) 'Language development of the pre-school child', Inst. for Child Welfare. Monog. No.4, Minneapolis: Univ. Minnesota Press.

438

McFIE, J. (1961) 'The effect of education on African performance on a group of intellectual tests', Brit. J. Ed. Psych., 31, 232-40.

McKEACHIE, W. J. et al. (1955) 'Relieving anxiety in classroom examination', J. Abnorm. Soc. Psych., 50, 93-8.

McKECHNIE, R. J. (1971) 'Between Piaget's stages: a study in moral development', Brit. J. Ed. Psych., 213-17.

McKECHNIE, R. J. (1971) 'The influence of story structure and behavioural area on the moral judgement of the child', MSc thesis, Leeds University.

McLAUGHLIN, K. L. (1935) 'Number ability of pre-school children', Child. Ed., 11, 348-53.

McMANIS, D. L. (1969) 'Relative thinking by normals and retardates', Dev. Psych., 1, 1, 69.

McMANIS, D. L. (1969a) 'Conservation and transitivity of weight and length by normals and retardates', Dev. Psych., 1, 4, 373-82.

MEALINGS, R. J. (1961) 'Some aspects of problem solving in science at the secondary school stage'. Unpub. MA thesis, Birmingham University.

MEALINGS, R. J. (1963) 'Problem solving and science teaching', Ed. Rev., 15, 194-207.

MEDINNUS, G. R. (1959) 'Immanent justice in children: a review of the literature and additional data', J. Gen. Psych., 94, 253-62.

MEDINNUS, G. R. (1961) 'The relation between several parent measures and the child's early adjustment to school', J. Ed. Psych., 52, 153-6.

MEDINNUS, G. R. (1962) 'Objective responsibility in children: a comparison with Piaget data', J. Gen. Psych., 101, 127-33.

MEDINNUS, G. R. (1966) 'Behavioural and cognitive measures of conscience development', J. Gen. Psych., 109, 147-50.

MEHLER, J. and BEVER, T. G. (1967) 'Cognitive capacity of very young children', Science, 158, 141-2.

MEHLER, J. and BEVER, T. G. (1968) Reply by J. Mehler and T. Bever, Science, 162, 979-81.

MEHRABIAN, A. (1968) 'An Analysis of Personality Theories'. Englewood Cliffs, New Jersey: Prentice Hall.

MERCHANT, R. L. and REBELSKY, F. (1972) 'Effects of participation in rule formation on the moral judgement of children', Gen. Psych., Monogr., 85, 287-304.

MERMELSTEIN, E. and MEYER, E. (1968) 'Number Training Techniques and Their Effects on Different Populations'. Final Rept. Contract No.0E0-1432, US Office of Economic Opportunity.

MERMELSTEIN, E. and SHULMAN, L. S. (1967) 'Lack of formal schooling and the acquisition of conservation', Child Developm., 38, 39-52.

MERMELSTEIN, E., CARR, E., MILLS, D. and SCHWARTZ, J. (1967) 'Training techniques for the concept of conservation', Alberta J. Ed. Psych., 13, 185-200, Project No. 6-8300.

MERRILL, B. (1946) 'A measurement of mother-child interaction', J. Abnorm. Soc. Psych., 41, 37-49.

MEYER, E. (1940) 'Comprehension of spatial relations in pre-school children', J. Gen. Psych., 57, 119-51.

MEYER, E. and MERMELSTEIN, E. (1968) 'Sequence and acquisition of conservation'. Paper presented to American Educational Res. Assoc., Chicago.

MEYER, W. J. (1964) 'Developmental Psychology'. New York: Centre for

Applied Res. in Education.

MEYERS, J. L. (1958) 'Secondary reinforcements: a review of recent experimentation', Psych. Bull., 55, 284-301.

MILLER, D., COHEN, L. B., and HILL, K. T. (1969) 'A test of Piaget's notions on object concept development in the sensori-motor period', Paper delivered at biennial meeting of the Soc. for Res. in Child Developm., Santa Monica, California.

MILLER, G. A., GALANTER, E. A. and PRIBRAM, K. H. (1960) 'Plans and the Structure of Behaviour'. Oxford: Pergamon Press.

MILLER, P. H. (1966) 'The effects of age and training on children's ability to understand certain basic concepts', unpub. PhD dissertation, Teacher's College, Columbia University.

MILLER, P. H. 'Attention to stimulus dimension in the conservation of liquid quantity', Child Developm., 44, 129-36.

MILLER, S. A. (1971) 'Extinction of conservation: A methodological and theoretical analysis', Merr. Palm. Quart., 319-34.

MILLER, S. A. (1973) 'Contradiction, surprise and cognitive change: the effect of disconfirmation of belief on conservers and non-conservers', J. Exp. Child Psych., 15, 47-62.

MILLER, S. A., SCHWARTZ, L. C. and STEWART, C. (1973) 'An attempt to extinguish conservation of weight in college students', Dev. Psych., 8, 2, 316.

MILNER, E. A. (1951) 'A study of the relationships between reading readiness in grade one school children and patterns of parent-child interactions', Child Developm., 22, 95-112.

MINICHIELLO, M. D. and GOODNOW, J. J. (1969) 'Effect of an action cue on conservation of amount', Psycho-Sci., 16, 4, 200-1.

MINNESOTA, University of, (1950) 'Scale for Paternal Occupations'.

MISCHEL, T. (1971) 'Cognitive Development and Epistemology'. New York: Academic Press.

MODGIL, S. L. (1965b) 'An investigation into the development of the concept of volume weight in a group of children aged ten', Part II, unpub. thesis, Newcastle University.

MODGIL, S. L. (1965c) 'An investigation into the development of the concept of volume in a group of children aged ten', Part III. unpub. theses, Newcastle University.

MODGIL, S. L. (1969) 'The relation of emotional adjustment to the conservation of number', MEd thesis, University of Manchester.

MODGIL, S. L. (1972 in progress) 'The relation of emotional adjustment to the conservation of number - a three-year longitudinal study', in collaboration with DUDEK, S. and STROBEL.

MODGIL, S. L. (1972) 'The relation of emotionality and socialization to Piaget's theory of cognitive development'. Paper presented to the Association of Guidance Teachers of Ireland, 14th-15th April at Marion College, Dublin.

MODGIL, S. L. (1972 in progress) 'The development of mental strategies in children aged three through five years in a London Borough'.

MODGIL, S. L. (1972 in progress) 'Developmental patterns of logical thinking in relation to maternal over-domination, over-protectiveness and over-possessiveness'.

MODGIL, S. L. (1973) The patterning of cognitive development and logical reasoning in relation to socialization in young children', (in preparation).

MODGIL, S. L. (1973) 'The relation of cognitive conflict, multiple classification, verbal rule instruction and language activation to Piaget's concept of conservation in children in an EPA school' (in press).

MODGIL, S. L. (1973, in progress) 'An investigation of reasoning ability in adopted and fostered children', (with the assistance of P. Dasen).

MODGIL, S. L. and DUDEK, S. (1973, in progress) 'Personality variables as predictors of cognitive development in young children'. (Tentative title).

MODGIL, S. L. and LUNZER, E. A. (1971) 'The patterning of educational performance in relation to parental attitudes'. Invited paper at the B.P.S. Easter Conference at Exeter University.

MODGIL, S. L. and TANDEY, J. (1974 in press) 'The validity of Shoben's parent-attitude survey'.

MODGIL, S. L. DIELMAN, T. and CATTELL, R. B. (1973 in press) 'A factor-analytic investigation of personality, attitudinal and cognitive variables in seven- and eight-year-old children.'

MODGIL, S. L. and DUDEK, S. and STROBEL, M. (1973, in progress) 'Child-rearing practices and cognitive stability'. (Tentative title).

MODGIL, S. L. (1973) 'A cross-cultural investigation of conservation', in GOLDSCHMID, M., BENTLER, P. KOHNSTAMM, G. et al., J. Cross-Cult. Psych., 4, 1, 49-75.

MOHSENI, N. (1966) 'La comparaison des réactions aux épreuves d'intelligence en Iran et en Europe', Thèse d'université, University of Paris.

MONTAGUE, E. K. (1953) 'The role of anxiety in serial rote learning', J. Exp. Psych., 45, 91-6.

MOORE, S. and UPDEGRAFF, R. (1964) 'Sociometric status of pre-school children related to age, sex, nurturance-giving and dependency'. Child Developm., 35, 519-24.

MOORE, T. A. (Private Communication, 1972) 'The relation of self-image to Piaget's theory of cognitive development', M.Phil. Thesis, Surrey University, (in progress).

MOORE, T. (1967) 'Language and Intelligence — a longitudinal study of the first eight years', Human Developm., 10, 88-106.

MORF, A. (1959) 'Apprentissage d'une structure logique concrète (inclusion). Effets et limites', Etudes d'Epistémologie Génétique, 9. Paris: Presses Universitaires de France.

MORF, A. (1963) 'Les relations entre la logique et la langage lors du passorage du raisonnement concret au raisonnement formel'. Cited by FLAVELL, J. in 'The Developmental Psychology of Piaget'. Princeton, NJ: Van Nostrand, 375.

MORRIS, J. F. (1958) 'The development of moral values in children', Brit. J. Ed. Psych., 94, 253-62.

MORRISSETT, I. (1966) 'Concepts and Structures in the Social Science Curriculum'. West Lafagette, Ind: Social Science Educ. Consortium.

MOSHER, F. A. and HORNSBY, J. R. (1966) 'On asking questions', in BRUNER, et al., 'Studies in Cognitive Growth' New York: Wiley and Sons Inc.

MOSS, H. A. and KAGAN, J. (1958) 'Maternal influences on early IQ scores', Psych. Rep., 4, 655-61.

MOYNAHAN, E. and GLICK, J. (1972) 'Relation between identity conservation and equivalence conservation within four conceptual domains', Dev. Psych., 6, 2, 247-51.

MURDOCK, B. B. (1957) 'Transfer designs and formulas', Psych. Bull., 54, 313-26.

MURRAY, F. B. (1965) 'Conservation of illusion – distorted lengths and areas by primary school children', J. Ed. Psych., 56, 62-6.

MURRAY, F. B. (1966) 'Some factors related to the conservation of illusion – distorted length by primary school children', unpub. PhD thesis, Johns Hopkins University.

MURRAY, F. B. (1967) 'Phenomenal-real discrimination and length conservation'. Paper read at Soc. Res. Child Developm., New York.

MURRAY, F. B. (1969) 'Reversibility on non-conservation of weight', Psycho-Science, 1-9.

MURRAY, F. B. (1970) 'Stimulus mode and the conservation of weight and number', J. Ed. Psych., 61, 4, 287-91.

MURRAY, F. B. (1972) 'Acquisition of conservation through social interaction', Dev. Psych., 6, 1, 1-6.

MURRAY, H. A. (1951) 'Toward a classification of interaction', in PARSONS, T. and SHILS, E. H. (Eds.) 'Toward a General Theory of Action'. Cambridge: Mass: Harvard Univ. Press, 434-64.

MURRAY, J. and YOUNNISS, J. (1969) 'Operational achievement of inferential transitivity and its relation to serial ordering in the child', Child Developm., 39, 1259-68.

MURRAY, M. M. (1961) 'The development of spatial concepts in African and European children', unpub. MSc thesis, University of Natal.

MUSS, R. E. (1967) 'Jean Piaget's cognitive theory of adolescent development', Adolescence, 2, 7, 285-310.

MUSSEN, P. H. (Ed.) (1960) 'Handbook of Research Methods in Child Development'. New York: Wiley.

MUSSEN, P. (Ed.) (1970) 'Carmichael's Manual of Child Development'. New York: Wiley.

MYCOCK, R. W. (1968) 'The relationship between spatial ability and performance on some Piagetian tests', MEd thesis, Manchester University.

NADEL, C. and SCHOEPPE, A. (1973) 'Conservation of mass, weight and volume as evidenced by adolescent girls in 8th grade', J. Gen. Psych., 122, 309-13.

NAIR, P. (1966) Cited in BRUNER, J. et al. 'Studies in Cognitive Growth'. New York: Wiley, 187-192.

NAJARIAN-SVAJIAN, P. H. (1966) 'The idea of immanent justice among Lebanese children and adults', J. Gen. Psych., 109, 57-66.

NASH, B. C. (1969) 'Some number and spatial concepts of junior school children with visual perceptual difficulties', PhD thesis, Exeter University.

NASS, M. L. (1955) 'The deaf child's conception of physical causality', J. Abnorm. Soc. Psych., 69, 669-73.

NASS, M. L. (1956) 'The effects of three variables on children's concepts of physical causality', J. Abnorm. Soc. Psych., 53, 191-6.

NATADZE, R. S. (1963) 'The mastery of scientific concepts in school', in SIMON, B. and J. (Eds.) 'Psychology in the USSR'. California: Stanford University Press, 192-7.

NEAL, G. (1959) 'The age-placement of science in a junior school', unpub. PhD thesis, Birmingham University.

NEFF, W. S. (1938) 'Socioeconomic status and intelligence; a critical survey', Psych. Bull., 35, 727-57.

NEIMARK, E. D. (1970) 'A preliminary search for formal operations structures', J. Gen. Psych., 116, 223-32.

NEISSER, U. and BELLER, H. K. (1965) 'Searching through word lists', Brit. J. Psych., 56, 349-58.

NEWTON, G. and LEVINE, S. L. (Eds.) (1958) 'Early Experience and Behaviour'. Thomas.

NICHOLSON, W. M. (1958) 'The influence of anxiety upon learning: interference or drive increment?', J. Pers., 26, 303-19.

NIXON, M. C. (1967) 'Development of classification skills in young children', unpub. PhD thesis, Melbourne University.

NORO, S. (1961) 'Development of the child's conception of number', Jap. J. Ed. Psych., 9, 230-9. (Child Developm. Abstr., 38, 115).

NORTHMAN, J. E. (1964) 'The effects of training on the concept of quantity conservation', Unpub. manuscript.

NORTHMAN, J. E. and GRUEN, G. E. (1970) 'Relationship between identity and equivalence conservation', Dev. Psych., 2, 2, 311.

MATHEMATICS PROJECT (1968) 'Check-ups'. London: The Nuffield Foundation.

NURCOMBE, B. (1970) 'Precausal and paracausal thinking. Concepts of causality in Aboriginal children', Austr. and New Zealand Psychiat., 4, 70-81.

O'BRIEN, T. C. and SHAPIRO, B. J. (1968) 'The development of logical thinking in children', Am. Ed. Res., 5, 531-43.

O'BRIEN, T. C. and SHAPIRO, B. J. (1970) 'Logical thinking in children ages six through thirteen', Child Developm., 41, 823-9.

O'BRYAN, K. G. and BOERSMA, F. J. (1971) 'Eye movements, perceptual activity and conservation development', J. Exp. Child Psych., 12, 157-69.

O'BRYAN, K. G. and BOERSMA, F. J. (1973) 'Movie presentation of Piagetian tasks', J. Gen. Psych., in press.

O'BRYAN, K. G. and MacARTHUR, R. S. (1967) 'A factor analytic study of Piagetian reversibility', Alberta J. Ed. Res., 13, 211-20.

O'BRYAN, K. G. and MacARTHUR, R. S. (1969) 'Reversibility, intelligence and creativity in 9-year-old boys', Child Developm., 40, 33-45.

ODIER, C. (1956) 'Anxiety and Magical Thinking'. New York: International University Press.

OGILVIE, E. (1970) 'Concept growth and creativity', PhD thesis, Southampton University.

OJEMANN, R. H. and PRITCHETT, K. (1963) 'Piaget and the role of guided experiences in human development', Percept. Mot. Skills, 17, 927-40.

OKONJI, M. O. (1970) 'The effect of spatial training on the classificatory behaviour of some Nigerian Ibo children', Brit. J. Ed. Psych., 40, 1, 21-6.

OKONJI, M. O. (1971) 'Culture and children's understanding of Geometry', Int. J. Psych., 6, 2, 121-8.

OKONJI, M. O (1971) 'A cross-cultural study of the effects of familiarity on classificatory behaviour', J. Cross-Cult. Psych., 2, 1, 39-49.

OKONJI, M. O. (1972) 'Cultural variables in cognition', PhD thesis. Jointly with Makerere University and Strathclyde University.

OLERON, P. and HERREN, H. (1961) 'L'acquisition des conservations et le

443

langage: étude comparative sur des enfants sourds et entendants', Enfance, 14, 203-19.

OLIM, E. G., HESS, R. D. and SHIPMAN, V. (1965) 'Maternal language styles and their implications for children's cognitive development'. Paper presented at the meeting of PAP, Chicago.

OLVER, R. and HORNSBY, J. (1966) 'On equivalence', in BRUNER, et al, 'Studies in Cognitive Growth'. New York: Wiley, pp.68-85.

OPPER, S. (1971) 'Intellectual development in Thai children', unpub. PhD thesis, Cornell University, New York.

O'REILLY, E. and STEGER, J. (1970) 'Children's use of context in judgement of weight', Child Developm., 41, 1095-1101.

OSGOOD, C. E., SUCI, G. and TANNENBAUM, P. H. (1957) 'Measurement of Meaning'. Urbana: University of Illinois Press.

OSLER, S. F. and FIVEL, M. F. (1961) 'Concept attainment: I. The role of age and intelligence in concept attainment by induction', J. Exp. Psych., 62, 1-8.

OSLER, S. F. and KOFSKY, E. (1966) 'Structure and strategy in concept learning', J. Exp. Child Psych., 4, 198-209.

OSLER, S. F. and KOFSKY, E. (1967) 'Free classification in children', Child Developm., 927-37.

OTAALA, B. (1971) 'The development of operational thinking in primary school children. An examination of some aspects of Piaget's theory among the Iteso children of Uganda'. Unpub. PhD thesis, Columbia University.

OVERHOLD, E. D. (1965) 'An investigation of elementary students' achievement in arithmetic as related to the attainment of the concept of the conservation of substance', PhD thesis, Kansas University.

OVERTON, W. F. and BRODZINSKY, D. (1972) 'Perceptual and logical factors in the development of multiplicative classification', Dev. Psych., 6, 1, 104-9.

OVERTON, W. F. and JORDAN, R. (1971) 'Stimulus preference and multiplicative classification in children', Dev. Psych., 5, 3, 505-10.

OVERTON, W. F., WAGNER, J. and DOLINSKY, H. (1971) 'Social class differences and task variables in the development of multiplicative classification', Child Developm., 42, 1951-58.

PAGE, E. (1957) 'Haptic perception', diploma dissertation, Birmingham University.

PAGE, E. (1959) 'Haptic perception: a consideration of one of the investigations of Piaget and Inhelder', Ed. Rev., 11, 115-25.

PAIVIO, A. (1970) 'On the functional significance of imagery', Psych. Bull., 73, 6, 385-92.

PALERMO, D. et al. (1956) 'The relationship of anxiety in children to performance in a complex learning test', Child Developm., 27, 333-7.

PAPALIA, D. E. and HOOPER, F. H. (1971) 'A developmental comparison of identity and equivalence conservation', J. Exp. Child Psych., 12, 347-61.

PARASKEVOPOULOS, J. and HUNT, J. McV. (1971) 'Object construction and imitation under differing conditions of rearing', J. Gen. Psych., 119, 301-21.

PARKER, D. J. (1963) 'An inquiry into the number concepts of some seven- to ten-year-old children with reference to other aspects of their attainment'. MEd thesis, Leicester University.

PARKER, R. K. and DAY, M. C. (1971) 'The use of perceptual, functional and abstract attributes in multiple classification', Dev. Psych., 5, 2, 312-9.

PARKER, R. K., RIEFF, M. L. and SPERR, S. J. (1971) 'Teaching multiple classification to young children', Child Developm., 42, 1779-89.

PARKER, R. K., SPERR, S. J. and RIEFF, M. L. (1972) 'Multiple classification: A training approach', Dev. Psych., 7, 2, 188-95.

PARSONS, C. (1960) 'Inhelder and Piaget's "The Growth of Logical Thinking," II. A logician's viewpoint', Brit. J. Psych., 51, 1, 75-84.

PARSONS, T. and SHILS, A. (Eds.) (1951) 'Toward a General Theory of Action'. Cambridge, Mass: Harvard Univer. Press.

PASCUAL-LEONE, J. and BOVET, M. C. (1966) 'L'apprentissage de la quantification de l'inclusion et la théorie opératoire', Acta Psychol. 25, 334-56.

PATERSON, H. (1965) 'Possible solutions to problems: an exploratory study with children and adults', BEd thesis, Edinburgh University.

PAYNE, D. E. and MUSSEN, P. H. (1956) 'Parent-child relations and father identification among adolescent boys', J. Abnorm. Soc. Psych., 52, 358-62.

PEARSON, H. J. (Ed.) (1968) 'A Handbook of Child Psychoanalysis'. New York and London: Basic Books.

PEARSON, V. (1963) 'An investigation into the nature of moral judgement in six-year-old children', BA dissertation, University of Durham.

PECK, R. F. and HAVIGHURST, R. J. et al. (1960) 'The Psychology of Character Development'. New York: Wiley.

PEEL, E. A. (1956) 'The Psychological Bases of Education'. London: Oliver and Boyd.

PEEL, E. A. (1959) 'Experimental examination of some of Piaget's schemata concerning children's perception and thinking and a discussion of their educational significance', Brit. J. Ed. Psych., 29, 89-103.

PEEL, E. A. (1960) 'The Pupil's Thinking'. London: Oldbourne Press.

PEEL, E. A. (1964) 'Learning and thinking in the school situation', in RIPPLE, R. E. and ROCKCASTLE, V. N. (Eds.) 'Piaget Rediscovered'. A report of the Conference on Cognitive Studies and Curriculum Developm. Ithaca: Cornell University, 101-4.

PEEL, E. A. (1965) 'Intellectual growth during adolescence' Ed. Rev. 17, 3, June 1965.

PEEL, E. A. (1966) 'A study of differences in the judgements of adolescent pupils', Brit. J. Ed. Psych., 36, 77-86.

PEEL, E. A. (1967) 'Programmed thinking', Programmed Learning, p. 151-7, July 1967.

PEEL, E. A. (1968) 'Understanding and judging' Unpub. Manuscript.

PEEL, E. A. (1971) 'The Nature of Adolescent Judgement'. London: Staples Press.

PEEL, E. A. (Ed.)(1972) 'The quality of thinking in secondary school subjects', Educ. Rev., 24, No. 3 Birmingham University School of Education.

PELUFFO, N. (1962) 'Les notions de conservation et de causalité chez les enfants prévenant de differentes milieux physiques et socio-culturels', Archives de Psychologie, 38, 75-90.

PELUFFO, N. (1964) 'N. la nozione di conservazione del volume e le

445

operazione de combinazione come indici di suiluppe del pensiero operatorio in suggetti appartnenti and ambienti fisici e socioculturati diversi', Riviste de Psicol Sociale, 11, 99-132.

PELUFFO, N. (1965) 'Problemi cognitivi strategie, piant di soluzione', Riviste de Psicol Sociale, 12, 91-103.

PELUFFO, N. (1967) 'Culture and cognitive problems', Intern. J. Psych., 2, 187-98.

PETERS, D. L. (1969) 'Piaget's conservation of number: the interaction of language comprehension and analytic style with three methods of training', PhD thesis, Stanford University.

PETERS, R. S. (1958) 'The Concept of Motivation'. New York: Humanities Press.

PETERS, R. S. (1971) 'Moral developments: a plea for pluralism'. Cited in MISCHEL, T. (Ed.) 'Cognitive Development and Epistemology'. London: Academic Press.

PETERS, R. S. (1972) 'Education and human development'. Cited in DEARDEN, R. E., HIRST, P. H. and PETERS, R. S. (Eds.) 'Education and the Development of Reason'. London: Routledge and Kegan Paul.

PETTIFOR, J. L. (1964) 'The role of language in the development of abstract thinking', dissertation abstract, Centre for Cognitive Studies, Wayne State University.

PETTIGREW, Y. F. (1958) 'The measurement and correlates of category width as a cognitive variable', J. Pers., 26, 532-44.

PHEMISTER, A. (1960) 'An investigation into children's understanding of number on school entry, and of the effectiveness of infant classroom teaching based on Piaget's theory'. DipEd thesis, Manchester University.

PHILLIPS, B. N. et al. (1960) 'Influence of intelligence on anxiety and perception of self and others', Child Developm., 31, 41-6.

PHILLIPS, J. L. (Jr.) (1969) 'The Origins of Intellect: Piaget's Theory'. San Francisco: Freeman.

PHILLIPS, L. (1968) 'Human Adaptation and its Failures'. New York: Academic Press.

PIAGET, J. (1923) 'The Language and Thought of the Child'. London: Routledge and Kegan Paul. Translated by M. Gabain. (First English Publication in 1926.) 319pp.

PIAGET, J. (1924) 'Judgment and Reasoning in the Child'. London: Routledge and Kegan Paul. Translated by M. Warden. (First English Publication in 1926.) 204pp.

PIAGET, J. (1926) 'The Child's Conception of the World'. London: Routledge and Kegan Paul. Translated by J. & A. Tomlinson. (First English Publication in 1929.) 424pp.

PIAGET, J. (1927) 'The Child's Conception of Physical Causality'. London: Routledge and Kegan Paul, Translated by M. Gabain. (First English Publication in 1930.) 309pp.

PIAGET, J. (1932) 'The Moral Judgment of the Child'. London: Routledge and Kegan Paul, Translated by M. Gabain. (First English Publication in 1932.) 418pp.

PIAGET, J. (1936) 'The Origin of Intelligence in the Child'. London: Routledge and Kegan Paul. Translated by M. Cook. (First English Publication in 1952.) 425 pp.

PIAGET, J. (1937) 'The Construction of Reality in the Child'. London:

Routledge & Kegan Paul. Translated by M. Cook. (First English Publication in 1955.) 386 pp. (Basic Books Inc., 1954).

PAIGET, J. (1941) 'The Child's Conception of Number'. London: Routledge and Kegan Paul. Translated by C. Gattegno and F. M. Hodgson. (First English Publicaton 1952.) 248 pp.

PIAGET, J. and INHELDER, B. (1941) 'Le Developpement des Quantités Chez l'enfant. Neûchatel and Paris: Delachaux & Niestlé. 339 pp.

PIAGET, J. (1946) 'Play, Dreams and Imitation in Childhood'. London: Heinemann, (1951) and Routledge and Kegan Paul (1967). Translated by C. Gattegno and F. M. Hodgson. 296 pp.

PIAGET, J. (1946) 'The Child's Conception of Time'. London: Routledge and Kegan Paul. Translated by A. J. Pomerans. (First English Publication in 1969.) 298 pp.

PIAGET, J. (1946) 'The Child's Conception of Movement and Speed'. London: Routledge and Kegan Paul. Translated by G. E. T. Holloway and M. J. Mackenzie. (First English Publication in 1970.) 306 pp.

PIAGET, J. (1947) 'The Psychology of Intelligence'. London: Routledge and Kegan Paul. Translated by M. Piercey and D. E. Berlyne. (First English Publication in 1950.) 180 pp.

PIAGET, J. and INHELDER, B. (1947) 'Diagnosis of mental operations and theory of intelligence', Am. J. Mental Deficiency, 5, 401-6.

PIAGET, J. and INHELDER, B. (1948) 'The Child's Conception of Space'. London: Routledge and Kegan Paul. Translated by F. J. Langdon and E. A. Lunzer. (First English Publication in 1956.) 490 pp.

PIAGET, J. and INHELDER, B. and SZEMINSKA, A. (1948) 'The Child's Conception of Geometry'. London: Routledge and Kegan Paul. Translated by E. A. Lunzer. (First English Publication in 1960.) 411 pp.

PAIGET, J., BOSCHER, B. and CHATELET, A. (1949) 'La genèse du nombre chez l'enfant', in Initiation au Calcul. Enfants de 4à 7 ans. Cahiers de pédagogie moderne. Paris: Bourrelier, 5-28.

PIAGET, J. (1950) 'The Psychology of Intelligence'. London: Routledge and Kegan Paul. (French Ed. 1947).

PIAGET, J. (1951) 'The right to education in the modern world', in UNESCO, 'Freedom and Culture'. New York: Columbia University Press, 67-116.

PIAGET, J. and INHELDER, B. (1951) 'Die Psychologie der Fruhen Kindheit', in KATZ, D. 'Handbuch der Psychologie'. Basle: Schwabe.

PIAGET, J. (1951) 'Play, Dreams and Imitation in Childhood'. London: Heinemann (French Ed. 1946). (Routledge and Kegan Paul, 1967).

PIAGET, J. (1951) 'The Child's Conception of the World'. London: Routledge and Kegan Paul. (French Ed. 1926).

PIAGET, J. (1952) 'The Origin of Intelligence in the Child'. New York: International University Press (French Ed. 1936). (Routledge and Kegan Paul, 1953).
Routledge and Kegan Paul. (French Ed. 1941)

PIAGET, J. (1953) 'Logic and Psychology'. Manchester University Press. 48pp.

PIAGET, J. (1955) 'The Construction of Reality in the Child'. London: Routledge and Kegan Paul. (French Ed. 1937).

PIAGET, J. and INHELDER, B. (1955) 'The Growth of Logical Thinking from Childhood to Adolescence'. New York: Basic Books. Translated by

447

A. Parsons and S. Milgram. (First English Publication in 1958.) 356 pp.

PIAGET, J. (1955) 'Les structures mathématiques et les structures opératories de l'intelligence', in PIAGET et al. (publication collective de la commission internationale pour l'étude et l'amélioration de l'enseignement des mathématiques): L'Enseignement des Mathématiques. Neúchatel and Paris: Delachaux and Niestlé, 11-34.

PIAGET, J. and INHELDER, B. (1956) 'The Child's Conception of Space'. London: Routledge and Kegan Paul. (French Ed. 1948.)

PIAGET, J., BETH, E. W. and MAYS, W. (1957) Epistémologie génétique et recherche psychologique. (Vol. I des Etudes d'épistémologie génétique). Paris: Presses universitaires de France.

PAIGET, J. and INHELDER, B. (1958) 'The Growth of Logical Thinking from Childhood to Adolescence'. New York: Basic Books. (French Ed. 1955).

PIAGET, J. (1959) 'The Language and Thought of the Child'. London: Routledge and Kegan Paul. (Paperback edition) 288pp. (French Ed. 1923).

PIAGET, J. and INHELDER, B. (1959) 'The Early Growth of Logic in the Child'. London: Routledge and Kegan Paul. Translated by E. A. Lunzer and D. Papert. (First English Publication in 1964.) 302 pp.

PIAGET, J. et al. (1959) Etudes d'épistémologie génétique, Vols. 7, 8, 9, 10. Paris: Presses universitaires de France.

PIAGET, J., INHELDER, B. and SZEMINSKA, A. (1960) 'The Child's Conception of Geometry'. New York: Basic Books. (French Ed. 1948).

PIAGET, J. (1961) 'The Mechanisms of Perception'. London: Routledge and Kegan Paul. Translated by G. N. Seagrim. (First English Publication in 1969.) 384 pp.

PIAGET, J. and BETH, E. W. (1961) 'Mathematical Epistemology and Psychology'. Dordrecht, Holland: Reidel. Translated by W. Mays. 326 pp.

PIAGET, J. (1961) 'The genetic approach to the psychology of thought', J. Ed. Psych., 52, 277.

PIAGET, J. (1962) 'The stages of the intellectual development of the child', Bull. of the Menninger Clinic, 26, 3, 120-8. Topeka, Kansas.

PIAGET, J. (1962) 'Will and action', Bull. of the Menninger Clinic, 26, 3, 138-45.

PIAGET, J. (1962) 'The relations of affectivity to intelligence in the mental development of the child', Bull. of the Menninger Clinic, 26, 3, 129-37. Topeka, Kansas.

PIAGET, J. (1963) 'Explanation in psychology and psycho-physiological parallelism', in 'Experimental Psychology: its Scope and Method. Vol. I'. Chap. 3, pp. 153-192. London: Routledge and Kegan Paul. Translated by J. Chambers.

PIAGET, J. (1963) In 'Experimental Psychology: its Scope and Method. Vol. 6'. 'Perception', Chap. 18, pp. 1-62. London: Routledge and Kegan Paul.

PIAGET, J. and INHELDER, B. (1963) 'Mental images', in 'Experimental Psychology: its Scope and Method. Vol. 7'. 'Intelligence'. Chap. 23. pp. 85-143. London: Routledge and Kegan Paul. Translated by Thérèse Surridge.

PIAGET, J. and INHELDER, B. (1963) 'Intellectual operations and their development, in 'Experimental Psychology: its Scope and Method. Vol. 7'. 'Intelligence', Chap. 24, pp. 144-205. London: Routledge and Kegan Paul. Translated by Thérèse Surridge.

PIAGET, J. (1964) 'Cognitive development in children', J. Res. Sci. Teach., 2, 176-86.

PIAGET, J. and INHELDER, B. (1964) 'The Early Growth of Logic in the Child'. London: Routledge and Kegan Paul. (French Ed. 1959).

PIAGET, J. (1964) 'Judgement and Reasoning in the Child'. Patterson, NJ: Adams & Co. (French Edition, 1924).

PIAGET, J. (1964) 'Development and learning', in RIPPLE, R. E. and ROCKCASTLE, V. N. (Eds.) 'Piaget Rediscovered'. Ithaca. School of Education, Cornell University, 7-20, 176-86.

PIAGET, J. (1964) 'Six Psychological Studies'. University of London Press. Translated by Anita Tenzer. First English Publication in 1968. 169pp.

PIAGET, J. (1965) 'Sagesse et Illusions de la Philosophie'. Paris: Presses Universitaires de France. (To be published in English in 1972 by the World Publishing Co. NY.)

PAIGET, J. and INHELDER, B. (1966) 'The Psychology of the Child'. New York: Basic Books, Inc. Translated by H. Weaver. (First English Publication in 1969.) 173 pp.

PIAGET, J. (1966) 'Biology and cognition', Diogène, 54, 3-26. Translated by Martin Faigel.

PIAGET, J. (1966) 'The concept of identity in the course of development', Newsletter, 8, 2-3.

PIAGET, J. (1966) 'How children form mathematical concepts', Voprosy Psikhol., 4, 121-126.

PIAGET, J. (1966) 'La psychologie, les relations interdisciplinaires et le systéme des sciences', Bulletin de psychologie, 20, 5, 242-54.

PIAGET, J. (1966) 'Qu'est-ce que la psychologie?' Université de Genève, séance d'ouverture du semestre d'hiver. Geneva: Georg. 21-9.

PIAGET, J. (1966) 'Lettre à Romain Rolland, écrite en 1917. Action étudiante, (Genève), No.69, p.7.

PIAGET, J. (1966) 'Necessité et signification des recherches comparatives en psychologie génétique', Journ. international de psychol., Vol.I, No.I, pp. 313.

PIAGET, J. (1966) 'La problème des mécanismes communs dans les sciences dl'homme'. Actes du 6e congrès mondial de sociologie, Evian, Vol.I. Association internationale de sociologie.

PIAGET, J. (1966) 'L'intériorisation des schèmes d'action en opérations reversibles par l'intermédiaire des régulations de feedbacks. 18e congrès international de psychologie, Moscou, Symposium 24: 'Psychologie de la formation du concept et des activités mentales'.

PIAGET, J. (1966) Response to Brian Sutton-Smith, Psych. Rev., 73, 111-12.

PIAGET, J. (1966) 'La situation des sciences de l'homme dans le système des sciences. UNESCO. Recherche internationale sur les tendances principales de la recherche dans les sceinces de l'homme'. 1ère version de l'étude, 1ère partie, Chap. I, 15 avril, Polycopié.

PIAGET, J. (1966) 'Time perception in children', in FRAZER, J. P. (Ed.) 'The Voices of Time', 202-16. New York: Braziller. Translated by E. Kirky.

PIAGET, J. (1966) 'L'initiation aux mathématiques, les mathématiques modernes et la psychologie de l'enfant.' L'enseignement mathématique, tome 12, fasc. 4, pp. 289-292.

PIAGET, J. (1966) 'Henri Pieron, 1881-1964', Am. J. Psych., 79, 147-50.

PIAGET, J. (1966) 'Logique formelle et psychologie génétique', in FRAISSE, P., FAVERGE, J. M. and BRESSON, F. (Eds.) 'Les Modèles Formels en Psychologie'. Paris: CNRS, 269-76.

PIAGET, J. (1966) 'Autobiographie. Jean Piaget et les sciences sociales', Cahiers Vilfredo Pareto. Geneve: Librairie Droz. 4, 10, 129-55.

PIAGET, J. and INHELDER, B. (1966) 'Mental Imagery in the Child'. London: Routledge and Kegan Paul. Translated by P. A. Chilton. First English Publication in 1971. 396p.

PIAGET, J. (1966) 'l'Epistémologie du Temps. (Vol. 20 des Etudes d'epistémologie génétique). Paris: Presses universitaires de France. Chap. 1 & 2. 'Problemes du temps et de la fonction', pp.1-66 and (with the collaboration of M. Meylan — Backs) 'Comparisons et opérations temporelles en rélation avec la vitesse et la fréquence', pp. 67-106.

PIAGET, J. (1966) Preface to ALMY, CHITTENDEN and MILLER 'Young Children's Thinking. Studies of Some Aspects of Piaget's Theory'. New York: Teachers' College Press, Columbia University.

PIAGET, J. (1967) 'Biologie et Connaissance. Essai sur les Relations Entre les Régulations Organiques et les Processus Cognitifs'. Paris: Gallimard, 'Avenir de la science', series edited by Jean Rostand. 430 pp. (English translation in preparation and to be published by the University of Chicago Press.)

PIAGET, J. (1967) 'Logique et connaissance scientifique'. 'Encyclopédie de la Pléiade', volume publié sous la direction de J. Piaget. Paris, Gallimard, 1345 pp.

PIAGET, J. (1967) 'Perception et Notion du Temps'. (Vol. 21 des études d'épistémologie génétique). Paris: Presses Universitaires de France — Introduction: p. 1.

PIAGET, J. (1967) 'Psychologie et philosophie'. Débat de J. Piaget avec P. Fraisse, Y. Galifret, F. Jeanson, P. Ricoeur, R. Zazzo, a propos de 'Sagesse et illusions de la philosophie'. Raison Présente, (Paris, les editions rationalistes), No.1. Expose: pp. 52-55, interventions: pp. 62-76.

PIAGET, J. (1967) 'Intélligence et adaptation biologique', in 'Les Processus d'Adaptation'. Symposium de l'association de psychologie scientifique de langue francaise, Marseille (1965). pp. 55-81. Paris: Presses universitaires de France.

PIAGET, J. (1967) 'Le développement des perceptions en fonction de l'age', in PIAGET, J. et FRAISSE, P. (Eds.) 'Traité de Psychologie Experimentale, Vol. 6'. 'La perception', Chapitre 18. Paris: Presses universitaires de France.

PIAGET, J. (1967) 'L'explication en psychologie et la parallélisme psycho-physiologique', in PIAGET, J. et FRAISSE, P. (Eds.) 'Traité de Psychologie Experimentale. Vol. 1'. 'Histoire et méthode', Chapitre 3. Adjonction à la deuxième édition. Paris: Presses universitaires de France.

PIAGET, J. (1967) 'Cognitions and conservations: two views (a review of "Studies in Cognitive Growth")', Contemp. Psych., 12, 532-33.

PIAGET, J. (1967) 'Psychologie du psychologue', in: 'l'Homme à la Découverte de Lui-même', encyclopédie 'L'Aventure humaine', Vol. 5, Genève, Kister and Paris: La Grange Batelère.

PIAGET, J. (1967) 'Logique formelle et psychologie génétique'. Colloques internationaux du Centre National de la Recherche Scientifique. 'Les modèles et la formalisation du comportement'. Paris, 5-10 Juillet, 1965, pp.269-276, des cussion: pp. 276-283. Paris:

PIAGET, J., INHELDER, B., SINCLAIR-de ZWART (1968). 'Mémoire et Intelligence'. Paris: Presses universitaires de France. 487 pp. English translation, 1973.

PIAGET, J. and FRAISSE, P. (Ed.) (1968) 'Experimental Psychology: its Scope and Method'. London: Routledge and Kegan Paul. (Seven volumes available in English translation).

PIAGET, J. (1968) Structuralism. New York: Harper and Row. (First English Publication in 1971.) 124 pp.

PIAGET, J. (1968) 'Epistémologie et Psychologie de la Fonction'. (Vol. 23 des études d'épistémologie génétique, publiées sous la direction de J. Piaget). Paris: Presses Universitaires de France. 238 pp.

PIAGET, J. (1968) 'Epistémologie et Psychologie de l'Identité'. (Vol. 24 des études d'épistemologie génétique, publiées sous la direction de J. Piaget.) Paris: Presses universitaires de France. 209 pp.

PIAGET, J. (1968) 'On the Development of Memory and Identity'. Translated by E. Duckworth. Massachussetts: Clark University Press with Barre Publ., 42 pp.

PIAGET, J. (1968) 'Le point de vue de Piaget', J. International de Psych., 3, 281-99.

PIAGET, J. (1968) 'Quantification, conservation and nativism. Quantitative evaluations of children aged two to three years are examined', Science, 162, 976-79.

PIAGET, J. (1968) 'Le Structuralisme'. Colloque de Geneve: 'Structuralisme et symbolisme'. Cahiers Internationaux de Symbolisme, 17-18, 73-85.

PIAGET, J. (1968) 'La genesi del numero nel bambino', Il Sedicesimo, (La Nuova Italia, Firenze), 14-15, p. 15.

PIAGET, J. (1968) 'Cybernetique et Epistémologie'. (Vol. 22 des études d'épistémologie génétique, publiées sous la direction de J. Piaget.) Paris: Presses Universitaires de France. Foreword, pp. 1-3.

PIAGET, J. (1968) 'Six Psychological Studies'. London: University of London Press. (French Ed. 1964).

PIAGET, J. (1969) 'Psychologie et Pédagogie'. Paris: Denoel (Bibliotheque 'Mediations'). English publication to be published by Grossman-Orion Press, New York.

PIAGET, J. (1969) 'Science of Education and the Psychology of the Child'. New York: Grossman. Translated by D. Coltman. (First English Publication in 1970.) 186pp.

PIAGET, J. (1969) 'Genetic epistemology', Columbia Forum, 12, 3, pp. 5-11.

PIAGET, J. and INHELDER, B. (1969) 'The gaps in empiricism', in KOESTLER, A. and SMYTHIES (Eds.) 'Beyond Reductionism'. London: Macmillan, 118-48.

PIAGET, J. (1969) 'The Theory of Stages in Cognitive Development', California Test Bureau Invitational Conference on 'Ordinal Scales of Cognitive Development', Monterey, Cal., Feb. 9, 1969. Maidenhead: McGraw-Hill, Translated by S. Opper. Now published in 'Measurement and Piaget'. GREEN, D. R., FORD, M. P. and FLAMER, G. B. (Eds.) New York: McGraw Hill, 1971.

PIAGET, J. (1969) 'Quelques remarques sur les insuffisances de l'empirisme', Studia Philosophica, Annuaire de la société suisse de philosophie, 28, 119-28.

PIAGET, J. (1969) 'L'epistémologie génétique', 'La Philosophie contemporaine, Chroniques'. (Ed: R. Klibansky, Firenze, La Nuova Italia), 243-57.

PIAGET, J. (1969) 'The Mechanisms of Perception', London: Routledge and Kegan Paul. (French Ed. 1961).

PIAGET, J. and INHELDER, B. (1969). 'The Psychology of the Child'. New York: Basic Books Inc. (French Ed. 1966).

PIAGET, J. (1969) Foreword to FURTH, H. G. 'Piaget and Knowledge — Theoretical Foundations'. Engelwood Cliffs, NJ: Prentice Hall, Inc.

PIAGET, J. (1970) 'The Childs Conception of Movement and Speech'. London: Routledge and Kegan Paul (French Ed. 1946).

PIAGET, J. (1970) 'Piaget's Theory', in MUSSEN, P. H. (Ed.) 'Manual of Child Psychology'. New York: Wiley, pp. 703-33.

PIAGET, J. (1970) 'Science of Education and the Psychology of the Child'. New York: Grossman (French Ed. 1969).

PIAGET, J. and INHELDER, B. (1971) 'Mental Imagery in the Child'. London: Routledge and Kegan Paul. (French Ed. 1966).

PIAGET, J. (1971) 'Structuralism'. New York: Harper and Row. (French Ed. 1968).

PIAGET, J. (1972) 'A structural foundation for tomorrow's education', Prospects, Quarterly Review of Education. UNESCO, II, I, 12-27.

PIAGET, J. (1972) 'Piaget now', Parts 1, 2, and 3. (Piaget in discussion with Hill B.), Times Ed. Supp., 11 Feb., 18 Feb. and 25 Feb., pp. 19, 19, 21, respectively.

PIAGET, J. (1972) 'Intélligence et mémoire'. Symposium de l'Association de Psychologie Scientifique de langue francaise, 'La mémoire', Geneve. Paris: Presses Universitaires de France.

PIAGET, J. (1972) 'L'Epistemologie Génétique. Paris: Presses Universitaires de France, collection 'Que sais-je?'

PIAGET, J. (1972) Problemes de Psychologie Gén'J. (1973) 'Comments on mathematical education'. Cited in: HOWSON, A. G. (Ed.) 'Developments in Mathematical Education'. Proceedings of the Second International Congress on Mathematical Education. London: Cambridge Univ. Press.

PICK, A. D. (1965) 'Improvement of visual and tactual form discrimination', J. Exp. Psych., 59, 331-9.

PINARD, A. and LAURENDEAU, M. (1964) 'A scale of mental development based on the theory of Piaget: description of a project', J. Res. Sc. Teach., 2, 253-60.

PINARD, A. and LAURENDEAU, M. (1966) 'Le caractère topologique des premières représentations spatiales de l'enfant: examen des hypothèses de Piaget', Intern. J. Psych., 1, 243-45.

PINARD, A. and LAURENDEAU, M. (1969) ' "Stage" in Piaget's cognitive-development theory: exegesis of a concept', in ELKIND, D. and FLAVELL, J. H. (Eds.) 'Studies in Cognitive Development'. New York: Oxford.

PITTEL, S. M. and MENDELSOHN, G. A. (1966) 'Measurement of moral values: a review and critique', Psych. Bull., 66, 1, 22-35.

PODD, M. H. (In press). 'Ego identity status and morality: the relationship between two developmental constructs'. St. Elizabeth Hospital, Washington.

452

POOLE, H. E. (1962) 'The effect of urbanization upon scientific concept attainment among the Hausa children of Northern Nigeria', Brit. J. Ed. Psych., 22, 50-61.

PORTER, B. M. (1954) 'Measurement of parental acceptance of children', J. Home Econ., 46, 176-82.

PORTER, B. M. (1955) 'The relationship between marital adjustment and parental acceptance of children', J. Home Econ., 47, 157-64.

PORTER, R. B. and CATTELL, R. B. (1960) 'Handbook for the Children's Personality Questionnaire'. Champaign, Illinois: Inst. for Personality and Ability Testing.

PORTEUS, B. D. and JOHNSON, R. C. (1965) 'Children's responses to two measures of conscience development and their relation to sociometric nomination', Child Developm., 36, 703-11.

POSNER, M. I. and MITCHELL, R. F. (1967) 'Chronometric analysis of classification', Psych. Rev., 74, 392-409.

PRAGER, B. (1962) 'The effect of cognitive conflict on the acquisition of the concept of conservation'. (Unpub. study).

PRATOOMRAJ, S. and JOHNSON, R. C. (1966) 'Kinds of questions and types of conservation tasks as related to children's conservation responses', Child Developm., 343-53.

PRIBRAM, K. A. (1960) 'A review of theory in physiological psychology', Ann. Rev. Psych., 11, 1-40.

PRICE, K. C. (1970) 'Structural balance and other biases in cognitive structuring', unpub. MA thesis, Georgia University.

PRICE-WILLIAMS, D. R. (1961) 'A study concerning concepts of conservation of quantity among primitive children', Acta Psychologia, 18, 297-305.

PRICE-WILLIAMS, D. R. (1962) 'Abstract and concrete modes of classification in a primitive society', Brit. J. Ed. Psych., 32, 50-61.

PRICE-WILLIAMS, D. R. (Ed.) (1969). 'Cross-cultural Studies'. Harmondsworth, U.K.: Penguin Books Ltd.

PRICE-WILLIAMS, D. R. and GORDON, W. (1968) 'Manipulation and conservation: a study of children from pottery-making families in Mexico'. (Unpub. paper.)

PRICE-WILLIAMS, D. R., GORDON, W. and RAMIREZ, M. (1969) 'Skill and conservation: a study of pottery-making children', Dev. Psych., 1, 6, 769. Also published in BERRY, J. W. and DASEN, P. R. (eds.) (1974). 'Culture and Cognition'. London: Methuen.

PRINCE, J. R. (1968) 'The effect of western education on science conceptualization in New Guinea', Brit. J. Ed. Psych., 33, 64-74.

PRINCE, J. R. (1969) 'Science concepts in a Pacific Culture'. Sydney: Angus and Robertson.

PRINCE, J. R. (1969) 'Views on physical causality in New Guinea students.' Paper presented at 41st ANZAAS Congress, Adelaide, August.

PRIOR, F. M. (1959) 'The place of maps in the junior school', unpub. PhD thesis, Birmingham University.

PROTHRO, E. T. (1943) 'Egocentricity and abstraction in children and in adult aments', Am. J. Psych., 56, 66-77.

PROTHRO, E. T. (1961) 'Child-rearing in the Lebanon'. Cambridge, Mass: Harvard University Press.

PUFALL, P. B. (1966) 'Acquisition and generalization of spatial order conservation in young children', unpub. PhD thesis, Catholic University.

PUFALL, P. B., SHAW, R. E. and SYRDAL-LASKY, A. (1973) Development of number conservation: an examination of some predictions from Piaget's stage analysis and equilibration model', Child Developm., 44, 21-7.

PUMFREY, P. (1967) 'The growth of the schema of proportionality', Brit. J. Ed. Psych., 202-4. Also MEd thesis of the same title, Manchester University (1965).

PURCELL, K. (1958) 'Some shortcomings in projective test validation', J. Abnorm. Soc. Psych., 57, 115-8.

RADKE-YARROW, M. (1963) 'Problems of methods in parent-child research', Child Developm., 34, 215-26.

RAINSBURY, E. (1965) 'Some aspects of social and moral concept growth and attainment in primary school children'. MEd thesis, Leicester University.

RAMON, C. (1953) 'Anxiety and task as determiners of verbal performance', J. Exp. Psych., 46, 120-24.

RAMSBURG, E. (1965) 'Some aspects of social and moral concept growth and attainment in primary school children'. MEd thesis, Leicester University.

RAPAPORT, D. (1950) 'Emotions and Memory'. New York: International Universities Press.

RAPP, D. W. (1961) 'Child-rearing attitudes of mothers in Germany and the United States', Child Developm., 32, 669-78.

RARDIN, D. R. and MOAN, C. E. (1971) 'Peer interaction and cognitive development', Child Developm., 42, 1685-99.

RAVEN, J. C. (1943) 'The Mill Hill Vocabulary Scale'. London: Hutchinson.

REDMAN, S. et. al. (1969) 'An approach to Primary Science: A Book for Teachers of Juniors and Infants'. London: Macmillan.

REIMER, A. (1968) 'A study of first grade mathematics achievement and conservation', unpub. Master's thesis, Alberta University.

REISS, P. R. (1968) 'Implications of Piaget's developmental psychology for mental retardation', Am. J. Ment. Def., 72, 361-9.

REITMAN, W. (1965) 'Cognition and Thought. An Information Processing Approach'. New York: Wiley.

RENNER, et. al. (1962) 'The validity of a method for scoring sentence completion responses for anxiety, dependency and hostility', J. App. Psych., 46, 185-90.

RESNICK, L. B. (1967) 'Design of an Early Learning Curriculum'. Pittsburgh: Learning Research and Development Centre, University of Pittsburgh.

REST, J. (1968) 'Developmental hierarchy in preference and comprehension of moral judgement', unpub. Doctoral Dissert., Univ. of Chicago.

REST, J. (to be published) 'Comprehension preference and spontaneous usage in moral judgement', in KOHLBERG, L. and TURIEL, E. (Eds.) 'Recent Research in Moral Development'. London and New York: Holt-Blond Ltd.

REST, J., TURIEL, E. and KOHLBERG, L. (1969) 'Relations between level of moral judgement and preference and comprehension of the moral judgement of others', J. Pers., 37, 225-52.

454

RHEINGOLD, H. L. (1960) 'The measurement of maternal care', Child Developm., 31, 565-75.

RHYS, W. T. (1964) 'The development of logical thought in the adolescent with reference to the teaching of Geography in the secondary school', unpub. MEd thesis, Birmingham University.

RICHARDSON, E. M. (1966) 'A study of the development of some spatial concepts in blind children', PhD thesis, Liverpool University.

RIPPLE, R. E. and ROCKCASTLE, V. N. (1964) 'Piaget Rediscovered'. Ithaca, New York: Cornell Univ. Press.

RIVOIRE, J. L. (1962) 'Development of reference systems in children', Percept. Mot. Skills, 15, 554.

RIVOIRE, J. L. and KIDD, A. H. (1966) 'The development of perception of colour, space and movement in children', in KIDD, A. H. and RIVOIRE, J. L. (Eds.) Perceptual Development in Children. London University Press.

ROBERTS, G. C. and BLACK, K. N. (1972) 'The effect of naming and object permanence on toy preferences', Child Developm., 43, 958-68.

ROBINSON, H. B. (1964) 'An experimental examination of the size-weight illusion in young children', Child Developm., 35, 1, 91-107.

ROBINSON, H. B. and ROBINSON, N. M. (1965) 'The Mentally Retarded Child'. New York: McGraw-Hill.

ROBINSON, H. B., KATSUSHIGE,ᵢ K. and McDOWELL, (1961) 'The size-weight illusion in young children', Am. Psych', 16, 364.

ROFF, M. A. (1949) 'A factorial study of the Fels Parent Behaviour Rating Scales', Child Developm., 20, 29-44.

ROLL, S. (1970) 'Reversibility training and stimulus desirability as factors in conservation of number', Child Developm., 501-7.

ROSE, S. A. (1973) 'Acquiescence and conservation', Child Developm., 44,4 , 811-14.

ROSEN, B. C. (1956) 'The achievement syndrome: a psycho-cultural dimension of social stratification', Am. Soc. Rev., 21, 203-11.

ROSEN, B. C. (1959) 'Race, ethnicity, and the achievement syndrome', Am. Soc. Rev., 24, 47-60.

ROSEN, B. C. and D'ANDRADE, (1959) 'The psychological origins of achievement motivation', Sociometry, 22, 185-218.

ROSENSTEIN, J. (1960) 'Cognitive abilities of deaf children', J. Speech Hear. Res., 3, 108-19.

ROSENTHAL, T. and ZIMMERMAN, B. (1972) 'Modelling by exemplification and instruction in training conservation', Dev. Psych., 6, 3, 392-401.

ROSS, B. M. (1966) 'Probability concepts in deaf and hearing children', Child Developm., 37, 917-27.

ROSS, J. E. (1959) 'An inquiry into the ability of junior and first-year secondary modern children to reason about sound', unpub. PhD thesis, Birmingham University.

ROSSI, E. (1964) 'Development of classificatory behaviour', Child Developm., 35, 137-42.

ROSSI, E. and ROSSI, S. I. (1965) 'Concept utilization, serial order and recall in nursery school children', Child Developm., 36, 771-8.

ROTHENBERG, B. B. (1969) 'Conservation of number among four- and five-year-old children: some methodological considerations', Child Developm., 40, 383-406.

ROTHENBERG, B. B. and COURTNEY, R. G. (1968) 'Conservation of number in very young children: A replication of and comparison with Mehler and Bever's study', J. Psychol., 70, 205-12.

ROTHENBERG, B. B. and COURTNEY, R. G. (1969) 'Conservation of number in young children', Dev. Psych., 1, 5.

ROTHENBERG, B. B. and OROST, J. H. (1969) 'The training of conservation of number in young children', Child Developm., 40, 707-26.

RUBIN, K. H. (1973) 'Egocentrism in childhood: a unitary construct?' Child Developm., 44, 1, 102-9.

RUSSELL, D. (1956) 'Children's Thinking'. New York: Ginn.

RUSSELL, G. W. (1968) 'An appraisal of Piaget's theory of moral development', DipEd thesis, Leicester University.

RUSSELL, J. (1964) 'Reversal and non-reversal shift in deaf and hearing kindergarten children', unpub. MA·thesis, Catholic University of America.

RUTTER, M. L. (1967) 'A children's behaviour questionnaire for completion by teachers: preliminary findings', J. Child Psych. Psychiat., 8, 1-11.

RUTTER, M. L. (1968) 'The reliability and validity of the psychiatric assessment of the child: I. Interview with the child', Brit. J. Psych., 114, 563-79. Child Scales A and B.

RUTTER, M. L. and BROWN, G. W. (1966) 'The reliability and validity of measures of family life and relationships in families containing a psychiatric patient', Soc. Psych., 1, 38-53.

RUTTER, M. L. and GRAHAM, P. J. (1966) 'Psychiatric disorder in 10 and 11-year-old children', Proc. Roy. Soc. Med., 59, 382-7.

SAINT-PIERRE, J. (1962) 'Etudes des différences entre la recherche active de la personne humaine et celle de l'object inanimé'. Master's dissertation, Montreal University.

SALLEE, S. J. and GRAY, P. (1963) 'Failure to confirm Piaget's formulation of number perception in children', Percep. Mot. Skills, 17, 586.

SARANOFF, I. and SARASON, S. B. (1958) 'A cross-cultural study of anxiety among American and English school children', J. Ed. Psych., 49, 129-36.

SARANOFF, I. et al. (1959) 'Test anxiety in the 11+ examination', Brit. J. Ed. Psych., 29, 9-16.

SARASON, I. G. (1960) 'Experimental findings and theoretical problems in the use of anxiety scales', Psych. Bull., 57, 403-15.

SARASON, S. B. (1958a) 'Classroom observation of high and low anxious children', Child Developm., 19, 187-95.

SARASON, S. B. (1958b) 'A test anxiety scale for children', Child Developm., 29, 105-13.

SARASON, S. B., MANDLER, G. and CRAIGHILL, P. G. (1952) 'The effect of differential instructions on anxiety and learning', J. Abnorm. Soc. Psych., 47, 561-5.

SAWADA, D. and NELSON, L. D. (1967) 'Conservation of length and the teaching of linear measurement: a methodological critique', Arithmetic Teacher, 14, 345-8.

SCAPLEHORN, C. (1971) 'The patterning of reasoning, moral judgement and moral behaviour in adolescents', MPhil (in prep.) Univ. of Surrey. (Tentative title).

SCHAFFER, H. R. (1963) 'Some issues for research in the study of attachment behaviour', in FOSS, B. M. (Ed.) 'Determinants of Infant

Behaviour, II'. New York: Wiley; London: Methuen, 179-99.

SCHALLENBERGER, M. (1894) 'Children's rights','Ped. Sem., 3, 87-96.

SCHOFIELD, L. and UZGIRIS, I. C. (1969) 'Examining behaviour and the development of the concept of object', unpub. manuscript, Clark Univ.

SCHONELL, F. J. (1965) 'Backwardness in the Basic Subjects'. Edinburgh: Oliver and Boyd. 4th Edition.

SCHONELL, F. J. (1966) 'The Psychology and Teaching of Reading'. Edinburgh: Oliver and Boyd. 4th Edition.

SCHONELL F. J. and SCHONELL, F. E. (1965) 'Diagnostic and Attainment Testing'. Edinburgh: Oliver and Boyd. 4th Edition.

SCHWARTZ, M. M. and KOFSKY, E. (1970) 'Scalogram analysis of logical and perceptual components of conservation of discontinuous quantity', Child Developm., 41, 695-705.

SCHWARTZ, M. M. and SCHOLNICK, E. KOFSKY (1970) 'Analysis of logical and perceptual components of conservation of discontinuous quantity', Child Developm., 41, 695-705.

SCIENCE CURRICULUM Improvement Study (1966) 'Teachers' Guide — Material Objects'. (Preliminary Edition.) Boston: Heath.

SEARS, P. S. (1951) 'Doll play aggression in normal young children', Psych. Mon., 65, 6.

SEARS, R., MACCOBY, E. E., and LEVIN, H. (1957) 'Patterns of Child-Rearing'. Evanston, Ill.: Row, Peterson.

SEGALL, M. H., CAMPBELL, D. T. and HERSKOVITS, M. J. (1966) 'The Influence of Culture on Visual Perception'. New York: Bobbs-Merrill.

SEILER, B. (1966) Die Reversibilität in die Entwick lung des Denkens. Stuttgart: Klett.

SELMAN, R. L. (1971) 'The relation of role-taking to the development of moral judgement in children', Child Developm., 42, 79-91.

SELMAN, R. L. (to be published) 'The importance of reciprocal role-taking for the development of conventional moral thought', in KOHLBERG, L. and TURIEL, E. (Eds.) 'Recent Research in Moral Development'. London and New York: Holt-Blond Ltd.

SELTZER, A. R. (1969) 'The relationship between moral development and the development of time perception and time conceptualization in lower class negro children', Diss. Abstr. Inter., 31, 1524.

SERGEANT, D. C. (1969) 'Pitch perception and absolute pitch: some aspects of musical development', PhD thesis, Reading University.

SEYMOUR, P. H. K. (1969) 'Response latencies in judgements of spatial location', Brit. J. Psych., 50, 31-9.

SHANTZ, C. U. (1967) 'A developmental study of Piaget's theory of logical multiplication', Merr. Palm. Quart., 13, 121-37.

SHANTZ, C. U. and SIGEL, I. E. (1967) 'Logical operations and concepts of conservation in children: a training study', Final Report, Office of Education Grant No. OEG-3-6-068463-1645, Merrill-Palmer Institute.

SHANTZ, C. U. and SMOCK, C. D. (1966) 'Development of distance conservation and the spatial co-ordinate system', Child Developm., 37, 943-8.

SHANTZ, C. U. and WATSON, J. S. (1970) 'Assessment of spatial ego-centrism through expectancy violation', Psychonomic Science, 18 (2), 93-4.

SHANTZ, C. U. and WATSON, J. S. (1971) 'Spatial abilities and spatial

457

ego-centrism in the young child', Child Developm., 42, 171-81.

SHAPIRO, B. J. and O'BRIEN, T. C. (1970) 'Logical thinking in children ages six through thirteen', Child Developm., 41, 823-9.

SHAPIRO, M. B. (1952) 'Some correlates of opinions on the upbringing of children', Brit. J. Psych., 43, 141-9.

SHAW, M. C. (1964) 'Note on parent attitudes toward independence training and the academic achievement of their children', J. Ed. Psych., 55 (6), 371-4.

SHERMAN, J. A. (1967) 'Problems of sex differences in space perception and aspects of intellectual functioning', Psych. Rev., 4, 290-9.

SHIELDS, J. B. (1966) 'A study of the gifted child', MEd thesis, Leeds University.

SHOBEN, E. J. (Jr.) (1949) 'The assessment of parental attitudes in relation to child adjustment', Gen. Psych. Mon., 39, 102-48.

SIEGEL, A. W. and KRESH, E. (1971) 'Children's ability to operate within a matrix: a developmental study', Dev. Psych., 4, 2, 232-9.

SIEGEL, L. S. (1971) 'The sequence of development of certain number concepts in pre-school children', Dev. Psych., 5, 2, 357-61.

SIEGEL, L. S. (1971a) 'The development of the understanding of certain number concepts', Dev. Psych., 5, 2, 362-3.

SIEGEL, L. S. (1972) 'Development of the concept of seriation', Dev. Psych., 6, 1, 135-7.

SIEGEL, L. S. and GOLDSTEIN, A. G. (1969) 'Conservation of number in young children: Recency versus relational response strategies', Dev. Psych., 1, 2, 128-30.

SIEGEL, S. (1956) 'Non-parametric Statistics for the Behavioural Sciences'. New York: McGraw-Hill.

SIEGLER, R. S., and LIEBERT, R. M. (1972) 'Effects of presenting relevant rules and complete feedback on the conservation of liquid quantity', Dev. Psych., 7, 2, 133-9.

SIGEL, I. E. (1953) 'Developmental trends in the abstraction ability of children', Child Developm., 24, (2), 131-44.

SIGEL, I. E. (1966) 'Child Development and Social Science Education'. Part 4, A teaching strategy derived from some Piagetian concepts. Detroit: Merrill-Palmer Institute.

SIGEL, I. E. (1968) 'Reflections', in SIGEL, I. E. and HOOPER, F. H. (Eds.) 'Logical Thinking in Children', New York: Holt Rinehart and Winston.

SIGEL, I. E. (1969) 'The Piagetian system and the world of education', in ELKIND, D. and FLAVELL, J. H. (Eds.) 'Studies in Cognitive Development: Essays in Honour of Jean Piaget'. NY: Oxford University Press.

SIGEL, I. E. and HOOPER, F. H. (Eds.) (1968) 'Logical Thinking in Children'. New York: Holt, Rinehart and Winston.

SIGEL, I. E. and McBANE, B. (1967) 'Cognitive competence and level of symbolization among five-year-old children', in HELLMUTH, J. (Ed.) Disadvantaged Child, Vol. 1, Special Child Publications, 435-53.

SIGEL, I. E. and MERMELSTEIN, E. (1965) 'Effects of non-schooling on Piagetian tasks of conservation'. Paper presented at APA meeting, Sept.

SIGEL, I. E. and OLMSTEAD, P. (1968) 'The development of classification and representational competence'. Paper presented at the meeting of Pre-school Conf., Ontario Studies on Education, Canada.

SIGEL, I. E. and PERRY, C. (1968) 'Psycholinguistic diversity among "culturally deprived" children', Am. J. Orthopsychi., 38, 122-6.

SIGEL, I. E., ANDERSON, L. and SHAPIRO, H. (1966) 'Categorization behaviour of lower and middle class Negro pre-school children', Negro Ed., 35, 218-29.

SIGEL, I. E., JARMAN, P. and HANESIAN, H. (1967) 'Styles of categorization and their intellectual and personality correlates in young children', Human Dev., 10, 1-17.

SIGEL, I. E., ROEPER, A. and HOOPER, F. H. (1966) 'A training procedure for acquisition of Piaget's conservation of quantity: a pilot study and its replication', Brit. J. Ed. Psych., 36, 301-11.

SIGEL, I. E., SALTZ, E. and ROSKIND, W. (1967) 'Variables determining concept conservation in children', J. Exp. Psych., 74, 471-5.

SILVERMAN, I. W. and GEIRINGER, E. (1973) 'Dyadic interaction and conservation induction', Child Developm., 44, 4, 815-20.

SILVERMAN, I. W. and MARSH, K. (1969) 'On the production of images within the conservation experiment'. Paper presented at the meeting of the Soc. for Res. in Child Development, Santa Monica, California.

SILVERMAN, I. W. and STONE, J. (1972) 'Modifying cognitive functioning through participation in a problem-solving group', J. Ed. Psych., 63, 6, 603-8.

SINCLAIR-DeZWART, H. (1969) 'Developmental psycholinguistics', in ELKIND, D. and FLAVELL, J. H. (Eds.) 'Studies in Cognitive Development: Essays in Honour of Jean Piaget'. New York: Oxford Univ. Press, 315-36.

(SINGER) SHARAN, S. and WELLER, L. (1971) 'Classification patterns of underprivileged children in Israel', Child Developm., 42, 581-94.

SKEMP, R. R. (1961) 'Reflective intelligence and mathematics', Brit, J. Ed. Psych., 31, 45-55.

SLATER, C. W. (1958) 'A study of the influence which environment plays in determining the rate at which a child attains Piaget's "operational" level in his early number concepts', unpub. Dissert., Birmingham University.

SLEIGHT, G. F. (1949) 'Sleight Non-verbal Intelligence Test — Manual of Directions'. London: Harrap.

SMEDSLUND, J. (1959) 'Apprentissage des Notions de la Conservation et de la Transitivité du Poids', in PIAGET, J. (Ed.) Etudes d'Epistémologie Génétique. Paris: Presses Universitaires de France, 9, 85-124.

SMEDSLUND, J. (1961a) 'The acquisition of conservation of substance and weight in children: I. Introduction', Scan. J. Psych., 2, 11-20.

SMEDSLUND, J. (1961b) 'The acquisition of conservation of substance and weight in children: II. External reinforcement of conservation of weight and of the operations of addition and subtraction', Scan. J. Psych., 2, 71-84.

SMEDSLUND, J. (1961c) 'The acquisition of substance and weight in children: III. Extinction of conservation of weight acquired "normally" and by means of empirical controls in a balance', Scan. J. Psych., 2, 85-7.

SMEDSLUND, J. (1961d) 'The acquisition of conservation of substance and weight in children: IV. Attempt at extinction of the visual components of the weight concept', Scan. J. Psych., 2, 153-5.

SMEDSLUND, J. (1961e) 'The acquisition of conservation of substance and weight in children: V. Practice in conflict situations without external reinforcement', Scan. J. Psych., 2, 156-60.

SMEDSLUND, J. (1961f) 'The acquisition of conservation of substance and weight in children: VI. Practice in continuous vs. discontinuous material in problem situations without external reinforcement', Scan. J. Psych., 2, 203-10.

SMEDSLUND, J. (1962) 'The acquisition of conservation of substance and weight in children: VII: conservation of discontinuous quantity and the operations of adding and taking away', Scan. J. Psych., 3, 69-77.

SMEDSLUND, J. (1963) 'Development of concrete transitivity of length in children', Child Developm., 34, 389-405.

SMEDSLUND, J. (1963) 'Patterns of experience and the acquisition of conservation of length', Scan. J. Psych., 4, 257-64.

SMEDSLUND, J. (1963) 'Patterns of experience and the acquisition of concrete transitivity of weight in eight-year-old children', Scan. J. Psych., 4, 251-6.

SMEDSLUND, J. (1964) 'Concrete reasoning: a study of intellectual development', Mon. Soc. Res. Child Developm., 29, 2 (Serial No. 93), 3-39.

SMEDSLUND, J. (1965) 'The development of transitivity of length: a comment on Braines reply', Child Developm., 36, 577-80.

SMEDSLUND, J. (1965) 'Performance on measurement and pseudo-measurement tasks by five- to seven-year-old children', Scan. J. Psych., 6, 1-12.

SMEDSLUND, J. (1966) 'Microanalysis of concrete reasoning: I. The difficulty of some combinations of addition and subtraction of one unit', Scan. J. Psych., 7, 145-67.

SMEDSLUND, J. (1967) 'Determinants of performance on double classification tasks. I. Effect of covered vs. uncovered materials, labelling vs. perceptual matching and age', Scan J. Psych., 8, 88-96.

SMEDSLUND, J. (1968) 'Conservation and resistance to extinction: a comment on Hall and Simpson's article', Merr. Palm. Quart., 14, 3.

SMEDSLUND, J. (1969) 'Psychological diagnostics,' Psych. Bull., 71, 3, 237-48.

SMITH, D. A. (1970) 'The construction of the object', unpub. PhD thesis, Leeds University.

SMITH, I. D. (1968) 'Effects of training procedures upon the acquisition of conservation of weight', Child Developm., 39, 515-26.

SMITH, I. M. (1964) 'Spatial Ability'. London: University of London Press.

SMITH, R. F. (1963) 'An analysis and classification of children's explanations of natural phenomena', Diss. Abstr., 24(2), 653.

SOCIAL SCIENCE RESEARCH COUNCIL (1969-70) Annual Report. London: HMSO.

SOCIAL SCIENCE RESEARCH COUNCIL (1970) 'Longitudinal Studies and the Social Sciences'. London: Heinemann.

SOCIETY FOR RESEARCH IN CHILD DEVELOPMENT (Five Monographs) (1970) Cognitive Development in Children. Univ. of Chicago Press.

SONSTROEM, A. M. (1966) 'Manipulation, labelling and screening in the learning of conservation', unpub. PhD thesis, Harvard University.

SPITZ, R. A. (1965) 'The First Year of Life'. New York: International Universities Press.

STEEDMAN, A. (1968) 'The task of moral education: a philosophical examination of the theories of Freud and Piaget', MA thesis, London University.

STEFFE, L. (1966) 'The performance of first-grade children in four levels of conservation of numerousness and three IQ groups when solving arithmetic addition problems'. Technical Report No.14, Res. and Developm., Centre for learning and re-education. Univ. of Wisconsin.

STEINER, G. L. (1965) 'A developmental study of children's concepts of life and death', unpub. PhD Dissert., Teacher's College, Columbia University.

STENDLER, C. B. (1965) 'Aspects of Piaget's theory that have implications for teacher education'. Teach. Ed., 16, 329-35.

STENDLER, C. B. (1967) 'The transition from the stage of concrete operations to formal thinking'. Paper read at Soc. Res. Child Developm., New York.

STENILD, M. (1970) En experimentel analyse af stadier i begrebsind-laering. (An experimental analysis of stages in the development of concepts.) Copenhagen.

STENILD, M. (1970) 'Pavirkning af spatial problem losning. En experimentel undersogelse. (On influencing spatial problem solving.) Copenhagen.

STEPHENS, W. B., MILLER, C. K. and McLAUGHLIN, J. A. (1969) 'The Development of Reasoning, Moral Judgement and Moral Conduct in Retardates and Normals'. Dept. of Health, Education and Welfare, Washington, D.C.

STEPHENS, W. B., MILLER, C. K. and McLAUGHLIN, J. A. (1972a) 'The Development of Reasoning, Moral Judgement and Moral Conduct in Retardates and Normals'. Phase II, Project No. 15-P-55121/3-02. Temple University, Philadelphia.

STEPHENS, W. B., PIAGET, J. and INHELDER (1966) 'Application of theory and diagnostic techniques to the area of mental retardation', Education and Training of Mentally Retarded, 1, 75-87.

STEPHENS, W. B., McLAUGHLIN, A., MILLER, C. K. and GLASS, G. V. (1972) 'Factorial structure of selected psycho-educational measures and Piagetian reasoning assessments', Dev. Psych., 6, 2, 343.

STEVENSON, H. (1962) 'Piaget behaviour theory and intelligence', in KESSEN, W. and KUHLMAN, C. (Eds.) 'Thought in the Young Child'. Mon. Soc. Res. Child Developm., 27, (2, whole No.83), 113-126.

STONES, S. K. (1965) 'An analysis of the growth of adolescent thinking in relation to their comprehension of school history material', Dip.Child Psych., dissertation, Birmingham University.

STONES, S. K. (1967) 'Factors influencing the capacity of adolescent to thinking in abstract terms in the understanding of History', MEd thesis, Manchester University.

STOTT, D. H. (1960) 'Delinquency, maladjustment and unfavourable ecology', Brit. J. Psych., 51, 157-170.

STOTT, D. H. (1958) (3rd Edition 1966) 'Social Adjustment of Children — Bristol Social Guides'. University of London Press.

STOTT, L. and BALL, R. (1965) 'Infant and pre-school mental tests: review and evaluation', Mon. Soc. Res. Child Developm., 30, 3, Serial No. 101.

STOUFFER, S. A. et al (1950) 'Measurement and Prediction'. Princeton, NJ: Princeton Univ. Press.

STRAUSS, A. L. (1954) 'The development of conceptions of rules in children', Child Developm., 25, 193-208.

461

STRAUSS, A. L. and SCHUESSLER, K. (1951) 'Socialization, log reasoning and concept development in the child', Am. Soc. Rev., 1 514-23.

STRAUSS, S. (1972) 'Learning theories of Gagné and Piaget: Implications for curriculum development', Teachers' College Record, 74, 1, 81-102.

STRAUSS, S. and LANGER, J. (1970) 'Operational thought inducement', Child Developm., 41, 163-75.

STUART, R. B. (1967) 'Decentration, age and intelligence in the development of children's moral judgement', Diss. Abstr., 27(8b), 2864-5.

SUCHMAN, J. R. (1961) 'Inquiry training: building skills for autonomous discovery', Merr. Palm. Quart., 7, 3, 147-69.

SUCHMAN, J. R. (1964) 'The Illinois studies in inquiry training', J. Res. Sci. Teach., 2, 230-2.

SUCHMAN, R. G. (1966) 'Colour-form preference, discriminative accuracy, and learning of deaf and hearing children', Child Developm., 37, 943-51.

SUCHMAN, R. G. and TRABASSO, R. (1966) 'Colour and form preference in young children', J. Exp. Child Psych., 3, 177-87.

SULLIVAN, E. V. (1967) 'Piaget and the School Curriculum'. Toronto: OISE.

SULLIVAN, E. V. (1969) 'Transition problems in conservation research', J. Gen. Psych., 115, 41-54.

SULLIVAN, E. V., McCULLOUGH, G. and STAGER, M. (1970) 'A developmental study of the relationship between conceptual, ego and moral development', Child Developm., 41, 399-411.

SUPPES, P. and GINSBERG, R. (1962) 'Experimental studies of mathematical concept formation in young children', Sci. Ed., 46, 230-40.

SUSSEX UNIVERSITY SCHOOL OF EDUCATION (1968) 'Piaget in Perspective'. Papers read at a Conference at the University, 5th-6th April.

SUTTON-SMITH, B. (1966) 'Piaget on play: a critique', Psych. Rev., 73, 104-110.

SVENSEN, D. (1972) 'Stability in cognitive processes in institutionalized mentally retarded adults'. Report No.5. The Institute of Psychology, Bergen University, Norway.

SZEMINSKA, A. (1965) 'The evolution of thought: some applications of research findings to educational practice', in MUSSEN, P. H. (Ed.) 'European Res. in Cognitive Developm'. Monogrs. Soc. for Res. in Child Developm., 30 (2, whole No.100).

TANAKA, M., CAMPBELL, J. T. and HELMICK, J. S. (1966) 'Piaget for first-grade teachers: written exercises for assessing intellectual development', Educ. Testing Service Res. Memorandum, July.

TANNER, J. M. and INHELDER, B. (1956) (Eds.) 'Discussions on Child Development, Vol. I.' London: Tavistock.

TAYLOR, J. A and SPENCE, K. W. (1952) 'Relationship of anxiety level to performance in serial learning', J. Exp. Psych., 44, 61-4.

TAYLOR, S. (1969) 'The musical development of children aged 7 to 11', PhD thesis, Southampton University.

TEECE, A. R. (1969) 'The relationship of certain aspects of oral and written language in eight-year-old children', MPhil thesis, Southampton University.

TEETS, J. (1968) 'A comparison of two socioeconomic classes on the performance of Piagetian tasks', unpub. MA thesis, West Virginian University.

TEPLENKAYA, K. H. M. (1966) 'The formation of logical structures in six-to seven-year-old children', Congrès intern. de Psychol., 18, Symposium 24.

TERMAN, L. M. (1946) 'Psychological sex differences', in CARMICHAEL, L. (Ed.) 'Manual of Child Psychology'. New York: Wiley.

TERMAN, L. M. and MERRILL, M. A. (1937) 'Measuring Intelligence'. Boston: Houghton, Mifflin.

TERRELL, G., DURKIN, K. and WIESLEY, (1959) 'Social class and the nature of the incentive in discrimination learning', J. Abnorm. Soc. Psych., 59, 270-2.

TEUBER, H. L. (1967) 'Lacunae and research approaches to them', in DARLEY, F. L. (Ed.) 'Brain Mechanisms Underlying Speech and Language'. New York: Grune and Stratton.

THOMAS, D. I. (1966) 'Children's understanding of archaeological material', unpub. research, Birmingham University, reported by Peel in BURSTON, W. H. and THOMSON, D. (Eds.) 'Studies in the Nature and Teaching of History'. Routledge and Kegan Paul, 1967.

THOMPSON, G. (1951) 'The Factorial Analysis of Human Ability'. London University Press.

THOMPSON, L. (1948) 'Attitudes and acculturation', Am. Anthrop, 50, 200-15.

THROWER, J. (to be published) 'Effects of orphanage and foster home care on development of moral judgement', in KOHLBERG, L. and TURIEL, E. (Eds.) 'Recent Research in Moral Development'. London and New York: Holt-Blond Ltd.

TISHER, R. (1962) 'The development of some science concepts: a replication of Piaget's studies with pupils in a New South Wales country high school', unpub. BA thesis, University of New England, Armidale, NSW.

TISHER, R. (1967) ' "My father told me . . ." Children's explanations of some natural phenomena', Aust. J. Ed., 11(3), 204-12.

TISHER, R. (1971) 'A Piagetian questionnaire applied to pupils in a secondary school', Child Developm., 42, 1633-6.

TIZARD, B. (1974) 'In defence of nurture', New Society 10th Jan., p. 73.

TOBIN, M. J. (1972) 'Conservation of substance in the blind and partially sighted', Brit. J. Ed. Psych., 4, 2, 192-7.

TOMLINSON-KEASEY, C. (1972) 'Formal operations in females from 11 to 54 years of age', Dev. Psych., 6, 2, 364.

TOWLER, J. O. (1966) 'Children's spatial concepts', unpub. MA thesis, Alberta University.

TOWLER, J. O. (1968) 'Training effects and concept development: a study of the conservation of continuous quantity in children'. Paper presented at the meeting of the American Educational Research Association, Chicago.

TOWLER, J. O. and WHEATLEY, G. (1971) 'Conservation concepts in college students: a replication and critique', J. Gen. Psych., 118, 265-70.

TRABASSO, T., BOWER, G., GELMAN, R. and SCHAEFFER, B. (1966). 'Selection and additivity of cues in concept formation'. Proceedings of the Am. Psych. Assoc., 35-6.

TRAPP, E. P. and KAUSLER, D. H. (1958) 'Dominance attitudes in parents and adult avoidance behaviour in young children', Child Developm., 29, 4, 507-13.

TUDDENHAM, R. D. (1966) 'Jean Piaget and the World of the Child', Am. Psych., 35, 831-41.

463

TUDDENHAM, R. D. (1968) 'New Ways of Measuring Intelligence'. American Educ. Res. Assoc. Conven., Chicago.
TUDDENHAM, R. D. (1968) 'Psychometricizing Piaget's Méthode Clinique'. Revised paper and cited in ATHEY, I. J. and RUBADEAU, D. O. (Eds.) 'Educational Implications of Piaget's Theory'. Ginn-Blaisdell Company, 317-24.
TUDDENHAM, R. D. (1969) 'A Piagetian test of cognitive development'. Paper presented at the Symposium on Intelligence. Ontario, Toronto, May. Published in The Toronto Symposium 1969 on Intelligence, DOCKRELL, W. B. (Ed.) 1970.
TURIEL, E. (1966) 'An experimental test of the sequentiality of developmental stages in the child's moral judgement', J. Pers. Soc. Psych., 3, 6, 611-8.
TURIEL, E. (1969) 'Developmental processes in the child's moral thinking', in MUSSEN, P., LANGER, J. and COVINGTON, M., (Eds.) 'New Directions in Developmental Psychology'. New York: Holt.
TURIEL, E. (1973) 'Stage transition in moral development', in TRAVERS, R. M. (Ed.) 'Second Handbook of Research on Teaching'. Chicago: Rand McNally.
TURIEL, E. and ROTHMAN, G. R. (1972) 'The influence of reasoning on behavioural choices at different stages of moral development', Child Developm., 43, 3, 741-57.
TURNER, C. (1970) 'Children's concepts of God and Religious denomination', MEd thesis, Sussex University.
TURNER, G. H. N. (1966) 'A re-examination of certain of Piaget's inquiries on children's moral judgements in the light of his later theory', MEd thesis, Manchester University.

UGUREL-SEMIN, R. (1952) 'Moral behaviour and moral judgement of children', J. Abnorm. Soc. Psych., 47, 463-74.
UNIVERSITY OF BRISTOL INSTITUTE OF EDUCATION (1968) 'An evaluation of the development of scientific concepts in children taking part in the Oxford Primary Science Project' (cyclostyled document).
UNIVERSITY OF OXFORD, INSTITUTE OF EDUCATION (1967) Report to the Dept. of Education and Science on an inquiry into the formation of scientific concepts in children (cyclostyled document).
UZGIRIS, I. C. (Unpub. Manuscript) 'Socio-cultural Factors in Cognitive Development'. Clark University.
UZGIRIS, I. C. (1964) 'Situational generality of conservation', Child Developm., 35, 831-41.
UZGIRIS, I. C. (1973) 'Patterns of cognitive development in infancy', Merr-Palm. Quart., 181-204.
UZGIRIS, I. C. and HUNT, J. McV. (1966) 'An instrument for assessing infant psychological development'. Paper presented at the 18th Intern. Congress of Psychology, Moscow.
UZGIRIS, I. C. and HUNT, J. McV. (1969) 'Toward Ordinal Scales of Psychological Development'. Illinois University, Psych. Develop. Lab. (Mimeo.)

VANDEVENTER, M. and JACOBS, P. I. (1971) 'The learning and transfer of double-classification skills: a replication and extension', J. Exp. Child Psych., 12, 240-57.

VERNON, P. E. (1951) 'Recent investigations of intelligence and its measurement', Eug. Rev., 43, 125-37.
VERNON, P. E. (1955) 'The assessment of children'. University of London Inst. of Education, Studies in Education, 7, 189-215.
VERNON, P. E. (1960) 'Intelligence and Attainment Tests'. London University Press.
VERNON, P. E. (1961) 'The Structure of Human Abilities'. London: Methuen.
VERNON, P. E. (1964) 'Personality Assessment'. New York: Wiley.
VERNON, P. E. (1965a) 'Ability factors and environmental influences', Am. Psych., 20, 723-33.
VERNON, P. E. (1965b) 'Environmental handicaps and intellectual development', Brit. J. Ed. Psych., 35, 1-12.
VERNON, P. E. (1966) 'Educational and intellectual development among Canadian Indians and Eskimos', Ed. Rev., 18, 79-91 and 186-95.
VERNON, P. E. (1967) 'Administration of group intelligence tests to East African pupils', Brit. J. Ed. Psych., 37, 282-91.
VERNON, P. E. (1969) 'Intelligence and Cultural Environment'. Methuen's Manuals of Modern Psychology. London: Methuen.
VERNON, P. E. (1969a) 'Abilities and educational attainments in an East African environment, J. Spec. Edu., 4, 335-45.
VICKERS, M. and BLANCHARD, B. (1973) 'The development of preference for cognitive balance', J. Gen. Psych., 122, 189-95.
VINACKE, W. E. (1951) 'The investigation of concept formation', Psych. Bull., 48, 1-31.
VINACKE, W. E. (1954) 'Concept formation in children of school ages', Education, 75, 527-34.
VINH BANG (1957) 'Elaboration d'une échelle de développement du raisonnement'. Proc. 15th int. congr. Psychol., 333-4.
VINH BANG (1971) 'The psychology of Jean Piaget and its relevance to Education'. Cited in RUSK, B. (Ed.) 'Alternatives in Education'. London University Press.
VYGOTSKY, L. S. (1962) 'Thought and Language'. Massachusetts Institute of Technology; New York, London: Wiley. 168 pp.

WACHS, T. D. (1970) 'Report on the utility of a Piaget-based infant scale with older retarded children', Dev. Psych., 2, 3, 449.
WACHS, T. D., UZGIRIS, I. and HUNT, J. McV. (1967) 'Cognitive development in infants of different age levels and from different environmental backgrounds'. Paper presented at the biennial meeting of the Society for Research in Child Development, New York.
WALKER, C., TORRANCE, E. P. and WALKER, T. S. (1971) 'A cross-cultural study of the perception of situational causality', J. Cross-Cult. Psych., 2, 401-4.
WADDELL, V. (1968) 'Some cultural considerations on the development of the concept of conservation'. Unpub. Paper presented to Genetic Epistemology Seminar, Austr. National University.
WAGHORN, L. and SULLIVAN, E. (1970) 'The exploration of transition rules in conservation of quantity (substance) using film mediated modelling', Acta Psych., 32, 65-80.

WALLACE, J. G. (1965) 'Concept Growth and Education of the Child'. Slough: NFER.

WALLACE, J. G. (1967) 'An inquiry into the development of concepts of number in young children involving a comparison of verbal and non-verbal methods of assessment and acceleration', PhD thesis, Bristol University.

WALLACE, J. G. (1972) 'Stages and Transition in Conceptual Development'. Slough: NFER.

WALLACE, J. G. (1973) 'Class-inclusion performance in children: information-processing theories and experimental studies'. Paper read at the British Psychological Society Conference, Liverpool University, Easter.

WALLACH, L. and SPROTT, R. L. (1964) 'Inducing number-conservation on children', Child Developm., 35, 1057-71.

WALLACH, L. WALL, J. A. and ANDERSON, L. (1967) 'Number conservation: the roles of reversibility, addition-subtraction, and misleading perceptual cues', Child Developm., 38, 425-42.

WALLACH, M. A. (1963) 'Research on children's thinking', in STEVENSON, H. W. (Ed.) 'Child Psychology'. (62nd Yearbook of Nat. Soc. Study of Educ. Part 1) Chicago, 236-76.

WALLACH, M. A. and KOGAN, N. (1965) 'Modes of Thinking in Young Children — a study of the Creativity — Intelligence, Distinction.' New York: Holt, Rinehart and Winston.

WANG, M. C., RESNICK, L. B. and BOOZER, R. F. (1971) 'The sequence of development of some early mathematics behaviours', Child Developm., 42, 1767-78.

WARD, J. (1972) 'The saga of Butch and Slim', Brit. J. Ed. Psych., 267-89.

WARD, J. and PEARSON, L. (1973) 'A comparison of two methods of testing logical thinking', Canad. J. Behav. Sci., 5, 4, 385-98.

WARD, L. O. (1965) 'An investigation into the attitudes of pupils in a girl's grammar school to the moral aspects of historical events', MA dissertation, University of Wales.

WARNER, W. L., MEEKER, M. and EELLS, K. (1949) 'Social Class in America'. Chicago: Social Science Research Association.

WASIK, B. H. and WASIK, J. L. (1971) 'Performance of culturally deprived children on the concept assessment kit-conservation', Child Developm., 42, 1586-90.

WEBB, R. A., MASSAR, B. and NADOLNY, T. (1972) 'Information and strategy in the young child's search for hidden objects', Child Developm., 43, 1, 91-105.

WECHSLER, D. (1949) 'Wechsler Intelligence Scale for Children'. New York: Psychological Corporation.

WECHSLER, D. (1958) 'Measurement and Appraisal of Adult Intelligence'. Baltimore: Williams and Wilkins.

WECHSLER, D. (1967) 'Manual for the Wechsler Pre-school and Primary Scale of Intelligence'. New York: Psychological Corporation.

WEI, T. T. D. (1966) 'Piaget's concept of classification: a comparative study of CD and MC children', PhD thesis, Illinois University.

WEI, T. T. D., LAVATELLI, C. B. and JONES, R. S. (1971) 'Piaget's concept of classification: A comparative study of socially disadvantaged and middle-class young children', Child Developm., 42, 919-27.

WEISBROTH, S. P. (1970) 'Moral judgement, sex and parental identification in adults', Dev. Psych., 2, 3, 396-402.

WEISKRANTZ, L. (Ed.) (1968) Analysis of Behavioural Change. New York: Harper and Row.

WERE, K. (1968) 'A survey of the thought processes of New Guinean secondary students', Unpub. MEd thesis, Adelaide University.

WHEATLEY, G. H. (1968) 'Conservation, cardination and counting as factors in mathematics achievement', Am. Ed. Res. Assoc., Feb. 1968.

WHEELER, L. R. (1942) 'A comparative study of the intelligence of East Tennessee mountain children', J. Ed. Psych., 33, 321-34.

WHITE, B. H. and SALTZ, E. (1957) 'Measurement of reproducibility', Psych. Bull., 54, 2, 89-91.

WHITE, B. L. (1969) 'The initial coordination of sensori-motor schemas in human infants — Piaget's ideas and the role of experience', in ELKIND, D. and FLAVELL, J. H. (Eds.) 'Studies in Cognitive Development: Essays in Honour of Jean Piaget'. New York: Oxford University Press.

WHITE, R. R. (1960) 'Test performance as a function of anxiety and type of task', reported in: SARASON, S. B., et al., 'Anxiety in Elementary School Children'. New York: Wiley.

WHITE, S. H. (1965) 'Evidence for a hierarchical arrangement of learning processes', in 'Advances in Child Development and Behaviour, 2'. New York: Academic Press.

WHITEMAN, M. and PEISACH, E. (1970) 'Perceptual and sensori-motor supports for conservation tasks', Dev. Psych., 2, 2, 247-56.

WHITEMAN, P. H. and KOSIER, K. P. (1964) 'Development of children's moralistic judgements: age, sex, IQ and certain personal-experimental variables', Child Developm., 35, 843-50.

WIENER, G., RIDER, R. V. and OPPEL, W. (1963) 'Some correlates of IQ changes in children', Child Developm., 34, 61-7.

WILDE, R. (in progress) 'Linguistic training for class-inclusion behaviour', DPhil thesis, Sussex University.

WILLIAMS, A. A. (1958) 'Number readiness', Ed. Rev., 11, 31-46.

WILLIAMS, A. A. (1968) 'Applications in the Classroom to the Development of Early Number Concepts', Cited in 'Piaget in Perspective'. Paper read at Sussex University Conference — 5th-6th April.

WILLIAMS, N. (1969) 'Children's moral thought. Parts I and II', Moral Education, 1, 1 and 2, May and September 1969.

WILLIAMS, P. (1961) 'A study concerning concepts of conservation of quantities among primitive children', Acta. Psych., 18, 297-305.

WILLINGTON, G. W. (1967) 'The development of the mathematical understanding of primary school children', MEd thesis, Manchester University.

WILLOUGHBY, R. H. and TRACHY, S. (1971) 'Conservation of number in very young children: a failure to replicate Mehler and Bever', Merr. Palm. Quart., 205-9.

WINER, B. J. (1962) 'Statistical Principles in Experimental Design'. New York: McGraw-Hill.

WINER, G. A. (1968) 'Induced set and acquisition of number conservation', Child Developm., 39, 195-205.

WISEMAN, S. (1964) 'Education and Environment'. Manchester University Press.

WITKIN, H. A., DYK, R. B., PATERSON, H. F., GOODENOUGH, D. R. and

KARP, S. A. (1962) 'Psychological Differentiation'. New York: Wiley.

WOHLWILL, J. F. (1957) 'The abstraction and conceptualization of form, colour, number', J. Exp. Psych., 9, (4) 253-62.

WOHLWILL, J. F. (1959) 'Un essai d'apprentissage dans le domaine de la conservation de nombre', in PIAGET, J. (Ed.) 'Etudes d'Epistémologie Génétique'. Paris: Presses universitaires de France, 9, 125-35.

WOHLWILL, J. F. (1960) 'Developmental studies of perception', Psych. Bull., 57, 249-88.

WOHLWILL, J. F. (1960a) 'Absolute vs. relational discrimination on the dimension of number', J. Gen. Psych., 96, 353-63.

WOHLWILL, J. F. (1960b) 'A study of the development of the number concept by scalogram analysis', J. Gen. Psych., 97, 345-77.

WOHLWILL, J. F. (1962) 'From perception to inference: a dimension of cognitive development', in KESSEN, W. and KUHLMAN, C. (Eds.) 'Thought in the Young Child' Monogr. Soc. Res. Child Developm., 27, 87-106.

WOHLWILL, J. F. (1966) 'Piaget's theory of the development of intelligence in the concrete operations period', Am. J. Ment. Defic. Mon. Suppl., 70, No.4.

WOHLWILL, J. F. (1968) 'Children's responses to class-inclusion questions with verbally and pictorially presented items', Child Developm., 39, 449-66.

WOHLWILL, J. F. (1968) 'Piaget's system as a source of empirical research', in SIGEL, I. E. and HOOPER, F. E. (Eds.) 'Logical Thinking in Children'. New York: Holt, Rinehart and Winston.

WOHLWILL, J. F. (1968a) 'A study of the development of the number concept by scalogram analysis', in SIGEL, I. E. and HOOPER, F. H. (Eds.) 'Logical Thinking in Children'. New York: Holt, Rinehart and Winston, 75-103. Originally in J. Gen. Psych., (1960) 97, 345-77.

WOHLWILL, J. F. and LOWE, R. C. (1962) 'Analysis of the development of the conservation of number', Child Developm., 33, 153-67.

WOLF, R. M. (1964) 'The identification and measurement of environmental process variables related to intelligence', unpub. doctoral dissertation, University of Chicago.

WOLF, R. M. (1964) 'The measurement of environments', in 'Proceedings of the 1964 Conference on Testing Problems', Princeton, NJ: Educational Testing Service.

WOLFENSTEIN, M. (1953) 'Trends in infant care', Am. J. Orthopsychiat., 23, 120-30.

WOLFF, P. H. (1960) 'The developmental psychologies of Jean Piaget and psychoanalysis', Psych. Issues, 2 (I) Monograph 5.

WOOD, M. E. (1968) 'A study of children's growing social and motivational awareness', PhD thesis, London University.

WOODWARD, M. (1959) 'The behaviour of idiots interpreted by Piaget's theory of sensori-motor development', Brit. J. Ed. Psych., 29, 60-73.

WOODWARD, M. (1961) 'Concepts of number of the mentally subnormal studied by Piaget's methods', J. Child Psychol. Psychiat., 2, 249-59.

WOODWARD, M. (1962) 'Concepts of space in mentally subnormal studied by Piaget's method', Brit. J. Soc. Clin. Psychol., 1, 25-37.

WOODWARD, M. (1962) 'The application of Piaget's theory to the training of the subnormal', J. Ment. Sub., 8, 3-11.

468

WOODWARD, M. (1963) 'The application of Piagetian theory to research in mental deficiency', in ELLIS, N. R. (Ed.) 'Handbook of Mental Deficiency'. New York: McGraw Hill.

WOODWARD, M. (1965) 'Piaget's theory', in HOWELLS, J. G. (Ed.) 'Modern Perspectives in Child Psychiatry'. Edinburgh: Oliver and Boyd.

WOODWARD, M. (1970) 'The assessment of Cognitive Processes: Piaget's approach', in MITTLER, P. (Ed.) 'The Psychological Assessment of Mental and Physical Handicap'. London: Methuen.

WOODWARD, M. (1971) 'The assessment of Cognitive Processes: Piaget's approach', in MITTLER, P. (Ed.) 'Handbook of Mental Deficiency'. New York: McGraw-Hill.

WOODWARD, M. (1972) 'Problem-solving strategies of young children', J. Child Psych. Psychiatr., 13, 11-24.

WOODWARD, M. and STERN, D. J. (1963) 'Developmental patterns of severely subnormal children', Brit. J. Ed. Psych., 33, 10-21.

WRIGHT, D. (1971) 'The Psychology of Moral Behaviour'. Harmondsworth, UK: Penguin.

YARROW, L. J. (1961) 'Maternal deprivation: toward an empirical and conceptual re-evaluation', Psych. Bull., 58, 459-90.

YARROW, L. J. (1964) 'Separation from parents during early childhood', in HOFFMAN, M. L. and HOFFMAN, L. W. (Eds.) 'Review of Child Development Research'. New York: Russell Sage Foundation.

YATES, J. and RICHARDSON, J. (1970 'An attempt to apply Piaget's theory of intelligence to the assessment and training of children in a special care unit.' Invited paper, BPS Conference at Nottingham University.

YOUNISS, J. (1964) 'Concept transfer as a function of shifts, age and deafness', Child Developm., 35, 695-700.

YOUNISS, J. and DENNISON, A. (1971) 'Figurative and operative aspects of children's inference', Child Developm., 42, 1837-47.

YOUNISS, J. and FURTH, H. G. (1965) 'The influence of transitivity on learning in hearing and deaf children', Child Developm., 36, 533-8.

YOUNISS, J. and FURTH, H. G. (1966) 'Prediction of causal events as a function of transitivity and perceptual congruency in hearing and deaf children', Child Developm., 37, 73-82.

ZAPOROZHETS, A. V. (1965) 'The development of perception in the pre-school child', in MUSSEN, P. H. (Ed.) 'European Research in Cognitive Development'. Mon. Soc. Res. in Child Developm., 30, (2, whole No.100) 82-101.

ZAPOROZHETS, A. V. and ZINCHENKO, V. P. (1966) 'Development of perceptual activity and formation of a sensory image in the child', in LEONTYEN, A., LURIA, A. and SMIRNOV, A. (Eds.) 'Psychological Research in USSR.', Moscow Press.

ZA'ROUR, G. I. (1971) 'Conservation of weight across different materials by Lebanese school children in Beirut', Sci. Ed., 55, (3), 387-94.

ZA'ROUR, G. I. (1971) 'The conservation of number and liquid by Lebanese school children in Beirut', J. Cross-Cult. Psych., 2, 165-72.

ZEMPLENI, A. and ZEMPLENI, J. (1970) 'Milieu Africain et développement'. Rapport présenté à la session de l'Assoc. de Psych. Sc. de Lang. Francaise, Lille, Sep.

ZIGLER, E. (1969) 'Training the intellect versus development of the child'. Paper presented at annual meeting of the American Educ. Res. Association, Los Angeles.

ZIGLER, E. and BUTTERFIELD, E. C. (1968) 'Motivational aspects of changes in IQ test performance of culturally deprived nursery school children', Child Developm., 39, 1-14.

ZIMILES, H. (1963) 'A note on Piaget's concept of conservation', Child Developm., 34, 691-5.

ZIMILES, H. (1966) 'The development of conservation and differentiation of number', Mon. Soc. Res. Child Developm., 31, No.6, Serial No.108.

ZINCHENKO, V. P. and RUZSKAYA, A. G. (1961) 'A comparative analysis of Touch and Vision', Psych. Abstr., 25, 99-102.

SUPPLEMENTARY REFERENCES

COWAN, P. A. (1966) 'Cognitive egocentrism and social interaction in children', Amer. Psych., 21. 623.

GESELL, A. (1940) 'The First Five Years of Life'. New York: Harper.

GESELL, A. and ARMATRUDA, C. S. (1951) 'Developmental Diagnosis'. New York: London.

GOTTESMAN, M. (1973) 'Conservation development in blind children', Child Developm., 44, 4, 824-7.

LEFEVRE, A. (1970) 'A propos d'un cas de "dyscalculie" de la rééducation à la psychothérapie', Perspectives Psychiatriques, 4, 30, 39-56.

MODGIL, S. L. (1965a) 'An investigation into the development of the concept of substance in a group of children aged ten', Part I. Unpub. thesis, Newcastle University.

NEALE, J. M. (1966) 'Egocentrism in institutionalized and noninstitutionalized children', Child Developm., 37, 97-101.

PEISACH, E. (1973) 'Relationship between knowledge and use of dimensional language and achievement of conservation', Dev. Psych., 9, 2, 189-97.

PILLER, M. (1971) 'Recherche de psychologie sur une population d'adultes analphabètes de la Côte d'Ivoire'. Unpub. report, University of Geneva.

PIMM, J. B. (1974) 'The performance of the emotionally disturbed child on Piaget's conservation tasks' (personal communication).

SIEGLER, R. S., LIEBERT, D. E. and LIEBERT, R. M. (1973) 'Inhelder and Piaget's pendulum problem', Dev. Psych., 9, 1, 97-101.

AUTHOR INDEX

472

473

Rest, J., 364
Rhys, W.T., 271
Richardson, J.N., 385
Rieff, M.L., 118, 124-5
Ripple, R.E., 259
Robbins, O., 81-2, 96-7
Roberts, G.C., 8, 22, 138
Rockcastle, V.N., 259
Roeper, A., 102, 117
Roll, S., 80, 93
Ross, B.M., 258
Ross, I., 152
Rothenberg, B.B., 34-7, 41-4, 48, 80,
    91-2, 217
Rothman, G.R., 366
Rowland, A.D., 193, 206
Rubin, K.H., 381
Rutter, M.L., 376
Ruzskaya, A.G., 178, 185

Sabharwal, V., 255
Saiga, H., 226-7
Saint-Pierre, J., 23
Sarason, S.B., 376
Sawada, D., 115
Scaplehorn, C., 275, 364, 386
Schallenberger, M., 281
Schoenfeld, E., 58
Schoeppe, A., 64
Schofield, L., 27
Scholnick, E.K., 57
Schroder, H.N., 365
Schwartz, J., 103, 236
Schwartz, L.C., 79
Schwartz, M.M. 57, 59-60
Sears, P.S., 320
Sears, R., 317
Selman, R.L., 354, 365
Seltzer, A.R., 309, 313, 334
Serpell, R., 229
Shanks, B.L., 34, 45, 81, 85-6
Shantz, C.U., 42, 44, 48, 125, 179, 180-2,
    187-8, 190
Shapiro, B.J., 159, 164
Shapiro, H., 145
Sharan (Singer), S., 250
Shaw, R.E., 13
Shields, J.B., 158
Shoben, E.J., 299, 375-6
Shulman, L.S., 226, 230, 236
Siegel, A.W. 141, 148-9
Siegel, L.S., 33, 37, 42, 44, 46-9, 52, 151,
    155, 232
Siegler, R.S., 111
Sigel, I.E., 79, 102-4, 117, 136, 145, 177,
    251, 369, 381, 386
Simonsson, M., 226, 244-5
Simpson, G.J., 79, 102
Sinclair, H., 111, 115, 126, 238
Slater, A., 193, 197
Smedslund, J., 35, 70, 76, 78-80, 83, 87,
    93, 101-7, 115, 126, 149, 151, 154,
    189, 213, 221, 265
Smith, D.A., 21, 23

Smith, E.C., 342, 344, 358
Smith, I.D., 105, 107
Smith, M.B., 362
Smock, C.D., 180-2, 187, 190
Sonstroem, A.M., 80
Sperr, S.J., 118, 124-5
Sprott, R.L., 48, 80, 83, 93, 102
Stager, M., 365
Steffe, L., 33
Steger, J., 151, 154
Stephens, W.B., 12, 168, 196, 214, 219,
    309, 325, 386, 390-1
Stern, D.J., 191, 210
Stewart, C., 79
Stones, S.K., 272
Stott, D.H., 310, 376
Stott, L., 215
Strauss, A.L., 291, 294
Strauss, S., 111, 114, 126-7
Strobel, M., 369
Stuart, R.B., 307, 309, 312
Suchman, R.G., 271
Sullivan, E.V., 79, 238, 263, 358, 365
Syrdal-Lasky, A., 13
Szeminska, A., 64, 170, 187, 189, 215,
    237, 247, 259, 317, 323, 388

Tanaka, M., 385
Taylor, S., 266
Teets, J., 57, 61
Teplenkaya, K.H.M., 235
Terman, L.M., 320
Thomas, D.I., 271
Thompson, L., 283
Thrower, J., 365
Tisher, R., 159, 171-2, 261, 385-6
Tizard, B., 257
Tobin, M.J., 220
Tomlinson-Keasey, C., 12, 118, 159,
    172-3, 260
Towler, J.O., 64, 71-2
Trachey, S., 36
Tuddenham, R.D., 13, 232, 370, 382-3
Turiel, E., 340, 343, 349, 352, 354,
    359-60, 362, 364, 366

Uğurel-Semin, R., 309, 314, 318, 324-5,
    327
Updegraff, R., 375
Uzgiris, I.C., 8, 20, 24, 27, 36, 45, 64-5,
    69-70, 196, 215, 228, 238, 254

Vandeventer, M., 117-8, 120-4
Vernon, P.E., 226-7, 231-3, 245
Vickers, M., 160
Vinh-Bang, 16, 387
Vore, D.A., 193, 216-7

Wachs, T.D., 9, 20, 196, 215-6
Waddell, V., 226
Wagner, J., 141, 145-6, 151, 232
Wallace, J.G., 14, 87-8, 90-1, 105
Wallach, L., 48, 60, 80, 83-4, 93, 101-2
Wallach, M.A., 251

475